A DIGEST

OF THE

LAWS, CUSTOMS, MANNERS, AND INSTITUTIONS

OF THE

ANCIENT AND MODERN NATIONS.

BY

THOMAS DEW,

LATE PRESIDENT OF THE COLLEGE OF WILLIAM AND MARY.

NEW-YORK:

D. APPLETON & COMPANY, 200 BROADWAY.

M.DCCC.LIII.

TABLE OF CONTENTS.

ANCIENT HISTORY.

CHAPTER I.

CHAPTER II.

CHAPTER III.

CHAPTER IV.

CHAPTER V.

MODERN HISTORY.

CHAPTER I.

CHAPTER II.

CHAPTER III.

CHAPTER IV.

CHAPTER V.

CHAPTER VI.

CHAPTER VII.

CHAPTER VIII.

CHAPTER IX.

PREFACE.

THE great body of this volume is the work of Prof. Thomas Dew, late President of the College of William and Mary. It was prepared originally in the shape of Lectures, in the Historical Department, over which he presided, and, during his lifetime, was printed for the use of his class, but never published. Its publication was prevented by his death.

The work is, what its title declares, a *Digest of History, Ancient and Modern.* It makes no pretensions to originality; but, as an Historical Manual, it is believed to possess decided advantages over all those compendiums of history now in use in our schools and colleges. Indeed, it was the imperfection of these compilations, and the necessity which the author felt for some proper text-book to be placed in the hands of the student, as an accompaniment to his historical lectures, that led to the preparation of this work. On examination, it will be found that more than ordinary labor has been expended upon it; and that the author has proceeded upon higher principles, and has had higher aims in view than compilers ordinarily propose to themselves. Instead of being, like most historical compendiums, a mere catalogue of events, chronologically arranged, it is a careful, laborious, and instructive digest of the laws, customs, manners, institutions, and civilization of the ancient and modern nations. The department of modern history particularly, in which such works are generally most deficient, has been prepared with unusual care and industry. In proof of this, reference is made to the chapters on the Reformation, the Papal Power, the English Constitution, and the French Revolution.

For a digest of history, prepared on these principles, it is believed that a demand exists, particularly in our schools and colleges, and it is to meet this demand that this volume is now presented to the public. It is believed that the schoolmaster will find in it an excellent substitute for the histories now in use, the historical lectures a desirable text-book to be placed in the hands of the student as an accompaniment to his lectures, and the general reader a useful manual.

ANCIENT HISTORY.

CHAPTER I.

ANTEDILUVIAN HISTORY.

SECTION I.

1. *What first subject which claims attention?* Cosmogony or the creation of the world.

2. *Opinions on the creation?* Ocellus Lucanus imagined the earth eternal and uncreated. Xenophanes and the Eleatic sect imagined the universe to be but one substance, and that God and the world are one and the same. Pythagoras and Plato contended that there were three causes—1st, intelligent, 2d, modellary, and 3d, material. Ovid adopts this partially.

3. *Why belief in an intelligent cause?* Order, harmony, and design, in the physical and moral world prove its existence.

4. *Where do we find the only authentic record of the creation?* In Genesis.

5. *Describe the order of creation?* First was created the vast chaos floating in the immensity of space. The Spirit of God moved on the face of the waters, and God said "let there be light, and there was light." This, the first period of creation. Second, the separation of the waters from the earth, and the creation of a *firmament.* Third, collecting the waters together, and formation of seas and lands. Fourth, sun and stars were created. Fifth and sixth, inferior animals. And lastly man, the master-piece of creation, created in the image of God.

6. *How was woman created? And where was placed this primitive couple?*

7. *What the character of this first pair?*

8. *Relate the story of the transgression and fall of man.*

9. *What the curse pronounced against them?*

10. *Who were the first born of Adam and Eve? Relate the story of Abel.*

11. *What the fate of Cain?* He was cursed, and a mark set upon him. He seceded from the tribe of Adam and retired into the land of Nod.

12. *Who the next mentioned son of Adam and Eve, and what the character of his descendants?* Seth; and his descendents were religious.

13. *How did this more righteous race at last become corrupted?* By intermarriage with the vicious descendants of Cain. *Were the men of those days of ordinary stature?* Moses says there were giants, and by intercourse with Sethites, begat mighty men.

14. *According to Moses, what ultimately became the state af morals?* Excessively depraved. "God saw," says Moses, "that the wickedness of man was great in the earth, and that every imagination of the thoughts of his heart was only evil continually. And he repented that he had made man, for all flesh had corrupted his way upon the earth." Hence the flood.

15. *Who was selected by God to be saved in the general deluge? And why was he selected, and how saved?* Noah, his family, and divers animals in pairs. Noah was righteous—saved by the ark.

16. *Describe the deluge.* See Genesis, ch. 7.

17. *How was the earth peopled again?* From Noah and his three sons, Shem, Ham, and Japhet.

18. *What was the average age of the antediluvians?* Excessively great. The lives of most of the patriarchs were prolonged beyond the ninth century, and Noah was 500 years old before he had either child who was with him in the ark, and was 600 at the period of the deluge, and 950 at his death! Methuselah, the oldest man on record, lived 969 years; Adam lived 930!

SEC. II.—COMMENTARY ON THE ANTEDILUVIAN HISTORY.

1. *Does the physical existence of this globe take its date from the Mosaic creation of man?* Certainly not. Geological researches prove, beyond a doubt, an antiquity greatly beyond the period at which Moses fixes the creation of man. The general deluge, which took place 1656 years after his creation, is, comparatively, a recent event.

2. *What then are we to understand by the Mosaic creation?* Only a mere formation or grouping of elements already in existence, and of the creation of man, animals, plants, &c. As to the first verse of Gene-

sis, one party contends that the "*beginning*" spoken of is the commencement of *our time*, and the creating is the mere *fitting* up, making it equivalent to "in beginning of our time God *fitted up* the heavens and the earth," &c. Others say, first verse distinct from the sequel, and relates to the original creation from nothing.

3. *Have we any reason to believe that animals and plants have existed previous to the creation of the present specimens?* Geology proves the affirmative. There are three strata of rocks mentioned by geologists, called Neptunian, because deposited from water, organic remains in each. Those of the primary transition stratum oldest and deepest in the earth, are totally different from those of the secondary stratum; and again those of the tertiary are totally different from the two former. Not a single specimen common to two strata; and the fossil remains of man are comparatively recent, and are never found among the old organic deposits. Geology and the Mosaic account both prove that man was among the last animals created.

4. *Do the extinct species of vegetables and animals, by their different formations, show a totally different set of laws by which they were governed?* No. Earth contains records of previous systems like the present in their outlines, but with totally different details. (Enc. Met. p. 550.)

5. *Do we find the same specimens remaining entire through the whole period requisite for the formation of one stratum?* No. Changes seem to have been gradual. The specimens at the bottom of a stratum are very much altered from those at top. *e. g.* M. Deshayes has shown that oldest tertiary stratum has only 3¼ per cent. of species identical with living. Second, more recent group holds 18 per cent., and third, 49, and the more recent, little else. (Enc. Met. 553.)

6. *Does the earth exhibit marks of violence and revolutions totally different from the deluge?* Yes. The principal source of these seems to have been internal heat, producing upheavings, the breaking up of stratified rocks, the injection into great fissures of melted Plutonic remains, the elevated position of the Plutonic rocks, the upheaving of one side of enormous rock, whilst the other side is below—vertical strata. *e. g.* Isle of Wight, Yorkshire, &c. (Enc. Met. 540,) contorted strata, &c., all prove it. The earth exhibits an alternating series of periods of repose and violent convulsions. Subject not yet well systematized. (798, Wiseman, 184.) Thus from gradual changes in the adaptations of the earth from climate, or by occasional violent convulsions, the whole animal and vegetable kingdom, of one period, have been entirely destroyed to make way for the new creations of another, *e. g.* mountain lime-stone of the north of England has 200 species of animal remains,

the lias 115, and the chalk 43, and of the 358 not any one is found in two of the strata. So that between the formation of the lime-stone, and that of the lias, the whole animal population of the sea had been entirely changed, and a similar complete renewal occurred before the chalk was deposited. (552.) And again, in south of England the chalk is covered by other more recent strata, filled with the reliquiæ of animals entirely different from those which lived and died before.

6. *In the Mosaic account, is the word "day" to be understood tropically, to mean an age, or literally, to mean one revolution of the earth?* Either supposition may be compatible with the authenticity of the account. If the first hypothesis be adopted, then the six days' creation may extend thousands of years back, and time be allowed for all the changes which geology proves to have taken place from the creation of man. If the second, then the six days' creation would be confined to the mere arrangement and adjustment of the earth, which had existed thousands, perhaps millions of years before, to the newly-created animals and plants. An event not at all incompatible with previous history of the globe. Arguments pro and con. (V. 47, Phi. Mag.) Prichard for "ages," &c., Horne for "days," Josephus and Philo among ancients for "ages," 115, 260, Hindoo tradition for "ages," Etruscan also, 113, 114.

7. *Are there any traditions among other nations than the Jews which serve to confirm the Mosaic account?* The Hindoos have very similar. The Spirit of God moving on face of waters almost literal. Menu, it is very singular, defines his days and nights, and makes them ages instead of common days. Age is 4,000 years, twilight preceding it is 400 years, and following it 400; and a day of Brahma is 1,000 times an age, and the night as long. (114.) The use of twilight and night, singular coincidence. Etruscans have another still more similar, preserved by Suidas. Creation divided into twelve departments, each of one thousand years—succession same almost with Genesis, (P. M. 114, to 6,000th year when man was made, 12,000th the consummation of all these. (Turner 34.)

8. *Is there any tradition or ancient belief which would admit long time and great revolutions, before man was created?* The institutes of Menu recognize this long existence and frequency of revolutions "There are creations also and destruction of worlds innumerable," and God performs all with as much ease as if in sport. The Birmese have similar traditions of destruction, both by fire and water. The Egyptians by great cycle or sothic period, record similar opinions. The early fathers of the Christian church, St. Gregory Nazianzen, St. Justin Martyr, St. Bazil, St. Cesarius, Origen, &c., all suppose an indefinite

period between creation of world, and ordering of all things as described by Moses. (W. 178.)

9. *Are we to suppose that the heavenly bodies were created on the 4th day, or that their functions were merely established in relation to the earth?* The latter. The word "create" in Genesis is sometimes used in the sense of "establish." In the book of Job we are told that when the foundation of the earth was laid "the morning stars sang together, and all the sons of God shouted for joy." (387.) Hence, formed before earth.

10. *How are first and fourth days' creation reconciled?* Various explanations, *e. g.* one says latent light created first day; another, that principle of light was created that day, and the substances in which it was to shine on fourth. Another that heat and light were made, which aided in the subsequent formations. (Turner, 24.) Another that *create* means to order—to make *appear;* that a dense vapor was cleared away on the fourth, which made lights *appear* to the earth, &c. No reason to think light was created even first day. "Let there be light," does not imply that it did not before exist, but that it was substituted for darkness at that time. Many animals, thousands of years before man, were furnished with eyes. (Buckland's Geo. 30 and 34.) The difficulty here is in favor of authenticity; for impostors would have no apparent clashing.

11. *Are there any traditions among nations which seem to corroborate the Mosaic account of the fall of man, and of the progressive corruption of the human race up to the period of their destruction?* All nations seem to have some traditions on this subject, *e. g.* Hesiod's Pandora, or the Grecian Eve, a modest virgin, adorned by Minerva, covered with jewels by *Graces*—crowned with flowers by Seasons—but, unluckily, gifted with *speech* filled with *falsehood* and *deceitful* manners by *Mercury.* Hence, she became corrupter of man. (T. S. H. v. 1, 424.) The nations of the east have some traditions very analogous to the Mosaic account, *e. g.* the two principles in the Persian religion, good and evil—Ormudz and Ahriman; conflict between them, fall and imperfection of man and all things else, owing to interference of Ahriman, the evil principle. In the traditions of the Indians, we have two races; one gigantic and corrupt, engaged in eternal wars with the race of Brahmin patriarchs, pious and holy. (Schlegel, 61.) The Chinese have similar traditions, and the wickedness of her emperors was represented as one cause of the deluge, whilst the good patriarchs labored for the benefit of the race. (121.) In a mountain range of Asia, abounding in metals, there is a people (Tschudes in French,) who have preserved the very names of Cain and Seth in tradition; but with change of character.

Cain is father of good race, the inventor of the arts, mechanic, miner, architect, &c. (Sch. 55.) The Greeks and old Romans had same traditions under different forms. Deterioration of race progressive. 1st. Golden age, when earth supplied all wants, life was sweet, and death a delightful sleep. Then 2d, silver age, 3d, brazen, 4th, iron. Wickedness so great in brazen age as to determine Jupiter to destroy the animal races by a flood. (See Ovid.)

12. *Is the great age, or gigantic stature of the antediluvians, any argument against authenticity of the Mosaic narrative?* Changes prove that we have no reason to make present races the standard by which to judge of others in primeval times. Geology proves that the animal and vegetable kingdoms have undergone several entire changes, *e. g.* Lizard or Saurian tribes, *Megalosaurus*, of Buckland, from 30 to 70 feet long, *Ichthyosaurus*, or fish-lizard—it has lizard head, fish's body, and four paddles for legs—size enormous. Enaliosaurus or sea-lizard, Pterodoltylus or flying-lizard. (Wiseman, 183.) Again—we find remains of animals belonging to families, though very different, of elephant, rhinoceros, hippopotamus, the largest animals known to us, which must have been many times larger than the modern. Again—we have horns of some animals, whose species are known, such as horns of a bull, still attached to the frontal bone; horns of the stag, and teeth of elephants, which must have belonged to animals four or five times as large as the largest of the modern breed. (Sch. 69.)

In the vegetable kingdom, the same differences are apparent. We have no reason, then, to wonder at size or longevity of antediluvians, because beyond our standard. Evident reason, besides, for size and age of antediluvians: 1st, the size of other animals, and 2d, the space and plenty of food would call for rapid multiplication of species, which longevity would favor, &c.

13. *Do the traditions of other nations favor the account of Moses, in regard to longevity and stature?* Eastern natives have such traditions, and so did the Greeks, especially in relation to size; *e. g.* the Titans, who made war on heaven, were supposed to be earth's offspring, and when at last conquered by Jove, their blood produced men--a race

> *Contemptrix superum sevæ avidiessima cædis,*
> *Et violenta.*—Ovid.

and their great wickedness was supposed to be the cause of the Deucalian Deluge. In all traditions, the giants are the most wicked portion of mankind, just as Moses makes them. In regard to the longevity of the primeval race of man, Hesiod says, of the silver age, it was much worse (*polu cheiroteron*) than the golden, and adds, the "growing child was nursed 100 years by his careful mother, very infantine in his home." He says, however, they frequently shortened their life by their follies and vices, &c. (T. Sacred His. v. ii. 234.) Cyclopean and Pelasgic structures, and those of Egypt, testify to herculean race. (Schl. 72.) And so do the traditions of the aborigines of America. (T. S. H. v. ii. 250.)

14. *Why is the subject of the general deluge of so much importance?* Because, being the greatest revolution since the formation of man, it must have left indelible marks upon the earth, and ineffaceable impression on the minds of the first inhabitants. Noah lived 350 years after the flood, his family much longer. He and his family must, therefore, have spread the interesting tale in that time to four quarters of the globe. Geology and tradition, then, must test the Noachian flood; and with this test the Mosaic account must stand or fall.

15. *Before geology was studied, how were the various irregular phenomena exhibited by the earth explained?* All derangements, marine deposits on continents, and in mountains, all misplaced organic remains, &c., were attributed to the deluge.

16. *May it not be possible for all those effects to have been produced by a deluge?* There are certain effects comparatively superficial and modern, which are attributed necessarily to some deluge—others more deep, and different, not effect of deluge, and much more ancient.

17. *Geological proofs of a deluge?* Effects are of disturbing rather than of shaping power; dislocations, removals, transports, scooping and furrowing. (W. 194.) 1st. Valleys of denudation, as on coast of Devon and Dorset, granitic prisms upon plains of Greiffenstein, in Saxony. 2d. *Bowlder stones* on sides and tops of mountains, *e. g.* Peaks of Otto in Virginia. 3d. Transportation of pebbles and rocks to distances, and in directions that ordinary action will not explain. *e. g.* Pebbles of Oxfordshire and London, (198,) rocks from Norway, in Yorkshire, (199.) Upon the lakes of our hemisphere are similar phenomena. All these bowlder stones too large for ordinary currents. *e. g.* Pierre á Martin, 10,296 cubic feet of granite; that at Neufchatel, 38,000 cwt.; Johannisstein, 24 feet in diameter, (201.) Again, remains of animals. *e. g.* Elephants and Rhinoceros, &c., of tropical climes, frozen up at north, or buried in diluvial gravel, and deposits. (Enc. M. 794.)

18. *Are there geological proofs of the oneness and generality of the deluge?* Inundation in whole northern hemisphere was from north to south. *e. g. Bowlders* of Durham and Yorkshire, from Cumberland, latter from Scotland, latter from Norway—pebbles of Thames, from Birmingham—erratic blocks of Poland and Germany, from Sweden and Norway. *Detritus* in North America, from same direction. Valleys

correspond with this direction. (210.) Partial inundations would not explain these phenomena.

19. *What are the proofs of a general flood from tradition?* Hesiod speaks of destruction of human race, without mentioning means. (T. S. H. ii. 234.) Ovid's description of Deucalian flood, taken from traditions of his day. Berosus in Chaldean annals gives account of deluge. Xisuthius king of Babylon, saved by warning of *Chronos.* The ark, the animals in pairs, the birds sent out, &c., all described. Similar tradition existed in Media and Assyria. In Egypt the Deucalian flood was believed in, this by Greeks was transferred to Greece. Egyptians made Deucalian an Egyptian, Greeks a Grecian. The Arundelian marbles have incribed this flood. Plutarch speaks of the dove as a tradition of his time. Curious Deucalion, son of Prometheus and grandson of Japetus according to Greeks—Japheth or Japet, son of Noah according to Moses. (T. S. H. 2 v. 243.) Pliny speaks of deluge as settled point, and of Joppa in Syria as older "*antiquior terrarum inundatione.*" Speaks, too, of the whale "*fabulosa ceta,*" as worshipped there. Here, too, a whale swallowed Andromeda. It is curious that Joppa is port whence Jonah embarked. Among the Persians, the Magi believed in a general deluge. Vanity of each nation fixed on one of its own mountains to rest the ark on, and some of its own people to be saved. China possesses traditions on the same subject, *e. g.* Confucius, 400 A. C., opens his history of China with country still under water. The Hindoos in Sanscrit commemorate same; it is a principal subject of a great poem Mahabharat, in which Manu a pious king is saved in vessel which rested on Himovan mountains. Eight persons were saved. The Koran preserves the same tradition. Magagines of Africa have same traditions, &c.

20. *Did the tribes of North and South America have any traditions on this subject?* Scarcely a single one without them! Mexicans had a tradition. Coxcox was their Noah, saved with his wife Xochiquatza on trunk of tree. The Chilians, Cholulans, and nations of Mechoacan, have traditions on same subject. The latter make Tespithin Noah. The incident of the bird is preserved, and, what is strange, eight persons were supposed to be saved. Humboldt says similar traditions among all the tribes of upper Oronoco about "*the great waters.*" The people of Cuba, of Kamtschatka, the Peruvians, the Brazilians, the Canadians, the Chippewayans, and even the South Sea Islands, &c., &c., all have similar traditions. So we say with Humboldt, all the nations of the earth possess these traditions, like the relics of a vast shipwreck. Besides all this testimony we have the Apamean medals representing ark, man and wife, dove, &c. (W. 290.)

CHAPTER II.

POSTDILUVIAN HISTORY.

1. *From whom was the earth replenished with people and animals?* From Noah and his family, and of animals saved by the ark. Noah lived 350 years after the deluge, and some of his immediate descendants to the fifth century.

2. *What is represented as the great cause of the dispersion of human race, and of variety of languages?* Building tower of Babel, and confusion of tongues.

3. *Object of tower of Babel?* Built by Nimrod the Cushite, who first aspired to be a great conqueror. End probably two-fold; made from principle of vanity, and for fortress, or for idolatrous purposes. Nimrod seems to have been the first to destroy the patriarchial system of government, prevalent after the deluge. His aim was probably universal empire.

4. *What are the two theories about origin of languages?* First, that it has arisen in a rude state among every people from necessity, and been gradually perfected. Second, that it was given to Adam and Eve, preserved by Noah, and finally separated into dialects at the confusion of Babel.

5. *What are the arguments for latter opinion independent of the Bible?* First, all the arguments going to prove the Mosaic deluge, prove the common origin of the present races of man. Second, all proofs in the various languages of the world of a derivation from common source establish the same.

6. *What are the principles of proof under second head?* It is said, if two languages formed perfectly distinct from each other, even chance that one word meaning the same thing should be common to the two, 3 to 1 against 2 words, 10 to 1 against 3, 1,700 to 1 against 6 and near 100,000 to 1 against 8. (W. 69.) Ergo, coincidence in words proves intercourse between nations, or a derivation of the languages from common parent, *e. g.* French and Latin words in English, *beef*, *mutton*, *pullet*, *liberty*, *necessity*, *proximity*, *expert*, *&c.* Again similarity in grammar may prove the same.

6. *What is the study which groups nations according to languages called?* Ethnography.

7. *How does the ethnographer proceed?* First, he reduces the

nations of the earth to certain great families as to language. *e. g.* Indo-European, Semitic, American families, &c. He then shows the common origin of the members of one family by similar words and grammar, then the common origin of different families by same process. *e. g.* Indo-European includes Latin, Greek, Persian, Sanscrit, Teutonic, Celtic, &c., &c. Coincidences in words striking. *e. g. Pader*, *Mader*, *Sunu*, *Dokhter*, *Brader*, *Maud*, all Sanscrit, or Persian, similar to our words. Persian has *beh*, *behter*, *bad*, *badder*, &c., evidently more regular than our positive and comparative. (33.) Again, similar coincidences among families. *e. g. Six*, in Sanscrit *shash*, in Persian *shesh*, in Latin *sex*, in Greek *ex*, in German *sechs*. It belongs thus to Indo-European family. In Semitic found likewise, *e. g. shesh* in Hebrew. Again, *seven*, in Sanscrit *saptan*, in old German *sibrin*. In Semitic, we have *shevang* Hebrew, and *Shebat* Arabic. (58.) The word *sack* in almost all families.

8. *How did Young endeavor to prove that the Egytians had once colonized Spain?* In the Biscayan or old Spanish, Humboldt found the words *beria* new, *ora* dog, *gachi* little, *oguia* bread, *otzoa* a wolf, and *shaspi* seven. In the old Egyptian *beri* is new, *whor* dog, *kredchi* little, *oik* bread, *ounch* wolf, and *shashf* seven. (60.) But this evidently might be the result of derivation from common language, as well as by intercourse among the nations.

9. *Have there been any coincidences discovered between the American family and others?* As far as researches have gone, about 170 coincidences have been discovered. In addition to which, there are very strong circumstances to prove the aborigines of America to be an off-shoot from Asiatic family of nations.

10. *What has been the result of these ethnographical studies?* That there was, probably, what Moses asserts, but one language at first, which, from the dispersion of our race, has broken into dialects, which have been converted into the actual living languages of the present day.

11. *What first nation to claim our attention after dispersion?* Jews.

12. *From whom sprang Abraham and the Jewish nation?* Shem.

13. *What the condition of the Abrahamic family when chosen as the people to transmit the true religion?* Pastoral. Singular that patriarchal hero of Moses should be so faithfully described according to Nomadic institutions. He is represented as migrating from place to place—stations marked with geographical accuracy; here pitches his tents by a tree, there by a fountain. He is nowise superior to his age or country in any thing except his religion. He is neither demigod or mighty conqueror. When he comes up from his visit to Egypt

he has "*sheep and oxen, and he asses, and men servants, and maid servants, and she asses and camels,*" a picture of wealth of pastoral chieftain. His point of honor not very high—twice made his wife pass for his sister lest his own life might be in danger. Again, had several wives according to custom of east; and the insolence of Hagar, and consequent ill treatment by Sarah, all perfectly natural.

14. Why does such a description as this prove the truth of Mosaic account? Because disposition generally to make founders of nations gods or demi-gods, and history is at first all fable. Not so here. Description is true to nature.

15. *What the character of succeeding patriarchs?* Isaac's life not eventful—happy and contented with Rebecca. Adventures of Jacob give a striking view of Nomadic habits; meets Rachael at the well—hospitality of Laban—works seven years for Rachael—cheated—works seven more—jealousies of the sisters on account of their barrenness—substitute handmaids—Laban and Jacob both striving to cheat each other—Jacob finally getting all the best of Laban's cattle—runs away from his father-in-law. (Mil. v. 1–29.)

16. *Describe state and progress of civilization under patriarchs?* Under Abraham peaceful pastoral Nomads—travel on camels, no horses—Abraham has no obstacle in settling wherever he got pasturage for his cattle—gives Lot choice of right or left—sinks wells wherever he goes—only burial place he gets a right to by purchase. Jacob has to buy land to pitch his tents on even. In Jacob's time caravan trade established. When Abraham receives celestial strangers, kills calf with his own hands, and offers nothing but *milk* to drink. Isaac had commenced agriculture—had meats, *wine*, &c. Moses' characters all characteristic. *e. g.* Isaac quiet and easy—Esau, hunter, bold, reckless, improvident—Jacob, herdsman, cautious, subtle and cowardly—Esau brave—Jacob crafty. Women not so jealous of husbands' affections as of each others fruitfulness. Great passion for having children.

17. *Points of interest in Jewish history?* Sale of Joseph into Egypt, and rise to power—descent of Jacob and his family to Egypt—settle in Goshen—became slaves—plagues of Egypt—exodus under Moses—delivery of the law from Mount Sinai—conquest of, and settlement in, Canaan, &c.

18. *When does the history of Israelites become most interesting afterwards?* With the reign of David, which exhibits a man from obscurity raised to the throne of Israel, fortifying his power by strong military force, extending his dominions and enriching himself and subjects by the spoils of his enemies. He established a monarchy which was tottering, and by civil and religious regulations, gave his people

prosperity and civilization. He built the city of Jerusalem, and made it the seat of his government.

19. *Who and what the character of his successor?* Solomon—mounted the throne at 20—fond of magnificence and show—built the Temple—laid heavy taxes on his people—which disposed the people to revolt under his son.

20. *What condition of his kingdom?* In height of prosperity. Extent from Egypt to foot of Lebanon, and from Euphrates to the sea—held balance between Assyria and Egypt. Its trade was great. He built Tadmor and Baalath, now Palmyra and Balbec, for caravan stations. "*Silver was in Jerusalem as stones, and cedar trees as sycamores?*

21. *What the subsequent history of Israel?* Under Rehoboham, son of Solomon, ten tribes revolted and elected Jeroboam king. The history of ten tribes full of wars, massacres and revolutions. But two tribes of Judah remained firm to the house of David. *Excision* of ten tribes by Shalmanesar, the king of Assyria, (719 B. C.) Jerusalem was first taken (601 B. C.) and destroyed by Nebuchadnezzar, (587 B. C.) Period of servitude was 70 years—restored by Cyrus the great. (Mil. 1, v. 221.) Daniel, Shadrach, Meshack, and Abednego, were carried to Babylon after the first conquest, (601 B. C.) at which period captivity began.

22. *Give some account of the government and changes which it underwent until the exodus.* Government was patriarchal. Abraham, Isaac, and Jacob were the chiefs of these tribes. This government always prevails among Nomads. The wealth of these emirs of Nomads very great, *e. g.* Abraham armed on one occasion 318 house-born servants. Fourth part only can bear arms, hence he had 1272 male, and perhaps as many female slaves. But although as individuals rich, yet as kings or chiefs not to compare with leaders of Nomads on great central table land of Asia. No great nation in or about Palestine, *e. g.* Chedarlaomer, first to attempt military expedition, was defeated with three other kings by Abraham with three hundred and eighteen of his servants. Single encampment a kingdom—five kings in vale of Sodom. Joshua defeated thirty-one kings—Adonizebec boasted of defeating three score and ten. Jacob had four wives, and by them twelve sons. Judah, Zebulon, Issachar, Joseph, Benjamin, Reuben, Levi, Simeon, Gad, Dan, Asher, and Naphtali. Hence 12 tribes of Israel. *Isaac* means one *who prevails with God*—name given to Jacob after having wrestled with him. Jacob adopted two sons of Joseph, Ephraim and Manasseh, in Joseph's place, which made 13. Then one tribe, that of Levi, was devoted to religion, leaving still 12 political tribes. This

government prevailed in Goshen up to period of Exodus, where country was favorable to Nomads. Then came the law from Mount Sinai. God became the king of Israel, every thing done to establish religion, (John H. C. 31.) Tabernacle made for his residence. Defection from religion high treason, (35.) Hence complete separation from all nations, *e. g.* Cicero condemns Jews, (37.) Moses was but a mediator between God and his people ; proper title *legislator of the Israelites and their deliverer from the Egyptians.* (J. Arch. section 220.) Hence no proper successor. Joshua was military leader for conquest of Canaan and had no successor. The Elders were heads of tribes, 6 from each made 72. Priests were at head of religious ceremonies. Before Moses, heads of tribes were priests, *e. g.* Cain and Abel, Noah, Abraham and Job, Abimelech and Laban, Isaac and Jacob, sacrificed personally, (Calmet.) Afterwards family of Levi was chosen for the services of religion, and priesthood was annexed to the family of Aaron. Kings no longer officiated, *e. g.* Uzziah, king of Judah, punished, (2 Chron. 26, 19.) Levites provided for by tithes from all other tribes, and they in turn paid tithes to the priests. For administration of justice Moses divided people in tens, fifties, hundreds, thousands, and placed judges over each. Mode taken from Egypt. Amongst the higher of these judges there was much political power likewise. The judges were rulers from Joshua to Saul, and some of them as Jair, Ibzan, Elan, Abdon, Eli, and Samuel, had almost kingly power. People desired a king under Samuel, and Saul was appointed. The assemblies of two kinds : 1st. Select, composed of princes of tribes, heads of thousands, &c. 2d. Assembly of the congregation—all the judges, and many of the people admitted, (J. H. C. 56.) To these assemblies Moses added himself when he delivered the law.

23. *What was the political relation existing between the tribes?* Each tribe had a sort of independent government, with its own magistrates and representatives ; sometimes acted without aid or sanction of others, *e. g.* tribe of Benjamin protected criminals of Gibeah and fought against others—tribe of Judah *alone* chose David king. Sometimes several tribes acted together without others, *e. g.* Judah and Simeon in war against Canaanites—Ephraim and Manasseh on same occasion—tribes of Zebulon and Naphtali with Barak to oppose army of Jabin—Manasseh, Asher, Zebulon, and Naphtali, chose Gideon leader against Midianites. The tribes east of Jordan chose Jephtha against Ammonites, &c. (H. C. 53.)

24. *What were the circumstances calculated to bind them together?* Necessity of union against common enemies. They came from a common ancestor, *Abraham*—divine promises—common religion—common

God and king—sacred tabernacle, and afterwards the temple, common oracle, urim and thummim—common high priest—common learned class, *Levites*—common law of church and state, and common general assemblies and festivals, *e. g.*—Day of Pentecost—feast of tabernacles, &c. (54.)

25. *What the influence of such a government?* Exceedingly favorable to development of character and individual energies. Not favorable for harmony or tranquillity.

26. *Civilization of Israelites.* Not superior to their neighbors except in religion. Character entirely Nomadic at first, then mixed. Uniform simplicity—every one either shepherd or husbandman, *e. g.* Gideon taken from threshing floor to deliver his country. Saul was tending his flocks when made king. David was brought up in sheepfold. *Ruth* beautiful expose of condition of people in those days.

27. *Amusements on festival occasions.* Music and dancing. They had stringed instruments, wind instruments, drums, cymbals, &c., and vocal music. We have canticles of joy, of thanksgiving, of praise, of mourning, *e. g.* Song of Songs, Psalm 45, Song of David on death of Saul and Abner, Lamentations of Jeremiah, &c. There were 24 bands of music for the temple. Kings had their own music, *e. g.* Asaph was master of music to David. Kings were sometimes musicians, *e. g.* David exquisite on the harp—drove off vapors of Saul by his music, and charmed Saul's messengers who came to take him, (Calmet.) Dancing was an essential part of the festal solemnities, and of the sacred worship, *e. g.* After passage of Red Sea, damsels of Israel, with Miriam at their head, playing on tabret, sang and danced. David danced at induction of ark into the tabernacle, and reproached by Michel *not for dancing*, but for mixing with the people, (2 Sam. 6, 16, 23.) At the feast of Shiloh, the damsels danced. Indeed in Psalms 149, 4, and 150, 4, the dance is ordered. Moses speaks of people at banquets as *rejoicing before Jevovah;* and in days of Solomon people are spoken of, by way of compliment, as numerous as the sands of the sea, "*eating, drinking, and making merry.*" (J. Arch. sec. 97.) (F. Lib. v. 25, 22.) Some commentators suppose every psalm had an appropriate dance. The dance was in Israel what Cicero says of it in his day, *Multarum deliciarum comes saltatio.*

28. *Literary character of the Israelites?* Purely national, but of high order. Three most distinguished persons, Moses, David, and Solomon, three splendid poets and writers. Sacred poetry of other nations contemptible when compared. Finest specimens of the beautiful and the sublime are found in the Bible. Isaiah sublime in the extreme. Koran, Zendevesta, Vedas, and all other religious codes, sink into in-

significance by the side of the Old Testament. The sublimity of the prophets a proof of inspiration.

29. *Arts, manufactures, and commerce?* Arts considerably advanced but not equal to Egyptians. Each one made his own instruments for tillage. Women spun, wove, embroidered, and made clothes for their families, and for sale. Chariots were built, stones hewed, instruments made of gold, silver, and brass, and there were vessels of clay, &c. In time of David and Solomon, there were good carpenters and masons, though not equal to Tyrians. Seals, rings, pendants, necklaces, bracelets, amulets, mirrors of brass, &c., all spoken of at early period, (Arch 144.) At later date artificers in high repute, *e. g.* Joseph a carpenter, Simon a tanner in Joppa, Alexander, learned Jew, a copper-smith, Paul and Aquila were tent makers, &c. (89.) In time of patriarchs, commerce was by caravans. In days of David and Solomon both by caravans and sea. Tyrians in those days were carriers of the world.

CHAPTER III.

MONUMENTAL HISTORY.

1. *What is the principal source from which the history of the earliest periods of Egypt, and of most of the great Asiatic nations, is derived?* Monuments.

2. *Objects of raising monuments?* Raised by kings and nations through a principle of mere vanity, or to commemorate great events, or to serve useful purposes. Hence, monuments of all descriptions from a pile of stones, to the temple, pyramid, canal, &c. *e. g.* Pillar of Jacob at Hebron—heap of stones, mark of reconciliation with Laban. (P. 1. 75.)

3. *How are monuments historical?* First, they indicate state of the arts and civilization. (H. Af. v. 2. 8.) *e. g.* Pantheon, sewers, wall of China, Apollo Belvidere, pyramid, &c. Second, excites inquiry—a history, a tradition or *mythus* attached to them, *e. g.* Botetourt, old magazine here—column of Trajan, of Vendome, temple of Fortuna, Mulubris origin of tale of Coriolanus, house of Loretto, Coliseum, &c. When covered with inscriptions much more instructive. *e. g.* Arundelian and Capitoline marbles, (p. L. 80.) obelisks of Egypt, &c.

4. *Character of a monumental history?* 1st, Fragmentary. 2d, Too many things ascribed to founders. *e. g.* Tarquinius Priscus, builder of pyramids, &c. 3d, Not chronological unless full of dates. 4th, Mar-

vellous, especially if monuments are large and extraordinary—tales of superstition or vanity link with them.

5. *May not names have historic importance?* Yes. *e. g.* All the names of persons and places in Old Testament of historic importance—name of this state, name of this place, college, Pittsburg, *Le Champ du Mensonge*, when Gregory treated with Louis feeble.

6. *Historic importance of national customs and ceremonies?* *e. g.* Paschal supper among Jews, Lord's supper among Christians, annual ship sent by Athenians to Delos, the ceremony of wedding Adriatic sea at Venice, celebration of 22d February and 4th July in United States, Anaximander's petition to magistrates of Lampsacum that boys might play on anniversary of his death. (P. L. 77.) All have a tendency to perpetuate history of events.

7. *Historical importance of coins and medals?* Portable monuments—generally have date—some king or emblem—you learn state of arts. *e. g.* Hercules Farnese, Venus de Medicis, Apollo, and Marcus Aurelius, all have been found on coins. (85.) You find out too customs in dress, &c., and often character of princes. *e. g.* Nero has his fiddle, Commodus lion skin. Medals have been struck expressly to commemorate events. *e. g.* All events of reign of Louis XIV. on medals—whole history of Balbec and Palmyra gathered from medals. (82.)

8. *Why are the Egyptian monuments so interesting?* Because they are numerous, large, and often covered with hieroglyphics, which enable us to guess at their history.

9. *How many kinds of hieroglyphics?* Three. Figurative, symbolic or ideographic, and phonetic.

10. *Figurative?* 1st, Imitates object completely. *e. g.* Sun, moon, &c. 2d, Abridged imitation. *e. g.* Ground plot of a house for the house. 3d, Imitation conventional. *e. g.* Firmament by section of blue ceiling with or without stars.

11. *Symbolical or ideographic?* Must go to rhetoric for the idea—expression of abstract ideas by physical objects. *e. g.* By *synecdoche*—two arms lifted up was *an offering*—perfuming pan and grains of incense, *adoration.* By *metonomy*—crescent of moon for *month*—writing materials for *writing.* By *metaphor*—bee for *an obedient people.* Four legs of lion for *strength;* asp for *power of life or death.* (Greppo, 42.) The symbolical were the *only true* hieroglyphics according to ancients.

12. *Phonetic?* Hieroglyphics for letters corresponding to our alphabet.

13. *In what did great discovery of Young and Champollion consist?* In proving the existence of this class, and furnishing key by which it might be read.

14. *In what manner were they led to this discovery?* Upon general principles, they supposed that the Egyptians must have had an alphabet. Fact first proved by *trilingual* monument dug up by the French troops at Rosetta, in Egypt, containing a decree in honor of Ptolemy Epiphanes, *in Greek* on one side, *in hieroglyphics* on the other, and *enchorial* on the third. Supposed the same decree on each side, but in different languages—Greek translated the other two. Supposed further, that the hieroglyphics encompassed in an elliptical *bas-relief*, called *cartouche*, must be the name of the king, *Ptolmes.* In same manner on another monument the name of Cleopatra was deciphered. The correspondence of five letters common to the two names proved the truth of the conjecture. (G. 15, 21 and 196.) In this way the names of numerous kings were quickly deciphered, and great light was shed over the Egyptian history.

15. *Are these different kinds of hieroglyphics found entirely distinct, or are they all seen on same monument?* The latter. The Phonetic constituted about two-thirds of all found on the monuments.

16. *What the principle on which the Egyptians chose signs for their letters?* That hieroglyphic of any object might be used to signify initial letter in the name of the object; *e. g.* picture of eagle stood for A, because *ahour* is Egyptian for eagle; a mouth stood for R, because *ro* is Egyptian for mouth.

17. *How, on this principle, could the signs be prevented from indefinite increase?* Merely by arbitrary limitation. No letter has more than eight or ten signs for it. But all that were selected were chosen on the principle stated.

CHAPTER IV.

EGYPT.

1. *Why is the history of Egypt so interesting?* Because it lays claim to antiquity surpassing that of any nation we know of—because it has been rendered famous by its connection with the Israelites—because it is the land of grand and interesting monuments—the mother of the ancient civilization, &c., &c.

2. *Who supposed to be the founder?* Ham, son of Noah, and was anciently called Misraim, after son of Ham.

3. *Situation and boundaries?* In Africa, stretching along the Nile

—about 600 miles in length—varying in breadth from 30 to 300; bounded on south by kingdom of Sennaar and cataracts of the Nile; north by Mediterranean sea; east by Red sea; on west by Marmorica. Egypt almost as small as England.

4. *Divisions of Egypt?* Three—upper, middle, and lower. Thebais from city Thebes, Heptanomis, or seven nomes, and the Deltas. Of these parts, the upper first civilized, then middle, &c.

5. *Character of government?* Three estates—king, priests, and soldiers. The priests controlled the king to great extent, *e. g.* Diodorus says early in morning king attended to state affairs—then sacrifices and prayers—then priest rehearsed his praises and reminded him of his duties, and read to him from lives of the great kings. Amusements, meats, drinks, &c. were all prescribed. [H. A. v. 2, 155.]

6. *How was Egypt divided for political purposes?* Into nomes.

7. *Origin of nomes?* Most probably a division first made for religious purposes. Each one had its own temple, and was under its own governor, and worshipped often gods *of its own*, not only distinct from, but frequently hostile to those of its neighbors.

8. *Was the government of Egypt always a consolidated despotism?* Egypt at first seems to have been divided into tribes, and afterwards into nomes—each having government of its own. This government was probably consolidated by the expulsion of the Hyksos or Shepherd kings, and partly by the policy of Joseph during the years of famine—when the king became a sort of feudal proprietor of all the lands. But the priests never lost *their* power.

9. *Would not Egypt have been greater with a more consolidated government?* Great consolidated empires unfavorable to individual energy and greatness; they are without a history, *e. g.* history of India or Hindostan in the east most interesting, because government less consolidated than that of China, and the other great eastern despotisms.

10. *Division of lands in Egypt?* Principal portion belonged to the three ruling castes—kings, priests, and soldiers.

11. *What the law in regard to trades, occupations, &c.?* All hereditary; son followed business of father. These castes originated in all probability from tribes, each one preserving its peculiar occupations, customs, &c.

12. *What degree of consanguinity allowed of in marriage?* Even brothers and sisters. Causes—1st, Isis and Osiris married; 2d, Brothers and sisters kept separate from each other.

13. *Religion?* Divided into two branches—*Esoteric* and *Exoteric*—*mystical* and the *popular*. Former, religion of the priests, not known to the people.

14. *Egyptian mythology?* *Mind* and *matter* co-eternal—latter originally chaos, by action of former generated all forms. This supreme mind, called Demiurgos or Ammon. Theory of Orpheus that the world was hatched from an immense *egg* by fiery nature of spirit, taken from this. Ammon, under a modification, represented the male spirit of the universe, called Nef or Nour—the good genius—vivifying principle, *vis vivica*, described so well by Virgil:

> "Spiritus intus aliit, totamque infusa per artus,
> "Mens agitat nolem, et toto se corpore miscet."

Female principle, goddess Neith, another emanation from Demiurgos, presided over moral attributes—wisdom, philosophy, and military tactics attributed to her—prototype of Minerva, both created from supreme god. Her chief temple at Sais. Inscription on her temple, "I am all that has been, all that is, and all that will be." Priests of Sais regarded her as *mens eterna ac opifex.* In Vedas, Vishnou is spoken of in similar strain, "All which has been, all which is, and all which will be, are in Vishnou." Like God in scripture, "Which was, and is, and is to come." "The same yesterday, to-day, and forever," &c. The god Phtha—architect of the world—the *Hephaistos* of Greeks, and *Vulcan* of Latins. Besides these, the *Sun* and *Moon* were worshipped—*Sun* was made son of *Phtha*, and succeeded to him on throne of Egypt; hence titles of Pharaohs, "offspring of the Sun—son of the Sun," &c. [Grep. 230.] *Sate*, daughter of Sun, answers to *Hera* of Greeks, and *Juno* of Latins—protectress of Egyptian monarchs, especially of the 18th dynasty. *Sme*, goddess of justice, answers to *Themis.* Gods of second rank—*Osiris and Isis*—*Sol inferus* and *Luna infera*—like *Diana* and *Hecate* among Latins. Osiris answers to *Pluto*, Isis to *Proserpine* and *Ceres* both. [233] *Amenti* of Egypt is *Hades* of Greeks, and *Tartarus* of Latins—governed by Osiris as chief, with many inferior divinities. Whole world divided into three zones. 1st, *Earth*, or zone of trial; 2d, *zone of air*, agitated by winds and storms, zone of temporal punishment; 3d, above these two, zone of rest; these three subdivided into thirty-two. God *Pooh* presided over second zone, where bad spirits were tormented, till they came either to earth, to animate a new body (according to doctrine of transmigration of souls), or passed to third zone, into pure ether of rest.

15. *Origin of Grecian notions about Acheron, Charon, Cerberus, &c.?* For city of Memphis is common place of burial beyond the lake *Acherjsia* or *Acharejish*, meaning *last state or condition of man.* On border of this lake sat a tribunal of forty-two judges, who decided whether deceased should be buried beyond the lake; virtuous entitled

o burial, vicious thrown into a large ditch called *Tartar*, meaning *lamentation*. The good carried over in a boat, for which a stated sum was paid. *Cemetery* was large plain, surrounded by trees intersected by canals, called *elisant* or *elisiœns*, meaning *rest*. Hence lake *Acheron*, *Tartarus*, *Charon*, and the *elysian fields* of the Greeks. Again, after interment, three cries or farewells were uttered by the attendants. On *tomb*, *horse of the Nile* was engraved, or placed on the *mummy*. Greeks mistook this for a *dog*, and connecting it with three farewell shouts, represented a triple-headed dog called *Cerberus*, from Egyptian *ceriber*, meaning *cry of the tomb*. (235.)

16. *Second branch of Egyptian religion?* Animal worship. Cats, rats, wolf, lion, crocodile, ichneumon, ox, goat, &c., all worshipped. *e. g.* *bull* at Memphis and Heliopolis—*goat* at Mendes, *lion* at Leantopolis, &c. Animals worshipped kept in consecrated inclosures, attended by higher classes, and buried with royal pomp. *e. g.* Apis at Memphis, whose burial cost 50 talents, or £13,000. Fire terrific, says Herodotus, because of the danger to cats, and not to children. Cry, save the cats. Roman ambassador who killed a cat.

17. *Puzzle of Hume?* What kept these cats from multiplying to an alarming extent, with such kind treatment? Thinks the kittens were not gods, and therefore destroyed before deified.

18. *Causes for this worship?* 1st, Gods pressed in battle had taken refuge in these animals, hence veneration for them 2d, They had been painted on standards, and success deified them. 3d, Because of great use, *e. g.* sheep, cow, goat, &c. We acquire love for animals in certain situations. *e. g.* Tartar for his horse, and the Arab for his camel. 4th, These animals had properties sometimes emblematical of divinity; *e. g.* keen sight of the hawk, of omniscience. 5th, Transmigration of souls made them reverence animals that might have souls of men in them. 6th, Hieroglyphics—by using figures of animals to denote certain properties might produce this worship.

19. *Learning of Egyptians?* Surpassed rest of the world in early times. *e. g.* Moses was said to possess the wisdom of Egyptians, and Solomon *hyperbolically* spoken of as possessing more than the boasted wisdom of Egypt. Geometry was first studied in this country. Annual inundation produced annual processioning. Derivation of the term—*ge*, *terra*, and *metron*, *mensura*. Anecdote of Thales, and the discovery of the mode of inscribing right angled triangle in a circle—of Pythagoras and the 47th Euclid; former sacrificed an ox, the latter one hundred; the latter doubted, because Pythagoras believed in transmigration of souls. In medicine, profession divided physician for each great division of human system. Theory about the duration of human life—astrology

deeply studied. The horoscope of each individual was cast at birth, and this superstition threw great power into hands of priests. (H. A. 157.)

20. *Why was Egypt never very warlike?* Because almost cut off from world by sea and desert, she was left to her own resources for aggrandizement. Sesostris was her most warlike monarch. Hieroglyphics have proved his existence and mighty power.

21. *What did her wealth and civilization depend on?* Upon the development of her internal resources.

22. *Physical character of Egypt?* Soil finest in world—the gift of the Nile. Nile commences rising about summer solstice, and continues till about autumnal equinox; caused by periodical rains in the mountains of Ethiopia; a rich slime is deposited, which renews every year the powers of the soil. Water is spread over the country by canals, and if the inundation does not reach a certain height, a famine or scarcity is sure to ensue; for in Egypt it rarely rains, hence perfect preservation of monuments and paintings.

23. *Different appearances of Egypt in July, August, &c., when under water, and in January, February, &c., when covered with vegetation?* (H. A. 61.)

24. *How is Egypt protected against the great desert on the west?* By the Libyan chain of mountains, a stony ridge covered with sand. On the west it sinks down into the great desert; on the east into the fertile valley of the Nile; guards Egypt against invasions of sands—you have here the region of fertility bordering on the *waste.* Again, in valley you have the habitations of the living; at foot of Libyan chain, and in the sides of mountains, you have countless graves and sepulchres—you have *empire of life* bordering on *empire of death.* This circumstance powerfully influenced the character of the nation. (H. 65.)

25. *Character of the country on the eastern side of the Nile from the valley to the Arabian Gulf?* Totally different from western side—stony mountainous tract—unfit for agriculture—good for pasturage—possesses marble of every variety of color, granite, porphyry, &c. From this district came the materials for all the splendid monuments of Egypt. (H. 66.)

26. *Monuments of Egypt?* Valley of Nile, in whole course through Upper and Middle Egypt, was covered with succession of cities and monuments; those of Upper Egypt (Thebais) most magnificent. Pyramids belong to Middle Egypt. As you ascend the Nile, *Tentyris*, now *Dendera*, on west side, is first city in Upper Egypt to strike beholder with its gigantic and massive architecture, so different from any thing on globe. Here is the temple with the famous Zodiac. Twenty miles higher up, come to great city of Ammon—mighty Thebes—whole width

of valley, nine miles from east to west, both sides of stream, is covered with the most magnificent ruins; and where the habitations for the living cease, commence those of the dead, extending into western mountains. Temples towering like mountains, surrounded by scattered colossi, sphinxes, and obelisks. The great temple of Jupiter Ammon yet exists at Carnac—stately palaces of Pharaohs stand at Luxor and Medinet Abou; colossus of Memnon, wonder of the ancient world;* other temples and colossi, and royal sepulchres, with paintings fresh as yesterday, all remain. Ascending the Nile, link after link of this chain of monuments follows in rapid succession. Just beyond the bounds of Thebes, ruins of Hermanthis present themselves—then beautiful temple of *Esneh*, ancient Latopolis—then *Edfu*, the ancient *Apollinopolis Magna*, with the most magnificent temple, except that of Thebes; then come monuments of Eliethyca, Silsilis, and Ombos. Twenty-five miles farther we come to limits of ancient Egypt, and here are the most splendid monuments. At *Philæ* they show the tomb of Osiris—on the isle of *Elephantis*, Greeks, Romans, and Arabs, erected monuments here which are now scattered in the dust; but those of old Egypt, thousand years older than the oldest, defy destruction! (70.) No wonder that travellers have supposed sometimes that a race of giants must have built these great monuments. The lake Mœris, 400 miles in circumference, was to great extent artificial, intended to receive waters of the Nile for the dry season. Near this was the Labyrinth, of which Herodotus said, "all the buildings of the Greeks together could not have cost so much." This Labyrinth had 12 palaces, 3,000 chambers, and ways and passages innumerable! On these monuments, especially of Upper Egypt, we see much that became the model to the Israelite. The tabernacle, the temple, the sacred utensils of the Jews, had all their *prototypes* in this monumental land. The *ark of the covenant*, the *cherubim* with their extended wings, the holy candlesticks, the show bread, and many parts of the Jewish sacrifices, all appear in the engravings of Thebes. Architecture of Jews was that of Egyptians on a small scale; they had more wood, because Egypt had no Lebanon with cedars. (H. A. 297.) (77.) But most enduring monuments are Pyramids, found only in Middle Egypt, generally built on square or triangular bases, well fitted to resist effects of time and flood. Largest is that of Cheops, height 481 feet (height of St. Paul's steeple), square base, each side 693 feet; surface covered 480,259 square feet, or about 11 acres! Casts no shade at mid-day.

* It was 29 feet to knee from bottom of the foot; to the instep 4 feet, and thence to ankle 2 feet 6 inches; the foot 5 feet broad, and the leg 4 feet deep.

This Pyramid has been variously estimated, because of the collection of sand about the base, *e. g.*

	Feet.			Feet.
Herodotus,	height 800	-	length of side	800
Strabo,	do. 625	-	do. do.	600
Pliny,	do. ——	-	do. do.	708
French Savans,	do. 440 470 (Eng.)		do. do.	704

It was covered over with upwards of 200 steps of marble, receding until you arrived at top, about 13 feet square. These pyramids have all one side *due north*, and others of course fronting cardinal points. Some distance up on north side, there is a small opening, often concealed by marble fitting it, which leads down by a slope, of little more than 26 degrees with the horizon, to a great distance. In the interior always a well at great depth—a small chamber with sarcophagus sometimes containing bones belonging to bovine species, probably of *sacred bulls.*—Great Sphinx, near Memphis, now buried in sand, another prodigy: head and breast, woman, body and tail, lion, in *cumbent* posture, huge paws stretched 50 feet before the body, length of body 130 feet, 63 feet high, breast 33 feet wide! [R. E. 116.] The object of these sphinxes is conjectured to be a representation of Divinity, which must combine the male and female nature, for purposes of creation. (122.)

27. *Object of the Pyramids?* Some say for granaries. Aristotle says they were the works of tyrants—Pliny thinks built for ostentation, and to divert public mind; all refer them to shepherd kings. True cause, for purposes of religion, for burial, and perhaps for astronomical purposes. The sloping way descending at angle of 26 just suits for observation on north star when it passes the meridian below the pole. Their belief that the soul would again unite with the body after 3000 years, made them wish to preserve body; hence art of embalming, and great care in burying; hence dread of the sea; hence splendid sepulchral monuments.

28. *Origin of Egyptian style of Architecture?* 1st, Climate hot—sun vertical—stone and marble plenty—people superstitious—hence porticoes, colonnades, and temples of most massive character, totally different from any graceful architecture of Persepolis, where there was no necessity to guard against excessive heat. 2d, Architecture of *Troglodytes* in a measure suggested this—introduced from Ethiopia. [H. A. 280.] Describes cave of Egypt.

29. *Character of sculpture and painting?* First, grand without grace—latter remarkable for freshness of colors after thousands of years.

30. *What race probably inhabited Egypt when centre of the*

world's civilization? Herodotus says a black race with woolly hair. (H. A. 85.)

31. *Are we to conclude they were negroes?* No, his expression may be interpreted *dark brown* with *curly hair.* Ammianus Marcellinus says, *plerique subfusculi sunt et atrati*—color of present *Copts.*

32. *May not this question be decided by monuments?* Yes, *e. g.* historical *bas-reliefs* on temple of Thebes. Figure of king several times—*always same*—nothing of negro—more than 100 attendants, nothing still—seem to have rather Grecian profile. Representations on obelisks, heads of sphinxes, and deities, have nothing of the negro. Painting in sepulchres, fresh as yesterday, prove that the ruling caste was not negro, *e. g.* in sepulchres at Eluthias, men are red, women yellow, hair of both black and curled, not *woolly!* Again, in royal sepulchre at Thebes, explored by Belzoni, there are decapitated persons, all Negroes; those destroying them, red. In this sepulchre we have white, red, and black, most accurately drawn. Two contracts exist, one at Paris, fac-simile of the other at Berlin—in latter Parmenthes, seller, called of *darkish brown* color, and buyer, *honey colored* or yellowish; same color of buyer, Osarreres, in Parisian. Nose and face described, but *no negro features.*

33. *Conclusion?* That different races in Egypt, and that one approaching to white was the ruling race, while negroes were always subjects and slaves.

CHAPTER V.

ASIA.

SECTION I.

1. *General description of Asia?* It stretches from the Frozen Ocean through the temperate zone almost to the equator. Europe stops in Mediterranean—Asia four times as large as Europe—its productions more varied and superior to those of Europe—land more fertile—more incommoded by deserts than Europe. *e. g.* Arabia and Cobi; not so much as Africa.

2. *Describe the two mountain ranges which form the grand divisions of Asia?* They are the Atltaic and the Tauric. 1st. From west to east, beginning just above the Caspian sea—sends off branch to north under name of Ural mountains, stretches to the Arctic

Ocean. The main chain, with mean elevation of 6 or 7000 feet, crosses southern Siberia—widening as it goes east, fills the territory of the Tungusians, and the shores of Siberia, losing itself on the shores of the Pacific. 2d, Tauric range rises in Asia Minor, passes through Armenia, thence through the countries south of the Caspian, through Media and districts of Hyrcania, Parthia and Bactriana, till it reaches east of Great Bucharia, or ancient Sogdiana; here it divides into two, one going south-easterly, the other north-easterly, forming an inclosure of great *sea of sand*, called by Herodotus Sandy Desert (modern Cobi); northern branch unites with Altaic range on confines of Siberia—southern passes north of Hindostan through Great and Little Thibet, losing itself in central China near Pacific. This, the branch called Himalaya, rising to enormous height of 25,000 feet; higher than Chimborazo of the Cordilleras of South America.

3. *Rivers?* They flow from these two chains of mountains; *e. g.* Irtish, Yenesei and Lena, three of largest rivers in old world, rise in Altaic range, and empty their waters in Arctic ocean, through north of Siberia. Four great rivers of southern Asia rise Tauric range, and empty into Persian and Indian oceans—Euphrates, Tigris, Indus, and the Ganges. Out of the same range rise the Oxus and Iaxartes, flowing into the sea of Aral. On the eastern side rise the great rivers of China, Hoangho and Keangkhu, flowing into eastern ocean.

4. *Grand divisions made by the two chains of mountains?* 1st, Northern or hyperborean regions beyond the Altaic range to Frozen ocean; intense cold—thin, hunting population, little known to history. 2d division includes vast regions of Central Asia lying between Altaic and Tauric ranges; vast tracts of level *steppes*, under names of Mongolia and Tartary, stretching from Caspian across Asia to Pacific. This great table land of Asia, lying between 40 and 50 degrees north latitude, colder than similar latitudes in Europe.

5. *Physical character of this region?* Whole region a sort of prairie—very few trees—too far from market for agriculture—generally fertile—covered with a luxuriant growth of herbage, equal to height of cattle which feed on it.

6. *Third great division of Asia?* Third or southern division, partly filled up by ramifications of Mount Taurus, partly to south of this range—extends in shape of a continent to tropic of Cancer; beyond which three great peninsulas Arabia, Hindostan, and Malacca, reach far into torrid zone; comprises the richest and most fertile regions of globe—temperate climate—large rivers—grandest and choicest pro-

ductions of earth—animals of all kinds—fruits, cotton, silk, sugar, tea, coffee, rice, wheat, spices, aromatics, gold, silver, precious stones and pearls.

7. *Character of the people on great central plains of Asia?* Nomads, with tents and encampments, instead of cities and houses. Wealth in sheep, cattle, horses, and camels. Milk and flesh constitute their diet—skins, fleece, and hair constitute their clothing. Constantly in motion—always on horseback.

8. *Character of the people of third division?* With few exceptions, agricultural. Includes the most populous and *stationary* empires on the face of the globe. These were earliest *magazines* of wealth and civilization.

9. *Military character of second division?* Life of nomads fits them for war; always in open air—untiring horsemen—wants limited—baggage light—move from region to region with all their flocks and families. They have been the scourge and renovating power of the nations of the earth. Their history uniform; true descendants of Ishmael—eternal depredators on civilized nations. Most all the conquests in ancient times, except Macedonian and Roman, came from that quarter.

10. *Governments which they formed?* Patriarchal and military—sometimes *immense; e. g.* Saracen kingdom extended from Morocco and Spain to Hindostan; and successors of Genghis-Khan had armies at same time in Silesia and under wall of China. Government partakes of nature of a military encampment.

11. *Commerce of Asia?* Of two kinds; by water and land—the latter principally by caravans.

12. *Nature and cause of the caravan trade?* Vast extent of Asiatic continent—predatory habits of nomads—want of navigable rivers, and of timber for boats on table-land—number and extent of deserts—all make large associations necessary for commerce. These associations are caravans; large military escort—camels principal beasts of burden—have stations of rest called caravansaries—have great routes—cities built and kingdoms enriched by their trade; *e. g.* Babylon, Persepolis, Palmyra, Balbec, and parts of Egypt, &c. (H. Asia, 22.)

13. *Commodities carried by caravans?* Not bulky—such as 1st, Precious commodities, *e. g.* gold, silver, precious stones and pearls. 2d, Articles of clothing, *e. g.* wool, cotton, silk, and furs. 3d, Spices and aromatics. (40.)

14. *What nations best situated for commerce?* Those that could enjoy both land and sea; *e. g.* Phœnicia, Tyre, Carthage, and Asia Minor, formed the two *termini* of the caravan and sea trade. (39.)

SEC. II.—BABYLON.

1. *Where was this kingdom, and whence the name?* In Asia, between Euphrates and Tigris, and derives its name from tower of Babel.

2. *Climate?* Very warm—rains rarely—requisite moisture supplied by overflowing of the Euphrates, caused by melting of snow and ice in the mountains of Armenia.

3. *How is the country irrigated?* By help of canals and lakes, by which the whole plain is filled. This, one cause of persevering energy of Babylonians. (143.) These canals so broad as to impede invasion of nomads. Xenophon with 10,000 men could only cross them on bridges. (133.)

4. *Soil?* Herodotus said it was one of the most fruitful countries on the globe, especially in corn. (140.) But like steppes generally, no wood, nor stone, or marble.

5. *Who founder?* Nimrod who seems to be the first to aspire to empire, and to break up patriarchal government. After this Babylon vanishes, and Assyrian monarchy appears, until finally overthrown by Babylonians.

6. *Period of Babylonish history most interesting?* Brilliant epoch during latter part of 7th century, 630 B. C., 70 years before the rise of Persian monarchy.

7. *Origin of Babylonio-Chaldean empire?* The Chaldeans a nomad people from mountains of Taurus and Caucasus, overwhelmed southern Asia, conquered the Syrian and Babylonian plains—made Babylon the seat of empire. With these Chaldeans, Nebuchadnezzar conquered Assyria, overthrew Pharaoh Necho, king of Egypt, at Cercesium on Euphrates—destroyed Jerusalem, carried the Jews in captivity to Babylon, besieged Tyre, and established the greatest empire in the world. These things occurred in the reigns of Jehoiakim and Zedekiah in Jerusalem, and were foretold by the prophets Jeremiah and Ezekiel. Jeremiah favored by Nebuchadnezzar.

8. *Dream of Nebuchadnezzar and interpretation by Daniel?* Epitome of great empires. See Daniel, ch. 2.

9. *Government?* Such as nomads form when they become stationary—despotic. Kings never associated familiarly with subjects—showed themselves but seldom, and then surrounded by pomp and magnificence.

10. *Does not the splendor of Babylon seem incompatible with the condition of the people supposed to have built it?* It is a peculiarity of Asiatic despotisms, that they concentrate power and magnificence

on a single spot. The conquered are slaves, forced to work at will ot the despot. All the artists, mechanics, carpenters, and workmen of skill, were engaged at Babylon from the four quarters of the world. All the world was robbed by Nebuchadnezzar, to beautify and enrich Babylon. Hence results here which could not have taken place under other circumstances. (149.)

11. *Description of Babylon?* Built after the model of a regular encampment; square form, 15 miles to the side, surrounded with a ditch and walls 350 feet in height, and 87 thick, 25 gates on each side, 3 towers between every two gates; corresponding to the gates, 25 streets cut at right angles, 25 streets running in opposite direction, making 625 squares; counting some of outer squares, 676. Walls made of brick and bitumen taken from ditch. Euphrates runs from north to south, and guarded by walls on banks similar to outer walls, in which 25 great gates opposite the streets.

12. *Was the population of Babylon as large as the dimenions of the city would indicate?* No, city was very open—streets 150 feet wide—each square of buildings was three-fifths of a mile in length, and all the inner space was in gardens—this one reason of its capacity to stand a long siege. The population at most flourishing epoch was not computed at more than 1,250,000; less than the population of London, and several of the cities of Asia.

13. *Hanging gardens of Nebuchadnezzar?* Were in front of the royal palace, consisted of terraces raised one above another, with stairs 10 feet wide—these terraces supported by large buttresses covered with pebbles and earth—then with a platform of lead to prevent water from passing—then with earth sufficient to produce largest trees—on the top was an aqueduct supplied with water from river; height 350 feet.

14. *Cause of their erection?* Amyite the Mede, wife of Nebuchadnezzar, wanted something to break dull monotony of plain, and like the mountains of her native land; hence these gardens.

15. *Mention some other monuments of Babylon?* There were two splendid royal palaces, one three and the other seven and a half miles in circumference, besides the temple and tower of Belus, supposed to have been the celebrated tower of Nimrod mentioned in scripture. Tower of Belus or Baal, *i. e.*, planet of Jupiter, built of burnt bricks dipped in bitumen—320 feet high—eight stories with slanting stairs on exterior—pyramidal in shape. Nebuchadnezzar enlarged the temple with immense buildings, more than a mile in circumference—surrounded it with walls two and a half miles in circuit, supplied with brazen gates—which were made in part of the *brazen sea*, the *brazen pillars*, and the *brazen vessels* taken from the temple of Jerusalem. (Calmet.)

The heap of ruins now called *Birs Nimrod*, supposed to be on site of this tower. All the buildings in Babylon were of brick, and Moses says tower of Bable was of brick, and on plain of Shinar. (Gen. 11, 3.)

16. *Character of Babylonish architecture?* Influenced by their building materials—had neither stone nor wood, and therefore all monuments were of *brick;* hence the absence of the *column*, which stamps character in Grecian architecture—hence ruins are but heaps of broken bricks. Upon many of the bricks inscriptions are found—supposed by some to be contracts. Sculpture scarcely existed here, because of want of marble and stone.

17. *General character of the city under Nebuchadnezzar?* Most magnificent city on earth. Called in scripture, *the great—the praise of the whole earth—the beauty of the Chaldees' excellency—the glory of kingdoms—the golden city—a lady—the lady of kingdoms—a queen for ever!* &c.

18. *Has any city been erected in modern times similar to Babylon, and which can to any extent illustrate the account given of Babylon by Herodotus?* Marco Polo has given an aceount of the city of Taidu, built by successor of Ghenghis Khan, near Pekin, which is entirely on the model of Babylon, without *intending it;* square—six miles to the side—surrounded by a square wall—streets wide and straight—cut each other at right angles—city like a *draught-board*—several palaces with large gardens and spacious courts, &c. (H. 187.)

19. *Was the situation of Babylon favorable to commerce?* Exceedingly so; spoken of in scripture as *a land of traffic—a city of merchants.* (Ezekiel 17, 4.) Euphrates poured into Persian gulf, infinitely superior to Arabian gulf for commerce, which is long, narrow, and rocky, [H. 220;] had whole of southern Asiatic trade—Babylon formed the centre of trade between north and south of Asia—again the great depot for caravan trade between east and west—it formed the point for "the confluence of nations." In modern Bagdad and Bassora, we have *now* every variety of human beings. Porter says sounds of voices and rustling of silks remind one of swarms of bees. Bagdad is still great *caravansary* of Asia. [195.]

20. *May it not be doubted whether Euphrates was navigable below Babylon?* It is not now; but from Isaiah, we suppose it was under Nebuchadnezzar and his successors. Chaldeans are spoken of as exulting in their ships. Æschylus in the "*Persians*," speaks of Babylon sending forth a promiscuous multitude who embark in *ships*, &c. [232.]

21. *Religion of the Babylonians?* Of the most idolatrous character. Three stages of idolatry: 1st, worship of sun, moon and stars; 2d, image worship; 3d, hero worship.

22. *Explain origin of the first?* Heavenly bodies naturally arrest attention of the mind and produce devotion, *e. g.* caution of Moses to Israelites, lest when they should lift up their eyes to heaven and behold sun, moon and stars, they should be *driven* to worship them. Again, wide plain of Babylon, pastoral life, flat roofs, &c., calculated to produce it. Great observatory on tower of Belus increased this propensity.

23. *Origin of second stage, image worship?* We require something to strike senses—hence *materialism* of most religions—hence the denunciations in the Bible against worshipping *stocks, and stones, and graven images.* Again, this image worship produced more complexity, and favored priestcraft.

24. *Principal images worshipped in Babylon?* Those of the *Sun*, and six planets, *Saturn, Jupiter, Mars, Mercury, Venus*, and the *Moon*, Temple of Belus or Baal was supposed to have been erected to the *Sun*, but after time of Nebuchadnezzar it was in honor of the planet Jupiter, and the *golden image*, more than 40 feet high, in sitting posture, was probably of the divinity, supposed to reside in the planet. The temple of *Mylitta or Venus*, was to the deity of that beautiful planet, &c.

25. *Origin of third stage of idolatry, hero worship?* Great love and gratitude, especially after death, which we have for those who have rendered great services to their country.

26. *What kind of learning in Babylon?* Principally judicial astrology.

27. *What naturally leads to this study?* A belief that the stars are instinct with *divinity*, and that it is their province to supervise the affairs of this world.

28. *Famous regulation in regard to marriage?*

29. *State of morals in Babylon?* Excessively corrupt—their banquets were the most disgusting debauches, *e. g.* Belshazzar and his nobles were drunk when handwriting appeared upon the wall; women disgustingly profligate—required to prostitute themselves once in their lives to strangers in the temple of *Mylitta* or *Venus*—appeared sometimes at feast almost in a state of *nudity;* hence Babylon is represented in scripture under the figure of a *lascivious woman*, of a *harlot, a whore*, &c.

30. *Military character of the Babylonians?* Under Nebuchadnezzar and his father, best soldiers in the world—appropriately styled in scripture, *the hammer of the whole earth—the battle-axe—the weapons of war, proper to break in pieces nations, and to destroy kingdoms.* In 70 years totally changed, and far inferior to the hardy mountaineers under Cyrus from Persia and Media.

31. *How came the Chaldeans, a nomad race, simple in their habits, and hardy warriors, thus to degenerate in so short a time in both moral and military point of view?* Universally the case with great empires formed by shepherd kings. A rude, ignorant people, suddenly acquiring immense wealth, are sure to indulge in every extravagance and vice; they can only enjoy their possessions as *sensualists*—all self-government is lost—the most shameless extravagance prevails. Herodotus tells us that certain districts were condemned to furnish certain things. *e. g.* one the queen's *head-dress*, another the *girdle*, &c. We are told that Tritontœchmus, the satrap of Babylon in Xerxes' time, devoted four cities to the maintenance of his dogs. Again, the levying of taxes *in kind* is calculated to produce *beastly* enjoyments; *eating, drinking, and making merry*, must be the result of eastern mode of levying revenue in *corn, meat, wine*, &c. Hence Jeremiah calls Babylon the *golden cup* that made all the earth drunken, and all the nations mad. (Ch. 51, 7.)

32. *Do wealth and luxury now produce the same effects as formerly?* Modern *civilized* nations are not injured by these—they are benefited; it is a semi-barbarous, rude, unenlightened people alone who are corrupted by them.

33. *Successors of Nebuchadnezzar?* 1st, His son Evil-Merodach, murdered by his brother-in-law Neriglissar for his intolerable wickedness. Neriglissar ruled four years; followed by son, a minor, who was murdered after nine months. Nabonid or Laby Netus (the Belshazzar of Daniel), and grandson of Nebuchadnezzar, was placed on throne: his mother Nitocris, wife of Evil-Merodach, regent during his minority. (Cal. Art. Babylonia.)

34. *How was war with Medes and Persians brought on?* By hunting excursion of Evil-Merodach, and an attack he made on some Medes with a garrison sent to the relief of a frontier town of Babylon.

35. *Character of Medes and Persians?* A hardy race north of Babylonish empire, led on by Cyrus, the greatest general of his day.

36. *Stratagem by which Babylon was taken?* The river Euphrates was turned, and on a night of feast and drunkenness Cyrus marched his army down channel of river—entered the gates which had been left open, and surprised Belshazzer in his palace, just after the famous writing had appeared on the walls—*Mene, Mene, Tekel Upharsin!* Thus was founded Medo-Persian empire on the ruins of the Babylonish.

37. *Fate of the Jews?* In the first year of Cyrus's reign (536 B. C.), and three years after overthrow of Babylon (Cyaxares or Darius the Mede ruled three.) went forth a royal edict inviting the Jews from all parts to return to Jerusalem to rebuild the city and the temple;

and Cyrus delivered to exiles 5,400 sacred vessels of gold and silver, which Nebuchadnezzar had carried to Babylon from Jerusalem.

38. *Fate of the city of Babylon?* It has realized the awful prophecies of Isaiah (ch. xiii. 19, 20, 21, 22), and of Jeremiah (ch. l. 40, 41, and ch. li. 57, 58.) All modern travellers represent it as a haunt for wild beasts and owls, and the inhabitants of the east regard it as as a place visited by spirits, and are very fearful of passing the night there—*literally* verifying the prophecies. (R. on Prophecies.)

39. *What became the capital of Medo-Persian emprie?* Susa, and Bablyon began immediately to decline.

SEC. III.—PHŒNICIA.

1. *Importance of history of Phœnicia?* Most interesting in consequence of her great trade, peculiar government, and peaceable policy.

2. *Why are the defects in her history so much more lamented than those of Persia, Babylon, Assyria, &c.?* Because history of one of latter is the history of the others. History of Phœnicia can be made out from no other nations.

3. *Who were the Phœnicians supposed to be descendants of?* Ham—originally divided into 11 families. Sidon son of Canaan, the founder of Sidon, the most powerful city at first.

4. *Situation and extent?* Phœnicia proper very small—on the eastern shore of the Mediterranean, about 120 miles in extent from south to north—from Tyre to Aradus—never more than 20 in breadth.

5. *Physical character?* Full of bays and harbors—in some places high mountains covered with fine timbers—used in ships and houses; many islands near the shore almost as celebrated as the main land.

6. *What were the principal cities?* Sidon and Tyre; and besides these there was such a number of other cities, as that the whole territory was dotted with them, exhibiting appearance almost of an unbroken city. Sidon was oldest, and no doubt founded Tyre on main land, which became greater than parent. Tyre on the island, near the old city, was early founded, but did not attain its greatest size till old Tyre was ruined by Nebuchadnezzar; then grew up as Venice did when Huns drove the Italians into island on which it is situated. New Tyre was taken by Alexander, and finally ruined by trade centring in Alexandria of Egypt.

7. *Military character of the Phœnicians?* Not very warlike; territory too small; dwelt in cities from the earliest times—depended on commerce for wealth—used mercenaries in war, as Carthage did at later period.

8. *Government of Phœnicia?* A sort of federative system—an al-

liance of cities, each of which with adjacent territory had its own king. Tyre became the undoubted head of the alliance in flourishing period between time of Solomon and Nebuchadnezzar (Ezekiel, ch. 27). She was to Sidon, Arvath, Tripolis, &c., what Carthage became afterwards to Utica, Leptis, Adrumetum, &c.; and what Gades in Spain became to Phœnician colonies, planted there. Although government of each city was kingly, not despotic—commerce requires liberty, and small communities are sure to obtain it. Magistrates in each city—met sometimes in general congress at Tripolis, to treat of common affairs.

9. *Religion and priesthood?* Hercules was principal God—there was a numerous and powerful priesthood, *e. g.* Sichæs, husband of Dido, and brother-in-law of king Pygmalion being put to death, caused the revolution, which ended in planting colony at Carthage (H. 20.) We are told in I. Kings, xviii. 22, that there were 450 priests of Baal, who had great influence even among the Jews.

10. *What did the power of the Phœnicians depend on?* On immense wealth created by their commerce. This well described by Ezekiel in his denunciation against Tyre (ch. xxvii. 4, 5, 12, 13, 14, 16). Tyre represented as enriched by traffic with gold and silver, and precious stones—as clothed with fine garments, and sinning in consequence of her ill-gotten wealth. With her wealth Phœnicia subsidized other nations, and procured her soldiers by hire, *e. g.* (Ezekiel, xxvii. 10, 11.) "They of Persia and of *Lud* (*Lydia*) and of *Phut* (*Lycia*) were in thine army, thy men of war, they hanged the shield and helmet in thee," &c.

11. *Character of their commerce?* Both sea and land trade; situated at eastern terminus of the Mediterranean, they of course pushed their sea trade west, whilst they enjoyed a caravan trade with both Asia and Africa.

12. *What their policy for extending their maritime trade?* They planted colonies along the coast of the Mediterranean, and in the islands, and by means of these they extended their commerce even to Spain and England. They had colonies in Cyprus, Crete, in the islands of the Archipelago, in Greece, at Carthage, at Utica, Leptis, at Gades, &c. So that in the language of Ezekiel, the cities of Phœnicia were "replenished and made very glorious in the midst of the seas."

13. *What kind of alliance between the mother country and her colonies?* Phœnicia not in midst of her colonies, as Carthage was; moreover, she was never very powerful in consequence of small territory, hence her colonies were free, but traded with her because of the immense market which she possessed in Asia and Africa.

14. *Which the most important of her colonies in a commercial point of view?* Gades in Spain. Curious fact that nearly a thousand years before Christ, Spain was to Phœnicia what Mexico and Peru became in modern times to Spain. "*Tarshish*" (Spain,) says Ezekiel, "was thy merchant, by reason of the multitude of all kinds of riches: with silver, iron, tin and lead, they traded in thy fairs." Spain was considered the only country on the globe at once rich in metals, corn, wine, oil, wax, fine wool, and fruits. (H. 66.)

15. *What the western terminus of the trade of Phœnicia?* They traded beyond the straits of Gibraltar to the tin and amber islands. England is conjectured to be the former; the latter not exactly known —they certainly went far into the Atlantic. "Thy rowers have brought thee," says Ezekiel, "into *great waters*." Conjectured by some that they reached the Madeira and Canary Islands. (69.)

16. *Trade on the Arabian Gulf or Red Sea?* This trade rose out of connection with the Jews—carried on through the ports of Eloth and Ezion-Geber (1 Kings, ix. 26,) which had originally belonged to Edomites, or to Idumeans, and fell into hands of Jews during the reign of David or Solomon.

17. *What was the celebrated trade of the Jews to the land of Ophir, mentioned in the Scripture?* Some suppose it trade to the East Indies, or to Ceylon, others to Arabia Felix, and Bochart to eastern coast of Africa. Heeren thinks *Ophir* general name for the rich countries of the south, on the African, Arabian and Indian coasts. (73.) This trade carried on chiefly by the intervention of Phœnicians.

18. *Political relations between Phœnicia and the Jews?* Of the most amicable character. Palestine was an agricultural country, and raised corn and other products for Phœnicia, whilst latter was manufacturing and commercial, and supplied former with her luxuries, &c. Hence no wars between them.

19. *Have not some supposed that the Phœnicians circumnavigated the continent of Africa?* Herodotus tells us that Necho, king of Egypt, having finished his canal to Red Sea, sent some Phœnician mariners through that sea to Indian ocean, with orders to double Cape of Good Hope, and came in at Gibraltar, which was accomplished in three years—they stopped each year to raise supply of provisions—they told what Herodotus did not credit, that sun passed to *right hand*, or north of them—this strongest argument now for the truth of statement. If this voyage was made, no good resulted, for short time after Nebuchadnezzar ruined the great Tyre.

20. *Give an account of the land trade of Phœnicia?* Almost as great as sea trade; three branches, 1st, Arabian, East Indian and

Egyptian; 2d, Syrian and Assyrio-Babylonian; and 3d, that of North-Armenio-Caucasian. First very important—Arabia immense country; large portion desert; but Arabia Felix in southern part one of the richest countries of the ancient world, and as large as France. This country traded with East Indies—spices, gold and precious stones, native products, suited to caravan trade. Job supposed to have been Arabian; well acquainted with *mining*. (xxviii. 1–12.) In trade with Egypt Phœnicians supplied wine; Egypt supplied cotton, embroidered work, &c. *e. g.* "Fine cotton and embroidered work (says Ezekiel,) spreadest thou over thy pavilions; dark blue and purple from the Peloponnesus were thy coverings." (114.) This trade carried on by caravans, first to Thebes and then to Memphis. Second branch includes trade with Syria, Palestine, Babylon, and Assyria, by land—that with Babylon greatest—supposed that Balbec and Palmyra were two caravan stations in the Syrian desert, and were built up by this trade. These two cities in Jewish annals are ascribed to King Solomon, under the names of Baalath and Tadmor, and although their most celebrated ruins belong to a more modern epoch, yet there is no doubt they were great caravan stations in the time of the Jews and Phœnicians, in trade between these latter countries and the Babylonians and Assyrians. Third branch of trade, with Armenia and the north, not so great as the other two, but important.

21. *Did the Phœnicians carry on this trade by their own caravans and traders, or did they employ other nations?* They hired other nations. Prophet in speaking of Tyre always speaks of other nations *coming and bringing* their wares to the Tyrians. (ch. 27 Ezekiel.)

22. *Manufactures of Phœnicia?* Her dyes purest in ancient world. Tyrian purple most beautiful; beautifully colored garments of Sidon celebrated by Homer; their manufactures of wool, fine; produced glass, ornaments of all kinds, utensils, baubles, gewgaws, &c.

23. *Decline and downfall of Phœnicia?* First, conquered by Nebuchadnezzar, then by Alexander—her trade injured by rise of the Grecian cities, and power of Carthage, and subsequently by the great trade of the Mediterranean centring at Alexandria, under successors of Alexander.

24. *Influence of Phœnicia on the condition and civilization of the world?* She was one of the most civilized nations of her day—supposed to be inventor of alphabet, which Cadmus carried into Greece. Voltaire says a trading people like the Phœnicians, who first carried on commerce upon a large scale, must learn to write, if only to keep their accounts and traffic with others. By means of immense trade and colonization, Phœnicians acquired and disseminated all the civilization of their age. Thirl-

wall thinks they did more than all other nations for the infant civilization of Greece. (v. i. 76.) Phœnicia stands, too, an almost solitary instance in the ancient world of a nation rising to wealth and splendor, and pushing her religion, her institutions, and her civilization, over the known world, by the pacific means of trade and colonization.

CHAPTER VI.

EUROPE.

1. *Physical character of Europe compared with Asia and Africa?* Not more than one-fourth of Asia in size; much smaller than Africa; in number and grandeur of natural productions, inferior to both; cultivable soil less fertile.

2. *How stands the comparison in other respects?* Europe far surpasses the other two in character of people, and in all productions of art. Asia presents one unbroken chain of grinding despotisms from earliest times. In Europe, always struggling for liberty and best forms of government—simple inventions in Asia, complex in Europe, *e. g.*—*hand-loom*, *sun-dial*, *wind-mill*, *canal* in Asia—*chronometer*, *power-loom*, *steam-mill*, *rail-car* in Europe—Asia invents the *boat*, Europe produces formidable *man-of-war*. When Asia has first invented, she has rarely made any valuable use of the invention, *e. g.* China had art of printing, had gunpowder, and mariner's compass, long before Europeans, but never printed a book; made nothing but fire-works out of powder, and never applied the *compass* to navigation! (Schl. 97.) In arts, compare *Indian Idol* with *Jupiter* of Phidias; *transfiguration* with Chinese paintings, &c. In philosophy, no Aristotle, Socrates, Plato, Bacon, Locke, or Bentham, &c., in Asia. In history, no Herodotus, Tacitus, Hume or Gibbon. No orators like Demosthenes, Cicero, Chatham and Burke. In war, great conquerors have come from East, and by mere numbers and *physical force*, have overthrown empires. But no such generals as Alexander, Hannibal (Carthage, although in Africa, was European in character), Cæsar, or Bonaparte. Soldiers of Europe have been better than those of Asia, *e. g.*—Marathon, Salamis, Platæa, &c. Macedonia ruled on Indus and Nile, and the Romans conquered known world. In modern times, when Europe was degenerated, the Saracens were stopped by Charles Martel, and the Mongo-

lians were stopped in Silesia. The *Turk* had gotten foothold in Europe, but Russian would soon drive him out if Europe would permit it. In mercantile adventure, nothing like European, he finds new continents—pushes his trade to the earth's limits, and civilizes, rules, or destroys wherever he goes, *e. g.* England has more than 150,000,000 of subjects at a distance of a three months' voyage. In North America the red man has almost disappeared. In South America, aborigines still numerous, but every general, statesman, man of power, &c., is European. Armies inferior, *e. g.*, battle of Saint Jacinto, &c.

3. *Whence proceeds this undoubted superiority of Europe over the other quarters of the globe?* It results not from superiority of body, but of mind; and this results from following causes:—First, Caucasian or the *white race* inhabiting Europe seems to be a superior race. It is proved so by uniform testimony of history, and other races seem intellectual in proportion to *likeness* to European, *e. g.*, races of Asia and Africa.

A second cause is the physical character of Europe—stretching through the northern temperate zone, it terminates on the Mediterranean before it reaches the tropics. Principal countries lie between 40 and 60 degrees of latitude. Does not run far enough south to have enervated lazy races of the tropics; nor is there much of it near the pole, requiring whole exertion for mere subsistence. Not so fertile as Asia and Africa, but sufficiently so if cultivated. Unsuited to nomadic life—no European nation ever lived in tents, and therefore never subject to internal migrations, the *curse* of Asia. Has great water frontier in proportion to its magnitude—has more bays, rivers, and not so much uniformity as to favor *large* empires like China or Hindostan—no great desert like *Sahara*, or *Arabia*, or *Cobi.* Had Mediterranean been a desert, the whole character of Europe would have been changed. Again, chain of Alps connects with Pyrenees by Cevenus of France, with the Carpathian and Balkan mountains, running to the Black Sea on the east. This chain constitutes the bulwark to the three great peninsulas of Europe—Spain, Italy, and Greece. Against it, the wave of barbarism has generally been broken, and these countries had a breathing time for starting forward in career of civilization—had this wall been thrown down, neither Greece nor Rome could have been civilized—the Gauls and Scythians would soon have overrun them. Happened too, that countries thus protected were choice spots of Europe—sky, air, mountains, vegetation, all change on southern side of the Alps.

A third cause—Polygamy everywhere in Asia, nowhere in Europe. Civilization in Greece commenced with marriage of one man to one woman—a law of Cecrops. One man to one woman among our German ancestors.

4. *Disadvantages of polygamy?* First, destroys all family harmony, and delightful sympathy which constitutes the charm of marriage. Second, degrades woman and makes her a slave—her chastity to be guarded only by the *lock* and *key*—hence her influence so necessary to progress of civilization is lost. Third, in every family some wives will be preferred—children of those will be treated as superiors—hence system of despotism in every family—races of children unfit for free government—*hence no region in constant practice of polygamy has ever enjoyed a free government!* No people can possess *rational liberty* when one half the race is under *surveillance* of hateful eunuchs, and a system of despotism reigns in every household!

CHAPTER VII.

GREECE.

SEC. 1.—TO DOWNFALL OF TROY.

1. *Situation, boundaries, and extent of Greece?* In south-eastern corner of Europe. On the north bordered by Epirus and Macedonia, with no exact limits. On east by Hellespont and Egean sea, dividing it from Asia. On south by Mediterranean, and on the west by the Ionian and Adriatic seas, separating it from Italy. This country less than Portugal in extent. Contrast startling between speck of earth, scarce visible on map of world, and immense influence exercised over destinies of our race. To us mother of arts, of sciences, of law, and of republicanism; besides all this a military people, who finally conquered under Alexander almost known world.

2. *Physical character?* It is to Europe what Europe is to Asia and Africa—has more water frontier in proportion to size than any country in Europe—it fronts most beautiful and fertile regions of Africa—Egean filled with fruitful islands—main land as it advances south terminates in peninsula of Peloponnesus like outspread palm of the hand—country everywhere intersected by bays, rivers and mountains, which was principal cause of division into so many small states—soil in the valleys fine—climate delightful—region volcanic, &c.

3. *Who were the first inhabitants of Greece, and what their char*

acter? Pelasgi, a name supposed to be general, like that of Saxon, Frank, &c. (Thirl. 41.) They were in comparatively barbarous condition—in hunting and shepherd state—dwelt in caves, and are reported to have been unacquainted with use of fire.

4. *Origin of this race?* All that is known is that they were first settlers of Greece; whether descended from Inachus or Pelasgus, or supposed to be *Autochthones*, is a matter of very little importance now.

5. *Architecture of Pelasgi?* Masonry, Polygonal—stones fit without cement; not to be confounded with Cyclopean, composed of immense blocks of stone with small pebbles in the interstices. (Bul. 18.) Most ancient architectural monuments of Europe supposed to be raised by them.

6. *Hellenic races, or Hellenes?* A race supposed to be descended from Hellen, son of Deucalion, and who overran Greece—after their day Pelasgi disappear or are absorbed—not much superior to Pelasgi in civilization—supposed to have come from Thessaly and the west. This race stamped its character on Greece, and became true *Greeks;* a name bestowed by foreigners.

7. *Circumstances favorable to civilization of Greece?* Her situation was accessible to some of the most civilized nations of antiquity; *e. g.* Crete, Egypt, Phœnicia, Phrygia, &c. These nations are supposed to have colonized Greece at early period; *e. g.* Cecrops and Danaus settled Athens and Argos with Egyptians; Cadmus, a Phœnician, settled Thebes in Bœotia; and Pelops, a Phrygian, settled in Peloponnesus.

8. *Have we not reason to doubt the reality of these colonies?* That of Cadmus seems well authenticated; others, particularly those of Cecrops and Danaus, doubtful. History of these individuals less distinct as we go farther back into antiquity; but no reason for supposing there were *no* colonies.

9. *General circumstances proving such colonies?* First, the great population of Egypt often visited by famine and by civil wars, which drove out large numbers. Secondly, great revolutions happened in these countries about time of colonization in Greece; *e. g.* arrival of Egyptian colonies corresponds with expulsion of Hyksos.

10. *Most important institutions and arts introduced?* Institution of marriage, main pillar of social edifice attributed to Cecrops. Agriculture attributed to the Egyptians, and writing to the Phœnicians—Cadmus introduced alphabet of sixteen letters—Duplicates omitted *zeta, theta, eta, xi, phi, chi, psi, omega.*

11. *Circumstances which had a tendency to retard progress of civilization?* 1st, Topography—Greece is intersected in every direc-

tion by mountains and rivers; hence, divided into very small states, unable to form society on scale large enough for civilization or energetic government, and therefore, infested with robbers—again, numerous islands and bays were infested by pirates. 2d, Greece liable to invasion from north, especially from Thrace, and this supposed by some main reason for amphyctionic council.

12. *What period is embraced in the heroic ages of Greece?* Between the first appearance of the Hellenes in Thessaly and the return from siege of Troy.

13. *Why called heroic age?* Because seems to have been the period of individual prowess and heroism. Everywhere in Greece a class of elevated characters, devoted to arms, possessing wealth, &c., constituting a nobility, performed feats of courage and patriotism similar to knights in feudal kingdoms; they were called *heroes;* a term of honor always embracing idea of courage, and generally of immense physical strength.

14. *Different modes by which heroes distinguished themselves?* 1st, by killing wild beasts; 2d, by works of improvement; 3d, by destroying robbers and pirates; 4th, by national enterprises.

15. *Explain the reason why killing wild beasts should confer such honors.* First, number of wild beasts very great; secondly, arms used not like our guns and rifles; man not far above the beasts in the conflict. Herodotus says, not long before he lived, Mysians, subjects of Crœsus, sent formal deputation to their king for aid against *monstrous boar.* To this day, when tiger appears near villages of India, they apply to Europeans for aid. (M. 1. 59.) Cannot wonder, therefore, that conquest of *Nemæan lion* and of the *boar* of Erimanthus among the great feats of Hercules.

16. *How distinguished by second mode?* Every infant society stands in need of physical improvements, as turning streams, building dams, erecting walls, &c.

17. *How by third mode?* Robbers and pirates infested seas and lands of Greece, and were, from feebleness of government, too strong for police—hence the hero who could break up these banditti, as much distinguished, as man who could conquer a country at more civilized age. In all these feats both courage and physical strength were necessary with the imperfect weapons of antiquity. Not so much so now. In new countries, however, we see something of the same thing now-a-days, *e. g.* on our western borders, and in portions of South America, courage and strength still great accomplishments. Individuals rely on themselves, because society is bad and protection of government uncertain—hence armed with pistols, bowie-knives, dirks, Arkansas toothpicks, &c.

18. *Fourth, by national undertakings?* When successful, would of course confer renown, as at present day.

19. *Exemplify all these modes of obtaining renown by traditions of Hercules?* He clears country of noxious animals, cuts off heads of hydra, kills lions, cleaves rocks, turns rivers, opens or stops subterraneous outlets of lakes, kills robbers and giants, punishes wrong, &c. All these peculiar to society in infancy. Again, punishes tyrants, subdues countries, exterminates his enemies, bestows kingdoms on his friends, &c. All these seem of a national character.

20. *By traditions of Theseus?* Three great feats. First, journey from Trœzen to Athens; second, victory over the *Minotaur?* third, political revolution in Attica. First, in going to Athens from Trœzen, to claim the crown, he did not cross Saronic gulf, but went by land—road haunted by monsters and savage men. In Epidaurus won brazen mace, with which Periphetes had surprised unwary—he killed the robber himself. In Isthmus tore Sinis to pieces by two pines, he had killed travellers with, and destroyed the wild *sow* of Crommyon, named Phœa, supposed by some, female robber. In Megara, stopped at narrow pass, hewn in cliff by Sciron, from which he threw travellers into sea—Theseus conquered Sciron and threw him into sea, clearing Scironian route of all monsters and robbers. On this same journey he stretched *Procrustes* on his own bed. After becoming king of Attica took alive celebrated bull near Marathon, &c. (Mit. i. 55, Thirl. i. 132.) Second, *Minotaur of Crete*, half man and half bull, creature of unnatural intercourse—fed upon boys and girls sent from Athens and confined in Labyrinth. Theseus goes himself to Crete—is well received by king Minos, and procures exemption from tribute. Third, in his journey to Crete, becomes acquainted with foreign institutions and laws, and on his return to Athens remodels the government and laws.

21. *Were the feats of the heroes performed in companies or by solitary individuals?* Hercules and Theseus perform their feats alone, or with only one comrade—in the Theban wars we find a union of seven chiefs—confederacies became frequent in latter part of heroic age—numerous band combined against the *Caledonian boar*—many chiefs united in the Argonautic expedition, and subsequently in the siege of Troy—*individuality*, however, characteristic of this age, as of chivalry.

22. *Meaning and end of the Argonautic expedition?* A great puzzle; some interpret to be purely allegorical; that *golden fleece* was the plunder that was taken in Colchis; that the *dragon*, the *fire-breathing bulls*, the *armed men*, &c., are nothing more than emblems of the difficulties to be encountered. Some think that the gold flowing down the streams in Colchis was caught in fleeces, and that gold alone

was the object of the expedition. The *bulls* have been supposed to be a savage race of people called *Tauri*, who made war on the Greeks; others give a purely religious character to the whole affair. (T. vi. 145.)

23. *Who were the heroes in this expedition, and why called Argonautic?* Jason, Orpheus, Tydeus, Telamon, and in general, fathers of the heroes at siege of Troy—name taken from the great ship *Argo;* first fifty oared galley the Greeks ever built.

24. *Against whom was the next great combination of the Greeks?* Troy.

25. *Where situated?* In Asia Minor, at the foot of Mount Ida, near the Hellespont, on the two streams, *Simois* and *Scamander*.

26. *Who the founder, and what order of succession to king Priam?* Dardanus of Greek origin, with a colony of Greeks and Phrygians, supposed founder, who built city on the mountain. His son Erichthonus, rich in blooded horses, owning 3,000, was second; his son Tros, third, gave name to *Troy;* son of Tros, Ilus, fourth, gave name to *Ilium* after building it in the plain; Laomedon, son of Ilus, fifth. In his reign Homer says it was taken and sacked by Hercules. Sixth, Priam, son of Laomedon, in whose reign it was besieged and taken by the Greeks.

27. *What the causes of the war?* Paris, son of Priam, attracted by reputation of Helen, wife of Menalaus, king of Laconia, paid a visit to that court, and carried off Helen—hence league of all states of Greece against Troy. Again, jealousies and animosities existed between Greeks and Trojans on account of stealing boys and girls for slaves, *e. g.* story of Ganymede, and on account of stealing cattle. Neighboring states half civilized, always depredating on each other in this way.

28. *What the superior civilization of Troy attributed to?* First, *topography*—an extended plain near 200 miles in extent, not cut up into small states. Second, proximity to more civilized nations—Phrygia, Phœnicia, &c.

29. *Number of ships and troops raised against Troy?* 1000 ships, 102 men to each galley, making an army of 102,000 men.

30. *In what port did they rendezvous?* Aulis.

31. *Length of siege, and causes of the duration?* First, difficulty of taking fortified towns with arms then used; second, neighboring nations being depredated on by Greeks, lent assistance to the Trojans; third, quarrels among chiefs, especially between Agamemnon and Achilles.

32. *Is the Trojan war, as related by Homer, an historical event which may be relied on?* Very little reason to doubt its existence; no confidence, however, can be placed in mere details. All the circum-

stances being in accordance with the character of the times, no proof of accuracy of details, because fiction possesses this trait in eminent degree, *e. g.* novels of Scott.

31. *Does history of modern times furnish any thing analogous?* Ireland furnishes very curious analogous case, producing a most important revolution. Dermot, the king of Leinster, by force and fraud, succeeded in carrying off Dervorghal, celebrated beauty, wife of O'Ruark, king of Leitrim. Latter raised a confederacy of chieftains with king of Connaught at their head—invaded Leinster, expelled Dermot, and carried back the princess. Dermot fled to England, obtained an army of 500 men from Henry II., &c. Hence conquest of Ireland by the English. (M. 81.)

SEC. II.—GOVERNMENT, ARTS, MANNERS, &c. OF EARLY GREEKS.

Homeric poems have given great interest to those ages, at the same time that they afford almost the only knowledge we possess on the above mentioned subjects, to the downfall of Troy.

1. *Government of the states of Greece before the siege of Troy? Kingly*—Aristotle thinks first *elective*, soon, however, became hereditary.

2. *Prerogatives of the king?* Commanded armies in war—performed sacrifices—administered justice—not absolute—called councils of the chiefs, and, on great occasions, whole army was convened—did nothing of importance without advice—were very little more than first among equals, *e. g.* Alcinous, in Odyssey, is king of all the Phœacians, and yet twelve other chiefs with same title. Though Ithaca had an acknowledged head, several others bore same title, and might aspire to the throne in a vacancy. (T. 167.) No account of any thing like regular legislation. In administration of justice, king was not absolute—indeed, in celebrated case of manslaughter, in Homer, parties first appeal to the bystanders—then the elders are called in, who seat themselves on the marble benches in a circle, with two talents of gold placed by litigants in centre. The litigants then pleaded by turns, and the award of gold is made, and all without mention of king. (M. 113.) Principle of *pecuniary compensation* for murder seems to have prevailed among Greeks, *e. g.* above instance. Again, when Ajax would show how unreasonable was Achilles' wrath, he says that men are used to accept compensation from the murderers of their *brothers and sons even.* Kings had a portion of lands considered as national domain. *Presents,* too, were common, *e. g.* in towns which Agamemnon proposed to give Achilles, he mentions *presents* as chief profit. Presents were always made by the litigants to the judges, (T. 168.) *e. g.* Judicial office

mentioned as a source of honor and *profit* to Telemachus, while administering his father's government. (166.)

3. *Qualifications requisite for a great prince?* Both physical and mental accomplishments—robust frame, lofty stature, majestic mien, skill in arms, patience under hardships, undaunted courage, love of enterprise—also, prudence in council, readiness of invention, and fluency of speech. Supposed by some, Homer wrote Iliad to exemplify advantages of physical accomplishment, and the Odyssey the still superior advantages of mind. But no superiority of mind could compensate for want of *bodily abilities.* Hence monarchs in old age were obliged to resign in favor of more athletic successor, *e. g.* Ithaca well governed under Laertes and Ulysses, yet when son was absent, father in old age could not maintain his authority. Again, when Achilles sees Ulysses in Elysian fields, he asks with anxiety whether his father, Peleus, was still obeyed by the Myrmidons, or whether in the decrepitude of age the sceptre had been snatched from him.

4. *Size of states of Greece?* States very small then, as they always continued. This a striking feature in Grecian history, *e g.* Thessaly alone contained ten small states, each with a separate chief; Bœotia had five; besides which, in central Greece, were the Mynians, Locrians, Athenians, Phocians. In Peloponnesus, were Argos, Mycenæ, Sparta, Pylus, four states in Elis, and Arcadia, all governed by independent chiefs, &c.

5. *What prevented some one of the states from conquering all the rest?* Topography of country, and political equilibrium.

6. *Why were the Greeks necessarily a warlike people?* Because of division into so many states, and proximity to each other, always liable to attack from neighbors.

7. *State of military art?* Although Homer speaks of the importance of steadiness in the soldier, of drawing up the army in ranks and files, and in *phalanxes*—and speaks of the orderly, noiseless march of the Grecians, contrasted with disorderly march of Trojans—yet, upon the whole, must infer a low state of military art. *Personal prowess* and skill of the chief of more importance than *art of directing.* No men so important as *Hector* and *Achilles*, yet neither appears very distinguished as a leader. Fate of battles determined by *individual* courage; one great warrior like *Achilles* or *Ajax*, an over-match for whole squadrons of half-armed common troops; just as in days of chivalry. Had not regular sentries; *e. g.* Diomed praised for sleeping on his arms outside tent, to be in readiness. Turks, to late period, had none.

8. *Arms?* *Defensive*—helmet, breast-plate, and greaves of brass—

shield of bull's hide strengthened with brass; common soldiers did not have this armor, and consequently inferior to chiefs. *Offensive*—in time of Hercules and Theseus, the club and mace; in time of siege of Troy, darts, javelins, and swords were all in constant use; bows and arrows were used by the light armed. *e.g.* Locrians under Oilean Ajax never engaged in close fight.

9. *Manner in which horses were used?* Homer makes no mention of horses used for cavalry; used altogether for chariots; strange, as the country of Greece was not well suited to chariot. Same thing in Britain when invaded by Cæsar. Mitford supposes horses used were from north Danube, too small to carry man and armor. (p. 140.) In one of Homer's battles, where Nestor draws up army, he puts a line of chariots in front, worst of the infantry in next line, and best troops in rear.

10. *Laws of war?* Such as usually prevail among uncivilized nations—no quarter except for ransom; *e. g.* Agamemnon reproaches Menelaus with effeminacy for wishing to spare a fallen enemy, and puts the suppliant to the sword, and Homer approves the deed. Armor and property of slain a part of spoils of victor—dead body was treated with indignity, and exposed to vultures; *e. g.* dead body of Hector dragged around Troy, and obtained with great difficulty by Priam. When city was taken, men were put to death, and women and children made concubines and slaves, and distributed like other spoil; *e. g.* dispute between Agamemnon and Achilles about two female captives; again, even Ulysses wept at a woman being torn from her slain husband, and beaten by the soldiers upon her neck and shoulders to make her advance.

11. *Light in which piracy was regarded?* Not dishonorable. *e.g.* Telemachus, after enjoying hospitality of Pylians, is asked by Nestor, with no view to insult, whether he is voyaging with a particular object, or roving over sea as a pirate, and for sake of indiscriminate mischief. In barbarous states of society, robbery and piracy are looked on as very little different from other kinds of warfare; and the divided states of Greece, the islands, and the number of bays and rivers, made these vices more common in Greece than elsewhere.

12. *Condition of females?* Much more elevated than at later period—Helen and Andromache frequently appear in company of the chiefs, and enter into conversation; Penelope appears among her suitors. Character of Penelope in Odyssey a handsome panegyric on the sex. Parting of Hector and Andromache, exquisite; even Helen gains wonderfully upon us in spite of failings. Homer very courteous to the fair sex; Pope not so, and has misrepresented speech of injured Agamemnon, by his translation of it in the 11th book of the Odyssey, v. 433, and of translation 540. But in spite of Homer's praises, we infer fre-

quent corruption of the sex—stories of loves of gods, of such heroines as Tyro, Œthra, Creusa, and Coronis, show female purity not properly valued; again, tales of Helen, Clytemnestra, Antæa, Phædra, and Alcmena, prove the infidelity of wives. Helen in Troy was treated with affection and respect; and when carried back to Greece, and made the mistress of Menelaus' household, she neither loses the esteem of her husband, nor does she herself feel any disgrace at her conduct. One duty sometimes discharged by women a little surprising; attended and waited on men in bath, and virgins of highest rank even performed this office for distinguished chiefs; *e. g.* Telemachus at court of Pylus was aided in bathing, anointing and dressing himself, by the beautiful Polycaste, virgin daughter of old Nestor. Penelope directs her young maids to attend Ulysses to the bath, not knowing who he was: even the modest Nausicaa, the interesting Phœacian princess, orders her female attendants to perform same office for Ulysses, who declines, from feelings of delicacy, and yet immediately after accepts similar services in the house of Alcinous. Similar customs, it is said, exist to this day among the Arabs. (M. 169.)

13. *Employments of ladies?* Those of highest rank ever employed in needle-work, spinning and weaving, and superintending slaves; *e. g.* after parting between Andromache and Hector, former goes back to her apartment to direct labors of maid-servants. The directions which Penelope's housekeeper gives the maid-servants would still answer in east—to sweep and sprinkle the floors, to spread the crimson carpets on the seats, to rub the tables with sponges, to wash the bowls and cups, and go to the fountain for water. In these duties fifty maid-servants engaged, and twenty went to the fountain for water! Not degrading for princess even to go with urn for water, as Rachel did in time of Jacob, nor for her brother to tend his father's flocks and herds, as Jacob did those of Laban. Besides all these duties, women ground corn with a hand-mill; eleven ground for Ulysses' family. Ladies of first rank, too, are washerwomen; *e. g.* Nausicaa, daughter of king of Phœacia, went in a carriage drawn by *mules*, with her maids to a fountain at distance from the city to wash the clothes of the family.

14. *Do we meet in the heroic times, so nearly resembling the age of chivalry, any thing like the romantic love of the knight for his mistress?* No: love has reference, both in cases of mortals and immortals, *always* to sensual enjoyment—no traces of refined sentimental love flowing from higher principle than lust; no semi-barbarians, except the Germanic nations, have ever been characterized by such refinement of the passion.

15. *Friendship among the men?* This tie of closest character,

almost equal to devotion of knight to his mistress; *e. g.* Hercules and Ioalaus, Theseus and Pirithous, Orestes and Pylades. Argument of Iliad turns on affection of Achilles for Patroclus, and is guilty of horrible cruelty of sacrificing twelve Trojans to the manes of his friend. Idea of a Greek hero not complete without brother in arms; such friendship common among people of warlike character, and who rely more on themselves than the government for protection.

16. *Hospitality of Greeks?* Unbounded. No question asked until banquet is finished, and then even if pirate or robber, still safe, *e. g.* question of Nestor to Telemachus. Same thing among the Europeans of middle ages, and among Arabs and Tartars of present day.

17 *Repasts of the Greeks?* At meals, guests took seats along the walls of the apartment, after having undergone an ablution. Fare simple, *e. g.* in luxurious palace of king Alcinous, preparation for great feast consisted only of sheep, hogs, and oxen slaughtered for the occasion. Wine was drunk after the meal was finished, not to excess however, as among our German ancestors, *e. g.* suitors of Penelope, always feasting at expense of Ulysses, are *never* represented as drunk. Among the most abusive epithets applied by Achilles to Agamemnon, the foremost is "*heavy with wine.*" A *bard* was indispensable to the feast. After meal the dance and gymnastic exercises were common, *e. g.* Alcinous leads out guests to open place, where they amuse themselves with trials of strength in gymnastics, then they dance, and finally at king's command, two of great activity perform feats of leaping and dancing.

18. *Were there not frequent murders in those days?* Very frequent; caused either by deliberate treachery or violent passion; *e. g.* suitors of Penelope propose to kill Telemachus and divide his property, and only *one* hesitates, and proposes to consult the *gods first*, as killing a person of royal race was no *light matter.* Some of the favorite personages of the Iliad and Odyssey had committed murder, *e. g.* Patroclus at very early age killed his playmate in a passion, caused by a quarrel about a game. Phœnix has great difficulty in refraining from killing his own father. Ulysses, in fictitious narrative, lies in wait with a companion in the dark, and assassinates a man, wishing to deprive him of his share of booty brought from Troy! We find a parallel to this in Europe, and especially in Italy during the middle ages, when private revenge was so frequent, those treacherous murders are related by the historians of the day as quite natural, and seem to excite no horror, *e. g.* murders of Cæsar Borgia.

19. *State of agriculture?* Had begun to advance in time of Homer. Cicero says Hesiod makes no mention of *manuring land.* Homer speaks of *dunging land*, *of ploughing*, *sowing*, *reaping corn*,

and mowing grass ; vine raised and wine made, *e. g.* Nestor had wine at a sacrifice 11 years old; and in Alcinous' garden the vineyard is main feature—olive was raised and oil expressed. In Alcinous' orchard we have *olives, apples, pears, pomegranates, and figs.*

20. *What the principal items of wealth?* Herds and flocks—hence we know Greeks had not passed entirely from shepherd state. *e. g.* Eumeus in Odyssey, speaking of Ulysses' wealth, tells neither of his *lands nor movables*, but altogether of his *herds and flocks.*

21. *Circulating medium? Cattle.* Precious metals bought and sold *by weight* like other commodities—not used as money, *e. g.* golden armor of Glaucus valued at *one hundred oxen ;* brazen armor of Diomed at nine; tripod, first prize for wrestling at funeral of Patroclus, at twelve; female slave, second prize, at four. Commerce carried on almost all by *barter, e. g.* in Iliad we have supply of wine sold in Grecian camp; some buy with *brass*, some with *iron*, some with *hides*, some with *cattle*, and some with *slaves.*

22. *State of commerce?* Rather low. Phœnicians had the commerce of Mediterranean. Sidon the great manufacturing and commercial city of world in Homer's day. Business of sailor not in very high repute, *e. g.* Ulysses taunted by a Phœnician for looking like a man engaged in *mercantile business*, instead of athletic sports.

23. *Useful arts?* Impression left by Homer that those arts were considerably advanced. Dwellings, furniture, clothing, armor are described as costly and magnificent, *e. g.* houses of wealthy, of polished stone with several apartments below. In Odyssey, following are presents to young lady: a large tunic, with twelve golden hooks nicely fitted to well bent eyes; a golden necklace, set with amber; a pair of three-drop ear rings, exquisitely brilliant; and another ornament for the neck, for which we want a name. Some of these, however, were brought from Sidon. In description of Phœnician vessels coming to Greek island freighted with trinkets, we see immense difference between Greeks and Phœnicians in arts; a woman of quality with her maids, represented as handling and gazing on the ornaments, like a South Sea Islander does at this day.

24. *Carpentry?* The Greeks were behind the eastern nations in this respect. The business, however, was held in high esteem. The carpenter classed with soothsayers, physicians, and bards, and sent for to great distance. This trade is practised by most illustrious chiefs, *e. g.* Ulysses builds boat in which he leaves island of Calypso; and in his own palace, in midst of his opulence, made his own bedstead, and adorned it with gold, silver, and ivory. The celebrated *wooden horse* of the Greeks was built by Epeus, one of the Grecian chiefs.

25. *Art of navigation?* Greece, in consequence of its bays, rivers, islands, and numerous seas, was more favorable to a sort of boat navigation than to that of large vessels. Compass, to this day, is hardly used in the Ægean sea, and indeed, on the coast of the Mediterranean generally; sails were used, but oars were most relied on—hence Grecian vessels were light, slender, half-decked boats—ran near the shore and were principally worked by oars. Thucydides calculates 120 oarsmen to largest galley mentioned by Homer, and only 20 as usual complement. The mast was movable, and only hoisted in fair wind—at night taken down and stored away. In sailing in daytime, followed windings of the coast, or shot from headland to headland, or from isle to isle—at night, vessel put up in port, or hauled up on beach. No anchor—vessel tied to some object on shore when not taken out of water. Hempen cordage unknown—leathern thongs were used instead. Winter stopped all navigation. Hesiod speaks of laying up merchant ship, covering it with stones, taking out rigging, and hanging the rudder up by the fire. Says fair sailing season not more than fifty days. Sea fights must have been very rare, as Homer makes no mention of them.

26. *Tools mentioned by Homer?* Hatchet, wimble, plane, and level; saw, square, and compass seem unknown to him—hence supposed that the Grecian fleet was built without *saw!*

27. *Imitative arts?* Difficult question—representations on small scale frequent; *e. g.* garment woven by Helen had a number of *battle scenes;* another, given to Ulysses by Penelope, had picture of a *chase*, wrought with gold threads; shield of Achilles had several compartments, containing groups of figures. By the door of the palace of king Alcinous, we are told there were rows of dogs in gold and silver, and in his hall, upon pedestals, golden statues of boys holding torches, &c. The Iliad, however, contains only one allusion to a statue as work of art: *e. g.* robe offered by Hecuba, queen of Troy, to Minerva in her temple, is placed by priestess on *knees of goddess.* No mention of painting as an art, though he speaks of coloring of ivory, in which Carian and Mœonian women excelled.

28. *Was the art of writing known to Homer?* Although colony of Phœnicians is point well established, and the introduction by them of an alphabet, yet doubted whether this was before Homer, and *if so*, whether any practical use was made of the letters. Only one passage in Iliad which has any bearing on the subject; it is where the calumniated Bellerophon is sent by Prœtus, king of Argos, to his ally, the Lycian king, Iobates, with a closed tablet, in which Prœtus had *traced many deadly signs;* that is, had given instructions to kill Bellerophon; contended that the word *signs* rather expressive of *pictorial* than *alpha-*

betic writing; on other hand urged, that Phœnicians were notoriously in possession of the practical art; that their dealings with the Greeks were very frequent before Trojan war; that they first communicated the art to the Ionians, whom Herodotus represents as calling their books *diptheræ* or *skins*, because the plant of the biblos, or papyrus, being scarce, they used sheep and goat skins to write on; that writing is so essential to preservation of important documents, that rudest materials would be used, rather than suffer them to be lost; *e. g.* Koran at a much later date was transcribed on leaves and mutton bones. (B. v. 1. 158.) That moreover, testimony of antiquity supports it; *e. g.* Euripides exhibits Agamemnon *writing a letter to* Clytemnestra, that Æschylus describes shield of chief at siege Thebes as bearing *inscription in letters of gold*—Plutarch tells us that Lycurgus collected and transcribed poems of Homer, and latter supposed by many to have been nearly cotemporary with former. Upon the whole, extremely doubtful, whether Homer committed his own poems to *writing*.

29. *Extent of knowledge in Homer's time?* Very limited. Homer has been praised for geographical knowledge; but it must have been very small, confined almost entirely to Greece and Ægean sea; *Black sea* was regarded as ocean; some think he has given even a false position to Ithaca. Earth was regarded as plain surface, circular like horizon, begirt with deep river, flowing gently around the orb, separating the world of life and light from realms of darkness, dreams, and death. Hence he makes Vulcan terminate shield of Achilles with a *circular stripe*, representing great *oceanic river;* beyond this river lay *Hades* and the deep pit of *Tartarus*—sun, moon and stars descend into this ocean, but how they come back to the east, at the rising, Homer has not told us. Thirlwall supposes Mimnermus more than 600 years (B. C.) may have given us the belief of Greeks when he sang of *golden bowl* wrought by Vulcan, and furnished with wings, as a floating couch for repose of Phœbus after finishing his diurnal journey, in which he is rapidly carried through the waters of the encircling sea from the abode of Hesperides to land of Ethiopians, where a new chariot and fresh steeds await him. (T. v. 1, 216.) Epithets which Homer applies to vault of heavens seem to show he considered it of *solid metal.* Atlas described as holding lofty pillars which kept heaven and earth apart. Vulcan, when hurled from *heaven*, is represented as falling from *morn to noon, from noon to dewy eve*, before dropping on Lemnos.

30. *Did one man produce the Iliad and Odyssey?* Those for negative say that writing was not practised by Homer; that, therefore, it would be impossible for *one man*, without that art, to produce, after all expungings and curtailments, a poem of upwards of 15,000 hexameter

lines; that if you add the Odyssey, the improbability is doubled; that the parts of the Iliad, and again those of the Odyssey, are not so connected as to prove unity of authorship; that they were nothing more than rhapsodies of several poets improved and added to, till Pisistratus finally collected and published them in present form. Those for affirmative join issue as to art of writing; but even if Homer could not write, still he might have produced the Iliad. Bards were frequent in those days, and the times were exciting; that poetry does not, like philosophy, require high civilization to perfect it; that it may be most beautiful at the very dawn of literature; *e. g.* the poetry of Moses, Solomon, and David; that the difficulty of remembering would not be great with a bard who relied entirely on his memory; that recent facts illustrate this remark; *e. g.* the *Dschangariade* of the Calmucs surpasses the poems of Homer in length, as much as it falls short in beauty, and yet exists only in the *memory* of the people. (H. 101.) The songs of a nation are last things committed to writing, because so well remembered. Many negroes in the United States, who cannot read, know as many songs as would amount to Iliad. Lastly, it is contended that there is a unity in both poems, which prove the unity of authorship; that the differences between the books of the Iliad are not greater than between the plays of Shakspeare, and that the supposition of one Homer is much more credible than of twenty.

31. *Effect of the Homeric poems on Greece?* They formed in some measure character of Greeks; founded on best feelings of human nature; on love of wife, children, and country—on love of glory. Again, they infused a national spirit into the divided system of Grecian government; they formed a sort of political constitution for those states, binding them together, warning them of the evils of discord, and of benefit of harmonious intercourse.

SEC. III.—RELIGION OF THE GREEKS.

1. *Importance?* Most polished and elegant religion of ancient world, and belonged not only to the Greeks, but was the religion of the Romans, and is that which came in conflict with, and was finally overthrown by, the Christian religion.

2. *Character?* Polytheistical—a god for almost every department of nature, for physical accomplishments, and even for most of the passions and propensities of the heart; *e. g.* Apollo or Phœbus was god of *sun*, Diana of *moon*, Neptune of the *sea*, Ceres of *agriculture*, Minerva of *wisdom*, Aglaia, Euphrosyne, and Thalia, were the three *Graces*, Venus was goddess of *beauty*, Cupid of *love*, Nemesis of *vengeance*, Pan

of *shepherds*, &c. Every river had its god, and every grove its nymphs —gods, as numerous as multitudes assembled at Olympic games.

3. *Government of the gods?* Sort of limited monarchy—Jupiter king of kings; shakes Olympus by his nod—not powerful as god of *monotheist*—under control of *Fates*—under apprehension of danger from the gods; *e. g.* Thetis in preferring the prayer of Achilles, pleads the service she had rendered, when Jupiter was threatened by the other gods; he relies mainly on physical strength to keep the gods in due subjection—he had not the *omnipresence* and *omniscience* of the God of the Christian; hence, numerous stratagems by which he was deceived; *e. g.* trick of Juno, when she enticed him aside on Mount Ida, whilst Neptune was sent into Grecian camp to fight against Troy, contrary to command of Jove.

4. *Did the gods yield a ready obedience to their king?* By no means—they obey, not because he is wise and good, but because they *fear* him. Juno was always discontented and disposed to thwart him—never did couple quarrel more than this heavenly pair. Minerva speaks of him as "raging with an evil mind, in perpetual opposition to her will." And even when Vulcan on one occasion made peace in heaven, he urges implicit obedience to the great thunderer's will, because of his strength and power, as evidenced by his own lameness, caused by Jupiter putting him out of heaven, on the isle of Lemnos, for his insolence. On one occasion nearly all the gods combined against Jupiter, but he overawed them. Sometimes represented as exceedingly positive, and even tyrannical; *e. g.* in 8th book of Iliad, when he threatens to hurl the god who shall dare to interfere between Greece and Troy, as far beneath the "infernal centre, as from that centre to the upper world."

5. *Were all the gods together omnipotent?* No—when giants made war on heaven, the whole of the gods were alarmed, although all combined. Again, there was as much faction in heaven of polytheist, as on earth; *e. g.* conflict between Greece and Troy, produced two parties among gods; this opposition destroyed their power.

6. *Character of the gods?* Supposed *material* to some extent, having physical wants of man—fed on *ambrosial food* and drank the delicious *nectar*, and were regaled by the *savory odor* which ascended to heaven in the sacrifices. Not perfect; had all foibles and imperfections of human nature; *e. g.* Mercury was most accomplished hypocrite, and the very prince of rogues; Jupiter was represented as very loose in morals—supposed that play of *Amphytrion* was pleasing to him, as every rake likes to hear of his lecherous feats. Their code of morality in many respects detestable; *e. g.* Minerva is represented on one occasion as advising Pandarus to bribe Apollo with *promise* of a hecatomb, to aid him in assas-

sinating Menelaus, contrary to faith of solemn treaty; even Jupiter and Juno join in promoting so foul a murder. Again, instance before quoted, where suitor of Penelope proposes to consult gods, and *particularly* Jupiter, before he would *consent to murder* of Telamachus. The women in polytheistical heaven, on whole, no better than other gods; *e. g.* Minerva is rather a sour unattractive old maid, in spite of all her wisdom—Juno is a morose, scolding, cruel goddess—Venus is beautiful, but dissolute, &c. Individually, gods were like to, but more powerful than men; hence, often engaged in battle with each other, and with men, and sometimes overcome by mortals. In 20th book of Iliad, Jupiter revokes his interdict, and permits the gods to take sides as they choose, with Greece or Troy—general fight between the gods ensues, one *pitted* against another: *e. g.* Phœbus against Neptune; Minerva against Mars; Juno against Diana; Vulcan against Xanthus, &c.—and no one is represented as more formidable than Minerva, who knocked down Mars with a huge rock; a most *unfeminine feat!* In this same battle mortals are represented as daring to contend with immortals, and even triumphantly; *e. g.* Diomed wounds Venus in hand, and sends her weeping to heaven, and in same day comes successfully into conflict with the god of war. Perhaps there is no one of the gods on the field of Troy represented so terrible as Achilles, the great hero of the Iliad. It was in consequence of limited power of gods that certain things were practised which would be inconsistent with our notions of divinity; *e. g.* Spartans prayed *early* in the morning to be beforehand with their adversaries; and Seneca says it was customary to bribe the sexton to give the votary a place as near the god as possible, to be certain of being *heard.* When Alexander besieged the city of Tyre, the Hercules of the temple was bound with chains for fear of his *desertion* to the Greeks. It is said, when Augustus lost his fleet by storm, he refused to let Neptune be carried in procession with the other gods, by way of *disgrace;* and on the death of Germanicus, who was extremely popular in Rome, the gods were taken down and chastised!

7. *Why was polytheistical religion so much more sociable and tolerant towards other religions, than the Jewish and Christian religion?* Because difference in gods worshipped did not argue difference of religion: different religions might contain some gods under different names; or if really different gods, as the multitude was so great, it would only prove that there were some departments of nature to be presided over in one country which did not exist in another. With *monotheism*, case very different, all systems of polytheisms must be false, there can be no compromise; *e. g.* Tiberius proposed, it has been said, to place statue of Christ in Pantheon among the gods; proposition

most scornfully rejected by Christians. Polytheists readily allowed statues of their emperors to be placed in their temples; but Agrippa, king of the Jews, is reported to have fainted when he heard of the order of Caligula to set up his statue in the temple of Jerusalem, and whole city would have perished rather than have seen Caligula's statue placed in the *sanctum sanctorum*.

8. *Origin of the Grecian religion?* Supposed to have been derived in great measure from the religion of Egyptians, as before explained; still large portion was of Grecian origin, and that even though taken from Egypt, became *Grecian* in character.

9. *Which supposed to be most natural, and prior in point of time, theism or polytheism?* If we go back to creation of man or even to human race just after the deluge, we find monotheism first. But if the question be, which would most naturally arise among a set of barbarians without any religion, then it becomes more doubtful. Those who suppose monotheism prior in point of time, say, that providence of god takes its character from peculiar circumstances in which it is employed; *e. g.* in maritime situations the people will have a god of *sea*, a Neptune; a forest people will have a *hunting god;* an agricultural people will have *god of tillage*, &c. By, and by, those tribes having each but *one* god, enlarge and mix by conquest and colonization, and give and receive each other's gods; hence *polytheism*. To this theory Mitford and Fergusson incline—on other side, Mr. Hume contends that polytheism is most natural, and prior in point of time; first, he makes appeal to facts, that polytheism exists among all semi-barbarous nations; that there was a constant tendency to it among the *Jews;* that the Christian religion during the middle ages did, in fact, degenerate into sort of polytheism—that throughout world, nearer you get to state of nature, the more divided you find divinity, &c. Explanation of the fact—large and comprehensive minds take in whole view of nature at once—there appears unity of design throughout, and harmony in all its parts—not so with mind of *savage;* he sees nature in part; hence diversity, and even contradiction, apparent throughout—supposes a number of independent or even opposing divinities to account for the results; *e. g.* tiller of soil plants his grain, by genial influence of sun and moisture it is reared to maturity, when the storm arises and prostrates all his hopes—he is apt to think *good* spirit presided over the seasons that were propitious, and that an *evil* one presided over the destroying hurricane—thus, throughout physical world, element seems at war with element, principle with principle; *e. g.* fire to water, heat to cold, rest to motion, &c.—again, in mental world, same apparent opposition; thousand motives seem to operate at once, and every principle seems to have antagonist; *e. g. selfishness* courses one way,

benevolence another—*love of glory* pushes us into the battle-field, and *fear* makes us tremble when we get there—the *love of virtue* imposes restraints on our inclinations, the *love of pleasure* makes us disregard them. In view of these manifold oppositions and inconsistencies, the savage supposes as many supernatural agencies or intelligences at work in the physical and moral world; hence he has his *good* gods and his *bad* gods—he has his god of the *sun* and his god of the *sea*, he has god of the *winds*, and god of the *mountains*—he has his god of *wisdom* and his god of *battle*, his god of *vengeance* and his god of *love*, the god of *marriage* and the god of *celibacy*; he has the Graces and the Furies, an Elysium and a Tartarus, a Jupiter and a Pluto. It is only the large philosophical mind that can leap at once the vast chasm that separates the human from the divine nature; and can see amidst the apparent contradictions and elemental strife of nature's parts, a unity and harmony which demonstrate existence of but *one architect* for the whole system of the universe; hence, diffusion of intelligence best guarantee for preservation of true religion. Again, capacious mind most struck by constancy of nature's laws and orderly arrangements of universe;

> "The regular return of genial months,
> And renovation of a faded world."

Not so with limited mind of a savage; he is most struck with the erratic movements of nature; the meteor, the comet, the eclipse, the earthquake, the prodigy of every description, are what strike him most forcibly, and these are not so apt to be looked on as result of some unchanging intelligent cause. But again, says Mr. Hume, we are in perpetual suspense—balancing between our *hopes and fears*, between life and death, health and sickness, plenty and want. While thus in constant apprehension without understanding causes of events—*causas rerum*—imagination is at work, conjuring up supernatural agencies to account for these results; hence this kind of superstition in compound ratio of ignorance and liability to accident; *e. g.* negroes more superstitious than whites, because more ignorant; sailors more superstitious than landsmen of same intelligence, because more liable to accidents on an unsteady element; for same reason soldiers, gamblers, &c., are apt to be superstitious.

10. *Other reasons which operated in production of Grecian polytheism?* There is disposition in man to give attributes of mind to material objects; *e. g.* veneration for *Holy Land*, love for *plank* that has saved us in shipwreck, a choleric man curses the *stone* that hurts him, and even a dog barks at it—hence, frequency of the *prosopopœia.* This disposition in unenlightened age quickly leads on to deification of ob-

jects of nature—no land so well calculated as Greece to produce this effect. Rivers, bays, mountains, rocks, islands, all under the influence of genial clime and a brilliant sun, well calculated to produce a multitude of *local divinities.* Besides all the above-mentioned causes, hero-worship might have become a very fruitful source of deification, as before explained.

11. *Character of the priesthood?* No regular organized priesthood as in Egypt. In armies there were priests; *e. g.* Calchas, Chryses, Maro, Dares, &c., and there were afterwards local oracles, but never had organized power of a regular priesthood in army; generals sacrificed as well as priests, and in temples officers taken from people, and served but a short time generally.

12. *Effect of this?* Religion left to people—few *mysteries* except those introduced from Egypt. A regular priesthood sure to link philosophy with religion, and make an incomprehensible mystery of whole; *e. g.* Egypt, where *esoteric* religion was always a mystery. Philosophy tied to religion never advances—hence, no advance in the east; in Greece left free, consequently pushed to high state of perfection. Again, when regular priesthood, with regular support and leisure to construct their system, they make a *symbolical religion;* manage to give a symbolical meaning to all their gods; *e. g.* Egyptians represented *Ammon* with *ram's head*, because sun is in *Aries* when Egyptian spring commences, and Ammon was a sort of type of spring, being the *vis vivica* of the Egyptian. Upon similar principles, the *sphinxes* have been explained, representing *male and female natures.* Hence, in following out symbols, it was no matter how much nature was outraged; *e. g.* Indian will give his god twenty arms, Phrygian represents his Diana with as many breasts, the Egyptian puts heads of animals on man's body—or *vice versa*—human form subordinate—great object symbolical. Absence of priesthood has powerful tendency to destroy *symbolism*—people have not leisure and time to perfect such things—hence, the gods introduced into Greece soon lost symbolical character. In Hesiod and Homer we have traces of *symbolism; e. g.* Jupiter sometimes designates *pure ether*, Juno *atmosphere*, and even in matching the gods, in 20th book of Iliad, some suppose Homer to be symbolical; *e. g.* Mars against Minerva, *i. e. rashness* vs. *prudence;* Neptune *vs.* Apollo, *i. e. water* vs. *sun;* Juno *vs.* Diana, *i. e. marriage* vs. *celibacy*, &c. But we find even in Homer a disposition to throw off *symbolism* and to make gods *moral persons; e. g.* to make Jupiter true *ruler of gods and men*, Juno *queen of heaven*, the god of war a *real terrible warrior*, &c. The later Greeks completely succeeded, and hence, gods everywhere, *moral persons*, under human shapes.

13. *Did the Greeks believe in a hereafter, and a system of rewards and punishments in another world?* They did, but their notions were indistinct; when body perished, soul escaped like a dream; went to invisible world or *Hades*, and had no rest until body had received rites of burial; hence, desperate effort of Priam to obtain corpse of Hector. In *Hades*, soul without the body, has nevertheless same form, but little strength; pursues same avocations as on earth, but in a joyless, unprofitable manner; *e. g.* Orion, like spectre of North American hunter, pursues *disembodied beasts*, which he had killed in mountains, over the Asphodel meadow—Minos holds mock trials—Achilles still pre-eminent in world of spirits; but in spite of all this the prospect was gloomy and cheerless, and spirit losing its body, lost its energy and mental vigor. Achilles tells Ulysses he would prefer to return to earth, and he says that *the ghost* is all that is left in Hades, *the mind* is gone. As far below Hades, as from latter to upper world, was the deep gulf of Tartarus, to which the enemies of the gods were condemned; locked in with iron gates and a brazen floor. On other hand, a *very few* favored heroes were wafted to a delicious island of ocean, cooled by perpetual zephyrs, &c. Such is the *hereafter* of Homer.—In succeeding ages it was stripped of most of its revolting features, and the *Elysium* of Virgil is infinitely superior to the *Hades* of Homer.

14. *For offending the gods what punishment was most dreaded?* Punishment in this world, not hereafter. No actions so meritorious in the sight of gods as pious munificence and liberal sacrifices; pride and insolence, and neglect of gods were unpardonable.

15. *Influence of religion on Grecian character?* 1st, The gloomy existence in Hades was calculated to make the Greeks endeavor to enjoy themselves in this world; "make the most of existence," said the poets, for soon comes the *dreary Hades*." 2d, On the moral character, effect rather pernicious—exmples of the gods were corrupting; Heeren says, however, that gods did not set themselves up as *examples*; their doctrine was, do as we *order*, and not as *we do*; some truth in remark. Society of gods was but an expose, on a larger scale, of the society of men; good and bad; but all not worthy of imitation; *e. g.* foibles of Jupiter, and lewdness of Venus, not worthy of imitation, but their nobler qualities were; and it was office of *Furies* to punish transgressions, whether in imitation of gods or not; their dwelling place in depths of invisible world; an object of horror to wicked; shrouded themselves in darkness when executing work of retribution, and unlike other gods, could not be propitiated. But in spite of all this, the examples of the gods must have had a pernicious moral influence, on principle that the vices of superiors are readily imitated by inferiors; and because too, the mortal

who was most virtuous was not most acceptable, but one who sacrificed most liberally, and because greatest of gods could be bribed to aid in foulest of crimes. 3d, Influence on character in other respects was great —gods had human forms and human tempers. When Epicurus said gods were *indifferent* to human events, he virtually robbed man of the divinity; but this not creed of the Greek, he believed his gods took deep interest in human events, therefore could be approached more easily. Sympathy more complete—idea of *one dread eternal God* under no human form, is an abstraction not easily realized; hence, Christ, who was clothed with human form, and died on the cross, has made christian religion much more attractive to mass of mankind. Catholic approaches his saint, or virgin, more confidently than he does his God because not so far removed from himself; in same manner polytheist of old lived upon familiar terms with his gods; depended upon them in his difficulties—he was made a more energetic being by their aid and example, whether for good or bad; *e. g.* the warrior was made more sanguinary and active by the stimulating example of god of war; whether the votary imitated the virtues or the vices of Jupiter, with such an example, he was sure to become the more energetic. Gods produced same effect on Greece, that such men as Alexander, Cæsar, Alfred, Bonaparte, and Washington produce now upon the human family.

16. *Although polytheism was the creed of the Greeks and Romans, are we to suppose that the philosophers were incapable of arriving at the conclusion of one supreme God?* Unity of the divinity was certainly the *philosophical belief*, *e. g.* Cicero speaks of one law and *one* God governing the universe, as the human soul governs the body which it animates. Seneca tells us that the different names given to the deities were only descriptive of the different characters in which the God of nature appears to us in his works. Plutarch expresses himself to same effect—as *sun* is common to all the world, though called by different names in different places, so there is but *one supreme mind* that governs the world, though worshipped under different names, and has *inferior powers* for his ministers. (S. Ac. and Mo. Pow. vol. 2, 51.) Socrates and Anaxagoras, among the Greeks, are both supposed to have been impressed with the unity of divinity. Thus we clearly see how philosophy is the ally of the true religion, while ignorance leads on to idolatry and superstition. Ignorance scatters the divine nature into countless multitudes of gods, whilst philosophy and reason concentrates it into one eternal sublime supreme God, such as the Christian adores.

17. *May not the number of gods that have been worshipped in different ages, and the different forms in which religion has appeared in dif-*

feret countries, be considered as formidable argument against the existence of any God, or of any true religion? Las Cases reports Bonaparte as saying that this argument was considered by him, at the age of thirteen even, as unanswerable. Bonaparte's conclusion illogical; diversity in forms rather proves truth of great points in which there is coincidence. The more overwhelming is truth, the more liable we are to connect absurdity with it, and to believe that absurdity, because of its connection with the splendid truth which the mind cannot reject. Thus the belief in an intelligent cause is so strong, so necessary to human nature, that man will not reject it, although it may often be presented to the mind by the various superstitions in a thousand different forms, connected with startling absurdities; a truth not deeply impressed, or of little importance, can never produce such an effect; we will believe it independently, but we will reject it if accompanied by absurdity; it is only the great truth stamped indelibly upon the human heart, which can produce conviction not only of *its own* reality, but of *that* even, of the absurdity which becomes connected with it. Achilles may love Patroclus so much that even his vices may appear as virtues. Some one of the ancient world is reported to have said that he would rather believe *drunkenness no vice*, than that Plato could do wrong. Only intensest admiration can produce this effect; so it is only great convincing truth that can cover and protect revolting absurdity; and in view, no doubt, of this fact, Lord Bacon exclaimed that he "had rather believe all the fables in the *Legend*, and the *Talmud*, and the *Alcoran*, than that this universal frame is without a *mind*;" (p. 60.) that is, that there is nothing, however absurd, springing out of religion, to which it would not be easier to *give* his assent than to *withhold* it from this great truth proclaimed by every part of the universe. Absurd forms then, in which religion has so often appeared and been received as truth by its votaries, only the stronger proof of those great truths which belong to all religions. Hume says, "examine the religious principles which have prevailed in the world, you will scarcely be persuaded they are any thing but sick men's dreams," "or playsome whimsies of monkeys in man's shape;" and hence, concludes that "the whole is a riddle, an inexplicable mystery," &c. Conclusion *non sequitur*.

18. *Are there any general tenets belonging to all religions?* All religions agree in a system of rewards and punishments either *here* or *hereafter;* in the belief of a Tartarus and an Elysium; in the belief of a first great cause, or a number of superhuman intelligences, who order and govern the universe. "In such a contest and disagreement (about mere forms) you may see," says Maximus Tyrius, "this one law and speech acknowledged by common accord, that there is one God, the

king and father of all, and many gods the children of gods, and ruling together with him. This the Greek says, and this the barbarian says, and the inhabitant of the continent and the islander, and the wise and the unwise." Again, all nations agree in having some religion. "If you search the world," says Plutarch, "you may find cities without walls, without letters, without kings, without money; but no one ever saw a city without a deity, without a temple, or without some form of worship." (57.)

SEC. IV.—GREECE AFTER THE TROJAN WAR.

1. *In what condition did the Grecian chiefs find their countries after the siege of Troy?* Siege of Troy, by drawing off most efficient men from states of Greece, had a tendency to throw governments into great confusion; as a few individuals of character are much more important in a small semi-barbarous state than in a large civilized kingdom—hence, chiefs on return had great difficulties to surmount; *e. g.* Ulysses after his wanderings found his kingdoms disordered and impoverished; Agamemnon had scarce set foot on Argive territory before he was murdered by Egystheus, who had married Clytemnestra, and usurped throne of Argos in his absence. Old Nestor found a more quiet kingdom, &c.; but generally, states of Greece were thrown into disorder.

2. *What next great event which claims attention of historian?* Return of the Heracleidæ, or the descendants of Hercules. Driven from Peloponnesus, some time before the Trojan war, they had retired beyond Isthmus of Corinth, and about eighty years after Trojan war are supposed to have returned at the head of the Dorians, and dispossessed the Pelopidæ, or descendants of Pelops, of the principal portion of the Peloponnesus.

3. *Condition of Greece for nealy* 400 *years after the return of Heracleidæ?* By the conquests of the Heracleidæ and other causes, Greece was re-plunged almost into her original barbarism. Her history for a long period is obscure and uncertain; civil wars, internal and external migrations and colonizations were very frequent during the whole of this period; *e. g.* the Eolic, Ionic, and Doric migrations, and colonies in Thrace, Macedon, Africa, and Magna Græcia.

4. *Change in the governments of Greece during this period?* From south of Peloponnesus to north of Thessaly, with the exception of Sparta, monarchy seems to have expired, and to have been succeeded every where by either an oligarchy or democracy.

5. *Immediate effect of this change?* Plunged Greece into still greater disorder, and caused her territories to be divided into yet smaller

states than before. But the remote effect of this change was to make the Greeks, at the same time, the most energetic and most turbulent people which the world has ever seen.

6. *Causes which produced change in Grecian governments?* It is impossible now to find out the particular causes which operated in each state of Greece; but easy to point to circumstances favoring the change. First, frequent migrations and conquests; stability of monarchy rests on undisputed title, and quiet succession for ages; no such monarchy in Greece; kings too often dethroned by conquest, or from decrepitude of age, or imbecility, &c. Second, colonization was another cause of change; have already seen in time of Homer that government, although kingly, was not despotic, chiefs and people had power and liberty. Now suppose a colony sent out by such a state; as king stays at home, colony would naturally assume either the oligarchical or democratic form; *e. g.* all the colonies of Great Britain on becoming independent, naturally assume republican form. Even colonies of Spain have same tendency—not proper materials in colony to organize *regular monarchy*. Third circumstance, and most important, was the smallness of the Grecian states. Government much easier overthrown in small states than in large one; an organized power becomes more formidable in proportion to *absolute*, and not to *relative* strength. This a principle of great importance, and may be thus illustrated: Government is the *organized power*, the subjects constitute the *disorganized power;* the latter is in all monarchical states the greater numerical force, but rendered less efficient by disorganization. Chance for a revolution depends on a successful combination of the disorganized against the organized party, which is always more easy in small than large community; *e. g.* suppose the parties are as 1 to 10 in numbers—it is evident if you suppose a community of 11, one man could never maintain himself against 10 if dissatisfied; in state of 110, 10 would more easily rule 100 than one would 10; in 1100, 100 would rule 1000 more easily than 10 would 100; but even here in course of a single night a conspiracy might be formed among the 1000 which would break into rebellion on next day, and completely revolutionize the government. If now you will suppose 1,000,000 of men, 100,000 would rule much more easily than in the other cases, and still more easily would 1,000,000 rule 10,000,000; because 1,000,000 being the organized party, always on the alert, and determined of course to maintain their authority, could not be overcome unless by combination of sufficient force against them. Now probability would be against such a combination, for before it could be formed, the secret would transpire, and government would strike at and conquer the conspirators in detail. Again, for precisely the same reasons, a standing army is powerful in a state,

more in proportion to *absolute* than *relative* numbers; *e. g.* let us adopt Gibbon's supposition that 100th man in a community is as much as the people can maintain for keeping up regular army. In community of 100, one man is the military; in that of 1000, 10 men would be, and in that of 1,000,000, 10,000 would be; but one man would have no influence on 100, 10 would have but little on 1,000; but 10,000 would strike terror into largest city on the globe. Wellington says, up to time of Louis Philip, 4,500 soldiers were amply sufficient to keep Paris quiet, and more than enough for London. Paris has 1,000,000 and London 1,500, 000 souls. Army great engine of despotism everywhere. Hence from above we see why revolutions are so frequent in small states and so rare in large ones; *e. g.* states of Greece in ancient, and of Italy in modern times, oftener revolutionized than any other countries in Europe. They represent principles of *mobility;* great southern countries of Asia rarely revolutionized, represent the principle of *immobility.* For above reasons, we have nothing to fear from increase of *blacks,* if the *whites* increase in any thing like the same proportion, because whites are dominant organized power.

7. *What states in Greece are supposed to have taken lead in abolishing monarchy?* Thebes and Athens. Latter supposed to have formally abolished monarchy because Athenians would not be ruled by any king after Codrus, their last king, had so nobly devoted himself to death for his country.

8. *Tyrants and their influence on the Grecian governments?* They answer to our term *usurper*—no legitimate title. Sometimes princes of great mildness and friends of learning, *e. g.* Pesistratidæ at Athens. Their occurrence natural at the transition period of Grecian governments; favored tendency to democracy; first rose to favor by taking democratic side. Machiavel has said truly, sometimes cause of liberty best promoted by putting all power in one hand. (B. 149.) These tyrants in Greece answered to the Cæsars and Bonapartes of larger countries; they rode into power on the triumph of the popular party, and maintained themselves against higher classes by support of the lower. But their dynasties soon terminated; it required but short reigns to make them fall into the obnoxious systems of other monarchs. They were finally driven out of most of the states of Greece. Longest period for any one of these dynasties not more than 100 years, (H. 156,) and this happened only of dynasty of Orthagoras at Sicyon, and of Cypselus at Corinth; both remarkable for great mildness and continued popularity.

9. *What the institutions supposed to have had most effect in remedying the disorders in Greece, and binding states together in a sort of*

federative union? Amphictyonic Council, the Oracle at Delphi, and the Olympic Games.

Amphictyonic Council.

1. *Origin of the term?* Some suppose derived from Amphictyon, son of Deucalion, first founder—all conjecture. Thirlwall says the term almost identical with word which signifies a body with a local centre; (iv. 374.) that there were probably many Amphictyonics with their local centres of union; *e. g.* Strabo mentions one held at Onchestus in Bœotia—no account of states comprising it—another in Island of Calauria, including seven states. Object of these partial unions was to secure the peace and safety of the states, and was something like the *truce of God*, so frequently proclaimed by the popes in modern Europe. But that most celebrated of all, was that known simply by the name of *the Amphictyonic Council*, including largest portion of Greece.

2. *Members, and places of session?* Thessalians, Bœotians, Dorians, Ionians, Perrhœbians, Magnetes, Locrians, Œtians, Phthiots or Achæans, Malians, and Phocians. At the head of Dorians was Sparta, and at head of Ionians was Athens. The council held sessions alternately at Delphi and Thermopylæ. Thirlwall explains this by supposing originally two Amphictyonics, one at Delphi, other at Thermopylæ, and in union it was agreed to sit alternately in each place. (376.)

3. *Object of this larger association?* Same as that of lesser. Object described in oath taken by members—to refrain from utterly destroying any Amphictyonic city, to refrain from cutting off supply of water, and to defend temple and treasure of Delphic oracle from sacrilege.

4. *Did this association accomplish all its ends?* Not perfectly. Members could not be restrained from war and rapine. Hence, only efficient when some powerful states would execute the decrees; *e. g.* punished the Dolopes of Scyrus for piracy by hands of Athenians, who coveted their island. Most legitimate sphere was for honor and safety of Delphic sanctuary; *e. g.* when procession passing through Megara to Delphi was insulted by Megarians, Amphictyonic council punished offenders with death or exile. Again, in celebrated case of Crissa on the Crissean gulf, for insult to strangers returning from the oracle, Amphictyons proclaimed a sort of sacred war against the city, and by the aid of Thessalians under Eurylochus, and Sicyonians under the tyrant Cleisthenes, Crissa was razed and the whole Circhæan plain laid waste. Thus it was in cases where Amphictyonic council could call in a powerful state to execute, or when it attempted something calculated to excite the sympathies of all Greece, that its action was efficient.

5. *Moral effects of the council?* Drew most talented men together from all Greece—interchanged ideas and notions about government—hence, a more rapid diffusion of knowledge and laws. This advantage augmented after establishments of democracies, because a greater number of delegates were sent from each state. It had the effect of infusing a national spirit among the Greeks, of supporting a sort of *law of nations* among them, and rendering the character more homogeneous. This council, and others like it, furnish almost only instances of regular representative government in ancient world.

6. *Age of Amphictyonic council?* Supposed to have been before Trojan war, though Homer makes no mention of it.

Delphic Oracle.

1. *General cause for the establishment of oracles?* Desire of man to look into futurity. This ardent desire renders him liable to imposture. In ancient time, soothsayers and prophets were more generally credited, because of greater ignorance of people, and the greater superstition inspired by polytheistical religion. At present day, even negroes and ignorant persons have great faith in *fortune-tellers and conjurers;* among our Indians, every tribe has its prophets, who are always men of great influence.

2. *Particular cause?* Supposed that a Phœnician captain carried off woman attendant in the temple of Jupiter Ammon, at Thebes, and sold her as slave in Epirus; woman discovered her superiority to Epirots; said she possessed the power of foretelling, from priests of Egypt; her pretensions excited curiosity; she took her station under large oak near Dodona, and gave her responses to multitudes who consulted. Hence fiction preserved by priests of Dodona, that black pigeon flew from Thebes to Dodona, and perching upon oak, proclaimed in foreign dialect that oracle should be established there. A temple was built, a priest proclaimed, and hence *oracle of Dodona.*

3. *Two kinds of oracles?* Persons who travelled and attended the camps and armies, like Calchas and Chryses at siege of Troy, or local oracles, like those of Olympia and Delphi.

4. *Objection to moving oracles attached to armies?* Were overawed by chieftains; *e. g.* Calchas was afraid to tell the real cause of Grecian disasters on one occasion, lest he might offend Agamemnon, and did not venture till Achilles promised he should receive no injury—hence Euripides says prophecies should be delivered by Apollo alone, who respects nobody. For this reason local oracles were preferred.

5. *Where would these oracles be naturally established?* At any place which from any cause was supposed to be honored by special grace

and frequent presence of a god; *e. g.* oracle at Olympia in honor of Jupiter.

6. *Origin of the oracle at Delphi?* On southern side of Mount Parnassus, dividing Phocis from Locris, was a profound cavern with crevices emitting a mephitic sulphureous vapor, powerfully affecting brain of those who inhaled it. Said to be first discovered by a goat-herd, whose goats came out leaping and skipping after breathing the gas—the goat-herd went in and came out like his goats, leaping and dancing. Soon supposed that this vapor was the breath of inspiration from the god of the place. Even in more enlightened times in Greece, frenzy of every kind was supposed result of inspiration, and incoherent speeches of frantic men were thought prophetic. Whole scenery calculated to foster the idea; projecting ridges of Mount Parnassus hung over chasm from north like a canopy; two immense rocks flanked it on east and west, and rugged Mount Cirphis guarded it on south. This almost inaccessible spot, called *Delphi*, (*solitary*, *alone*,) rendered more romantic by numberless echoes that multiplied every sound, and inspired visitor with intensest veneration for god of the place. At first every individual wishing to consult the god inhaled the vapor; but this attended often with fatal consequences, a priestess was then chosen, a temple built, and the Pythia or priestess was seated on a tripod, when she inhaled the gas, and her response was given under the excitement produced by it.

7. *Who was selected for priestess?* At first a *young*, *ignorant* virgin. In consequence of the defilement of Pythia by a votary, one of 50 years was afterwards chosen?

8. *Why ignorant?* Because supposed less mind the priestess had, the more certainly would she utter the inspirations of the god.

9. *Reputation and wealth of the oracle?* Soon became the most celebrated oracle in world; occupied central position in Greece; in a city honored by meeting of Amphictyonic council, which was its protector; objects collected in groves and temple, to astonish admiring multitude; *e. g.* splendor of marble, gold and silver statues, and the magic of painting, seemed to introduce beholder to actual Olympus in presence of the gods. Rich magnificence proverbial even in Homer's day.

10. *Sources of wealth?* First, all who came to consult the god paid liberally for the response. Second, being a place of great sanctity, and under especial protection of Amphictyonic council, in time of trouble and conquest both private and public treasure was deposited in temple—hence became a sort of *bank of deposit* for all Greece. In time of Xerxes wealth of oracle hyperbolically spoken of as equalling revenue

of Persian monarch. Under these circumstances, not to be wondered that city of Delphi, fronting the chasm in amphitheatrical form, should become one of the richest and most celebrated cities of Greece.

11. *Responses?* Before given, sacrifices were made, and if not favorable, pythoness could not be inspired; this one way of putting off or denying answers. Again, only a few days in year, under any circumstances, when god could be interrogated. When answers were given, priestess was led to tripod by the priests of temple, and by some means, she was thrown into convulsions—broken accents, uttered in phrenzy, were collected and arranged as responses of gods. These responses were often ambiguous or figurative, so as to admit of an interpretation either way, when events were doubtful. In some cases, however, when decisive answer could be risked, it was given.

12. *Faith reposed in ancient oracles, especially that at Delphi?* Implicit among the ancients. Even some of earlier Christians admitted the power of vaticination, but supposed it came from *Devil.* Some modern philosophers are far from considering common explanation of impositions of ancient oracles as satisfactory; *e. g.* Niebuhr said oracles were strange things, and that it was easier to *say* that it was all artifice of priests than to *prove* it. (L. R. 188.) He rather leaves the impression that he did not consider them as impositions.

13 *Why was not the imposition detected?* For following reasons: Priests gave the answers to those who applied, not the pythoness; they were of course among the most learned and intelligent men of the times; they could delay the answer, or even refuse altogether, if sacrifices were unpropitious; in doubtful cases they could give ambiguous answers; in cases where a judgment about the result could be easily formed, they gave clear answer. The very response of the oracle had a tendency to produce the result predicted; it discouraged one side, whilst it inspired confidence in the other; in case the event happened differently from what was anticipated, it was easy to give a figurative sense to the prophecy, and thus save credit of oracle. In many cases, prophecies could be safely made, because sure to happen somewhere, or to satisfaction of some people; and lastly, there is a wonderful disposition to believe the marvellous and miraculous.

14. *Illustrations of the above?* In celebrated response of oracle to Pyrrhus, "*Æaciden posse vincere Romanos*," he might interpret either way. It was predicted that Vespasian and Titus would become emperors; so might any man of sense have predicted, seeing a madman on the throne, and these two men adored by the army. In celebrated case of Joan d'Arc, her predictions inspired new courage in the French, and dispirited the English, hence success of the French. Tell a super-

stitious man that he will die before a given day, and the first spell of sickness will be apt to prove fatal. Voltaire in his "*Essai sur les Mœurs*," says it was predicted in the Leige Almanac, that a *people* would come from the north that year that should destroy every thing. No people came, but there came a *cold north wind* which destroyed vineyards, and prophecy was fulfilled. Again, in same almanac there was a prediction that a *great man* would die, and that there would be a *shipwreck*. The *village judge* died, and some *fishermen* sunk in a little vessel near the shore, and Mons. Laensborgh was immediately looked on as the great prophet of Leige. For same reason, the *vials* mentioned in scripture have been identified with the great warriors of every age; and several Anti-Christs have been clearly pointed out by knowing ones. As to disposition of human mind to believe in extraordinary coincidences, and superhuman powers, all writers have noticed it. Even the highest order of intelligence is not always exempt from this weakness. Bacon and Sir Matthew Hale believed in witchcraft; Tycho-Brahe in astrology, and even Queen Elizabeth sent to Dr. John Dee, the astrologer, to consult about the most lucky day for her coronation. So prone are we to believe in the marvellous, that it is with reluctance we surrender our belief even when the fraud is detected. To this day, one half the world believes in the existence of a *Upas tree*. This same propensity causes any extraordinary coincidence to be circulated widely while contrary is not noticed; *e. g.* one dream which comes to pass, is told of, and remembered, while the thousands of failures are never mentioned, or soon forgotten.

14. *Effects of the oracle of Delphi upon Greece?* Under the especial protection of Amphictyonic council, therefore, interested in keeping the peace of Greece. Its great authority enabled it to compass many differences. Cicero says, such the reputation of oracle, that no expedition was undertaken, no colony sent out, and often no affair of any distinguished family or individual entered on without its sanction. It often inspired Greeks with courage against foreign foe. It made the priests of Delphi study profoundly the politics of the whole world, and particularly of every state of Greece; in infant state of civilization, of great advantage to have an institution which compels a certain class to become profoundly imbued with political philosophy; it is well to make a lodgement of learning some where. True, that this desire for information, led the priests often to get their information by dishonest means; *e. g.* they bribed attendants to communicate the secrets of those who came to consult oracle; they took advantage of secret confessions in the mysteries, and they no doubt had a regular system of *espionage* over all Greece, by which they were made acquainted with all that was going on.

Besides all this, the oracle was often bribed to get a favorable answer. Upon the whole, however, an institution tending to remedy disorders of times, and push forward civilization more rapidly in Greece.

Olympic Games.

1. *General cause for establishment of games in Greece?* All people have sports of some kind; generally determined by circumstances. Those of antiquity were well calculated to strengthen the body and prepare for war, particulary so in Greece, because, first, in use of arms of antiquity bodily strength was indispensable; and second, states of Greece small and always engaged in war. At the funeral of Patroclus, in Iliad, are mentioned the following games: chariot race, foot race, boxing, wrestling, throwing the quoit and the javelin, shooting with the bow, and fencing with the spear, nearly the same as those at Olympia.

2. *Origin of Olympic games?* In first place, particular gods honored particular spots; *e. g.* Apollo, Delphi; Neptune, Isthmus of Corinth; and Jupiter, Olympia, in Elis. Hence supposed from earliest times there had been games in honor of Jupiter, but had been discontinued; and in time of Iphitus, in consequence of the dissensions of Elis, oracle at Delphi was consulted, and response was that the games should be re-established, and that a truce should take place during the five days of the festival.

3. *Describe the Gymnasium where these sports took place?* A spacious edifice surrounded by a double range of pillars, with an open area in the middle; adjoining were various apartments containing baths and other conveniences for the combatants; near to these were shady walks and groves, interspersed with seats and adorned with porticoes, for the recreation of the combatants, the lectures of the sophists, the exhibitions of the poet, the historian, &c.

4. *What did these games, in their most perfect form, consist of?* First, those of the Stadium; second, of Hippodrome.

5. *Stadium?* Consisted of an elliptical terrace, arranged principally with a view to the foot race. That at Athens, of a later period, was 120 geometrical paces in length, and 27 in breadth. It lay along the Ilissus and was lined on both sides with white marble. That at Olympia was of same dimensions, and contained at one end, called the goal, an elevated throne for the judges, whilst at the other end was the tomb of Endymion, the favorite of Diana, in beautiful white marble.

6. *Games of the Stadium?* First, the foot race; second, leaping; third, wrestling; fourth, exercises of the arm; fifth, boxing, and fighting with the cestus. Besides these compound sports; *e. g. pancration*, boxing and wrestling; *pentathlon*, all five, &c. First, for running, combatants were naked and passed the goal twice, and sometimes twelve times;

then the race was more than a two-mile heat; sometimes ran with weights. Olympiad generally distinguished by him who won the foot race; *e. g.* first Olympiad "*when Chorœbus won the foot race.*" Second, in leaping, object to surpass in length, not height; carried leaden weights with holes through them for fingers; weights not thrown behind as now-a-days. Report concerning the leaping of antiquity incredible; *e. g.* Phaulus of Crotona, leaped 55 feet, and Chinos of Sparta, 52. Third, wrestling—rubbed with oil and sand; victory adjudged to him who threw adversary three times in five—best three in five. Fourth, exercises of arm, in pitching quoit and throwing javelin; quoit, a large disc of metal—object, distance, not exactness of aim; in throwing javelin both distance and exactness. Fifth, boxing not in very high repute, especially among the Spartans; because supposed necessary to cultivate large amount of flesh to protect the ribs, which led on to a luxurious mode of living, at war with Spartan abstemiousness, and voluntary hardships. As to cestus, it was a leathern thong loaded with lead, and was introduced at 23d Olympiad—an exceedingly dangerous weapon, and therefore not in high repute, especially after Damoxenus slew his adversary by foul play, so that he was driven from the stadium in disgrace, and the wreath solemnly adjudged to his dead victim. In this game combatants had headpiece of brass for protection, but in spite of all precaution, mutilation or death was the frequent consequence. Lucilius tells of a cestus fighter so battered that he could not prove his identy, and lost his inheritance in consequence.

> "For by his brother sued—disowned—at last,
> Confronted with his picture, he was cast."—(F. G. & A. 66.)

7. *Hippodrome?* Of same form as Stadium, though much larger, so that forty chariots could go abreast. These chariots open vehicles, generally on two wheels, drawn by two or four horses, connected with yokes abreast; (*byjugæ* and *quadrijugæ.*) Charioteer stood erect, and generally drove twelve times around the Hippodrome, making several miles. Often a scene of perfect confusion; difficult to prevent being turned over or knocked out of the track; *e. g.* in Electra of Sophocles, he represents every one of the ten competitors as being overthrown or knocked out of his chariot, in consequence of the running away of the hard-mouthed steeds that drew the Thracian car. Only wealthy men could join in the sports of the Hippodrome. On one occasion, Alcibiades entered seven charriots, and won with three of them. At a later period, Nero, the emperor, drove a chariot drawn by ten horses on the Hippodrome, and was tumbled out of his chariot and lost the race. Ladies could appear here by proxy.

8. *Qualifications of those who contended?* Open to all the Greeks,

whether rich or poor, who had never been slaves or disgraced; but not to foreigners, not even kings and princes; *e. g.* Alexander, son of Amyntas, king of Macedon, not permitted to enter lists until he proved his Argive descent.

9. *Comparison of these games, as mere amusements, with the Roman and other games?* Infinitely preferable to the gladiatorial sports and combats with the wild beasts in a Roman amphitheatre—which were nothing but "gratuitous ferocities," and "graceless butcheries." (B. 111.) The tilts and tournaments of the chivalrous age were very little better than barbarous shows; and only a few, those of royal and noble blood, or knightly honors, could enter the lists; but in Greece, no restriction. Olympic games have been called "knighthood of a whole people." (113.)

10. *Prize and honors to the Olympic victors?* In games described by Homer and Virgil, valuable prizes were given to victor; but at Olympia after seventh Olympiad, a simple garland of the leaves of the wild olive was placed upon his head. Honors—a statue in the *Altis*, erected by his friends or his country; his name was inscribed in the public register; odes in honor of him composed by the poets; shouts and praises of assembled Greece; showers of flowers and a banquet; all these honors received at Olympia. On returning home, he passed through a breach in the walls, (metaphor denoting walls unnecessary, when there were such citizens;) first seat in public spectacles; at Athens was entitled to 500 drachmas, and a place by magistrates in Prytaneum; at Sparta to prominent station in field. (112.) Even greatest cities were proud of victor; *e. g.* Hiero, Syracusian tyrant, prevailed on Astylus of Croton, who won the foot race in three successive Olympiads, to transfer honor of the two last to Syracuse, which Crotonians resented by taking down his statue, and turning his house into a prison. (T. v. i. 389.)

11. *Effects on the condition of Greece?* First, on the body—training for games increased the mere physical accomplishments of the Greeks; kept them in health and vigor, whilst it prepared them for war, developed all the muscles, and produced finest forms; *e. g.* combatants generally finely formed men, as statues in the Altis prove. Hence one reason for the favorable influence of the games on statuary. On other hand produced too intense an admiration of display of mere animal powers, and in training individual, neglected too much duties of citizens. Second, an union of states, doubtful, opened only to Greeks, therefore drew a line between them and the barbarians; but at same time produced intense rivalry between states. Many states had separate treasuries at Olympia for reception of their offerings, which were

often so many monuments of their enmity. (T. 391.) But although in some respects unfavorable to national spirit, yet in third place contributed to harmony, because truce was declared during the time of holding the games, and as there were three other places at which games were holden, there was an armstice throughout all Greece every year—even a short suspension of arms is favorable to peace. Again, stood in place of the modern establishment of resident ambassadors ; the leading citizens of Greece met at the games ; could make treaties of peace there, or amicably settle their disputes. Fourth, these games brought together the first men of the age ; intercourse between them favorable to civilization ; the philosophers and sophists gave their lectures ; poets and historians read their works ; *e. g.* Pindar read his poetry and Herodotus his history—last not well authenticated—but still such things were done ; stood in the place of the press, in communication of thought, invention, and discovery ; at some of these games, particularly the Pythian, regular prizes were adjudged in poetry, song, and music, as well as for the gymnastic feats. Fifthly, effect important in a politico-economical light ; acted as *fairs* in modern times, where all things could be bought and sold, and enriched greatly territories in which the games were holden.

12. *Where were the other games holden in Greece?* At Delphi, Isthmus of Corinth, and in Argos—called the Delphic, Isthmean, and Nemean games—sacred to Apollo, Neptune, and Juno. These alternating with Olympic games, made the period of Olympiad four years, and the celebration of some one of the games every year.

Spartan Laws.

As the laws of Lycurgus and Solon are supposed to have had a great influence on Greece, and are reckoned, especially the former, to have contributed very powerfully to the establishment of order and tranquillity, it becomes necessary to explain these two celebrated codes.

1. *How came Sparta to remain monarchical when other states changed their governments?* Supposed by some to have been the result of *diarchy*, or double executive. After return of Heraclides, Laconia fell to Aristodemus, who had twins, Eurysthenes and Procles ; mother either would not or could not tell the elder, and consequently both permitted to rule. Mutual jealousies weakened the royal prerogative so much, as to throw great power into hands of people, and therefore they did not desire change. Whether the accident of birth produced the diarchy in Sparta, cannot be positively told. Legends of Thebes, as well as the catalogue of the Iliad, prove this double executive familiar to ancients. (T. 318.)

2. *Story of Lycurgus?* Fifth in descent from Procles. His brother Polydectes, king of Sparta, dying, left widow pregnant, who informed Lycurgus if he would promise to marry her, the issue, if male, should be destroyed; feigned compliance; had the boy after birth brought to him, and proclaimed king under name of Charilaus (joy of the people). Queen enraged, raised a faction against him; spread the report that he had attempted life of child; consequence was, Lycurgus travelled abroad; visited Crete and Phrygia, some say Egypt and India. In this journey he was enabled to look into laws of various countries. His travels did for him what the press and books do for modern legislators. He returned home with an unsullied name and great reputation; found his country in the utmost disorder; a new system of legislation called for by all, and himself looked to as the saviour of his country; procured sanction of Delphic oracle for his laws; promulgated them; then obtained promise from people that no change should be made in them till his return; left Sparta and *never returned.*

3. *Is the story of Lycurgus generally believed to be correct?* History of world has never furnished us with a parallel instance of one man at once introducing and carrying through an entire system of laws, impressing a distinct character upon a whole people, and enduring for ages afterwards. Moreover, similar laws it is known existed in Sparta and other portions of Greece and her colonies, before the time of Lycurgus; hence many have not only doubted the sole agency of Lycurgus in the promulgation of Spartan system, but have even doubted his existence. We have no grounds for this conclusion, and must therefore admit his existence. Although he did not originate the entire system, yet he digested the code, thus acting the part of Edward the Confessor, or of Edward I., in England.

4. *Estates in the government of Sparta?* First, kings; second, a senate; and third, assembly of the people; fourth, ephoralty.

5. *Kings?* There were two; at home in time of peace, power small; ex-officio presidents of the senate; united priestly with regal power; their garb was simple like other citizens; could be reprimanded, deposed, or even put to death; in war, when abroad at head of army, their power absolute, like as in heroic times; *e. g.* Agamemnon bears reproach and insult in council, but in field absolute—"death in his hand." No responsibility until they returned and relapsed into mere kings; this supremacy in war necessary in a state situated like Sparta; want of this power in field reason why modern states of Italy have been beaten by other nations; said that "a baggage cart could not be moved, or a cannon planted, without order from senate."

6. *Senate or gerusia?* Composed of thirty members, correspond-

ing to thirty *obes* into which Sparta was divided; each at least sixty years old before election. Elected by the people in whimsical manner; judges were shut up in room invisible to the people; candidates presented themselves one by one to people, and received their plaudits; he who got the greatest applause was elected first, and he who obtained next greatest, next, &c.; judges forming their judgments entirely from the applauses given, not knowing who were the individuals applauded at the time; (T. 317,) elected for life; no responsibility to the people; functions deliberative, judicial, and executive; was the originating branch of legislature, no business being taken up by the people without first being prepared by the senate. They exercised a criminal jurisdiction with power of degrading and even inflicting death, and formed a sort of advisory council for the kings.

7. *Public assembly of the people?* Met at full moon, and sometimes oftener when necessary. Its sanction necessary to give validity to the decrees of senate; resolutions passed by the senate were not altered or amended in this assembly and sent back to senate as now-a-days, but were passed or rejected in the shape in which they came from the senate. In fact, the modern mode of making amendments to original resolutions seems to have been practised in none of the deliberative bodies of antiquity. In the assembly there was no debate allowed, only simple affirmative or negative; hence there was no eloquence in Sparta.

8. *Ephori?* Five in number; chosen annually by the people; most democratic feature in Spartan government; not designed so by Lycurgus; in fact, doubted whether Lycurgus's laws originally had this feature at all; at first designed alone for civil causes; soon began to encroach; being representatives of people, arrogated to themselves right to inquire into the conduct of all officers, except councillors; every eighth year, selected dark night, when they watched aspect of heavens, and if signs unfavorable, kings were adjudged to have offended the deity, and were suspended from office till acquitted by oracle of Delphi, or priests of Olympia; in fact, soon arrogated to themselves power of trying kings; *e. g.* before Persian war, sat in judgment on King Cleomenes on accusation of bribery; after Persian war, ordered execution of regent Pausanias; all this done in concert with the senate. In lesser matters, acted independently, fined or reprimanded kings for too much affability of manners, and on one occasion, rebuked Archidamus for marrying too small a wife; they pushed their authority over education, social habits, over the discipline of armies and raising troops, and at last became almost as powerful in Sparta as the tribunes were in Rome. Ephoralty was to Sparta what the house of commons has been to England. Aristotle says one cause of stability of Spartan institutions; it tempered

stern aristocracy with such infusion of democracy as made the people contented with government. (B. 126.) But after all it was a sort of democracy among the Spartans *alone*, not extending to the Laconians and Periœci, who composed the great mass of the free Lacedemonian population. Hence, on whole, we must pronounce Spartan government eminently aristocratical.

9. *In what light must we regard Sparta, in order to form a just idea of her whole system?* We must look on Spartans as a little band of soldiers, supporting themselves over a people that detested them. On one side they had to contend with their neighbors in arms, on the other with the hatred of their slaves. Under the penalty of destruction, they were obliged to be brave, temperate and hardy; they must be forever on the alert, and must have all the virtues of sentinels to guard them against sword of Messenian, or the revenge of the Helot. Hence their system apparently at war with nature. (127.)

10. *Agrarian law?* It was division of land into equal portions. Laconia is supposed to have been divided into 39,000 shares, of which Sparta had 9,000. This account of Plutarch probably incorrect, as both Aristotle and Socrates suppose the Spartans had the richest and largest shares. There are supposed to have been three Helots for every Laconian, and as these belonged to Spartans they would have required most land. (T. 303–4.) But although equality not so complete as Plutarch imagines, yet law of Lycurgus no doubt remedied great inequality before complained of in Laconia.

11. *Does there not appear to be a sort of contradiction in the system of Lycurgus?* It is supposed his great object was to give stability to his government by establishing an aristocracy in the senate that would uphold the decaying power of the kings, and yet no measure could be conceived more democratical than an agrarian law. This is a great puzzle in the system, and will perhaps be never satisfactorily answered. We may conjecture then that it must have been a sort of compromise. There were three orders of citizens—first, Spartans; second, Laconians; third, Periœci—the latter a sort of provincials. Now probable that the Heracleidæ, at head of the Dorians, when the country was conquered, suffered a few to take too large a portion of conquered lands, as happened in Rome; that this was complained of, and that the agrarian division may have been a sort of resumption of the crown lands, to be re-divided among the descendants of the conquerors. Such a division might harmonize all parties, and give additional vigor to the state. Upon this hypothesis there was a popular and aristocratical party in Sparta. In diarchy, one king would probably take one side, whilst colleague would take the other; *e. g.* Eurypon's (grandson of

Procles) ambition of popularity was nothing more than his taking the popular side, while Charilaus's tyranny might be the result of taking opposite side. Before the time of Lycurgus there were frequent commotions in Sparta which probably resulted from the clashing of two parties; *e. g.* by one of these commotions death of Enomus, father of Lycurgus, was caused. Lycurgus's senate and agrarian law were then, in all probability, a system of compromise between the two parties, like the senate and house of representatives in our system, was a compromise between little and big states; and this idea, supported by fact, that agrarian law is represented as very popular with one party, while it was exceedingly odious to another—so much so as to endanger the life of Lycurgus.

12. *Circulating medium?* Iron, a native product of Laconia. Use of gold and silver in this respect abolished. Doubtful whether the precious metals had been used as money before time of Lycurgus; but if they had, Lycurgus abolished their use under popular belief that money, the then measure of value, produces most of the evils flowing from institution of property.

13. *Meals?* In Sparta were public tables and citizens dined together. Meal at expense of those who shared it; head of family providing for his whole family; tables had fifteen persons each; vacancy filled by election of the members, like vacancy in a volunteer company. Unanimity required at elections to fill vacancies. (T. 331.)

14. *In what light was a citizen of Sparta regarded by this system of laws?* As born for his country alone.

15. *Women?* Whilst in other countries men take pains to improve breed of horses, sheep, dogs, &c., Sparta seems to be only country where the attempt was made by the laws to breed strong, able-bodied men. To this end, the women were made by their education as hardy and robust as possible; they boxed, wrestled, ran races, pitched quoits, &c., in order to bring forth hardy men. When Gorgo, wife of Leonidas, heard Spartan women accused of governing husbands, answered they alone knew how to bring forth men. When child was deformed and sickly, and not likely to be a defence to his country, the laws enjoined infanticide by exposing it to wild beasts. Some historians praise the Spartan women very much, but after all they exhibited all the frailties of the sex without any of the feminine graces. Aristotle makes out the Spartan with all his bravery the most henpecked of men. He and Plato both speak of the women as unchaste; and even Plutarch, with all his admiration of them, says, Spartans were permitted to lend their wives to one another; jealousy in the men was unmanly and ridiculed. The Spartan was taught to sink the feelings of the lover and the husband

in a cold principle of utility; and it mattered but little who was the father of a child, provided it was a strong healthy one, fit to make a soldier.

15. *Education?* Spartan taken at age of seven, and subjected to a sort of public education, lest indulgence of parents might make him soft and effeminate. The most ardent patriotism was instilled into his mind; in every case the love of self was made to yield to the welfare of his country; he was early inured to hardship, discipline, and patriotism; "he was starved into abstinence," and "beaten into fortitude;" he was no student of science, for the mere soldier cares not for science; he was taught to be gay, witty, and laconic, to say little, and to the point; a few aphorisms constituted the whole of Spartan wisdom; result of such an education was athletic frame, and hardy habits; as he approached age of manhood, discipline more and more harsh; city was scene of hard labor, low diet, and severest discipline; when he became a soldier, camp was a place of comparative recreation; hence Spartan was eager to join the army.

16. *Law permitting Spartans to steal?* If the theft was with such address as to pass undetected, it was applauded; if not, it was punished; *e. g.* Spartan boy mentioned by Plutarch, who stole a fox, and permitted it to eat to his bowels rather than discover the theft.

17. *Paley and other moralists, have seized on this and similar facts, to prove non-existence of moral faculty—can such an inference be drawn?* By no means. Lycurgus did not give permission to steal for the sake of the *vice*, but for nobler purposes. His great object to make every Spartan complete soldier; cunning as necessary as bravery; supposed that the boy who could rob his companion's wardrobe, or steal dexterously, could with equal address rob an enemy's camp; hence stealing was permitted for what was considered a patriotic purpose, and not for sake of the vice, and as proof of it, when detected at the time, it was severely punished. Again, in Sparta, where an agrarian law existed, stealing was not the same thing as elsewhere. Where there is community of goods, men of course have not the same sacred regard for property; *e. g.* when Captain Cook first landed on Sandwich islands, natives came aboard his vessel and took every thing they could lay their hands on, without considering it an offence; reason, in island there was community of goods.

18. *Helots?* Supposed by some to be the Achæans, made slaves after their country had been conquered by Dorians; by others that they were the slaves of the Achæans, who only changed masters; by others that they were the inhabitants of a conquered island, Helos. Origin, matter of no consequence, as slavery was prevalent throughout ancient

world, and generally was the condition of the conquered in war. Helots were *real property*, attached to the farm, *adscripti glebæ*. A certain amount of produce was exacted from them—hence the Helot, miserable as he was, could sometimes accumulate property. All antiquity bears testimony to harsh brutal treatment which they received from the Spartans. Not permitted even to sing Spartan songs.

19. *Cryptia?* We are told by Plutarch that this was an institution designed for purpose of ridding state of the most dangerous of the slaves, whenever they became too numerous. Picked men were armed and sent through the country, to murder secretly such numbers as should lessen danger. Probable that this institution was a sort of *patrol* sent through the country for the double purpose of inuring to the hardships and practices of war, and to keep the Helots in subjection. As their authority was complete over the slaves, they would often abuse it by assassinations, especially in time of alarm from apprehended insurrection. We are told by Plutarch, that on one occasion, Sparta was fearful of insurrection, and proclaimed to the Helots that all whose services entitled them to it, should come forward and receive their liberty; 2,000 came, and were all secretly murdered, as being dangerous men. (T. 312.)

20. *Success of Lycurgus's system?* Described as almost complete even where all other legislators have failed; *e. g.* prescribed sobriety, and they were sober; he prescribed mirth, and the Lacedemonians were both sober and merry—but it was mirth tempered with wisdom; he prescribed even a peculiar style of conversation, and immediately the style of the Spartan became laconic and witty; he prescribed modesty and deference to the aged, and Sparta exhibited a band of youths pre-eminent for these amiable traits. Now all legislators have wished the same things, but in vain. (M. 275.)

21. *Causes?* First, the peculiar position of the Spartans, already explained, which required Sparta to be a camp of soldiers, under the penalty of destruction. Second, smallness of the territory, which gave a man of notoriety the same advantages over the Spartans that a father has over his family. In large country impossible for one man to produce so great an effect; whilst one part may be with you, another is against you; whilst one part is heating, another is cooling, &c. But third, the institution of slavery was the main pillar on which the whole fabric rested.

22. *Explain the influence of slavery?* First, without slavery Spartans could not have that leisure which was essential condition of all their institutions. Agriculture, mechanic arts, and all menial services performed by Helots, left Spartans leisure to lead the lives of soldiers.

Second, slavery was the condition *sine qua non* for that fundamental regulation of the whole system, the *agrarian division.* Such law generally unwise, not only because of its injustice, but because it produces idle, worthless population. No freeman will labor when others are to share with him the fruits of his industry. The number of slaves in Sparta in a measure superseded this objection, for Helots could be made to work their lands under all circumstances. Again, without an agrarian division there is much greater equality among the freemen where there are numerous slaves, than without them—ordinary difference of rank is laid in difference of occupation; *e. g.* we will not associate upon a footing of equality with the man who cleans our shoes and stands behind our backs at table; but where there are slaves they perform all menial services, and leave the freemen as nearly equal as is possible for men to be in this world; *e. g.* greater equality among freemen of the southern than northern states; and Bryan Edwards says still greater in West Indies than in any part of world besides. Slavery then may be pronounced absolutely necessary for the fundamental regulation of Lycurgus, the agrarian division.

23. *Show how the social part of the system of Lycurgus flowed from the agrarian division as a sort of corollary?* After such a regulation there was no difficulty in establishing public tables, because after taking away the distinction of property, none other was left but the distinction of age and talent. But aristocracy of talent likes publicity, because it can show off the more brilliantly. A great man is forgotten in solitude, he shines with splendor before multitude—hence no objection to public tables. Again, man who must appear several times a day in public will take care to remain sober where drunkenness would be disgrace, for he would certainly be detected at the public tables. Being together at public tables it was easy to train themselves and the young in brevity of conversation, and the youths being always in the presence of their superiors would naturally become modest and deferential towards them. Equal associating with equal, without a feeling of salutary restraint, naturally generates rough and unpolished manners—hence woman so necessary to polish off manners. For same reason, where different orders in state, manners are rather more polished than in democracies.

24. *Remarks on Lycurgus's system?* First, mistook the great end of government—happiness the great object of all our exertions in this world. We should be patriotic, because it conduces to our happiness. Lycurgus's system sacrificed the happiness of individuals to make them patriotic and hardy—converting the *means* into the *end;* he endeavored to conquer nature, which can never be permanently done—*naturam expel-*

las furca tamen usque recurret; he would abolish gold and silver, and feed his citizens on black broth, and denounce the acquisition of property, to conquer the grovelling propensities of the human heart, and yet, the history of Greece proved that no people were more open to bribery than the Spartans. He would bring men and women into each others' presence in a state of nudity, that the Spartan's self-command might triumph over his passions; but, as Gibbon says, insulted nature would vindicate her rights, and Spartan women were the most gracelessly dissolute of all Greece. Second, this system violated every principle of morality for mere political ends; *e. g.* infanticide enjoined, adultery was winked at, the *cryptia* established, &c. Third, upon the whole, government of Sparta must be pronounced aristocratical, although the Spartans of the city were all equal, and, therefore, *quoad* themselves, were a democracy, yet when we remember the Laconians, the Periœci, and the Helots, who formed the great bulk of population, we see at once a close oligarchy. The senate, too, was composed of aged men elected for life, who would naturally favor the oligarchical tendency of these institutions. Hence, whilst we shall see Athens heading the democratical party in Greece, we find Sparta at head of aristocratical—Sparta lived for the past, Athens for the future—the one was change and activity, the other fixed and stationary. Music and dancing were cultivated among the Spartans, but they were to be only of one kind—it was a crime to *vary* an air or *invent* a measure. One produced great philosophers and great orators; the other hardy men and short sentences. The institutions of Sparta have been the theme of praise in every age; but few great men and noble deeds have illustrated them; the Spartan was selfish, grave, and taciturn; born to command others, he was elevated in manner, and haughty in his bearing—he possessed a sort of stern, sullen dignity under the coarsest garb. There was more hauteur about the poorest Spartan citizen, than in the wealthiest noble of Corinth, or the most voluptuous courtier of Syracuse, and it was the *attaché* of a character untempered by benevolence, amiability, or mercy.

Laws of Solon.

As the character of the Spartan laws was supposed to be derived from Lycurgus, so those of Athens are generally traced back to Solon as the most important lawgiver in the Athenian history.

1. *Character of Solon?* So learned and philosophic as to be entitled to rank among seven wise men of Greece. Less bold and daring, but more virtuous and attentive to established rights of individuals than Lycurgus; belonged by character to those who might be styled moderates; unambitious of power; when urged to make himself tyrant of

Athens, refused with that noted saying, "tyranny is a fair field, but it has no outlet." He was, however, a warrior, orator, poet, philosopher and legislator, and possessed faculty of accommodating himself to circumstances; went not so much for *beau ideal* in the abstract, as for *practical* utility; when asked about his own laws, said they were the best the people were *capable* of receiving.

2. *State of Athens during his time?* It had three parties; 1st, the inhabitants of the mountains; 2d, of plain; 3d, of coast: 1st, democratic; 2d, oligarchical—here lay the large estates of the higher orders; 3d, *moderates*, wishing liberty enough to promote commerce, but not so much license as would endanger property. It was these parties that kept Athens in constant commotion. At one time they had recourse to Draco to frame a code of laws, at another time as late as Solon a man named Epimenides, an inspired philosopher of Crete, was sent for to act as a sort of umpire—but all in vain.

3. *Character of Draco's code?* Supposed to have been very sanguinary, hence said to be written in blood; represented as having no grades in punishment, since Draco was wont to say, that the smallest crime merited death, and the greatest could not be punished more. He must however have had a sort of scale or gradation in punishment, since there were lesser punishments than death; *e. g.* loss of franchise for an attempt to change one of his laws; again, for a particular offence, we read of an individual being mulcted ten oxen. (T. 2. 20.)

4. *Effect of such a code?* Too severe to be executed, inspires the criminal with hope, and defeats its end. Hence first measure of Solon was to abolish it.

5. *Regulation of Solon in regard to property?* Not certainly known. Did not abolish property; some supposed all debts cancelled; others that interest was forfeited; others that interest was lessened, and money debased, &c. This regulation commemorated by feast of *Seisachtheia* or delivery from burthens. The lands too were released from pledges or mortgages; it is said before this release that *stone posts*, considered as monuments of aristocratical oppression, everywhere met the eye throughout Attica; these posts marked the land as a pledge for debt, and had the amount of debt and name of creditor inscribed on them.

6. *Government?* Extremely democratic; composed of three orders: 1st, popular assembly; 2d, council of 500, or senate; 3d, judiciary.

7. 1*st*, *Assembly of the people?* Composed of all the freemen of mature age. This like as in Sparta waited for the action of the senate; but could modify a resolution which had come from senate without send-

ing it back; meeting once a month, sometimes oftener; no regular number required for *quorum;* except on some occasions where 6000 were necessary. Those citizens who were seen going in a different direction at the hour of meeting were *marked* and fined; every man above 20 could speak; those above 50 were called on first; votes generally taken by show of hands, except in cases of mal-administration, when balls or ballots denoting *condemnation* or *acquittal* were cast secretly into an urn, and the fate of the accused decided by majority. All votes equal; president of the assembly had power of repressing and punishing all breaches of order.

8. *Freemen?* Included free population of Attica as well as of city; two polls taken, one in time of Pericles, other of Demetrius Phalerius —according to 1st, 14,040 voters; according to 2d, 21,000, and at some period 10,000 paid capitation taxes without rights of Athenian citizens, being aliens, or of foreign extraction or freedmen. Supposing the whole number of freemen five times the number of voters, we have 105,000 the whole Athenian free population at last period, and 72,000 at first.

9. *Slaves?* Generally computed at 400,000; hence although Athenian government was democratical in regard to freemen, yet, taking entire population, it was aristocratical.

10. *Reason of great number of slaves in Greece?* Laws of war gave captor right to put prisoner to death or to enslave him. When nations are in hunting state, they uniformly gratify principle of revenge by putting prisoners to death by most cruel torture; *e. g.* Indians of North America; but as soon as they become agricultural, prisoner is made slave, because his labor is valuable; hence slavery is first cause of mitigation of horrors of savage warfare; in time of Herodotus, a tradition was preserved of a time when there were no slaves in Greece, and when prisoners consequently were all put to death; again, where states, like those of Greece, were constantly engaged in war, unless there had been a large body of slaves in each state, freemen could not have devoted themselves to civil and military life; all history has shown that the nation with most slaves in ancient times was, *ceteris paribus*, the most powerful in war; and if there had been a state in Greece without slaves, the probability is, it would quickly have been overthrown by the neighboring slave states. Heeren admits that without slaves in Greece the upper classes would never have obtained great mental pre-eminence.

11. *Distribution of citizens into ranks?* Four ranks according to property; 1st, had yearly income of 500 measures (*medimni*) called *penta cosiomedimnians;* 2d rank, all those whose yearly income was less than 500 and more than 300; 3d, all less than 300 and more than 200; 4th, all under 200.

12. *Value of these estates?* The *medimnus* exceeded our bushel by six pints and a fraction; medimni were either of dry or liquid produce of the farm, of corn, barley or wine, oil, &c.; hence difficult to ascertain value; medimnus valued at one drachma by Solon, consequently lowest estate of first rank was 500 drachma, 12th part of talent; property at 12 times income would be one talent. [38.]

13. *Duties, privileges, and prerogatives of the several classes?* First and second class bound to keep a horse properly equipped for service; hence called *Hippeis* or *Hippodatelountes*, these were the Athenian *knights;* 3d, kept heavy armor, and had privilege of serving only among heavy armed troops; called *zengites* from a yoke of oxen supposed to be required for such a farm, these were the yeomanry of the country; 4th, class generally poor, called *thetes*, because principally employed as hired laborers on farms; they were excluded from all offices; served as light-armed troops, and in later times manned fleets. In voting and on juries all were equal; but magistrates and high order of military were taken from three first. This division of Solon reminds us of similar division in Europe during middle ages, into nobles, knights, burgesses and vassals.

14. *Senate?* Solon at first divided the people into four tribes or wards; each ward elected 100 councillors, making 400 in all. Afterwards, wards were increased to 10 with a representation of 50 each, making senate 500. In election, 1st, by *dokimasia* or *scrutiny* it was determined what citizens were eligible, and then the number of senators was chosen from those who passed the scrutiny *by lot*, no one under 30 was thus eligible; went out of office every year, and were responsible for conduct; hence not so aristocratic a body as the *gerusia* of Sparta.

15. *Powers and functions?* Designed to restrain popular assembly—originated all laws—divided into sections of 50 councillors each—one section from each ward—called *prytanes*—each section represented whole senate for 35 days at a time, and during its term assembled every day in its session-house (*prytaneum*) to consult on state affairs. Prytanes had a different president every day, each one serving in turn. President during his day of office had custody of the public seal, keys of the treasury and of the citadel. These prytanes formed a sort of executive committee for the whole senate. All matter was first prepared by them as by modern committees; then transmitted to senate, if approved was called a *proboulema*, was then written on tablet exposed to public view, and brought after several days before assembly of people for approval or rejection. (M. 366.)

16. *Judiciary?* A body of 6000 citizens, each 30 years old, was chosen *by lot* every year to form supreme court (Heliæa) divided into

several smaller ones, not limited to any particular number; this supreme court had very extensive political powers; it was to guard the democracy and punish all attempts to overthrow it; any person causing a law to be passed contrary to one in existence, or even injurious to public interests, might at once be dragged before this court, which decided the law and the fact of the case. Solon considered his laws as simple, and that every citizen might decide on them; he thought every citizen should be interested in administration of justice; there was here no nice distinction between the province of judge and juror; every magistrate presided over court in his district for trial of offences there, without reference to his legal knowledge; hence law was not studied as a profession at Athens. Solon looked on his *Heliastic* courts as representatives of the democracy; their numbers made them irresponsible, and it was hoped would place them above bribery; but experience proved numbers no guarantee against corruption. These popular courts were less feared, because of the Areopagus—a highly revered court in Athens from earliest times—composed of members elected for life from the body of archons, of which there were nine acting as presidents of the courts of justice. Murder, maiming, poisoning, and arson, were tried in the Areopagus; it was held in open air; criminal was generally tried in night, that his appearance might excite neither prejudice nor favor; very little pleading, except simple narration, and no appeal to the passions; no appeal could be taken to other tribunals; at first, could stop the effect of judicial decrees of the people. It was moreover a censorial court; guardian of public morals and religion; superintended education; punished idleness, and every citizen was obliged to account to it for his means of livelihood. This body never interfered in politics except on rare and great emergencies, and then they acted with a weight of character like that of our ex-presidents; their demeanor was of the gravest character; it was an offence to laugh in their presence when in session; no archon who had been seen in a tavern could be elected; an Areopagite was forbidden to write a comedy, as being too undignified.

17. *Object of that regulation which required every man in civil broils and commotions to take part with one side or other?* Supposed that good men were apt to hold themselves aloof on such occasions, while the wicked and selfish would take the field and prevail by energy; if, however, the good were bound to take sides, they would espouse virtuous cause, and render it triumphant. Again, as Athens was a democracy, it became necessary that every man should act his part, and take a due interest in the affairs of state; otherwise the power would soon steal into the hands of the few.

18. *Provisions for changing the laws?* At the first meeting of the

popular assembly in each year a committee of 1000, called *nomathetes*, were appointed to propose alterations in the laws; when proposed, five advocates were chosen (*Syndics*) to defend the old law; besides this six of the nine archons were officially vested with the power of noticing defects and incongruities in the laws, and reporting to the *nomathetes;* these six archons were called *thesmothetes*, and were of course well versed in the laws.

19. *Why were all the law-givers of Greece so prejudiced against changes in the laws?* Because change and revolution are the besetting sins of small democratical states; hence celebrated law of Charondas that the man who proposed to change a law, or abolish an institution, should come on the *Bema* with a rope about his neck, and if his proposition were rejected, he should be hanged.

20. *Remarks on the laws of Solon?* By making all the citizens legislators and judges, bad laws, bad decisions, and a capricious tyranny of the multitude not unlike that of a Turkish sultan, were but too frequently the results. Hobbes says such government is but aristocracy of orators, interrupted sometimes by temporary monarchy of a single orator. But in midst of disorder and insecurity of both persons and property, there were some advantages. Such a government produces exuberance of energy, genius, and real greatness. Great men illustrated Athens; every man in state was stimulated by government to do his best; no one folded his arms in inglorious repose. In the assemblies, and in the Heliastic courts, business of every variety and importance were attended to by multitudes; questions of peace and war, of ships and songs and theatres, the reception of ambassadors, the carving of statues, the bridling of aristocracies, the making of laws, &c., were all discussed; it was popular assembly and popular court that educated the Athenian; the very caprice of the multitude created the splendid oratory of Athens; the dream of Milton was, at least in part, realized; the Athenian became a legislator and a judge in peace, (although a bad one,) in war a formidable soldier; at all times acute in judgment and resolute in action; here the people were the state; theirs were the *portico* and the *school*, the *theatre*, the *gardens* and the *baths*. "Lycurgus made machines, and Solon made men; and in Sparta this machine was wound up by the tyranny of a fixed principle; it could not dine as it pleased, nor walk as it pleased." Solcn's laws were not severe, he every where appealed to a sense of honor and a fear of shame; to be styled *atimos*, or unhonored, was a severe punishment to the Athenian. Lastly, the slaves of Athens were treated with a mildness in perfect contrast with the brutality of the Spartan.

SEC. V.—MEASUREMENT OF TIME. NEWTON'S CHRONOLOGY.

Present course of lectures does not require strict attention to chronology, therefore mere dates have been little attended to. Proper, however, to explain mode of computing time, and Newton's correction of ancient chronology.

1. *How would time be naturally measured?* By regular return of certain appearances or phenomena in the heavens and the earth, which strike the senses of all persons; three of these conspicuous; *day* and *night*, *course of the moon*, and *return of the seasons;* 1st, one revolution of earth, 24 hours, a day; 2d, from one new moon to another, *lunar month;* 3d, revolution of earth around sun, *solar year*.

2. *Difficulties in this measurement of time?* The smaller periods do not exactly divide the larger; hence difficult to accommodate the different periods to one another; *e. g.* one *lunation* is about 29½ days, one year is more than 12 lunar months, and more than 365 days.

3. *Days?* Commence at different hours; *e. g.* ancient Babylonians, Persians, Syrians and modern Greeks, with some other countries, commence at *sun rising;* ancient Athenians and Jews, with Austrians, Italians and Chinese, reckon from *sun setting;* ancient Umbri and Arabians, with modern astronomers, from *noon;* Egyptians and Romans, with English, Americans, French, Dutch, Spaniards, &c., from *midnight;* Jews, Romans, and most ancient nations, divided day into 12 hours and night into 4 watches. Each watch contained 3 hours; 1st watch extended to third hour before midnight, called *opse*, the *even;* 2d, to midnight *mesonuction* (*midnight*); 3d, to third hour before sunrise, *alectorophonia* (*cock crowing*); and 4th, to sunrise, *proi* (*the dawning*) *e. g.* Mark, ch. xiii. 35. "watch ye, for ye know not at what hour the master of the house cometh, (1) at *even*, or (2) at *midnight*, or (3) at *cock crowing*, or (4) at dawning" (morning). As this division was relative to rising and setting sun, the watches and the hours of the day and night varied in length with the seasons. Now the day is universally divided into 24 equal hours. Most nations divide into twice 12; some, as Italians, Bohemians and Poles, count 24 hours without interruption.

4. *Month?* Complete lunation about 29½ days; hence ancients made them alternately 29 and 30 days, and in clear weather any considerable variation could be rectified by adding an intercalary day, or substracting one. When months came to be considered as twelfth part of a year, it was necessary to allow 30 and 31 days to the month. Whenever months are divided by days in scripture, 30 days are allowed to month, and 12 months to year, making 360 days; this particularly to be observed in interpreting prophetical books of Daniel and St. John.

5. *Year?* Great variety as to commencement; *e. g.* Jews began year for civil purposes, with month *Tizri* (September); for ecclesiastic purposes, with *Nisan* (April) at period of passover. Athenians began with first new moon after summer solstice. Romans at first had only 10 months, commencing with March and ending with December; Numa added January and February. In England, till 1752, there were two beginnings of the year, one in January the other on 25th March. In 1752 present arrangement was adopted by act of parliament. Supposed by some that Antediluvians up to 160th year of Enoch computed by weeks and not years.

6. *Methods of accommodating year to months and days?* This has been great puzzle; 12 lunar months want about 11 days of making the year; appears from Herodotus' account of interview between Solon and Crœsus, that in time of Solon they got over the difficulty by intercalating a month every other year; but as this mode too much, probably rectified it by omitting intercalation from comparison of seasons with festivals; *e. g.* if first fruits were to be carried in procession on particular day of a certain month, they would see the necessity of intercalating, if fruits were not ripe; or would see the necessity of omitting, if in average season, they were ripe before the time. Various *cycles* were introduced to give a fixed rule for intercalating, of which *Metonic* invented by Meton the astronomer, and afterwards corrected by Calippus of Athens, was most perfect; this cycle was 19 years, with 7 intercalary months. By this, not only do the new and full moons return on the same day of the year, but very nearly on same hour; accordingly it generally prevailed in Greece, and was adopted by Christians at council of Nice, for purpose of settling time for keeping Easter and other movable feasts. This cycle, however, is not perfect, as it falls short of 19 years by nearly 1½ hours, consequently the new and full moons in the heavens had anticipated, in time of Dr. Priestley, the new and full moons in the calendar of the Book of Common Prayer, by nearly four days and a half. In some countries they count altogether by lunar months, allowing 12 to year; *e. g.*, Mahommedans—hence beginning of year with them moves through all the seasons, at rate of about 11 days per annum. As long as nations computed by lunar months, they did not so much regard number of days in year. But at an early period Egyptians were not satisfied with this, and divided year into days. Athenians divided civil year into 10 *prytaniæ*, corresponding to division of their tribes, some 35 and others of 36 days. The difficulty here is, that year cannot be evenly divided by days; it is 365 days, 5 hours and 49 minutes nearly. In time of Julius Cæsar the present arrangement was adopted, and therefore called the *Julian year*, the year was divided into 12 months

some 30, some 31, and one 28 days; this arrangement makes exactly 365; to allow for 5 hours and 49 minutes, the excess of solar year over 365 days, every fourth year was made leap year, and one day added to February. This, however, allowed a little too much, being 6 hours instead of 5 hours and 49 minutes; and Pope Gregory XIII. in 1582, perceiving that vernal equinox, which at Council of Nice in 321 fell on 21st March, now come on 10th, ordered 10 days to be dropped between 4th and 15th October. Here commences the *new style* as distinguished from the *old;* and to make solar correspond with civil year, ordained that every hundredth year (of course leap year) should drop the extra day in February, excepting the 400th, when it should be retained; this so near as not to vary more than a day in 5,200 years. Parliament in 24th Geo. II., in 1752, adopted this regulation of Pope Gregory XIII., and dropped 11 days between 2d and 14th September; and beginning of year was changed from 25th March to 1st January, 1752; here commenced *new style* in Great Britain.

7. *Origin of names of the months?* Of Roman origin; Romulus divided year into 10 months; *Martius* (March), from his supposed father, *Mars;* 2d, *April is* (April) either from *Aphroditê*, Greek name of Venus, or because trees and flowers then open (*aperiunt*); 3d, *Maius*, (May) from *Maia*, mother of Mercury, or as some suppose in honor of *the old* (*majorum*); 4th, *Junius* (June), in honor of *Juno*, or as some suppose of *the young* (*Juniorum;*) rest named, from their number, Quintilis, Sextilis, September, October, November, December. *Quintilis* was changed to *Julius* (July) in honor of Julius Cæsar, and Sextilis to *Augustus* (August), from Augustus Cæsar, because in it he had first been made consul; in it gained several battles; *e. g.* took Alexandria in Egypt (A. U C. 724), and 15 years after (*lustro tertio*), on same day probably, the 29th August, conquered the Rhæti. Numa added two months called *Januarius* (January), from god *Janus*, and *Februarius*, because people were purified (*Februabatur*, *i. e. pergabatur* or *lustrabatur* by an expiatory sacrifice (*Februalia*) from the sins of the whole year, this being anciently last month of year.

8. *Roman division of the month?* Into *Kalends*, *Nones*, and *Ides*. 1st day of the month called Kalendæ (*a calando*, *vel vocando*), priest then calling out that it was new moon; the 5th day was the *nonæ*, the nones; the 13th was the Idus, *Ides* from obsolete verb *iduare*, to divide, because ides nearly divided the month; the *nones* so called because counted inclusively, they were 9 days from the *ides*. The division by *weeks* was Jewish, and arose from the commandments; was not introduced among Romans till nearly the time of emperor Severus. Country people were in the habit of going to the cities to buy and sell

every *9th day*, and consequently on those market days the comitia were forbidden to be holden. (A. 80 and 280.)

9. *Eras or epochas?* Memorable events, which may be useful as points from which to date, *e g.* Greeks who for a long time had no fixed eras, found, at last great convenience in counting by Olympiads (4 years); from the 1st Olympiad about 776 years (B. C.) Romans, dated from the building of Rome; Athenians named years by archons, Romans by consuls; Mahommedans reckon from flight of Mahomet from Mecca, called the *Hegira.* About 360 years after birth of Christ, Christians began to count from that era.

10. *Difficulties in chronology?* Without utmost caution, mistakes innumerable; all the varieties of days and months to the years in different nations must be allowed for; *e. g.* in dating from the Hegira or flight of Mahomet (622 A. D.), as the months are lunar and only 12 to year, we must subtract 11 days from every Julian year to get the Mahommedan; not only, however, must all these varieties be allowed for, but in absence of registers and printing press, tradition is relied on, which can never be accurate in mere dates. Moreover when different nations refer to different epochs, hard to compare them; hence some historians refer generally to time without designating, *e. g.* Herodotus often refers to events about 1, 2, 3, or 400 years ago, which might be often fifty years wide of true time of epoch. When, however the historian would be accurate, he was obliged to give a specification almost as minute as Mrs. Quickly's in 'Merry Wives of Windsor,' *e. g.* Thucydides thus designates the time of the march of Thebans on Platæa; "and in the 15th year of the 30 years' truce, when Chrysis was in the 48th year of her priesthood at Argos, Ænesias ephor at Sparta, and 2 months were yet wanting to complete the archonship of Pythodorus at Athens, in the sixth month after the battle of Potidæ, the spring then beginning, an armed body of somewhat more than 300 Thebans marched on Platæa about first sleep." With our present mode of computing time, and with our epocha, the birth of Christ, to refer to, mere chronology has become a very simple matter. Not so anciently. So palpable are the mistakes made by ancient historians, that Newton undertook to lay down principles for its own correction.

11. *Mode of correcting ancient chronology by the reigns of kings, and by successive generations?* Principle is that nothing can be inferred from *one* reign, or *one* generation; it may be very long, or very short; but take a great number, and the average duration will be very near the same. From many cases Newton found that when kings succeeded each other regularly, they reigned on average, from 18 to 20 years each; again, in generations of men, the interval is fixed at 33 to

34; the reason of greater time between generations of men, than succession of kings, is that in former we always count from father to son, while in latter, one brother often succeeds another on the throne, and kings are besides more liable to violent death. If we count generations by the eldest son instead of the whole family, the average period is reduced from 28 to 30 years. In history, then, if we know the number of kings, multiply by 18 or 20, and we have the years. If we know the generations, by 28 or 30, for intervals between father and eldest son, and by 33 or 34 for generations in general; *e. g.* between return of Heraclidæ and battle of Thermopylæ, whose date is known, there reigned 17 kings in each royal line at Sparta, multiply by 20 we have 340 the time—corresponding to year 159 after the death of Solomon, and 46 before 1st Olympiad. Again, between return of Heraclidæ and Argonautic expedition, we have 4 generations of father and eldest son, which multiplied by 30, would give 120 years for the interval. By this computation, taking of Troy is placed about 76 years after Solomon, and the Argonautic expedition about 43. Upon same principles, Sir Isaac Newton decided against the chronology of Roman kings; average reign of 35 years not probable. Hook says 19 or 20 years apiece, make the most consistent series of facts. From Roman history Newton thus fixes date of Trojan war; from Latinus to Numitor inclusive, 16 kings reigned in Longa Alba, 7 in Rome; but as Romulus was contemporary with Numitor, add 6 to 16 equal 22 kings. As these reigns were turbulent, take 18 years for each, and we have, from the *regifuge*, or consulship of Brutus and Poplicola, 396 years to Latinus, who received Æneas in Italy; this places Trojan war 78 years after death of Solomon. This synchronizes almost exactly with the similar computation through the line of Spartan kings and generations, between the return of Heraclidæ and taking of Troy, mentioned above. This chronology makes Dido contemporary with Æneas, and Solon with Crœsus. It makes too, the courses of descents and generations mentioned in scripture, parallel to those in fabulous period of Grecian history fall within the same intervals of time with those which have occurred since history has become authentic, &c.

12. *Use which has been made of eclipses in eorrecting ancient chronology?* Fears and superstition of mankind have made them note, in all ages, these phenomena, with many attendant circumstances; and as the time of an eclipse can always be ascertained, we are enabled to tell the very hour at which it must have happened; *e. g.* we are told by Thucydides that an eclipse of the moon took place just as Nicias and the Athenians were preparing to sail from the harbor of Syracuse; they considered it a bad omen, staid three days, and were all destroyed. Now by looking into astronomical tables, we find that the moon was at

the full about midnight in London, and one o'clock at Syracuse, on the morning of 27 August (413 B. C.) when the sun was only 4° 48′ from the node, far within 12°, the limit of lunar eclipses; it was therefore totally eclipsed at Syracuse on that night. Many other eclipses have been mentioned, all of which can easily be verified, and their dates fixed.

13. *Use made of the precession of the equinoxes?* Quantity of precesssion has been acertained to be one degree in 72 years, *i. e.* sun crosses ecliptic so much farther west every year, that in 72 it amounts to a degree; this is regular, hence, knowing the point of intersection at a former period, we can easily calculate the time; *e. g.* have every reason to believe that the constellations were invented at time of Argonautic expedition, and that equinoctial colure at that time passed through middle of Aries, and the solstitial through middle of Cancer; if so, Newton found at the end of 1689 that the equinoctial and solstitial points had gone back 36° 44′; at 72 years to 1°, time 2645 years; which places Argonautic expedition 25 years after Solomon. But if we place cardinal points by the stars through which colures passed in primitive sphere described by Eudoxus, the recession will be 36° 29′ answering to 2627 years, placing the expedition about 43 years after Solomon, almost identical with the results obtained by methods already described. Again, Pliny tells us that Thales fixed the equinoxes and solstices in the 11th degree of their respective signs, making the recession since Argonautic expedition 4° 26′ 52″ answering to 320 years; which counted back from 41st Olympiad, at which Thales wrote, places Argonautic expedition 44 years after Solomon. Meton, year before Peloponnesian war, and in 316th year of Nabonassar, placed the summer solstice in 8th degree of Cancer, which makes 7° recession, answering to 504 years, which places Argonautic expedition 44 years after Solomon. Lastly, Hipparchus in 602d year of Nabonassar, fixed vernal equinox in 4th degree of Aries, making recession 11° or 792 years since Argonautic expedition, placing that event in 43d year after Solomon! These four coincidences extraordinary, and undoubtedly fix the expedition after Solomon, instead of 300 years before, in time of Gideon, as was the common opinion.

14. *Rising and setting of the stars?* When mentioned in relation to rising or setting of sun, enable us to calculate the time, because this depends on precession of the equinoxes; *e. g.* Hesiod tells us that 60 days after winter solstice the star Arcturus rose just at *sun set;* from which easy to calculate that he lived about 100 years after Solomon, or in the age just after the Trojan war; corresponding to Hesiod's own account of the time at which he lived.

SEC. VI.—PERSIA.

As it was the contest with Persia which forms the most brilliant feature in Grecian history, at the same time that it produced a most important influence on the Grecian character, necessary to give here some account of Persia, in order that we may better understand the character of this contest.

1. *Rise of the Persian Empire?* Have already seen that the Persians were half agricultural, half nomadic people, from mountainous country, who under Cyrus the Great overran the Assyrian, Babylonish, and Median empires, bringing about one of those great revolutions so frequent in the east. Crœsus, the King of Lydia, the most powerful monarch who perhaps ever reigned in Asia Minor, stimulated by an equivocal response from the Delphic oracle* declared war on Cyrus, and consequence was overthrow of Lydia by Persians; thus Persian empire was brought into immediate contact with the Greeks.

2. *Religion of the Persians?* Interesting to us because bearing an analogy to the Jewish; because it has subsisted for ages with but little alteration, &c.

3. *The two principles?* To reconcile the existence of evil with the omnipotence and benevolence of God, has been a great puzzle with all nations; Persians tried to get over difficulty by introducing two divine principles, one of *good*, called Ormuzd, the other of *evil*, Ahriman. At first, these gods were supposed eternal, but were subsequently represented as the creatures of time. These two principles rule, one in kingdom of *light*, the other in that of *darkness;* throne of Ormuzd is surrounded by 7 *amshaspands*, the *princes of light*, of whom Zoroaster or Zerdusht was first; under these are the Izeds, the *genii of good.* Kingdom of darkness similarly organized; throne surrounded by 7 great *Deevs*, *princes of darkness*, under these infinite number of inferior deevs; these two kingdoms eternally at war, the evil principle and evil genii with good principle and good genii. At the expiration of 12,000 years, Ormuzd will prevail, and kingdom of light will be established over universe. These principles extend their influence to animal and vegetable kingdoms; all plants that are noxious, all animals ferocious and cruel, belong to kingdom of Ahriman; he is source of all evil, while Ormuzd is source of all good, both in vegetable and animal kingdoms.

4. *Heeren's account of the origin of this part of Persian religion?* Eastern nations have no idea of any government but absolute monarchies; even in dreams of imagination they do not dare to emancipate

* "If Crœsus crosses the river Halys, a great empire will be overthrown."

themselves; hence while European always imagines himself *exalted and free*, when he sketches ideal happiness, Asiatic always imagines himself under *absolute sway* of some benevolent being. Zoroaster lived in a country bordering on Nomads; had an opportunity of seeing difference between rule of an established monarch in agricultural country and of the roving chief of Nomads; his kingdom of light was realized in Iran, the Medo-Bactrian kingdom subject to Gustasp; while *Turan*, the land of the Nomads, of which Afrasiab was king, was the picture of kingdom of darkness, (H. 379.) Turan lay to north of Iran; so kingdom of Ahriman was to north of that of Ormuzd; so the *Deevs* or evil genii come always from north.

5. *Worship of sun, moon, stars, and the elements?* These Mr. Gibbon supposes were venerated at first as *emblematical* of divinity, as the Catholic revered the image of his saint or of the virgin; of all productions of Ormuzd, the sun (*mithras*) was supposed the noblest and mightiest antagonist to Ahriman. As the Mahommedan turns to Mecca, so the Persian in his prayers always turned towards the sun, especially the *rising sun*. The moon and sun, the most brilliant luminaries of the heavens, have always tempted the adoration of mankind; even Job confesses the danger of the temptation. "If I beheld the sun when it shined, or the moon walking in brightness, and *my heart hath been secretly enticed, or my mouth hath kissed my hand*, this also were an iniquity," &c. After heavenly bodies, terrestrial elements have greatest claim to worship; *e. g. fire* as symbol of sun and of original heat which pervades all nature, was particularly worthy of adoration; fire has always been looked on as an emblem of great purity, and it is known that the Jews regarded it with veneration. A never-dying fire was kept on altar of burnt offerings in Jerusalem. God revealed himself to Moses by a flame in the bush, and testified his presence to children of Israel, in the wilderness, by a pillar of fire by night, which became a cloud of smoke in the day. The Romans had six vestal virgins, whose duty it was to keep up an undying fire in the temple of Vesta. Air, earth, and water, were holy, and worshipped, and every effort made to keep them pure. The Persians were as particular as the Egyptians in the burial of the dead; according to Zoroaster there was a resurrection for the dead, to take place at the destruction of the kingdom of Ahriman, when there would be a restoration of all things under the triumph of Ormuzd; hence the splendor and durability of the royal sepulchres; intermediate state of the same was looked on as prolongation of present life; each monarch was allowed sepulchral treasury, protected by bodies of soldiers and sentinels: thus Persepolis became depot of immense treasures. (209.) The *Zendevesta* was the book of Zoroaster, containing moral and reli-

gious creed; about three centuries ago the *Sadder* was compiled from Zendevesta, containing moral precepts.

6. *Character of morality of the Sadder?* A sort of epicurism, indulgence of passions recommended when it did not injure society; no merit annexed to mortification and abstinence, &c. Souls of men were supposed at first to be unembodied spirits, but Ormuzd in order to make use of them in warring against Ahriman clothed them in flesh, the better to sustain the combat, promising that light should not forsake them till Ahriman was conquered. When any foul deed or wicked act was invoked, Persian prayed to Ahriman; *e. g.* when Xerxes prayed that his enemies might always banish their best citizens, as the Athenians had Themistocles, he addressed his prayer to Ahriman.

7. *Feroohers?* According to tenets of Zoroaster, not only all men but all animals have their archetypes, purest efflux of the creative thought of Ormuzd; name of these ideal essences was *Ferooher;* were conceived to resemble the beings made after their model, only purer, more glorious and immortal; these essences varied like mortals, some more perfect than others; *e. g.* the Feroohers of Zoroaster and Brahman, and of the kings, were esteemed most perfect. These Feroohers are frequently found amid Persian sculpture. (H. 206.)

8. *Analogy of Persian religion to the Jewish?* Striking; *e. g.* fall of man, kingdom of Satan, reign of Christ. Hence many suppose that Zoroaster was acquainted with the Jewish religion, and founded his own on it.

9. *Character of the Persians under Cyrus?* A semi-barbarous warlike people, inured to hardship and used to abstinence; *e. g.* Herodotus makes Sandams the Lydian say to Crœsus, when projecting invasion of Persia, "what will you gain by waging war with such men; their clothing is skins, their food wild fruits, and their drink water. If you are conquered, you lose a cultivated country; if you conquer, you take a barren region."

10. *Government of Persians?* Such as the Nomads of Asia generally establish; before their conquest like all Nomads were divided into tribes, three of these were noble, called the Pasargadæ, the Maraphii and the Maspii; 1st, most noble of three, and from noblest family of this tribe (*Achæmenidæ*) was always taken the king and the principal wife. (H. 332.) When country was conquered, the provinces were left in possession of armies under generals who answered for the security of conquests; joined with these, were the receivers of the king's tribute; in the large cities there were separate independent commanders. Thus a sort of military government like that of a camp was established; such precisely was government under Genghis-Khan. (H. 838.) In order to secure conquests, citizens of one district were

often transplanted to another; *e. g.* Jews to Babylon, by Nebuchadnezzar; 6000 Egyptians to Suza, by Cambyses; and the Egyptian colony which Herodotus met at Colchis, were transplanted probably in time of Nebuchadnezzar.

11. *Character of Persian kings, and changes in government from Cyrus to Xerxes?* The kings of the east have always been of the most absolute character; considered as proprietors of the whole soil, as the complete masters of their subjects; none, not even their children, dared address them by any other title than *Lord*, *great king*, *king of kings;* latter title given to Nebuchadnezzar by Daniel. Parthians adopted this style from the Persians, and as late as the time of Constantius, Persian monarch thus signed himself in a letter to Roman emperor, "*Sapor*, *king of kings*, *allied to the stars*, *brother of the sun and moon*, &c. Cyrus is supposed by craft to have got at head of all the armies of Persia, and thence became monarch, like Genghis-Khan; his name changed from Agradates to Cyrus (Sun) (336.) Government as above described; his son Cambyses successor; great tyrant, according to Herodotus, who got all his information from Egyptian priests; Ctesias is less severe on his character; Cambyses conquered Egypt, made no alteration in government; with Cambyses ended line of Cyrus. Attempt made to restore Median dynasty; failed, and Darius Hystaspes of the family of Achœmenidæ elevated to throne; developed Persian government; empire organized into 20 satrapies; military and civil power separated. Xerxes was a weak, vainglorious monarch, calculated to bring on the last stage of effeminacy and bad government.

12. *Change in the character of the people?* Under Cyrus, Persians were hardy and valorous; best soldiers in the world. Under Xerxes, effeminate and infinitely inferior to Greeks. Already have pointed out causes which change manners of conquering Nomads; pleasures, carnal; no mental enjoyments. Luxury fatal to uncivilized people; not to civilized.

13. *Manners and morals, of the court of Persia?* Nomads always adopt, as far as possible, habits and luxuries of those they conquer, *e. g.* Tartars in China; so Persians adopted manners and luxurious habits of Medes. Polygamy existed; every thing determined by eunuchs and favorite wives. Kings, except Cambyses, not naturally cruel; but their wives occasionally perfect fiends, *e. g.* Amytis, Amestris and Parysatis. Harem filled from provinces, under surveillance of eunuchs; wearisome etiquette even in king's pleasures; a year to be spent in purification, before noviciate beauty was admitted to royal presence. (See Esther ii. 12.) Hence, the kings had generally as many concubines as days in year, *e. g.* Darius Hystaspes had 360, corresponding to days in Persian

year; and Artaxerxes is said to have had 115 children; 15 more than old Priam. *Wives* generally of family of Cyrus, or of Achœmenidæ, were on higher footing than *concubines*, though latter were sometimes elevated to dignity of former, *e. g. Esther*. The life of queen consort as rigidly confined and watched, as that of concubines; *e. g.* mentioned as extraordinary, that Statira, wife of Artaxerxes, appeared in public without a veil. Jealousy among the women intolerable; *e. g.* when Amestris, wife of Xerxes, got her sister-in-law, wife of Masistes, whom she suspected, in her power, she caused her breasts, tongue, nose, ears and lips, to be cut off! (Rol. 232.) Another consequence of the *Harem*, was to produce uncertainty in succession. Oldest son of the queen, was the heir apparent, but he might be defeated often by intrigues of the mother, or of favorite concubines, or by poison of a treacherous eunuch, and the selection of successor was left to monarch. Another consequence of the Harem, was utter insignificance of any thing like a *council of state;* all matters discussed in interior of Seraglio, under influence of queen-mother, favorite wife, and the eunuchs. The three capitals, Babylon, Susa (in Persia,) and Ecbatana (in Media,) were the places of residence for court; spring at Ecbatana, three summer months at Susa, and autumn and winter at Babylon. King's palace in Persia, as now at Constantinople, was called *the Porte; ai pulai* frequently occurs in the Cyropœdia; palaces were surrounded by spacious parks, called *paradises*, so large as to admit large armies. King could only be approached through his great officers; his courtiers, his masters of ceremony, his guards, &c., formed an immense body. According to Ctesias, there were daily fed at the king's table, 15,000 persons, and Xenophon says, that a considerable body of men, was required solely to make up the king's bed! These attendants were marshalled, like the army, into tens, hundreds, &c. All had titles which betokened their relation to king; *i. e.* one called *king's ears*, another the *king's eyes*, &c. The *table* of the monarch was of course of most sumptuous character; nothing but most costly could be touched by him; *e. g.* he could drink only the water of the Choaspes, conveyed to him in silver vessels, whenever he journeyed; his *salt* came from near temple of Jupiter Ammon, in the centre of African desert; his wine from Chalybon, in Syria; his bread was made of the wheat of Æolia, &c. The best fruits of each province were presented to monarch, on his royal journeys, and Xenophon speaks of bodies of men whose sole business it was to search throughout the empire for luxuries for the royal table. The chase was among the most noble of royal pleasures, and was considered best preparation for war. Whole armies were sometimes engaged in this way. (H. 392—405.) As every thing king said, or did, was worthy of record, he had always a number of *scribes* about his person, who attended him at the festival, public review, and even in battle, and noted down all the words that fell from him. (Esther iii. 12 and viii. 9, also Ezra vi. 1.) To these scribes was committed task of writing down the commands, or edicts, of king, which was sealed with the king's signet, and dismissed to its destination; *e. g.* when king Ahasuerus, by advice of Haman, ordered a general massacre of Jews, the king's scribes were called in to take down the order, and it was sealed with his signet. (See Esther iii. 12 and 13.) This practice prevails throughout east; *e. g.* king's scribes are mentioned in earliest records of the Mongol conquerors. Hyder Ali, too, in modern times, was always attended by 40 *scribes.* In this way were formed the *chronicles* of Persia, or the court history, which the king consulted, when he wished to review his past acts; *e. g.* (Esther vi. 1 and 2,) when the king could not sleep, and ordered the *chronicles* to be brought, that he might read the part relating to Mordecai, the Jew. It was probably by help of these chronicles that Herodotus was enabled to give so many details and anecdotes of the kings, and to furnish that celebrated catalogue of the army of Xerxes, with dress and arms of different nations, and names of their leaders.

14. *Revenue—financial system?* We must dismiss the idea of a public treasury like those of modern times; with our notions of finance, we look too exclusively to the *money* revenue, and imagine a public exchequer from which *money* payments are made to the public functionaries. Such a state of things *was*, and *is* now, unknown in the east. Public officers received no appointments in the European sense of the word; tribute in money furnished nothing more than *private* revenue of the monarch; taxes were levied in *kind*, proportioned to the fertility of soils. Payments in *money* were only made to limited extent in the maritime districts, whilst those in *kind* were always made in the interior provinces; *e. g.* Media contributed 100,000 sheep, 4,000 horses, &c., and the like of Cilicia, Armenia, &c. Best productions of every province were the king's; hence the abundance of luxurious provisions which flowed in upon the court, producing habits of waste and sensuality so notorious. Persian monarch was regarded as proprietor of the whole soil; not only, however, was the court of the king, but of the satrap also maintained in the manner above described; particular spots provided particular luxuries; *e. g.* Herodotus says Masistius, satrap of Babylon, reserved four villages of Babylonia to support his *Indian hounds.* And in similar manner, Tritontœchmus was furnished with his 800 stallions and 16,000 mares, without counting his war horses. Thus Themistocles received the city of Magnesia to supply him with his *bread*, Lampsacus, to supply his *wine*, and Myus the *side dishes* of his

table. Great officers received no money, but had towns and provinces assigned them, just as the Autocrat of the Russias assigns over whole districts of *serfs ;* such assignments were usually for life. Besides supplying the courts of the kings and satraps, the provinces were further burthened with the support of the armies stationed in, or marching through them. For this purpose magazines of corn and provisions were prepared, and all the contributions were in *kind* not *money.* Hence we are not to wonder at the desolation caused by march of a great army like that of Xerxes; nor that the citizens of Abdera should return thanks to the gods, because Xerxes made but *one meal* a day! Now-a-days, if army is under proper discipline, and does not ravage the country which it passes through, it may act like a great market, and even diffuse prosperity around it. Not so in the Persian empire, when each district was burthened with the support of the army as long as it remained in it. The *original Persia* was exempt from all taxes and burthens of a general character, because the conquering country.

15. *Satrapies?* We have seen that these resulted from the military government of Cyrus; the civil was separated from the military power, and by the side of the satrap, was the general of the satrapy. But in time the two powers came frequently to be united, and likewise many satrapies were run into one, with a single head; *e. g.* Cyrus the younger was satrap of Mysia, Phrygia, and Lydia, and generalissimo of all the forces which mustered at Castolus. Same the case with Pharnabasus, and after Cyrus, Tissaphernes received all his provinces, besides retaining his own. Hence one main cause of downfall of Persia. Satraps became powerful, and of course rebellious; several became founders of monarchies, which, like Cappadocia, Pontus, &c., became more or less independent; their courts were modelled after those of the king, and they had guards about their persons; *e. g.* Orœtes, satrap of Mysia and Phrygia, had 1000 Persian guards about him; hence the satraps were frequently at war with each other; *e. g.* Tissaphernes and the younger Cyrus were at war previous to the expedition of latter, and their enmity was viewed with satisfaction by the court.

16. *Military organization?* Nomad conquests are migrations; hence they move with wives, children, and flocks; again their strength is always in cavalry; these two points to be borne in mind in attending to military organization; while the former encumbers, the latter insures speed in movement. In every province there were two kinds of forces, those for the cities and garrisons, and those for the open country. In a nation of conquerors every man is a soldier; hence internal organization of Persia upon the decimal system; people divided into tens of thousands, with a general over each (*myriarch*), then into thousands,

with a commander (*chiliarch*), these into hundreds, and again into tens, with separate officers to each division; such a division common to Nomad conquerors; *e. g.* Mongols of modern times. Hence rapidity with which immense armies can be gotten together; *e. g.* orders are issued to commanders of ten thousands, these issue to the chiliarchy and commanders of hundreds and tens; thus in a few days a great Mongol prince will assemble several hundred thousand of cavalry. Persian empire was divided into *military cantons*, irrespective of civil administration, termed *nomoi* by Herodotus; each canton had its centre or place of military *rendezvous ; e. g.* Castolus was the muster place for the canton in the satrapy of Cyrus the younger; Thymbria for the army of Syria, and Aleius Campus for that of Cilicia. For cavalry, Nomad nations to south and east of Caspian were preferred; Hyrcanians, Parthians, and Sacœ. Soldiers were only paid *in kind*, and never in *money*, except the Greek mercenaries, who were better than Persian soldiers. Before time of younger Cyrus their pay amounted to a daric per month (about £1 0 4d. sterling); Cyrus increased it to 1½ darics. Besides these, none had pay in money; in fact in many of the satrapies there was no coined money. Darius Hystaspes was the first to coin money in Persia, hence the name *Daric.* Soldiers often *billeted* on particular villages, which were compelled to furnish them with all they wanted.

SEC. VII.—WAR BETWEEN GREECE AND PERSIA, AND ITS CONSEQUENCES.

1. *Rise of the war between Greece and Persia?* As soon as Lydian kingdom was conquered, Persia was brought into contact with Greece and her colonies; *the democratic principle* which prevailed through Greece, was thus brought into contact with *that of despotism*, which prevailed in Persia, and in the east. Again, Persia was divided into satrapies, many of which were really powerful countries; hence while by working of democratic principle, many efficient Greeks would be driven from their homes, take refuge in Persia, and excite the Persian monarch against the Greeks, and the discontented satraps on the other hand in Asia, would naturally form alliances among the Greeks, and foment dissensions in Persia, that they might gain their purposes. Thus, the relation of the states of Greece towards Persia, was like that of Italy towards Germany, during period of Italian republics; as on incursion of a Frederic or a Henry, some crafty noble of a free state often joined the imperial standard that he might gain the rule over a city; thus in Greece we find the ambitious and the discontented, flocking to Persian standard, to gain the tyranny of an island or a city; *e. g.* Coes, private citizen, thus raised to tyranny of Mitylene; Histiæus was confirmed in Mi-

letus, &c. And hence, although a war with Greece was for a long time avoided on account of the utter insignificance of the Greeks in the eyes of the Persian monarchs, yet sooner or later such a conflict was unavoidable.

2. *Immediate cause?* Owing to the intrigues of Aristogoras, tyrant of Miletus, and Histiæus, a distinguished Greek, who was detained in Persia by Darius, contrary to his inclinations. Aristogoras was anxious to annex Naxos to Miletus; prevailed on Darius to aid him with a Persian fleet; enterprise failed from dissensions of the commanders, and whole expense was thrown on Aristogoras. Just in this dilemma, Histiæus sent secret message to him, to revolt from Persia, in order that Darius might send him (Histiæus) to quell the revolt. Aristogoras, to render himself popular, in accordance with spirit of age, laid down tyranny, and established democracy in Miletus; this example spread through Ionia, and soon the tyrants were forced everywhere to abdicate, or fly from their cities. Aristogoras went then into Greece, failed to bring Sparta over to his designs; inflamed the more democratic Athenians; obtained a fleet which sailed to Asia Minor, debarked the troops at Coressus, marched suddenly on Sardis, the capital of Artaphernes, the satrap of Lydia, and burnt it down. Hence the Persian war. As soon, however, as the Persian armies could be gotten under weigh, one after another of the Ionian cities was reduced, till all Ionia was subjugated—then many of the islands, as Chios, Tenedos, Lesbos, &c., were reduced, and all Asia Minor fell under Persia. Mardonius was then placed at head of Persian fleet, and sent to take vengeance on Greece His fleet was almost entirely lost in doubling the promontory of Mount Athos, and the expedition failed. Datis and Artaphernes were then put at head of the Persian forces, and sent into Greece, and here commences the brilliant exploits of Athens, with the great battle of Marathon.

3. *Armaments of Persia?* Those under Xerxes are reported to have been so great as to induce great skepticism. Herodotus has described the Persian army under Xerxes, on the plain of Doriscus, as made up of the soldiers of 56 nations. He states the total amount of fighting men at 2,500,000; and including all the attendants, wives, concubines, servants, &c., the total is placed by him beyond 5,000,000.

4. *Can any confidence be placed in the statement of Herodotus?* Bonaparte did not believe these statements; he doubted whole of this brilliant period; he regarded Persian war as a series of indecisive actions in which each party claimed victory; thinks Xerxes burnt Athens, and returned triumphant in *his* estimation, while Greeks claimed victory, because they *had not surrendered* at Salamis; says the Greeks were a "vain hyperbolical people, and consequently exaggerated and perverted

every thing to their own praise; and we now have no Persian chronicle to correct their falsehoods. He thought the whole aspect of this narrative *suspicious.* He therefore doubted it, whilst he professed great faith in Roman history; for here he pronounced the facts "as clear as daylight." He believed too, in the great armies of Genghis-Khan and Tamerlane, because they were followed by gregarious nations, and he even thought that such armies might again scourge Europe. (L. C. J. v 1. 211.) Besides all this, it is well known that *provisioning* a large army is extremely difficult, and was not so well understood in ancient as modern times; and that at this day it may be pronounced almost impossible to provision under the most favorable circumstances, so large a body of men as 5,000,000, concentrated on a limited territory. On the other hand, all the historians who have investigated this subject, although they may admit exaggeration, are yet satisfied that the statement of Herodotus is *substantially* correct. The more his writings have been investigated, the greater the confidence which the learned have in their truth; he was credulous in some things, but exceedingly exact when he himself could investigate; he lived so near these times that he could have gotten all his statements from actors in the scene. Again the period of the Persian war was one of great men, of great orators, and what may be called a *historical period.* Nothing substantially false could obtain general credence in such an age. As regards the numbers in the armies, it is further remarked, that what Bonaparte calls gregarious nations, can assemble larger armies than any others; they do not *pay* the troops, and they levy their taxes in kind, and thus provision their armies without the intervention of a *circulating medium.* Besides all this, a large fleet attended the movements of the Persian army, and supplied it with necessaries. France at one time, under Napoleon, had a million of men under arms, who were entitled to *pay;* and under Louis XIV. the military establishment amounted for many years in succession, to 400,000 men. These forces for France it has been argued, were *relatively* as large as the forces of Persia. Again, as to the issue of the expedition, it is impossible to doubt that the Persians were most *decisively* beaten—the rapid conquests of the Greeks immediately after the great expedition, and the new station which we find them occupying in the politics of the world, most conclusively prove it.

5. *Effects of the Persian war on Greece?* Just before this war, states of Greece had advanced most rapidly in civilization and power, and perhaps the period of internal wars had come. Invasion of Persia, although it could not unite the Greeks into one nation, came just in time to prevent these wars among themselves. It produced a closer union, and a more national spirit among them than had existed since

the Trojan war—it produced rapid development of character, and was the era of great men and great energy—it gave the ascendency to the democratic principle, through the instrumentality of Athens, and was the means of the rapid increase in wealth, in luxury, in the fine arts, &c. Thus the states of Greece were the more rapidly pushed to their *zenith*, and perhaps the sooner thereby prepared for their downfall.

6. *Effect on Athens particularly?* As Athens had been the leading state against Persia, and had decidedly the ablest generals and the wisest statesmen, she reaped, by common consent, the greatest harvest of *glory*. As her country was ravaged and houses burnt, the aristocracy was more completely prostrated than elsewhere. She had too the finest fleet in Greece, which was decidedly favorablo to triumph of democratic principles. It became necessary for Greece to have a common treasury and a common fleet. Athens, from her energy, her glory and her former merits, became the administrator and arbiter of that treasury and fleet, and soon thereby acquired a dangerous ascendency in Greece. Sparta, on the other hand, being the next most powerful state, naturally became the centre of that party opposed to Athens. Her position, even if her institutions had not prepared her for it, would have forced her to take the oligarchical side in politics—hence the origin of those dreadful internal wars which so long ravaged Greece. But although the effect of the Persian war was to give the ascendency to Athens, to make her despotic among her allies, and often the promoter of most intolerable injustice, and thereby sooner to prepare Greece for her downfall, yet was all this attended by such a powerful stimulus to greatness, of every description, in Athens, that the world can scarcely regret the general result. When Athens was thus made the first state in Greece, her ambition, of course, roused her to the exertion necessary to maintain her ascendency. The city was to be every thing which could make it illustrious in the eyes of the Greeks—hence her splendid temples, her noble works of art, her brilliant festivals and theatres. It was this supremacy alone which could give to Pericles a theatre of action worthy of him—it was this which awoke the genius of a Phidias, a Polygnotus, a Sophocles and an Herodotus. Without it, Athens might have been more just, but not so great—she might have prolonged the reign of democracy, but she could not have illustrated it with so much glory. It was, in fine, the Athenian supremacy which made the Athenian democracy the most extraordinary multitude—the most *singularly constituted mob*, recorded on the page of history.

7. *Effect on the world?* As has been before observed, Persian war brought principle of *despotism* into collision with that of *democracy*, with most fearful odds in favor of the former. And Marathon, Ther-

mopylæ, Salamis, Platæa, &c., demonstrated to the world the mighty difference between the man who fights for his freedom and his country, and him who fights for a master. It is this war which has stood, and perhaps will stand, as long as the world shall endure, the most glorious monument that ever was erected to the cause of freedom. From the days of Themistocles down to the present moment, what writer has ever written on the influence of republican government, without drawing copious illustrations from this portion of Grecian story. What orator has ever spoken of patriotism without the mention of Marathon and Thermopylæ—and hence, even if those celebrated battles could be proved to have existed in fable alone, yet would it be beyond the power of human intellect to calculate the immense influence which they have exercised over the destinies of this world, from the mere fact that for ages past they have been mingled with the exhortations of the patriot, have been constantly heard on the field of battle, have been introduced into the anthem of the poet, and have been consecrated to the cause of free institutions everywhere, until they have become the very *watchwords* of liberty and independence throughout the world.

SEC. VIII.—MISCELLANEOUS HISTORY.

1. *Sculpture and Painting.*

1. *What was the condition of these arts during the flourishing period of Grecian history?* They rose to a degree of perfection rarely if ever attained before or since.

2. *Origin of these arts?* Founded on both a principle of utility and of vanity, *e. g.* pictorial representation is the first step in *writing.* Sculpture too has always been a means of transmitting important events to posterity—the first writing was probably on stone. Monuments are early erected to commemorate important events, as the *hill of stones* by Jacob and Laban; or to satisfy principle of vanity, as was probably the case with the *tower of Babel.*

3. *To what power of the mind do these arts principally address themselves?* To the *imagination*, and consequently have generally been carried to greatest perfection where the imagination was most cultivated.

4. *When the moderns are compared with the ancients, in regard to the imagination, how stands the comparison?* Ancient had more imagination, but less reason. The progress of science rather unfavorable to the cultivation of a highly wrought imagination. (*Cognoscere causas rerum,*) the knowledge of causation leaves too little play for the imagination, *e. g.* when the philosopher hears *thunder*, and sees *light-*

ning, he knows to what to refer these phenomena, and ceases consequently to wonder or to conjecture. But in the absence of science, the imagination is thrown into full action. Hence easy to explain how many of the arts have risen to their acme in the early stages of the world. Homer, David and Solomon, in poetry, and Phidias, Praxiteles, Zeuxis, Apelles, &c., in sculpture and painting, may never be surpassed; but Pythagoras, and Thales, and Plato, and Aristotle have long since been not only surpassed, but superseded in the cultivation of *philosophy*.

5. *In accounting for striking national characteristics, what circumstances are we to regard mainly?* The religion and government.

6. *Influence of religion on the arts of sculpture and painting in Greece?* The Greeks were *polytheists and anthropomorphites* thorefore each devotee would like to have images of his favorite gods; and as the gods had human forms, the sculptor would of course give to them the utmost perfection of muscle, limb, expression, symmetry of proportion, &c. Among all other polytheists of the ancient world, the religion was more or less symbolical, and the object of the sculptor was to give you the symbol, and not a human form; hence it mattered not how much nature was outraged, *e. g.* Indian would give his god 20 arms; the Phrygian would give his Diana 20 breasts; the Egyptian would place a human head on a lion's body. In the pagoda of Elephantis, near Bombay, is a colossal statue of Brama, represented sitting, arms crossed, with face and figure of man in front, female face and form behind; upon right breast is the *sun*, upon left *moon* and *stars;* waters, mountains, animals and plants are exhibited upon it. This is one reason of the low condition of arts in those countries. Although the Greek religion was symbolical at first, it soon cast off its symbolism, and gods became *moral persons*, to be represented under human forms. The belief, too, so prevalent among the Greeks, that the divinity resided in the statue, was of itself calculated to give a powerful stimulus to the arts. Voltaire (Tom. xv., p. 129) thinks such a belief impossible on account of its absurdity. It is most true that such belief is absurd; but that does not prove its non-existence. We are told that Stilpo was banished from Athens by a decree of the Areopagus, for asserting that the *Minerva* in the *Parthenon* did not contain the divinity. Again Horace represents God Priapus as saying that he was formerly a *trunk of a tree*, and the workmen doubted whether he would make a *god* or a *block* out of it. Voltaire says Horace intended *ridicule;* but where would be the point in the ridicule, *if no one* had ever believed divinity in the statue, and it would be difficult to explain the erection of the *molten calf* in the wilderness on any other principle. The fact is, throughout all ages there has been a tendency to *idolatry; e. g.* Jews under Moses,

and the Catholics of the middle ages, exemplify this proclivity of the human heart. Besides all this, the polytheistic religion operated much more powerfully on the imagination (that power of the mind to which these arts address themselves principally), than a Monotheistic religion. When *we* wonder abroad, we contemplate in the objects around us nothing but their mere *materialism*, *e. g.* mountains, groves, rivers, &c., are to us mere material substances. Not so with the ancient Greek; these things were *animated* by the supposed presence of divinity. Nymphs were in their groves, gods in their rivers, and the senate of the gods was convened on their mountains. Such belief as this operated strongly on the imagination, and was calculated to perfect the arts. Under all these circumstances, easy to conceive the difference between ancient and modern sculptor, *e. g.* Phidias and Canova: when former sculptured a Jupiter or a Minerva, he made a statue in which divinity was to reside, and which multitudes would adore. Hence the mighty stimulus to his imagination. Canova had no such belief, and knew that his statues of the gods were mere imitations, and would draw adoration from no one.

7. *Influence of government?* There are two main springs of action with man—love of fame, and love of money. Now the governments of Greece, so far as arts were concerned, operated most powerfully on both of these. Governments were democratic. Hence statues, paintings, &c., were for the people; and it is well known that the plaudits of an enraptured multitude are much more intoxicating than those of an autocrat. Again, specimens of art in Greece were for the public places, where they constantly met the gaze of the multitude, *e. g.* Minerva of the Parthenon, would not only spread the reputation of Phidias through Athens, but it was the object of adoration to thousands of strangers who visited the city; and his Jupiter at Olympia was visited quadrennially by thousands who came from the four quarters of the world to the great Olympic festival. In Greece, too, the history of the people was linked with the arts. Their tombs, temples, altars and consecrated places—their shields, helmets, breastplates, &c., all made, by the artist's skill, to perpetuate the memory of their fathers. Homer and Hesiod sang at the dawn of Grecian history of the artistic labors of Vulcan, and the sculptured shields of Hercules and Achilles. Let the Greek wander where he would, he beheld the history of his country embodied in marble by the chisel of the sculptor. What are our galleries in comparison with the temples, groves, and public places of Greece? We visit the former in an hour of leisure under the impulse of idle curiosity; but the latter were filled with the memory of her heroes and her gods.

The second principle of action, *love of money*, operated on with equal power by the Grecian democracies. Generally supposed that democracies are unfavorable to arts, because too niggardly in their expenditures. Not so with the Grecian. Every democracy had its public buildings, for the assembly of the people, for the public treasure, for gymnastic exercises, for national festivals, &c., *e. g.* the Prytaneum, the Odeon, Pynx, Gymnasium, Theatres, Galleries, &c., of Athens. As Greece was divided into a number of small states, these naturally strove to excel one another, and consequently were more lavish in their expenditures.

But the defeat of the Persians, and the subsequent conquests of the Greeks, suddenly poured such a stream of wealth into these little democracies, that they forthwith became most efficient patrons of the fine arts. Athens took the lead, because she had the largest fleet, had been the most efficient in overthrowing the power of the Persians—had consequently obtained the supremacy or *Hegemony* ("Ηγεμονια) in the Grecian confederacy, and the final management of that joint treasure of the confederates originally intended for the benefit of all against the common enemy. This treasure Athens most unjustly squandered for her own particular purposes, and was main cause of the magnificent patronage which Pericles bestowed on the arts. As Athens usurped the *Hegemony* of the democratic portion of Greece, her citizens became proud, and thought that the leading state should erect buildings and monuments worthy of her supremacy. She was to be clothed in magnificence and splendor, such as would dazzle the beholder and reconcile tho other states to her supremacy. Hence the people themselves always voted the most magnificent mode of executing the public works, no matter how costly; *e. g.* when Phidias submitted two plans for a statue, one to be executed in marble, and the other of gold and ivory, with a recommendation of the first, because cheapest, the people at once decided in favor of the latter. And even if public men were accused of too much extravagance on these monuments, people were easily reconciled by appeal to their vanity; *e. g.* when Pericles, charged with extravagance, replied that the commonwealth might be exonerated from the burthen, if he might be permitted to inscribe the works with *his name*, proposition rejected at once, and no more said about the expenses.

8. *Preceding remarks exemplified by modern sculpture and painting?* During latter part of the 15th, and the whole of the 16th centuries, arts in a most flourishing condition—more so than they have ever been since—causes similar to those that operated on ancient Greece. 1st, Catholic religion had degenerated into a sort of Polytheism. Image

worship was revived, and the Catholic churches were everywhere filled with paintings and statues. 2d, The Italian republics which had been the first to take the lead in commerce and manufactures, became most wealthy at that period, and consequently were in condition to bestow the most liberal patronage on the arts.

9. *Influence of the gymnastic festivals?* It is supposed that the games holden in some portions of Greece every year had favorable influence on the arts. First, the youth being so thoroughly trained in gymnastic exercises, the forms of the Greeks were thereby more perfectly developed. Second, the exercises were performed in a state of nudity, and the artiste had every opportunity to select most perfect models. Third, high honors were paid to the victor, and a statue was generally erected to him by his city or his friends, which at Olympia was placed in the Altis; and thus gallery of statues was formed at each of the places where the games were celebrated.

10. *Art of painting among the Greeks?* The Greeks attained to great eminence in this art, and some have supposed they even excelled moderns; *e. g.* Aristides, Theban, painted the sacking of a city, and represented a dying mother with infant at the breast, and the countenance of the mother exhibited fear lest the child should suck her blood, instead of milk, when she was dead; so that no one could doubt the peculiar cause of the mother's dread. Again, we are told by Pliny that Parrhasius of Ephesus painted the people of Athens under a female figure, which represented them at once as harsh, unjust, and fickle—at the same time mild, clement, pitiful, noble, brave and generous—and at same time mean, cruel, and cowardly, and that the spectator could not fail to see in the female countenance all those opposite qualities. Zeuxis is said to have painted grapes so perfectly, as to have deceived the birds.* From these and such other instances, the admirers of antiquity have come to the conclusion, that painting among the ancients was as perfect as sculpture, and both far beyond the reach of the modern arts. In spite, however, of such instances, from which no general conclusion can be drawn, there is little doubt that art of painting among the ancients was far behind that of sculpture. The management of colors was not so well understood as now; and it has been said only four were

* After all, this trite anecdote about the bunch of grapes argues very little for the skill of Zeuxis, as the grapes appear to have been held up by a child, whose resemblance was not striking enough to scare the birds away. These tricks betoken no high skill, even if successful. A dog will recognize his master's picture, and the more readily, when of that sort of *daub* called a *staring likeness*. Bassano played off a trick of the kind on the great painter, Annibal Carracci. He painted a book on a picture which Carracci tried to remove in order to examine the picture.

used by Grecian painters—white, red, yellow, and black. The art of painting has reached much higher perfection since introduction of Christianity. Sentiment and feeling have become more predominant in the works of art, and these are expressed more easily by colors, than by the rigid forms of sculpture. Hence modern or Christian period has been termed *romantic* in respect to the fine arts, in contradistinction to *classic;* and the art of painting is called pre-eminently romantic. Such painters as Michael Angelo, Corregio, Raphael, Titian, &c., presented the beautiful in the noblest forms, and transferred the ideal of the antique to the art of painting.

11. *Difference between condition of the arts in Greece and rest of the ancient world?* In some of the great monarchies, Egypt for example, their monuments were of a more colossal size, but were devoid of that beauty, grace, harmony of proportion, belonging to arts of Greece. Mysterious structures of Egypt display vastness and simplicity, but after all are but what Strabo calls "the barbarous monuments of painful labor." In them we behold rather the record of power, of patience, and of labor, than the creation of mind, of taste, or of genius. They are gloomy and grave, and at same time stiff and motionless, as their mummies—more nearly allied to the dead than the living. But when we look to the monuments of the Greeks, we find the proof of their refined intellects. All is grace, and harmony, and complete development. They were the first to separate the ideas of perfection and purity of taste from those of mighty masses. It was they who first learned the art of breathing *life* into statuary, and of inspiring marble with sentiment and feeling. What a mighty difference between the Jupiter of Phidias, and an Indian idol, or an Egyptian Isis!—between the spiritualized art of an Apelles and the childish fancies of a Chinese painter! Again, no artists of antiquity understood the influence of association so well as the Greek. Painting and sculpture differ widely from poetry in the latitude which they enjoy. The poet can commence at the inception of the event, and trace it through all its stages to its consummation. Not so the painter or sculptor. The latter must seize on some one position or state of things and trust to association of ideas for the effect. The poet is neither trammelled in *time* nor in *space;* the painter and sculptor in both. The poet may trace an emotion from its origin to its termination. The sculptor and painter must seize on some one stage and trust to association for the rest. Now one great art of the latter must consist in the selection of that particular position which may produce happiest effect by association. This is rarely the one that expresses most violence or most lamentation, but some one of more moderation. Poetry has no trammel of this character. *e. g.* When So-

phocles describes Philactetes with his wounded foot, he makes whole isle of Lemnos resound with his lamentations. The same Philactetes has been the subject of the sculptor; and here there is no expression of effeminate lamentation, but we behold the patient concentrated woe of a suffering hero. So likewise in the dying Gladiator, how much more impressive to behold him leaning on his shield, his head drooping, his manly brow consenting to death, and his resolution rising superior to the agony, than if the sculptor had exhibited him in all the violence of the combat when mortal wound was received. Now Grecian artists have never been excelled in this, the happy selection of that particular state which would, by association, produce the finest effect.

12. *Progress of the arts in Greece?* Four periods; first, from the rude beginnings to the time of Pericles; second, age of Pericles or Phidias, when the ideal sublime prevailed; third, to the death of Alexander—*beautiful style;* fourth, age after Alexander.

13. *First period? Ideal style.* Pausanias tells us that, in primitive ages, deities of Greece were represented by stones and trunks of trees unformed by art. As late as Adrian's time, blocks of stone, representing Apollo, Juno, and Bacchus, were to be seen at Thebes, Argos, and Delphi, and the celebrated Cupid of Praxiteles was sent by Phryne to Thespia to replace a *stone* worshipped there from earliest times. As skill advanced, some regularity of form was given to these signs of the gods, the blocks were hewn into columnar shapes, next they were fashioned into a sort of rude outline of human figure, but arms were not separated from the body, and drapery was stiffly marked in deep lines upon the surface. Such the condition of sculpture, when arrival of Dædalus (1234 B. C.) fixed new era in the arts. About same time Dibutades invented *coroplastic art*, or application of soft materials to modelling the representations of sculpture—name from Cora, his daughter, who, according to romantic fable of the poets, traced by a lamp upon the wall the shadowed profile of her lover as he slept, in order to get a rude likeness to solace the hours of his absence. Struck with likeness, her father carefully filled up the lines with clay, and thus formed a *Medallion* long preserved at Corinth; and to this have the poets traced the art of painting, (E. E. v. 17, 16.) For the several centuries during this period the arts slowly advanced until arrived at the stage in which they existed in time of Pericles. The reign of Pisistratus was the most favorable portion of this time to arts. He collected around him most esteemed artists, *e. g.*, Eucharis, son of Eubulides, and Callon of Elis. These two made famous statue of Bacchus, in which were preserved the lineaments of their patron, the most beautiful as well as accomplished man of his age. Callimachus, inventor of the Corinthian

Capital, supposed by some to belong to this reign. After time of Pisistratus, three most distinguished artists were Polycletus, Pythagoras, and Myron. Latter made celebrated Iconic statue of Ladus, the foot-racer, poised on one foot, with the body springing forward; and it was said "breath seemed to agitate his lungs; and the form was gazed upon as if flying from its pedestal to snatch the crown of victory." (E. E. 24.) Myron brought mere imitative art to great perfection; represented external nature well, but could not touch the heart or elevate imagination like the sculptors of age of Pericles.

13. *Second period—Age of Pericles. Ideal sublime?* Every circumstance combined to make this age famous for the arts. First character of Pericles, whose lofty conceptions were in unison with exalted tone of feeling in his native city. Athens too had been despoiled by the Persians of ancient monuments, but now with magnificent resources at the head of the Grecian confederacy, with cultivated taste, she became the abode of splendor and the nursery of elegance and art. Above all appeared Phidias, most renowned artist of this period, and it is doubtful which most profited by the connection, the patron or the artist. Works of this Homer of sculpture of three kinds—1st, *Toreutic, i. e.*, statues of ivory and other materials; 2d, statues of bronze; 3d, sculptures in marble.

First, Olympian Jupiter supposed to be his masterpiece. This statue placed in a temple at Olympia in Elis; 230 feet long, 95 broad, from ground to decorations above the gateway 68 feet, covered with Pentilican marble cut into shape of tiles. God represented as sitting on a throne, in repose, one hand supporting a figure of victory, other resting upon burnished sceptre of precious metals—body naked to the cincture, was composed of ivory, hair of gold, with an enamel crown on the awful head—lower limbs clothed in flowing vestment gemmed with golden flowers and animals—throne rising above head of the god most exquisitely sculptured, composed of ivory and ebony inlaid with precious stones.

Another work of the *Chryselephantine* order, scarcely inferior to the Jupiter, was the Minerva of the Parthenon—the glory of Athens—figure of the goddess stood upright, armed, one hand grasping a spear, other holding an image of victory. At her feet lay a shield covered with most beautiful sculpture, representing on the convex the Amazonian war, the Athenian leader being a portrait of Pericles, which, with the representation of himself under the figure of bald old man, rolling a stone as emblematic of his art, was subsequently the cause of his banishment. On concave were the giants warring against heaven. On golden sandals was portrayed battle of the Centaurs. In the figure itself the nude was of ivory, and the robes and ornaments of gold. Parthenon, in which this statue was placed, was most magnificent temple, 217 feet 9 inches in length, most beautifully decorated in *bas-relief.* Much of this has been transferred to London by Lord Elgin. These two statues were so grand and sublime that they were supposed to have had no slight influence on the religion of the Greeks, and he was deemed unfortunate, who once in his life at least, had not been able to behold these divinities.

2d. Works of Phidias in bronze numerous, and generally colossal. His Minerva Poliades surpassed in this respect the Minerva of Parthenon, of such majestic proportions, that the spear and crest could be seen, towering above the Acropolis, by mariner as he rounded promontory of Sunium, 25 miles off. This statue and its ornaments were painted by Parrhasius.

3d. We are able fully to appreciate labors of Phidias in marble, by examination of *Elgin marbles* in the Museum in London. In these remains we have both statues and relievos—former ornamented the tympana of Parthenon. On eastern pediment was birth of Minerva, on western her contest with Neptune. Of these two compositions, fourteen pieces remain, consisting of seventeen figures more or less mutilated, all of heroic size, double the natural. In 1676, all these were entire; in 1687 destruction commenced by blowing up a Turkish magazine, during siege of Athens by the Venetians, which laid the Parthenon in ruins. Among the relievos, the combat between Theseus and the Centaurs, a subject most interesting to the Athenians, is exhibited. These designs, of which fifteen are preserved, exhibit bold relief approaching to roundness. These remains are memorials of sculpture in great perfection. Grandeur is the prevailing character; but mixed with simplicity and true nature; yet the finishing is delicate and even minute; chiselling facile, vigorous, and flowing; the touch broad; shadows deep and firm; style strictly learned; muscles, and marking of the bones, decidedly pronounced; anatomical science of those fragments equal to any that have come down to us; expression of action complete. West said we could not view the equestrian Athenians, without conviction that they and their horses actually existed such as we see them in the marbles.

15. *Chryselphantine sculpture, mode of executing it, its character, &c.?* In these colossal works of combined materials, like the Jupiter and Minerva, first step was a full-sized model; then a copy in wood, which was the nucleus to which the ivory and the gold were affixed. This frame work was not solid; within the cavity were the irons and supports for fixing whole to pedestal, and for holding together the parts,

as head, arms, &c. Necessary too to get into the work for taking care and repairing. This frame work was then veneered over with ivory, *i. e.*, by closely fitting small pieces or plates of ivory upon the wood by means of pins and cement. In the Olympian Jupiter, Pausanius tells us that Phidias worked the ivory in pieces in his study. Ivory part completed, attachment of drapery and ornaments in gold or other metal, either east or beaten out, was easily executed.

Chryselephantine sculpture was not so durable as the bronze and marble; for besides the wood work always subject to decay, the ivory was likewise affected either by dryness or moisture, and the expansion and contraction of the wood work were always injuring the joints. Hence difficulty of preserving this kind of sculpture. Charge of preserving Olympian Jupiter was intrusted to set of artists under the title of *Phœdruntia*, who were obliged to sacrifice to *Minerva Ergane* before commencing these functions. Original expense of this kind of work, and difficulty of preserving it may have been the main cause of the gradual disuse of the Chryselephantine order, and the substitution of marble and bronze. Some have doubted whether this kind of statuary could ever have imposed on the imagination unless from size, and consequently that, for artistic expression, it could never have been comparable to marble or bronze. The preference however given to this order by Phidias, whose judgment, as to *expression*, is placed beyond all doubt by the Elgin marbles, and the rapturous praises of the ancient world, accustomed to the most magnificent specimens of the art in every department, conclusively prove the high character of this order for expression as well as grandeur.

16. *Third period to death of Alexander. Beautiful style?* Agoracritus of Paros, and Alcamenes, the Athenian, were favorite pupils of Phidias. These executed principally in the heroic style, in imitation of their master; but the two most celebrated statues of Alcamenes, the Venus of the gardens, and the Cupid of Thespis, mark a slight change from the heroic towards the beautiful. But style of Scopas more clearly shows transition of the school of Phidias into that of Praxiteles. He was of Paros. Grace, softness and truth his characteristics. Two of his statues extant: Venus in the Townly collection, and the group of the Niobe at Florence—former more allied to the beautiful style—latter assimilates more closely to the Phidian. This latter statue has been attributed by some to Praxiteles; and Pliny was in doubt between the two.

Lysippus and Praxiteles were the great artists of this period, and perfected the style. Former, favorite of Alexander, worked principally in bronze; said to have produced 610 statues—some say 1500.

Doubtful whether any remain;—bust at Portici is doubtful. The horses brought from Chios to Constantinople, by Theodosius the younger, and, after 1204, placed on the façade of St. Mark's in Venice, are not supposed quite equal to Lysippus' reputation. Some of his works of Phidian order, *e. g.*, Tarentine Jupiter, 60 feet high, of cast metal, and 21 equestrian statues of Alexander's body guards, who fell at the Granicus in defence of their prince. To Chares, his favorite pupil, Cicero ascribes the Colossus of Rhodes. But Lysippus was also the sculptor of works the most beautiful and delicate—his finishing exquisite, and his imitation of nature was most faithful. His education was most complete of all the artists. Praxiteles of Cnidos worked in both brass and marble. He chose subjects generally requiring soft, elegant style. For most part they were female figures or youths. First who made statue of Venus entirely naked—considered indecorous, but pardoned for the beauty of performance. Most feeling of all sculptors, formed the ideals of Diana and Bacchus; the latter the contrast to the Satyrs and Fauns, who express rudenses and licentiousness. Former expressed virgin modesty with bold activity. Homer's Nausican his model, his Cupid supposed the most beautiful ever executed. His Apollo, *Sauroethonos*, or Lizard killer, exhibited all simplicity and elegance which could be given to youth. First who gave perfect union of intellectual charm with feminine grace in his representations of the "queen of soft desire," his draped and nude, or Coan and Cnidian Venus, fixed each a standard, from which invention has not since departed.

17. *Comparison of the third with preceding period?* Some have supposed latter more perfect than the former. Not so; Elgin marbles have rarely been surpassed for beauty even. But without actual decay of talent, various causes combined to operate this change from the combination of the grand and beautiful, to the beautiful simply. First, colossal statues, like Jupiter and Minerva of Phidias, were too expensive for any but rich states. Artists naturally adopted by degrees the style that would enable them to supply the most extensive market. In the progress of the arts the sculptors became as much indebted to private as to public patronage, and the colossal order was too expensive for the former. 2nd, It must be admitted that in all the departments for the exercise of mind, there is not found in any nation lengthened display of highest genius. A few elevated spirits only are placed in the solitary majesty of general eminence. Succeeding aspirants contented to select some particular province to cultivate and render their own. Thus Praxiteles resolved to woo exclusively milder graces of his art. Over his composition he has diffused a perfect grace, a voluptuous beauty, an expression at once spiritual and sensual, confessed by coldest heart,

satisfying most fastidious taste, and admired by most trembling modesty.

18. *Fourth period—Age after Alexander. Decline?* The schools of Lysippus and Praxiteles conclude history of Greek sculpture in its greatest perfection. Many names of great respectability occur afterwards, but there were no longer the genius and invention of the preceding periods. They were but imitators of great masters who preceded.

19. *Progress of the art of painting in Greece?* Cannot divide into regular periods as in case of sculpture. It must have been coeval with the formation of society. Pictures were used for writing among the Mexicans, *e. g.* Montezuma was apprised of invasion of Spaniards by rude pictures on a sort of cloth. We know that painting was familiar to Jews at an early period, *e. g.* figures of Cherubim embroidered on curtain of the Holy of holies. (Ex. xxvi. 32.) Same on hangings of the sanctuary. Diodorus tells us that the bricks in Babylon were frequently painted, and prophet Ezekiel is desired "to take him a tile, and lay it before him, and portray upon it the city, even Jerusalem." In like manner Homer, who does not make distinct mention of painting, speaks of embroidery, which implies of course the art of design. The history of Philomela, although wrapt in fable, shows the practice of tapestry pictures at very early period. Homer represents Helen, in third book Iliad, as embroidering pictures of those misfortunes and battles her beauty had caused. When Hector was killed, Andromache was found in small chamber embroidering colored flowers on cloth. Virgil too has indicated his belief in high antiquity of painting, when he represents Æneas as beholding the whole Trojan war painted on the walls of temple of Juno at Carthage.

First step in art of painting was to give durability to colors. Polygnotus, the elder, first who subjected his works to fire for this purpose, doubtful whether he invented the *encaustic* method, mode of painting in enamel, or whether first adopted use of wax with his colors, which would require heat, or whether he merely invented style of drawing by burning the surface of wood with hot iron—*poker drawings.* Next step was *Monochromatic* style, or use of single color—*Chiaro Oscuro.* Next step was to give attitude and posture to animate figures. First painters made their figures stiff and upright in thin lines. Great step to represent them with their heads looking up, or down, or sideways, (the *Catagrapha* of the ancient writers,) this improvement due to Cimon of Cleone, who was first to represent muscles and veins, and the folds of garments. Next painter of great distinction was celebrated Phidias. His *Medusa's* head was a wonderful painting, according to Pliny. Apollodorus next perfected the *shading* with all its gradations.

Parrhasius studied symmetry of human figure, gave improved expression to the countenance, formed the curls with grace, and carefully finished extremities of hands and feet. Aristides, of Thebes, said by Pliny to be first who expressed various emotions of mind in delineating human countenance. He depicted passion and sentiment faithfully—paintings mainly historical, *e. g. Bacchus and Ariadne, sacking of a town*, battle between *Greeks and Persians, &c.* Zeuxis did much for painting. One of the vainest and greatest of artists. Instead of crowding the canvas with incidents, he had few, but made them perfect; was fond of the beautiful, therefore chose female figures principally. Was proudest of his Helen, composed of beauties of five most beautiful girls of Crotona, who sat for him. He painted Jupiter surrounded by all the deities, the infant Hercules strangling the serpent, &c., &c. He was of age of Pericles. But painter of most reputation was Apelles, of age of Alexander. He was the Raphael of Greece—in character like to Raphael. His master, Pamphilius, was very like to Petro Perugino, master of Raphael. He had no self-conceit like Zeuxis—enjoyed friendship of Alexander as Titian did of Charles V.; in painting his Venus, fell in love with beautiful Pancaste, one of the concubines of Alexander, who sat for the painting. Alexander then presented her to the painter. Had custom of exposing his paintings to public view to hear criticisms, and profit by them. In this way originated with him the well-known proverb, "*Ne sutor ultra crepidam*," (E. E. No. 29, 282.) Seems to have studied pleasing illusion of *fore-shortening*, which was but little understood by ancients. *Thunderbolt*, held in the hand of Alexander, in the character of Jupiter, was said to *advance* beyond the picture. His allegorical picture of *Calumny* was subject of much praise. His other greatest works were *Venus rising out of the sea*, *Procession of Megabysus, The Priest of Diana at Ephesus, Clytus arming for battle, &c.* Protogenes of Rhodes was cotemporary with Apelles, and of great merit. He it was who made the *foam* at the mouth of the horse, by dashing the sponge in a lucky fit of passion on his painting. It was his picture of *Temperance*, of which Apelles said it was worthy to be carried to heaven by the Graces; and with him we close the account of Grecian painters, as the art began henceforth to decline.

20. *Ancient paintings which have come down to us?* Pictures in the Museum at Portici, taken from excavations of Pompeii and Herculaneum, are the best preserved specimens of ancient art; and if a fair specimen, as they probably are not, would place art of painting among ancients far below modern, in both color and general effect, and yet some of these have purity and elegance of design which none but such

as Raphael and Corregio have ever equalled, *e. g.*, *Dancing girl of Herculaneum*, *The Nereid riding on a sea monster*, the two sitting female figures in picture representing *sale of Cupids*, *Visit of Juno and Minerva to Venus*, *&c.* So also the *Europa* wrought in Mosaic in the Barberini palace, and the *Apollo giving chaplet to a poet*, taken from the baths of Titus. From bright colors, red, yellow, &c., still visible on walls of Pompeii, it seems coloring matter has lost little of its freshness or vigor. Yet there is no science in their coloring, no richness of tint. Real excellence in these particulars could scarcely have been reached before the invention of oil painting, which seems to have been unknown to the ancients.

Upon whole, plastic art and painting bore to each other opposite relation to that of modern times; former most cultivated. More public arts are among a people, more certainly will sculpture surpass painting. Both may be public, but former far better for public monuments than latter. Paintings are more destructible, besides they must be placed on walls. Works of plastic art, statues, busts, &c., are more independent, easily placed wherever there is room for them—hence better suited to public places and buildings. Now, in Greece, all these were for public. We have no instance of a statue belonging to private man. Individuals often paid for them, but always for purpose of setting them up in public places, as temples, porches, market-places, gymnasia, theatres, &c., (H. G. 288.) Even in Rome, arts were not introduced into private life before time of Lucullus, Verres, &c. And it is doubtful whether their example was ever widely followed. Verres plundered Sicily of works of art, and they were all public with one exception, the four statues of Heius, and even these were in a chapel, (*sacrarium*,) and were therefore somewhat public. Pausanias, as late as second century after Christ, travelled through Greece, which had been several centuries under dominion of Romans, and every work of art which he describes was found in public places, makes no mention of any work belonging to individual. (292.)

2. *Literature—Philosophy—History—Drama—Eloquence.*

The democratic governments of Greece did not found and support great literary institutions as in modern times. It was not till after the age of Alexander, when monarchical governments were established, that provision was made for such institutions; the museums of Alexandria and Pergamus were then founded. Yet Heeren says it is great mistake to suppose that Grecian states did nothing for education and improvement—they only did it in different way from moderns. We measure civilization by state of *scientific* knowledge, ancients by that of the *arts.* We patronize *schools of science*, they the *schools of art*. (H. 244.) The latter was closely connected with their literature; the most sublime statues of Phidias did but embody the conceptions of Homer, and the masterpieces of sculpture and painting often furnished the best commentary on the tragedians. (273.) Even where the persons were different, sculptor could yet draw from the poet, or vice versa, his conception of ideal forms; *e. g.*, sublime figures of the Niobe and Laocoon can easily represent to mind an Electra or Œdipus, such as they floated before imagination of the poet.

1. *Thales of Miletus?* Lived more than 600 years B. C., first of Grecian philosophers, deeply imbued with Egyptian knowledge, celebrated for geometry and astronomy, progress in former very limited, first to demonstrate that every diameter *bisects* the *circle*, and first to find out method of inscribing right angled triangle in circle. On discovery of latter, in excess of joy, sacrificed an ox to Minerva. These propositions known to freshmen of our colleges—supposed to have made some fortunate conjectures about stars and our solar system, first to calculate eclipses, and predicted that of 601 B. C., which separated armies of the Medes and Lydians at moment of engagement. (T. U. H. v. i. 261.) Did not pretend to regular system in morals, but taught after manner of the Gnomic poets by maxims and precepts. One of his maxims, "not to do to others what, if done to us, we should resent," supposed by Gibbon same with great Gospel precept, "to do as you would be done by." Maxim of Thales, however, only forbids *evil doing* —Christian commands *universal charity*—Xenophon in Cyropædia, commending benevolence to enemies, makes nearer approach than Thales to Christian precept. (Mit. 4. 122.) His school called the Ionic.

2. *Anaximander?* Disciple of Thales, committed his master's tenets to writing, taught that all things are changing, that there is a succession of worlds, said to be first constructer of the sphere, first delineator of limits of sea and land, first inventor of the *Gnomon* for painting hours by shadow on *sun dial.*

3. *Pythagoras?* Soon after the Ionic rose the Italic sect, so called from country where Pythagoras first taught. He, like Thales, travelled for knowledge, particularly in Egypt—said even to have visited India to study doctrines of gymnosophists—returning to his native Samos political disturbances drove him into Italy—established his school at Crotona —like Egyptian priests, had two kinds of doctrine, *exoteric* and *esoteric;* one for public, other for his private and initiated pupils. Object of former general morality, latter consisted of mysteries—said that five years of silence were required to prepare his scholars for these secrets. (T. U. H. ii. 263.) Wonder then that he should have had a school of

females—had great respect for women; his wife was a philosopher, and no less than fifteen of others of his female disciples rose to great distinction; his disciples formed a sort of secret society ramified into all the cities of Magna Græcia; at one time this society all powerful at Crotona; offices of state filled by its members; they combined gymnastics with philosophy. So distinguished were Crotonians for gymnastic feats that six prizes were won by them at one Olympiad, and the great wrestler, Milo, who led the armies of Crotona against Sybaris, was one of his most distinguished disciples. (H. 248.) But a secret society with power always excites opposition party—this happened with Pythagoreans. Cylon headed the opposite party, and succeeded in destroying the society of Pythagoras.

Pythagoras was in politics a decided friend of oligarchy, which was bad policy for an innovator, as democracy is much more favorable both to literary and political revolutions. (B. 2. 231.) *Self-command* was the great virtue inculcated in his morals. Arithmetic, astronomy, music and geometry were all cultivated—he taught the occult properties of numbers, by which he explained origin and substance of all things, thus forming a union between arithmetic and magic; to him is ascribed the demonstration of the 47th proposition of Euclid, which caused him to sacrifice a *hecatomb*—latter part at least doubted, because he believed in transmigration of souls, and consequently would not sacrifice oxen in which the soul of men *might* dwell. Pythagoras held sun to be central fire, the seat of Jupiter, the stars were divine, &c.; his disciple, Ocellus Lucanus, gave a treatise Περι το παντος, or of the universe, which has come down to us; contending for eternity of mundane system, and impossibility of change from failure or corruption of parts. Aristotle and Plato both borrowed largely from him.

4. *Anaxagoras?* But the philosopher who exercised the most influence on Athens before Socrates, was Anaxagoras of Clazomene, called, by way of distinction, "*the intellect of his age.*" He was of the Ionian school—flourished from B. C. 480 to B. C. 450, a period falling between battle of Thermopylæ and the five years' truce of Sparta, one year before Cimon's death. To him attributed first conception of one eternal, almighty, and all-good being—gods of Greece stood low in his estimation—sun and moon were mere matter—doctrine at war with popular superstition, and so repugnant to system on which depended the festivals, processions, sacrifices and oracles, which fascinated vulgar mind, was viewed with horror. Even his astronomical knowledge, which enabled him to calculate eclipses, lowered the importance of priests, augurs, interpreters and seers; hence accusation of impiety against him, and all the power of Pericles could only secure him the means of escape

from Attica to Lampsacus, where he passed the remainder of his days in exile. This was the commencement of the contest between philosophy and the popular religion. Anaxagoras meddled but little with politics, yet influence was great through Pericles, his friend and patron. He freed Pericles, says Plutarch, from superstition proceeding from false judgments respecting auguries and prodigies, by explaining their natural causes, and this produced no slight political effect among a people addicted to this kind of superstition. Archelaus, a pupil of Anaxagoras, was first *native Athenian* who taught philosophy at Athens, and from him we date those schools which so much illustrated that famous city. It was in his school that Socrates was trained.

5. *Sophists?* It was just after the time of Anaxagoras that the sophists arose in such numbers in Greece—these the first who gave instruction for pay—they taught both philosophy and rhetoric—the former in their hands degenerated into art of confounding opponent by syllogisms and sophisms; and the subjects on which they were fondest of speculating were those respecting which we ought to learn that we know nothing at all. This kind of reasoning, when disputation and speaking were taught, was closely connected with rhetoric. They thus reduced eloquence to a mere art of disputing, and became a theme of reproach among philosophers and comic poets, until at last the precepts and the very name of the sophists became odious to ancients. They rose however in their day rapidly in numbers and importance, and must therefore in some manner have been closely connected with the wants of the times.

6. *Causes which produced them?* 1st, After Persian war, and the attainment of *hegemony* by Athens, and consequent multiplication of business before the popular assembly, and of lawsuits before the courts, an intense demand sprung up in Athens for knowledge on one hand, and the art of communicating it on other. Sophists endeavored to satisfy this demand—when there was so much to manage and talk about, and where all subjects were discussed orally, instructors in logic and rhetoric could not fail to be acceptable; and these sophists are entitled to the glory at least of having shown the necessity of liberal education. With the Athenians philosophy was not the monopoly of a few studious minds, it was interwoven with the manners, pursuits and glory of the *Demus;* it was not apart from the occupations of life—the Agora and the courts were to them in the place of academies and colleges—there was no free man, however low, but what felt necessity for instruction. Sophists were thus the fruit of their age. They came from all parts of Greece to teach in this great city, in which, after Persian war, there was so great demand for knowledge. Gorgias, who begins series, came

from Leontium in Sicily, Protagoras from Abdera, Hippias from Colophon, &c. They taught for money, and orally, without the use of books, which were too dear. None without some sort of eloquence could undertake this—they frequented places of public resort, the Agora, public walks, gymnasia and porticoes, and recommended themselves by most ostentatious displays of their abilities in disputing with one another, or with any one who would converse with them.

2dly. The sycophants who infested Athens, and rendered the lives and fortunes of individuals so insecure, by the prosecutions which they gave rise to, produced a strong necessity for rhetoric and eloquence. It was necessary for each man, if possible, when charged by the sycophants, to be able to defend himself, and, if he could not make his own defence, he applied to the sophists for aid, who were in the habit of writing for pay (M. 4. 78), and thus supplied place of professional lawyer.

7. *Abuses to which they gave rise?* At Athens, where value of eloquence as a weapon or shield was felt more and more every day, youths who flocked round sophists cared less for solid knowledge than for the art of display, which would enable them to shine in the assembly and in the courts; hence they were so anxious to learn the whole art of dialectics, to confound and perplex the adversary. It was this art, the *quidlibet per quodlibet ars probandi*, which inflated the disciples of the sophists with so much self-conceit, which thrust them prematurely into public life, when they supplanted older and graver citizens on the Bema or in the courts—and hence they were regarded as great evil; *e. g.* in last scene of the knights of Aristophanes the first resolution which *Demus* adopts, after coming to his senses, is to bar the Agora and Pnyx against beardless youths, and make them go a hunting instead of speaking. (T. iv. 260.)

Another abuse which they gave rise to was tendency to unlimited skepticism. When the pupil is trained to disputation, and taught, as Gorgias taught, to speak on any thesis and argue on either side, he soon loses the faculty of judging, he has no settled conclusions, doubt prevails every where. Not to wonder that this *Pyrrhonism* should have extended itself to religion; men who can argue for or against every thing, will soon attack the system of religion, and deny all its dogmas; hence the sophists of Athens were noted for irreverence towards the popular superstition, and this is one of the most serious charges urged against them by comic writers. No one watched more closely all the tendencies of the sophistical spirit than Aristophanes; he had sagacity to see that it pervaded every province of thought and action; he traced it in music, in lyrical poetry, but, above all, in the tragic drama; it was the true cause of earnestness with which he assailed Euripides, the last of the great tragic writers—he thought he saw in him the most dangerous of sophists; *e. g.* Aristophanes attacks him with great force for a line he puts into mouth of one of his most pious heroes, in which he draws distinction between an oath of *the tongue* and of *the mind*, in terms which would seem to justify any perjury. He contrasts his irreligion with the piety of Æschylus, shows that he makes the speeches of his heroes too often the vehicle for rhetorical display, and in his philosophical reflections too often shake belief in matters of highest importance. (T. 264.) No wonder then that he should represent Euripides in the infernal world as hero of a class composed of *foot-pads*, *cut-purses*, *parricides* and *house-breakers*, who are delighted with his rhetorical artifices. (262.)

8. *Socrates?* Whilst it was tendency of sophists to run wild and cause contempt to be thrown on philosophy by their abuses, it was to be expected that now and then great reformers would appear, to expose absurdity and bring the mind back to the right channel of investigation. Such was Socrates the son of Sophroniscus. No man has ever lived to whom philosophy is more indebted, and yet we have none of his writings. No man whose name has filled a larger space among mankind, and yet he was void of ambition. He has been fortunate in having two such scholars as Plato and Xenophon, who have given the world such an intense interest in their master. Not necessary to describe his system of philosophy minutely. It made its way because connected with highest interest of man. Whilst sophists brooded over their speculations and indulged in mere conquests of words, Socrates taught man to look into himself, γνωθι σεαυτον, know thyself, was his great maxim—his influence connected with forms of social life at Athens. He gave instruction neither in his house nor in any fixed place; the public squares and porches were the scenes of his conversation. Xenophon tells us that he went to the walks and Gymnasia early in the morning. When the Agora was filling he was there, and in afternoon, wherever there was most company—generally principal speaker. His manner amusing and instructive—was most patient hearer. Such method of teaching could only succeed in such a place as Athens, among a people who spent large portion of their time in public. He took no private scholars, nor would he consent, although a poor man, to receive compensation for any instruction he gave in public. In this respect, as in many others, he is misrepresented by Aristophanes, in the *Clouds*, who exhibits him as poor, and teaching for money. It was his delight in all places, and under all circumstances, to meet and refute the sophists. Against them he used the most cutting irony; and in most of his disputations,

he was fond of making his adversary refute himself by the answers which he gave to interrogatories propounded.

9. *Beneficial result of Socratic method?* To Greeks belongs the praise of first separating *philosophy* from *religion*, and the appearance of Socrates, noblest result of that separation. He could not have been produced in any of the great eastern despotisms. In all of these, without exception, philosophy is the slave of religion. Improvement is impossible; for to innovate in philosophy, would be to attack the system of religion. The tyranny of the inquisition over the great Galileo illustrates the danger of such an alliance. Socrates threw off these shackles; he investigated man as a social being, and deduced his conclusions from principles of nature, and not from arbitrary dogmas of absurd religion. Hence he himself was purer than any one of the gods of antiquity, and his morality was of a sterner character than that found in the heavenly hierarchy.

10. *Charge of irreligion?* The Socratic method of investigation, by neglecting the popular superstition, gave occasionally an air of irreligion to his speculations, which became offensive to the superstitious; and although there is no proof that he disbelieved the popular superstition, yet he appears to have been deeply impressed with the theology of Anaxagoras, which maintained existence of *one infinite being.* Moreover, he was himself imbued with superstitious belief that he was divinely impelled to the employment which he followed; that a divine spirit constantly attended him. Such notions were frequently construed into hostility to the polytheistic creed, by introducing new divinities.

11. *The "Clouds" of Aristophanes?* It is well known that Aristophanes in comedy called the "Clouds," introduces Socrates by name, and held him up to the scorn and ridicule of the Athenians, as the arch sophist, the master of the free-thinking school. Story is of young spendthrift who has involved his father in debt by passion for horses—becomes pupil of Socrates, who teaches him art of defrauding creditors, of considering filial obedience, piety to gods, &c, as antiquated prejudices. This spendthrift answers well to Alcibiades, one of the most profligate, and greatest of Socrates' disciples. Besides representing Socrates as inculcating the most dangerous doctrines, and as being irreverent towards God, he ridicules his investigations in physics, by representing him as engaged in most ridiculous inquiries, such as measuring a flea's jump, and accounting for a gnat's noise. (M. 4, 140.)

12. *How came Aristophanes to mistake the character of Socrates?* It would seem that Aristophanes must stand convicted by this comedy either of foulest motives or grossest mistake. His character precludes the former; therefore must conclude he was mistaken. He saw So-

crates often in public places, and disputing with sophists, and therefore he took him to be one. He knew that Euripides, who introduced sophistical spirit into the drama, and Alcibiades who illustrated it in his life, were among his most intimate friends. He suspected him of belief in the theology of Anaxagoras. Besides all this, the absence of mind which sometimes made Socrates appear ridiculous, his diverting method of arguing, by which there was scarcely a mechanic in Athens that had not been amused as well as puzzled, in his mien and gait, and his singularly ludicrous features so capitally suited for a comic mark, all made him a fit person for comedy.

13. *Accusation of Socrates?* Generally supposed that the Clouds had no little effect in bringing this about. Although his accusation was more than twenty years after the appearance of Clouds, during which time four revolutions in government had taken place. We must know political condition of Athens to investigate this subject. The time at which he was brought to trial was highly unfavorable. It was at a time when revulsion was taking place in public feeling; when the Demus were once more rallying around their ancient institutions, civil and religious. Under the odious reign of the 400, and afterwards under still more abominable tyranny of the 30 headed by Critias, public morals had become more and more infected. Skeptical opinions had spread among the higher classes. New rites and ceremonies were introduced of a mystical and immoral nature. All these things in the minds of the people naturally associated themselves with the odious misrule which had prevailed in Athens. As the aristocracy were running into one extreme, democracy were driven into other. They began to regard with warmer devotion the old system of polytheism, to look on the sophist with more horror. In one word to cleave with more pertinacity to all that seemed connected with past greatness of Athenian democracy. The proceedings and disclosures following the mutilation of the Hermes' busts are but illustrations of popular feelings. Add to all this, it appeared that Socrates had been the instructor of Critias, the bloodthirsty tyrant, the deadly enemy of the people, who had introduced his cousin Charmides to the philosopher—the same who was associated in the tyranny of the 30 with Critias, and died by his side (T. 4, 278.) Although Socrates despised the developed character of Critias, and had incurred the enmity of the tyrant, still these facts produced their effect, and, along with other causes, disposed public mind to condemnation of Socrates. Melitus before the king-archon delivered information to following effect. "Socrates is guilty of reviling the gods whom the city acknowledges, and of preaching other new gods. Moreover he is guilty of corrupting youth. Penalty, death." This charge,

brought in name of Melitus, was urged by Anytus, who had been banished by the 30, and one Lycon, an orator. All three were supposed to be excited by resentment provoked innocently by the philosopher in his ordinary conversations. He was condemned.

14. *Death of Socrates, and its effect?* Xenophon says Socrates might have averted his fate by condescending to supplication, but disdained to do it. Execution at Athens followed quickly on the condemnation, commonly next day. But Socrates was condemned on eve of the departure of the *Theoris*, the sacred vessel that carried the yearly offerings to Delos, and immemorial tradition forbade all executions till the vessel's return. Thirty days elapsed before the Theoris returned. Some of his friends pressed Socrates to take advantage of this respite and escape. But he refused to prolong a life already verging on 70, by a breach of the laws which he had never violated. (T., 4, 280.) He awaited the arrival of the ship, and when his hour came, with utmost composure drank fatal cup, and died.

All writers, from Plato down, have dwelt on the pathos of this tragic tale. But magnanimity of Socrates, however admirable, is not that in which he has most outshone other men. Mitford thinks Lord Russel's fate was far more trying. Singular merit of Socrates was in purity and usefulness of manners and conversation, and the steadiness with which he practised in a corrupt and blind age all moral duties. In his acts he anticipated the sublime morality of the New Testament. His death under these circumstances produced as important consequences as his life. It sanctified and canonized his philosophy. Had he been snatched away by sickness, he might have been remembered by his disciples, but not with devotional enthusiasm. The poisoned cup insured him immortality. He presented what before had been wanting, the example of a philosopher who could die for his principles. His death was the triumph of philosophy.

15. *Progress of philosophy after death of Socrates?* From his disciples proceeded a number of philosophers who differed widely from one another. This arose from fact that Socrates had no system, and laid no chains on spirit of inquiry. His great object was to excite mind to investigation and self-examination. Therefore not to wonder that Antisthenes, who made self-denial, and Aristippus, who made pleasure the basis of morals, a Pyrrho who doubted, and a Euclid who demonstrated, were all his friends. Plato was most distinguished of all his disciples. In him the poetic character of the Greeks expressed itself philosophically. None but a poetical nation could have produced a Plato. (H. 259.) Hence Diogenes used to call him a *Socrates run mad.* Demosthenes, Isocrates, and Aristotle, were all the disciples of this great man. He

established his school in a place called the Academy, hence called Academic. His philosophy found opponents in four great sects—those of Aristotle, of Pyrrho, of Zeno, and Epicurus—called the Peripatetic, the Skeptic, the Stoic, and the Epicurean.

The philosopher of the ancient world whose writings have produced the greatest effect on posterity is undoubtedly Aristotle. Born at Stagira, a Thracian city. After youth of dissipation, took to intense study. Was twenty years favorite of Plato. His father was Philip's physician, and he became so reputed for learning, that he was made tutor of Alexander the Great. After Alexander grew up, he established a school in the Lyceum. He lectured his pupils while walking. Hence his school was called the *Peripatetic.* Aristotle had one of those great and masterly minds which, having the advantage of coming late in age of inquiry, is enabled to survey all the departments of knowledge, and to extend the limits of each during a single lifetime. Hence his writings form the great text-book in the study of the ancient world. His labors were commensurate with the whole range of literature. To give an account of his works is to describe all which was known to the ancients.

16. *Connection of philosophers of Greece with active pursuits of life favorable to true philosophy?* Generally supposed in republican governments that men are too much engrossed by politics to cultivate philosophy. Great mistake. Philosophy most frivolous where it dares not penetrate into institutions which surround it. Nothing so cheers literary man as hope to increase happiness of human race. When thought may be the forerunner of action, when happy reflection may be transformed into a beneficent institution, then do speculations of man of genius ennoble philosophy. Hence custom of ancients to blend together military, legislative, and philosophic pursuits, produced intense mental activity, and great improvement. Even Socrates, whose disposition was averse to politics, could not escape its influence. We find him fighting at Potidea, Amphipolis, and Delium. We find him in civil office. At one time president of the General Assembly, at another member of council of five hundred. In latter capacity, when a *Prytan*, we see him obstinately resisting the popular tyranny in the trial of the six generals, when his colleagues yielded to the storm. Xenophon was one of the greatest generals of his age. Thucydides was chosen as the leader of the party opposed to Pericles, and how much more deeply philosophical is the work of that great historian, because of his connection with politics. And even if the philosopher was not personally connected with the political movements of the times, still his mind could not be wholly immersed in mere impracticable abstractions; for the Agora, the forum, and the camp, with all their bustle and turmoil, were constantly calling

it back to the contemplation of all the exciting and turbulent realities of Grecian life.

3. *History.*

17. *Early history of the Greeks?* Consisted entirely of traditions. These supplied poets with their themes. Hence early history all poetic. Feats of Hercules, exploits of Jason, siege of Troy and founding of colonies, most interesting themes for poetic historians. Even when historians first wrote in prose did not discard poetic character, *e. g.* Cadmus of Miletus, Pherecydes, Hecatæus, &c., preserved poetic character, though not the measure of verse. Cicero thought these like Fabius Pictor and Cato among Romans. No similarity; for latter were wholly prosaic. (H. 263.) Most celebrated of legendary historians lived not long before Persian war, in latter half of sixth century B. C.

18. *Effect of Persian war on history?* Before this war, few subjects to inspire historian. Trojan war, Argonautic expedition, &c., belonged to tradition, and were half included in region of poetry. There existed no great national theme of universal interest, and undoubted historic truth. Persian war supplied this. It awakened national spirit of Greeks, battles of Marathon, Thermopylæ, Salamis, Platæa, &c., glorious themes for historian.

19. *Herodotus?* First who undertook to treat of a purely historical subject, and thus gave to history rank as independent branch of literature; called therefore *father* of history. Although Persian war main subject gave such a range to his narrative as to be sort of universal history, took every opportunity of interweaving his narrative with history of those countries which he had to mention. Visited greater part of them himself, and collected his information from the most credible sources; and although he tells many marvellous tales on the authority of others, yet few writers have received greater confirmation by the advances of geographical and historical researches than Herodotus.

20. *Thucydides?* While Herodotus read his history to the assembled multitudes at Olympia, Thucydides, a boy, has been represented as listening and catching the enthusiasm which made him the successor of Herodotus. Although this tale is discredited, yet we cannot doubt the influence of the example of Herodotus. Whilst latter wrote history of past, Thucydides wrote that of his own times. His work eminently critical, which distinguishes him from Herodotus. Age of Thucydides one of grandeur, but full of difficulties. Not an age of war only, but of revolutions with all their horrors. Whether a man were an aristocrat or democrat, a friend of Athens or of Sparta, was the question on which depended fortune, liberty, and life. After Amphipolis was captured by

Brasidas, the Spartan general, Thucydides was accused of coming too late to the rescue, and was banished by the Athenians to Thrace, where he spent twenty years in exile, during which he composed his great work, that has conferred on him an immortality, which the relief of Amphipolis could never have given him. He was eminently qualified for his task—perfectly calm and unprejudiced amid conflict of the passions. How nobly has he done full justice to the character of his great rival, Pericles, by a delineation of his character which nothing can surpass. Has been said to be only exile that ever wrote an impartial history. Writing about passing events he ascertained every thing by personal inquiry. His subject was entirely prosaic. His whole object was truth. In this respect he rose above his age. Neither his own nor the following could reach him, *e. g.*, Theopompus and Ephorus, whenever heroic age was to be discussed, drew their materials from mythographers and poets, as if Thucydides had never written.

21. *Xenophon?* Took third great step in history. Wrote of his own exploits—for his Anabasis is his greatest historical work.

22. *Decline of history?* In period of their freedom, all principal kinds of history were developed among Greeks. Afterwards made hardly any progress, although subjects of history grew more extensive and various with Macedonian and Roman age. Idea of philosophical and universal history was developed by Polybius, and his continuator, Possidonius. But after downfall of liberty, when rhetoric became prevalent, and was applied to history, higher kind of criticism ceased to be employed in it. The essence was forgotten in disputes about the form. Proofs of this are manifest even in the writings of Dionysius of Halicarnassus, although considered among the first of ancient critics. (H. 272.)

4. *Drama*

Was the species of literature which peculiarly signalized age immediately following Persian war. It belongs, too, as much to the political as the literary history of those times.

23. *Origin?* Earliest lawgivers of the Greeks considered poetry as chief means of forming character of youth, and even of influencing riper years. Poetry was not separate from song, and was generally accompanied by an instrument. Hence not to wonder that in Sparta, where every thing was controlled by law, *ancient music* was *legally protected*, and certain tunes were established by law. At every festival in Greece it was customary to sing the songs of the poets. By-and-by the choral songs were introduced, and choruses became chief ornament of the festivals, composed of persons of all ages, who replied to each other alter-

nately in song. As festivals were public concerns, so too were the choruses. Choral song as old as the days of Homer. Drama was the result of these choruses. In the islands of the South Sea, especially the Society Islands, travellers give an account of spectacles which remind us of earliest times of Greece. (H. 275.)

24. *Connection with the state?* Dramatic poetry exhibits lively representation of action, requires scenic decorations, and is exhibited before an assembly. Hence its character is more public than any other kind of poetic composition. Of all kinds of verse it concerns the state the most. Among the Greeks, besides, it was an affair of religion, and therefore essential to all the festivals. But these festivals were state matters. Here then is a reason why the state should encourage dramatic representations. A Grecian state could not exist without festivals, and festivals without choruses and plays. Hence plays were one of the civil burthens or *liturgies*, (λειτουργιαι.) Theatres were built and decorated at public expense. No instance of their erection by private persons as at Rome. From their size and number, they required vast sums of money to erect them.

25. *Rise of tragedy?* Dramatic performances would soon be divided into the tragic and comic, according to the nature of the representation. Æschylus was the father of the finished drama. He fought in the battle of Salamis, and it was not till after the Persian war, that a theatre of stone was erected at Athens. It was for him that Agatharchus painted first scene which ever agreed with the rules of linear perspective. It was after his time that the decorations became so heavy a charge. Sophocles and Euripides were his successors, and added perhaps to the grace, beauty, and variety of the characters, but did not reach the sublimity and grandeur of Æschylus.

26. *Character and subjects of the Grecian tragedy?* Æschylus sometimes ventured to bring cotemporary characters and events into his tragedies, *e. g.* play which celebrated battle of Salamis, and another in which he used the drama as a political engine to support sinking power of the Areopagus. With such exceptions, however, scene of Greek tragedy was always laid in heroic ages, and its subjects confined to the circle traced by the epic poets. The characters of Æschylus are too far above sphere of real life to awaken the full moral sympathy. His prominent figures are all colossal. Homeric heroes even appear more terrible and majestic in his plays. (T. 3, 75.) Tragic drama had but few points of relation with the state. With few exceptions forms of monarchy alone were introduced on the stage. Nor was this for political effect. Violent commotions in ancient royal families, and their extinction, were not introduced to make them objects of contempt, and to

quicken the spirit of democracy, but solely because no other actions possessed so eminently the sublimity of the true tragic character. The great effect of these tragedies was to elevate the Grecian mind, by accustoming it to contemplate the lofty specimens of the heroic ages. (H. 281.)

27. *Difference between ancient and modern drama?* A tragedy among the Greeks was a spectacle for the whole people, furnished by the state at great cost. The promiscuous crowd assembled in an immense unroofed amphitheatre, of which the architecture and decorations were magnificent. The actors declaimed with great violence in order that they might be heard by so large an audience. A numerous chorus was present through all the acts, singing with great loudness. Masks were used for the double purpose of counterfeiting and enlarging the person, and to give greater force to the voice, by means of a contrivance which acted like a speaking-trumpet. Our modern theatres are much smaller than the ancient, the audience much more select. They are so near the actors as to make loud speaking unnecessary. The modern actor models himself by nature's standard in every particular. He knows how to vary and multiply the emotions more than the ancient. In ancient tragedy there is great vigor, and often the most agitating sublimity; but moderns have more variety, more grace, and give characters to their *dramatis personæ* much more consonant to nature in all their parts than the ancients, *e. g.* Æschylus, in the Agamemnon, makes Clytemnestra kill her husband in most atrocious manner, and yet we can scarcely divine from the play her real motives. It seems to be from neither love, jealousy, nor ambition. All that she says is that Agamemnon consented to the sacrifice of Iphigenia, therefore he deserves death. A great crime, says La Harpe, is only theatrical when instigated by some great passion, or when it is followed by great remorse; and we have neither in the Clytemnestra of Æschylus. (Tome 1, 317.) Upon the whole, the same writer concludes that the Voltaires and Racines are more rare than the Sophocles and Euripides. (307.) Bulwer has much higher opinion of ancient tragedy. Considers the play of Agamemnon, so much criticised by La Harpe, as a masterpiece. Nothing more impressive than the opening with the solitary watchman on the tower, who for ten long years had watched nightly for the beacon fires to announce the fall of Ilion, and beholds them blaze at last. The character of Cassandra is drawn with a master's hand, &c. He considers Æschylus, on the whole, superior both to Sophocles and Euripides, and in point of grandeur and sublimity, unrivalled in the modern world.

28. *Rise of comedy—its peculiar sphere?* In midst of deep-rooted

corruption, when legal authorities were growing powerless, when the Sophronistæ and the Areopagus had lost all their weight, and the licentious multitude followed precipitately the dictates of their own headstrong will, there arose in the domain of art a frank and vigorous censorship, which castigated vices and follies of the age, joining poignant ridicule and wit to the deep earnestness of high-minded patriotism. The old comedy, with all its defects, supplied one of the great wants of the age. It was to Athens what the liberty of the press is to modern republics. When Athens was in her meridian glory, both tragedy and comedy were encouraged at public expense; but their effects on the political system were widely different. In tragedy, the Athenian beheld the old heroic monarchy in its independence on fate, the nothingness of human pride and earthly presumption, crushed by the wrath of the gods. Although the tragedy was copiously interspersed with political reflections, yet these could only be applied to the Athenian democracy as figurative allusions, or as moral maxims. Tragedy and real life were separated by wide gulf. Athenians would not allow an allusion to their real misfortunes in tragedy, *e. g.*, Phrynicus was fined because he represented destruction of Miletus by the Persians.

The *old* comedy, on other hand, sprung from wantonness of the democracy of Megara, and was transferred to Athens. Comic poets not only permitted, but enjoined to level their satire against all who deserved it. Comedy was thus a great political engine; a genial tribunal of public morals springing out of real life; a mirror which reflected the realities of the world we live in. The dim warnings of mysterious power of fate in Greek tragedy little adapted for deep impression on popular mind, as crimes and sorrows of supernatural kings and heroes were not applicable to spectators. But aim of comedy, says Aristophanes, was to make men better in the state, to admonish and instruct, and at same time to lampoon and ridicule the foibles and vices of individuals. (Wach. 2, 205.)

29. *Comic poets of the old school?* *Old* comedy flourished from Persian to end of Peloponnesian war, most renowned poets were Cratinus, Eupolis, Plato, Pherecrates, and Aristophanes. Aristophanes, almost our only authority, as but little remains of the others. His poetical career commenced about the beginning of Peloponnesian war, and lasted about ten years after. His pieces exhibit just and striking picture of Athenian people, and give an insight into manners and morals superior to any thing which has come down from ancient world.

30. *Licentiousness of the old comedy?* There were no bounds set to the license of the comic poets. Their shafts were levelled at dress, manners, morals, deformities, political vices, *e. g.*, Aristophanes ridicules

Epicrates, who prided himself for his comely beard. He lashes the dissipation of Æschines, calls Pisander coward with a daring aspect. Callias, the prodigal who moults away his goods and chattels like a bird does its feathers, and who is a coward in spite of the lion skin which he wore. He is still more severe upon the voluptuous and the unchaste, such as Cleonymus, who disgraced himself by throwing away his shield, committed perjury, and cajoled the people.

The beardless and incontinent Clisthenes whom he introduces in the *Thesmophoriazusæ* as ambassador to the women; in the Birds, he carries a weaver's shuttle, &c. Even bodily infirmities do not escape him, *e. g.*, ridicules Archidemus and Neoclides for being blear-eyed; calls Melanthus a leper; jeers Ctesiphon about his fat belly; laughs at Cleigenes for his small monkey figure; calls Chœrophon the owl, &c.

But commonly took a bolder stand, when it even ventured to attack the most powerful leaders of the democracy. Even the great and powerful Pericles himself was obliged to submit to the castigations of the comic poets. Cratinus, Teleclides, Hermippus, Eupolis, and Aristophanes, all ventured to attack him. He was apostrophized as *Zeus*, the Jupiter. Aspasia was called Juno, Omphale,* or Deianira,† but at the same time a courtezan. His sons were called simpletons, and that by Aspasia, a bastard. They laughed at big head of Pericles; they ridiculed the slowness with which he built the walls and Odeum, and the cautious policy in avoiding a battle, after first irruption of the Peloponnesians, was bitterly derided. His friends were called Pisistratides, &c. No demagogue, no matter how dangerous he might be, could escape, *e. g.*, Aristophanes inflicted severest castigation on that malicious, covetous, and sanguinary idol of the populace, Cleon; and when he could get no actor to perform the part, he took the mask and appeared himself in the character of Cleon. He pursued him with most untiring zeal; he lashed him in the "*Babylonians*;" in the *Knights*, speaks of his dog-like effrontery, his sycophantic snarling and barking, his greediness for a bribe. In the *Clouds* he again brings the detested *tanner* upon the stage; in the *Wasps*, he is made to play part of a devouring sea-monster, &c. (W. 2, 214.) Aristophanes even ventured to attack the principal tyrants among the thirty who had subverted the democracy. He denounced the equivocal and time-serving Theramenes; he wishes Cleophon, with his interminable prate about war, was in Hades. Speaks of the admiral Adimantus, as one for whose death every one should pray, &c.

* A queen of Lydia, with whom Hercules was so much enamored, that she made him submit to spinning, and other sedentary offices.

† Wife of Hercules.

But most remarkable fact is that the comedians ridiculed the sovereign *Demus* themselves, and Aristophanes was actually crowned for having done so in the *Knights*, where he introduced the people under their proper name, *Demus*, as an old dotard, with some cunning, but incapable of governing himself. Cleon is represented as his favorite, under the mask of a Paphlagonian slave, described as lying, thievish, greedy, fawning, &c. As in the *Knights* he ridiculed the popular assembly, so in the *Wasps* he attacked the other strongholds of power, the courts of justice, with still keener ridicule. (T. 4, 251.) He depicts their love of acting as judges, ascribes it to covetousness, &c., and in the *Clouds* displays a picture of the mischievous power of the sycophants and brawlers, which is embodied in the speech of Adicœologas, &c. (W. 221.)

31. *What was the influence of the comedians?* Judging from the nice sensibilities of the moderns, and their extreme attention to the point of honor, we should conclude that the *old* comedy must have been intolerable. We are at a loss to know how individuals could have borne to be burlesqued before the assembled people, in a manner far more harassing than is now done by the public press. Our press, with all its licentiousness, is not to be compared with the satire of the old comedy. Moreover, it would seem that the comic poets must have produced great political results by the freedom with which they charged the leading statesmen of the times.

As to the first, it is certain that the ancients had not the same keen sensibilities that we have. Subjects, the bare mention of which would shock every feeling of delicacy and shame in our nature, seem often to have been regarded by the Athenian as merely ridiculous, and as for the point of honor which every gentleman now attends to so scrupulously, it was scarcely regarded by the ancients. It is one of the fruits of chivalry.

As to second point, the political influence, we are astonished that it did not produce more. It is true the death of Socrates has been ascribed to the Clouds, but that play produced at the time very little excitement against the philosopher, and it was not till twenty years after that he was condemned. The worthless Cleon preserved all his popularity and power in spite of the violent attacks of Aristophanes, and Pericles submitted patiently without any injury, as far as we know, resulting from the attacks of the comic poets. The fact seems to be, that people of Athens went to comic representations to laugh and be amused, and it mattered but little at whose expense the laugh was raised. During the hour of mirth they discarded all thoughts of business, and the moment the representation was over, they returned to serious occupations with minds wholly unbiased by what had transpired at the theatre. Hence it has been said, great as the comic muse was, it could not deprive the beggar of his obol, or a scavenger of his office; and this perhaps may be one of the strongest examples in favor of the full liberty of the press, when there is no restraint. Virtue is apt at last to prevail, because her cause is good, and her weapons powerful.

32. *Middle and new comedy?* As the democratic principle gradually wore out in Greece, the *old* comedy became more and more unpopular, until it was forbidden to introduce any one on the stage by his proper name. The comic poets then adopted method of describing living persons and passing scenes under fictitious names, so that they could not easily be mistaken, and this was called the *middle comedy.* At last the poets were forbidden under any circumstances to introduce the living in their plays, and this was called the *new comedy.* Menander, among the Greeks, was at once the creator and model of this species of dramatic representation, and it was he who was so closely imitated by Terence.

5. *Ancient Eloquence.*

Eloquence of the Greeks one of the most interesting subjects connected with their history. It has generally been considered far superior to that of modern times. Mr. Hume has deliberately pronounced the orations of Demosthenes as the models which, of all human productions, approach nearest to perfection. (V. 1, 109.)

Some have gone so far as to assert that the mighty eloquence which once shook whole democracies, can no more return than the prowess which, single-handed, ran upon embattled armies clad in iron, and put them to rout, than the shout of Stentor, or the blast of the dread horn of Fontarabia. (S. R. 4, 514.)

33. *Interest excited by the orators of Greece?* We are told by Cicero, that when Demosthenes was to speak, men flocked to Athens from the remote parts of Greece, as if to witness the most splendid spectacle which could be exhibited. Whereas at London, says Hume, men saunter in the Court of Requests, whilst the most important debate is going on in the two houses. That eloquence of best speaker does not compensate for loss of dinner; that even when old Cibber was to act, more curiosity was excited than when the prime minister was to defend himself against a motion for removal or impeachment. (104.)

34. *Style of ancients supposed more sublime?* Mr. Hume says Demosthenes and Cicero attempted flights successfully, which would be ridiculous in modern speakers, because they could not sustain them, *e. g.*, the *Apostrophe* of Demosthenes to the *manes* of heroes who fought at

Marathon, Platæa, &c., whilst justifying the battle of Chæronea,* or the bold figure of Cicero, when he represents rocks and mountains as moved with horror at the bare recital of the enormities of Verres. Suitable too to the vehemence of thought and expression was the vehemence of action. The *supplosio pedis*, *stamping of the foot*, *percussio frontis et pectoris*, *striking of the forehead and chest*, were all usual, and considered but moderate gestures, whereas at present they are almost banished, except from the theatre.

35. *Explanations which have been offered for difference between ancient and modern eloquence?* Some have supposed that the genius and energy of the ancients were superior to that of the moderns. Others maintain, that with the same races there is no reason to think that the genius has been at all lessened, that we are physically and mentally equal to both the Greeks and Romans, and that all the difference between ancient and modern eloquence can be explained by reference to the difference of circumstances which called it forth. Many who maintain this latter position, say that it is difficult to adjudge the palm to either; for each is suitable to the circumstances under which it was developed—the difference being more in *kind* than *degree*.

36. *Most prominent causes of difference?* 1. Difference of theatre for the display of oratory. 2. Paucity of laws anciently, and character of pleadings. 3. Exciting topics, such as revolutions, oppression of provinces, &c. 4. Invention of printing press. 5. Superiority of Latin and Greek languages.

37. *I. Character of the theatre on which the Grecian eloquence was displayed?* Almost all the tribunals before which the Grecian orator appeared, were of the popular character. The popular assembly was sovereign, and before it all political matters were discussed. Here was the finest arena for the orator, the πανηγυρις, or great festival meeting, such as the Olympic games, was occasionally another arena.

The Heliastic courts too were so numerous and promiscuous as to be fairly entitled to appellation of popular tribunals—much more so than the Roman courts; composed of the prætors and judices selecti. When Socrates was condemned, by what court is uncertain, we are told that no fewer than 280 voted against him. Even in the Areopagus,

* This splendid passage, which for more than 2,000 years has been deemed the greatest effort of oratorical power, was suggested by a stroke of eloquence scarcely less grand and beautiful, and almost as bold, from his antagonist, Æschines, who in his speech against Ctesiphon calls up the illustrious dead of Athens, and plants them around himself, and bids his hearers listen to the groans that the crowning of the man (Demosthenes) who had conspired with the barbarians, draws from the tombs of those who fell at Marathon and Platæa.

the least popular of all the courts, never fewer than 50 were present. In the palmy days of Grecian eloquence this court had lost most of its power and influence, and the more popular courts, sometimes numbering more than 1000 *dicasts*, or jurors, judged all the cases of importance.

38. *Influence of the popular assembly on the Grecian oratory?* The *ecclesia*, (εκκλησια,) or popular assembly of Grecian states, was generally sovereign. No appeal from its decrees—not divided into two branches like modern deliberative assemblies. Its decisions were prompt, and generally under the influence of excited feelings—hence finest imaginable theatre for display of impassioned eloquence. Orator felt an awful responsibility, and most laboriously prepared himself before such a powerful, but at the same time tumultuary and excitable multitude—wayward, fitful and refractory—alternately slave and tyrant—now passive instrument of demagogue, then "like a devilish engine back recoiling" upon the rash hand that aspired to direct. In modern deliberative bodies questions of great importance are debated for weeks, and sometimes months, and it rarely happens that much can be achieved by one speech, no matter how powerful. Speeches have now very little more effect than spinning out the time, and giving to the parties an opportunity to arrange and compromise the matter. After several weeks debate a result frequently takes place from the arrangement of leaders wholly uninfluenced by the debates, *e. g.*, celebrated tariff compromise in 1832. Not so in Greece. Orator knew full well that, if powerful impression could be made on his audience, his cause would be gained. There was no delay—decree went forth immediately—hence not only was the judgment to be convinced, but passions were to be aroused. The triumph of the moment was final victory. No waiting for another tribunal to pass upon the measure, for an executive to give his sanction, nor for voters to communicate with their constituency; for here the sovereign people themselves were present in primary assembly.

39. *Must not the popular assemblies of Greece have been deficient in that critical taste necessary to form the accomplished orator?* Mr. Hume thinks the Athenian assembly, composed often of lowest vulgar, must have been inferior to Roman senate or a British parliament, and consequently that the great orators of Greece were rather formed in spite of, than by means of such an audience. That orator, in measure, formed the taste of his audience in Greece, there can be no doubt, *e. g.*, Diodorus says Gorgias of Leontinus was very taking with his figures of speech, his antithesis, &c., until the introduction of better style taught the people to despise his. But that this taste, when once formed, reacted on the orator, there can be as little doubt. From various

causes, Athenian assembly, though composed of many of the *beggarly ragamuffins* so admirably burlesqued by Aristophanes, was nevertheless one of the most critical audience which the orator has ever been called in any age to address. Its taste strange to say was fastidious to a fault. Demosthenes himself several times failed before such an audience, and that too from defects which would not have been objected to by any but an Athenian assembly. At every failure, however, he returned with more vigor to his studies, and ever after, by closest application, his fame was established. He was once hooted off the *Bema* for laying the acute accent on the ή in ασκληπιος. This extraordinary tact in regard to language pervaded whole Athenian people. Illustrated by anecdote of the elegant Theophrastus, who had lived many years at Athens, and prided himself for speaking with all the purity of *Attic style*, and was one day mortified by an old woman whom he was attempting to beat down in the sale of some articles, finding out from his language his foreign origin, and addressing him ὦξενε. (B. 4, 425.) In both Greece and Rome, the passages in the orations which seem to have produced most magic effect, were those of most exquisite finish in thought and words, and such as the most refined taste of after ages has uniformly admired.

40. Attic taste in eloquence similar to Italian taste in music. Extraordinary taste of Athenians in eloquence no doubt arose from the intense interest they took in political matters, and the constant practice of hearing the best speakers, so that the whole nation became imbued with this taste. The meanest citizen had a *nice ear for eloquence*, which most intelligent of other countries did not possess. We see now something similar in the taste of the Italians for music. You may get together the most refined assemblies of Americans, Englishmen, or Frenchmen, and bring before them Catalina, or Pasta, or Paganini, and although they may talk well, yet they cannot feel like the Italians, nor display that sense of music, that acute discrimination and nicety of ear which even a company of Lazzaroni will exhibit in Italy. Bad music to an Italian is worse than *unpleasant;* it is *painful.* Hence exclamation of the poor Italian at the French opera, when almost agonized by the bad music, "*I Francesi hanno le orecchie di corno.*" These Frenchmen must have ears of horn!

41. *Error of supposing that the popular assembly gives rise to loose and diffuse speaking?* This effect ascribed to popular assemblies because supposed to be ignorant, and to require that the speaker should dwell on each point so as to make himself understood. Facts against the theory, *e. g.*, speeches of Demosthenes are the most condensed on record, so much so, that we are almost constrained to suppose that the

spoken speeches must have been rather more dilated. With him there is no coming back on the same ground, or lingering over it. All is done at once. There is nothing superfluous, nothing for mere effect. He is never scattered, never stagnant, never sluggish; nor can the hearer ever stop for an instant to admire or throw away a thought on the great artist, till all is over, and he has time to recover his breath. This is the effect of true eloquence, and not of argument alone. Demosthenes combined the two. In Rome, the speeches before the *comitia*, or popular assemblies, were much more condensed than those before the senate, or the prætors. It has been well said, that three or four of the Philippics of Demosthenes, put together, would hardly equal in length an average congressional harangue *de lanâ caprinâ.* (S. R. 4, 531.) Fact is, the popular assembly is highly favorable to production of energetic, rapid, and condensed speaking, which is only kind that can command the attention of promiscuous audience. When there are first-rate speakers, a multitude will not tolerate one that is tedious and prolix. Whilst in the senate the order and decorum of the body insures patient attention to worst speakers, *e. g.*, Roman senate was patient audience, and would listen to the speaker all day. Not so with Athenians. They often restricted their orators in time. Pregnant brevity of Lysias is attributed by Dionysius to the necessity of conforming his speeches to scanty contents of *Clepsydra.* Sometimes they would not listen to the speaker at all, at others compelled him to omit what was disagreeable, and sometimes forced him to begin where they chose. Even Demosthenes himself, in all his speeches, shows utmost anxiety about being heard—begs them not to disturb him until they have heard all. In his great oration for Ctesiphon, Æschines exhorts the people not to let him have his way, for if they did, he would hurry their feelings off by torrent of irrelevant declamation.

42. *Immense labor of the Athenian orators before they appeared before the people?* No wonder that the orator of Greece prepared himself with minute care before appearing in public; the exquisite structure of the sentences, the balanced period, the apt and perfect antithesis, the neat and epigrammatic turn, the finished collocation, says Lord Brougham, who is best of judges, all indicate an extreme elaboration, that could hardly have been the suggestion of the moment. The orations of ancients were eminently *artistic.* Every word seemed selected with skill, and in its proper place. Dionysius, speaking of exquisite finish given by Isocrates and Plato to their styles, compares their works to pieces of fine *chasing* or *sculpture.* (E. R. v. 36, 84.) This one reason why orators of Greece so frequently repeat whole sentences and paragraphs which had been spoken on a former occasion, *e. g.*, nearly the whole of 4th

Philippic of Demosthenes is made up of passages from other speeches, principally from that on affairs of the Chersonese. Reason of this was no doubt that the style had been brought so near perfection, that orator could not change but for the worse, and where slight alterations have been made, the critic can see at once the causes which led to them. Now all this seems strange to us, for such repetitions would now be intolerable. But whilst they mark the finish given to style by ancients, they at same time show that an Athenian audience were like spectators at a play; the orator was not only to convince and instruct, but to amuse and delight. Hence, as the modern Italian will listen with rapture to the same opera thirty nights in succession, so the Athenian never tired of the fine passages of Demosthenes or Domades. Most of the great speeches of antiquity were written out beforehand, and committed to memory. Pericles commenced this practice, and it is well known how adverse Demosthenes was to extempore speaking. He knew too well the Athenian audience, and the difficulty of pleasing, to trust often to the impulse of the moment. This elaborate preparation was not on the logic and argument, for in this respect the moderns are superior to the ancients. The argument was always good, but did not consist of long and elaborate chains of reasoning. Variety of topics were handled in succession, in manner calculated to strike; predominant passions were appealed to; excitable feelings were aroused by skilful allusions, glaring inconsistencies exposed, &c. Sometimes a word sufficed. The naming of a town or man to an audience, well acquainted with all the circumstances, would frequently produce an electrical effect, which no chain of reasoning, however close, could achieve. Every orator, who has addressed a popular assembly, is aware of such influences.

43. II. *The second cause?* It is well known that the legislation of modern times is much more complete than formerly. There were then comparatively few laws. Cicero says that he could make himself acquainted with the laws of Rome in three months. The beautiful science of *pleading*, too, which occupies so important a place in the *common law* of England, was comparatively unknown to the ancients.

44. *Effect of the paucity of the laws on the ancient speakers?* In proportion as the laws are few in number, so does the judicial power, wherever vested, become more and more important; for, in the absence of law, the judge is left to decide the case according to his notions of natural equity. In such a state of things, the orator will have a much finer field for display. He may not only address himself to the understanding of his judges, but arouse the feelings. When, however, there is a law which will fit every case, the advocate is then reduced to the

necessity of showing the application of the law. Every effort to arouse the passions is viewed with distrust—it is regarded as a species of trick to divert the mind from the true issue. Not only, however, in the ancient republics did they have few laws in comparison with modern nations, but the few which they had were not so scrupulously observed, particularly where the sovereign people were the judges, *e. g.*, when six commanders were brought to trial after the battle of Argusinæ, according to law of Canonus, each case should have been decided separately. But the people voted on all together; and when the law was urged, they exclaimed that it would be monstrous if the *Demus* could not do what they liked. Something of the same kind occurred in trial of Socrates, and it is well known, that in case of the conspirators, for whose death Cicero pleaded, he succeeded in palpable violation of a well known law of the Roman commonwealth. The ancient orators, particularly the Athenian, were then in truth scarcely ever trammelled by laws. The judges were consequently exposed to all the influences of oratory. How different in modern times. We are comparatively *a law-making*, *law-loving*, and *law-obeying* people. Let the most splendid orator now make the finest appeals to the passions, and prove too by the most ingenious logic that what he urges is consonant with reason, and built on natural justice; still the most clumsy debater will demolish him at a blow, if he can only prove that the *law* and the *constitution* are against him. It has been well observed, that administration of public justice is now a strict logical syllogism. Written law is the major, verdict of jury the minor proposition, and the sentence of judge is conclusion, *e. g.*, *law* says he who commits murder shall be hanged. The *jury* say A. B., prisoner at bar, has committed murder. Therefore says the *judge*, let A. B. be hanged.

45. *Effect of separating the dispensing or pardoning power from the judicial?* In early ages all powers are blended, and judicial and executive are concentrated in same hands. King David sat in the gate and dealt out justice. St. Louis and Louis XII. administered justice under an oak. German emperors travelled from place to place to hold courts, &c. In Greece and Rome, these different powers of government were blended, and never could be separated. And hence, whilst in modern times all civilized nations vest the *dispensing* or *pardoning* power in the executive, in Greece and Rome it remained with the judicial power wherever exercised. The effect of the separation has been to confine the courts exclusively to the law. A *merciful* judge is now a criminal judge, and a jury who would save the guilty prisoner by their verdict, must be perjured. The whole scene in which Sir W. Scott has so touchingly described the intercession of Jeannie Deans to save the life

of her sister Effie, would have been wholly out of place in a modern court. It is inimitable, however, when brought to bear on the king, who has the pardoning power. In ancient times, all these influences might be exerted on the court; for, first, there might be no law to govern the case, and the judges would be left to follow their inclinations; or if there was a law, it might be dispensed with. When a charge of peculation was brought against Scipio, the only answer he returned was, "This day, last year, I won the battle of Zama." And we must agree with Edinburgh reviewers, that not only such reply would be wholly inadmissible in court, but that Mr. Tierney would look a little awry at even the Chancellor of the Exchequer who should make such a reply to his calculations. But such a consideration might well have great weight with a king who had the pardoning power, if such a man as Scipio had been previously condemned.

46. *Means used in ancient times to influence the tribunals?* From all that has been said, we can see that formerly the orator had full range in his discourse. He looked to the whole nature of man, to all his passions, prejudices and emotions, as well as to the reasoning faculties. He endeavored to operate on all. Man is like a many-stringed instrument, upon which he alone can play with success, who can touch with skill *all the chords.* And Hume, with all the ancient critics, has pronounced in favor of the orator who can produce most powerful effect on the passions. Quinctilian says logicians can be found everywhere. An able argument is not rare; but seldom has that orator appeared whose eloquence could carry the judge out of his depth, who could throw him into what disposition of mind he pleased, fire him into resentment, or soften him into tears. (Q., 1, 397.) Many have constructed arguments as logical as those of Demosthenes and Cicero, but none ever arrayed them before their audiences with such magic power. The greatest men of the age acknowledged the resistless force of such oratory. Even Julius Cæsar once confessed himself subdued by the eloquence of Cicero, and absolved a criminal contrary to his settled purposes.

Under these circumstances, we see at once why orators anciently paid so much attention to gesture. We all know the persevering efforts of Demosthenes to cure all his natural physical defects. He studied rhetoric under Isæus, delivery under the comedian Satyrus, and afterwards under the actor Andronicus, and was in the habit of constant declamation. It is well known that besides paying such attention to delivery, Demosthenes arranged his dress with studied care. Cicero studied under Molo, the rhetorician. Even after coming out at the bar, went into Greece, attended schools of oratory, and afterwards, when in full practice, continued habit of declamation by way of exercise, frequented the school of Gnipho, and studied delivery under two great actors, Roscius and Æsop. (B. 4, 422.) Cicero tells us that Gracchus kept man behind him with pitch-pipe to regulate his voice before the people. Hortensius, celebrated rival of Cicero, prepared all his attitudes before a mirror. When about to go into forum, like Demosthenes, he chose and put on his dress with a view to oratorical effect; and Macrobius says he once instituted a suit against a man for ruffling his toga after being elaborately adjusted. Quinctilian, who was one of the best speakers of his day, gives particular directions for dress of the orator, how to manage the folds of his gown, and the rings upon his fingers. Orator in Quinctilian's time had large space to move in. This *travelling oratory* carried to such extent on a particular occasion, that the orator was asked by his antagonist how many *miles he had spoken?*

Ancient orators practised every art which could operate on the feelings or on the prejudices, *e. g.*, Antonius, when pleading for old Aquilius, tore open his tunic and exposed his wounds, and then made a pathetic appeal to Marius, which brought tears even from that stern chieftain, with whom Aquilius had served. Hyperides saved the beautiful Phryne from just condemnation, by laying bare her bosom before the judges. When Cicero was about to be impeached by Clodius, he went in mourning with the whole equestrian order. Accused party, says Quinctilian, may sometimes appear in worn and tattered garments, indicative of wretchedness and despair. He may even prostrate himself before his judge and embrace his knees. His wife and children may be brought into court, and appeals made in their behalf. Hence effort of opposing counsel to counteract, *e. g.* Quinctilian was counsel for young man, of whom a large estate was claimed for a young girl, on the plea of being his sister. The lawyer of girl directed her at certain part of his pleading, to go over to her supposed brother and clasp him around the neck. This move was understood as soon as made, by Quinctilian, and young man, by getting out of the way, totally disconcerted the advocate for the girl. When Glycon brought a child into court that he might excite compassion by his crying, he asked in his speech, why he wept? The child answered, because my schoolmaster *pinches* me. On another occasion when number of boys were brought into court, opposing lawyer threw handful of marbles among them, which set them all to scrambling. (Q. 1, 394.) In Greece it is certain that the same arts were practised, as we learn from Aristophanes, who, in one of his plays, ridicules the courts by introducing the mock trial of a *dog* for stealing a cheese. He brings in a *litter of puppies*, whose yelping is urged by counsel, as the wailing of helpless orphans over the fate which is to befall their parent.

47. *Difference between ancient and modern systems of pleadings, and its effect on oratory?* By the genius of the common law, a great proportion of every trial, civil or criminal, consists of the *pleadings*. Every charge must be *precise*, *specific*, *single*. Every fact must be related with minutest accuracy of *time*, *place*, and *circumstance*. Answer must be drawn with some logical acuteness. Every fact charged in violation of law, must be met by direct denial in terms adapted to nature of the charge. Every accusation in vague or general terms must be repelled by an appeal to the judge, whether the party is bound to answer. In this manner, the *declaration* or *allegation*, on the one side, and the *answer* on the other, lead to *issue* involving generally a single question, either of *fact* to be decided by *jury*, or of *law* to be decided by judge. This beautiful science of pleading has been somewhat altered in England by some little abatement from its original strictness, and in this country still more. It nevertheless yet remains in sufficient force to make it one of most important branches of the law, and it has produced an essential difference between ancient and modern judicial oratory. Pleadings among the ancients were very loose. Forms of process, both civil and criminal, were very simple and general. Cicero speaks of whole system of pleadings with contempt, derides it as compilation of verbose and unmeaning pedantry, and asserts, with all the pressure of his business, he would make himself master of the science in three days. Owing to this difference in the pleadings, the modern advocate is hedged in and prevented from taking that wide range in the discussion which a loose system would allow, *e. g.*, Cicero *vs.* Verres makes apology for passing over the licentious debaucheries of his youth, because too shocking for his modesty; then he proceeds, "fourteen years have elapsed, since you, Verres, held the office of quæstor. *From that day to this, I put in judgment every thing you have done!* Not an hour of your life will be found unpolluted by some theft, some baseness, some cruelty, some villany. During those years you successively disgraced the offices of quæstor, of delegate in Asia, of prætor in the city, and prætor in Sicily. *From the functions of these several stations will arise the fourfold distribution of my whole accusation.*" This celebrated oration would never have been delivered before an English or American judge. For, although in criminal cases the defendant is allowed the fullest latitude, it is not so with the prosecutor. His pleadings must be of strictest character. He must have a written declaration of charges penned with most technical accuracy. A sweeping accusation against 14 years of a man's life would be totally inadmissible. He could not rake up the undefined crimes of a dissolute youth for purpose of increasing the measure of his guilt—not a witness could

he call to prove a single offence not specified in the bill of indictment—not one word could he utter unconnected with the allegations and the proofs. Had he lifted his torch on the midnight revels of his adversary's boyish days, the judge would have told him that he must not proceed. Had he attempted that beautiful apostrophe to the Alban groves and lakes and fountains which has immortalized Cicero, he would have been told that he was travelling out of the record. The various specified misdemeanors too would have been cognizable before different tribunals. Official misdemeanors would have been tried by one, private wrongs by another, and perhaps thefts and acts of cruelty by a third; and before each every offence charged must have been drawn up in most precise language by an *article of impeachment*, *a writ of trespass*, or an *indictment*, and these, like the stakes and floating buoys of an expansive but shallow river, would have continually reminded him that he could not proceed a foot beyond them without stranding. (A. 1. 288.)

When Cicero defends Publius Sectius from charge of riot, grounded on a special law, not one-tenth of his long oration is at all to the point in issue; and that most exquisitely composed speech for Archias the poet could never have been delivered before an American court. Archias was on his defence against charge of being an alien. Not one-sixth part of the speech has any bearing on the real question involving the construction of the Roman law of naturalization; it is mainly taken up with the literary merits of his client. If an American barrister, says Mr. Adams, should undertake, by an elaborate argument, to prove that the Abbe Delille was an American citizen, because he was an excellent French poet, if all the muses should combine to compose his oration, not five sentences of it would he be suffered to deliver; the judges would stop him in his oratorical career, by asking for the *certificates of naturalization*. Cicero's notions of pleading are exemplified by remarks which, in one of his dialogues, he puts in the mouth of the old orator Anthony. Pontius had a son supposed to be killed in war with Cimbri; under this belief father left his property to another son—soldier returned after the death of his father. "Had you been employed," says Anthony, "to defend his cause, you would not have discussed the doctrine as to priority or validity of testaments; you would have raised his father from the grave, made him embrace his child, and recommend him, with many tears, to the protection of the centumviri." (D. 2. 140.) In a British or American court nothing would have been discussed but the validity or priority of the wills, all the rest would have been cut off by the rigor of the pleadings. In our own country, in different states, and even in different courts of the same state, the rules of pleading are enforced with different degrees of rigor, and it is uniformly observed, that where the pleading is most strict, there is least declamation on part of lawyer—strict pleadings always rein up the counsel to the stern *logic* of the law.

48. III. *Third cause of difference between ancient and modern eloquence?* It is evident that, all other things being equal, the more agitating and important the subjects are which call forth the orator, the more grand and imposing will be his oratory. He will be stimulated by the responsibility which devolves on him to the utmost exertion of all his powers, whilst the importance and grandeur of his subjects will impart force to his eloquence and an impressive interest to his counsels.

49. *Political events of ancient times more agitating than those of modern?* Governments of modern nations are much more settled and stable than those of ancient times. Revolutions are much more rare than formerly. Invention of gunpowder has rendered wars more expensive, and therefore given a decided advantage to civilized over barbarous nations. Power now depends on wealth, and barbarous nations are unable to support the expense of war. Hence conquest *now* moves in opposite direction. The civilized man conquers the savage every where, whilst in ancient times, when the sword, javelin, bows, arrows, &c., were the instruments of war, the hardy barbarians could easily supply themselves with those cheap weapons, and thus were enabled often to overthrow the wealthy but more effeminate nations. Conquests generally were much more easily achieved in ancient than in modern times. Amongst equally civilized nations, since the invention of gunpowder, and the perfection of the modern system of the *political balance*, it is almost impossible for any nation to achieve the conquest of its neighbors, *e. g.*, since days of Charles V. of Germany, nations of Europe have been engaged in almost constant wars, and yet scarcely any of the large states have been blotted out from the political system, nor has the territorial integrity of even the smaller been materially impaired. Nation on the defensive has decided advantage over the offensive. Hence very rarely case that one can be surprised by another. War now a matter of science, of deliberate calculation. Not so anciently. No conquest now by a *coup-de-main.*

50. *Circumstances which rendered the political events of Greece so interesting and imposing?* First, the little states of Greece formed a sort of confederacy against the barbarian powers, particularly the great empire of Persia. Secondly, there was rivalry, negotiation, and frequent wars among the Grecian states themselves, *e. g.*, Peloponnesian war of 27 years' duration. Thirdly, after the Persian war Athens obtained the *Hegemony* of the democratic states, and she soon usurped the right of coercing the refractory members, and of deciding all the great

questions of political importance in the courts of Athens. This brought the great and agitating questions of all her allies to her courts, and thus opened the finest field for the display of oratory. Fourthly, there was that important class of subjects growing out of the relation of the conquering states of Greece to their subject islands and provinces, including cases of malversation in office, and oppression on part of governor, &c. Now we must remember that all these agitating topics, whether tried before the assembly or in the courts, were in fact discussed before a *popular* tribunal; for in Athens the *Heleastic* courts were all of the popular character; and thus the orator enjoyed full range for the display of his powers.

51. Demosthenes appeared at a time particularly favorable to oratory. First, in formation of great orators necessary to have the *trade* of speaking separate and distinct, so that the orator confines himself to his profession alone; and secondly, not only must the topics be great and agitating, but the country must be in the condition to make the orator the most important character. Both of these circumstances concurred in favor of Demosthenes.

52. *Explain first circumstance?* Easy to trace relative importance of eloquence and statesmanship on one hand, and military skill on the other. At time of Persian war, military skill most important, *e. g.*, Miltiades, Themistocles, &c., rose to power more by military skill, than by eloquence or statesmanship. Great change at time of Pericles. He was both statesman and orator, and likewise general. In former capacity acquired more power than in latter. In time of Demosthenes we find the orator and statesman rising to great influence *without* military skill. The cause of this seems to be that Athens, by drawing to herself after the Persian war all the principal lawsuits from the democratic states, gave rise at once to the profession of the lawer; and the Peloponnesian war, during the time of Pericles, and after, brought so many great political causes before the courts, gave rise to so many state trials, that the labors of the advocate and statesman became united. Effect of this was to give to the orator a power of speech which is rarely acquired except by practice. A proper training is requisite for the full display of the mental powers in debate, *e. g.*, Dumont tells us that, in national assembly of France, only orators who possessed any talent for improvisation were Maury, Clermont-Tonnere, Barnave, and Thouret. Of these, Barnave was only one who could extemporize a speech of any length. Mirabeau could not. Most of his great passages are short, rapid, electrical, flashing out from between trains of argument most laboriously prepared. It was the want of training which produced this

anomaly—one that would never occur in England or the United States, where we are so much accustomed to public speaking.

53. *Explanation of the second circumstance?* A state of peace with great and agitating questions, with imminent dangers threatening the state, is most favorable to the orator. Reason evident—in war, events are great and agitating, but force then more important than persuasion—military chieftain greater than the orator. Not so in time of peace, with dangers impending. Then the orator is the great man of the age—he nerves his countrymen for the coming contest—he inspires fortitude under trials, *e. g.*, When the children of Israel were about to leave Egypt, Moses was afraid to take the command, because he felt the want of eloquence at such a time; and Jehovah acknowledged its importance when he answered, "Is not Aaron, the Levite, thy brother? I know that he can speak well, and he shall be thy spokesman unto the people." When the great and agitating questions of the crusades were preached up, such men as Peter the Hermit and St. Bernard were the great men of the age; but when Peter joined the army, he soon sunk into utter contempt, because the general was here more important than the orator, and the man who had shaken all Europe by his preaching, lost his reputation in the camp. In the national assembly of France, just before the commencement of the continental wars, in spite of all the disadvantages resulting from want of training among the speakers, there were occasionally great displays of oratory, and perhaps Mirabeau has hardly been excelled in modern times. But when force became predominant, eloquence ceased. Such men as Pichegru, Moreau and Bonaparte became the men of the age. And in our own country we had fine theatre for eloquenee in those provincial assemblies which heralded our revolution, when the orators of the day were arming the people intellectually for the great battle of independence—it was then that the eloquence of Henry was called forth.

Now what condition can we imagine more favorable to eloquence than age of Demosthenes. Every thing conspired to produce the great orator. Form of government had long made public speaking customary; political and forensic eloquence were united, as before explained, and in the north of Greece there had risen up a power with the most wily statesman and able general at its head, who bade fair to conquer the liberties of Greece. Philip, it has been said, formed Demosthenes. The dangers, which he created, inspired the eloquent warning of the orator; *e. g.* what speaker ever had a more agitating theme than Demosthenes, when he made the great speech that brought about the alliance between Thebes and Athens, and led to the fatal battle of Cheronæa. He had warned his countrymen against Philip, but hireling orators had calmed the popular excitement. At length, late one evening, news arrived that Philip had seized Elatea, the key of Phocis and Bœotia, and might soon be expected before the walls of Athens. On the morrow, at dawn of day, the senate met, and the people crowded into the assembly. Prytanes reported the news. Herald himself was produced and made to recite from his own lips. Then the crier called aloud to the assembly, "Does any one wish to speak?" None answered to the call; and it was repeated over and over again, until Demosthenes mounted the Bema, and delivered that soul-stirring speech, which made the assembly cry out, with one voice, "Let us march against Philip." Such a case could not occur in modern times, nor even in the Roman republic.

54. *Character of the subjects which called forth the Roman oratory?* Mr. Dunlop says that "Cicero had a wider, and perhaps more beautiful field than Demosthenes; the wide extent of the Roman empire, the striking vices and virtues of its citizens, the memorable events of its history, supplied an endless variety of great and interesting topics, whereas many of the orations of Demosthenes are on subjects unworthy of his talents." (2. 193.) We can scarcely imagine more glorious opportunities for display of oratory than those afforded by complaints of oppressed and plundered provinces against their governors, *e. g.*, impeachment of Verres; here the clients of Cicero were the injured people of a great province. When he pleaded their cause, not Sicilians only, but persons of distinction from all Italy flocked around him in the forum—glaring guilt of Verres, and nature of his crimes, made the subject most copious, interesting, and various. "Such a wonderful assemblage of circumstances," says Mr. Dunlop, "never yet prepared the course for the triumphs of oratory. So great an opportunity for the exhibition of forensic art will, in all probability, never again occur." (160.) From extensive ramifications of Roman power, numerous cases arose of description rarely to be met with in modern times. There is but one case in all British history at all comparable to the case of Verres—the impeachment of Warren Hastings—and that called forth perhaps as great a display of oratory as has been witnessed in modern times. It is true that the subjects of forensic eloquence in Rome perhaps excelled in importance and interest those of Greece or of any other nation which has ever appeared; and hence most of Cicero's master-pieces were delivered in the *forum*. But great as those subjects were, they could not compare in interest with the important subjects debated before the assemblies of Greece. Bar does not admit

the most sublime eloquence. The highest order can only arise "on occasions calculated to shake and agitate the human soul." When consternation prevails, when even the brave are mute with astonishment, then the man who can stand forth undismayed, and point out the means of deliverance, or lead the way to a noble self-devotion, like Patrick Henry, when he exclaimed, "whatever others do, I'll fight," is the truly eloquent man. Such situations as these oftener existed among the Grecian democracies than in the Roman empire. The extent of the latter, its power, mixed character of its government, with predominance of the senate, all conspired to prevent the occurrence of these crises, in which the very existence of the commonwealth was threatened, and the great state matters were not always debated before a tribunal so favorable to eloquence as popular assemblies of Greece. The Roman senate materially modified Roman oratory.

55. IV. *Fourth cause of difference between ancient and modern eloquence?* The invention of the printing press, without doubt, is most important of modern events—has fixed an era in history of mankind—has given to government, to literature, to civilization, a new aspect; and not to wonder, therefore, that it has powerfully contributed to change character of eloquence.

56. *Effect of printing press on the mass, and consequent influence on eloquence?* Formerly books were necessarily so dear that few could be produced, and consequently very few could purchase or read them, *e. g*, in time of Louis XI. supposed that about 6000 persons in all France were employed as copyists, whilst, at this time, with that powerful engine, the press, in motion, 60,000 persons in the city of Paris alone obtain their living, either directly or indirectly, from the business of the press. The consequence has been a greater diffusion of knowledge among the people. This has contributed to destroy that immense inequality which formerly existed among individuals; even the lucky few, who had wealth and talent, could procure but a scanty supply of the imperfect works that existed—the deficiency was to be supplied by travel and personal inspection; *e. g.*, Herodotus obliged to travel most extensively before he could write his history. The very few, therefore, who could amass knowlēdge, and cultivate their talents, enjoyed a monopoly which gave them undue power over the illiterate mass. Voltaire has compared the great men of antiquity among the people to few tall cypresses amid a thick undergrowth of shrubbery. The printing press has elevated the mass, and perhaps brought down somewhat the more gifted few—to pursue the simile of Voltaire, it has lowered the tall cypresses and elevated the shrubbery. "The *noble* has gone down on the social ladder, and the

roturier has gone up." Public opinion is every thing, individual influence is nothing. The orator now does not possess that commanding superiority over his audience which will enable him to sway it by his eloquence. There is too much light in the world to make the orator ever the principal instructor.

57. *Periodical press and its influence?* It has been well observed by Lord Brougham that the orator of old was the parliamentary debater; the speaker at public meetings, the preacher, the newspaper, the published sermon, the pamphlet, the volume, all in one. Not to be wondered at, that when such a being was to speak, all Greece should assemble to hear him. Great change since invention of printing—periodical press is now the organ of communication, and the potent engine that controls the popular will—it is periodical press which first discusses every matter of importance; and, when the orator now rises to speak on any great subject, in a deliberative body, or even in a court of justice, he finds that the novelty of his subject has been worn off by the newspapers—his arguments are stale, and he feels like one rehearsing the thrice told tale. How different from the Greek and Roman orator, who monopolized all the functions of the press, the senate, the school, and the pulpit, and was even a rival of the stage actor. Surprise has always been found a powerful coadjutor of eloquence; but what orator can now operate a surprise on his audience, either as to matters of fact or of argument. He finds that busy, sleepless organ, the press, eternally ahead of him.

58. *Influence of the press on eloquence, through its influence on society and government?* With progress of civilization and advancement of arts, manufactures and commerce in modern times, men are divided into more varied professions and occupations than formerly. We are too busy, each with his own concerns, to exercise directly all the political functions—we delegate management of political interests to those who have the leisure and ability to attend to them. But whilst the system of representation thus throws the immediate action of the government into the hands of a few, the diffusion of knowledge by the press secures to the people an irresistible influence over the government—sectional interests are better understood—and it is well known that large masses will generally pursue their interest—representatives feel themselves responsible to their constituents, and hence, in all great deliberative bodies, legislation becomes a matter of compromise and balancing between the great and jarring interests of the body politic Every thing must now be done by calculation, by previous arrangement, by party combination. It has been justly said that, even in the greatest storm of debate, you may perceive the speaker under the do-

minion of a spirit of calculation—in his boldest flights he is still bound in the fetters of political combinations. No orator now can, by the energy of his single voice, sway the deliberations of modern parliaments to the issues of peace or war. But, in the democracies of antiquity, war was often declared, alliances formed, revolutions achieved, by the single influence of one potent tongue. The assemblies of Greece and Rome were supreme, and on their judgments depended the fate of empires. It was the population of the metropolis that ruled unconditionally and irresponsibly all the other parts of the body politic. But in the modern representative assembly, the capital in which it deliberates may not have a single representative. All the discordant interests of a widespread territory are here represented—the pulse that beats within the senate chamber may not be in unison with that which beats around it. It is not on the multitude of the metropolis, not even on the assembly seated in the capitol, that the orator must produce his effect. He must in fact address, through the medium of the press, the distant provinces of the empire, and wait for the slow returns of popular will, before he can persuade to action. Before the orator can operate on an American Congress, it is necessary first to operate on American people. Congress is but the mirror that reflects the popular will. When an immediate effect is to be produced, the stronger passions of our nature must be appealed to. But when time is an element in the calculation, the principle of self-interest predominates over every other. When Demosthenes addressed the Athenian assembly, or Cicero the Comitia of Rome, the audiences did not wait to hear from the islands of the Ægean, nor from the province of Gaul, or from the more distant Britons, their decisions were immediate and irresponsible. Hence every effort was made to rouse the stronger passions of our nature. But he who addresses the modern parliament knows full well that it cannot be by a mere stroke of oratory that his effect must be produced. He knows that the speech which he delivers, to be efficient, must be such a one as will bear the closest scrutiny. He knows that the editor and reviewer will sit in judgment on it, the leaders of the opposite party will analyze it, but, above all, the wise men of that constituency which he represents will sit in solemn judgment on its merits. Such a speaker must be exact in his information, accurate in his principles and details, comprehensive in his views. His plans and his principles will be of infinitely more importance than the mere rhetoric with which he enforces them. However, at the moment of delivery, the substance may be concealed by the skill of the orator, he may be sure that when the wand of criticism is applied, every principle and every plan will be made to stand forth to public view in all their nakedness. When a gentleman was once asked, how he liked the speech of one of the finest orators of our country, he answered that he had been greatly disappointed, but that it was impossible for human power to produce eloquence upon 14¾ *cents to the square yard.* For all that, however, our speaker must not neglect cents and quarters of cents, no matter how unfavorable to oratorical display. He is very sure that the great interests of this country will not be cheated out of their wealth, or reconciled to dangerous schemes of policy, by the mere jugglery of oratory. Thus substance is every thing, ornament nothing. The modern science of political economy has of itself operated a powerful change in public speaking.

59. V. *The fifth cause of difference between ancient and modern oratory?* Superiority of classic languages for the great ends of oratory is acknowledged by every scholar; take it all in all, no language has ever equalled the Greek. Lord Brougham, when speaking of Demosthenes, says that the adoration of ages has consecrated his place at the head of the mighty masters of speech, and the loss of the noble instrument, with which he forged and launched his thunders, is sure to maintain it unapproachable for ever. Peculiar structure of ancient languages, whilst it dispensed with the larger proportion of those little words which Dr. Campbell has aptly called the *luggage of language*, gave much more latitude to the collocation of the related words in a sentence; and, consequently, enabled the speaker so to arrange, as to place the important words in that position which would give greatest force or beauty to the sentence. Even in most common prose, the utmost attention was sometimes paid to the arrangement of words; *e. g.*, in note-book of Plato, after his decease, it was found that the first sentence of his treatise, De Repub., had been written several times over with different arrangements, so as to select the best; and yet the sentence translated is simply, "I went down yesterday to the Piræus with Glaucon, the son of Ariston." It would be ridiculous to bestow such pains on the collocation of the words of such a sentence in any modern language. Yet we cannot charge Plato with sacrificing force and dignity to the polish and miniature beauties of language, whose diction Cicero compares to the inspiration of poetry, and Quinctilian to the responses of the Delphic oracle, and of which it was said, had the father of the gods spoken in Greek, he would have used no other language than Plato's. It was by means of this liberty in collocation, and the more musical character of the words, that the effect of many a sentence in the ancient orations must be mainly attributed; *e. g.*, Cicero's description of Verres, he tells us, produced an electric effect on his audience—*stetit soleatus Prætor Populi Romani, cum pallio purpureo, tunicaque tulari, muliercula nixus, in littore.* Again, he says he was present when

Carbo in a speech pronounced the following words, *Patris dictum sapiens temeritas filii comprobavit;* in which the metre of the word *comprobavit* drew forth a shout which it was wonderful to hear. Ancient rhetoricians gave rules for composition of "numerous" prose, scarcely less nice and complex than those of metrical harmony. It is owing mainly to the superiority of the ancient languages, that no translation can do justice to the orations of Demosthenes and Cicero. Hence the Edinburgh Review was justified in saying of the translations of Demosthenes' speeches by the Abbe Auger, that, when the bullion and substance of the athletic and ponderous orator was spun into French wire, it bore very little more resemblance to the original than the slim figure of one of their skipping posture-masters to the muscular frame of old Milo of Crotona, or one of their lean kine to a well-fed bull of the Crowland or Bedford level. (36, 487.)

In the preceding remarks I have not insisted particularly on free institutions as a cause of eloquence, because these were common to the ancient and modern world, and all history has shown that genuine eloquence can only flourish under institutions of a republican character. Under arbitrary governments, where one governs and the rest obey—where the despot, like the Roman centurion, has only to say to one, Go, and he goeth, and to another, Come, and he cometh—persuasion is of no avail. Wherever submission is the principle of government, eloquence can never arise. Hence, in modern times, we can only look for eloquence in states with popular institutions, like England and America. Or, if it appear in despotisms, it will be in times of great popular excitement, as in the commencement of the French revolution. Among the ancient nations, Greece and Rome only, and these merely during the existence of popular institutions, furnish us with the great specimens of oratory. The vast despotisms of Asia, either in ancient or modern times, have furnished not one single great and acknowledged orator.

60. *Conclusion of the comparison between ancient and modern eloquence?* Will be seen from foregoing remarks that difference between ancient and modern eloquence is owing mainly to difference of circumstances, and hence difficult to assign the palm to either. The ancient had perhaps more force, more passionate appeals, and produced greater effect on the audience. Ours has more logic, more learning, more thorough regard to all the great interests of the body politic. If, upon the whole, it be asserted, as Hume and Quinctilian, and most of the critics have done, that the rarest and noblest specimens of oratory are those that appeal to the strong passions, and carry away the hearer a passive instrument in the hands of the orator, we must never forget that

this advantage was due to circumstances that no philanthropist could ever wish to return. It was the forms of procedure, character of the courts or assemblies, before which questions were tried, and, above all, the nature of those questions themselves, that gave to Greek and Roman oratory such dazzling splendor, and surrounded it with a glory which can never shine on the efforts of rhetoric in better regulated communities, under a more sober dispensation of justice, and with that invaluable engine, the press, giving ubiquity to intellect, by pouring its floods of light over the world.

61. *Demosthenes and Cicero compared?* These two orators generally compared, because they stand first in their respective countries. Theophrastus, it is true, is represented by Plutarch as saying Demosthenes was worthy of Athens, and Demades above it, thus giving preference to latter.* But, in spite of this, we must give to Demosthenes first place in Greece. In making this comparison between two great orators of antiquity, we must remember that we cannot compare the manner and elocution of the two, but must judge mainly from what has come down to us from each, and this, in case of eloquence, is but an imperfect test. There is generally something in the *manner* of the great orator for which no language can compensate. Hence we can never adequately determine true oratorical merit by even the most accurately reported speeches; *e. g.*, Mr. Burke's speeches are incomparably the best that have ever been delivered in parliament, judging from the printed reports, and they will probably survive all other specimens of British parliamentary eloquence, and yet it is a well known fact, that Burke was not an orator—he could not produce an effect on the house. On the evening when he delivered his great speech on the Nabob of Arcot's debts, so faint was the impression, that Pitt and Grenville, after consultation, decided not to answer it; and yet both were obliged afterwards, when it appeared in print, to acknowledge it to be one of the most perfect models of oratorical compositions to be found on record. (M. 1. 251.)

Demosthenes and Cicero have been compared, 1st, as *business* speakers; 2d, as regards *vehemence* and *moral sublimity;* 3d, as to *learning* and *philosophy;* 4th, as to *morals.*

62. First, speeches of Demosthenes have more of the business character than Cicero's. They are always to the point, no digressions—no common-places—nothing for mere ornament. Demosthenes combined lofty declamation of Lord Chatham, with close, business-like,

* Demades was said to be a good *extempore* speaker, and this was probably cause of preference given by Theophrastus.

rapid debating of Fox. He is almost painfully concise, even to the reader; whereas, Cicero often amplifies and deals in philosophical reflections, some of which are mere common-places. He was accused by his cotemporaries of being rather florid and *Asiatic* in his style.

63. Second, have more of the moral sublime. Heeren has pronounced Demosthenes the most sublime and purest tragic character with which history acquaints us. From his first appearance to moment when he swallowed the poison in the temple, we see him struggling against destiny—sometimes thrown to the ground, but never subdued. How natural that the lines of melancholy and indignation, which we behold in his bust, should have been imprinted on his austere countenance. His political principles emanated from depth of his soul. He remained true to feeling and conviction amid all changes and dangers; and hence that vehement sublimity which made him the most powerful of orators. When Cicero spoke, the *man* was admired, the *oration* was praised. When Demosthenes had spoken, the crowd went away denouncing Philip.

A great deal of this difference between the two orators must, however, be attributed to difference of subject. Cicero, on a suitable theme, sometimes made near approach to the Greek; *e. g.*, his speech against Piso was extremely vehement. His second Philippic against Anthony has more *Demosthenean* vehemence than any of his orations. In latter part of his speech for Milo he rises into the moral sublime; so likewise in many parts of the speeches against Verres—in all these instances his subject was of such a nature as to call forth the vehemence. But Cicero would often weaken, by digression or philosophical reflection, in midst of the most powerful eloquence; *e. g.*, in oration for Milo, in midst of most vehement declamation, he digresses suddenly into dissertation about order of Divine Providence—beautiful, but ill-timed. Eloquence with Demosthenes was an *instrument* to attain his ends; with Cicero it was an accomplishment—a branch of finished education.

64. Third, Demosthenes less learned. Rochefoucault has remarked that no man ever exerted his faculties to the fullest extent of which they were capable. Great critic has observed, if ever there was an exception to this remark, it was Cicero. Perhaps most perfect example of universal genius, combined with untiring study, presented in annals of history. Some men may have equalled him in genius, some in labor, but never was there so illustrious an instance of the "*mutual league* between nature and study, between the ethereal spirit and terrestrial toil," as this wonderful man presents. He was poet, historian, philosopher, moralist, epistolary writer and critic, and, in every character, except the first,* he

* It is said we appreciate compliments most highly upon *doubtful* accomplish-

is pre-eminently great. From 26th year of his age, when he first appeared in public, in defence of Quinctius, to the last year, when he delivered his Philippics against Anthony, his labors in his profession and his studies in the closet were without intermission. Demosthenes labored as intensely as Cicero, but it was all for one purpose—it was not to be an elegant scholar, but an irresistible orator—in him, consequently, we behold nothing but the one great talent. Demosthenes, therefore, produced greatest effect on *auditor*, Cicero on the *reader*. Burke, of all modern speakers, most resembles Cicero in his matter, and therefore has generally been regarded as an imitator. Cicero is always ethical and deeply philosophical.

65. *Morals?* The moral character of Demosthenes has suffered from having taken a bribe, as was asserted, from Harpalus, a creature of Alexander, whose prosecution was commenced by Demosthenes, but afterwards discontinued, because of the present of a golden cup, made by Harpalus. This charge, however, rests on insufficient grounds, and is now discredited by best historians. Of the private character of the Greek we know but little; but the noblest impulses alone could give rise to that immortal eloquence, by which he so often roused the democracies of Greece. With Cicero much more familiarly acquainted—was undoubtedly one of the best men of his age. Mr. Adams thinks that his system of morals was the most perfect ever promulgated before the glad tidings of Christianity. No one has ever more beautifully delineated the pleasures, or prescribed the duties of friendship—no one with more soothing hand has extended consolations of virtue to the waxing infirmities of age.

After all these bright points, we can but regret that last infirmity of great minds—an overweening vanity; Cicero's fulsome praises of himself are sometimes disgusting to modern reader. Demosthenes was entirely free from this weakness. We must, however, remember that ancients generally had but little of that delicate sensibility which would blush at praise, particularly *self-praise*. Cardinal Wolsey defended his usual style of address, *ego et meus rex*, by the custom of the ancients, who always, in the spirit of selfishness and candor, put themselves first. Demosthenes was no doubt the firmest man, and perhaps the most uncompromising patriot—sternness was his characteristic. Cicero was sometimes wavering, and his party always feared his want of firmness.

ments. Upon that principle we can explain the reason why Julius Cæsar, when trying to win Cicero, praised his poetry as much as his eloquence. So likewise under Cardinal Richelieu, applicant for office was more likely to obtain it by calling cardinal a greater poet than Corneille, than if he had told him he was the greatest statesman of the age.

He vacillated between Cæsar and Pompey, and it was thought the artful praises of the former, operating on his vanity, too often weakened his exertions for his party. Both were banished from their countries, and Cicero wept over his fate like a child. Demosthenes bore it with manly fortitude. Both have been charged with cowardice—Demosthenes ran away at the battle of Cheronæa, (no proof, by-the-by, of cowardice, as the whole army fled ;) and Cicero was always accused of being deficient in nerve; it was said the presence of Pompey's troops, at the time he defended Milo, so agitated him as to produce a perfect failure. He always, however, had resolution to attack his enemies with great fierceness; *e. g.*, his attacks on Catiline and Mark Anthony. Both behaved with great firmness in the hour of death, and both fell, the patriotic victims of despotism.

66. *Laborious preparation of Demosthenes and Cicero before speaking?* Both not only prepared themselves, but wrote out carefully their speeches before speaking, whenever they had an opportunity. Demosthenes was extremely adverse to speaking without this preparation, and generally the mode of doing business allowed of it. When, however, there was a necessity for it, he spoke extemporaneously, and Plutarch says, with great power; *e. g.*, celebrated reply to Pytho was unpremeditated; and he spoke on the capture of Elatea after a single night's reflection. Cicero too was capable of splendid extemporaneous display, whenever the exigency demanded, as in the case of great riot in theatre on account of Otho's law; yet he too pronounces the pen to be most effectual teacher of eloquence.

It was this constant habit of writing out speeches, which will explain the anomaly of so many *written* speeches, never delivered; *e. g.*, oration against Midas by Demosthenes was never spoken; five out of seven of orations against Verres were never spoken; 2d Philippic *vs.* Mark Anthony was not even *designed* to be spoken. Oration for Milo was not delivered, at least not as it now appears. And in the written speeches reference is often made to circumstances which would now appear ridiculous. In speech for Milo, Cicero makes reference to things which could only happen whilst in the rostrum; *e. g.*, alarm occasioned by presence of armed men, attention of audience, effect on adversary by certain passages, &c., all these were put in at random. But in second Philippic, never delivered, he speaks as if delivering it on particular day, which day is spoken of as bearing on the argument; affirms that certain parts make Anthony feel as if torn in pieces; and actually asserts that he is *at the moment* growing pale with fear, and perspiring. In Greece it was very customary for the pleaders to write speeches and give them to others to deliver. The celebrated Isocrates, after his first failure, never could command resolution to appear again in public, but wrote many admirable orations delivered by others.

67. *Demosthenes and Cicero not supposed to be good debaters—reasons?* Moderns are so much in habit of extemporaneous speaking that we have acquired a sort of contempt for *written* speeches—we consider them unfit for modern mode of debating; and hence the two great orators of antiquity, it has been supposed, would have cut no great figure in the struggle of a modern debate, where the subject is argued stringently with an antagonist, "hand to hand and foot to foot." As mode of doing business anciently allowed of preparation, it is probable that Cicero and Demosthenes were not good debaters in our sense of the term; but that is no objection to them. Theirs was the highest kind of eloquence.

68. *Laborious preparation produces best oratory?* History has shown that the greatest speeches cannot be struck out at a heat. Finest displays have been those most studied, where the orator, as has been happily said, refines into simplicity, and elaborates into ease. Generally supposed, orator cannot feel the impulse of inspiration except with the audience before him—great mistake. In closet his imagination may picture the scene, and thus inspire him as effectually as if the speech were delivering. Facts prove this theory; *e. g.*, two greatest orators of ancient world preferred writing, and without doubt the two speeches of Cicero, the one for Milo and the other the second Philippic against Anthony, which were never delivered, were his greatest; the last particularly remarkable as a vehement oratorical effort. Speech, too, of Demosthenes against Midas is one of his best, although never spoken. In modern speeches, even, there is little doubt but that most of the passages of overpowering eloquence are most elaborately wrought out beforehand. The most powerful orator that England has ever produced, Lord Chatham, most laboriously prepared himself. He is said to have read Bailey's Dictionary twice over, to have articulated before a glass to perfect himself in use of language. Every reason to believe that all his most celebrated passages, even that splendid allusion to the tapestry, were concocted beforehand. The very folding of his flannel around him like a toga, and that sweep of his crutch, by which he awed his adversary into silence, were all pre-arranged.

Of all the orations of modern times, that of Sheridan in the trial of Warren Hastings seems to have produced the most magic influence on his audience,* and yet we know that it was most laboriously prepared—

* Mr. Hume considers effect produced by Cicero on so cool a head as Cæsar's, an evidence of great power. Judging by similar rule, we should pronounce speech

all the decorative passages were worked to a full polish beforehand by most artistic skill. Industry of his whole family, from Mrs. Sheridan down to Edwards, his servant, was put in requisition—some with pen and scissors making extracts, while some were pasting and stitching his scattered memoranda in their proper places. (M. 2, 31.) Our American orators too generally prepare finest passages. In late presidential canvass (1840 it was proved by the fact, that the same speech would be delivered in different places almost *verbatim et literatim*—several of most successful of our popular orators have confessed that their finest declamatory passages were wrought out beforehand and committed to memory. Well known that Mr. Randolph, one of our greatest orators since time of Henry, most laboriously prepared himself, as has been proved by his notes. About Patrick Henry there is some doubt, but still, when we reflect how little learning he had, and yet how complete and perfect were his oratorical efforts, we must suppose that he too made

of Sheridan on the Begum charges as pre-eminently eloquent. Bisset, the continuator of Hume and Smollett, tells that Logan, an accomplished scholar, and who himself wrote a masterly defence of Hastings, went into House of Commons prepossessed in favor of accused, and against the accuser. At end of first hour of Sheridan's speech, he pronounced it all declamation without proof—at the end of the second, he said "this is a most wonderful oration,"—at close of third, said "Mr. Hastings has acted very unjustifiably"—after the fourth, "Mr. Hastings is a most atrocious criminal"—and at close of speech, which lasted five hours, he said, "of all the monsters of iniquity the most enormous is Warren Hastings!" Sir William Dolben moved the adjournment of the debate, confessing it was impossible to give a determinate opinion after such a speech. Mr. Stanhope seconded motion—his opinion had inclined to side of Mr. Hastings, that now, nothing but information almost equal to a miracle, could prevent him from sustaining the charge; but he had just felt the influence of such a miracle, and therefore he mnst avoid an immediate decicision. Mr. Matthew Montague made similiar confession. Burke, Fox and Pitt immediately paid compliments which proved that all were overwhelmed by the display. It may be well here to add, before closing note, that the result in this case marks difference between ancient and modern theatre. Had decision been made immediately, as would have been done in Athens, or even as quickly as in Rome, Hastings would certainly have been hanged or sent to the galleys. But in England the prosecution was spun out through several years—influence of great interests were brought to bear on the trial. The success of Mr. Hastings in his government in spite of all his enormities, moderated the public censure—public opinion turned in his favor, and thus was this great state criminal not only preserved unharmed, amid all that perilous lightning which flashed around him from lips of Burke, Fox and Sheridan, but his trial came to be regarded as unworthy persecution of a meritorious and successful statesman, he was discharged, and lived to see the day when a British House of Commons thought themselves honored by his presence, and actually welcomed him with cheers, when called as a witness on East India Company's charter. (1813)!! (M. S. 2. 32.)

elaborate preparation. With the learning and study of the Earl of Chatham, he would have surpassed all modern orators; with all his defects, however, he equalled any man that has appeared since the days of Cicero.

69. *Extemporaneous debating requires most perfect preparation?* All other things being equal, the man who possesses a thorough and complete knowledge of a whole subject, will be the most ready debater. You cannot take such a man by surprise, because he is prepared at all points; and this explains why men of great reputation almost always fall below expectation, when suddenly transferred to great deliberative bodies, before which they have not been regularly trained; *e. g.*, Lord Erskine went to parliament with an unrivalled reputation as a forensic speaker, yet he was no match for Pitt and Fox, very much to his chagrin—it was remark of distinguished senator some years since, that the greatest debater of the world might be suddenly translated to the senate of the United States, and for the first year at least he would find himself unequal to some three or four in that body. The reason is not that the new speaker has intellect less powerful, but because, in first place, he is not so thoroughly master of all those topics which may *by possibility* engage attention of the house, as he who has been longer trained on that arena, and therefore he is much more subject to surprise; 2dly, he is not so thoroughly acquainted as older members with the temper of the house, and therefore, even if he could deliver as good speech as any one, yet it would not be so effective; he could not throw his shot between *wind* and *water* with that precision which a more thorough knowledge of the temper of the body alone could enable him to do.

70. *Presidential canvass of* 1840 *presented a scene somewhat analogous to popular speaking in Greece?* During the entire summer, and the months of September and October, people throughout the United States became so interested in the presidential contest as to gather from day to day in large assemblages, before which best speakers of the districts engaged in debate. The greatest orators, too, in this country, travelled from county to county, and state to state, like Peter the Hermit, visiting even the most inaccessible regions, that they might everywhere awaken the public mind to a due sense of the importance of the crisis—the subject too was great and agitating; the public mind became deeply excited, and perhaps it may be asserted, that never since the period just before the American revolution, had a finer field been presented for the display of oratory—it was not the schoolmaster, but the orator, who "was abroad in the land." By the success of this experiment we may assert that a new era has been introduced into this country, and perhaps a "*new leaf* turned over in the world's history." Henceforth,

whenever the public mind shall be deeply agitated, and parties not *geographically* divided, we may calculate on the recurrence of similar scenes. The *stump* and the *steam engine* will become, as was asserted by one of Virginia's most gifted sons, the means of disseminating knowledge, and breaking down the influence of central dictation, and caucus juggling. And thus will the oratory of modern times be made more analogous to that of the ancients. By this means the orator once more is made the successful rival of the press.

What will be the influence of this on future character of American eloquence? Decidedly beneficial. It is feared by some that these promiscuous assemblies will increase all the defects of American oratory; that our speakers will become more turgid, prolix, declamatory, and their style more rude and unpolished than ever. This is not to be apprehended—history of ancient republics has most conclusively proven that no audience is so favorable to production of close, concise, and powerful oratory, as the popular assembly. People, says Mr. Hume, may sometimes be imposed on by false taste in rhetoric; but, uniformly, when the true orator makes his appearance, his superiority will be acknowledged, and the palm adjudged to him. Lord Brougham justly remarks that speaker who lowers his composition in order to accommodate himself to habits and taste of the multitude, will find that he commits a grievous mistake. All the highest powers of eloquence consist in producing passages which may at once affect most promiscuous assembly. Best speakers of all times have ever found that they could not speak too well, or too carefully, before popular assembly. "*Mirabile est*," says Cicero, "cum plurimum in faciendo *inter sit inter doctum et rudem, quam non multum differat in judicando*." Clear, strong, terse, natural style has always been that which most delights the people; and these remarks are confirmed by all most effective speakers in late presidential canvass.

It is true our popular assemblies are inferior to that of Athens, because in hands of latter dwelt all political power; it was addressed on all the great topics of the day, by the first orators of Greece, and therefore its taste and tact must have been greater than that which can be generated among the millions spread over our boundless region, any portion of whom, when assembled together, must feel that they are but a microscopic fragment of the sovereign *demus*, with a share of power less than the widow's mite. This great popular mass will ever be too broken and varied to be wrought in all its parts to that high polish, taste, and tact which characterized an Athenian assembly. Every multitude which assembles cannot have the training which the first orators of the country alone can give. But, although on no point can we bring all the influences to operate which formed the Athenian audience, yet we are compensated by the wider theatre on which we are practising. We are *enacting Greece*, if I may use the expression, on a grander scale; and if, from any equal portion of our population, we may expect fewer great orators, we must remember that we shall have millions of freemen where the Athenians had thousands, and that the multiplication of our chances may more than compensate for the want of that concentrated influence which operated so intensely within the walls of Athens and Rome. Our multitudes are now the most intelligent in the world, and, from the interest they take in public matters, more susceptible of improvement. No observer could fail to mark, during the late presidential campaign, the rapid improvement achieved in the popular mind by a few months of *oratorical labor*. Even the most uncultivated became at last possessed of the main points in the argument, and contracted an intense relish for the higher kinds of eloquence Mr. Hume said in his day few would go without their dinners to hear the finest speech that could be made in Westminster Hall. But some of our best speakers have not only addressed crowds who went without their dinners, but were willing to brave the burning sun, or the pelting rain, rather than lose any portion of the intellectual repast prepared for them. The critical taste of the whole American people has been wonderfully improved in the period of a few short months; but particularly in those districts where they have enjoyed the advantage of hearing in quick succession some of the finest orators of our country. It is but fair, therefore, to conclude that a continuance of such scenes, whilst it would improve the critical taste of the people, would react on the speaker, and produce the most vigorous species of popular eloquence.

SEC. VI.—WOMEN, MANNERS, MEALS, &c.

1. *Change in condition of women after the establishment of the democratic governments?* Have already observed that condition of women was comparatively elevated during the Homeric period; but after change to democracy we almost lose sight of them, until we are ready to believe that the Greeks had some other mode of continuing their race, and that they were the real αυτοχθονες, which they claimed to be in the commencement of their history, springing from the ground ready made, women were kept in the utmost seclusion. "The best woman," says Thucydides, "is she of whom least is said, either in the way of good or harm." Tragic theatre proclaimed silence to be greatest ornament of woman—"Thy wife abroad," cried the comic theatre, "'sdeath and furies! what does she from home?" The *owl*, a *muzzle*,

and a *pair of reins*, were the fittest emblems on sepulchre of the accomplished housewife. Owl emblem of her *watchfulness*, muzzle of her *silence*, reins of the *skill* with which she managed the servants, like the charioteer with his studs. Even this domestic seclusion might not have been so degrading to woman, if she had equal standing with her husband; but this was not the case, she was his inferior, as the following account of Ischomacha by Xenophon clearly proves.

2. *Ischomacha, an Athenian bride?* Xenophon, in one of his dialogues, introduces Socrates conversing with Ischomachus, a rich *Athenian gentleman*, in his usual inquisitive manner. Socrates soon interrogates him about his household establishment, and the answers give great insight into female education—wife of this gentleman was married at 15; she had lived under a *surveillance* equal to that of nunnery—during which time care of her friends seems to have been to make her see as little, hear as little, and ask as few questions as possible—she was temperate and sober, and, as the rough Greek expressed it, "in matters which concerned the belly she had been well disciplined"—when all the materials were put into her hands, she could make a vest—such the being who was to make the wife of an Athenian gentleman. He speaks of training this woman precisely as he would of a young horse. "When he found her well in hand, supple and tractable, so as to be conversable," he asks if she knew why her parents had given her in marriage, and he had accepted her. Whereupon he enters into philosophical inquiry as to causes which impose marriage-yoke, &c. He then teaches her the duties of good wife: to abide within doors; to send to their labor the out hands; to superintend those within. All that was brought in she was to receive, she was to distribute what was necessary, and when there was surplus to take care of it, that what ought to be consumption of a year might not be the waste of a month. She was to see that the wool brought was converted into cloth, and that the corn was ready to make bread, &c., &c. These mere animals were of course highly decorated; before her marriage Ischomacha painted both white and red, and wore high-heeled shoes. (L. Q. 22.)

3. *Reason for the seclusion of females in Greece?* Mitford attributes it to the democratic institutions. Turbulence of these little democracies made it often disagreeable, and sometimes hazardous for ladies to be even in the streets. Again, universal suffrage, and the political equality of all the freemen, made the higher orders pay the utmost court to the lower, even to the most ill-bred and worthless of them. Not only those who sought honors, but those likewise who would protect their property, were obliged to associate familiarly with the rabble. The ladies, to avoid a society which their husbands and fathers could not, lived with fe-

male slaves in secluded part of the building, and seldom appeared in public except at those religious festivals, at which ancient custom required them to bear a part, and sacerdotal authority could guard them from insult.

4. *Influence of female seclusion on the literature of Greece?* It wants that refinement, variety and sentiment which educated women alone can impart—*sentimental* love which pervades modern romance was not known to the ancients. Even in their plays woman acts subordinate rôle—it is all men, all business, all public matters. In the comedies we have ever before our eyes, gymnasium, senate, general assembly, courts of law, &c.; there is bustle, pursuit, energy, activity, but none of that pleasing variety "which wanders from the camp to the court, from philosophy to the boudoir, from the enterprises of the field to the courtesies of domestic life." All that class of writing denominated *polite literature*, among the Greeks, suffered greatly from the want of the female impress.

5. *On female chastity?* Montesquieu asserts that Grecian women were conspicuous for virtue. If so, it was because system of education made them too uninteresting to be objects of desire, or seclusion deprived them of the temptation. They were rather negatively than positively virtuous—it was rather *want* of temptation than *power* to resist. If such a character as Alcibiades was less dangerous in Greece than he would be in modern Italy, it was only because opportunity was less frequent, or woman was less attractive. From the writings of comic poets we should not form high estimate of morals of Athenian women, either married or unmarried. Seclusion is but a sorry substitute for intelligence and liberty. Lock and key are but poor guaranties of the chastity of woman—virtuous principle, fortified by mental culture, is best guardian of connubial fidelity, when woman, the equal of man, enjoys his entire confidence and love, in possession of a full liberty, which but the more attaches her to her family and fireside, where she feels that she is the true divinity.

6. *Courtesans?* So far we have been speaking of Athenian women of the better classes. There was a class of females in Greece called *hetæræ*, (ἑταιραι,) or female friends, usually translated *courtesans*, who deserve particular mention, from their character and influence. These women were highly accomplished; that education which was denied the woman of character was bestowed on the *hetæra;* she was taught to sing, dance, play upon the lyre, blow the single and double flute. One or two of these were generally present at the entertainments, and amused and delighted company by their performances. They cultivated powers of conversation, improved their minds in every particular, and endeavored to make themselves fit companions for most intelligent of

the Greeks; *e. g.*, Aspasia was the mistress and companion of Pericles, with intellect highly cultivated; even Socrates himself confessed that he was charmed by her conversation; Plato says she was the author of a celebrated funeral oration which Pericles delivered, and which Mitford has pronounced unrivalled. Thus, whilst modest and unlettered housewife sank into oblivion, the hetæra became subject of history; her birth was object of curiosity; her fortunes were traced; her bon mots and sallies of wit were noted; and, when she died, a monument sometimes was placed over her.

7. *Extraordinary reputation of distinguished courtesans?* A modern can scarcely comprehend the eclat which sometimes attended the career of the hetæra, unless indeed the applauses and money lavished on a Taglione or an Ellsler might help to explain it. "Have you heard of the new beauty that is training by Apelles?" write sisterhood of Corinth to their friends in Athens. "Oh, prodigious ignorance, if you have yet to hear of it! There is but one woman in Greece, and Lais carries all before her. Lais is the theme of the perfumer's shop. Lais is the talk of the theatres. In the ecclesia, in the courts of justice and in the senate-house, nothing is heard but Lais. In all places, and among all descriptions of persons, nothing but Lais. The very dumb nod to one another the praises of her beauty, and Lais is a tongue to those who possess not the power of speech."

The political influence of the hetæra was sometimes very great. Pericles was accused, and perhaps with reason, of listening to the counsels of Aspasia. At time of Xerxes' invasion, more than one Grecian city was brought over to Persian side by influence of Thargelia, a distinguished courtesan, who afterwards became queen of Thessaly. (M. 2. 282.) The celebrated Phryne became so wealthy that she offered to rebuild the walls of Thebes. This woman, although of very low origin, had great public spirit.

8. *Virtues and vices of this class.* Sometimes possessed great benevolence, and sustained their peculiar relations with devoted attachment. Aspasia was sincerely loved by Pericles, and as far as we know she was exclusively attached to him. Meneclides, in a letter to his friend, Euthycles, on the death of Bacchis, a courtesan, shows most devoted love. "She is gone; the beautiful Bacchis is no more. Never, never shall I forget her. What feeling, what sensibility, what humanity she possessed!" "You remember that Mede, who lately landed here from Syria, his pomp and his retinue; you have heard too of his ostentatious promises and offers to Bacchis: eunuchs, maid-servants, dress and finery —nothing was to equal her establishment. To his great indignation, and despite of it, she would not admit the prodigal promiser. She pre-

ferred reposing under my little every-day mantle; and, satisfied with my sparing and humble presents, she spurned the satrap and his splendid donations. The Egyptian merchant and his mountains of silver fared no better. Never, surely, was there so excellent a creature," &c.

These women, however, often plundered their lovers to greatest possible extent, and became deeply corrupt; *e. g.*, Petale writes to her lover, Simalion, who used to tell her he had spent night in tears, when he had nothing to give her, "Would to heaven that one of my profession could support her establishment on tears; I might then live in splendor, for you have an inexhaustible fountain. But, alas! we must have other accompaniments—money, dress, equipage, attendants. One whole year I have devoted to poverty and you. During that time not one single box of perfume has crossed my eyes, and my head is perfectly dry; as for the old tattered Tarentine mantle, 'sdeath! I feel my cheeks burn whenever I appear in it. What! have you no such thing as a drinking cup at home? Is your mother without jewels; has your father no little bills or bonds, *on which you can lay your hands?*" Of course a profession like that of the courtesan would be liable to great reverses. She who habitually breaks the great moral law, in one or two particulars, is but too apt ultimately to throw off its whole restraint and become abandoned. Latter part of the life of Lais, already mentioned as filling all Greece with her fame, illustrates this observation. She became at last the mark for the coarsest ribaldry, a "slut and wine-bibber;" her only care to supply the cravings of appetite—"to eat, drink, masticate and tipple." She who, in the days of her youth and freshness, was said to be as inaccessible as the proudest satrap of Persia, became at last "companion to the common streets."

"Want her who will, a stater, a three obol piece,
Or a mere draught of wine brings her to hand."—(L. Q. 22. 201.)

We can now see why many of these hetæræ, in a place like Athens, should obtain nicknames which would stick to them through life; *e. g.*, Lais was called the *hatchet*, because of her severity in exacting price of her favors; Gnathæna was called the *cistern;* Nico was called the *she goat;* Callisto *the sow*, and her mother *the crow*, &c.

9. *Low state of female education in Greece—main cause of the profession of the hetæra?* Whenever the virtuous woman is secluded and uneducated, in a country as intellectual as Greece, she ceases to be a fit companion for man. His home becomes a place of *ennui*, and is deserted for the public places and houses of entertainment. The hetæra in her splendid establishment formed a resource for those who found no pleasures at home. "By means of wives," says Demosthenes, in his oration for Neæra, "we become the fathers of legitimate children, and

maintain faithful guardians for our houses, the hetæra was meant to promote the enjoyment of life." Man naturally wishes most ardently for the sympathies of the opposite sex—woman's praise has inspired a large proportion of the noble achievements which have been accomplished in this world. Hence the great moral beauty of those matrimonial connections where the woman can comprehend the whole character of her husband, and sympathize with him in all the vicissitudes of his fortunes. How touchingly has Pliny described his intelligent wife, and the solicitude which she manifested in his pleadings at the bar—it is this that constituted the great charm in the wife of Peter the Great, and made Mrs. Sheridan so suitable a companion for her husband. But in Greece, at the period now under review, no great man had wife with those qualities which could enable her to comprehend the individual with whom she was united; he met not with that sympathy which he so much coveted in the female bosom. Under such circumstances can we wonder that a man like Pericles, harassed and worn down by the toils of government, should turn from the legitimate companion of his bosom to her whose whole soul was attuned in unison with his—who had a mind to comprehend, and a heart that could beat responsively to his. The hetæra of Greece, therefore, must ever be regarded as a melancholy memorial of that corruption which must ever result from that injustice to woman which would systematically degrade her, by neglecting her mental culture.

10. *Love of ideal beauty generated by the fine arts had some influence in producing the hetæræ?* No people ever enjoyed the contemplation of so many splendid models of female beauty, as the Athenians did in their public places. The chisel of the sculptor and the brush of the painter had filled the city with forms, on which the Athenian could gaze till the mind became "dazzled and drunk with beauty." This was constantly leading the mind to the contemplation of that ideal excellence which existed in the mind of the artist. It produced a distaste for the ordinary specimens of female form and accomplishment; and it is supposed that Grecian women were not generally handsome. Nothing could satisfy, therefore, the fastidious taste of the Greek but beauty of an *artistic* character, such as was met with in the hetæra, who, to exquisite form and feature added all the accomplishments that art could bestow to render her fascinations complete. The hetæra of Greece was, to the admirer of the beautiful, just what Fanny Ellsler now is, to the admirer of graceful movements, each endeavoring to realize the beau ideal in her peculiar department; while the modern *danseuse* exhibits to our view the very *poetry* of motion—the ancient hetæra endeavored to realize the poet's dream about the queen of beauty.

11. *Example of Pericles, and its influence?* It is supposed that example of so great a man as Pericles gave to the hetæræ of Greece a countenance and support which wore away the little odium still attached to them. Certain it is that the first men in Greece were proud of the acquaintance and notice of Aspasia, and thus, by losing its deformity, this vice appeared to lose its guilt.

12. *Advantages which the law gave to virtuous woman over the hetæra?* In spite of all the fascinations of the hetæra, the Greek could not but feel the advantages of chastity in the mother of his children, with an intensity sufficient to make him guard by law her predominant rights. Greeks had intense love of country, and, to be citizen of such a state as Athens, was an honor which kings even coveted, but none but the descendants of Athenian women were entitled to citizenship, the hetæra of foreign origin was not, and the native Athenian, the moment she became a courtesan, lost it, and ranked, as to rights, with the wife or daughter of a metic or sojourner in Athens. She was, moreover, obliged to wear dress of a particular kind, not to wear certain ornaments; she was excluded from the services and sacrifices of the temple; all the great objects of Athenian ambition too were closed against the son of such a mother, no matter who might be the father. And thus did the law attempt to compensate for the great wrong which custom had inflicted on the virtuous portion of the sex in Greece.

13. *Habits of the Athenians?* Rose generally at daybreak—spent short time in devotion—soon after six in the morning the *dicasts* took their seats on the tribunals, and those employed in agriculture, commerce and manufactures went to work at 12, refreshed themselves with short sleep, then spent few hours in hunting, or in exercise of the Palæstra, or in walking through the delightful groves on banks of the Illyssus and Cephisus, or still more frequently in discussing in the Agora the interests of the state, conduct of magistrates, news of the day, &c. They sometimes filled up a leisure hour before dinner by playing at κυβεια and πεττεια, the first of which resembled hazard, and the second either backgammon or chess. (L. 2, 23, 269.)

14. *Meals?* Three meals usually taken. First called by Greeks ακρατιϛμα—answers to our breakfast, and was taken immediately after rising. Very light—usually bread dipped in wine. Second, the αριϛτον, or luncheon, taken about mid-day—an informal meal. Third, the Δειπνον, answering to our dinner, and the Roman *cœna*, taken about sunset. Homer describes guests always as *sitting* at table, but in later times it was usual to *recline* on couches: except as to women or children, who more generally sat. Two usually reclined on one couch, (κλινε,) each upon left arm, with the right free. At a banquet, given

by Attaginus of Thebes, to fifty Persians and fifty Greeks, one Persian and one Greek reclined on each couch. (Deip. 320.) Somewhat similar to the feast of middle ages, where the knight and his lady-love ate off the same plate. Before the guests reclined, their shoes were taken off and feet washed by slaves. A table or tripod, with provisions on it, was placed before each couch, somewhat in the style of a French restaurant. In eating, Greeks used their fingers altogether, except in eating soups they used a spoon or a piece of bread hollowed out. They wiped their fingers on pieces of bread, called *απομαγδαλιαι*; and it is on bread that had been wiped on that Aristophanes makes one of his dicasts to subsist.

15. *Food?* Bread, cheese, fruits, beef, mutton, hog's and goat's flesh, principal articles of food in Homeric age. Meat was roasted in very large pieces; *e. g.*, at marriage feast of Hermione, Menelaus commences by taking in his hands the *side of roasted ox*, and placing it before his friends. Many sorts of wine too were in use—some of Nestor's was eleven years old. (Deip. 319.) Hercules, who understood, no doubt, art of putting himself into what we call *condition*, fed solely on *beef and green figs.*

Herbs, pottage, salt fish, a barley cake, a bottle of wine and figs for a dessert, formed the repast of the common Athenians in the days of the democracy. Of course a more sumptuous provision would appear on the tables of the rich, though the number of dishes was fewer than upon the tables of the wealthy in Rome. The frumenty, a sort of soft cake prepared of wheat, and the wheaten or barley bread, were the most common farinaceous preparations. Vegetables most used were *mallows*, lettuces, cabbages, beans, lentils, &c. Pork was most favorite animal food, as among Romans—sausages were much used.

Plato remarks that Homer's heroes never ate fish. In later time fish were in highest repute of all kinds of food. This taste was a passion instead of an appetite; and eels were considered most delicious of fish. The worst thing which one epicure could wish of another was, that there might be Copaic eels in market, and all sold before he arrived. This eel said to rank among fish in estimation of epicures, as Helen among women with amatory poets. Not to wonder that *fishmonger* was one of the most important characters in Athens. Lynceus of Samos wrote a book, teaching art of making fishmongers tractable and civil. They were great politicians too. When Aristophanes raises the cry, *a tyranny on foot! the democracy in danger!* he puts it in the mouth of the fishmonger, and the herb-woman whose stall supplied the fish sauce of the day. (L. 2, 23, 262.) Antiphanes declared that a fishmonger had same effect on him as Gorgon's head—that he became a petrifaction and not a man at bare sight of one of them. The ancients were remarkable for their sauces; though not quite so numerous as the French, which are estimated at *four-score.*

16. *Cooking and preparing the food?* Memorable dinner given by classical doctor in Peregrine Pickle has produced aversion to ancient cookery. D'Israeli, however, says their cooking must have been superior to ours, since they could make dainties out of tough membraneous parts of *matrices* of a sow, and the flesh of young hawks and young asses. If a modern prize ox would surprise a Roman or a Greek, we should be equally surprised at prodigious pains which they bestowed in fattening some of the smaller animals, *e. g.*, Pliny says that one man studied the art of fattening snails till some were so large as to have shells holding several quarts; goose was fattened so as to have enormous liver; their peacocks were stuffed; the most exquisite hog flesh was fattened on whey and figs; flesh of young foxes fed on grapes is praised by Galen; and the great doctor, Hippocrates, thought flesh of *puppies* equal to that of birds. (3, 204.) Hired cooks carried art to most whimsical perfection, *e. g.*, serving up a pig roasted on one side and boiled on the other, without having been split. Sometimes by mixtures could give to vegetables the taste of fish or meat, *e. g.*, King of Bithynia had longing for small fish, called *aphy.* His cook cut a turnip to the shape of one, then cooked it with a number of ingredients so as to deceive the nice palate of the monarch. D'Israeli says the English are the greatest gorgers of mere animal food in the world; that the art of preparing vegetables, pulse and roots may be said to be scarcely known to them, and even the peasant, for want of this skill, sometimes treads under foot the finest food. Same remark applicable to our own country.

Ancient cook master of his profession—considered himself judge of individual character, and often prepared his dishes to suit; *e. g.*, Athenæus, in his work on cookery, introduces a cook descanting on the metaphysics of his trade; for young man in love, he would prepare scuttle fish and crabs, with exquisite cordials filtered—for the philosopher, a *voracious animal*, he would prepare solid ham and bulky feet—for the financier, with costly niceness, the rare glociscus—for old men, with more insensible palate, he would put much mustard in their dishes, and provide the stimulating sauces to lash the lazy blood through their veins. (210.) Certain cooks had great reputation through Greece in certain departments; *e. g.*, in the culinary Pleiades, Agis of Rhodes excels all Greece in *broiling* fish. Aphonetus, in making *sausages and hog's pudding.* Nereus, the Chion, *boiled a conger eel*, in manner to satisfy the gods. Ariston was pre-eminent in laying out the contributions to a club feast, &c. (L. 2, 23, 270.)

17. *Athenians at dinner?* The Greeks had great horror of what the French call the *diner d'ami*, *the family dinner*, which it said always draws from an Englishman's cellar his oldest bottle of wine, and from his heart his oldest story. "Defend me," says Menander,

"From family repasts,
"Where all the guests claim kin—nephews and uncles,
"And aunts and cousins, to the fifth remove," &c.

Most common kind of entertainments were the club or picnic parties, where each man contributed his share of eatables, or subscribed so much money to undertaker who provided the feast. Richer Athenians, however, often gave entertainments at which only a few were generally present. It used to be a sort of maxim with elegant Romans, never to have at a dinner party a number less than the *graces*, nor more than the *muses.* The Athenians allowed greater number than this, though a special law forbade more than 30. It was expected that the guests should come dressed with more than ordinary care, and have bathed and perfumed themselves just before starting. Hence, Plato tells us, when Socrates was going to dine at Agathon's he both *washed and put on his shoes*, things which he seldom did.

At dinner the Greeks indulged to excess both in eating and drinking—dinner was brought in very hot, particularly the fish, and epicures sometimes resorted to means to harden their hands and mouths; *e. g.* Philoxenus used to confess that in hot bath he held his hands in hot water, and gargled it in his throat, that he might be able to devour hottest dishes. "He is an oven, not a man," exclaimed a grumbling fellow-guest. (D. 3. 215.) Pithillius, it seems the most eminent of gluttons, guarded his hands against heat by finger stalls, and encrusted his tongue with an armor, which has puzzled the learned not a little. *To drink like a Greek* became a proverb. They sat long at table and drank deep. "Long may you live" was salutation to the person who drank off a large cup without taking breath. We are assured that three officers were elected in Athens, whose business it was to attend entertainments and see that each one drank his portion. From excesses in eating and drinking Greeks were often made sick, and hence the frequent call for the physician on those occasions. But ancient dinners were no sinecures, either bodily or intellectually—to touch a lute, to bear a part in a catch or scolium, to enliven the board, to narrate a fable or tell a tale similar to those found in the old Fabliaux, were among the lighter contributions to a Greecian feast. Hence at the club feast, those who could amuse the company were not contributors in money or provisions. These termed ασυμβολοι, among whom were placed poets, singers, &c. At the entertainments of private individuals, those who could amuse often went uninvited; *e. g.*, in the Xenophontic banquet Philip, *the jester*, goes without invitation. Besides these lighter intellectual amusements they sometimes entered into disquisitions on grave and philosophical subjects, especially when such men as Socrates were present.

18. *Four banquets?* History has brought down to us a particular account of four banquets: one described by Plutarch, one by Aristophanes, one by Plato, and the fourth by Xenophon. That by Plutarch is in time of Solon, given by Periander, king of Corinth, at which seven wise men of Greece were all present. There are women at this banquet, who are neither flute-players nor dancers; they are silent at dinner, and retire as soon as the *large goblet* begins to circulate. Anacharsis at his toilet, and his rude locks made decent by Periander's daughter running her fingers through them, (there were no combs,) and this grateful beau all the time talking to her about the diet and *purgations* which his countrymen underwent in sickness, bear a close analogy to the simple manners of Homeric times.

The kings of Egypt and Ethiopia interchange a number of conundrums, and stake whole villages and towns on the success of these little problems, and the wise men now and then clubbed together for a solution when the royal heads were incompetent. (L. 2, 24, 423.)

We will pass over banquet of Aristophanes, described in one of his comedies, for purposes of burlesque, to the Platonic and Xenophontic banquets, so interesting to us, because both introduce a *convivial* Socrates. Former given by Agathon, the successor of Euripides, in commemoration of the success of his first tragedy—principal characters present—Pausanias, Phœdrus, beautiful pupil of Socrates, Aristophanes, Alcibiades and Socrates. Socrates makes more preparation than usual, saying that, "to a handsome man's house I make it a point to go in the handsomest manner"—took the liberty of carrying his friend Aristodemus, although not invited—as soon as Socrates had introduced his friend he took seat by Agathon, the handsomest man in company; for, if possible, he always sat by handsomest man. Supper ending, Pausanias proposes, as company had suffered by a preceding debauch, that each one should be allowed to drink as he chose; proposition defended by Eryximachus, a physician, with professional reasoning—passed. Except as to Socrates—all one to him whether he drank *gallons* or *nothing*. A second resolution dismissed the female flute player, so as to leave gentlemen alone. Conversation at Greek table not interchange of casual thoughts, but discussion of some topic. Love is proposed—each one gives his opinion on this subject in succession—not to wonder before all had finished that *love* had been treated in every way, mythically, politically, historically, physically, metaphysically, enigmatically, scientifically, poetically, sophistically. Socrates of course makes a labored display, at times a little mystical. His interrogatory style of handling topics reminds one of the ventriloquist, who furnishes a set of speakers out of himself; his, however, was the crack speech of the company.

Aristophanes was about to explain something, when there is violent knocking at door, caused by Alcibiades, with a female fluter and a company of revellers, asking for admission to crown Agathon—it was granted, and Socrates was then seated between the two beautiful men, Agathon and Alcibiades. Hard drinking now commences. Alcibiades, already intoxicated, leads the way by tossing off a flagon of nearly seven pints, and Socrates follows. A revel then begins; as the scene heightens the prudent physician and one or two others sneak off. Socrates, Agathon, Aristophanes, towards day, are still swallowing large potations, but the two last fall asleep before sunrise, and Socrates, after having seen them all out, rises with his little Boswell (Aristodemus) to pass through the ordinary routine of the day, as if *nothing had happened.*

In the works of Plato, body is always subordinate to mind; in those of Xenophon they are on a par; former was a closet student, latter was a soldier as well as scholar. Plato's banquet celebrates a triumphant tragedy, Xenophon a victory gained in wrestling. Hero of Xenophon's banquet is a young *pancratist*, patronized by the wealthy Callias, who gives the feast. Account of the effect of the beauty of Autolycus on the company gives some idea of the Grecian admiration of beauty. His appearance, says Xenophon, was like brilliant phenomenon in the heavens at night. Every eye was turned on him, and none gazed without feeling a perturbation of soul. In some it interrupted speech, in others it caused fidgety restlessness, and continual change of position. A modern could well understand all this if it had been a woman instead of a man, *Autolyca* instead of *Autolycus.* Supper dispatched and tables removed, libation of wine to the gods succeeds, and a pæan is sung to Apollo; then enters a Syracusan with a company, among whom are a female fluter and dancer, and beautiful boy who can play on the cithara. These regale the company with music, dance, songs, juggling tricks, and with sword-diving, *i. e.*, springing in and out of circle formed with swords, sharp points upwards. Socrates ever and anon complimenting the banquet for regaling so many of the senses, besides the palate. Afterwards comes the intellectual part. Each has to tell on what he most valued himself. Callias begins by taking ground on power he has of making fellow-creatures better by giving money. Niceratus (son of Micias) valued himself most on his memory; could repeat whole Iliad and Odyssey by heart. Critobulus prided himself on his beauty. Antisthenes, who had not an obol in his pocket, on wealth (of course mental). Charmides boasted of his poverty. While Socrates, drawing up his countenance very much to the amusement of the company, pompously declared that *his* talent lay in *pimping*, &c. Elaborate reasons given for most of these opinions. During these explanations, Critobulus pronounces his master, Socrates, uglier than any of those fantastic persons, who, in the satiric drama, were represented as companions of Bacchus. Socrates, instead of getting mad, offers to contest the palm of beauty with Critobulus himself, and they agree to make the flute and cithara players the umpires. Judgment in favor of Critobulus, in spite of the ingenious argument of Socrates. Socrates appears to have been a sort of *butt* at this entertainment; for, besides this attack of Critobolus, Antisthenes rallied him about his wife, Xantippe, and the Syracusan spouted to him from the "Clouds" about the flea's hop, &c.

After this, female in character of Ariadne, is introduced, then comes Bacchus fuddled—a dally between these two not a very decent scene; and shortly after the company break up.

19. *Platonic and Xenophontic banquets a sort of high comedy?* Because regulated by canons somewhat like those for comedy—a little buffoonery at the commencement—a strong view taken of some important political or moral subject in the middle, and a revelry almost amounting to *ruffianism* of enjoyment towards the end. (L. 2, 24, 441.) These two banquets, sketched by fancy of Socrates' great disciples, have made many doubt whether Socrates could have been what the moderns would call a *gentleman*. A writer of great ability in London Quarterly insists he was not, and that his manners must have been such as to shut him out of the first society even in Athens. However waggish he may be represented, and however large his potations may have been without affecting him, his philosophy and morals are nevertheless of a very superior character in his remarks at the banquets. And he seems to have been what we would call in convivial phraseology the *life and soul* of the company. He is evidently the convivial hero at both the banquets.

SEC. IX.—EXTERNAL AND INTERNAL CONDITION OF ATHENIAN DEMOCRACY AFTER PERSIAN WAR.

In order to understand the causes which produced the decline and downfall of the Grecian republics, we must again advert to the position of Athens after the Persian war.

1. *Athenian Hegemony?* Before the Persian war Sparta was the most powerful and perhaps the most renowned of the Grecian

states; and although her conduct, during that war, was often tardy, and sometimes disgraceful, yet she was generally permitted to take the principal station in the Grecian confederacy. Athens, however, by universal consent, was acknowledged the most efficient power against Persia. To her was due the great victories at Marathon and Salamis; she inspired the confederates with courage and constancy; she furnished the heads that could plan as well as the arms that could execute; she became to Greece what Greece was to rest of world, an eminently *naval* power. The history of Greece had been always linked with the sea. Homer draws up his armies on the sea-shore; it is by seaside, and in solemn act of purification by its waters, that first movements of the army take place; it is by side of far-sounding sea that Chryses addresses his sad prayer to Apollo for vengeance; it is from ocean's bosom that Thetis rises like a mist to dispel the sorrows of her warlike son. The 2d book of the Iliad, containing the long catalogue of Grecian ships, was always the most delightful to the Grecian reader. Now what the sea was to the old Greek generally, it became to Athens in after times more particularly—she was the great freebooter of the Grecian seas—it was the element that suited her character; it was on the sea that she first checked the proud Persian; it was on the sea that she nourished her democratic spirit and her commercial enterprise; it was on the sea that she acquired that ascendency which placed her above her ancient rival, and gave to her the first station in Greece. Such had been her services in the Persian war, that by universal consent she was permitted to enjoy the *hegemony*, or controlling direction of the confederacy of the demoratic states.

2. *Common treasury, and its removal to Athens?* During the Persian war and afterwards it became necessary to have a common treasure, to which all the allies contributed for purpose of forwarding the war. As Athens did most, she would have naturally most control over this common purse. But it was owing to the character of one man that its complete control was unwisely surrendered to her, and the case stands forth a prominent example of the importance of resisting the first step of usurpation, particularly when the usurper wields his power so beneficially and equitably as to lull all apprehension. It was owing to confidence, inspired by stern integrity and justice of Aristides, that the allies agreed to surrender into hands of Athens the management and direction of the common treasury; it was to her that was given by common consent the exclusive appointment of the directors of this treasury, called Hellenotamiæ, (Ἑλληνοταμιαι.) The amount of the contribution was at first fixed by Aristides at 460 talents,* and was distri-

* As the Athenian coins will often be mentioned, well to subjoin in a note the

buted among the parties with such impartiality as to give universal satisfaction, and to obtain for him the appellation of the *just*. The treasure was first deposited at Delos, the place of meeting for discussion of common interests of Greece. Afterwards, on the proposal of the Samians, it was transferred to Athens, and thus placed completely in Athenian hands.

3. *Tyranny exercised by the Athenians over their allies?* Political philosopher might well have predicted the consequences of intrusting Athens with the imposition of tribute on her allies, and its exclusive management when collected. The *tax-layer* being separate from the *tax-payer*, of course it became the interest of the former to assess the tax as high as possible, in order that the highest profit might be derived from the disbursement. Does not belong to human nature to be just for any length of time in the position occupied by Athens. This league soon became the *Societas Leonina*, in which Athens of course played the lion's part. By means of this common treasury allies were compelled to become servile instruments of Athenian aggrandizement. The principle was maintained at Athens that she was not bound to give an account of the disbursements. Athenians practised on the principle that stronger might command the weaker. The refractory allies were forced into compliance. Nothing more prominent in the administration of Pericles than distrust of the allies. Sixty Athenian triremes cruised about Grecian seas whole year round to keep the allies faithful; and citizens did duty on board by rotation. Allies regarded the rapidity of their movements with a sort of superstitious terror. Athenians became daily more overbearing and insolent. When Pericles took direction of affairs, Athens had not extended her authority over the surrounding states; but before Peloponnesian war her empire was established over her allies, and many were reduced to absolute subjection. Aristophanes, in the Knights, puts down the subject states in round numbers at 1000. The tribute money, too, which Aristides fixed at 460

account of them by Bockh. (Econ. Athen.) In Attica, and most of Greece, *talent* contained 60 minæ, the mina 100 drachmas, the drachma 6 oboli. Down to the half obol the coins were silver. As to value of the talent there has been variety of opinions, owing to fact that it varied in weight and fineness; the earlier talents being rather heavier than the later. Bockh rates the Attic drachma at 65 troy grains of pure silver, nearly equal to 9⅜d. sterling. Whence the mina amounts to £4 0*s.* 6¾*d.*, and the talent to £241 13*s.* 4*d.*, about $1160, putting the pound sterling at $4 80. We must remember that silver was relatively much dearer in ancient times than at the present day, a multiple of 3 or 4 being required to convert ancient values in to modern, same weight and fineness—this rule would make the Attic talent estimated in our money about $4640 by the latter multiple, or $3480 by the former.

talents, was rapidly increased, until at last, by the advice of Alcibiades, it was raised to 1300. In some instances whole cities and districts were stripped of their possessions, and the land parcelled out into portions called *cleruchias*, held by citizens or colonists sent out from Athens, called *cleruchi*. Such was the treatment of Naxos and Eubœa, and, at a later period, of Mytilene. (W. 2, 102.)

4. *Liturgies?* But while Athenian democracy oppressed the allies, the government was no less formidable to the rich at home. One means of practising this oppression was by the liturgies, which were a sort of extraordinary taxation, by which certain burthens were thrown off the common treasury upon individuals of wealth. These were of two classes—one for the promotion of the pleasures of the people, the other for the exigencies of state; the first called regular or *encyclic*, including expenses of theatre, games, sacred missions, festivals, &c.; namely, the Choregia, Gymnasiarchy or Lampedarchia, Architheoria and Hestiasis, or feasting of the tribes, were compulsory on all who possessed property to the amount of three talents. But these expenses fell on the rich individuals of each tribe in regular rotation, except when voluntarily undertaken by individuals out of turn. (Her. 323.)

The *Trierarchy* was most important of second class of liturgies. Under the old system there was a classification of the people into 48 divisions, called naucrariæ, subsequently increased to 50, each of which furnished a vessel for public service. As naval power of Athens increased, this provision became inadequate to public wants; and then the custom arose for the *strategi*, or military commanders, to name annually, from among the richest, as many as were required to act as trierarchs, each being compelled to equip a trireme, and keep it in constant repair—the state furnishing the *hull* of the vessel and the pay for the crew. Subsequently two persons might combine to furnish one trireme, as was allowed in case of Choregia. At last the institution of the *Symmoriæ* arose; according to which 1200 of the wealthiest citizens were saddled with whole expense of the trierarchy—to which end they were divided first into 20 symmoriæ, and each symmoria into *synteliæ*, each containing at most 16 members, and bound to equip a vessel, though at less expense than formerly, for the state furnished the rigging.

Whenever any of the above expenses were furnished by an individual, he had all the honor which could accrue from it; *e. g.*, he was either the commander of the trireme, or could appoint the commander at his pleasure; and, in case of the theatre or festival, the splendor of the fête always insured reputation to the donor. Hence, as long as these expenses were incurred by individuals, such was the emulation excited, that it rather required the intervention of law to limit than to stimulate the generosity of each. But the institution of the symmoriæ had a decidedly injurious influence on naval architecture, and on the general equipment of the fleets; for when the syntelia, a club of 16 or less, furnished a trireme, they would naturally endeavor to build and equip at the cheapest rate, entirely regardless of the welfare of the state. Demosthenes at last had a law passed requiring every ten talents of wealth to furnish a trireme, so that individuals not possessing that amount clubbed until the amount was reached, and thus the tax became general. (Her. 324.)

5. *Exemplification from one of the speeches of Lysias?* In the 21st speech of that celebrated lawyer, put in the mouth of his client, he endeavors to recommend himself by an enumeration of his services to the commonwealth. His first appointment was as choregus to the tragedy—expense 30 minæ—three months after, at Thargelia, he exhibited a male troop, which won the victory—cost, 2000 drachmæ. In archonship of Glaucippus, at great festival of Minerva, he exhibited troop of dancers in arms—800 drachmæ. In same archonship a male troop at festival of Bacchus—victorious—including a tripod dedicated on the occasion—5000 drachmæ. In archonship of Diocles at lesser festival, a troop to dance around the altar and sing in a circle, 300 drachmæ. Seven succeeding years had office of *trierarch*—6 talents. In spite of these heavy expenses he made beside, in periods of exigency, two contributions, one of 30 minæ, other of 4000 drachmæ. In archonship of Alexias, having returned home, had the honor of superintending bodily exercises of a chorus, in the festival of Prometheus—gained the victory—12 minæ. Immediately after was choregus to a troop of boys—15 minæ. In archonship of Euclid was choregus to the comedies, employed Cephisodotus as teacher to the troop—victorious—17 minæ—to which add 7 minæ for troop of beardless dancers, at the lesser Panathenæa. In naval contest at Sunium his vessel gained victory—15 minæ. Besides all this, his offices as leader of a sacred embassy (*Architheorus*), as Arrephorist, &c., all cost more than 30 minæ. (L. 2. 26, 257.)

6. *The liturgies of Greece bear close analogy to the forced loans and contributions, under the name of benevolences, which modern potentates have sometimes had recourse to?* During the reign of Edward IV., and afterwards under the Tudors, rich individuals were singled out, and required to contribute to the government according to their means. We have heard of the famous *logical fork* of Archbishop Morton, one of the *privy* council of Henry VII. He exacted benevolences from those who lived *extravagantly*, for their opulence was proved by their *style of living;* and also from those who lived *economically*, for

their *economy*, he said, made them rich. In 1545, Henry VIII. had recourse to a general exaction, miscalled benevolences. The commissioners for the levy are instructed to incite all men to a *loving contribution*, according to their substance—it is intimated that 20 pence in the pound on the yearly value of land, and half that sum on movables, is as little as his majesty can reasonably accept. Commissioners are to use "good words and amiable behavior," to induce men to contribute, and to dismiss the obedient with thanks. They must summon but few to attend at *one time*, and to commence with every one *apart*, "lest some one unreasonable man among so many, forgetting his duty towards his God, his sovereign and his country, may go about by his malicious frowardness to silence all the rest, be they never so well disposed."

Lord Herbert has recorded case of one Richard Reid, an alderman of London, who refused; it was deemed necessary not to overlook this disobedience. Reid was soon drafted as a soldier to serve in the army, then on the borders of Scotland, at his own expense; and Sir Ralph Ewer, the general, received intimations to employ him on the hardest and most perilous duty, and subject him to the greatest privations—the letter concluding, "finally, you must use him in all things according to the sharp disciplyne militar of the northern wars." Poor Reid was soon taken by the Scots, and his ransom amounted to much more than the benevolence demanded of him. (H. C. H. 1, 33.) The analogy of these benevolences to the liturgies cannot fail to strike every one, and proves the great similarity that will ever exist in arbitrary power, no matter where exercised, whether by numbers or by a despot.

The liturgies of Greece, however, had one decided superiority over benevolences, they conferred distinction on those who sustained them; *e. g.*, he who equipped vessels had a right to command them; he who feasted the tribes, or exhibited spectacles, rendered himself conspicuous, and at the same time popular. Such means as these have always been resorted to by wealthy aspirants for the purpose of obtaining popularity. The law in Athens only rendered that compulsory which ambition is so ready to prompt. It was a sort of legalization of the very policy by which Cymon, in Athens, and the old Duke d'Orleans (*Egalité*), in France, won their popularity. It is for this reason that some have contended that the liturgies in Greece were aristocratic in their tendency, and threw more political power into hands of wealth, than its proper share; they formed the high road to public office.

7. *Similarity of the trierarchy to the famous ship-money under the Stuarts?* It is well known that in the reign of Charles I. the monarch claimed the privilege, in case of necessity, of issuing his writ to London and other sea-port towns, enjoining them at their expense to provide a

certain number of ships of war, of a prescribed tonnage and equipage, empowering them to assess all the inhabitants for a contribution according to their substance. This demand on the sea-port towns bears a close analogy to the liturgy called the trierarchy in Greece. Cities under Charles representing rich individuals among the Greeks. But as the difficulties of Charles increased, he not only directed his writ to the seaport towns, but to the whole kingdom, and of course instead of demanding the ships he called for the equivalent in money. The sheriffs were directed to assess every individual according to their judgment of his means, and to enforce the payment by distress. It was in regard to this ship-money that Hampden stood the celebrated suit for 20 shillings which has immortalized his name.

8. *Antidosis, or exchange of fortunes?* In regard to liturgies, it was possible for any one to throw off his burthen if he could point out a *richer* man, who was free from it, by proposing the *antidosis*, or exchange of fortunes. Person thus pointed out was obliged in three days to give an inventory of his property; a seal in mean time being placed on his doors, to prevent fraud or evasion. On proof of superior wealth, the denounced was obliged to take the place of his accuser, or to exchange estates with him. Amusing to see the arts practised on such occasions; to witness the keenness with which he who was saddled with the liturgy hunted up a richer man, and the great quickness of memory with which the latter seemed immediately endowed, the long list of debts in which he was suddenly involved, and the kindness of heart which had occasioned them. It was proposition to exchange made by Lysimachas that caused Isocrates to undertake third of the three trierarchies performed by him; and in similar manner a liturgy was imposed on Demosthenes.

9. *Athenian courts?* Have already seen that Athenians, after obtaining *hegemony* of Greece, soon decreed that all the principal lawsuits of the allies should be tried in their courts. Constitution of these courts exceedingly unfavorable to impartial justice. The *jurors* or *dicasts* for the trial of causes amounted in all to 6000 persons, being citizens above age of 30, selected annually by the nine archons and their secretary, probably 600 from each tribe. They were called *Heliasts* from *Heliæa*, the place of assembly. They were formed into 10 divisions, complement of each division being strictly 500,* although it varied according to circumstances, sometimes diminishing to 200 or 400, whilst at others it was raised to 1000 or 1500, by the union of two or three divisions.

* The other 1000 consequently must have acted as supernumeraries.

Every one to whose lot it fell to serve as a juryman received, after taking the oath, a tablet inscribed with his name and the number of the division to which he was to belong during the year. On the morning of every court day recourse was again had to lots, to decide in which courts the divisions should respectively sit for that day, and the suits of which they should take cognizance, since there were many which could only be decided in certain courts. The number of these courts is uncertain; most of them were in the Agora, and distinguished by numbers and colors. Stones with corresponding marks were handed to the dicasts at the entrance of each court, as symbols of judicial power, and at same time tickets, on presentation of which, after the institution of pay, each one would be entitled to receive his compensation from the treasury. Courts were generally in session except on festival days, and when the popular assembly met. (Her. 265.)

Proceedings before the courts were simple—each party might speak twice, generally the senior first; length of speeches depended on the number of *clepsydræ*, which the magistrate had assigned to each according to importance of the subject—water was stopped only whilst quotations from the laws or other documents were reading.

Judges gave their votes as soon as pleading ended, *without* consultation, by white or black pebbles, or such as were solid or perforated. Equality of votes, as in modern times, was an acquittal. *Appeals*, strictly speaking, were not possible, for the public tribunals were committees of persons representing sovereign power of the state. A reversion of judgment was *sometimes* obtained from the court, where condemned person could prove that his sentence was result of false testimony. Although no appeals could take place from the regular courts, yet complaints could be lodged and suits instituted against officers for misconduct in the discharge of judicial functions. The cases of appeal in Athenian jurisprudence were from decisions of the public *arbiters*, (διαιτηται,) a set of men chosen by lot from the tribes, each above 50 years of age, before whom private suits might be brought for *arbitration*. These διαιτηται were rather arbiters than judges, not a regular court, and hence an appeal lay beyond them to Heliastic courts. (H. 289.)

Besides the *Heliæa* and *Diætetæ*, there were courts or juries chosen from persons of same profession or craft; *e. g.*, breach of military law was tried by court martial, profanation of mysteries by the *initiated*, and the *nautodicæ*, although chosen by lot, was of similar kind, charged with settlement of disputes concerning commerce and navigation. Finally there was a sort of court of rural judges, composed first of 30, afterwards of 40, to decide all petty cases not exceeding 5 drachmæ—

all beyond this amount were sent up to the courts in Athens. (292.) Pericles is supposed to have been the first to institute pay to the dicasts, being one obol per diem, which was afterwards raised by Cleon to three (about 4 pence sterling of modern money).

10. *Character of the administration of justice in Athens?* We can scarcely imagine a judicial system worse calculated for attaining the great end of justice than that of Athens. In first place, the pay which was given to the dicasts had most injurious influence; it was too small to attract any but the poorest; men of standing would naturally shun the juries on which were placed multitudes of the rabble. These last would look to the courts as source of pleasure and profit—the more litigation the more regular the pay. "I sold sausages," says Agoracritus, in the *Knights*, "but I got the best part of my livelihood by judging causes." "If the archon should not order the court to sit to day," says the boy in the *Wasps*, "how are we to have victuals?" "Alas!" answered his father, "I fear we must go supperless." Besides the fixed pay, which was small, there was the hope of bribes, which might be large. Again, fine and confiscation, ordinary punishments of the Athenian law, conveyed property into the treasury, to be thence distributed in various ways for gratification of the people. This state of things produced first a bias in favor of litigation. The more lawsuits, and the longer they were continued, the better the pay; hence the prepossession in favor of the most uncompromising litigant and the man who brought most cases for trial. Again it produced a decided leaning in favor of the prosecution, for every condemnation swelled the public fisk. Life and property were insecure to an extent that would be intolerable to the moderns. Glorious security of the English law, requiring sanction of grand jury to the merit of an accusation before a man can be brought to trial, was unknown at Athens. Any man could accuse, and the archon was bound by his office to bring the accused to trial. The glorious privilege of the *habeas corpus* was unknown, and when the cause came before the jury there was no right of challenge to guard against partiality.

The great number on the juries, too, had a tendency to destroy that responsibility, and the salutary influence of public opinion, which would have operated on smaller bodies. It gave undue pride and self-importance to the lowest classes, and organized a sort of agrarian spirit in the courts—"We are as great as kings," says an old dicast—"the principal men of the commonwealth watch our rising in the morning. Presently one of those who have embezzled money approaches me, bows humbly, and begs favor. If ever you yourself, in any office, or even in the management of a military mess, robbed your companions, pity me.

He stands trembling before me as if I was a god." Besides all this, these large irresponsible *mob* juries could never have really business habits; the dicast liked to be amused whilst deciding causes; he went into court as a man does to a spectacle. This fostered habit of viewing judicial business as pastime. In their best moods Athenians came to hearing of a cause, as they would take their seats at theatre to compare compositions of rival poets—more dazzled by eloquence than they were careful of justice.

11. *Sycophants?* The tyranny of numbers bears a strong analogy to that of one man—a system of espionage will be sure to exist under both. Where justice is administered as at Athens, the profession of *sycophancy* arises as a matter of course. The rapacious appetite for confiscations and fines will be catered for by those who will make a business of hunting up the game. Sycophancy was a trade at Athens. The sycophants or informers counted the lowest people, and became the terror and scourge of the rich. They singled out generally the opulent citizens of timid natures and quiet habits, and threatened them with prosecutions; to avoid which the accused often paid large sums of money, unless where they could follow the advice of Socrates to his friend Crito, to fight them with their own weapons, that is, by hiring other sycophants to denounce the informers. (M. 4. 25.) The resident aliens were very much exposed to this annoyance. But, above all, the noble and affluent citizens of the subject states had particular reason to tremble at the thought of being dragged before the Athenian tribunals, and were generally anxious to stop the mouths of the sycophants by gold. Even whole states often found it necessary to bribe the sycophant or to purchase the protection of a powerful demagogue, as we know that Cleon was once bribed by some of the islands to relieve them from an extraordinary impost. (T. 4. 226.) It was as dangerous to be rich under the Athenian democracy as under a Turkish despotism. Same subterfuges were used to conceal wealth, the same bribery and flattery to preserve it. In Xenophon's Banquet, Charmides is made to speak in favor of poverty; he had been wealthy, but lost all. "While I lived a rich man," says he, "I had reason to fear the attacks of house-breakers; I was under the necessity of courting the sycophants, knowing it was in their power to do mischief which I could not return. I received continually orders from the people to undertake certain expenses for the commonwealth; and I was not allowed to go anywhere out of Attica. But now that I have lost all, I sleep anywhere fearless; I am considered faithful to the government; I am not threatened with prosecutions, but can make others fear; I am a free man, I can stay in the country or go out at pleasure. The rich rise from their seats for me as I approach,

and make way for me as I walk. I am now like a tyrant, whereas before I was an absolute slave. Before I paid tribute to the people, now a tribute from the public maintains me." Proper to remark in regard to this oft-quoted defence of poverty, that, in conclusion, when host asked Charmides if he did not pray that he might never be rich again, he answered no, he was very ready to run the risk.

12. *Exemplification of the maladministration of justice in Athens by the pleadings of the lawyers?* It will be found in the forensic speeches which have come down to us, that the courts of Athens were not regarded as impartial tribunals sworn to maintain justice, but were actually and avowedly considered by counsel as interested parties, whose claims were never to be disregarded. And hence we find arguments and considerations urged on the courts implying a state of things which would be considered as intolerable in modern times. The celebrated orator, Lysias, whom we have before introduced, belonged to democratic party, and therefore his speeches may well be taken as evidence against the courts. You see him constantly urging in behalf of his client, that the people will gain nothing by his condemnation; *e. g.*, "should you confiscate the property of Timotheus, it is only in the view of some *extraordinary benefit* to the city that such a measure can be *recommended.*" In defence of man accused of bribery, he makes his client say, "None of you can doubt that I shall make a better steward than they who administer your finances. If you deprive me of this property, you will not enrich yourselves; you will only give up this fund to be squandered like every other. You had much better give me yours than take mine. I have lived with the strictest economy, that I might have more to spend on you, and hold my fortune only to your use." It was powerful argument that public officers embezzled or mismanaged confiscated property, and therefore state lost it; *e. g.*, says Lysias, "If it were seen that the property confiscated by these persons was preserved for the city I could put up with it; but you are well aware that part of it disappears before it is brought to the hammer; and that of the rest, what ought to go for a great price, is sold for a mere trifle." In another place, "So far were these guilty proceedings from commanding a supply of money for the mercenaries, that to the public nothing resulted but hatred and disgrace, while all the benefit merged in the contrivers of the scheme." (L. 2, 26, 265.) But in spite of all this, a deficiency in the revenue was a formidable argument against the accused, and the counsel did not hesitate to speak openly of its influence. Lysias again says, "And this he did with the perfect knowledge, that when the senate have funds *sufficient* they are guilty of no delinquencies; but when these funds *run low* they are compelled to receive accusations, to confiscate

property, and to *give way* to such of the orators as recommend the most infamous proceedings." (Cont. Nicom.) Again, he quotes the language of certain orators, who urged the condemnation of the accused because there was want of money in the treasury—"If you acquit them, observe there is no more money in the military chest, and the mercenaries must go without their pay."

When an individual was condemned and his property confiscated, they often went against the nearest of kin, if it did not hold out to their expectations; *e. g.*, Nicophemus and Aristophanes, father and son, were condemned, and their estates proved less than expected, courts went against the next of kin. Defendant complains the case is hard, that he knew nothing of the affairs of the condemned—how could he answer the items one by one? On such a day, your relative received so much from such a banker or ship owner; what is become of it? At such a time had large fund; where is it? &c. In conclusion, defendant says, "I know how difficult it will be effectually to refute the received opinion of the great riches of Nicophemus. The present scarcity of money in the city, and the wants of the treasury, which the forfeiture has been calculated on to supply, will operate against me." (M. 4. 87.)

Lastly, one powerful consideration, which we find all the orators urging in behalf of their clients, is the liberal manner in which they have performed their liturgies; and this is *openly* pressed as reason why the judges should lean to them in their decisions. An appeal of this kind in fact generally formed the peroration of the Athenian pleader. "Whatever expenses the law enjoined, (says a defendant,) I had defrayed, and more too. Why?—that I might stand higher in your estimation, and that, *in case of any misfortune*, I might stand a trial upon secure grounds." Besides all this, we have abundant evidence that the judges were open to bribery, and that the multitude of the jury was no guaranty against it. "It is now a matter of perfect safety, (says Lysias,) to rob and pillage you. If the delinquents escape discovery they enjoy fearlessly the fruits of their guilt; if detected, they either buy off danger by a part of the theft, or, brought to trial, they possess weight and authority sufficient to force an acquittal." Again, "Should you acquit these men, they will acknowledge no obligation to you—all will be due to their disbursements, and to the money which, originally taken from you, they now lay out in bribes." Once more, "Since that last decree, which passed the ecclesia, I see Ergocles and his companions no longer sparing their money, but buying their very souls from the orators, from their opponents, and from the Prytanes, and carrying corruption in a numerous body of the citizens to boot." In a subsequent speech it was asserted, that on this occasion more than 2000 persons were bribed. The *euphemism* used on such occasions was πειθειν, to persuade, to *make a man understand reason*, &c. (L. 2, 26, 267.)

13. *Heavy fines?* We can now see why fines imposed in Athens were so heavy; it was as much to swell the public treasure, as to promote justice, and few of the popular favorites ever could escape these fines—Miltiades, Themistocles, Aristides, Timotheus, Demosthenes, were all fined at some period of their lives most heavily. The two fines imposed on Miltiades amounted to 80 talents, which his son Cimon paid after his death. Cimon himself was fined 50, and Demosthenes was fined 50 on action for bribery, besides being banished. Pericles himself was fined, what amount is uncertain; and that because he was accused of surrendering the country to the Lacedemonians improperly, and thereby inflicting a severe injury on the owners of the land.* Many of these fines were inflicted for bribery and corruption, and the public officer who oppressed and plundered often found himself obliged to disgorge his ill-gotten wealth by one of these judicial decrees. The following graphic account is scarcely exaggerated. "Wheel within wheel showed the affair of corruption at Athens. The public first robbed the individual (by the liturgies); the individual reimbursed himself from the public; bribery from abroad was allowed to aid peculation at home; the victim's treasures were allowed to swell, till he became ripe for the public orator; and then, through the courts of justice, he drops a full and fattened morsel into the mouth of the insatiable *demus*."

14. *Analogy in this respect between the tyranny of one man and of the multitude?* When that odious engine of despotism, the *star chamber*, was in existence in England, its maladministration of justice made the monarchy of England bear a close analogy to the democracy of Athens. It was a tribunal, says Hallam, which reaped gain from the punishment inflicted, and therefore they "sat, like famished birds of prey, with keen eyes and bended talons, eager to supply for a moment, by some wretch's ruin, the craving emptiness of the exchequer;" and hence the evils became enormous under Charles I., because he always wanted money, and his parliaments would not furnish him; *e. g.*, gentleman of name of Allington was fined £12,000 for marrying his niece. Another £4000 for saying Earl of Suffolk was a base lord, and a like sum was forfeited to the king. Sir David Forbes had to pay £5000 to the king, and £3000 to the party, for opprobrious words against Lord

* On one occasion, when the Lacedemonians invaded Attica, they abstained from injuring the lands of Pericles; and Pericles, who well understood the suspicious temper of the populace, immediately surrendered the lands to the public, in order to stand above suspicion.

Wentworth. Bishop Williams, of Lincoln, once lord keeper, and the man who advanced Laud to public favor, became at last one of Laud's victims. The only charge proved was, that he had received certain letters from one Osbaldiston, master of Westminster school, wherein some contemptuous nickname was used to denote Laud. And although Williams had never divulged these letters, yet was he made to pay £5000 to the king, and £3000 to Laud. Osbaldiston was sentenced to still heavier fine, to be deprived of all his benefices, and to stand in the pillory, before his school in Dean's Yard, with his ears nailed to it. Again, Prynne, a lawyer of great erudition, and a zealous puritan, wrote a large volume, called *Histriomastix*, on the theatre, and was particularly severe against the actresses, likening them to the courtesans on the Roman stage.* Six weeks *after* the publication the queen performed a part in a mask at court. Peter Heylin, by the instigation of Laud, brought Prynne and his big book before the star chamber. He was sentenced to stand twice in the pillory, to be branded in the forehead, to lose both his ears, to pay a fine of £5000, and to suffer perpetual imprisonment. (2, 47, 51.) These are some of the beauties of monarchy, when monarch is not properly restrained, with a miscalled court of justice at his command, each member of which is appointed by himself and responsible to him alone. They bear but too striking a resemblance to the arbitrary exactions practised in the multitudinous courts of the Athenian *demus*. So certain is it that the same temptations will operate alike on all mankind, and that, to have justice impartially administered it is indispensably requisite that the judicial tribunals should have no personal interest in the results.

15. *Regular taxes not oppressive in Athens?* Where all power was practically exercised by the *demus* not to be expected that they would be partial to general taxes, which would operate on the poor, who had a numerical majority in the ecclesia. Direct taxes, and particularly the poll tax, were regarded with great horror. Bockh mentions four sources of ordinary revenue—1st, that arising from public domains and the mines, from the customs and excise, and some taxes on industry and persons, extending only to slaves and aliens; 2d, fines, forfeitures, confiscations, &c.; 3d, tribute of the allies; 4th, the liturgies.

Of these four kinds of taxes only a portion of the first could be regarded in light of a uniform tax on the Athenian people. All the rest exemplify that principle of human nature which will ever make men, whether few or many, with unlimited power in their hands, shift the burthens from their own shoulders upon the defenceless classes, while

* In Prynne's index to this part of the work, he has the unfortunate expression, "women actors notorious whores."

they appropriate the disbursements to their own benefit. In ten years' time we know that Demosthenes' property paid only 2 per cent. tax, while the same property well managed yielded 100 per cent. profit. The mines were the most important part of the public property, and the silver mines of Mount Laurium were the most productive. In Themistocles' time the product was between 30 and 40 talents, but decreased regularly afterwards, till they were shut up, in the time of Strabo. The import and export duties were only 2 per cent. ad valorem, an exceedingly moderate tax, yielding, according to Bockh, some 30 or 36 talents. As regards the μετοικιον, or *protection money* of resident aliens, this was tax of 12 drachmæ a head, upon every alien domiciled in Attica. They were compelled to put themselves under care of guardian or patron, προσατης—had no *persona standi in judicio*, and were in a state of perpetual pupilage. This *metic* tax was exacted with most unmerciful rigor. As we learn from noted example of Xenocrates, a disciple of Plato, and his second successor, in the academy, who, in spite of his philosophy and his exemplary morals, was sold as a slave, for default in the payment of this tax.* Yet, in spite of all these hardships, 10,000 foreigners were computed to be generally in Athens, such was the irresistible fascination of this great capital. The tribute of the allies and the liturgies, particularly the former, were mainly relied on; and even in extraordinary exigences, every shift would be resorted to before a general tax would be recommended; *e. g.*, Thucydides' account of that celebrated speech of Pericles, in which he exhibits his financial budget to the people, and urges them to perseverance in the Peloponnesian war—no direct tax recommended.

16. *Report of Pericles on the ways and means for carrying on the Peloponnesian war?* That the citizens should move with their property from the country to the city; that they should equip the fleet in which they were superior; that they should retain in their hands the affairs of the allies, and keep them to their duty; that the power of Athens depended on the tribute paid by the allies, being then nearly 6,000 talents per annum, besides other revenues; that there were 600 talents in the treasury—there had been 9,700, but a large amount had been spent on the Propylæa of the citadel, and at Potidea. Next comes the extraordinary resources in case of exigency. All the gold and silver that had been deposited in private and public places of deposit, with the sacred vases used in shows or in the games, and the Median spoils, all these he estimates at 500 talents. He added, that much money could be procured from other temples, and, if all this should fail, they

* Demetrius Phalerius bought and emancipated him.

might use the golden ornaments with which the statue of Minerva was adorned, estimated at 400 talents; but this was to be replaced as soon as public safety would allow. In this whole report, the accomplished statesman does not, under any circumstances, recommend recourse to a direct uniform tax on the Athenian population.

17. *Ordinary disbursements?* In examining the disbursements we shall find the writer in the London Quarterly to be about *half* right, when he pronounced Athens a great *mad-house* as well as *poor-house.* Bockh divides the regular expenditures under the following heads: 1, public buildings; 2, police; 3, festivals; 4, donations to the people; 5, pay for certain public services; 6, maintenance of the poor; 7, public rewards; 8, providing arms, ships and cavalry in time of peace. Of those the 1st, 3d, 4th, 6th, 8th, redounded almost exclusively to the benefit of the Athenians and the others mainly. Upon the 1st have already spoken at large, while on subject of sculpture and painting. These public buildings, statues, paintings, &c., could never have been produced by Athenian resources alone; the bare cost of keeping them in repair was enormous. The Pyræus, with its fortifications, the Acropolis, the Docks, &c., were all built and kept up at a most lavish expenditure.

2d. Democracies never have strong police, in the modern sense of the term; every man is considered a sort of police officer, and is bound to guard the public safety. In Athens there was always readiness enough to prosecute, and the city swarmed with sycophants; but a *preventive* police scarcely existed, except as to a city guard, composed of from 300 to 1,200 public slaves, who lived in tents in the market place, and afterwards on the Areopagus, and kept watch and ward over the peace of society.

3d. Public festivals caused prodigal expenditure. Splendid pageantry of the procession and the chorus, the decorations of the temple, the music and the gymnastic games, the intellectual pleasures and the scenic pomp of the theatre, the sacrificial banquets, at which whole hecatombs were slaughtered, costly perfumes that smoked on the altars, golden crowns and tripods bestowed on victors at the games, such the items of luxurious, but refined profusion, that beguiled the leisure hours of that wonderful antithesis, "the Demus of Erectheus." Theatre particularly was a source of enormous expense. They laid out on it sums sufficient to equip fleets and armies. "If it were calculated (says a Lacedemonian in Plutarch), what sum each play cost the Athenians, it would be found that they had spent more treasure upon Bacchuses Phœnissæs, and Edipuses, and Antigones, and the wars of Electra and Media, than for wars undertaken for empire and freedom against the barbarians." When the dreadful news of the disaster of the Athenian army in Sicily arrived, the people were at the theatre, and such was their passionate enjoyment of this kind of amusement, that, after a moment's pause, they ordered the actors to go on with the play. There were, however, some peculiar benefits attendant on the expenditures included under the third head; they cultivated sentiments of natural religion, the elegant humanity of social intercourse, and the genius and taste for literature and the arts, and were no doubt one main cause of the generation of that peculiar character in the Athenian people which none other have ever possessed. (S. R. 16, 294.)

4th, 5th, 6th, 7th. We have already seen that dicasts in the courts received 3 obols a day when engaged in trying causes; so likewise the ecclesiasts, or members of the popular assembly, received 3 obols each, when the assembly sat, and pay was given to the army after the time of Pericles. Now, although this pay was trifling for each member, yet so great were the multitudes in the assemblies and on the courts, that the aggregate was enormous in the course of the year. Bockh supposes that nearly a third part of the citizens sat as judges every day. The number of paupers or pensioners, on account of poverty alone, is estimated at about 500. As for gold crowns and other rewards of merit or success, they were of course occasional, and not therefore susceptible of accurate calculation; they were more rarely bestowed when there were many deserving, than in a later and more degenerate age. As to the popular donations—the distributions of corn, the division by lot of the lands in conquered countries (*cleruchiæ*), together with the public revenues of the mines, and the *theoricon* or *theatre money*, a fatal innovation of Pericles, were the principal, and of these, the most important was the latter.

18. *Theoricon?* This took its origin from entrance money to the theatre. Entrance was at first free; but crowds and tumults having arisen, from concourse of many who had no right of entrance, the scaffolding of the theatre, which was of wood, gave way. Afterwards it was determined, to prevent similar evil, to sell the seats for two obols. But that this regulation might not exclude the poor, the entrance money was *given* to them, on the payment of which each one would be entitled to his seat. This entrance money, it seems, was paid to the lessee of the theatre, who was bound to keep it in repair, and who generally paid a rent to the state, as we know to have been the case with the theatre at the Piræus. The application of theorica was soon extended, and money was distributed on other occasions than at the theatre, though always at the celebration of some festival. Under the head of theorica were comprised sums expended upon sacrifices and other solemnities. Not only at the Panathenæa, but at all the great festivals, theorica were

distributed. Bockh thinks that at an early period, 3,000 citizens out of 20,000 received this largess, making it amount to a talent a day, and as there were 25 or 30 days on which the distribution took place, it would make annual expenditure amount to as many talents. In process of time it was greatly increased; it became to Athens what the poor-rate system has become in modern nations, absorbing a large portion of the funds of the state. Eubulus caused a law to be passed solemnly appropriating to this purpose the receipts of other branches of the revenue, and actually denouncing the punishment of death against any one who should *propose* the repeal or alteration of the law. Preservation of the commonwealth was thus postponed for the pleasures of the Athenians. It was this extraordinary law which so hampered Demosthenes, when he was urging his countrymen to war with Philip, and it was not until after the fatal battle of Chæronea, that he finally succeeded in causing these funds to be restored to the military chest to which they originally belonged. It was the theoricon which had so pernicious an effect on the foreign relations of Athens; for her citizens preferred remaining at home, in midst of revelry and idle pursuits of pleasure and novelty, whilst military affairs were given up into the hands of mercenaries, who, being badly paid, pillaged the allies whom they were sent to protect, or undertook expeditions on their own account. This mercenary system had besides unfavorable influence on patriotism; the offer of an obol more was sufficient to make whole ship's crew desert from one fleet to another. (H. 352. W. 2, 397. S. R..16, 296.)

19. *Estimate of the amount?* Bockh says the lowest estimate cannot be placed below 400 talents, and making allowance for occasions of extraordinary profusion, 1000 talents he does not consider too high for the yearly estimate; and this does not include the war expenditures. Now it must ever be remembered that all this was spent on rather more than 100,000 freemen, including men, women and children, or if we number the voters alone, on a little more than 20,000. Well, then, may we say, if Athens by these disbursements was made a great *poor, house*, her citizens were in truth the most *lordly paupers* that the history of the world affords. It was no caricature when Aristophanes, in the Wasps, makes one of these lorldly plebeians propose that every twenty of the citizens should at once be maintained by a subject city, in a style worthy of the trophy of Marathon. With regard to war expenditure, we must remember that, although Athens was almost constantly at war, yet in consequence of the great cheapness of the *materiel* and munitions of an army, and the manner of waging war, the actual expenditures of *money* were trifling, when compared with modern wars. Until time of Pericles, the soldiers received no pay, and provided their own

arms and accoutrements, and by the *trierarchy* the rich were compelled to bear the heaviest part of the expense of equipping the fleet. Their campaigns were generally made between seed-time and harvest. This was the case with the Greeks until the second Persian war, and with the Romans until the siege of Veii. After the introduction of pay, and the employment of mercenaries, the war expenses were sometimes very great; *e. g.*, single item of pay for the troops in Sicilian expedition amounted annually to 3,600 talents, exceeding greatly the average revenue of the state. This, however, was a distant expedition, for the sake of conquest, and was far more expensive than the ordinary Greek wars, in which the campaigns were usually very short.

SEC. X.—CAUSES OF THE DECLINE AND DOWNFALL OF THE GRECIAN REPUBLICS.

After foregoing remarks on internal and external condition of Athens, we can easily trace out the prominent causes of the decline and downfall of Grecian democracies.

1. *Interest of democracy to reduce the citizens to lowest number consistent with safety?* For every citizen having an interest in a certain public capital, increase of citizens would be increase of partners; the greater the number of *divisors* the less of course the dividend to each. But if the number became too small, the security of the commonwealth would be endangered. Combined consideration, therefore, of the means of subsistence and gratification, with the means of defence, would decide the degree of population to be desired in a Grecian republic. Now, unless the danger was pressing, general wish was against increase—the rich disliked it for the same reason that we dislike increase of the poorer class in our parishes; for there was not only a poor law at Athens similar to ours, but their whole system was virtually of same character. The poor objected to it, because it diminished their chances of advantage from sacrifices, from treats to their ward, from pay as dicasts, &c. The idea of common interest in a common stock was fundamental principle of every Grecian commonwealth. Hence Grecian politicians rarely supported increase of citizens; *e. g.*, Xenophon, in his political writings, recommends increase of slaves and resident aliens, but never of citizens. Now what was true of every Grecian state was eminently so of Athens. While she sat as a queen among a thousand subject cities, whose tributes were poured into her lap, it was her constant interest to guard against any extension of citizenship which would increase the number of partners in so profitable a concern.

3. *Hegemony of Athens contained the principle of its own destruc-*

tion? The supremacy which Athens obtained over the allied states, after the Persian war, was highly unfavorable to duration of democracy; it established a great government upon too narrow a basis; it was the pyramid seated upon the little end. Discontents and jealousies arose among the allies; they viewed the Athenians as masters and robbers, rather than as allies, and became anxious, of course, to throw off the yoke. Not only the desertion, but the active hostility of the allies was to be expected at every favorable crisis. Hence, after being so long tyrannized over, not to wonder that they should throw themselves into the arms of Sparta and the oligarchical interest.

4. *Internal division another source of weakness?* Whilst the democratic confederacy was becoming weaker and weaker every day, from the tyranny of Athens, and the consequent alienation of the allies, every state was a prey to the most violent internal factions of the poor against the rich, the democracy against the aristocracy. The rich man could never feel secure under the Grecian democracy; for if he escaped fines and confiscations, he was ever liable to be called on to fit out galleys, to get up plays, to make sacrifices to the gods,* to undertake sacred missions, &c., at his individual expense. This party spirit, engendered between the rich and poor, ran high in every state. During the Peloponnesian war, it attained such a pitch of fury, that in one of the states the oligarchy took a formal oath to work the demus all the mischief in their power, while, on other hand, we see the Samian demus forbidding its members to intermarry with the wealthier order, as well as that of same class in Corcyra, which, like the Florentine citizens of fourteenth century, excluded the dynasts from all offices and dignities. The murderous ferocity of the populace of Corcyra was scarcely paralleled during the bloody scenes of the French revolution. (W. 2, 188.)

5. *Influence of tribes—Sparta heads the Dorian race, Athens the Ionian?* A lasting union was never established among the Grecian states—a transitory but imperfect alliance was sometimes effected in times of common danger, as in the Persian war. The reason of this internal division was not altogether owing to geography and government—it was due in part to difference in character and disposition of the original races. There was a gulf of separation between Doric and Ionic races which never could be removed. A voluntary union for any length of time was impossible. 1st, These tribes were divided geographically—in the Peloponnesus the Dorians predominated—in Attica and the islands, the Ionians. 2dly, Their dialects were different. 3d,

* We must remember that every great sacrifice was equivalent to a feast to the people, for it was vulgarly but truly said, that the gods were offered only the *guts and smoke*, whilst men feasted on the carcass.

Their manners were different, particularly in regard to women; and their festivals were not the same. 3dly, Their governments were generally different.

Sparta aspired to the hegemony of the Dorian race, and her government was in every respect the opposite of that of Athens, who stood at the head of the Ionian. The Dorians were what we may denominate *conservatives*, the Ionians *progressives.* Sparta accordingly headed the oligarchical or *conservative* party of Greece, the Athenians the democratic or *progressive.* (H. 296.) The opposing party in every democratic state was therefore accused of leaning towards Sparta. And the *ultra* portion of them were called *Laconistæ.* Aristophanes speaks of this portion as chiefly fops, who aped the dress and manners of the Spartans; swaggering bullies, with *coats, sticks* and *mustaches.* (W. 2, 194.)

6. *Causes which led to the Peloponnesian war?* The interval between the battle of Marathon and the Peloponnesian war was the period of Grecian greatness, and of the resplendent glory of Athens. Causes, however, which we have adverted to, prepared the way for that great civil strife—that war of Greek upon Greek, which could terminate alone in woe to Greece, no matter which party was victorious. We have seen the heterogeneous elements banded together to resist Persia—the institution of a common purse, and the generous confidence reposed in Athens, making her its depository and manager. This trust, however, was soon violated, and the allies saw themselves plundered for the exclusive benefit of Athens. A general civil war in Greece became inevitable. The allies plundered and disgusted; the rich feeling themselves and property to be at the mercy of irresponsible multitudes; Sparta discontented and jealous, longing to regain her lost position at the head of Greece, which Athens had so proudly usurped—all portended a convulsive war, *ad, internecionem,* in which the two belligerent parties were to be marshalled under the banners of Athens and Sparta. Hence the famous Peloponnesian war, which lasted 27 years.

7. *Effects?* Consequence most melancholy. Gloomy destiny of Greece seemed revealed in the natural phenomena of the times—earthquake followed earthquake—Ætna disgorged its contents—eclipses terrified the people, drought, famine and plague swept off multitudes. But terrors of nature less dreadful than passions of men—covetousness and revenge, hatred and rage, sordid avarice and blood-stained cruelty vied with each other in working havoc and destruction. Towns were levelled, the vanquished and helpless were remorselessly butchered. Upon the Spartan side rests the infamy of commencing this system, The Megarians, against the law of nations, slew the Athenian herald,

Anthemocritus, just before the war. Athenians of course instantly declared war *of extermination* against Megara, and the generals were made to take oath that they would twice each year invade her territory. Soon it became custom to murder the prisoners on both sides—women and children were made slaves. This was the fate which Platæa experienced at the hands of the Spartans. The Athenians imbrued their hands in blood of Eginetans, who were expelled from the island. A similar fate befell the Scionæans and Melians. Recorded of Conon, as a most generous act, that he pardoned and liberated the noble Rhodian Dorieus, whom he took prisoner. The Syracusans condemned Athenians and their allies, whom they took prisoners, to die a lingering death in their stone quarries, or reduced them to slavery. Lysander, the Spartan, completed this long series of atrocities by murdering the 3000 Athenians taken prisoners at Ægospotamos, and the Spartans even murdered the traders of neutral towns whom they found in the captured vessels. No promises were binding—brave and noble-minded men did not scruple to use low artifice to get their victims in their power. The temples of the gods were no longer held sacred, the sanctuary was violated, and the altar of Jove was desecrated. In the bosom of every state the baneful flames of civil discord raged with devastating fury. All were occupied with traitorous designs, endeavoring to secure assistance from without, in order to overpower the adverse faction at home. Treason prevailed everywhere. (W. 2, 181-8.)

8. *Plague in Athens, its moral effects ?* In consequence of the crowds which the invasion of Attica drove into the city, a plague broke out in second year of the war, which raged with unabating fury during whole of third. This dreadful scourge forms a new era in history of Athenian people—from that moment it began to decline. Some idea may be formed of its ravages from fate of besiegers before Potidæa, out of 4000 heavy armed, 1050 perished in 50 days. The moral effects were equally disastrous—it seemed to extinguish all virtue. Thucydides tells us, that the people, deeming their property and lives to be theirs only for a day, determined to enjoy the present moment. The fear of the gods and the laws of man, did not restrain them. They became less religious when they beheld the devout and the wicked involved in the same destruction. None expected to live till they could be brought to justice and punished for their crimes. A boundless corruption of manners ensued. Meanwhile the citizens were reduced in number, and their ranks still further thinned by the drafts occasioned by the war. This led to extraordinary measures to supply the deficiency. But the motley crowd, which these new laws of naturalization generated, was never equal to that which was purely Athenian.

9. *Administration of the government?* There are three periods during which it is proper to examine the policy and character of the administration of the government of Athens, in order that we may rightly understand the causes of the decline of the Grecian democracies. These are, 1st, the period from Persian invasion to time of Pericles; 2d, the period of Pericles; 3d, from Pericles to time of Alexander.

10. *First period, from Persian invasion to time of Pericles, Themistocles, Aristides?* It has been well observed that the general spirit of thought and act which at a given epoch pervades great bodies of men, becomes as it were *incarnate* in certain great individuals, who are the master spirits of their age. Such undoubtedly was Themistocles during this first period. Will not now speak of his generalship, but merely his state policy. Aristides is generally looked on as his great political antagonist; and at first view we are apt to conclude that one headed the aristocracy, and the other the democracy. This is not so—both were democrats. The real cause of their antagonism resulted from their different views concerning the welfare of Athens. Aristides was against relying much on the navy—he seems not to have desired an Athenian maritime supremacy—he regarded it as perilous—it seemed a departure from the simplicity and rustic virtues of his forefathers. He did not like to trust resources of his country to a faithless element in pursuit of precarious advantages. Civic virtue and integrity in performance of public duties at home were in unison with his feelings. Themistocles, on other hand, wished Athens to develope her full power. He saw that the sea was the true theatre for her greatness. He was for bending all the resources of his country to this great object. The battle of Salamis and the general success of the Greeks, proved his superior statesmanship. Aristides himself was convinced of the policy of his administration.

Themistocles was determined to make Athens the first power in Greece. He was the instigator of that famous self-denying ordinance by which the people agreed no longer to distribute the silver from the mines of Laurium among themselves, but to apply it to building of a fleet. And this act shows how greatly superior he was to the mere time-serving demagogue, hunting after ephemeral popularity. He it was who projected the plan of fortification, that connected Athens with the Piræus, and made her at once a great fortified seaport town. He regarded all the glory which Athens had won, in the two Persian wars, but as means of farther aggrandizement. It was his policy which laid the foundation for the Athenian *hegemony*. Themistocles was no doubt unprincipled; he was but little scrupulous as to his means. Hence the opinion of Aristides had more moral weight; that of Themistocles was result of more enlarged views; the former was behind his age; the latter always with or in advance of it.

11. *Cimon?* During the latter part of what we may call the administration of Themistocles, Cimon rose to great notoriety. He was the leader of the aristocratic party in Athens, and one of the ablest generals of the age. Of course he leaned towards Sparta, and a conjuncture of circumstances enabled him to supplant Themistocles. A series of most splendid victories and a most princely liberality shown towards the lower orders, after coming into possession of his magnificent estates in the Chersonesus, upheld his power for a season, and contributed to place Athens into what perhaps may be termed a *false position.* A rupture with Sparta produced downfall of the aristocratic party in Athens, and although Cimon's victories still kept him in credit and power, yet circumstances soon brought forward, as the first actor in Greece, the most accomplished demagogue and ablest statesman which the annals of Greece have furnished. (Pericles.)

12. *Second period—age of Pericles?* The true and worthy successor of Themistocles was Pericles. He was the master spirit of his age, the true representative of the Athenian people; and hence he may be said to have ruled them, during the 40 years of his political life, with almost absolute sway, and his character and success have demonstrated to the world, that even fickle multitudes can best be won by real magnanimity of soul, ability in counsel, and fidelity in the discharge of duty. The annals of Greece present not his equal for intelligence, fortitude, and the qualities that enable men to rule others. He was the model of a hard-working statesman. "There was in the whole city (says Plutarch) but one street in which he was ever seen—the street which led to the market-place and the council-house. He declined all invitations to banquets, and all gay assemblies and company. During the whole period of his administration he never dined at table of a friend; he only just made his appearance at the nuptials of his nephew, Euryptolemus; but immediately after the libation he arose. He did not always appear even in the popular assemblies, but only when important business was to be transacted; smaller concerns he intrusted to his friends and the orators." Thucydides says he was most *notoriously* honest. He was a brave man, and the most skilful and cautious general of his age, while he was at same time the most powerfully eloquent man of Greece. The comic poets described him as bearing thunder and lightning on his tongue. His demeanor was of a character bordering on austesity, and he who without doubt was the most glorious demagogue, the most popular idol which the world has ever produced, seemed in his dignified demeanor to feel but little sympathy with the vulgar

multitude. His grave and majestic countenance was the index of a mind too proud to flatter and to cringe. He towered above the multitude which he governed, like a being of a higher order, presenting a perfect contrast to the truckling complaisance of the mere popularity hunter.

13. *General estimate of the administration of Pericles?* Shallow politicians and historians have been unable to comprehend the true character of this administration. Without doubt his main object was to render Athens not only the first but the governing city in Greece. He was for establishing an Athenian *supremacy*, instead of maintaining a mere balance of power between Athens and Sparta. This being his great end, of course all his means were to be directed to it. In the first place, then, which party should he espouse, the aristocratic or democratic? Evidently the last; for, in point of morality, it was the equal, generally the superior of the former, and in point of *state policy*, it was the party whose supremacy alone could give full development to Athenian greatness. The reason can easily be made manifest—there were two great races that divided Greece, the Dorians and the Ionians, and, corresponding with some exactness to this division of races, was that of governments into the aristocratic and democratic. At the head of the former was Sparta, at head of latter was Athens. Now Pericles knew full well, that whenever Athens gave up her democracy she fell as a matter of course into dependence on Sparta, who was the natural leader of the oligarchical party, whilst she at the same time lost her most efficient support, the democratic allies. When there are two rival powers in a great system of states, divided by antagonizing principles, if one has notoriously the lead in favor of one set of principles, the other is driven to advocate the opposite system, or to fall in a state of inferiority to its rival; *e. g.*, Bonaparte pronounced Francis I. to be *pigmy great man*, because he persevered in taking the Catholic side in the controversy, when it was evident that Charles V. was the natural head of that party. Supposing him to have had no more scruples, it was evidently his policy to have come out boldly as the leader of the Protestant cause. It was his only chance for placing France at the head of the European system. So likewise we observe in history of Athens, that the moment the oligarchy triumphed at any time, Athens was brought down to a state of inferiority to Sparta. The two parties in Athens were called *Philolacones* and *Antilacones*. The latter were more consistent, determined and independent; for the former in power could neither place firm reliance on Sparta, nor act with vigor and resolution by themselves.

Pericles has been reproached with ministering to the most glaring foibles of the Athenians, cupidity and the love of pleasure, and with thereby having corrupted the national feeling, whilst he exhausted the resources of the state; that he gratified the demus by *cleruchias* and judicial salaries; adorned Athens with the Propylæa, the Parthenon &c., and allowed the people the gratuitous indulgence of their love of dramatic exhibition, and of art, by instituting the *theoricon*—and all this for the purpose of winning the favor of the multitude. It has been supposed that not having as great wealth as Cimon to purchase favor with, his resource was in the public, to do that with the people's own money which he had not means to accomplish from his own private resources. That Pericles adopted most deliberately a system which eventually produced great corruption, there can be no doubt. But his character precludes the supposition that it was done with the purely demagogical interest of winning popularity. As Athens enjoyed the *hegemony* of the democratic states, Pericles supposed that she should be adorned in a style worthy so proud a station. And, as she was to maintain her democracy, all the monuments of the arts were to be for the public, *for* the people. The greatest men in Athens lived in dwellings no better than their neighbors'. The small houses of Themistocles and Aristides were long pointed out. Even as late as time of Demosthenes we find the orator reproaching Midias for his large house at Eleusis. The splendor of Athens was not perceived till the public squares and the Acropolis were approached.

Again, Pericles well knew that the arts, the theatre, the gymnasium, the ecclesia and the courts of justice were, in fact, the great schools of popular education in democratic states, and these means were used by him to educate the people, and make them capable of command. The institution of pay to the army, to the ecclesiasts and the dicasts, was necessary to the completion of the system. An army equipped at *its own expense* is necessarily aristocratic; in Athens such an army would be composed of the rich and the Eupatrides alone—*pay* produces a *civic* army—an army of the poor as well as the rich, an army penetrated with the spirit of the times, and capable of defending it. Upon the same principle it was necessary to pay the ecclesiasts and the dicasts. Otherwise the rich would have excluded the poor. De Tocqueville is correct in asserting that pay to all the officers of government is a highly democratic feature in our government; for without pay offices fall too exclusively into hands of the rich, who alone can afford to hold office.

The effects of this system were most baleful on the courts of justice; yet, even here, there was compensating advantage. Pericles knew that courts were public schools in which the public mind was trained, and, better still, restrained. There is something, it has well been said, in the very function of judicature, so important, so solemn, so elevated, that it impresses with a sense of peculiar responsibility even the lowest and most degraded of our species. There are men who would vote a bill of attainder in parliament, who would shrink from such a sentence on the bench of justice. Bad as the Athenians were in their courts, they were worse in the ecclesia. The sworn juror in the trial feels a high obligation to act justly, and consequently to listen to, and weigh well the pleadings. Every jury before whom an important cause is ably argued, if not tampered with, is likely to come out of court better and wiser, and it is precisely in this point of view that we hold in high reverence our own jury trial; it is admirable scheme of discipline; it is true school of republican liberty and knowledge. I agree with one of ablest writers of our country, that a single prætor, a high justiciary, might perhaps dispose of cases even of fact, as correctly in the long run as the juries, but we believe that our political institutions, well poised as they are, would perish with such an innovation.

Finally, we must never forget, in estimating the policy of Pericles, that the lower classes of Athens were superior in knowledge to the same orders in all other countries, for by his system they were almost as well instructed as the rich. The great objection to the very poor on the bench of justice is, not only that their poverty exposes to corruption, but that their ignorance subjects them to imposition. Now the whole polity of Athens was admirably calculated to make the poor man in point of intellect but little inferior to the rich, for he had the benefit of the same kind of education.

14. *Third period—from death of Pericles to the age of Alexander?* In the age of Pericles we have the meridian glory of Athens. The policy which he pursued was the one best calculated to develop quickly Athenian greatness; but the system was not framed for duration. In the hands of a man like Pericles evil might be staved off, and the progress of corruption stayed. But scarcely does he recede from our gaze before all these evils gather and close around the city. The misfortune of his system was, that it was of such a character as to enable the dishonest politician to take the short route to popularity by turning demagogue, and working the political machine more exclusively for the benefit of the poor, who constituted the numerical majority in Athens. Division of parties afterwards was not so much into aristocrats and democrats, as into friends of legality and order on one side, and base flatterers of the populace, the brawlers and disturbers of public peace, on the other. Henceforth you find no one man who can entirely compose all differences, and represent the whole Athenian people. You find generally one who is supported for his honesty and ability, whilst there is another running, if I may use the expression, for the *saleable interests*

of the commonwealth, interests which might be won by flattery and largesses.

15. *Nicias, Cleon, Hyperbolus?* Passing over Lysicles, the dealer in sheep, and Eucrates, the flax-seller, who were in favor but a very short time, we come to the two great rival candidates for first place in Athens after death of Pericles—Nicias and Cleon, whose characters completely illustrate foregoing remarks. These two men, though neither, in any respect, equalled Pericles, may be considered as representing, one the better, the other the worse side of, that great man. The wealthy Nicias was one of the most incorruptible patriots of his day whilst Cleon, the *tanner*, was a boisterous, impudent, ferocious, dishonest demagogue. We have not only the authority of Aristophanes, but that of Thucydides likewise, for the baseness and impudence of this man. It was he who instigated the murder of the Mytileneans. It was he who inveighed most violently against Nicias, as commander of the army, and caused that modest man to resign. He boasted that he could bring the Lacedemonians, besieged in Sphacteria, within twenty days, dead or alive, to Athens. The Athenians actually took him at his word, appointed him to the command of the expedition, and the fellow actually accomplished his promise.

The gross levity of this whole proceeding is unparalleled in history. The people assembled, and waited coming of Cleon, who was to bring forward a proposition. After some delay, Cleon came, with garland around his head, and requested assembly to adjourn till next day, as he had a feast at his house, and wished to be with the guests. The people laughed, and adjourned. His success against Sphacteria made him think himself a great general. He had the presumption to go against Brasidas and the rebellious Chalcidians, where he incurred contempt and hatred of soldiers, and was defeated and killed at Amphipolis.

Nicias had, after death of Cleon, a wider scope, and held for some time the first place in Athens. But Athens had now arrived at that state when there would be generally some representative of the baser and more corrupt elements of the body politic. Such a competitor soon arose in the person of Hyperbolus, the *lamp-maker*, an acknowledged knave, born of a father who had been branded, and had labored as a public slave in the mines, and of a mother whom the comic poets pursued with unsparing ridicule—a man convicted publicly of the fraud of mixing lead with the metal he used for his lamps. The cabals of this fellow against Nicias, Phæax and Alcibiades had nearly secured him the chief authority, when a union of the two former caused him to be expelled by *ostracism*. And the Athenians, when they came to reflect on his character, were so disgusted that they passed a decree that ostracism had been disgraced, and should for ever after be abolished. (W. 2, 237.)

16. *Alcibiades?* But the most complete type of the Athenian character, in its degenerate age, was Alcibiades—that great moral *antithesis*, in whom the virtues and vices of his country were so strangely blended—the warrior and the fop—the statesman and the voluptuary—the demagogue and the patriot—the orator and the drunkard. The man who would have made Athens mistress of the world, and yet did most to destroy her. He united all the corrupting arts of the sophists with the profound philosophy of Socrates, of whom he was a favorite pupil, and he had been the ward of Pericles. Vigor of his constitution enabled him to indulge, without restraint, the amorous propensities of his nature, and in drinking and wrestling he found but few competitors. He was a faultless model of beauty, no little distinction in Athenian eyes. He was the heir of immense wealth, and the descendant of an old and illustrious house, which the demus held in veneration. Birth, even in a degenerate age, was of more importance in Athens than superficial thinkers are apt to suppose. The occupations of Lysicles, the *cattle-dealer*, Eucrates, the *dealer in flax and bran*, Cleon, the *tanner*, Hyperbolus, the *lamp-maker*, and Cleophon, the *lyre-maker*, all of whom rose to power, was the theme of the most unsparing ridicule with the comic poets. These, too, seem to be the earliest specimens of men elevated from similar stations to influence, and the people joined heartily in the laugh raised on this ground. Even after the Peloponnesian war, Andocides deplored the dishonor which had befallen his mansion, because during his absence it was inhabited by Cleophon, the *lyre-maker*.

Alcibiades, being the incarnate image of the Athenian demus, might perhaps have attained a supremacy over the multitude equal to that of Pericles, had he not, whilst pliant and cringing to the people at large, treated individuals of all ranks with most unheard of insolence, and thereby incurred their eternal hatred. His conduct to individuals was as capricious and wanton as that of his native city; *e. g.*, detained by force, three or four months in his house, Agatharcus, the painter, until he had produced all the paintings required of him. Struck in sheer wantonness Hipponicus, whose daughter he married. Terrified his own brother-in-law, Callias, with threats of assassination; disturbed the Dionysiac festival by a rude assault on his competitor; protected Thasian poet, Hegemon, from lawsuit, by going openly to public archives and destroying the record—seized his wife, Hepparete, in presence of the archon, when suing for a divorce, in consequence of ill treatment, and dragged her home, &c. (T. 3, 332.)

Such was the strange being, who exercised so wonderful an influence over the Athenians, and was the cause of the Melean massacre, (one of the most disgraceful measures in Grecian history,) and the Sicilian war, in which the Athenian army perished, and Athens received a blow from which she never recovered. His influence at home but hastened on that career of degeneracy and corruption which prepared Greece for the Macedonian rule. It was the failure of the Sicilian expedition which set the oligarchy to plotting until they succeeded in establishing the government of the 400 in conjunction with 5000 citizens selected from all the Athenian population—a government soon overthrown, in consequence of its iniquity. But the effects were still most baneful. The democracy became more violent, as was manifested in the judicial murder of the generals that won the battle of Arginusæ. The intrigues of the oligarchy on the other hand, were unremitting; to their treachery without doubt is due the defeat of the fleet at Ægospotamos, (B. C. 405,) the last support of the sinking cause of Athens. In conjunction with Sparta, the oligarchy again achieved a revolution and the most odious tyranny of the Thirty was established—a tyranny so revolting as soon to produce a reaction—when a band of exiled democrats, headed by Thrasybulus, Archinus and Anytus, again succeeded in restoring the democracy to power. Such revolutions as these produce the most violent party feuds, and there was unfortunately no recuperative energy in the Athenian constitution. From the time of Pericles to Alexander, the regular tendency of the government was from bad to worse.

17. *From the Peloponnesian war to Alexander?* Athens was obliged to terminate the Pelponnesian war by a humiliating treaty with Sparta. Without allies, forts, fleets, or treasure, she became dependent on her great rival; stopped of the tribute which had flowed in from so many subject cities, the Athenians lost their importance, whilst the value of their property sank ruinously low. Sparta obtained the hegemony of Greece, but her rule was more oppressive still than that of Athens. She exacted the tribute of her allies, and this produced a still greater corruption in Sparta than it had ever done in Athens. Occasionally Athens would partially recover her lost greatness, but only for a season.

Thebes too became an important state, and in Epaminondas and Pelopidas we meet with heroes worthy the proudest days of Greece or Rome. But the glory of Thebes rose and sank with these two illustrious men. The democratic principle was rapidly wearing itself out by the greatest corruption; selfishness was usurping the place of patri otism, and the general degeneracy was fast preparing the way for despotism, when there arose in the north of Greece a most accomplished king, at the head of a semi-barbarous state, with a well disciplined mercenary army at his control, and a full treasury. The states of Greece were unable to withstand such a hero at the head of a nation in all the freshness of youth. The worn-out and corrupted democracies were unable to compete with the concentrated energies of a wily monarch. The crazy, rotten machinery of the old system could not work against the new. Where Philip's soldiers could not enter, Philip's ass, laden with gold, was sure to obtain admission.

The eloquence of Demosthenes was all in vain. He represented the spirit of the small cities and petty republics—a time past that could never return. His attempt to reanimate a by-gone and demolished age, says Monsieur Cousin, was a *real wager* against all possibility. His history is similar to that of all men who attempt impossibilities. After the performance of prodigies in the tribune, he found it necessary to run away at Cheronæa. That battle established the guardianship of Macedonia over the Grecian republics, formally acknowledged by the nomination of Philip to be the General of Greece in the Persian war. The history of Philip's son, Alexander the Great, is too well known. All Greece fell into a state of dependence on his colossal empire, and the *individuality* of the states was merged into the great whole: and thus terminated the career of the Grecian republics, leaving the student rather in wonder at the length of time that they had endured, than at the final termination of their existence.

SEC. II.—GENERAL ESTIMATE OF GRECIAN CHARACTER.

Shall conclude remarks of Grecian history by a general estimate of the Grecian character; and in order that this may be done fairly, necessary to point out the difference between the notions universally prevalent in ancient world, concerning the powers and functions of government, and those prevalent among modern civilized nations.

1. *Absolutism of the governments of the Grecian states?* Governments of antiquity, no matter of what kind, were considered as possessing every power. There were *no constitutions*, limiting their authority, no reserved rights to individuals. The state was every thing—the individual only became important through the state. The ancients started with the state and deduced all individual relations from that point. The moderns start with individuals, and deduce the state from them. To procure the safety of the state was the great problem to be solved anciently; to procure the safety of individuals, now. Ancient governments aspired to the regulation of every thing; they never withheld their action, except through policy. Difference in form of government

made no difference in its power; the democracies were just as omnipotent as the aristocracies and the monarchies.

2. *Examples?* Spartan laws best illustrate true theory of ancient governments. They think for the individual, feel for him, and act for him. They tell him whom he shall marry, when he *shall* repudiate his wife. They pay the same attention to the breeding of men that a Pennsylvania grazier does to the breeding of his cattle. Plutarch tells us that King Archidamus was fined for marrying too small a wife. This same system prescribed death to a certain portion of the offspring, when not likely to be serviceable to the state. It proscribed certain occupations to the freemen, regulated the music, and made man a mere machine to be wound up by the government. In other states we perceive recognition of the same plenary powers of government, *e. g.*, in Crete certain number of youths were picked out of the *Agele* (division of youth) to be married. To remain unmarried was punished in many Grecian states. A *psephisma* (decree) was passed, B. C. 400, to make Timotheus of Miletus use 7 instead of 11 chords on his lyre. It is this same absolutism of government which helps to explain the origin of *liturgies.* The sacredness of property in modern Europe, which rises superior to all the powers of the prince, was not known to the ancients.

3. *What constituted ancient liberty?* It consisted principally in the share a man had *in* the government, not freedom *from its* action. *Perfect equality was perfect liberty.* The government might be the most complete despotism on earth, but if each one had his equal share in that despotism, then he had liberty. With the moderns it is different. We regard freedom from personal restraint and security of property as the great essentials of liberty. The individual and his property both were looked on as belonging to the state in the ancient republics. Now-a-days the state is considered as created for *their protection.* Demosthenes in Athens could never have made an exclamation similar to that which fell from the elder Pitt, on the Middlesex election, when he asserted that the humblest cottage in England was an inviolable sanctuary, which "the winds may whistle through, and the rains of heaven may enter, but the king of England cannot."

4. *Lot.* As the ancients aimed at perfect liberty in perfect equality, not to wonder at the introduction of the principle of the *lot*, to do away, as far as possible, the inequality occasioned by talent and virtue. "This (says Lieber) has a deep meaning—the were naturally and consistently led to the lot." "Not only magistrates, but even generals and orators, were determined by lot." Herodotus makes *isonomy* (ισονομια) and lot the characteristics of ancient democracy, and the same thing is predicable of the Italian republics of the middle ages, particularly of Florence.

Their governments were perfect despotisms, but then the *people* were the despots; and lest the talented might prevail, the lot was introduced, to give each man a chance for the offices.

5. *Independent judiciary unknown to the ancients.* They did not separate distinctly the different departments of government; their theory was hostile to the administration of justice by a small, select, independent judiciary. In the democracies it was too important a branch of sovereignty to be surrendered by the demus. It was to be exercised by those who could do as they pleased. They had not yet arrived at that cardinal principle, growing out of feudalism and Christianity, that neither *one*, the *few*, nor the *many* have a right to do what they please; that unanimous millions have no right to do what is unjust; that absolute power is not for frail, mortal man.

6. *Socrates' refusal to escape from a notoriously unjust condemnation was correct with the ancient notion of political ethics?* The state being every thing, and the individual nothing, the latter of course is bound to abide the decision of the former. To question the justice of the sentence would have been to deny the omnipotence of the government. With the modern notions, however, he would not only have been right to make his escape, but morally bound to do it; because his innocent life was demanded, which the government not only had no right to sacrifice, but was bound to protect. No one but applauds Lavalette for accepting the deliverance offered by his intrepid wife. No one blames Grotius for being carried by his wife and maid-servant, in an old box, out of the prison in which he was unjustly confined by Maurice. And no one would have blamed John Russell, if he had exchanged clothes with Lord Cavendish, and fled from prison. Submission to the infamous sentence of such a judge as Jeffries would be wrong, if the condemned could make his escape. When Stubbe, a puritan lawyer, had his right hand cut off, for writing a pamphlet against the marriage of Elizabeth, he waved his hat with the left, and exclaimed, "Long live the Queen Elizabeth," and afterwards wrote against the Catholics for Lord Burleigh. Lieber says truly, that Stubbe "was either a man of uncommon elevation of mind, or the very meanest of slaves." (1, 428.)

7. *Ostracism?* We can now explain an anomaly in the Grecian democracies, which has been so often misunderstood by students of history. As government was omnipotent, and liberty consisted in equality, and equal participation in the government, the Grecian democracies felt the want of some method of getting rid of men who became so powerful or popular as to endanger the general liberty. Hence the institution of *ostracism*, at Athens and Argos, and *petalism* at Syracuse, by which the people could banish their dangerous men *before* the commission of

any offence. All nations have occasionally felt the want of ostracism; *e. g.* Niebuhr, in Roman history, speaking of Manlius, says, "Whether *guilty* or *innocent*, he became an extremely dangerous person, through a misfortune for which there was no cure; and matters could not fail to grow worse and worse. This knot might have been solved by *ostracism.*" No dishonor was attached to this punishment, on the contrary, it was often the highest compliment. Hermodorus, in Ephesus, was banished because he was considered *the best;* and all are acquainted with the anecdote in which the Athenian told Aristides, (*incog.*) that he voted to ostracise him because he could not bear to hear every body calling him *the just.* When Hyperbolus, the lamp-maker, a mean but dangerous citizen, was ostracised, the people formally abolished the punishment, because they considered it disgraced by its application to so despicable a character.

8. *Frequency of wars made the claim of the men without property to an equal participation in the government much stronger in ancient times than now?* The little states of Greece were so constantly at war, that hostility may be considered the rule, and a state of peace the exception. Hence the institutions of antiquity were all adapted to war, as being the prime concern of social life. The whole discipline and education of youth were directed to this purpose. "The infant warrior in the Myth was dipped by his mother in one of the rivers of hell; he was hardened by exposure, invigorated by exertion, made nimble and supple by exercise." The rendition of military service was therefore the great burthen of the state, and consequently we find, in both Greece and Rome, whenever the plebeians made a rally for liberty, it was always on this ground; *e. g.* the secession to Mons Sacer. In a government like that of the United States, this argument would have but little force in the discussion of the question of universal suffrage. Peace is here the rule, and a state of war the exception; and even during war, gunpowder has so enhanced the expenses, that national strength depends more on wealth than on men. Besides all this, our laws must be uniform; hence I feel as secure with a representative who has similar interests with mine, as if I were legislating in propria persona. Hence the men of property in our republics, for example, could not make a law against *persons*, which would not equally operate on themselves; and the man without property, therefore, may now be perfectly safe, even if he has no share in the government. But in ancient republics this might not always have been the case.

9. *Judging by our standard, Greece produced few models of the virtuous gentleman?* Moral depravity of the ancient world was greater than that of the modern. It is well remarked, by one of the most

learned scholars of our country, that there is scarcely a great man of Greece whose biography is free from some of those dark stains, which no virtues would now be thought sufficient to compensate, and no glory to conceal. Without citing the example of Themistocles and Lysander, notoriously unprincipled even for their own times, however gifted and celebrated, Plutarch has scarcely a hero who would pass muster as *a gentleman* now. Heeren has pronounced Timoleon the most perfect model of a republican in the history of the world; yet even he permitted as barbarous and wanton a murder as the mean vengeance of faction ever perpetrated. (Leg. 83.) The fact is, that the spread of the sublime precepts of the Gospel, together with the elevation of the female sex consequent on the establishment of the feudal system, have of themselves wrought a wonderful influence on modern civilization, and made it wholly different from the ancient.

10. *Energies of men fully developed in the Grecian democracies?* Never was system better calculated for the development of individual energy than the democratic system of Greece. According to theory of ancient government, it is true that the state was every thing, and the individual nothing; but then, in the democracies, each individual might exercise a great influence *through* the government. A man in Attica or Argos might be a very important part of the state, much more so than if he had been in a nation of 40,000,000 souls. The principle of the *lot*, and the constitution of the juries and assemblies made *every* man anxious to qualify himself for office. Hence there was no undeveloped talent. These little democratic caldrons were always boiling, and true genius and energy of soul were sure, sooner or later, to rise to the top. In the day of her greatest glory, Athens had more great men within her walls, than the rest of the world; and, in like manner, Machiavelli asserted of democratic Florence, that she had, within a population of 80,000 souls, more great men than were to be found in all the great empires north of the Alps put together.

11. *Grecian system not fitted for duration?* But if the democratic system was calculated for development, it was not fit for duration. Such a system can never be stationary; if it does not advance, it will retrograde; *e. g.* Any one who understands the true character of the administration of Pericles, will see that he could never have run his career a *second time.* With all the elements in intense action, the stationary condition is impossible. The elevated plateau of the Indo-Chinese world is the true empire of *immobility* and despotism, because all the elements are in repose. All is stationary there. All, as Monsieur Cousin expresses it, is in a state of *envelopment*, and it was perhaps well that the cradle of civilization should be firm and fixed. But Greece

was the child of progress, and therefore herself necessarily progressive. Thucydides, in his summary of character of the Athenians, says, "They were born never to be at rest themselves, nor to suffer others to be so." And if a short but crowded and energetic life is preferable to an age of noiseless slavery, we can never lament that civilization, in her progress westwardly, cast off, as soon as she reached the shores of the Mediterranean, that character of immobility which has enshrouded the endless generations that have lived in the great despotisms of Asia. These great empires, with all their durability, have no history: they are like the calm, boundless ocean, with no objects standing out above the great unbroken surface to arrest the gaze of the beholder. Two hundred years of Grecian democratic history presents more facts for the gratification of a laudable curiosity, more matter for deep philosophical reflection, than all the barren annals of Chinese history for thousands of years past.

12. *Comparison between Athens and Sparta?* Before concluding Grecian history, well to institute comparison between the aristocratic and democratic states, and as Sparta and Athens headed the two great parties, may at once take these two as samples. Plato and Xenophon both were great admirers of the Spartan system. But facts prove most conclusively that the democratic, with all its faults, was vastly superior to it. When we look to the administration of justice in Athens, and consider the kind of arguments addressed to the court, and the direct interest which the judges had in confiscations, the Athenians appear to be but little better than a horde of Usbecs or Algerines, and the mere theorist would at once conclude, that where property was so badly protected all accumulation would cease. Yet the fact is not so; Athens was, with all the defects in her government, the most flourishing state of Greece. Her citizens were the most enterprising, and accumulated wealth the fastest. You may ascribe this, no doubt, in part to *hegemony* which she possessed over the democratic states, thereby drawing the wealth of Greece into her lap. But then Herodotus says her career in wealth commenced immediately after the overthrow of the Pisistratidæ, and does not hesitate to ascribe it to the system of equality.* Sparta,

* It must not be supposed that little influence is meant to be ascribed to the fact that Athens possessed the *hegemony* of the democratic states. On the contrary much of her greatness was due to this; it made the whole city a sort of senate of kings, and inspired importance into the meanest of Athenian citizens. Much of the present greatness of the English nation is owing to a similar circumstance. Her political economists have long shown that her numerous colonies and foreign possessions cost more than they are worth, and hence speculative men have often recommended an emancipation. But the moral effect of these possessions on the nation is incalcu-

up to the conclusion of the Persian war, was considered the leading state in Greece. Yet what a singular contrast does she present with Athens. Historians have strangely conspired to praise her constitution, which seems fit only to make soldiers. Yet if we could forget Thermopylæ, how little could Sparta boast of even in war. In the great Persian conflict, how little do her political and military operations appear when compared with those of Athens. How narrow-minded the patriotism of a Spartan! How closely bordering on perfidy was Spartan indifference after completion of the Isthmean wall. Until time of Brasidas she never produced even a celebrated general; and Thucydides remarks, were she then to pass away, like other empires she would leave no monument behind to prove her grandeur, while Athens was covered over with the trophies of genius and power. In fine, I repeat the assertion of Pericles, Athens was the instructress of Greece, and every citizen seemed capable of dedicating his faculties to the most multifarious objects with dexterity and grace. At the conclusion of the Peloponnesian war, the tribute that had flowed in on Athens was seized by Sparta; yet it produced no greatness there in the arts, literature or statesmanship—it merely produced sensuality without refinement, corruption without greatness.

But not only was Athens crowned at home with prosperity and glory, but in spite of her injustice in her federal relations, and her occasionally barbarous and bloody cruelties, she was in truth, when compared with the rest of Greece, what Pericles asserted in his panegyrical oration, the *school of humanity and fraternity*. Foreigners were more mildly treated there than elsewhere. Slaves were better treated there than in any other city of Greece, and there was less cruelty in the execution of her laws, and her repentance of misdeeds was often candid and cordial; *e. g.*, after death of Socrates, how bitter was the remorse of demus, when they closed the Palæstras and Gymnasia, expelled several of his accusers, and put Melitus, the principal one, to death. (W. 2, 350.)

13. *Niebuhr's opinion of the Athenian demus?* Indebted to Bishop Thirlwal for translation of the impressive passage containing it. It is perhaps an exaggerated eulogy; but no opinion of that great man and cautious investigator can be without great weight. "Evil without end may be spoken of the Athenian constitution, and with truth—I should say, God shield us from a constitution like the Athenian! were not the

lable; it has made England a land of rulers and statesmen, and given to them a pride and loftiness of character, far beyond what we meet with in the continental nations. Hence, whilst England is most rapacious and unjust as a nation, she stands proudly pre-eminent in the sterling moral worth and the elevated practical character of her citizens.

age of such states irrevocably gone by. As it was, it shows an unexampled degree of noble-mindedness in the nation, that the heated temper of a fluctuating popular assembly, the security afforded to individuals of giving a base vote unobserved, produced so few reprehensible decrees; and that, on the other hand, the thousands among whom the common man had the upper hand came to resolutions of such self-sacrificing magnanimity and heroism, as few men are capable of, except in their most exalted mood. Let who will clamor and scoff, for myself, should trials be reserved for my old age, and for my children, who will certainly have evil days to pass through, I pray only for as much self-control, as much temperance in the midst of temptation, as much courage in the hour of danger, as much calm perseverance in the consciousness of a glorious resolution which was unfortunate in its issue, as was shown by the Athenian people, considered as one man. We have nothing to do here with the morals of the individuals: but he who, as an individual, possesses such virtues, and withal is guilty of no worse sins in proportion than the Athenians, may look forward without uneasiness to his last hour."

14. *German historians have best understood the true character of the Grecian governments?* Mr. Legaré, who is one of the most accomplished Greek scholars in this country, and is to be numbered among the very few who have seized the true spirit and character of Grecian civilization, attributes the superiority of German histories of Greece to the fact, that they have been governed in their speculations less by the writings of Plato and Xenophon, and more by those of Aristotle, than most others. Plato and Xenophon wrote in the spirit of a *reaction.* The abuses of democracy which they daily witnessed disgusted them with popular government. Men of their transcendent intellects even may be pardoned for despairing of the fortunes of humanity, when surrounded by the misdeeds of democracy. How many strong minds have conceived an uneradicable disgust for the whole cause and character of the French revolution, from the horrors which were perpetrated during its progress. Aristotle is not obnoxious to this charge. He is exempt from all passion or prejudice for or against democratic institutions. He writes always in the true spirit of philosophy. He studied twenty years under Plato in the Academy, and left Athens at age of 37. He was employed by Philip as preceptor to his son, Alexander the Great. Now although he had lived at Athens long enough to perceive all the deformities of democracy, yet he lived in Philip's court a sufficient time to spy out a few of the deformities of monarchy, and to see that "despotism is apt to love low company." He is a true and impartial witness, who reports after the most ample experience on both sides. He

does not, like Plato and Xenophon, when speaking of a perfect commonwealth, always imagine the reign of a patriot king. He does not entertain their extravagant admiration of Spartan institutions. After the most deliberate inspection of all kinds of government, he still has some faith in the *people.* He saw the great truth, that all governments perish by pushing to excess their peculiar principles; and the conclusion at which he arrives, after a survey of the whole ground, is that the best government is a *well-tempered popular* constitution, in which the popular element is strong and active. At the same time, no one saw more clearly all the defects of the Athenian democracy than he did, nor more earnestly deprecated them.

15. *Value of Grecian history to the American student?* De Tocqueville says that democracy is to be the inevitable condition of modern nations. He is no discoverer; he has uttered what has long been felt. It has been well asserted, that Paris is as much the capital of the *democratic*, as the *polite* world. The forms of royalty are still kept up, but the reverence that alone can sustain them is gone. Under these circumstances the inquisitive mind turns with new relish to Greece, which Heeren has well observed may be considered as "*a sample paper of free commonwealths.*" The activity of these commonwealths, and the frequency of revolution, present every combination of the social elements, and gave to the Greek politician a vast and diversified experience; *e. g.*, Syracuse, it has been affirmed, presents in its history alone a complete compendium of governments, having passed through more revolutions than occur in the annals of modern Europe, if Italy be excepted.

But the history of Greece is particularly important to the American student. He can there learn the true value of the democratic principle, and acknowledge its energizing influence, whilst he sees its corrupting tendency when not restrained. He may there be taught to appreciate the blessings of representative legislatures, and select, independent and disinterested judiciaries. But above all will he behold the great blessings of our federative system, which in our state governments secures all the stimulating influence of small independent commonwealths, whilst in the federal head we behold just power sufficient to keep the peace throughout the system: thereby preventing those family jars and civil wars which hastened the downfall of Greece. He will see the true value of an equipoise between the federal and state governments. He will learn above all things to dread the evil of consolidation, which extinguishes individual energy and greatness of soul, by grinding down all to the same ignominious level. And, lastly, should that evil hour ever arrive, (which may Heaven avert!) when this great union shall be sundered, and our confederacy separated into its original elements, the history of Greece will still shed a twilight over the dark scene—inspire some consolation amid the general gloom; by showing that, bad as is the system of small, divided, and hostile states, it yet produces a compensating energy, which generates more of what constitutes the true glory of man, than can ever be found in the greatest empires of the world.

CHAPTER VIII.

ROME.

SEC. I.—THE ORIGINAL ITALIAN RACES.

Although we cannot explain the origin of the early Italian races, it is a great point gained, to know, that they existed and preceded the Romans on the soil of Italy; for it was from the blending and fusion of these different races that the Romans sprang, and it is with the study of their civilization that the study of Roman history properly begins. Indeed, without knowing something of their character, laws, religion, government, and manners, it is impossible fully to comprehend the history of that mighty people who sprang from them. We shall therefore begin with some account of those early races who preceded the Romans on the soil of Italy.

1. *The Oscans.* The Oscans were probably the most ancient race which inhabited Italy—the original stock from which sprang several of its most powerful nations, such as the Sabines, Samnites, and others. Before the foundations of Rome were laid, the numerous tribes into which this race was split, seemed to have been bound together by a great national *league*, extending over the whole range of the Apennines. Of this league, the Samnites were the most powerful tribe, and formed its vital core and centre. What the precise terms of this league were, we do not know; but, from the case of the Sabines, who, at an early period, left this league and united with the Romans, we know that the tribes were not prohibited from forming separate alliances.

The Oscans were, in a high degree, a pastoral and agricultural people, devoted to its pursuits, both theoretically aud practically, inhabiting a hilly country, and scattered through numerous villages, instead of being crowded together in large cities. The existence among them of an agricultural priesthood (Fratres Arvales), devoted not exclusively to the performance of religious rites, but partly to the scientific practice of agriculture, shows in what estimation that pursuit was held among them. Their manners were simple, their habits industrious, they tilled their own ground, and fed their own flocks. Before the foundations of Rome were laid, their country was in the highest state of civilization; flourishing fields, rich pastures, stretched to the highest ranges of the Apennines, and their hills and valleys were studded with innumerable villages, the abodes of a great moral population; they were emphatically a brave, hardy, contented, and warlike race. To the latest time, Sabine virtue furnished the Roman poets and orators with an exhaustless theme for eulogy, and to the latest time, many of the most illustrious patrician houses of Rome reverted with pride to their Sabine ancestors.

The social and political institutions of this race, seem to have been rather *patriarchal* than *aristocratic*, in the modern acceptation of that term. The authority of the *pater*, or father, as the head, first of the family, and then of the tribe, seems to have been the first and most prominent element of their system. In wealth, power, influence, and privilege, the *Samnite pater*, the prototype of the great Roman patrician, was the greatest of aristocrats; but he was no aristocrat in that offensive sense in which the Tuscan Lucomon or the feudal baron was an aristocrat, begirt with trembling slaves, or ruling with the strong arm multitudes of submissive serfs and vassals. His power, however great, was *paternal*. It was imposed by no superior force, but grew naturally out of his position as the head of his family or tribe, to every member of which he was bound, by the bond either of blood or religion, and was therefore cordially acquiesced in. This patriarchal organization is a leading feature in the social system of the Oscan races, and enables us to explain many things in the subsequent history of Rome which would otherwise remain inexplicable.

The Oscans constituted one of the original tribes of Rome, and were the WARRIOR CASTE *of the new state.*

2. *The Latins.* The Latins belonged, in all probability, to that great race which, in very early times, overspread both Greece and Italy, under the various names of Pelasgians, Tyrsenians, Siculians, &c. The foundation for this opinion rests mainly upon the analysis of their language, which is different both from the Oscan and the Etruscan—thus distinguishing them from these two great nations of central Italy. It bears, on the other hand, the strongest affinities to the Greek, in the circumstance of many common words, and similarity in the declension of nouns and verbs. The Greek, however, is not the only element

in the Latin language. It has another element in common with the other languages of central Italy; and while this Greek element distinguishes the Latin from the Oscans and Etruscans, and connects them with the Pelasgians, this latter element distinguishes them from the Pelasgians, and connects them with the Oscans, *thus rendering it probable that the Latins were a mixed people, formed by a union between the Oscan and Pelasgian races.* Not only so, but it has been observed, that the terms relating to agriculture and domestic life are mostly derived from the Greek, while those relating to arms and war are mostly Oscan—thus leading to the inference that the Oscans were the ruling class, the Pelasgians subject, and that the fusion of these races arose out of the conquest of the Pelasgians by the Oscans.

The Latins inhabited that district immediately south of the Tiber, called Latium. The period of their greatest prosperity and power seems to have preceded that of authentic history. In these early times, that country, now so barren, desolate, and volcanic, seems to have teemed with a numerous, wealthy, and energetic population, and the infected region, now poisoned for many a league by the malaria of the Pontine Marshes, is supposed to have been the seat of flourishing towns and cities. There seem to have been thirty Latin municipalities, each having its own independent government, and living according to its own laws, usages, and customs, yet bound together, as in the case of the Oscan race, by a national league or federation, of which Alba Longa was the centre. Their cities seem to have been built on heights, crowned by a citadel, and gradually extended their domain around the central eminence. Their buildings were massive and gigantic, and would seem to indicate an hierarchical establishment, by whom alone such enormous works could have been erected.

3. *The Etruscans.* The Etruscans were the latest, but most inscrutable of all the Italian races—darker, says Niebuhr, than the Egyptians. Their origin is shrouded in impenetrable darkness. An age, which has brought to light the hidden treasures which, for thousands of years, have been wrapped up in the hieroglyphics of Egypt, has not been able to penetrate the deep obscurity which hangs around the Etruscan race. There are, however, the strongest reasons for believing that they were of oriental origin. Their religion, laws, language, social and political arrangements, all bear the oriental stamp. Some think them an Egyptian colony; but the reasons for thinking them of Phœnician origin are much stronger. And, should the dark problem of their origin ever be solved, it may perhaps turn out that they sprang from a race older even than the Phœnicians—that race from which the Phœnicians themselves derived their institutions.

Like the Oscans and Latins, the Etruscans were also bound together by a great national league of which Etruria Proper, or Royal Etruria, was the centre. Of this great league, in the days of its prosperity and power, we know nothing. Before Rome has any place in history, the bonds of its union had been weakened, its energies exhausted, its religion corrupted and its civilization worn out. Yet Etruria was great even in her ruins, and it is universally agreed that she was once a prosperous and powerful state, in the possession of an immense commerce, and much the most polished and civilized of all the nations which preceded the Romans on the soil of Italy.

The civilization of the Etruscans presents many remarkable and important peculiarities. Their institutions seem to have been based on a union between aristocracy and religion. The system of *castes* existed instead of that of *classes*, thus clearly indicating an Asiatic origin. All power seems to have resided in a patrician order, who, like those of Egypt, India, and other oriental nations, were also a *sacerdotal caste*, in whose families the priesthood was hereditary, and who were surrounded, not like the Samnite and Latin fathers, by tribes bound to them by the ties of common blood and a common religion, but by serfs and slaves bound up in the iron system of castes, born to hopeless servitude transmitted from sire to son, and swayed at pleasure by their lordly and priestly masters, through the combined influence of religion and fear. This marked division and want of community between the ruling caste and the great body of the people, has led to the belief that the Etruscans were not a homogeneous population; but that the Etruscan chiefs were a body of skilful and intelligent foreigners, who had, by force or policy, acquired the position of a ruling caste among a people inferior to them in civilization and inferior to them in race and blood. However this may have been, or whatever may have been the origin of the Etruscans, the existence among them of a ruling caste, in possession of the government, wielding all its powers with undisputed sway, and holding, as among the Slavonic nations the great mass of the population in complete subjection and serfdom, and who, at the same time that they thus concentrated in their order all civil power, were also a sacerdotal and priestly caste, having in charge all the offices of religion, clothed with its sacred sanctions, ministering at its holy altars, presiding over its awful mysteries, and transmitting those mysteries, not by written records whereby they might be divulged, but by oral instruction and tradition, from generation to generation, as the sacred and immemorial inheritance of their order—the existence of this lordly and priestly caste is the distinctive characteristic of Etruscan society, and one which came, in after times, to exert a vast influence over the destinies of Rome. So far as we can now ascertain, this powerful order had a senate for the ordinary administration of public affairs; but, in times of emergency, a king, or rather a regent was elected for a limited period. His title was that of *Lucomon.* His powers were both temporal and spiritual. Like the Roman king, of whom he was the prototype, he was not only the chief executive officer, executing the office of the senate and commanding its armies in time of war, but he was the high priest [Pontifex Maximus] or chief minister of religion, presiding over all its sacrificial rites and public offices. It was from these Tuscan kings or Lucomons, that the Romans derived much of their pomp and ceremonial, the purple robe, the golden crown, the curule chair, the eagle sceptre, the fasces, and the axe of the lictors—all which insignia were transmitted from the royal to the republican authorities. Never, perhaps, was there a people over whom religion exerted a greater influence, not even the Egyptians themselves. The ancient Etruscan lived, moved, and had his being in the midst of religion. It surrounded him on every side, in public and private, in his domestic life, and in the public institutions of the state. And this religion was no simple faith or belief—no primitive worship of nature and the elements, like that of the Oscans and Latins, but a religion of rites and ceremonies, veiled in pomp, shrouded in mystery, and administered by a patrician priesthood who were its hereditary guardians.

Such were the Oscans, Latins, and Etruscans, who preceded the Romans on the soil of Italy.

SEC. II.—THE ORIGIN OF ROME.

1. *Rome formed by the Union of Three Tribes.* Of the origin of Rome, we *know* nothing. The childhood and youth of this heroic city are shrouded in impenetrable myth and fable, and much of its early history is left to conjecture. In the absence of positive evidence, language is our best guide in seeking the origin of nations and races. Now, we know that the language of the Romans was Latin; this clearly shows their affinities with the Latin race. But we know that the Romans were not Latins, though speaking the Latin language; they were, politically, distinct from them. The Romans, then, were something which the Latins were not. What was this? Here language can lend us no aid; we must resort to *geography* and *tradition.* Upon reference to the early maps of Italy, you will see that Rome stands upon the confines of the three great confederacies, which I have described as occupying Italy before the foundation of that city, viz., the Oscans, Latins, and Etruscans. In the absence, then, of all tra-

dition, the mere geographical position of Rome would render it easily conceivable how a mixed population should form itself in this corner of the Latin territories. But fortunately we are not left to geographical probabilities. Tradition comes strongly in aid of geography; for it so happens, that the annals of Rome abound in legends and traditions, all pointing in the same direction, and leading to the conclusion, that the Roman state was formed by the union and ultimate fusion of the Oscan, Latin, and Etruscan races; and this conclusion may now be considered as established, as the result of the immortal labors of Niebuhr.

SEC. III.—THE SOCIAL SYSTEM OF ROME.

1. *The Original Roman Tribes.* Tradition informs us, that the founders of Rome were shepherds and herdsmen. It describes how these shepherds and herdsmen laid the foundations of the city on the Palatine Hill, and how, in a short time, their numbers were swelled by strangers from all the countries round about. In the very earliest times, it speaks of a division of the people into three distinct tribes—the Ramnences, the Titienses, and Luceres. The Ramnences are distinctly identified as the original shepherds and herdsmen who founded the city upon the Palatine Hill. The Titienses are also distinctly proved to have been Sabines, and their early union with the original people of the Palatine Hill cannot be doubted. In respect to the origin of the third tribe (the Luceres), as well as to the time of their establishment at Rome, more difficulty exists. The received opinion, however, is, that they were Tuscans, and that they did not settle at Rome until after the Titienses—perhaps not until the time of the Tarquins. However this may have been, it is certain that, at a time anterior to authentic history, the Roman state was formed by the union of these three tribes, viz, the Ramnences, Titienses, and Luceres.

2. *The Subdivision of the Tribes into Curiæ and Centuries.* The three original tribes were, for civil and religious purposes, subdivided into ten smaller bodies, called *curiæ;* so that the whole original Roman people consisted of thirty curiæ. The purposes of these curiæ were, as just stated, civil and religious. They formed centres of religious union, and of common sacrificial rites. They had nothing to do with war; there was another division of the people for the purposes of war, called *centuries*, and answering to the thirty curiæ, organized with reference to religion and civil affairs; there were thirty centuries organized with reference to war. In their military

system, the three tribes were represented by three centuries of horse, just as the thirty curiæ were represented by thirty centuries of foot, and this constituted the original Roman legion. Over each curiæ there presided a curion, who seems to have been both a magistrate and priest, while over each century there presided a centurion, who was a military commander. In time of peace, the centuries seem to have been subordinate to the curiæ; but in times of war this was reversed, when, according to the uniform usage of antiquity, armies in which various races served, were marshalled with reference to this variety of race; and, until the time of Servius Tullus, who overthrew the old constitution of Rome, and remodelled it on new principles, the Latin, Sabine, and Etruscan races fought in different bands.

3. *The Constitution of the Roman Gens or House.* We have said that the original Roman tribes were divided into thirty curiæ. It would be more proper to say, that the curiæ formed the tribes; for we shall now show that the original Roman state grew out of the union of certain elements, which were neither tribes nor curiæ, but *gentes* or *houses;* thus making the gentes, or house, the original element of the whole primitive Roman society and government. It is therefore of the greatest importance that we should understand what this gentes, or house, was. So far as we can now ascertain, the Roman gentes, or house, was formed, in the first instance, by the union of several families. But what was the bond of this union? Was it consanguinity or sameness of blood? Were all the families forming the gentes, or house, descended from a common ancestor? Originally, perhaps, this was so; but if so, in the course of time an artificial bond came to be substituted for the natural bond of blood. This artificial bond was *religion*—the joint performance of the same religious rites; and in later times, the artificial bond of religion having the place of the natural bond of blood, the gentes, or house, as it has existed within historical memory, may be described as an association of several families, bound together by the joint performance of the same religious rites and ceremonies; thus making the *altar* the centre of their union.

4. *The Roman Family.* The gentes, or house, being thus formed by the union of several families, bound together by the artificial bond of religion, the next step, in order to a more perfect understanding of the early social system of Rome, will be an analysis of that most primitive of all human associations—*the family*, as it existed at Rome. When we come to make this analysis of the primitive Roman family, we find it indelibly impressed with the patriarchal stamp. We find it consisting of two descriptions of persons; first, *members* of the family,

and secondly, *dependents* on the family. Now we have seen, according to the original Roman system, the state was divided into tribes; that these tribes were divided into curiæ, the curiæ into houses, and the houses into families. It follows from this arrangement that all who were *members* of a family, were members of a house, and if of a house then of a curiæ, and if of a curiæ then of a tribe, and if of a tribe then of the state, and so lastly a *Roman citizen.* The *members* therefore of the original Roman families, and they alone, constituted the earliest citizens of Rome—*the original Populus Romanus;* but if the *members* of the families alone were *Roman* citizens, how was it with that other description of population who were only *dependents* on the families? We have just seen that they could have no political connection with the state. Not being members of any family, they could not be members of any house, and if not members of a house then not of a curiæ, and if not of a curiæ then not of a tribe, and if not of a tribe then not of the state, and if not of the state then not citizens. There was therefore no place for them in the body politic. They were not recognized in any political capacity by the Roman constitution; their relation seems to have been wholly of a *private* nature, and confined to the houses formed by the union of the families on which they were dependent, and to which their allegiance was due. And these were the original Roman clients.

5. *The original Populus Romanus.* It thus appears that the original citizens of Rome were the *members* of the original Roman families, and the *members* of those families alone—the *dependents* of those families being *clients*, and excluded from all political rights and franchises. And, according to Niebuhr, these two classes (the *members* of the original families and their *clients*) constituted, in the earliest times, the entire population of Rome; and it is certain that the primitive constitution of the state contemplates the existence of no other class.

6. *The Roman Commons, or Plebs.* But in the course of time, partly by emigration, but principally by conquest, there came to be formed by the side of the original population of Rome an alien and foreign population, not contemplated by the original constitution of Rome, for whom no provision was made in that constitution—having no connection with either one of the three original tribes—related to none of the houses forming those tribes either by the tie of membership or clientage, and therefore excluded from all connection with the state—in a word, an anomalous population, uniting personal liberty with political subjection—*dependents* on no house and therefore freemen—*members* of no house and therefore disfranchised and not citizens of Rome. *Such were the plebs—the great Roman commons*—the

most illustrious commons the world has ever seen, unless the English be excepted. In the infancy of Rome, we see them poor, weak, disfranchised; connected with the state, but no part of it; compelled to fight its battles, but not permitted to share its privileges. They are not even allowed to live within the city—this is consecrated gronnd. The Aventine Hill, without its walls, is assigned them for their residence. Still less are they permitted to intermarry with any of the Roman houses. This would be, not only to admit aliens and foreigners within the pale of the constitution, but to taint the old patrician blood of Rome. For many generations the blood ran pure in the veins of those old patrician fathers of the city. No foreign alloy mingled with it, and the plebeians resided outside of the walls, a distinct community, regulating their own municipal affairs, and living according to their own laws, usages and customs. They were, as we have seen, for the most part, like the English commons, a conquered people; but they were also like that same commons an enterprising, energetic and intelligent people. Consequently they grew rapidly in wealth, and as they grew in wealth they grew in numbers, intelligence and power until, ultimately they came to be the most wealthy, most numerous and most powerful portion of the community. Added to this, there were in their ranks men as high-born, in whose veins the blood coursed as pure as in the veins of the haughtiest patrician of the city. The Scilii, the Decii, the Domitii and others, families as ancient and noble as the patrician Claudii or Quinctii, sprang from the bosom of the commons, and, in the latter days of the Republic, the majority of the illustrious historic names of Rome were of plebeian origin. That such a body of men should rest contented under their political disfranchisement and social inferiority, was not to be expected. Accordingly, in the very earliest times, we hear the mutterings of their discontent, and the early constitutional history of Rome is little else than the history of this illustrious body as it develops itself through incessant, though not bloody conflicts with the original Roman tribes—the growth of their demands always keeping pace with their growth in wealth, intelligence and power—the pride of privilege gradually yielding before the principle of equality, until ultimately the whole Roman plebs, like the English commons, fight their way within the pale of the constitution. The mantle of the high-born patrician descends upon the shoulder of the humble plebeian, and the entire Roman people, patrician and plebeian, are fused together in one homogeneous mass in the enjoyment of equal rights, franchises and liberties.

It thus appears that the *original Populus Romanus was a strictly privileged order*, in the exclusive possession of the government, while the *original Roman Commons were a degraded and disfranchised class.*

SEC. IV.—THE CONSTITUTION OF ROME DURING THE MONARCHY.

1. *The Constitution of the Patriarchal Tribe.* We have already seen that the Roman state was formed by the confederation of three tribes, and it is to the original principles of the tribe that we must look for the first elements of the Roman constitution. Not only so, but it is to the patriarchal tribe that we must look; for those tribes, out of a confederation of which Rome sprang, are indelibly impressed with the patriarchal character. So much so that, in perusing the early annals of Rome, we are irresistibly carried back to the time of the Hebrew patriarchs and the forms of society then existing.

The constitution of the patriarchal tribe, then, presents us with a patriarch, or chief who was the head of the tribe, and held his power by the common and immemorial consent of the tribe. He was its chief administrative officer, its judge, its general, and its high priest, thus uniting in his person executive, judicial, and sacerdotal functions. The patriarchal tribe also presents us with a council of elders, the chief men of the tribe, heads of the houses, and standing towards the houses in pretty much the same relation in which the chief stands towards the tribe. Lastly, we have the patriarchal family with its twofold division of members, and dependents—relations and servants—an association founded, not like the Feudal association, out of elements alien and hostile to each other, held together by force, but out of elements homogeneous, sympathetic, and united by the moral ties of common blood, common religious rites, and common traditions and remembrances.

2. *The Constitution of the Patriarchal Tribe a Miniature of the Early Constitution of Rome.* Such was the constitution of the primitive patriarchal tribe, and in it we have a faithful miniature of the early constitution of Rome. Indeed that constitution in its early stages, was little else than the organization and government of the tribe, enlarged, and extended so as to adapt it to a *confederation of tribes.* In the patriarchal chief, uniting in his person executive, judicial, and sacerdotal functions, we have the image of the early *kings of Rome.* In the council of elders who were the heads of the patriarchal families, we have the *Senate of Rome,* composed of the heads of the original Roman houses. Lastly, in the *members* of the patriarchal families, we have the primitive *Roman people,* and in the *dependents* on those families we have the original *Roman clients.* In this patriarchal system you will observe there was no place for aliens—men connected with the state either by membership or clientage. Hence the anomalous

position of the Roman plebs, or commons. There was no room for them in the early constitution of the state, and they remained, as we have described them, for many centuries, a disfranchised and inferior order.

3. *The Kings.* The early kings of Rome, like the chiefs of the patriarchal tribes, were at once chief magistrates, judges, generals, and high priests. Their power varied, in all probability, as in the Feudal monarchies of Europe, with the measure of their abilities and popularity. Over the *commons*, it seems to have been absolute; but over the *Roman people*, it was only absolute in *war*, and beyond the walls of the city. Within the walls of the city, every Roman citizen was entitled to appeal to his peers, assembled in their curiæ. The truth is, that the government of Rome, during the time of the Monarchy, as well as that of the Republic, was essentially aristocratic, and the kings, though invested with executive, judicial, and sacerdotal functions, were held in check by the nobility, and exerted, during times of peace, but small authority over the Roman people proper. The chief power of the government resided permanently in the Senate, where the aristocracy were represented.

4. *The Senate.* We have seen that the Roman state was formed by the confederation of three sovereign tribes. Each of these tribes was represented by a hundred chiefs, the heads of the great houses, thus making in all three hundred chiefs, and these constituted in the earliest times the *Roman Senate.* It is easy to understand that in a patriarchal form of society, a body thus constituted must have wielded vast power. And such we know was the fact. The Roman Senate gradually, and progressively engrossed all the powers of the state. It declared war, made peace, raised armies, levied taxes, declared a dictator when necessary, had the administration of the public lands, farmed out the revenues, and granted or withheld from the soldiers all booty taken in war. Not only so, but it came in later times, though under the nominal control of the people, to exercise the supervision of religion and its ceremonies, the distribution of the governments of provinces, and command of armies, together with the custody and appropriation of the public moneys. It exercised jurisdiction over all Italy, had the administration of all foreign affairs, sent and received ambassadors, determined the time of holding assemblies of the people, and prepared the business to be discussed and disposed of there. It could grant or refuse the *triumph* to the victorious general, and could, by means of the terrible *dent operam—ne quid est* (their suspension of the habeas corpus), clothe the consuls, prætors, and tribunes with absolute power. In addition to all this, the *judicial power* was, until the time of the Gracchi, exclusively in the Senate, and the *selecti judices*, answering to

our juries, were drawn from the Senatorial order. In a word, the Roman Senate was the great executive council of the nation, made up in the first instance of the old patrician nobility, but in later times, of the whole nobility both patrician and plebeian, in whom resided for the greater part of the time almost the entire power of the state.

5. *The Comitia Curiata.* Great, however, as was the power of the Senate, supreme power, according to the theory of the Roman constitution, did not reside in that body, but in the *Roman people*, assembled in their curiæ—called *Comitia Curiata.* These assemblies were composed exclusively of the *members* of the Roman houses. Neither the *clients* nor the *plebs* or *commons* were admitted in them. Politically, their existence was not required by the constitution. In the *Roman people*, then, as thus restricted, in their *comitia curiata*, resided sovereign legislative and judicial authority. In times of peace, all the edicts of the king and all the decrees of the Senate must be *ratified* in the *comitia curiata*, in order to give them validity; and to this assembly, in the last resort, an appeal always laid for a *Roman citizen*—not, however, for a *common* or a *client.*

6. *Change in the original constitution of Rome necessary.* From the account which has been now given of the primitive constitution of Rome, it will be seen that the Roman People were originally a strictly privileged order—indeed, *a caste*—in the exclusive possession of the government. This may have done well enough as long as the population of Rome was confined to the original tribes. But when, in the course of time, a rich, warlike, and noble body of commons grew up by the side of the original tribes, then it became manifest that the state had outgrown its original constitution, and that this patrician caste must either be recruited from the commons, or degenerate into a miserable oligarchy, and so be ultimately overwhelmed by the pressure of that great, powerful, and augmenting body. *It was so recruited.* The patrician order was constantly reinforced by accessions from the commons. This is the point upon which the political destinies of Rome turned. It enabled the patrician order to sustain itself for so many centuries in their great struggle with the commons, to maintain their ascendency to the very last, and to impress upon the government of the commonwealth those high aristocratic features which every where distinguished it. It now remains for us to explain in what manner the original patrician order was recruited and reinforced from the commons, and thus strengthened for the fulfilment of its high and mighty destiny.

7. *The Reform of Tarquin.* We have described the original Roman plebs, or commons, as a robust, industrious, warlike yeomanry—altogether

unlike that poor, dissolute, and rapacious rabble which we have been in the habit of associating with the idea of plebeian. We have also seen that this great body of commons had its leaders; men as wealthy as warlike, and, in their original country, as noble as the patrician fathers of Rome. But yet, in their adopted country, they were disfranchised, and deprived of all the rights of citizenship. When, in the natural progress of events, the commons had grown in wealth and power, and the number of these noble but disfranchised families had multiplied, it became manifest that the time had come when the doors of privilege and prerogative must be unbarred, and the government remodelled on a wider basis. The only question was, What should be the nature of the change? How far should it proceed? Should the government be *revolutionized* or *reformed?* Should it be remodelled on new principles, or only enlarged upon its old? In this great crisis of their fortunes, the patrician order, by their moderation, their timely concessions, and that high practical wisdom which ever distinguished them, not only saved for the present the old constitution of Rome, and the privileges and prerogatives of their order; but established that order upon a basis which enabled it to maintain its ascendency to the very last, and preserve, throughout the whole period of the commonwealth, a *mixed government*, with a large infusion of aristocratic elements. A *revolution* was avoided. The constitution was enlarged upon its original principles. The number of senators was doubled, and the senate thus increased from three hundred to six hundred. The vacancies thus created were filled from the great and powerful houses of the commons, and thus were the commons for the first time admitted within the pale of the Roman aristocracy. It seems, however, that the plebeian houses thus ennobled, were distinguished from the old patrician houses by the title of the *lesser houses*, thus giving rise to the distinction of *majores* and *minores gentes.* It would also seem that the plebeian senators did not vote until after the patrician, and in the latest times, when every vestige of political inequality had been swept away, and patrician and plebeian were melted together into one undistinguished mass, the descendants of the *majores gentes* never forgot their patrician origin. It was always the haughty boast of the Claudian family, that the blood of the old patrician fathers of Rome flowed pure in their veins, unpolluted by the taint of any foreign alloy.

This reform of the old constitution of Rome is attributed by common tradition to the elder Tarquin, who, whether Latin or Sabine, is generally admitted to have been a foreigner, and to have forced his way to the throne by personal talent and influence. He seems to have been but little favored by the Roman people, but threw himself openly into the arms of the commons, by whose assistance he was enabled to carry out his reforms, and consolidate his power. According to the early traditions, he wished to push his changes farther than he did. His plan seems to have been to double the number of the *tribes*, in the same manner in which the number of the *senatorial houses* had been doubled, in this way to organize the commons into three new tribes, to stand side by side with the Roman tribes—viz.: the Ramnenses, the Titienses, and the Luceres, and thus to admit the great body of the commons to the rights and privileges of Roman citizenship, just as the *wealthy* and *powerful families* of the commons had been admitted to the rights and privileges of the Roman aristocracy. But in this Tarquin failed. "The interest of the old citizens," says Arnold, "taking the shape of a religious objection, was strong enough to force the king to modify his project." And the result was, that, while the barriers separating the patrician and plebeian nobles were removed, and the wealthy, powerful, and noble families of both orders were united together in one consolidated body, the old distinctions between the Roman people and the commons were maintained, and the commons remained a disfranchised and degraded caste.

8. *The Reform of Tarquin prejudicial to the Commons.* Thus appears that the reform of Tarquin was essentially an aristocratic reform. By it the basis of aristocratic order was enlarged, the old barrier of race broken through, the distinction between the patrician and plebeian nobles abolished in the main, and the foundations of the new aristocracy laid in principles broad enough and liberal enough to embrace the wealthy, powerful and influential families of the commons. But while the barriers excluding the great plebeian families from the pale of the constitution were removed, and the foundation of the greatness of the Roman aristocracy laid in the union of the patrician and plebeian nobles in one great order, no such union, as we have seen, could be effected between the great body of the commons and the Roman people. The line separating the *commons* from the *Roman people* was as deep as ever. The commons were still disfranchised as before, and excluded from all the rights of Roman citizenship, and that event which laid the foundation of the greatness of the aristocratic order is the darkest, and most calamitous in the history of the commons. They gained absolutely nothing in the great struggle in which they had engaged, but came out of it with the loss of the wealthiest, noblest, and most powerful members of their order, who were their natural leaders, around whose standards they had often rallied, but who had now gone over to recruit the hostile ranks.

The direction which this reform of Tarquin took is a key to much of the future history of Rome. It enables us to understand the ascendency which the aristocratic order maintained throughout the whole period of the commonwealth. The union of the wealthy and powerful plebeian families with the old patrician caste, laid the foundation of the greatness of that order deep and broad, while the exclusion of the Commons from all the rights and privileges of Roman citizens, perpetuated those rivalries and divisions which were the sources of the weakness of both. It was precisely in the same way, by breaking down the distinction *between* the Norman and the Saxon nobles, by constantly recruiting the aristocracy by the admission of the wealthy and powerful commons within its pale, that the aristocracy of England have been able to maintain their ascendency from the Norman conquest to the present time, and impress upon its government those high aristocratic features for which it is distinguished. Both the people of Rome and the people of England have been able to make but slow progress against an aristocratic order thus consolidated and recruited.

From this period, the division of parties at Rome seems to have been as follows:—On one side were the whole body of the aristocracy, patrician and plebeian, backed by the *Roman people proper*, and their *clients*—on the other was the commons, single-handed, and weakened by the desertion of their most powerful members.

9. *The old Constitution of Rome subverted.* We have seen that the effect of the reform of Tarquin was to strengthen the aristocratic order, and make that order predominant in the state. Against this condition of things, so far as we can rely on the traditions of those early times, there seems to have been a speedy and violent reaction. The great and increasing power of the aristocracy, while it arrayed against it the whole body of the commons, appears to have also excited the jealousy of the kings, and we soon find a union effected between the king and the commons against the aristocratic order. This gave rise to a new struggle, which resulted, not as the former one had done, in a *mere reform* of the old institutions of Rome, but in their entire *subversion and overthrow.* The change now effected was emphatically a *revolution*, and is. by common tradition, attributed to Servius Tullus, the great leader of the commons. Like Tarquin, he seems to have been a foreigner, unpopular with the Roman aristocracy, and resting on the commons for support. by whose aid he remodelled the government on principles entirely new.

10. *The Constitution of Servius Tullus.* We have seen that the early system of Rome was an aristocracy founded in *race*—the principle of which is equality within its own body, and ascendency over all the rest of the community. The revolution of Servius consisted in the entire subversion of this early system, the abolition of all distinction of

race—and the substitution of a new system based on *property*, giving a portion of power to all—not however an equal portion, but graduated according to property as the standard. The effect of this system, therefore, was to do away with old distinctions and create new ones—to do away with distinctions of *race* and create distinctions of *property*. This revolution does not seem to have been effected immediately—it seems to have been brought about gradually and indirectly. It seems to have commenced with the organization of the commons as a distinct and separate body. They were divided into THIRTY TRIBES, four for the city, and twenty-six for the country; thus showing that a large proportion of the commons were a rural people. These thirty tribes of the commons seem to have been organized so as to answer to the thirty *curiæ* of the Roman people, who, it will be remembered, were accustomed to assemble, not in their three original tribes, but in their thirty curiæ. The commons were now to meet in their thirty tribes to manage their affairs, just as the Roman people proper assembled in their thirty curiæ for the management of their affairs. Over each one of these thirty tribes there presided a magistrate, called a *tribune*, and there were also judges to decide private causes among the commons. For the purpose of appointing these officers, as well as for other purposes, the tribes held their own meetings, called *comitia tributa*, answering to the *comitia curiata* of the Roman people.

Here, for the first time, we have the commons as an *organized body*, and this is a most important epoch in their history, for organization gives strength and the consciousness of strength. The organization of the commons was, however, as yet, entirely independent of the Roman people, and now we have two organized bodies (the comitia curiata and the comitia tributa), side by side, and answering to the House of Lords and House of Commons, before they were united in one body. The truth is, the Roman commons and people were now two distinct estates of the realm, with their separate organization, and without the means of uniting as States General, or a Parliament.

For the Roman people, assembled in their comitia curiata, considered themselves entitled to the whole control of the government; and while they allowed the commons, assembled in their comitia tributa, to manage the affairs of their own order, they were not permitted to intermeddle with any thing affecting either the patrician order or the general interests of the state. Upon the other hand, the patricians had nothing to do with the domestic affairs of the commons, as an order; but the commons, assembled in their comitia tributa, managed the affairs of their order; and the patricians, assembled in their comitia curiata, managed the affairs of their order, each independently of the other. The whole control of the government, the management of all *national* affairs, all foreign relations, and every thing affecting neither of the orders as orders, but the state as a state, was under the jurisdiction of the patricians assembled in their comitia curiata. These bodies assembled in different places, the patricians in the Comitium, and the commons in the Forum near by.

11. *The Comitia Centuriata.* Though thus organized as distinct bodies, there was *one* relation in which they were compelled to act together, and to feel that they belonged to one common country. This was in time of war. It has always been that the distinctions of peace vanish amidst the dangers of war. When marching against the public enemy, banded together in one army, fighting under the same standards, and in the same cause, they felt that they were the same people, and that, whether patricians or plebeians, they were all Romans. Here, then, we have a point of union between the two orders—a common basis upon which they might be organized as one people. They were so organized. The whole people, patricians and plebeians, were assembled for *military purposes in comitia centuria*, and thus the basis upon which the different orders of the state were first organized as one people was purely military. Indeed, so entirely were the comitia centuria military assemblies, that they were not permitted to meet within the walls of the city, but met in the Campus Martius, and bore the name of *Exercitus Urbanus* (the army of the city). They were not even assembled like the comitia curiata and comitia tributa, by the lictors, but by the blast of a horn. On returning home from war, they always stopped outside of the walls of the city, to try in their military character all military offences committed in the field; for the moment they entered its consecrated precincts, all civil relations were resumed, and the jurisdiction of the comitia centuria annulled.

But it was not to be expected that the comitia centuria, though thus purely military in its origin, would long remain so. All experience demonstrates, that a great and powerful body, when organized for one purpose, will soon extend itself so as to embrace other purposes; and so far as we can judge by the twilight of those early times, such was the course of things at Rome. The Roman people and commons, once organized for military purposes, soon began to extend their jurisdiction to civil purposes; and the comitia centuria, from being in their origin purely military assemblies, soon became the great ruling body of the nation, overshadowing the old comitia curiata and comitia, tributa, leaving to them jurisdiction only over such matters as appertained exclusively to their respective orders.

When we come to look to the constitution of the comitia centuria, we find that it was based on property and the whole people, patrician and plebeian, distributed into classes, with reference to the amount of their possessions, thus making *property* the ruling element of the new, as *race* was of the old, constitution; and in graduating power among the different classes, such a rule was observed as to give the ascendency to wealth, thereby removing the government from a close oligarchy and an uncurbed democracy, with numbers for its ruling element. The effect of the revolution was, to admit the plebeians to the right of citizenship, and to transfer the government from the patricians into their hands, but at the same time to vest the sovereign power in the hands of the wealthy and influential classes.

Such was the famous constitution of Servius Tullus, the patriot king of Rome. To the latest times, and throughout the whole of that eventful history, the commons look back fondly to this constitution as their Magna Charta. And when, afterwards, after centuries of disfranchisement and oppression, we find them again struggling into power, they conscientiously believed and maintained that they were only claiming their ancient and immemorial rights and liberties, settled upon their order in those early times by the Servian constitution.

12. *The overthrow of the Servian Constitution.* But the Servian constitution, whatever may have been its merits, was of short duration. It is even doubtful whether it was ever fully carried into effect, and it is certain that it was overthrown a short time after its formation. In latter times, after long and eventful struggles, and amidst undying jealousies and rivalries, it was partly, though never wholly, restored. It is in vain, at this distance of time, to seek the causes of the overthrow of this constitution; perhaps it was premature; perhaps the plebeians were not yet prepared to take their place side by side with the Roman people, and exercise, intelligently and beneficially, their new rights and franchises. The voice of universal history testifies, that institutions, to be permanent, must be the growth of time and circumstances. The constitution of a great people cannot be formed in a day; and when, in latter times, the Servian constitution was in part restored, this was done gradually, by successive stages, and every step was warmly contested and dearly won.

The revolution which overthrew the Servian constitution, is generally attributed to the latter Tarquin. According to tradition, he entirely crushed the liberties of the commons, abolished the laws of Servius, destroyed the arrangement of the commons into classes, excluded them almost entirely from the rank of the army, employed them in servile works, such as building the Circus, the Capitoline Temple and the Cloaca; in a word, reduced them to a condition more servile than at any former period of their history.

13. *The overthrow of the Monarchy.* But Tarquin was a selfish and vulgar tyrant, preferring himself to his order. Having, with the aid of the patricians, crushed the plebeians, his next object seems to have been to crush the patricians, and thus make himself absolute. This caused him to be cordially hated by both orders, who now united against him to effect his overthrow. This was accomplished in the year 244 after the foundation of the city. Tarquin was expelled, the monarchy abolished, and the commonwealth established. But the evils of Tarquin's tyranny survived his downfall. It was not so easy to restore what he had destroyed, as to expel himself and his family. After his reign, the commons no longer stood side by side with the patricians, as an equal order, free, wealthy, well-organized, and well-armed; but we find them poor, disunited, and defenceless. Accordingly, they soon sank beneath the power of the nobility, and that revolution which expelled the dynasty of the Tarquins, established at Rome, not a free commonwealth, but the dominion of an exclusive and tyrannical aristocracy. This revolution dates some twenty years before the battle of Marathon.

SEC. V.—FROM THE FALL OF THE MONARCHY TO THE WARS WITH CARTHAGE.—B. C. 509–264.

1. *The establishment of the Consular Government.* The only direct consequence to the internal constitution of Rome, proceeding from the abolition of royalty, was, that that power, undermined as it had been while in the hands of the kings, was transferred to two consuls, annually elected. Meanwhile the struggle for liberty, in which the new republic was engaged with the Etrusci and Latins, contributed much to arouse the republican spirit, which henceforward was the main feature of the Roman character—the evils of popular rule being in times of need remedied by the establishment of the dictatorship. The party, however, which had deposed the ruling family, took wholly into their own hands the helm of state; and the oppression of these aristocrats shown principally towards their debtors, who had become their slaves (*nexi*)—notwithstanding the *lex de provocatione* established by Valerius Poplicola, insuring to the people the highest judicial power,—was so galling, that after the lapse of a few years it gave rise to a sedition of the commons (*plebis*), the consequence of which was the establishment of annually elected presidents of the people (*tribuni plebis*).

2. *The Tribunes.* The further development of the Roman constitution in this period turns almost entirely on the contest, which the new

chiefs of the commons conducted against the hereditary nobility, for, not content with protecting against oppression, they soon proceeded to measures of attack, and in a short time extended the object so far, that short of a perfect equality of rights no termination of the contest was to be expected. It was, therefore, necessarily a long one, since the aristocracy of the time had too firm supporters in the clientela and by means of the auspices in the religion of the state.

3. *The twelve tables.* The code of the twelve tables confirmed the ancient institutions, and was in part completed by the adoption of the laws of the Greek republics, among which Athens in particular is mentioned, whose counsels were requested by a special deputation. In this, however, two faults were committed; not only were the commissioners charged with drawing up the laws elected from the patricians *alone*, but they were likewise constituted sole magistrates, with *dictatorial* power (*sine provocatione*), whereby a path was opened to them for a usurpation, which could be frustrated only by a sedition of the people.

By the laws of the twelve tables the legal relations of the citizens were the same for all; but as that code seems to have contained very little in reference to any peculiar constitution of the state, the government not only remained in the hands of the aristocrats, who were in possession of all offices, but the prohibition, according to the new laws of marriage between patricians and plebeians, appeared to have raised an insurmountable barrier between the two classes. No wonder, then, that the tribunes of the people should have immediately renewed their attacks on the patricians; particularly as the power of those popular leaders was not only renewed, but even augmented, as the only limit to their authority was the necessity of their being unanimous in their acts, while each had the right of a negative.

4. *The provisions of the twelve tables.* From the fragments preserved, and restorations made, by distinguished civilians, we learn that the twelve tables covered the following ground:

Table 1, related to lawsuits; and embraced regulations upon citing to judgment, surety and the judgment.

Table 2, prescribed rules upon the subject of robberies, embraced restitutions and prescriptions relating to them, and referred also to breaches of trust.

Table 3, treated of loans, and the right of creditors over their debtors.

Table 4, related to the right of fathers over their children. And it may be here observed, that this table was taken entirely from the ancient laws of Rome, and cannot be a subject of reproach to Greece for its harsh and unnatural provisions.

Table 5, related to inheritances and guardianships, and prescribed successions and distributions.

Table 6, referred to property and possession; and treated of conveyances of estates and merchandise.

Table 7, related to trespasses and damages, in which were included injuries to the person or property of another, slanders and murders.

Table 8, under the title of estates in the country, embraced chiefly disputes about property in the country, and damages.

Table 9, related to the common rights of the people, such as forbidding privileges, restoring the rights of persons pardoned, bribery, etc.

Table 10, related to the regulation of funerals and ceremonies to the dead.

Table 11, treated of the worship of the gods and religion.

Table 12, of marriages and the rights of husbands.

5. *Dissensions between the Patricians and Plebeians.* The main subjects of the new dissensions between patricians and plebeians, excited by the tribune Canuleius, were now the *connubia patrum cum plebe*, and the exclusive participation of the patricians in the consulship, of which the tribunes demanded the abolition. The repeal of the former law was obtained as early as 445 (*lex Canuliça*); the right of admission to the consulship was not extended to the plebeians till after a struggle annually renewed for eighty years; during which, when, as usually was the case, the tribunes forbade the military enrolment, recourse was had to a transfer of the consular power to the yearly elected commanders of the legions; a place to which plebeians were entitled to aspire (*tribuni militum consulari potestate*).—Establishment of the office of CENSORS, designed at first for nothing more than to regulate the taking of the census, and invested with no higher authority than what that required, but who soon after, by assuming to themselves the *censura morum*, took rank among the most important dignitaries of the state.

6. *Wars with neighboring States.* While in the mean time Rome, as the head of the neighboring allied cities (socii), both of the Latini, especially since the victory on the lake Regillus, and of the other nations, oppressed them, or at least they thought themselves oppressed, their continual exertions to free themselves at every opportunity, gave rise to an almost uninterrupted succession of petty wars, which must have depopulated Rome, had not this been prevented by the maxims adopted of increasing the number of citizens by freedmen, and frequently even by the conquered. Little remarkable as these feuds are singly, they are very much so from having been the cause of making the nation a nation of warriors, and of establishing that supremacy of the Senate, the important consequences of which will be hereafter exhibited

7. *The burning of Rome by the Gauls.* Rome, nevertheless, was soon after almost entirely swept away, by a storm from the North. The Sennonian Gauls, penetrating as far as Etruria from Northern Italy, made themselves masters of the city, except the citadel only, and reduced it to ashes; an occurrence, which impressed itself so deeply on the memory of the Romans, that few others in their history have been more spun out by tradition. Camillus, then the preserver of Rome, and in general one of the chief heroes of the time, performed a double service to his paternal city, for he frustrated, after the victory, the project of an entire migration to Veii.

8. *The Contests between the Patricians and Plebeians revived.* Scarcely had Rome been rebuilt, when the ancient feuds between the patricians and plebeians were revived. This was produced by an increase of taxation consequent on the establishment of military pay, and by the introduction of gross usury. The tribunes, Sextius and Licinius, by prolonging their term of office to five years, had established their power; while Licinius, by an agrarian law, decreeing that no individual should hold more than five hundred *jugera* of the national lands, had insured the popular favor; so that at last they succeeded in obtaining, that one of the consuls should be chosen from the commons; and although the nobility, by the nomination of a prætor from their own body, and of *ædiles curules*, endeavored to compensate for the sacrifice they were obliged to make, yet the plebeians having once made good a claim to the consulship, their participation in the other magisterial offices, (the dictatorship, 353, the censorship, 348, the prætorship, 334,) and even the priesthood, (300,) quickly followed as a matter of course. Thus at Rome the object of political equality between commons and nobles was attained; and although the difference between the patrician and plebeian families still subsisted, they soon ceased to form political parties.

9. *The Samnite War.* Far more important than any wars in which Rome had hitherto been engaged, were those soon about to commence with the Samnites. In former contests the object of Rome had been to establish her supremacy over her immediate neighbors; but in these, during a protracted contest of fifty years, she opened a way to the subjugation of Italy, and laid the foundation of her future greatness.

10. *The war against the Tarentines and Pyrrhus.* But the attempts of Rome, after the subjugation of the Samnites, to strengthen its power in Southern Italy, gave rise to a war with a foreign prince; the Tarentines, too weak to protect themselves against Rome, inviting the assistance of Pyrrhus of Epirus. He came, not for their sake, but for his own; but even his victories taught him that the Macedonian art

of war gave him but a weak superiority, which the Romans were soon able to turn to their own side; (as a good army of citizen soldiers is always victorious over enlisted troops.)

11. *Roman Colonies.* The chief means to which, even from the earliest times, the Romans had recourse for the foundation of their dominion over the conquered, and at the same time for the prevention of the too great increase of the needy classes of Rome, was the establishment of colonies of their own citizens, which, being settled in the captured cities, served likewise as garrisons. Each colony had its own distinct internal constitution, modelled, for the most part, upon that of the mother city itself; hence to keep the colonies in perfect dependence naturally became an object of Roman policy. This colonial system of the Romans necessarily and spontaneously arising out of the rude custom of bereaving the conquered of their lands and liberty, assumed its main features in the Samnite war, and gradually embraced the whole of Italy. Closely connected with this system was the construction of military highways (*viæ militares*), one of which, the Appian way, was constructed so early as 312, and to this day remains a lasting monument of the greatness of Rome at that period.

12. *The relations between Rome and the Italian nations.* But the relations of Rome to the nations of Italy, remained very various. 1. Some cities and nations enjoyed the full privileges of Roman citizenship; in part, however, without a voice in the comitia (*Municipia*). 2. More strict was the relation of the colonies (*jus coloniarum*), since the colonists possessed indeed their city constitution, but had no farther participation, either in the comitia, or the magistracies in Rome. The rest of the inhabitants of Italy were, either allies (*Socii, fœdere juncti*), or subjects (*Dedititii*). The first retained *a.* their internal constitution; but were obliged *b.* to give tribute and auxiliary troops (*tributis et armis juvare rempublicam*). Their more minute relations to Rome rested on the conditions of the alliance. These were the most advantageous 3. for the Latini, though each of their cities had its own alliance (*jus Latii*). And also 4. the other single nations of Italy (*jus Italicum*). On the contrary 5. the subjects, *Dedititii*, lost their internal constitution, and were governed by Roman magistrates (*Præfecti*), who were annually renewed.

13. *The Roman Constitution at this epoch.* The internal constitution of Rome itself, now completed, bore the character of a democracy, inasmuch as equality of rights existed both for nobles and commons. Yet this democracy was modified by expedients so various and wonderful—the rights of the people, of the senate, of the magistrates, fitted so nicely into each other, and were so firmly supported by the national

religion connecting every thing with determinate forms—that there was no reason, at that time, to fear the evils either of anarchy, or, what is much more astonishing when we consider the warlike character of the people, those of military despotism.

The rights of the people consisted in the legislative power, so far as fundamental national principles were concerned, and in the election of the magistrates. The distinction between the *comitia tributa* (as independent of the senate) and the *comitia centuriata* (as dependent on the senate) still existed as to form, but had lost all its importance, the difference between patricians and plebeians being now merely nominal, and the establishment of the *tribus urbanæ*, 303, excluding the too great influence of the people (*forensis factio*) upon the *comitia tributa.* The rights of the senate consisted in administering and debating all transitory national affairs, whether foreign relations (war and peace only excepted, in which the consent of the people was requisite), financial concerns, or matters regarding domestic peace and security. But the manner in which the senate was supplied must have made it the first political body at that time in the world. The rights and rank of magistrates were founded on the greater or lesser *auspicia*, no public affair being entered upon except *auspicato.* Consequently he only who was in possession of the former could hold the highest civic and military power (*imperium civile et militare; suis auspiciis rem gerere*); as dictator, consul, prætor: such was not the case with those who had only the lesser *auspicia.* The union of civil and military power in the person of the same individual was not without its inconveniences, but military despotism was in some measure guarded against by the prohibition of any magistrate possessing military command within Rome itself. We must not dismiss this subject without observing, that as the Roman constitution arose merely out of practice, there never having been any completely written charter, we cannot expect that all the details should be clearly ascertained; to attempt, therefore, in default of such authority, to describe all the minutiæ would be the surest way to fall into error.

14. *The Consuls.* On the abolition of monarchy the constitution became aristocratical. Two magistrates were annually chosen, with the authority and influence, which the kings had possessed, and called *Consuls* (*consules*). No particular age was originally requisite for this office, but a law (*lex annalis*) was enacted 180 B. C., that it should be held by no person under forty-three. Those, who sought the office, were called *candidati*, from their peculiarly white shining robe (*toga candida*). The election took place, in the assembly of the people, voting by centuries, usually towards the end of July or the beginning of Au-

gust. From that time until January of the following year, the person chosen was called *consul designatus*, and then he entered upon his office under many solemnities. The two consuls had equal power. Their badges of office were the same as those of the kings, excepting the golden crown, and the robe with purple ornaments; the latter was allowed them on certain public solemnities, as *e. g.* a triumph. At first, both consuls were chosen from the patricians; afterwards, however, one was often taken, and sometimes both, from the plebeians.

The duties of the consuls consisted in taking the auspices, assembling the senate, declaring the votes, among which they first gave their own, in proposing business to the senate and the people, fixing the comitia, appointing the judges, and preparing declarations of war. They were also usually commanders of the army, and were required to attend to all its wants, and inform the senate of all important occurrences. After completing the year of their office they were usually proconsuls or governors of provinces. The power of the consuls was gradually diminished, partly by the institution of the office of dictator and tribunes, and partly by the law which authorized appeals from the decisions of the consuls to the people. Under the emperors nothing more than the mere name remained; they were merely the agents to execute the imperial will, to whom a few privileges were secured. In the latter ages also, their number was increased, and their term of continuance very short. The office was preserved until A. D. 541 (cf. P. V. § 215), when it was conferred upon the reigning emperor for life.

15. *The Prætor.* *Prætor* was in early times the name for any magistrate, signifying merely an overseer, superintendent, or leader (from *præire*). But, in the year B. C. 365, the name was appropriated to an officer appointed to attend to the administration of justice. The prætor was at first chosen from patricians, when the consulship was communicated to the plebeians. Two prætors were chosen after the year B. C. 243, one to attend to the business of the citizens (*Prætor urbanus*), the other the business of strangers (*Prætor peregrinus*). Afterward there were four prætors, and six, then ten, fourteen, sixteen, and even eighteen, until Augustus, it seems, limited the number to twelve.

(1.) The dignity of the city-prætor was next to that of consul, and his principal business was holding courts of justice in the *tribunal* (*in* or *pro tribunali*), a building appropriated to the purpose in the forum. The prætor on entering upon his office, always published a statement of the rules and principles, by which he should be guided in his trials and decisions; this was called his edict (*edictum prætoris*). The usual form in giving his decisions was *do, dico, addico.*—In the absence of the consul, the city-prætor took his place; he could also call meetings of the senate and hold comitia; he had the care also of some of the great public games. The insignia of the prætor were the *toga prætexta*, a sword and spear (*gladius et hasta*), and an attendance of six lictors. In the provinces the proprætors had similar rank and authority, in the same manner as the proconsuls took the place of consuls.

(2.) Besides the general edict above mentioned, the prætor published particular edicts from time to time. Such as he copied from those of his predecessors were termed *tralatitia;* those framed by himself, *nova.* An edict published at Rome, *edictum urbanum;* in a province, *provinciale;* sometimes named from the province, as *edictum Siciliense.* Other magistrates (*honorati*) published edicts also. The law derived from all the various edicts was termed *jus honorarium;* this term or phrase, in later times, was applied to a collection of prætor's edicts regularly arranged by order of the emperor Hadrian; the same was also called *edictum perpetuum.*

16. *The Ædiles.* *Ædiles* were the magistrates, whose principal duty was the care of the buildings (*ædes*). They were of two classes, *plebeii* and *curules*, two of each. The former were created first, B. C. 493; the latter, B. C. 266. At a later period, Julius Cæsar added two others, called *Cereales*, who had the oversight of the stores of grain and provision. The *Ædiles Plebeii* had originally the care of the public and private buildings; and were required to make arrangements for the public games, see to the preservation of the public roads, regulate the markets, prove the justness of weights and measures, and in short attend to the police of the city. The *ædiles curules* were distinguished from them by the *toga prætexta*, and the *sella curulis.* They were at first taken solely from the patricians, but afterwards also from the people. Their chief care was of the great public games. They had also the oversight of the temples, except that of Ceres, which always belonged to the plebeian ædiles, with whom the curules probably shared, without distinction, the business of the police. In the Roman provinces, also, there were ædiles, whose office was usually but for a year. The office seems to have continued until the time of Constantine the Great.

17. *The Tribunes.* Of the *tribunes* there were different kinds. The tribunes of the people (*tribuni plebis*) were the most remarkable. The office originated from the general disaffection and secession of the plebeians, B. C. 493. The number was first two, then five, finally ten. One of them always presided at the comitia for electing tribunes. Their proper object was the protection of the people against the encroachments of the senate and consuls. In order to obtain this office,

patricians allowed themselves to be adopted into plebeian families. In the earliest times, the tribunes could not enter the senate, but had their seats before the door of the senate-room, where they heard all the deliberations, and could hinder the passage of any decree by the single word *veto.* By the Atinian law, B. C. 131, it was decreed that the tribunes should be of the rank of senators. Their power and influence constantly increased, although it was confined to the city and the circuit of a mile around it, beyond which they could not be absent over night.

The tribunes had no lictors, nor any insignia of office, except a kind of beadles called *viatores*, who went before them. Their persons were regarded as inviolable. Sylla abridged their power; he took from them the right, which they had exercised, of assembling the people by tribes, and thereby passing enactments (*plebiscita*) binding upon the whole nation, and left them only the power of their negative or intercession (*intercedere*). Their authority, however, was afterwards elevated again, but under Julius Cæsar it was small, and became still more insignificant under the emperors, who appropriated to themselves the tribunitial power, so that the tribunes annually elected had but merely the name and shadow of it. The office was abolished in the time of Constantine the Great.

18. *The Quæstors.* The *quæstors* were among the earliest magistrates of Rome, first appointed by the kings, then by the consuls, afterwards by the people. They were charged with receiving and managing the revenues, and with the scrutiny of certain kinds of bloodshed. Those for the city were called *quæstores urbani*, those for the provinces *quæstores provinciales*, and those for the examination of capital offences, *quæstores rerum capitalium*, or *parricidii.* Originally there were but two, afterwards four, and then eight; Sylla raised the number to twenty, and Julius Cæsar to forty.

(1.) The quæstors had also the oversight of the archives, the care of foreign ambassadors, the charge of monuments, presents and other tokens of respect publicly authorized, and the preservation of the treasures acquired in war. They were at first taken only from the patricians, but afterwards partly from the plebeians.

Under the emperors there was a kind of quæstors, called *quæstores candidati*, who were, properly speaking, nothing more than imperial messengers or secretaries, and were afterwards called *juris interpretes*, *precum arbitri*, &c., from their employment. Still later there was another kind, of considerable importance, styled *quæstores palatii*, or *magistri officiorum.*

(2.) The age requisite for the quæstor was 30, or at least 25, until reduced by Augustus to 22. The office was one of the first steps to preferment in the commonwealth, although sometimes held by those who had been consuls.

19. *The Censors.* The office of the *censors* (*censores*) was established at an early period, B. C. 442. There were two at a time, holding their office originally for five years, but afterwards only a year and a half. Their duties were various; the following were some of the principal; to take the census of the people, an accurate account of the age, property and descent of each head of a family, to divide the people into their tribes and rectify existing errors in the distribution, to decide the taxes of each person, to enrol those who were obligated to military service, to make account of the revenues in the provinces, to inspect the morals of the citizens, to superintend the leasing of public lands, to attend to contracts respecting public works, such as streets, bridges, aqueducts and the like.

(1.) The censors were authorized to inflict marks of disgrace (*nota censoria*, *ignominia*) from any evidence and for any cause, which appeared to them suitable. The luxury of the Romans, which in later times became so excessive, was considerably restrained by the censors. In order to escape the censorial rebukes or punishments, the office seems to have been left vacant for some time.

(2.) The censorial power was, however, vested in Julius Cæsar, first with the title *Præfectus morum*, afterward, for life, with the title of *Censor*. Augustus also assumed the power, although he declined the title. The same was done by several of his successors down to the time of Decius, A. D. 250, when the corruption of morals was too great to allow any magistracy or power of the kind.

20. *The Dictator.* Among the extraordinary magistrates of Rome, whose office was not permanent, but necessary only in particular circumstances, the *Dictator* is especially to be noticed. The first dictator was created on occasion of the same sedition or insurrection which occasioned the appointment of tribunes of the people; and similar disturbances, difficult wars, and other important emergencies occasioned the appointment of the subsequent dictators. Sometimes they were appointed for less important reasons, *e. g.* for regulating the public games and sports in the sickness of the prætor, not by the people, but by one of the consuls. The dictator was indeed always appointed by the consul, by order of the people or senate, and must be a man of consular rank. The power of the dictator was very great, in some respects supreme. War and peace, and the decision of the most important affairs depended on him.

(1.) Citizens, who were condemned to death by him, could appeal to the people. The power and office of the dictator was limited to six months. He could not appropriate without consent of the senate or people any of the public money. As commander of the army, he was confined to the limits of Italy. No one ever abused the power of this office so much as Cornelius Sulla. Cæsar, by this office, opened his way to absolute power, and after his death the dictatorship was abolished. It was, however, offered to Augustus, who refused the odious name or title, although he exercised all the power.

(2.) Plutarch and Polybius state that the dictator was attended by 24 lictors; but in the epitome of the 89th book of Livy, Sylla is said to have unwarrantably assumed this number. The dictator appointed usually from among those of consular or prætorian dignity, an officer, styled *Magister equitum*, whose business was to command the cavalry, and execute the orders of the dictator; but this officer was sometimes appointed by the senate, or the people; he was allowed the use of a horse, but the dictator could not ride without the order of the people. Sometimes a consul, or other existing magistrate, was invested with the power of dictator, by decree of the senate (*ne quid detrimenti capiat respublica*).

21. *The Decemviri.* The discontent of the people under the use which the consuls made of their power, led to the creation of a new office in the year B. C. 451, that of the *Decemviri*, with consular authority (*decemviri consulari potestate*, s. legibus ferendis). They were appointed for the special purpose of forming a code of laws. This gave rise to the laws of the twelve tables. As they soon began to abuse their great power, the office was abolished B. C. 449, and that of consul restored. From the same cause originated the office of military tribunes (*tribuni militum consulari potestate*), who in the year B. C. 445, were appointed in the place of consuls; but were dismissed after three months. Originally they were six in number, three patricians, and three plebeians; afterwards the number varied, sometimes three, sometimes four, six, or eight; sometimes military tribunes, and sometimes consuls were elected, as the plebeian or the patrician interests prevailed, until the year B. C. 366, when the plebeians were quieted by the choice of a consul from among themselves. Among the magistrates not permanent, must be mentioned also the præfect of the city, *Præfectus urbi*, to whom the consuls in their absence, especially in war, intrusted the charge of the police. Under the emperors this became a regular and permanent office of great influence.

The *Interrex* was an officer created to hold elections when there was no consul or magistrate, to whom it properly belonged. The name was drawn from the title of the temporary magistrate appointed by the senate, when there was a vacancy in the throne under the regal government.

Less important magistrates were the following: the *Præfectus annonæ*, charged with the procuring and distributing of grain, in cases of scarcity; the *Quinqueviri mensarii*, whose chief business it was to reduce public expenses (*minuendis publicis sumtibus*); the *Quinqueviri muris turribusque reficiendis*, to see to repairs in the walls and fortifications; the *Triumviri ædibus sacris reficiendis*, to repair the sacred buildings; *Triumviri monetales*, having charge of the mint; *Triumviri nocturni*, to superintend the nightly watch; *Duumviri navales* (*classis ornandæ reficiendæque causa*), for equipping and repairing the fleet, &c. Some of these, however, were not magistrates in the proper sense, but they were chosen from among the most respectable men.

The servants or attendants of magistrates were called in general *apparitores;* under which were included scribæ, notarii, actuarii, accensi, præcones, lictores, viatores, &c. The *Carnifex* was the executioner or *hangman.*

22. *The Extraordinary Officers.* Besides the magistrates which have been named, falling under the denomination of ordinary (*ordinarii*) or regular and permanent, and the extraordinary (*extraordinarii*) or occasional, there were various magistrates whose authority pertained to the provinces of Rome. These were in part such as have been named. Among them were the proconsuls, proprætors, proquæstors, the legates, conquisitors, &c.

Proconsuls were either (1) such as being consuls had their office prolonged beyond the time fixed by law; or (2) such as were raised from a private station to govern some province or to command in war; or (3) such as having been consuls went, immediately on the legal expiration of their consulship, into provinces assigned to their charge under the commonwealth; or (4) such as were appointed governors of the provinces under the empire; as all these were called proconsuls. But the name and dignity properly belonged to the third of these classes.

The senate decided from year to year what provinces should be consular, and then the consuls, while only *designati*, agreed by lot which of them each should take, on the expiration of his consulship. A vote of the people afterwards conferred on them the military command in their provinces. Their departure to their provinces, and return to the city, were often attended with great pomp. They enjoyed very absolute authority, both civil and military; but it was limited to a year, and they were liable to a rigid trial on their return; the offences most commonly charged were (1) *crimen peculatus*, ill use of the public money, (2) *majestatis*, treachery, or assumption of powers belonging to the senate or people, and (3) *repetundarum*, extortion or oppression toward the inhabitants.

The *Proprætors* were such as, after their prætorship, received provinces, in which for a year they had supreme command, usually both civil and military. Their creation, administration, and responsibility were similar to those of proconsuls, only they had but six lictors, instead of twelve, and the prætorian provinces were usually smaller than the consular. The *legati* were the chief assistants of the proconsuls and proprætors. The number depended on the rank of the chief officer, and the circumstances of the provinces. They at length obtained important authority as military commanders. One *quæstor*, or more, attended each proconsul or proprætor. His business was, to superintend the public accounts and the supplies of the army. Proquæstors were such as the chief officer appointed temporarily, on the absence or death of the provincial quæstor. The duties of the quæstor were assigned, under the emperors, to the officer styled *procurator Cæsaris*. The *conquisitores* were inferior officers, not properly civil, who were employed to raise soldiers, and by force if necessary.

SEC. VI.—FROM THE COMMENCEMENT OF THE WAR WITH CARTHAGE TO THE SEDITIONS OF THE GRACCHI. B. C. 264–134.

1. *Struggle between Carthage and Rome.*—The political division of Italy laid the foundation for the dominion of Rome in that country; the want of union and political relations in the world, paved the way to her universal empire. The first step cost her much; the succeeding followed easily and rapidly; and the history of the struggle between Rome and Carthage only shows, on a larger scale, what the history of Greece exhibits on a smaller. The whole of the following history confirms the fact, that two republics cannot exist near each other, without one being destroyed or subjected; but the vast extent of this struggle, the important consequences which followed, together with the wonderful exertions made, and the great men engaged on both sides, gave it an interest which cannot be found in that of any other nations. Though the power and resources of both states were nearly equal in appearance, they were widely different in quality and circumstances. Carthage, besides her dominion over the seas, had also a better furnished treasury, by which she was enabled to enlist into her service as many *mercenaries* as she pleased: Rome, on the contrary, *strong in herself*, had all the advantages possessed by a nation of warriors over one partly commercial, partly military.

2. *The first war of twenty-three years, B. C.* 264—241. The first war of twenty-three years between the two republics, arose from very slight causes; it soon, however, became a struggle for the possession of Sicily, which in the end naturally extended itself to the dominion of the sea. Rome, by the aid of her newly-built fleet, having obtained for some time this power, was enabled to attack Africa, and succeeded in driving the Carthaginians from Sicily.

The occupation of Messina by the Romans, 264, gave rise to this war. The defection of Hiero, king of Syracuse, from the side of Carthage, and his joining the Romans, first gave the latter the idea of expelling the Carthaginians from the island. The victory near Agrigentum, and capture of that city in 262, seemed to facilitate the execution of this project; it also convinced the Romans of the necessity of their having a naval power. We shall the less wonder at their forming a fleet in Italy, where wood was then plentiful, if we remember their previous experience in naval affairs; these were not the first vessels of war which they constructed, but only the first large ones which they built upon a Carthaginian model. The first naval victory of the Romans under Duilius, by the aid of grappling machines, 260. The project then conceived of carrying the war into Africa, was one of the great ideas of the Romans, and from that time it became a ruling maxim of the state, to attack the enemy in his own territory. The second and very remarkable victory of the Romans, 257, opened the way for them to Africa, and shows their naval tactics in a very brilliant light; but the unfortunate issue of their expedition to Africa, restored the equilibrium; and the struggle for the dominion of the sea became the more obstinate, as success did not altogether favor one party. The result of the contest appears to have turned upon the possession of the western promontories of Sicily, Drepanum, and Lilybæum, which were in a manner the bulwarks of the Carthaginians, and seemed impregnable since Hamilcar Barca had taken the command of them, 247. The last naval victory of the Romans, however, under the consul Lutatius, 241, having cut off the communication between Sicily and Carthage, and the finances of both parties being completely exhausted, a peace was concluded upon the conditions: 1. That the Carthaginians should evacuate Sicily and the small islands adjacent. 2. That they should pay to Rome, by instalments, in ten years, for the expenses she had been at in carrying on the war, the sum of 2,200 talents. 3. That they should not make war against Hiero, king of Syracuse.

3. *Effect of these successes on the constitution.* The issue of this war placed the political connections of Rome in a new situation, and necessarily extended her influence abroad. The length of the war and

the manner of its conclusion had, moreover, inspired a national hatred, such as is only found in republics; the conviction also that they could not remain independent of one another, must have become much more striking, as the points of contact had greatly increased since the beginning of the war. Who does not know the arrogance of a republic after the first essay of her power has been crowned with success! Rome gave a striking example of this by her invasion of Sardinia in the midst of peace. These successes had also a sensible effect on the Roman constitution. For although in appearance its form was not in the least changed, yet the power of the senate now acquired that preponderance which the ruling authority of a republic never fails to do after long and successful wars.

4. *Chastisement of the Illyrian Pirates.* An opportunity was soon afforded the Romans, in the Adriatic Sea, of making use of their superior naval power, in chastising the pirates of Illyria under their queen Teuta. By effecting this, they not only secured their authority over that sea, but at the same time formed their first political relations with the Grecian states; relations which soon afterwards became of great importance.

Commencement of the first Illyrian war, 230, which ended with the subjugation of Teuta, 226. The war, however, again broke out, 222, against Demetrius of Pharus, who conceived himself inadequately rewarded by Rome for the services he had rendered her in the preceding war. The Romans found him a much more dangerous adversary than had been expected, even after his expulsion and flight to Philip, 220. Throughout this war, Rome appeared as the deliverer of the Grecian states, which had suffered extremely from the plunder of these freebooters; Corcyra, Apollonia, and other cities placed themselves formally under her protection, while the Achæans, Ætolians, and Athenians vied with each other in showing their gratitude.

5. *Relations with Greece.* In the mean time, while Carthage endeavored to make up for the loss of Sicily and Sardinia by extending her Spanish dominions, which the jealousy of Rome restrained her from carrying beyond the Ebro; Rome herself had a new war to maintain against her northern neighbors the Gauls, which ended after a violent contest with the establishment of her authority over the north of Italy.

From the first Gallic war to the burning of Rome, 390, the Gauls had repeated their attacks in 360 and 348, even to the conclusion of the peace in 336. But in the latter part of the Samnite war, a formidable confederacy having taken place among the Italian tribes, some of the Gauls enlisted as mercenaries in the service of the Etruscans, while others allied themselves to the Samnites. This led them to take part in these wars in 306, 302, and 292, until they were obliged, together with the Etruscans, to sue for peace in 284, before which time the Romans had sent a colony into their country, near Sena. This peace lasted till 238, when it was disturbed by the incursion of the transalpine Gauls; without, however, their coming to any war with Rome. But in 232, the proposition of Flaminius the tribune, (*lex flaminia*,) to divide the lands conquered from the Senones, became the cause of new disturbances. Upon this occasion, the Gauls entered into an alliance with their transalpine countrymen, the Gæsates on the Rhone, who had been accustomed to engage as mercenaries. These having crossed the Alps, the dreadful war of six years (226–220) began, in which, after defeating the Gauls near Clusium, 225, the Romans pursued them into their own territory, and encamped upon the Po, 223. The Gauls having been again completely overthrown by Marcellus, were obliged to sue for peace; when the Roman colonies of Placentia and Cremona were established. The number of men capable of bearing arms in all Italy subject to the Romans during this war amounted to 800,000.

6. *Hannibal takes the command in Spain, and makes Italy the seat of war.* Before this storm was totally appeased, in which it is probable that Carthaginian policy was not altogether inactive, Hannibal had obtained the chief command in Spain. From the reproach of having first begun the war, he and his party cannot be cleared; Rome, in the situation she then was, could hardly desire it; he however who strikes the first blow is not always the real aggressor. The plan of Hannibal was the destruction of Rome; and by making Italy the principal seat of the war, he necessarily turned the scale in his favor; because Rome, obliged to defend herself, left to him all the advantages of attack. The preparations she made for defence, show that it was not believed possible he could execute his enterprise by the route which he took.

The history of this war, 218–201, of which no later transaction has been able to destroy the interest, is divided into three parts: the history of the war in Italy; the contemporary war in Spain; and from 203, the war in Africa. Hannibal's invasion of Italy in the autumn, 218—engagement near the river Ticinus and the battle of Trebia, in the same year. Battle near the lake Thrasymenus, in the spring, 217. Seat of the war transferred to Lower Italy, and the defensive system of the dictator Fabius until the end of the year. Battle of Cannæ, 216, followed by the conquest of Capua and the subjection of the greater part of Lower Italy. The defensive mode of warfare afterwards adopted by the Carthaginian, arose partly from his desire to form a junction with his brother Asdrubal and the Spanish army, and partly from his expectation of foreign support by means of alliances, with Syracuse, after the death of Hiero, 215, and with Philip of Macedon, 216. These hopes, however, were frustrated by the Romans. Syracuse was besieged and taken, 214–212, and Philip kept employed in Greece. In addition to this, the Romans retook Capua, nothwithstanding the audacious march of Hannibal towards Rome, 211, and he had now no succor left except the reinforcement which Asdrubal was bringing from Spain. The latter, however, was attacked immediately upon his arrival in Italy, near Sena, by the consuls Nero and Livius, and left dead on the field, 207. From this time the war in Italy became only of secondary importance, as Hannibal was obliged to act on the defensive in Bruttium.

The war in Spain began nearly about the same time between Asdrubal and the two brothers, Cn. and P. Cornelius Scipio, and was continued with various success, till the year 216, the issue depending much upon the disposition of the Spaniards themselves. The plan of Carthage after the year 216, was to send Asdrubal with the Spanish army into Italy, and to supply its place by an army from Africa; two victories, however, gained by the Scipios near the Ebro, 216, and the Illiberis, 215, prevented this from being effected, till at last both fell under the superior power and cunning of the Carthaginians, 212. But the arrival of the youthful P. Cornelius Scipio, who did not appear merely to his own nation as an extraordinary genius, entirely changed the face of affairs, and the fortunes of Rome soon became attached to his name, which alone seemed to promise victory. During his command in Spain, 210–206, he won over the inhabitants while he defeated the Carthaginians, and for the furtherance of his great design, contracted an alliance with Syphax in Africa, 206. He was unable, however, to prevent the march of Asdrubal into Italy, 208, which nevertheless rendered it an easy task for him to subdue all Carthaginian Spain as far as Gades, 206, and thus procured him the consular dignity at his return, 205.

The carrying of the war into Africa by Scipio, notwithstanding the opposition of the old Roman generals, and the desertion of Syphax, who at the persuasion of Sophonisba again went over to the Carthaginians, (whose loss however was well repaid by Masinissa, whom Scipio had won over to his side in Spain,) was followed by an important consequence; for after he had gained two victories over Asdrubal and Syphax, 203, and taken the latter prisoner, the Carthaginians found it necessary to recall Hannibal from Italy, 202; and the battle of Zama terminated the war, 201. The following were the conditions of peace: 1. That the Carthaginians should only retain the territory in Africa annexed to their government. 2. That they should give up all their ships of war, except ten triremes, and all their elephants. 3. That they should pay, at times specified, 10,000 talents. 4. That they should commence no war without the consent of Rome. 5. That they should restore to Masinissa all the houses, cities, and lands that had ever been possessed by himself or his ancestors. The reproach usually cast upon the Carthaginians, of having left Hannibal unsupported in Italy, in a great measure vanishes, if we remember the plan formed in 216, to send the Spanish army into Italy, and to replace it by an African one: a plan formed with much ability, and followed with as much constancy. We may add to this, that the Barcine faction maintained its influence in the government even to the end of the war. But why they, who by the treaty of peace gave up five hundred vessels of war, suffered Scipio to cross over from Sicily without sending one to oppose him, is difficult to explain.

7. *Power of Rome increased by the war.* Notwithstanding her great loss of men, and the devastation of Italy, Rome felt herself much more powerful at the end of this war than at the beginning. Her dominion was not only established over Italy, but extensive foreign countries had been brought under it; her authority over the seas was rendered secure by the destruction of the naval power of the Carthaginians. The Roman *form* of government, it is true, underwent no change, but its *spirit* much, as the power of the senate became almost unlimited; and although the dawn of civilization had broken over Rome, since her intercourse with more civilized foreigners, the state still remained altogether a nation of warriors. And now, for the first time, appears in the page of history the fearful phenomenon of a great military republic; and the history of the next ten years, in which Rome overthrew so many thrones and free states, gives a striking proof, that such a power is the natural enemy to the independence of all the states within the reach of her arms. The causes which led Rome from this time to aspire after the dominion of the world, are to be found neither in her geographical situation, which for a conquering power by land seemed rather unfavorable, nor in the inclination of the people, who were opposed to the first war against Philip; but singly and entirely in the spirit of her government. The means, however, whereby she obtained her end, must not be sought for merely in the excellence of her armies and generals, but rather in that uniform, sharp-sighted, and dexterous policy, by which she was enabled to frustrate the powerful alliances formed against her, notwithstanding the many adversaries who at that time sought to form new ones. But where could be found such another council of state, embodying such a mass of practical political wisdom, as the Roman senate must

have been from the very nature of its organization? All this, however, would not have been sufficient to have subjugated the world, if the want of good government, the degeneracy of the military art, and an extremely corrupt state of morals among both rulers and people, in foreign states, had not seconded the efforts of Rome.

View of the political state of the world at this period. In the west, Sicily, (the whole island after 212,) Sardinia, and Corsica, from the year 237, and Spain, divided into citerior and ulterior, (the latter rather in name than in fact,) had become Roman provinces, 206; the independence of Carthage had been destroyed by the last peace, and her subordination secured by the alliance of Rome with Masinissa; Cisalpine Gaul, formed into a province, served as a barrier against the inroads of the more northern barbarians. On the other side, in the East, the kingdom of Macedonia, and the free states of Greece, forming together a very complicated system, had opened a connection with Rome since the Illyrian war, 230, and Philip's alliance with Hannibal, 214. Of the three powers of the first rank, Macedonia, Syria, and Egypt, the two former were allied against the latter, who, on her part, maintained a good understanding with Rome. The states of secondary rank were, those of the Ætolian league, the kings of Pergamus, and the republic of Rhodes, with some smaller, such as Athens: these had allied themselves to Rome since the confederacy against Philip, 211. The Achæan league, on the contrary, was in the interest of Macedonia, which Rome always endeavored to attach to herself, in order to make head against those of the first rank.

8. *War against Philip, B. C.* 200, *lays the foundation of Roman power in the East.* A declaration of war against Philip, notwithstanding the opposition of the tribunes of the people, and an attack upon Macedonia itself, according to the constant maxim of carrying the war into the enemy's country, immediately followed. They could not, however, drive Philip so soon from the fastnesses of Epirus and Thessaly, which were his bulwarks. But Rome possessed in T. Quintius Flaminius, who marched against Philip as the deliverer of Greece, a statesman and general exactly fitted for a period of great revolutions. By the permanency of his political influence he became indeed the true founder of the Roman power in the East. Who could better cajole men and nations, while they were erecting altars to him, than T. Quintius? So artfully indeed did he assume the character of a great genius, such as had been given by nature to Scipio, that he has almost deceived history itself. The struggle between him and Philip consisted rather in a display of talents in political stratagem and finesse than in feats of arms: even before the battle of Cynoscephalæ had given the finishing stroke,

the Romans had already turned the balance in their favor, by gaining over the Achæan league.

The negotiations between Rome and Macedonia, from the year 214, give the first striking examples of the ability and address of the Romans in foreign policy; and they are the more remarkable, as the treaty with the Ætolians and others, 211, was the remote cause of the transactions which afterwards took place in the East. The peculiar system adopted by the Romans, of taking the lesser states under their protection as allies, must always have given them an opportunity of making war on the more powerful whenever they chose. This in fact happened in the present case, notwithstanding the peace concluded with Philip, 204. The chief object of the Romans in this war, both by sea and land, was to drive Phillip completely out of Greece. The allies on both sides, and the conditions of peace, were similar to those concluded with Carthage. The destruction of the naval power of her conquered enemies became now a maxim of Roman policy in making peace; and she thus maintained the dominion of the seas without any great fleet, and without losing the essential character of a dominant power by land.

9. *Conquest of Greece.* The expulsion of Philip from Greece brought that country into a state of dependence upon Rome; an event which could not have been better secured than by the present of liberty which T. Quintius conferred upon its inhabitants at the Isthmian games. The system of surveillance, which the Romans had already established in the West over Carthage and Numidia, was now adopted in the East over Greece and Macedonia. Roman commissioners, under the name of ambassadors, were sent into the country of the nations in alliance, and were the principal means by which this system of espionage was carried on. These however did not fail to give umbrage to the Greeks, particularly to the turbulent Ætolians; more especially as the Romans seemed in no hurry to withdraw their troops from a country which they had declared to be free.

Liberty was expressly granted to the state which had taken the part of Philip, namely, to the Achæans; to the others it was naturally understood to belong. It was nevertheless three years, 194, before the Roman army evacuated Greece, and withdrew from the fortified places. The conduct of T. Quintius during this period fully shows what he was. The Greeks indeed had much want of such a guardian if they wished to remain quiet: his conduct, however, in the war against Nabis, 195, shows that he had not really at heart the tranquillity of Greece.

10. *War with Syria and danger of a formidable league against Rome.* The treaty of peace with Philip contained the seeds of a new and greater war with Syria; but though this seemed inevitable at that

time, it did not break out till six years afterwards; and in but few periods of the history of the world is so great a political crisis to be found, as in this short interval. The fall of Carthage and Macedonia had shown the rest of the world what it had to expect from Rome; and there was no lack of great men sufficiently endowed with courage and talents to resist her. The danger of a formidable league between Carthage, Syria, and perhaps Macedonia, was never so much to be feared, as when Hannibal, now at the head of affairs, labored to effect it with all the zeal which his hatred of Rome could inspire; and they might calculate with certainty beforehand on the accession of many smaller states. Rome, however, by her equally decided and artful policy procured Hannibal's banishment from Carthage, amused Philip by granting him some trifling advantages, and gained over the smaller states by her ambassadors. By these means, and by taking advantage of the intrigues in the court of Syria, she prevented this coalition from being formed. Antiochus was therefore left without assistance in Greece, except from the Ætolians and a few other unimportant allies; while Rome drew from hers, especially the Rhodians and Eumenes, advantages of the greatest consequence.

The first cause of contention between Rome and Antiochus was the liberty of Greece, which the former wished to extend to the Grecian cities of Asia, and to those in particular which had belonged to Philip, and afterwards to Antiochus; while the latter contended, that Rome had no right to intermeddle with the affairs of Asia. The second cause of dispute was the occupation of the Thracian Chersonesus by Antiochus, 196, in right of some ancient pretensions; and Rome, on her part, would not tolerate him in Europe. This quarrel therefore commenced as early as 196, but did not become serious till the year 195, when, in consequence of Hannibal's flight to Antiochus, together with the turbulence and excitement of the Ætolians, whose object it was to embroil the rival powers, the political horizon was completely overcast. What a fortunate thing it was for Rome that such men as Hannibal and Antiochus could not understand each other!

11. *Battle of Magnesia.—Conditions of Peace.* This war was much sooner brought to a termination than the Macedonian, owing to the half-measures adopted by Antiochus. After having been driven from Greece by Glabrio, and after two naval victories had opened to the Romans the way to Asia, he felt inclined to act on the defensive; but in the battle near Magnesia, at the foot of Mount Sipylus, L. Scipio gathered the laurels which more properly belonged to Glabrio. The total expulsion of Antiochus from Asia Minor, even before this victory, had been the chief object of the war. The conditions of peace were

such, as not only weakened Antiochus, but reduced him to a state of dependence.

During this contest in the East, a sanguinary war was going on in the West—from the year 201, in Spain, where the elder Cato commanded, and from 193, in Italy itself, against the Ligurians. Whatever may be said upon the means made use of by Rome to increase the number of her citizens, it will always be difficult to comprehend, not only how she could support all these wars without being thereby weakened, but how, at the same time, she could found so many colonies!

12. *Moderation of Rome.—War against the Gauls in Asia Minor.* Even after the termination of this war, Rome refrained, with astonishing moderation, from appearing in the light of a conqueror; it was only for the liberty of Greece, and for her allies, that she had contended! Without keeping a foot of land for herself, she divided, with the exception of the free Grecian cities, the conquered Asia Minor between Eumenes and the Rhodians; the manner, however, in which she dealt with the Ætolians, who, after a long supplication for peace, were obliged to buy it dearly, shows that she also knew how to treat unfaithful allies. The war against the Gauls in Asia Minor was not less necessary for the preservation of tranquillity in that country, than it was injurious to the morals and military discipline of the Roman army. They here learned to levy contributions.

13. *Rome the Arbitress of the World.* Thus, within the short space of ten years, was laid the foundation of the Roman authority in the East, and the general state of affairs entirely changed. If Rome was not yet the ruler, she was at least the arbitress of the world, from the Atlantic to the Euphrates. The power of the three principal states was so completely humbled, that they durst not, without the permission of Rome, begin any new war; the fourth, Egypt, had already, in the year 201, placed herself under the guardianship of Rome; and the lesser powers followed of themselves—esteeming it an honor to be called the *allies of Rome.* With this name, the nations were lulled into security, and brought under the Roman yoke; the new political system of Rome was founded and strengthened, partly by exciting and supporting the weaker states against the stronger, however unjust the cause of the former might be, and partly by factions which she found means to raise in every state, even the smallest.

Although the policy of Rome extended itself every where, by means of her commissioners or ambassadors, yet she kept a more particular guard against Carthage, by favoring Masinissa, at her expense; against the Achæan league, by favoring the Spartans; and against Philip of Macedon, by favoring every one who brought any complaint against him.

14. *Internal corruption of Rome.* Although these new connections, and this intercourse with foreign nations, greatly aided the diffusion of knowledge and science, and was followed by a gradual improvement in her civilization, yet was it, nevertheless, in many respects, detrimental to the internal state of Rome. The introduction of the scandalous Bacchanalia, which were immediately discovered and forbidden, shows how easily great vices may creep in among a people who are only indebted for their morality to their ignorance. Among the higher classes, also, the spirit of intrigue manifested itself to an astonishing degree, particularly by the attacks directed against the Scipios by the elder Cato, whose restless activity became the instrument of his malignant passions. The severity of his censorship did not repair the evils caused by his immorality and pernicious politics.

Voluntary exile of Scipio Africanus to Linternum, 187. He dies there, 183, the same year in which Hannibal falls under the continued persecution of Rome. His brother, Scipio Asiaticus, is also unable to escape a trial and condemnation, 185. One would have expected a sensible effect from the exile of these two great men; but in a state where the ruling power is in the hands of a body like what the Roman senate was, the change of individuals is but of little consequence.

15. *New broils with Philip.—His death.—Open war.* Fresh disputes arose as early as 185, with Philip of Macedon, who soon found that they had spared him no longer than it suited their own convenience. Although the intervention of Philip's youngest son, upon whom the Romans had formed some design, prevented the powers from coming to an immediate rupture, and war was still further delayed by Philip's death, yet the national hatred descended to his successor, and continued to increase, notwithstanding an alliance concluded with him, until the war openly broke out.

The first circumstance which gave umbrage to Philip, was the small portion they permitted him to conquer in Athamania and Thessaly, during the war against Antiochus. But what sharpened his animosity much more than the object in dispute, was the conduct of the Roman commissioners, before whom he, the king, was called upon to defend himself as an accused party, 184. The exclamation of Philip, that "the sun of every day had not yet set," showed his indignation, and at the same time betrayed his intention. The interval previous to the breaking out of the war was any thing rather than a time of peace for Rome; for besides that the Spanish and Ligurian wars continued almost without intermission, the revolts which broke out in Istria, 178, and in Sardinia and Corsica, 176, produced much bloodshed.

16. *Second Macedonian War, ends with the ruin of the Kingdom.* In the second Macedonian war, which ended with the destruction of Perseus and his kingdom, it required the active efforts of Roman policy to prevent a powerful confederacy from being formed against her—as Perseus used all his endeavors to stimulate not only the Grecian states, and Thrace and Illyria, but also Carthage and Asia, to enter into alliance with him. Where was it that Rome did not, at this crisis, send her ambassadors? She did not, indeed, succeed so far as to leave her enemy quite alone, but prepared new triumphs for herself over the few allies she left him. The devastated Epirus, and Gentius, king of Illyria, suffered dearly for the assistance they had lent him; the states, also, which had remained neuter, the Rhodians and Eumenes, were made to feel severely that they were the mere creatures of Rome.

Beginning of the Macedonian war, 171, before Rome was prepared; a deceitful truce, which raised the indignation even of the elder senators, was the means resorted to for gaining time. Notwithstanding this, the war at first, 170 and 169, was favorable to Perseus; but he wanted resolution and judgment to enable him to turn his advantages to account. In 168, Paulus Æmilius, an old general, against the usual custom of the Romans, took the command. Bloody and decisive battle near Pydna, June 22, 168. So completely may one day overturn a kingdom which has only an army for its support! Contemporary with this war, and highly fortunate for Rome, was the war of Antiochus Epiphanes with Egypt. No wonder that Rome did not, till 168, through Popilius, command peace between them!

17. *Its consequences.* The destruction of the Macedonian monarchy was attended with consequences equally disastrous to the conquerors and the conquered. To the first, it soon gave the notion of becoming the masters of the world, instead of its arbiters; and it exposed the latter, for the next twenty years, to all the evils inseparable from such a catastrophe. The system of politics hitherto pursued by Rome, could not last much longer; for if nations suffered themselves to be brought under the yoke by force, it was not to be expected that they would long be held in dependence under the specious name of liberty. But the state of things after this war, was such as contributed to hasten a change in the form of the relations which existed between Rome and her allies.

The republican constitution given to the already ruined and devastated Macedonians and Illyrians, and which, according to the decree of the senate, "showed to all people that Rome was ready to bestow liberty upon them," was granted upon such hard conditions, that the enfranchised nation soon used every endeavor to procure themselves a king. Greece, however, suffered still more than Macedonia. Here, during the war, the spirit of faction had risen to the highest pitch; and the arrogant insolence of the Roman party, composed for the most part of venal wretches, was so great, that they persecuted not only those who had espoused an opposite faction, but even those who had joined no faction at all. Rome, nevertheless, could not believe herself secure, until she had destroyed, by a cruel artifice, all her adversaries.

18. *Foreign policy of Rome.* Entirely in the same spirit did Rome proceed against the other states from whom she had any thing to fear. These must be rendered defenceless; and every means of effecting that purpose was considered justifiable by the senate. The quarrels between the successors to the throne of Egypt were taken advantage of to cause dissensions in that kingdom; while Syria was retained in a state of tutelage, by keeping the rightful heir to the throne at Rome; and its military power neutralized by means of their ambassadors.

19. From these facts we may also conclude, that the injuries now meditated against Carthage were not separate projects, but rather formed part of the general system of Roman policy at this period, although particular events at one time retarded their execution, and at another hastened it. History, in recounting the incredibly bad treatment which Carthage had to endure before her fall, seems to have given a warning to those nations who can take it, of what they may expect from the domination of a powerful republic.

Cato was chief of the party which sought the destruction of Carthage, both from a spirit of envy against Scipio Nasica, whom he hated for his great influence in the senate; and because, when ambassador to Carthage, he thought they did not treat him with sufficient respect. But Masinissa's victory, 152, and the defection of Utica, brought this project into immediate play. Beginning of the war, 150, the Carthaginians having been previously inveigled out of their arms. The city, however, was not captured and destroyed till 146, by P. Scipio Æmilianus. The Carthaginian territory, under the name of Africa, was then made a Roman province.

20. *A new war with Macedonia and Greece.—Terminated by the destruction of Corinth*, 146. During this third war with Carthage, hostilities again broke out in Macedonia, which brought on a new war with Greece, and entirely changed the state of both these countries. In Macedonia, an impostor named Andriscus, who pretended to be the son

of Philip, placed himself at the head of that highly disaffected people, assumed the name of Philip, and became, particularly by an alliance with the Thracians, very formidable to the Romans, until overcome by Metellus. Rome wishing to take advantage of this crisis to dissolve the Achæan league, the Achæan war broke out. This war was begun by Metellus, and terminated by Mummius with the destruction of Corinth. By reducing both Macedonia and Greece to the form of provinces, Rome now gave evident proof that no existing relations, nor any form of government, can prevent nations from being subjugated by a warlike republic, whenever circumstances render it possible.

It might have been expected, that the destruction of the two first commercial cities in the world, in the same year, would have been followed by important consequences to the course of trade; but the trade of Carthage and Corinth had already been drawn to Alexandria and Rhodes, otherwise Utica might, in some respects, have supplied the place of Carthage.

21. *War in Spain.* While Rome was thus destroying thrones and republics, she met in Spain with an antagonist—a simple Spanish countryman named Viriathus—whom, after six years' war, she could only rid herself of by assassination. The war, nevertheless, continued after his death against the Numantines, who would not be subjected, but were at last destroyed by Scipio Æmilianus.

The war against the Spaniards, who of all the nations subdued by the Romans defended their liberty with the greatest obstinacy, began in the year 200, six years after the total expulsion of the Carthaginians from their country, 206. It was exceedingly obstinate, partly from the natural state of the country, which was thickly populated, and where every place became a fortress; partly from the courage of the inhabitants; but above all, owing to the peculiar policy of the Romans, who were wont to employ their allies to subdue other nations. This war continued, almost without interruption, from the year 200 to 133, and was for the most part carried on at the same time in Hispania Citerior, where the Celtiberi were the most formidable adversaries, and in Hispania Ulterior, where the Lusitani were equally powerful. Hostilities were at the highest pitch in 195, under Cato, who reduced Hispania Citerior to a state of tranquillity in 185–179, when the Celtiberi were attacked in their native territory; and 155–150, when the Romans in both provinces were so often beaten, that nothing was more dreaded by the soldiers at home than to be sent there. The extortions and perfidy of Servius Galba placed Viriathus, in the year 146, at the head of his nation, the Lusitani: the war, however, soon extended itself to Hispania

Citerior, where many nations, particularly the Numantines, took up arms against Rome, 143. Viriathus, sometimes victorious and sometimes defeated, was never more formidable than in the moment of defeat; because he knew how to take advantage of his knowledge of the country, and of the dispositions of his countrymen. After his murder, caused by the treachery of Cæpio, 140, Lusitania was subdued; but the Numantine war became still more violent, and the Numantines compelled the consul Mancinus to a disadvantageous treaty, 137. When Scipio, in the year 133, put an end to this war, Spain was certainly tranquil; the northern parts, however, were still unsubdued, though the Romans penetrated as far as Galatia.

22. *Attalus III. leaves his kingdom to the Romans.* Towards the end of this period, the Romans obtained at a much cheaper rate the possession of one of their most important provinces; for the profligate Attalus III., king of Pergamus, bequeathing them the whole of his kingdom (on what account is uncertain), they immediately took possession of it, and kept it in spite of the resistance of the legitimate heir Aristonicus, merely ceding, as a recompense, Phrygia to Mithridates V., king of Pontus. Thus, by a stroke of the pen, the largest and finest part of Asia Minor became the property of Rome. If this extraordinary legacy was the work of Roman policy, she paid dearly enough, in the long run, for this accession to her power and riches, by the destruction of her morals, and the dreadful wars to which this legacy gave rise under Mithridates.

23. *Roman Provinces—how governed.* The foreign possessions of Rome, besides Italy, comprised at this time under the name of provinces, a name of much higher signification in the Latin language than in any other, Hispania Citerior and Ulterior, Africa (the territory of Carthage), Sicily, Sardinia, and Corsica, Liguria, and Cisalpine Gaul, in the west; and in the east, Macedonia, Achaia, and Asia (territory of Pergamus). The inhabitants of these countries were entirely subject to Rome. The administration of them was carried on by those who had enjoyed the office of consul, and by prætors, subordinate to whom were the quæstors, or collectors of the revenue. The highest military and civil powers were united in these governors; a principal cause of that horrible oppression which was soon felt. Troops were always kept up in the provinces; and the Latin language every where introduced (except only where Greek was spoken), that the inhabitants might be made as much like Romans as possible.

Till nearly the end of this period, prætors were expressly appointed to each province. It was not till after the origin of the *quæstiones per-*

petuæ, that it became the custom for the prætors who had vacated office, to succeed to the provinces (*proprætores*), a principal cause of the degeneracy of the Roman constitution.

24. *Roman Revenue.* The acquisition of these rich countries naturally had great influence in augmenting the revenue of the Romans. Though Rome was not indeed a state like Carthage, altogether dependent upon finances, yet she kept these adjusted in a wonderful manner; a spirit of nice order being observed in this as well as in every other department of her administration. If in extraordinary emergencies recourse were had to native loans, to a change in the value of money, or a monopoly of salt, order was soon restored; while the booty obtained from conquered countries was also a great source of the public income, so long indeed as it was reserved for the state, and did not become the prey of the generals.

Sources of the Roman revenue (*vectigalia*) were: 1. Tribute (*a*) from the Roman citizens; that is to say, a property-tax imposed by the senate according to the urgency of the case (which, however, was remitted for a long time, after the war with Perseus, 168, being no longer necessary). (*b*) Tribute of the allies (*socii*) in Italy: which seems also to have been a property-tax; differing in different places. (*c*) Tribute of the provinces: in some a heavy poll-tax, in others taxes on property; in all, however, they were paid in natural productions, mostly ordinary, though sometimes extraordinary, as well for the salary of the governor as for the supply of the capital. 2. The revenue from the national domains (*ager publicus*), both in Italy (especially Campania) and in the provinces; the tithes (*decumæ*) of which were paid by means of leases for four years, granted by the censors. 3. The revenue from the customs (*portoria*), collected in the seaports and frontier towns. 4. The revenue arising from the mines (*metalla*), particularly the Spanish silver mines; the proprietors of which were obliged to pay a duty to the state. 5. The duty upon enfranchised slaves (*aurum vicesimarium*). All receipts flowed into the national treasury, the *ærarium;* all outgoings were exclusively ordered by the senate; and the people were consulted as little with regard to them as they were respecting the imposts. The officers employed were the *quæstores*, under whom were the *scribæ*, divided into *decurias*, who, though certainly subordinate, had nevertheless great influence. Their services, as they were not yearly changed, must have been indispensable to the *quæstores* for the time being; and the whole management of affairs, at least in detail, must have fallen into their hands.

SEC. VII.—FROM THE SEDITIONS OF THE GRACCHI TO THE FALL OF THE COMMONWEALTH. B. C. 134–30.

1. *Civil wars.—Power of the Senate creates an Aristocracy, which is opposed by the Tribunes of the People.* The foregoing period is composed of the history of foreign wars alone; in this, on the contrary, Rome appears in a continual state of internal commotion. And if foreign hostilities interrupted this state of things for a short time, it is only that it may be renewed with more violence, till at last it ends in a furious civil war. As the almost boundless power of the senate had laid the foundation of an exceedingly hateful family aristocracy, against which the tribunes of the people arrayed themselves in the character of powerful demagogues, there arose a new struggle between the aristocratic and democratic parties, which almost immediately grew into two powerful factions. This contest, from its extent and its consequences, soon became much more important than the ancient one between the patricians and the plebeians.

The family aristocracy gradually arose from the power of the magistrates, who now not only enjoyed a very high political importance, but, by the government of the provinces, acquired immense wealth. The present aristocracy, then, consisted of the ruling families (*nobiles*) concentrated in the senate. The struggle with the opposite party, the people (*plebs*), became so much the more violent in consequence of the great abuses which had crept into the administration, particularly in the division of the lands of the republic; the ruling families securing to themselves the fruits of all the victories and conquests, while the power of the democracy, by the vast accumulation of people, (without the means of livelihood, although voting in the *comitia*,) especially of enfranchised slaves, who, though strangers, mostly without power or property, formed, nevertheless, the greater part of what was then called the Roman people.

2. *First disturbances under T. S. Gracchus, B. C.* 133.—*He desires to relieve the distress of the lower orders, and dies in the attempt.* Commencement of the disturbances under the tribunate of Tib. Sempronius Gracchus, whom former connections had long made the man of the people. His desire was to relieve the distress of the lower orders; and the means whereby he hoped to do this was a better division of the lands of the republic, now almost exclusively in the hands of the aristocracy. His reform, therefore, naturally led at once to a struggle with that party. Tib. Gracchus however soon found, by experience, that a demagogue cannot stop where he would, however pure his intentions may be at first; and no sooner had he obtained a prolongation of his term

of office, in opposition to the usual custom, than he fell a sacrifice to his undertaking.

The first agrarian law of Gracchus was confirmed by the people, notwithstanding the fruitless opposition of his colleague Octavius, who was deposed; it decreed that no person should possess above five hundred acres of land, nor any child above half that quantity. This law was, in fact, only a renewal of the ancient *lex Licinia;* in the condition, however, in which Rome now was, it bore much harder upon the property usurped by the great families, than it did in former times. Appointment of a committee for dividing the national lands, and for inquiring also at the same time which were the property of the state (*ager publicus*) and which were not. New popular propositions of the elder Gracchus, especially that for the division of the treasures left by king Attalus of Pergamus, with the view of securing his continuance in office; great insurrection of the aristocratic party under Scipio Nasica, and murder of Tiberius Gracchus, on the day of electing the new tribunes of the people.

3. *His fall does not destroy his party.* The fall of the chief of the new party, however, occasioned any thing rather than its destruction. Not only was there no mention of an abrogation of the agrarian law, but the senate was obliged to allow the place in the commission, which had become vacant by the death of Gracchus, to be filled up; and Scipio Nasica himself was sent out of the way, under the pretext of an embassy to Asia. The party of the senate did, indeed, find a powerful support for a short time in the return of Scipio Æmilianus (*d.* 129) from Spain; but its greatest support was found in the difficulties of the law itself, which prevented its execution.

Great revolt of the slaves in Sicily under Eunus, 134–131. This contributed not a little to keep alive the dissensions, as it showed the necessity of a reform.

4. *The Tribunes endeavor to increase their power, B. C.* 130. Evident endeavors of the tribunes of the people to increase their power, Gracchus having now awakened them to a sense of it. Not satisfied with a seat and voice in the senate, Carbo wished that the renewing of their dignity should be passed into a law. By the removal, however, of the chiefs of the lower party, upon honorable pretexts, new troubles were put off for some years.

First establishment of the Roman power in Transalpine Gaul by M. Fulvius Flaccus, on the occasion of his being sent to the assistance of Massilia, 128. Southern Gaul became a Roman province as early as 122, in consequence of the defeat of the Allobrogi and Averni by Q. Fabius, who had been sent against them to support the Ædui, the allies of Rome. Capture of the Balearian isles by Metellus, 123. Quæstorship of C. Gracchus in Sicily, 128–125.

5. *C. Gracchus.* These palliative remedies, however, availed nothing after the return of C. Gracchus from Sicily, with a full determination to tread in the footsteps of his brother. Like him, it is true, he fell a victim to his enterprise; but the storm that he raised during the two years of his tribunate, fell so much the more heavily, as the popular excitement was more general, and from his possessing more of the shining talents necessary to form a powerful demagogue than his brother.

First tribunate of C. Gracchus, 123. Renewal of the agrarian law, and rendering its provisions more strict. Nevertheless, as he increased the fermentation by his popular measures, and by acting the demagogue, and obtained the renewal of the tribunate for the following year, 122, he so far extended his plan, as to render it not only highly dangerous to the aristocracy, but even to the state itself. Establishment of distributions of corn to the poor people. Plan for the formation of the knights (*ordo equestris*) into a political body, as a counterbalance to the senate, by conferring on it the right of administering justice (*judicia*), which was taken from the senate. Still more important project of granting to the Italian allies the privileges of Roman citizenship, and also the formation of colonies, not only in Campania, but also out of Italy, in Carthage. The highly refined policy of the senate, however, by lessening this man of the people in the eyes of his admirers, through the assistance of the tribune Livius Drusius, prevented his complete triumph; and, once declining, Gracchus soon experienced the fate of every demagogue, whose complete fall is then irretrievable. General insurrection, and assassination of C. Gracchus, 121.

6. *Victory of the Aristocratic Faction.* The victory of the aristocratic faction was this time not only much more certain and bloody, but they turned the advantages it gave them to such good account, that they eluded the agrarian law of Gracchus, and indeed, at last, completely abrogated it. But the seeds of discord already disseminated, especially among the Italian allies, could not be so soon checked, when once the subjects of these states had conceived the idea that they were entitled to a share in the government. How soon these party struggles might be renewed, or indeed a civil war break out, depended almost entirely upon foreign circumstances, and the chance of a bolder leader being found.

Agrarian law evaded: at first, by repealing an act which prohibited the transfer of the national lands already divided, whereby the patricians were enabled to buy them again;—afterwards by the *lex Thoria;* complete stop put to all further divisions, a land-tax, to be distributed among the people, being instituted in its stead; but even this latter was very soon annulled.

7. *Effects of this party spirit in corrupting the Nation.* Visible effects of this party spirit upon public morals, which now began to decline the more rapidly in proportion to the increase of foreign connections. Neither the severity of the censorship, nor the laws against luxury (*leges sumtuariæ*), nor those which now became necessary against celibacy, could be of much service in this respect. This degeneracy was not only to be found in the cupidity of the higher ranks, but also in the licentiousness of the lower orders.

Luxury in Rome was first displayed in the public administration (owing to the excessive accumulation of wealth in the treasury, especially during the Macedonian wars) before it infected private life; and the avarice of the great long preceded the latter. The sources from whence they satisfied this passion, were found in the extortions of the governors of provinces, their great power, and the distance from Rome, rendering the *legis repetundarum* of but little effect. Probably the endeavors of the allied princes and kings to gain a party in the senate, was a still more fruitful source, as they could obtain their end only by purchase, and so gave a new impulse to the cupidity and intriguing disposition of the members of that council. But private luxury requires everywhere some time to ripen. It attained its height immediately after the Mithridatic wars.

8. *The African war against Jugurtha, B. C.* 118–106.—*C. Marius.* This corruption was manifested in a striking manner in the next great war that Rome entered into, which was in Africa, against Jugurtha of Numidia, the adopted grandson of Masinissa; and soon after against his ally Bocchus of Mauritania. This war, kindled and maintained by the avarice of the Roman nobles, which Jugurtha had already had an opportunity of knowing at the siege of Numantia, paved the way to the aggrandizement of C. Marius, a new demagogue, who, being also a formidable general, did much more harm to the state than even the Gracchi.

Commencement of the quarrel of Jugurtha with the two sons of Micipsa, and assassination of Hiempsal, one of them, 118. When the other, Adherbal, arrived at Rome, 117, the party of Jugurtha had already succeeded, and obtained a partition of the kingdom. New attack upon Adherbal, who is besieged in Cirta, and, notwithstanding the repeated embassies of Rome to Jugurtha, is compelled to surrender, and is put to death, 112. The tribune C. Memmius constrains the senate to declare war against Jugurtha; but Jugurtha purchases a peace of the consul Calpurnius Piso, 111. Nevertheless Memmius hinders the ratification of the peace, and Jugurtha is required to justify himself at Rome. He would probably, however, have bought his acquittal, if the murder of his kinsman Massiva, 110, by the help of Bomilcar, had not rendered it impossible. The war is renewed under the consul Sp. Albinus and his brother Aulus, 110, but with very little success, until the incorruptible Q. Metellus took the command, 109, who would have put an end to it, notwithstanding the great talents now displayed as a general by Jugurtha, and his alliance with Bocchus, 108, had he not been supplanted by Marius, who obtains the consulship by his popularity, 107. Marius is obliged to have recourse to perfidy to get Jugurtha into his hands, who is betrayed by Bocchus, 106. Numidia is divided between Bocchus and two grandsons of Masinissa, Hiempsal and Hiarbas.

9. *C. Marius obtains the Consulate.—Defeats the Cimbri and Teutones.* The elevation of Marius to the consulate not only humbled the power of the aristocracy, but also showed, for the first time, that the way was open to a man of low birth (*homo novus*) to the highest offices; the method, however, which he had taken to form his army, entirely against the Roman custom, that is, of composing it of the lower orders (*capite censis*) must have rendered him doubly formidable. Nevertheless, he would scarcely have effected so great a change in the constitution, if a new and terrible war had not rendered his services indispensable:—this was the threatened invasion of the Cimbri and Teutones, the most powerful nations of the north, during which a new and violent rebellion of the slaves was raging in Sicily; for, after the defeat of so many Roman armies, the people believed that no one but the conqueror of Jugurtha could save Italy; and Marius knew so well how to turn this to account, that he remained consul during four successive years.

The Cimbri, or Cimmerians, probably a nation of German origin, from beyond the Black Sea, originated a popular migration, which extended from thence as far as Spain. Their march was perhaps occasioned or accelerated by the Scythian war of Mithridates; and their course, like that of the most momad races, was from east to west along the Danube. They had already, in 113, defeated the consul Papirius Carbo, near Noreia in Styria. In their progress towards the west, they were joined by German, Celtic, and Helvetic tribes (the *Teutones*, *Ambrones* and *Tigurians*). Attack Roman Gaul, 109, where they demand settlements, and defeat Junius Silanus, the consul. Defeat of L. Cassius Longinus and M. Aurelius Scaurus, 107. Great defeat of the Romans in Gaul, 105, occasioned by the disagreement of their generals, the consuls, Cn. Manlius and Q. Servius Cæpio. Marius obtains the command, and remains consul from 104–101. The migrations of the Cimbri—a part of whom reach the Pyrenees, but are driven back by the Celtiberians, 103—give Marius time to complete his army. In 102, after dividing themselves, they first attempted to penetrate into Italy—the Teutones through Provence, and the Cimbri by Tyrol. Great defeat and slaughter of the Teutones by Marius, near Aix, 102. The Cimbri, on the contrary, effect an invasion and make progress, till Marius comes to the help of Catulus. Great battle and defeat of the Cimbri, near the Po, July 30, 101.

10. *Marius buys his sixth Consulate.* Although, during this war, the power of the popular party had sensibly increased, yet the storm did not break out until Marius *bought* his sixth consulate. Now, even in Rome itself he wished to avenge himself upon his enemies; and what could the senate do, when it had at its head a demagogue in the consul himself? His league with the tribune Saturnius, and the prætor Glaucias, forming already a true triumvirate, would have overthrown the republic, after the expulsion of Metellus, if the unbridled licentiousness of the rabble connected with his allies had not obliged him to break with them, lest he should sacrifice the whole of his popularity.

The measures of this cabal, who wished to appear as if treading in the steps of the Gracchi, were principally directed against Q. Metellus, the chief of the party of the Senate, and who, since the African war, had been the mortal foe of Marius. After the exile of Metellus, occasioned by his opposition to a new agrarian law, this faction usurped the rights of the people, and lorded it in the committees; until at a new election of consuls, a general revolt, favored by Marius himself, took place of all the well-disposed citizens against them; Saturnius and Glaucias were besieged in the capitol, forced to surrender, and executed. The return of Metellus from his voluntary exile soon followed, 99, much against the will of Marius, who was obliged to retire into Asia.

11. *Conditions of Rome, B. C.* 98–91. The few years of tranquillity which Rome now enjoyed, brought to maturity many benefits and many evils, the seeds of which had been already sown. On one hand the rising eloquence of Antonius, Crassus, and others, was employed with effect against the oppressors of the provinces in the state trials (*questiones*); and some generous spirits used all their endeavors to heal the wounds of Sicily, Asia, and other provinces, by a better administration; while, on the other hand, the power of the *ordo equestris* became a source of much abuse: for besides their right to sit in the tribunals, (*judiciis,*) which C. Gracchus had conferred upon them, they had also

obtained the farming of the leases, and thereby the collection of the revenue in the provinces; by which means they were enabled not only to oppose every reform that was attempted in the latter, but even at Rome to hold the senate in a state of dependence. The struggle which now arose between them and the senate respecting the *judicia* (or right to preside in the tribunal) was one of the most fatal to the republic, as this right was abused by them for the purpose of satisfying their personal rancor, and oppressing the greatest men. The tribune M. Livius Drusus the younger, it is true, wrested from them half their power; but, alas! the manner in which he did it kindled into a flame the fire which had been smouldering from the time of the Gracchi.

Acquisition of Cyrene by the testament of King Apion, 97; notwithstanding which it maintained its independence, although probably by paying a tribute. Adjustment of the differences between the kings of Asia Minor by the prætor Sylla, 92.

12. *War of the Allies, B. C.* 91–88. Revolt of the Italian tribes, who desire to obtain the right of Roman citizens; whereupon the bloody *war of the allies* ensues. Although the oppression of Rome had been preparing this war for a long time, yet it was an immediate consequence of the intrigues of the Roman demagogues, who, since the law of the younger Gracchus, had, with the view of making themselves popular, continually flattered the allies with the hope of sharing the privileges of Roman citizenship. It was, however, soon seen that the allies were not at a loss among themselves for leaders, capable of forming great plans and executing them with vigor. Italy was about to become a republic, with Corfinium for its capital instead of Rome. Neither could Rome have saved herself from such an event, but by gradually permitting the allies to enjoy the complete freedom of the city.

After the civil wars of the Gracchi, large bands of the allies were continually flocking to Rome. These were in the pay of the demagogues, whom the *lex Licinia*, 95, had banished from Rome, and thereby laid the foundation of the revolt. From that time the conspiracy among these tribes began, and attained without interruption such a degree of maturity, that the carelessness of Rome can only be accounted for from the party fury which then existed, and which the *lex Varia*, 91, enacted against the promoters of rebellion, served only to inflame the more. The murder of the tribune Livius Drusus, 91, a very ambiguous character, brought the affair to an open rupture. In this alliance were the Marsi, Picentes, Peligni, Marrucini, Frentani, the Samnites, who played a principal part, the Hirpini, Apuli, and the Lucani. In this war, which was so much the more bloody, as it was mostly composed of separate contests and sieges, especially of the Roman colonies,

Cn. Pompeius the elder, L. Cato, Marius, and, above all, Sylla, particularly distinguished themselves on the side of the Romans: and among the generals of the allies Pompadias, C. Papius, etc. Concession of the freedom of the city, first to such allies as remained faithful, the Latins, Umbrians, etc., by the *lex Julia*, 91; afterwards, by degrees, to the remainder by the *lex Plotia*. Some, nevertheless, still continued in arms.

13. *Change in Constitution.* The war now just ended, essentially changed the constitution of Rome, as she no longer remained, as hitherto, the exclusive head of the whole state; and although the new citizens were only formed into eight tribes, yet their influence must soon have been felt in the committees, on account of the readiness with which they promoted factions. Besides this, the long-cherished private hatred between Marius and Sylla was greatly strengthened by this war, as Sylla's fame was considerably raised thereby, while that of Marius was proportionably diminished. An opportunity was only wanted, like that which the first Pontine war soon furnished, to stir up a new civil war, which threatened to destroy the liberty of Rome.

14. *Alliance of Marius with Sulpicius against Sylla, B. C.* 88. Alliance of Marius with the tribune Sulpicius, with the view of wresting from Sylla the command of the forces against Mithridates, already conferred upon him by the senate. The ease with which Sylla, at the head of an army on which he could depend, expelled the chiefs of this party, seems to have left him ignorant of the fact, that the party itself was not thereby destroyed. However judicious may have been his other measures, the elevation of Cinna to the consulship was an error in policy of which Italy had still more reason to repent than himself. How much blood might have been spared if Sylla had not unseasonably wished to become popular!

Proposition of Sulpicius for an indiscriminate distribution of the new citizens and freemen among all the tribes of Italy, that he might thereby gain a strong party in his favor, which, by a violent assembly of the people, transfers the command from Sylla to Marius. March of Sylla upon Rome, and expulsion of Marius, who, by a series of adventures almost surpassing belief, escapes to Africa, and is proscribed, with his son and ten of his partisans. Re-establishment of the power of the senate, whose number is made up by three hundred knights. Sylla after having caused his friend C. Octavius and his enemy L. Cinna to be elected consuls, hastens back to Greece.

15. *First war against Mithridates*, 89–85.—*His great power: that of Rome divided.* First war against Mithridates the Great. Sylla gains several victories over that king's generals in Greece; wrests from

him all his conquests, and restricts him to his hereditary dominions. Rome since the time of Hannibal had met with no such powerful opponent as the king of Pontus, who in a few months had become master of all Asia Minor, Macedonia, and Greece, and threatened even Italy itself; we must besides consider, that the war on the side of Rome was carried on in a manner altogether different from that of any previous one; as Sylla, after the victory of the opposite party, being himself proscribed in Rome, was obliged to continue it with his own army, and his own private resources. The unfortunate countries which were the theatre of this war, felt as many calamities during the struggle, as Italy was doomed to suffer after its close.

Commencement of the war by Mithridates before the termination of that of the allies, 89, by taking possession of Cappadocia and Paphlagonia. He was not less formidable by his alliance with the tribes along the Danube, and his navy, than by his land forces; and the irritation of the people of Asia against Rome rendered his enterprise still more easy. Double victory over Nicomedes, king of Bithynia, and the Roman general M. Aquilius, followed by the conquest of all Asia Minor except the isle of Rhodes. Massacre of all the Roman citizens in the states of Asia Minor. Expedition of the king's army into Greece, under the command of his general Archelaus, who makes Athens the theatre of the war, 88. Siege and capture of that unfortunate town by Sylla, 1st March, 87. Repeated great defeats of Mithridates's army under the command of Archelaus, near Chalcis, and afterwards near Orchomenus, by Sylla, 86, whose general plan was formed upon the entire destruction of his enemies. Negotiations for peace commenced by Archelaus, and finally settled at a personal conference between Sylla and Mithridates. The adverse party in Rome, however, had in the mean time sent a new army into Asia Minor, to act as well against Sylla as against Mithridates, under the command of L. Valerius Flaccus, who, however, is assassinated by his lieutenant Fimbria. The latter gains some advantages over the king, but being shut up by Sylla, kills himself. Owing to the licentiousness of his army, which Sylla dared not restrain; and the heavy contributions exacted by him in Asia Minor after the peace, in order to carry on the war in Italy, 84; together with the bodies of pirates formed out of the fleet disbanded by Mithridates, these unfortunate countries were almost ruined; the opulent cities more especially.

16. *New Revolution in Rome under Cinna and Marius.* But during this war a new revolution took place in Rome, which not only overthrew the order re-established by Sylla, but also, by the victory of the democratic faction under Cinna and Marius, gave rise to a wild

anarchy of the people, and which the death of Marius, alas, too late for Rome! only rendered more destructive; as the leaders themselves could no longer restrain the savage hordes of their own party. However dreadful the prospect of the return of Sylla might seem, it was nevertheless the only hope that remained for all those who had not joined the popular faction, or had not some connection with its leaders.

Revolt of Cinna, brought on by the proscriptions, soon after the departure of Sylla; Cinna, by distributing the new citizens into all the tribes, hoped to raise himself a party; but C. Octavius, at the head of the senate and ancient citizens, drove him from Rome, and forced him to give up the consulship, 87. He, however, soon raised a powerful army in Campania, and recalled Marius from exile. Capture and pillage of Rome, already weakened by famine, and horrible massacre of the inhabitants; after which Marius and Cinna name themselves consuls and banish Sylla. Death of Marius, 13th Jan., 86. C. Papirius Carbo succeeds him in the consulship. The mediation of the senate is useless, as the chiefs of both parties can only hope for security by the annihilation of their adversaries. The murder of Cinna by his own soldiers, 84, entirely deprives the dominant faction of a competent leader. Neither the cowardly Carbo, although he remained consul alone, nor the stupid Norbanus, nor the youth C. Marius (the son), had sufficient personal authority for that purpose; and Sertorius leaves Italy in good time to kindle a new flame in Spain.

17. *Sylla's return, and bloody civil war*, B. C. 83.—*Sylla's proscription.* Return of Sylla to Italy, and a terrible civil war, which ends only with the extermination of the democratic faction, and his own elevation to the perpetual dictatorship. Although his enemies had so much advantage over him in point of numbers, yet their party was so little consolidated, that he with his veterans could not fail to obtain an easy victory. The slaughter during this war fell for the most part upon the Italian tribes, who had joined the party of Marius, and this afforded Sylla the means of giving settlements to his own soldiers; but most of the horrors of this revolution which fell to the share of Rome, were reserved till the day of victory was past. Sylla's proscription, which should only have punished his personal enemies, was the signal for a general massacre, as every one took that opportunity to rid himself of his private foes: and avarice did as much as vengeance. Who in these days, so terrible to Italy, was sure of his life or property? and yet, when we consider the dreadful circumstances which attended the foregoing dominion of the people, deduct all that was done without Sylla's knowledge, and consider how much he was

obliged to do in order to satisfy his army, we shall find it difficult to say how far he deserves the reproach of wanton cruelty.

Sylla's arrival; victory over Norbanus immediately after and seduction of the army of the consul Scipio, 82. After this almost every person of distinction declared in his favor, and the young Pompey having brought to him an army which he had himself raised, his party acquired more consideration, and himself more power. Victory over the younger Marius, near Sacriportum, who throws himself into Præneste, where he is besieged. But the great and decisive battle gained before the gates of Rome, over the Samnites under the command of Telisinus, is followed by the fall of Præneste and the capture of Rome. After the proscription which immediately ensued, Sylla is created perpetual dictator, and secures his power in Rome by the emancipation of ten thousand slaves, whose masters he had proscribed; and in Italy by colonies of his veterans, whom he establishes at the expense of his enemies.

18. *Reform in the Constitution*, B. C. 81–79.—*Power of the Senate restored.—Sylla's Abdication*, 79. Great reform in the constitution during the two years' dictatorship of Sylla. The aristocracy of the senate, which he filled up with knights, was not only re-established, but he also stopped the sources from which the great disorders of the democracy had hitherto proceeded. It seems probable that his natural indolence, which led him to prefer a life of luxurious ease to one of laborious activity, when he was no longer spurred to the latter by his passions, was the chief cause of his voluntary abdication. He had, however, the great advantage over Marius, of not being the sport of his own feelings. The conduct of Sylla, indeed, was so consistent throughout, that it satisfactorily shows he knew very well what was his ultimate aim—which Marius never did.

Internal regulations of Sylla by the *leges Corneliæ.* 1. Law to restrain the influence of the tribunes, by taking from them their legislative power. 2. Law respecting the succession to the magistracy; the number of prætors fixed to eight, and the quæstors to twenty. 3. *Lex de majestate*, especially to limit the power of the governors of provinces, and to abolish their exactions. 4. *Lex de judiciis*, whereby the *judicia* were again restored to the senate. 5. Several police regulations, *de sicariis*, *de beneficiis*, etc., for the preservation and tranquillity of Rome, upon which every thing depended. 6. The *lex de civitate*, taking from the Latins and several Italian cities and tribes the privileges of Roman citizens, upon which they set so much store, although we scarcely know in what they consisted. *Foreign wars:* war in Africa against the leaders of the democratic faction, Cn. Domitius and King Hiarbas, which is ended by a triumph to Pompey, 80. Second war against Mithridates begun by Murena, in hopes of obtaining a triumph, to whom Archelaus came over; but which, under the command of Sylla, terminates in an accommodation.

19. *A state like Rome exposed to convulsions.* Nevertheless it was impossible that the enactments of Sylla should be long observed; as the evil lay too deep to be eradicated by laws. A free state like that of Rome, with no middle class, must, from its nature, be exposed to continual convulsions, and these will be more or less violent in proportion to its greatness. Besides, as in the last revolution almost all property had changed hands, there was spread over all Italy a powerful party, who desired nothing so much as a counter-revolution. And to this we may add, that there were many young men, such as Lucullus, Crassus, and above all Pompey, who had opened to themselves a career during the late troubles, which they would scarcely yet wish to bring to a close. It will not then appear strange, that immediately after the death of Sylla (88), a consul, M. Æmilius Lepidus, should form the design of becoming a second Marius; a design which could only be frustrated by the courage and activity of such a patriotic citizen as Q. Lutatius Catulus, his colleague.

Attempt of Lepidus to rescind the acts of Sylla, 78. Defeated, first before Rome and again in Etruria, by Catulus and Pompey, 77, after which he dies in Sardinia.

20. *Civil war of Sertorius in Spain.* But much more dangerous for Rome might have been the civil war kindled by Sertorius in Spain, if the plan of that exalted republican to invade Italy had succeeded. Even Pompey himself, after a six years' struggle, would hardly have prevented it, had it not been for the worthlessness of the Roman vagabonds who surrounded him, and his assassination by Perpenna. The rapid termination of the war after the fall of its conductor, is a circumstance much more creditable to Sertorius than to the conqueror Pompey.

The forces of Sertorius in Spain, consisted not only of the party of Marius which he had collected, but more essentially of the Spaniards, particularly the Lusitanians, whom he had inspired with an unbounded confidence in himself. Very variable success of the war against Metellus and Pompey, who receive but very little support from Rome, 77–75. Negotiation of Sertorius with Mithridates the Great, and interchange of embassies without any important result, 75. Sertorius assassinated by Perpenna, 72.

21. *The third Mithridatic war; combined with the servile war, and that of the pirates, threaten the downfall of Rome.* Before,

however, the flame of war was totally extinguished in the West, Mithridates kindled a new and much fiercer one in the East; at the same time a war of slaves and gladiators was raging with terrible fury in Italy itself; and whole fleets of pirates not only ravaged the Italian coasts, but threatened Rome herself with a famine, and obliged her to have recourse to a mode of naval warfare altogether peculiar. All these enemies were not without intelligence with one another; and colossal as was the power of the republic at that time, and rich as Rome was in distinguished men, it seems probable that the storm which beat on every side between 75–71, would have razed her to the ground, if a stricter alliance could have been formed between Sertorius, Spartacus, and Mithridates. But the great difficulty of communication which at that time existed, and without which probably a republic such as the Roman never could have been formed, proved of more assistance at this crisis than at any other.

The third Mithridatic war, occasioned by the will of Nicomedes king of Bithynia, who had bequeathed his kingdom to Rome, was carried on in Asia Minor, first by Lucullus, 74–67, and afterwards by Pompey, 66–64. Mithridates, being better prepared, had already concluded an alliance with Sertorius in Spain, 75. But the deliverance of Cyzicus by Lucullus, 73, and the defeat of the king's fleet, intended to act against Italy, not only frustrated all his original plans, but were followed by the occupation of his own dominions, 72 and 71, by the enemy, notwithstanding a new army which Mithridates collected, mostly from the nomad hordes of Northern Asia. Flight of Mithridates to Tigranes, 71, who positively refused to deliver him up, and formed an alliance with him, 70; while the Parthian, Arsaces XII., held both parties in suspense by negotiations. Victory of Lucullus over the allied sovereigns, near Tigranocerta, 69, and Artaxata, 68; but the mutinies which now broke out among his troops not only hindered him from following up these advantages, but turned the scale so much in Mithridates' favor, that in 68 and 67 he quickly regained almost all his dominions, even while the Roman commissioners were on their route to take possession of them. Lucullus by his reform in the finances of Asia Minor, raises a powerful party against himself in Rome, and thereby loses his command.

22. *The Servile war*, B. C. 73–71; *terminated by Crassus.* The war of the slaves and gladiators, which happened nearly at the same time, was, from the theatre of action being in its neighborhood, equally dangerous to Rome; it became still more terrible from the violence with which these outraged beings sought to revenge their wrongs, and more formidable from the talents of their leader, Spartacus; and the conclusion of

this struggle seemed, therefore, of so much importance to Rome, that it gave M. Crassus a much higher influence in the state than he could ever have obtained by his riches alone.

Commencement of this war by a number of runaway gladiators, who, being strengthened by an almost general revolt of the slaves in Campania, 73, soon became very formidable. The defeat of four generals, one after the other, throws open to Spartacus the road to the Alps, and enables him to leave Italy; but the greediness of booty manifested by his hordes, who wished to plunder Rome, obliged him to return. Crassus takes the command and rescues Rome, 72; upon which Spartacus retires into Lower Italy, hoping to form a junction with the pirates, and to carry the war into Sicily, but is deceived by them, 71. His complete overthrow near the Silarus, 71. Pompey then returning from Spain, finds means to seize a sprig of the laurel chaplet which by right should have adorned only the brow of Crassus; hence arises a misunderstanding between these two commanders, during their consulate, 70, which threatened to be dangerous to the state.

23. *The war against the Pirates terminated by Pompey.* The war against the pirates of Sicily and Isauria was not only very important in itself, but still more so in its consequences. It procured for Pompey a legal power such as no Roman general had ever before enjoyed; and the quick and glorious manner in which he brought it to a close, opened for him the way to the great object of his ambition—the conduct of the war in Asia against Mithridates.

The extraordinary power acquired by these pirates was owing partly to the great negligence of the Romans in sea affairs, partly to the war against Mithridates, who had taken the pirates into his pay, and partly also to the Roman oppressions in Asia Minor. War had been undertaken against them as early as 75, by P. Servilius; but his victories, though they procured him the title of *Isauricus*, did them but little harm. They were to be dreaded, not only for their piracies, but because they also offered an easy means of communication between the other enemies of Rome from Spain to Asia. The new attack of the prætor M. Antonius upon Crete, proved a complete failure; but it was the cause of that hitherto independent island being again attacked, 68, by Metellus, and reduced to a Roman province, 67. Pompey takes the command against the pirates with extraordinary privileges, obtained for him by Gabinius, and finishes the war in forty days, 67.

24. *Fall of Mithridates.* After these triumphs over so many enemies, Mithridates was the only one which now remained; and Pompey had here again the good fortune to conclude a struggle already near its end; for, notwithstanding his late success, Mithridates had

never been able completely to recover himself. His fall undoubtedly raised the power of Rome in Asia Minor to its highest pitch; but it brought her, at the same time, into contact with the Parthians.

Pompey obtains the conduct of the war against Mithridates, with very extensive privileges, procured for him by the tribune Manilius (*lex Manilia*), notwithstanding the opposition of Catulus, 67. His victory by night, near the Euphrates, 66. Subjection of Tigranes, while Mithridates flies into the Crimea, 65, whence he endeavors to renew the war. Campaign of Pompey in the countries about the Caucasus, 65; he marches thence into Syria, 64. Mithridates kills himself in consequence of the defection of his son Phraates, 63. Settlement of Asiatic affairs by Pompey: besides the ancient province of Asia, the maritime countries of Bithynia, nearly all Paphlagonia and Pontus, are formed into a Roman province, under the name of Bithynia; while on the southern coast Cilicia and Pamphylia form another under the name of Cilicia; Phœnicia and Syria compose a third, under the name of Syria. On the other hand, Great Armenia is left to Tigranes; Cappadocia to Ariobarzanes; the Bosphorus to Pharnaces; Judæa to Hyrcanus; and some other small states are also given to petty princes, all of whom remain dependent on Rome. The tribes inhabiting Thrace during the Mithridatic war, were first defeated by Sylla, 85, and their power was afterwards nearly destroyed by the proconsuls of Macedonia: as by Appius, in 77; by Curio, who drove them to the Danube, 75–73; and especially by M. Lucullus, while his brother was engaged in Asia. Not only the security of Macedonia, but the daring plans of Mithridates rendered this necessary.

25. *State of Rome; changes in her Constitution; the restoration of the Power of the Tribunes.* The fall of Mithridates raised the republic to the highest pitch of her power: there was no longer any foreign foe of whom she could be afraid. But her internal administration had undergone great changes during these wars. Sylla's aristocratic constitution was shaken by Pompey, in a most essential point, by the re-establishment of the power of the tribunes, which was done because neither he nor any leading men could obtain their ends without their assistance. It was by their means that Pompey had procured such unlimited power in his two late expeditions, that the existence of the republic was thereby endangered. It was, however, a fortunate circumstance for Rome, that Pompey's vanity was sufficiently gratified by his being at the head of affairs, where he avoided the appearance of an oppressor.

Reiterated attempts of the tribune Sicinius to annul the constitution of Sylla defeated by the senate, 76. But as early as 75 Opimius obtained that the tribunes should not be excluded from honorable offices, and that the judgments (*judicia*) should be restored to the knights (*equites*). The attempts of Licinius Macer, 72, to restore the tribunes to all their former powers, encountered but a short opposition; and their complete re-establishment was effected by Pompey and Crassus during their consulate, in 70.

26. *This victory of the Democrats leads to an oligarchy*, 70.—*Catiline's Conspiracy.—Cicero.* This victory of the democratic faction, however, in consequence of the use made of it by some leading men, necessarily led the way to an oligarchy, which after the consulate of Pompey and Crassus became very oppressive. Catiline's conspiracy, which was not matured till after several attempts, would have broken up this confined aristocracy, and placed the helm of state in the hands of another and still more dangerous faction—a faction composed in part of needy profligates and criminals dreading the punishment of their crimes, and partly of ambitious nobles. It occasioned a short civil war; but procured Cicero a place in the administration. With what pleasure do we forgive the little weaknesses and failings of one so gifted with talents and great virtues! of one who first taught Rome, in so many ways, what it was to be great in the robe of peace!

Catiline's first conspiracy, in which Cæsar and Crassus seem to have been implicated, 66, as well as in the second, 65: failure of the former by chance—of the latter through Piso's death. The third broke out in 64, as well in Rome, where the conspirators, having no armed force, were soon suppressed by the vigilance and activity of Cicero, 63, as in Etruria, where a victory of the proconsul Antonius over Catiline, who was left dead on the field, concluded it, 62.

27. *Effects of the Asiatic war on the Roman manners.—Great men of this period: Cato, Pompey, Crassus, Cæsar.* The suppression of this conspiracy, however, did not stay the effect which the recently concluded Asiatic war had upon Roman manners. The luxury of the East, though united with Grecian taste, which had been introduced among the great by Lucullus; the immense riches poured into the treasury by Pompey; the tempting examples of unlimited power, which single citizens had already exercised; the purchase of the magistracy by individuals, in order, like Verres, after the squandering of millions, to enrich themselves again in the provinces; the demands of the soldiers upon their generals; and the ease with which an army might be raised by him who had only money enough to pay it; all these circumstances must have foreboded new and approaching convulsions, even if the preceding storms in this colossal republic, in which we must now judge of virtues and vices, as well as of riches and power,

by a very magnified standard, had not formed men of that gigantic character they did:—men like Cato, who struggled alone to stem the impetuous torrent of the revolution, and was sufficiently powerful to retard its progress for a time; or, like Pompey, who by good fortune and the art of acquiring influence, arose to a degree of authority and power never before attained by any citizen of a free state; or, like Crassus, "who only considered him as rich that could maintain an army by his own private means," founding their pretensions on wealth; or, finally, like the aspiring and now powerful Cæsar, whose boundless ambition could only be surpassed by his talents and courage, "who would rather be the first in a village than the second in Rome." The return of Pompey from Asia, threatening the senate with a new dictator, appeared an eventful moment.

Attempt of Pompey, through the tribune Metellus Nepos, to be allowed to return to Rome at the head of his army, frustrated by the firmness of Cato, 62.

28. *Pompey's return revives the struggle between him and the senate, B. C.* 61.—*Cæsar's return from Lusitania*, 61. The arrival of Pompey in Rome renewed the struggle between the senate and that powerful general, although he had disbanded his army on landing in Italy. The ratification of his management of affairs in Asia, which was the chief point of contention, was opposed by the leading men of the senate, Cato, the two Metelli, and Lucullus, which induced Pompey to attach himself entirely to the popular party, by whose means he hoped to obtain his end; Cæsar's return, however, from his province of Lusitania, entirely changed the face of affairs.

29. *Triumvirate of Cæsar, Pompey, and Crassus*, 60.—*Cæsar's consulate*, 59, *obtains him the government of the two Gauls and Illyria for five years.* Close union between Cæsar, Pompey, and Crassus; that is, a secret alliance, formed by the interposition of Cæsar. That which formed the height of the ambition of Pompey and Crassus was only regarded by Cæsar as the means by which he might be able to effect his. His consulate—a kind of dictatorship under the mask of great popularity—necessarily paved the way to his future career, as by giving him the government of the two Gauls and Illyria for five years, it opened a wide field for conquest, and gave him an opportunity of forming an army devoted to his will.

Cæsar's abode and campaign in Gaul from the spring of 58 till the end of the year 50. By arresting the emigration of the Helvetians, and by the expulsion of the Germans, under Ariovistus, from Gaul, 58, Cæsar gained an opportunity of intermeddling in the internal affairs of that country, and afterwards of subduing it, which was completed by his victory over the Belgæ, 57, and the Aquitani, 56; so that Cæsar was at liberty to undertake his several expeditions, as well in Britain, 55 and 54, as in Germany, 54 and 53. But the repeated revolts of the Gauls, 53–51, especially under Vercingetorix, 52, occasioned a war no less obstinate than their first conquest. Roman policy continued the same throughout. The Gauls were subdued, by the Romans appearing as *their deliverers;* and in the country they found allies in the Ædui, Allobroges, etc.

30. The triumvirate, in order to establish their power upon a solid foundation, took care, by the management of the tribune Clodius, to get rid of the leaders of the senate, Cato and Cicero, before the departure of Cæsar; and this they did by giving the former a kingdom to govern, and by procuring the banishment of the latter. They must, however, soon have discovered, that so bold a demagogue as Clodius could not be used as a mere machine. And, indeed, after Cæsar's departure he raised himself so much above the triumvirs, that Pompey was soon obliged, for his own preservation, to permit Cicero to return from exile, which could only be effected by the most violent efforts of the tribune Milo. The power of Clodius, however, was but little injured thereby, although Pompey, to put a stop to the source of these disorders, and revive his own popularity, procured the nomination of himself as *præfectus annonæ*, or superintendent of provisions.

Exile of Cicero, the greater part of which he spent in Macedonia, from April, 58, till 4th Sept. 57. Ptolemy king of Cyprus deposed, and that island reduced to a Roman province by Cato, on the proposition of Clodius, 57. The personal dislike of Clodius and the riches of the king were the causes that brought upon him this misfortune.

31. *Jealousy of the Triumvirate.* A jealousy arises between the triumvirate, as Cæsar, though absent, still found means to keep up his party at Rome in such watchful activity, that Pompey and Crassus considered it impossible to maintain their own influence, except by procuring such concessions as had been made to him. Harmony once more restored by an accommodation at Lucca, as the parties found it necessary to preserve a good understanding with each other.

The terms of this accommodation were; that Cæsar should have his government prolonged for another five years; and that Pompey and Crassus should enjoy the consulship for the ensuing year, the former receiving the provinces of Spain and Africa, and the latter that of Syria, for the purpose of carrying on a war against the Parthians. In proportion as these conditions were kept secret, there remained less secrecy respecting the alliance itself.

32. *Second consulate of Pompey and Crassus, B. C.* 55. Second consulate of Pompey and Crassus. It was only amidst violent storms that they could effect their purposes; as it depended upon which faction should first gain or keep possession of the forum. The resistance they met with from the inflexible disposition of Cato, who in his austere virtue alone found means to secure himself a powerful party, shows how unfairly those judge who consider the power of the triumvirate as unlimited, and the nation as entirely corrupted.

Campaign of Crassus against the Parthians, undertaken at his own expense, 54. Instead, however, of gathering laurels like Cæsar, he and his whole army were completely overthrown in Mesopotamia, 53; and the Parthians from this time maintained a powerful preponderance in Asia.

33. *Pompey aspires to become head of the Republic; is appointed sole consul*, 52. As the triumvirate by this failure of Crassus was reduced to a duumvirate, Pompey, (who remained in Rome, and governed his provinces by lieutenants,) in the midst of continual domestic broils, which he cunningly took care to foment, was evidently aiming to become the acknowledged head of the senate and republic. The idea that a dictator was necessary prevailed more and more during an anarchy of eight months, in which no appointment of a consul could take place; and notwithstanding the opposition of Cato, Pompey succeeded, after a violent commotion, in which Clodius was murdered by Milo, in getting himself nominated sole consul; a power equal to that of dictator.

Consulate of Pompey, 52, in which, at the end of seven months, he took as colleague his father-in-law, Metellus Scipio. The government of his provinces, which afterwards became the chief seat of the republicans, is prolonged for five years.

34. *Civil War inevitable.* From this time civil war became inevitable; for not only the chiefs of the parties, but also their adherents desired it. The approach of the time when Cæsar's command would expire, necessarily hastened the crisis. Could it be supposed that the conqueror of Gaul would return to a private life, and leave his rival at the head of the republic? The steps taken on both sides towards an accommodation were only made to escape the odium which would attach to him who struck the first blow. But Pompey, unfortunately, could never understand his opponent, who did all himself, all completely, and all alone. The brilliant light in which Pompey now appeared, as *defender of the republic*, delighted him so much, that it made him forget what belonged to its defence: while Cæsar avoided, with the great-

est care, every appearance of usurpation. The friend, the protector of the people against the usurpations of their enemies, was the character which he now chose to assume.

Commencement of the contest upon Cæsar's demand to be allowed to hold the consulship while absent, 52. Cæsar, by the most lavish corruption, had increased his adherents in Rome, gained the tribunes, and among them especially the powerful speaker C. Curio (whom he did not think too dearly purchased at the price of about half a million sterling); by this man it was suggested to Cæsar that he should give up his command, and leave a successor to be appointed in his place, 51, if Pompey would do the same; a proposition which created a prejudice much in his favor. Repeated, but insincere offers of both parties for an accommodation, 50, till at last a decree of the senate was passed, Jan. 7, 49, by which Cæsar was commanded "to disband his army under the penalty of being declared an enemy to the republic," without regard to the intercessions of the tribunes, whose flight to him gave an appearance of popularity to his party. Cæsar crosses the Rubicon, the boundary of his province.

35. *Civil War between Cæsar and Pompey.* The civil war now about to break out, seemed likely to spread over nearly all the countries of the Roman empire; as Pompey, finding it impossible to maintain himself in Italy, had chosen Greece for the principal theatre of the war; while his lieutenants, with the armies under their command, occupied Spain and Africa. Cæsar, by the able disposition of his legions, was everywhere present, without exciting beforehand any suspicion of his movements. A combination of circumstances, however, carried the war into Alexandria, and even as far as Pontus; indeed it might be called rather a series of six successive wars than merely one, all of which Cæsar, by flying with his legions from one quarter of the world to the other, ended, within five years, victoriously and in person.

Rapid occupation of Italy in sixty days (when the troops under Domitius surrendered at Corfinus), which, as well as Sicily and Sardinia, were subdued by Cæsar almost without opposition; Pompey, with his troops and adherents, having crossed over to Greece. Cæsar's first campaign in Spain against Pompey's generals, Afranius and Petreius, whom he forces to surrender; this, however, is counterbalanced by the loss of the legions under Curio in Africa. In December, 49, however, Cæsar is again in Italy, and named dictator, which he exchanges for the consulate. Spirited expedition into Greece with the ships he had been previously collecting together, Jan. 4, 48. Unfortunate engagements at Dyrrachium. Removal of the war into Thessaly, and decisive battle of Pharsalia, July 20, 48; after which,

Pompey flies to Alexandria, where he is killed on his landing. Cæsar arrives three days after him at Alexandria.

36. *Cæsar again Dictator.* Cæsar, after the victory of Pharsalia, again nominated dictator, with great privileges. The death of Pompey, however, does not destroy his party; and the six months' war of Alexandria, as well as the expedition into Pontus against Pharnaces, gave them time to rally their forces both in Africa under Cato, and in Spain under the sons of Pompey.

During the Alexandrine war, and the expedition against Pharnaces, the son of Mithridates, who had obtained the kingdom of his father, but was slain by Cæsar immediately after his arrival, 47, great disorders had broken out in Rome, caused by the tribune Dolabella's flattering the people with the abolition of debts (*novæ tabulæ*), notwithstanding the military power of M. Antony, whom Cæsar had sent to Rome as master of the horse (*magister equitum*), as this abandoned sensualist at first actually favored the projects of the tribune. Cæsar's return to Rome, December, 47, put an end, it is true, to these disorders; but the increase of the opposite party in Africa, and an insurrection among his soldiers, obliged him to set out for Africa immediately, January, 46. Victory near Thapsus over Scipio and Juba; after which Cato kills himself at Utica. Numidia, the kingdom of Juba, becomes a Roman province. Cæsar, after his return to Rome, in June, is only able to stay there four months, as, before the end of the year, he is obliged to set out for Spain, to crush the dangerous efforts of Pompey's two sons. Bloody battle at Munda, March, 45, after which Cneius is killed, but Sextus escapes to the Celtiberians.

37. *Inquiry into the views of Cæsar.* Nothing seems more evident, than that Cæsar did not, like Sylla, overthrow the republic for the purpose of re-establishing it; and it is perhaps impossible to say, what could be the final views of a childless usurper, who, throughout his whole career, seemed only to be guided by an inordinate ambition, springing from a consciousness of superior powers, and to satisfy which, no means seemed to him difficult or unlawful. The period of his dictatorship was so short, and so much interrupted by war, that his ultimate plans had not time for their development. He endeavored to establish his dominion by popular measures; and although his army must still have been his main support, yet no proscription was granted to satisfy it. The re-establishment of order in the distracted country of Italy, and particularly in the capital, was his first care; and he proposed to follow that by an expedition against the powerful Parthian empire. His attempts, however, to obtain the diadem, seemed to place it beyond a doubt that he wished to introduce a formal monarchy.

But the destruction of the form of the republic was shown to be more dangerous than the overthrow of the republic itself.

The following were the honors and privileges granted to Cæsar by the senate. After the battle of Pharsalia, 48, he was nominated dictator for one year, and consul for five years; and obtained the *potestas tribunicia*, as well as the right of making war and peace, the exclusive right of the committees, with the exception of the tribunes, and the possession of the provinces. The dictatorship was renewed to him, 47, for ten years, as well as the *præfectura morum*, and was at last, 45, conferred upon him for ever, with the title of *imperator*. Although Cæsar thus became absolute master of the republic, it appears to have been done without laying aside the republican forms.

38. *Conspiracy formed against him, B. C.* 44, *by Brutus, Cassius, etc.—His death, March* 15. Conspiracy against Cæsar, formed by Brutus and Cassius, and terminating in the death of Cæsar. Men so exalted as were the chiefs of this plot, easily understand one another; and it was quite in accordance with their character not to meditate upon the consequences of their deed. Cæsar's death was a great misfortune for Rome. Experience soon showed that the republic could not be re-established thereby; and his life might probably have spared the state some of those calamities which now, by its change to a monarchy, became unavoidable.

We still want a discriminating life of Cæsar, who in modern times has been as extravagantly praised as Alexander has been unjustly censured. As generals and conquerors, both were equally great—and little; as a man, however, the Macedonian, in the brilliant period of his life, to which Cæsar never attained, was superior; to the great political ideas which developed themselves in Alexander, we know of none corresponding in Cæsar; who knew better than any how to attain dominion, but little of preserving it.

39. *Amnesty declared, but not approved by Antony and Lepidus.* Notwithstanding the amnesty at first declared, the funeral obsequies of Cæsar soon showed, that peace was of all things the least desired by his generals, M. Antony and M. Lepidus, now become the head of his party; and the arrival of Cæsar's nephew, C. Octavius (afterwards Cæsar Octavianus), whom he had adopted in his will, rendered affairs still more complicated, as every one strove for himself—Antony's particular object being to raise himself into Cæsar's place. However earnestly they sought to gain the people, it was in fact the legions who decided, and the command of them depended, for the most part, upon the possession of the provinces. We cannot, therefore, wonder, that while they sought to revenge the murder of Cæsar, this became

the chief cause of the struggle, and in a few months led to a civil war.

At the time of Cæsar's death, M. Antonius was actual consul, and Dolabella consul-elect; M. Lepidus, *magister equitum* (master of the horse); M. Brutus and Cassius, prætors (the first, *prætor urbanus*). Cæsar had given to the former the province of Macedonia, and to the latter that of Syria, which had been confirmed to them by the senate. M. Lepidus had been nominated to Transalpine, and D. Brutus to Cisalpine Gaul. But soon after the murder of Cæsar, Antony obtained, by a decree of the people, Macedonia for himself, and Syria for his colleague Dolabella, with whom he had formed a close connection; instead of which, the senate decreed to Cassius, Cyrene, and to Brutus, who now had the important charge of supplying Rome with provisions, Crete. But soon after (June 1, 44), Antony desired, by a new change, to obtain Cisalpine Gaul for himself, and Macedonia for his brother, C. Antony, both of which he procured from the people.

40. *Antony endeavors to establish himself in Cisalpine Gaul.* As M. Antony sought by force to establish himself in Cisalpine Gaul, and D. Brutus refused to give it up to him, and retired into Mutina, a short, indeed, but very bloody civil war arose (*bellum mutinense*). The eloquence of Cicero had caused Antony to be declared an enemy of the republic; and the two new consuls, Hirtius and Pansa, together with Cæsar Octavianus, were sent against him. The defeat of Antony compelled him to seek refuge beyond the Alps with Lepidus; but the two consuls being slain, Octavianus, at the head of his legions, was too important to be refused the consulship, and soon convinced the defenceless senate how impossible it was to re-establish the commonwealth by their powerless decrees. The employment, moreover, of the *magistratus suffecti*, which soon after arose, was in itself a sufficient proof that it was now no more than the shadow of what it had formerly been.

The Mutine war begins in December, 44, and closes with the defeat of Antony at Mutina, April 14, 43. Octavius obtains the consulate, Sept. 22.

41. *Formation of a triumvirate by C. Octavianus, M. Antony and Lepidus.* Octavianus, deserting the party of the senate, enters into a secret negotiation with Antony and Lepidus; the consequence of which is a meeting of the parties at Bononia, and the formation of a new triumvirate. They declare themselves the chiefs of the republic for five years, under the title of *triumviri reipublicæ constituendæ;* and dividing the provinces among themselves according to their own pleasure, they make the destruction of the republican party their prin-

cipal object. A new proscription in Rome itself, and a declaration of war against the murderers of Cæsar, were the means by which they proposed to effect it.

The agreement of the triumvirate was concluded Nov. 27, 43, after which the march of the triumvirs upon Rome gives the signal for the massacre of the proscribed, which soon extends all over Italy, and in which Cicero perishes, Dec. 7. The cause of this new proscription was not party hatred alone, but was as much, perhaps more, owing on the one hand to the want of money for carrying on the war they had undertaken, and on the other to a desire of satisfying the turbulent demands of the legions. Where is to be found a time so full of terror as this, when even tears were forbidden?

42. *Civil war between the Oligarchy and Republicans.* The civil war now on the eve of breaking out, may be considered therefore as a war between the oligarchy and the defenders of the republic. The Roman world was, as it were, divided between the two; and although the former had possession of Italy and the western provinces, that advantage seemed counterbalanced to the chiefs of the opposite party by the possession of the eastern countries, and the naval power of Sextus Pompey, which seemed to assure them the dominion of the sea.

M. Brutus had taken possession of his province of Macedonia as early as the autumn of 44; while Cassius, on the contrary, had to contend for that of Syria with Dolabella, who by the murder of the proconsul Trebonius had possessed himself of Asia. Being, however, for this offence, declared an enemy by the senate, and shut up in Laodicea by Cassius, he killed himself, June 5, 43. From this time Brutus and Cassius were masters of all the eastern provinces, at whose expense they maintained their troops, though not without much opposition. S. Pompey, after the victory of Munda, 45, having secreted himself in Spain, and afterwards become a chief of freebooters, had grown very powerful; when the senate, after Cæsar's assassination, having made him commander of the sea-forces, he with them took possession of Spain, and, after the conclusion of the triumvirate, of Sicily, and then, very soon after, of Sardinia and Corsica. It was a great thing for the triumvirate, that C. Pompey did not know how to reap half the profit he might have done from his power and good fortune.

43. *Its seat in Macedonia.* Macedonia became the theatre of the new civil war, and together with the goodness of their cause, superior talents, and greater power both by land and sea, seemed combined to insure the victory to Brutus and Cassius. But in the decisive battle at Philippi, fortune played one of her most capricious tricks, and with the two chiefs fell the last supporters of the republic.

Double battle at Philippi towards the close of the year 42; voluntary death of Cassius after the first, and of Brutus after the second engagement.

44. *Quarrels of the oligarchy among themselves.—Fulvia causes a civil war.* The history of the eleven years intervening between the battle of Philippi and that of Actium, is little more than an account of the quarrels of the oligarchy among themselves. The most subtle was, in the end, victorious; for M. Antony possessed all the sensuality of Cæsar without his genius; and the insignificant Lepidus soon fell a sacrifice to his own vanity and weakness. While Antony went into Asia to arrange the affairs of the eastern provinces, and from thence with Cleopatra to Alexandria, Octavianus returned to Rome. But the famine which then reigned in that city through Pompey's blockade of the sea-coast; the misery spread throughout Italy by the wresting of patrimonial lands from the proprietors to distribute among the veterans; and the insatiable covetousness of the latter, rendered his situation as dangerous now as it had been before the war. Besides all this, the hatred of the enraged consort of Antony, who had entered into an alliance with her brother-in-law, the consul L. Antony, brought on, towards the end of the year, a civil war, which ended with the surrender and burning of Perusium, in which L. Antony had shut himself up, and which was already much weakened by famine.

The *bellum Perusinum* lasted from the end of the year 41 till April, 40.

45. *Peace, B. C.* 40. This war, however, had nearly led to one still greater; for M. Antony, as the enemy of Octavianus, had come to Italy in order to assist his brother, and with the intention of forming an alliance with S. Pompey against the former. But fortunately for the world, not only was harmony restored between the triumvirs, but on account of the great famine which prevailed at Rome, a peace was also concluded with Pompey, although it lasted but a very short time.

The principal object of the peace between the triumvirs was a new division of the provinces, by which the city of Scodra, in Illyria, was fixed upon as the boundary. Antony obtained all the eastern provinces; Octavianus all the western; and Lepidus Africa. Italy remained in common to them all. The marriage of Antony with Octavia, Fulvia being dead, was intended to cement this agreement. In the peace concluded with S. Pompey at Misenum, he obtained the islands of Sicily, Sardinia, and Corsica, and the promise of Achaia.

46. *Pompey recommences the war, which causes his destruction,* 38; *and Lepidus's expulsion,* 39. Pompey, however, was not long in finding that an alliance between him and the triumvirs would only end

in his own destruction; and the war which he soon commenced, and which Octavianus could not bring to a close but with the assistance of Agrippa, was of so much the more importance, as it not only decided the fate of Pompey, but by leading to dissensions, and the expulsion of Lepidus, reduced the triumvirate to a duumvirate.

After a doubtful engagement at sea, 38, and the formation of a new fleet, Pompey was attacked on all sides at the same time; Lepidus coming from Africa, and Antony sending also some ships. Final overthrow of Pompey, who flies to Asia and there perishes. Lepidus wishing to take possession of Sicily, Octavianus gains over his troops, and obliges him to retire from the triumvirate.

47. *Foreign wars prevent Augustus and Antony from coming to an open rupture, B. C.* 35–33.—*Antony offends Rome and divorces Octavia*, 32. The foreign wars in which Octavianus as well as Antony were engaged in the following years, prevented for some time their mutual jealousy from coming to an open rupture. Octavianus, to tame his unruly legions, employed them with some success against the nations of Dalmatia and Pannonia; whilst Antony undertook an expedition against the powerful Parthians and their neighbors. But in offending Rome by his conduct in these wars, he only armed his opponent against himself; and his formal separation from Octavia, loosened the only tie which had hitherto held together the two masters of the world.

After his first stay in Alexandria, 41, Antony returned to Italy, 40, and then, having made peace with Octavianus, he carried his new wife Octavia with him into Greece, where he remained till the year 37. Although his lieutenant Ventidius had fought with success against the Parthians, who had invaded Syria, Antony determined to undertake an expedition against them himself, 36. But although in alliance with Artavasdes, king of Armenia, (whom he soon after accused of treachery,) in seeking to effect an entrance into Parthia, by passing through Armenia and Media, a different route from that taken by Crassus, he was very nearly meeting with the same fate, and the expedition completely failed. He then revenged himself upon Artavasdes, who fell into his hands in a fresh expedition which he made, 34, and deprived him of his kingdom. After his triumphal entrance into Alexandria, he made a grant of this as well as other countries to Cleopatra and her children. In 33, he intended to renew his expedition against the Parthians, in alliance with the king of Media; but having, at the instigation of Cleopatra, ordered Octavia to return home, when she had already come as far as Athens on her way to meet him, Octavianus and Antony reciprocally accused each other before the senate, and war was declared at Rome, though only against Cleopatra.

48. *Greece the seat of war between Antony and Octavianus.—Antony defeated at Actium, 2d Sept.*, 31 ; *his death*, 30, *leaves Octavianus without a rival.* Greece became again the theatre of war; and although the forces of Antony were most considerable, yet Octavianus had the advantage of having, at least in appearance, the better cause. The naval victory of Actium decided for Octavianus, who could scarcely believe it, till he found that Antony had forsaken his fleet and army, the latter of which surrendered without striking a blow. The capture of Egypt followed, and that country was reduced to a Roman province; the death of Antony and Cleopatra ended the war, and left Octavianus absolute master of the republic.

SEC. VIII.—FROM THE DEATH OF AUGUSTUS CÆSAR TO THE DEATH OF COMMODUS, B. C. 30.—A. C. 193.

1. *Augustus Cæsar*, B. C. 30.—A. C. 14. Octavianus Cæsar, on whom the senate conferred the honorable title of Augustus, which they periodically renewed, and which descended to his successors, possessed the sole dominion of the empire during forty-four years. The government, notwithstanding the great revolutions by which the republic had been converted into a monarchy, was not yet, either in fact or in form, altogether a despotic one. The private interest of the ruler required that the republican form should be preserved to the utmost, as without that he could not make an entire change; and the rest of his history sufficiently shows, that the cruelty with which he may be reproached in the early part of his career, was rather owing to circumstances than to his natural disposition. But during a reign so long, so tranquil, and so fortunate, could it be otherwise than that the republican spirit, which at the beginning existed only in a few individuals, should evaporate of itself!

The forms under which Augustus held the different branches of supreme power (dictatorship excepted) were; the consulate, which, till B. C. 21, was annually renewed; and the *potestas consularis*, which, in B. C. 19, was settled on him for ever; the *tribunicia potestas*, which was, 30, granted him for ever, rendered his person sacred (*sacrosancta*), and prepared the way to the *judicia majestatis* (accusations of high treason). As *imperator*, 31, he continued commander of all the forces and obtained the *imperium proconsulare* (proconsular power) in all the provinces. He assumed the *magistratura morum* (censorship), 19; and became *pontifex maximus* (high priest), 13. To avoid all appearances of usurpation, Augustus at first accepted the sovereign power only for ten years, and afterwards had it renewed from time to time, for ten or five years, which, at a later period, gave rise to the *sacra decennalia.*

2. *The Senate.* The senate, indeed, remained a permanent council of state, and Augustus himself endeavored to increase its authority by more than one purification (*lectio*); but the connection between him and that assembly seemed of a very fragile nature, as it was undetermined, and could not at this time be settled, whether Augustus was over the senate, or the senate over Augustus. All matters of state could not be brought before the senate, as even the most important often required secrecy. It naturally followed, that a prince, as yet without a court, and who had no proper minister, but only his friends and freedmen, should consult with those whom he thought most worthy his confidence, a Mæcenas, or an Agrippa, &c. Hence afterwards was formed the secret council of state (*concilium secretum principis*). Among the republican magistrates the highest lost most; and as so much now depended upon the preservation of peace in the capital, the offices of præfect of the city (*præfectus urbis*) and præfect of provisions (*præfectus annonæ*) were not only made permanent, but became, especially the former, the principal offices in the state.

The spirit of monarchy shows itself in nothing more than in its strict distinction of ranks; hence, therefore, the magistrates, especially the consuls, lost nothing. Hence also the long-continued custom of nominating under-consuls (*consules suffecti*), which in time became merely a formal assumption of the *ornamenta consularia et triumphalia* (consular and triumphal ornaments). Other offices were created for the purpose of rewarding friends and dependents.

3. *Introduction of standing armies.* The introduction of standing armies, already long prepared, naturally followed a dominion acquired by war; and became, indeed, necessary to guard the frontiers and preserve the newly-made conquests; the establishment of the guards and militia of the city (*cohortes prætorianæ* and *cohortes urbanæ*) were measures equally necessary for the security of the capital and the throne. The creation of *two* prætorian præfects, however, instead of *one*, diminished for the present the great importance of that office.

Distribution of the legions over the provinces in *castra stativa* (fixed camps), which soon grew into cities, especially along the Rhine, the Danube, and the Euphrates (*legiones Germanicæ, Illyricæ, et Syriacæ*). Fleets also were stationed at Misenum and Ravenna.

4. *The Provinces divided between the Emperor and the Senate.* The government, as well as the administration and revenue of the provinces, Augustus willingly divided with the senate; keeping to himself those on the frontiers (*provinciæ principis*), in which the legions were quartered, and leaving to that assembly the others (*provinciæ senatûs*). Hence his deputies (*legati*, lieutenants) exercised both civil and military

authority in his name; while those of the senate, on the contrary (*proconsules*), only administered in civil affairs. Both were, in general, attended by commissioners (*procuratores et quæstores*). The provinces were unquestionably gainers by this new arrangement, not only because their governors were more carefully looked after, but because they were paid by the state.

The fate of the provinces naturally depended, in a great degree, upon the disposition of the emperor and governor; but there was also an essential difference between the provinces of the emperor and those of the senate (*provinciæ principis et senatûs*): in the latter there was no military oppression as there was in the former; and to that may be ascribed the flourishing state of Gaul, Spain, Africa, etc.

5. *Finances: the private and military chest of the emperor; the state chest swallowed up by the former.* There is little doubt but that the finances of the treasury remained, upon the whole, much the same as before; but in its internal administration Augustus made many alterations, of which we have but a very imperfect knowledge. Of course there would be at first an obvious difference between the privy and military chest of the emperor (*fiscus*), which was at his immediate disposal, and the state chest (*ærarium*), which he disposed of indirectly through the senate, though it must afterwards follow as a natural consequence of increasing despotism, that the latter should progressively become merged in the former.

The great disorder into which the treasury had been thrown during the civil wars, and especially by giving away the state lands in Italy to the soldiers, together with the heavy sums required for the maintenance of the standing army now established, must have rendered it much more difficult for Augustus to accomplish the reform he so happily executed, and in which it seems to have been his chief aim to place every thing, as far as possible, upon a solid and lasting foundation. The principal changes which he made in the old system of taxation seem to have been: 1. That the tithes hitherto collected in the provinces should be changed into a fixed quota, to be paid by each individual. 2. The customs, partly by re-establishing former ones, and partly by imposing new ones, as well as an excise (*centesima rerum venalium*), were rendered more productive. The possession of Egypt, which was the dépôt of nearly all the commerce of the East, rendered the customs at this time of great importance to Rome. 3. All the state lands in which the provinces were, by degrees, changed into crown lands. Of the new taxes, the most considerable were the *vigesima hereditatum* (the twentieth of inheritances), though with important restrictions; and the fines upon celibacy by the *lex Julia Poppæa*. The greater part of these state revenues most likely flowed, from the very first, into the *fiscus:* that is, the whole revenues of the *provinciæ principis*, as well as of those parts of the *provinciæ senatûs* which were appropriated to the maintenance of the troops; the revenues arising from the crown domains; the *vigesima*, etc. To the *ærarium* (now under three *præfecti ærarii*) remained a part of the revenues of the *provinciæ senatûs*, the customs and the fines. Thus it appears that Augustus was master of the finances, of the legions, and thereby of the empire.

6. *Extension of the Empire.* The extension of the Roman empire under Augustus was very considerable; being generally of such a nature as conduced to the security of the interior, and to the safeguard of the frontiers. The complete subjugation of northern Spain, and western Gaul, secured the frontiers on that side; as did the threatened but never executed expedition against the Parthians, and the one actually undertaken against Armenia, A. C. 2. But the most important conquest in this quarter, was that of the countries south of the Danube, viz., Rhætia, Vindelicia, and Noricum, as well as Pannonia, and afterwards Mœsia. To counterbalance these, the expedition against Arabia Felix completely failed; and that against Ethiopia was of no further consequence than to strengthen the frontiers.

7. *Unsuccessful attempt to subdue Germany.* All these conquests together, however, did not cost the Romans so much as their fruitless attempt to subjugate Germany, first, by the sons-in-law of Augustus, Drusus, and Tiberius Nero, and afterwards by the son of the former, Drusus Germanicus. Whether or not this undertaking was a political fault, must always remain a problem, as it is now impossible to say how far the security of the frontiers could be preserved without it.

Rome commenced her hostile attack upon Germany under the command of Drusus, B. C. 12; Lower Germany (Westphalia, Lower Saxony, and Hesse) being in general the theatre of the war; while the Lower Rhine was attacked both by sea and land at the mouths of the Ems, the Weser, and the Elbe, on account of the great assistance afforded the Romans by their alliance with the nations on the coasts, the Batavi, Frisii, and Chauci. The intrepid Drusus, in his second expedition, 10, penetrated as far as the Weser, and, 9, even as far as the Elbe, but died on his return. His successors in the command (Tiberius, 9–7, Domitius, Ænobarbus, 7–2, M. Vinicius, 2—A. C. 2, then again Tiberius, A. C. 2–4, who was followed by Quintilius Varus, A. C. 5–9), endeavored to build on the foundation laid by Drusus, and, by erecting forts and introducing the Roman language and laws, gradually to reduce into a province the part of Germany they had already subdued; but the craftily organized revolt of the young Arminius (Hermann), a prince of the Cherusci, son of Siegmar, and son-in-law of Segestes, a friend of the Romans, together with the defeat of Varus and his army in the Teutoburg wald, or forest, near Paderborn, A. C. 9, rescued Germany from slavery, and its language from annihilation. It moreover taught the conquerors (what they never forgot) that the legions were not invincible. Augustus immediately dispatched Tiberius, who had just quelled a furious insurrection in Pannonia, together with Germanicus, to the Rhine; but these confined themselves to simple incursions, till Germanicus, A. C. 14–16, again carried his arms further into the country, and certainly penetrated as far as the Weser. Yet, notwithstanding his victory near Idistavisus (Minden), the loss of his fleet and part of his army by a tempest, on his return, and the jealousy of Tiberius at his victory, obliged him to give up his command. From this time the Germans were left at rest in this quarter.

8. *Reign of Augustus—a brilliant period for Rome.* The long and, for Italy itself, peaceable reign of Augustus, has generally been considered a fortunate and brilliant period of Roman history; and, when compared with the times which preceded and followed, it certainly was so. Security of person and property were re-established; the arts of peace flourished under the benign patronage of Augustus and his favorite Mæcenas; and we may add, that, as the formal restoration of the republic would only have been the signal for new commotions, the government of Augustus, if not the very best, was, at least, the best that Rome could then bear. Should it be said his private life was not blameless, it may be replied, that he inflexibly maintained an outward decency, to which, indeed, he sacrificed his only daughter; and if laws could have bettered the public morals, there was no lack of decrees for that purpose.

Among his most important laws to this end are, the *lex Julia de adulteriis* and the *lex Papia Poppæa* against celibacy. The latter excited many murmurs.

9. *Augustus's family.* Nearly all that remains of the history of Augustus, is an account of his domestic troubles; the most unhappy family being that of the emperor. The influence of Livia, his second wife, was very great, but does not seem to have been perverted to any worse purpose than raising her sons, Tiberius and Drusus, to the throne. The naturally unsettled state of the succession in a government such as that of Rome now was, became much increased by circumstances. After the untimely death of his nephew and son-in-law, Marcellus, whom he had adopted, his widow, Julia, the only child of Augustus by his wife Scribonia, was married to Agrippa. The two eldest sons of this marriage, C. and L. Cæsar, were adopted, upon the death of their

father, by the emperor, who showed so much fondness towards them as they grew up, that Tiberius, who, in the mean time, had married their mother, Julia,—afterwards banished by Augustus for her licentious conduct,—left the court in disgust. The death of the two young princes, however, again revived the hopes of Tiberius, who was adopted by Augustus, upon the condition that he should also adopt Drusus Germanicus, the son of his deceased brother, Drusus; after which Augustus, with the consent of the senate, formally associated him with himself in the government, making him an equal partner in the imperial privilèges: called by his successors, *lex regia*.

10. *Changes in the Constitution.—Power of the Comitia reduced.—Despotism introduced by the Judicia Majestatis.—Degraded character of the Senate.*—The reign of Tiberius Claudius Nero, or, as he was called after his adoption, Augustus Tiberius Cæsar, from his fifty-sixth to his seventy-eighth year, changed rather the spirit than the form of the Roman constitution. He succeeded quietly to the vacant throne at Rome, although the legions in Pannonia, and still more in Germany, felt that they could make emperors. Under him the *comitia*, or assemblies of the people, were reduced to a mere shadow; as he transferred their duties to the senate, which also became the highest tribunal for the state crimes of its own members: this assembly, however, had now been so much accustomed to obey the will of the prince, that every thing depended on his personal character. Tiberius founded his despotism upon the *judicia majestatis*, or accusations of high treason, now become an engine of terror, the senate also sharing his guilt with a pusillanimity and servility which knew no bounds. This degraded assembly, indeed, from the moment that it ceased to be the ruling authority of a free state, necessarily became the passive instrument of the most brutal tyranny. Notwithstanding the military talents and many good qualities of Tiberius, his despotic character had been formed long before his fifty-sixth year, when he mounted the throne; although exterior circumstances prevented him from entirely throwing off the mask which he had hitherto worn.

The foundation of the *judicia majestatis*, which soon became so terrible by the unfixed state of crime, had been laid during the reign of Augustus by the *lex Julia de majestate*, and the *cognitiones extraordinariæ*, or commissioners appointed to take cognizance of certain crimes: it was, however, the abuse of them by Tiberius and his successors, which rendered them so dreadful.

12. *Ruin of Germanicus and his family.* The principal object of Tiberius's suspicion, and therefore of his hate, was Germanicus, a man almost adored by the army and the people. This brave general

he soon recalled from Germany, and sent into Syria to quell the disorders of the East. After having successfully put an end to the commotions which called him there, he was poisoned by the contrivances of Cn. Piso and his wife; and even that did not shelter the numerous family which he left behind, with his widow Agrippina, from persecution and ruin.

13. *L. Ælius Sejanus, the cruel minister of Tiberius*, 23–31.—*Tiberius retires to Capreæ*, 26.—*Fall of Sejanus attended with great carnage*, 31.—*Tiberius becomes a despotic monster.* Rome, however, soon experienced to her cost the powerful ascendency which L. Ælius Sejanus, the præfect of the prætorian guard, had acquired over the mind of Tiberius, whose unlimited confidence he possessed the more, as he enjoyed it without a rival. The eight years of his authority were rendered terrible not only by the cantonment of his troops in barracks near the city (*castra prætoriana*), but (having first persuaded Tiberius to quit Rome for ever, that he might more securely play the tyrant in the isle of Capreæ) by his endeavoring to open a way for himself to the throne by villanies and crimes without number, and by his cruel persecution of the family of Germanicus. The despotism he had introduced became still more dreadful by his own fall, in which not only his whole party, but every one that could be considered as connected with it, became involved. The picture of the atrocious despotism of Tiberius is rendered doubly disgusting by the horrid and unnatural lust which he joined to it in his old age.

Tiberius's misfortune was, that he came too late to the throne. His early virtues made no compensation for his later cruelties. It is properly the former which Vel. Paterculus praises, whose flattery of Tiberius, in whose reign he flourished, is more easily justified than his praise of Sejanus.

14. *Caligula*, March 16, 37.—Jan. 24, 41. At the age of twenty-five Caius Cæsar Caligula, the only remaining son of Germanicus, ascended the throne; but the hopes which had been formed of this young prince were soon woefully disappointed. His previous sickness and debaucheries had so distorted his understanding, that his short reign was one tissue of disorder and crime. Yet he did still more harm to the state by his besotted profusion than by his tiger-like cruelty. At length, after a career of nearly four years, he was assassinated by Cassius Chærea and Cornelius Sabinus, two officers of his guard.

15. *Claudius*, Jan. 24, 31.—Oct. 13, 54, *the weak tool of his wives and freedmen.—Messalina; Agrippina procures the throne for her son, with the assistance of Burrhus, and poisons Claudius.* His uncle Tiberius Claudius Cæsar, who, at the age of fifty, succeeded him, was

the first emperor raised to the throne by the guards; a favor which he rewarded by granting them a *donative.* Too weak to rule of himself, almost imbecile from former neglect, profligate, and cruel from fear, he became the tool of the licentiousness of his wives and freedmen. Coupled with the names of Messalina and Agrippina, we now hear, for the first time in Roman history, of a Pallas and a Narcissus. The dominion of Messalina was still more hurtful to the state by her rapacious cupidity, to which every thing gave way, than by her dissolute life; and the blow which at last punished her unexampled wantonness, left a still more dangerous woman to supply her place. This was Agrippina, her niece, widow of L. Domitius, who joined to the vices of her predecessor a boundless ambition, unknown to the former. Her chief aim was to procure the succession for Domitius Nero, her son by a former marriage—who had been adopted by Claudius, and married to his daughter Octavia—by setting aside Britannicus, the son of Claudius; and this she hoped to effect, by poisoning Claudius, having already gained Burrhus, by making him *sole* præfect of the prætorian guard. Notwithstanding the contentions with the Germans and Parthians were only on the frontiers, the boundaries of the Roman empire were in many countries extended.

Commencement of the Roman conquests in Britain (whither Claudius himself went) under A. Plautius, from the year A. C. 43. Under the same general, Mauritania, A. C. 42, Lycia, 43, Judæa, 44, and Thrace, 47, were reduced to Roman provinces. He also abolished the præfectures which had hitherto existed in Italy.

16. *Nero.* Oct. 13, 54.—June 11, 68.—*His education and character.—Destroys Britannicus and all the Julian family: his vanity also makes him cruel: murders his wife and mother; plunders the provinces to support his profligacy,* A. C. 68. Nero Claudius Cæsar, supported by Agrippina and the prætorian guard, succeeded Claudius at the age of seventeen. Brought up in the midst of the blackest crimes, and, by a perverted education, formed rather for a professor of music and the fine arts than for an emperor, he ascended the throne like a youth eager for enjoyment; and throughout his whole reign his cruelty appears subordinate to his fondness for debaucheries and revelry. The unsettled state of the succession first called into action his savage disposition; and after the murder of Britannicus the sword fell in regular order upon all those who were even remotely connected with the Julian family. His vanity as a performer and composer excited in an equal degree his cruelty; and, as among all tyrants, every execution gives occasion for others, we need not wonder at his putting to death every one that excelled him. His connection, how-

ever, in the early part of his reign, with Agrippina, Burrhus, and Seneca, during which he introduced some useful regulations into the treasury, kept him within the bounds of decency. But Poppæa Sabina having driven him on to the murder of his mother and his wife Octavia, and Tigellinus being made his confidant, he felt no longer restrained by the fear of public opinion. The executions of individuals, nearly all of which history has recorded, was not, perhaps, upon the whole, the greatest evil; the plunder of the provinces, not only to support his own loose and effeminate pleasures, but also to maintain the people in a continual state of intoxication, had nearly caused the dissolution of the empire. The last years of Nero were marked by a striking and undoubted insanity, which displayed itself in his theatrical performances, and even in the history of his fall. It appears that both around and upon a throne like that of Rome, heroes were formed for vice as well as for virtue!

Discovery of the conspiracy of Piso, 65, and the revolt of Julius Vindex in Celtic Gaul, 68, followed by that of Galba in Spain, who is there proclaimed emperor, and joined by Otho, in Lusitania. Nevertheless, after the defeat of Julius Vindex in Upper Germany by the lieutenant Virginius Rufus, these insurrections seemed quelled, when the prætorian guard, instigated thereto by Nymphidius, broke out into rebellion in Rome itself. Flight and death of Nero, June 11, 68. Foreign wars during his reign: in Britain (occasioned by the revolt of Boadicea), great part of which was subdued and reduced to a Roman province, by Suetonius Paulinus; in Armenia, under the command of the valiant Corbulo, against the Parthians; and in Palestine against the Jews, 66. Great fire in Rome, 64, which gives rise to the first persecution against the Christians.

The principal cause why the despotism of Nero and his predecessors was so tamely submitted to by the nation, may undoubtedly be found in the fact, that the greater part of it was fed by the emperors. To the monthly distributions of corn were now added the extraordinary *congiaria* and *viscerationes* (supplies of wine and meat). The periods of tyranny were very likely the golden days of the people.

17. *Extinction of the Julian family causes many troubles.—Galba, June* 11, 68—*Jan.* 15, 69, *killed by the prætorian guard.* By the death of Nero the house of Cæsar became extinct, and this gave rise to so many commotions, that in somewhat less than two years, four emperors by violence obtained possession of the throne. The right of the senate to name, or at least to confirm, the successors to the throne, was still indeed acknowledged; but as the armies had found out that they could create emperors, the power of the senate dwindled into an empty

ceremony. Servius Sulpicius Galba, now seventy-two years of age, having been already proclaimed emperor by the legions in Spain, and acknowledged by the senate, gained possession of Rome without striking a blow, the attempt of Nymphidius having completely failed, and Virginius Rufus voluntarily submitting to him. Galba, however, having given offence both to the prætorian guard and the German legions, was dethroned by the guards, at the instigation of his former friend Otho, at the very time when he thought he had secured his throne by adopting the young Licinius Piso, and had frustrated the hopes of Otho.

18. *Otho, Jan.*, 69—*April* 16. M. Otho, aged thirty-seven, was indeed acknowledged emperor by the senate, but wanted the sanction of the German legions, who proclaiming their general, A. Vitellius, emperor, invaded Italy. Otho marches against him, but after the loss of the battle of Bedriacum kills himself—whether from fear or patriotism, remains uncertain.

19. *Vitellius, April* 16, *Dec.* 20, 69.—*Vespasian proclaimed emperor.* Vitellius, in his thirty-seventh year, was acknowledged emperor not only by the senate, but likewise in the provinces; his debaucheries and cruelty, however, together with the licentiousness of his troops, having rendered him odious at Rome, the Syrian legions rebelled and proclaimed their general, T. Flavius Vespasian, emperor, who, at the solicitation of the powerful Mutianus, governor of Syria, accepted the imperial diadem. The troops on the Danube declaring for him shortly after, and marching into Italy under their general Antonius Primus, defeated the army of Vitellius at Cremona. Vitellius was immediatly hurled from the throne, though not till after some blood had been spilt by the commotions that took place at Rome, in which Flavius Sabinus, the brother of Vespasian, was slain, and the capitol burnt.

20. *Vespasian, Dec.* 20, 69—*June* 24, 79. *Fixes the power of the senate; improves the treasury; founds public buildings, and promotes education; banishes the Stoics; and annuls the judicia majestatis.* Flavius Vespasian ascended the throne in his fifty-ninth year, and became thereby the founder of a dynasty which gave three emperors to Rome. The state, almost ruined by profusion, civil war, and successive revolutions, found in Vespasian a monarch well suited to its unhappy condition. He endeavored, as far as he could, to determine the relations between himself and the senate, while, by a decree, he restored to it all the rights and privileges which had been conferred upon it by his predecessors of the family of Cæsar, and settled and added some others (*lex regia*). He made a thorough reform in the completely-exhausted treasury, which he recruited in part by reducing the countries Nero had made free, together with some others, into provinces; partly by restoring

the ancient customs, by increasing others, and by imposing new ones; without this it would have been impossible for him to have re-established the discipline of the army. His liberality in the foundation of public buildings, as well in Rome as in other cities, and the care with which he promoted education, by granting salaries to public teachers, are sufficient to free him from the reproach of avarice; and although, on account of their dangerous opinions, he banished the Stoics, (who since the time of Nero had become very numerous, and retained nearly all the principles of republicanism,) the annulling of the *judicia majestatis* and the restoration of the authority of the senate show how far he was from being a despot.

Rhodes, Samos, Lycia, Achaia, Thrace, Cilicia, and Commagene, were brought by Vespasian into the condition of provinces. Foreign wars: that against the Jews, which ended with the destruction of Jerusalem, A. C. 70; and a much greater war against the Batavians and their allies under Civilis, who, during the late civil wars, sought to shake off the Roman yoke, 69; but were reduced to an accommodation by Cerealis, 70. Expeditions of Agricola in Britain, 78–85, who not only subdued all England, and introduced the Roman manners and customs, but also attacked and sailed round Scotland.

21. *Titus, June* 27, 79—*Sept.* 13, 81. *Dreadful fire and plague*, 79. His eldest son, Titus Flavius Vespasian, who in the year 70 had been created Cæsar, and reigned from his thirty-ninth to his forty-second year, gives us the rare example of a prince becoming better on the throne. His short and benevolent reign was, indeed, only remarkable for its public calamities; an eruption of Mount Vesuvius, overwhelming several cities, was followed by a destructive fire, and a dreadful plague at Rome. His early death secured him the reputation of being, if not the happiest, at least the best of princes.

22. *Domitian, Sept.* 13, 81—*Sept.* 18, 96*; a complete and cruel despot; unsuccessful in war; raises the soldiers' pay; employs informers.* His younger brother and successor, L. Flavius Domitian, who reigned from his thirtieth to his forty-fifth year, gives an example quite opposite to that of Titus; beginning with justice and severity, he soon degenerated into the completest despot that ever swayed the Roman sceptre. His cruelty, joined to an equal degree of pride, and nourished by suspicion and jealousy, made him the enemy of all who excelled him by their exploits, their riches, or their talents. The mortifications to which his pride must have been subjected in consequence of his unsuccessful wars against the Catti, and more particularly the Daci, increased his bad disposition. His despotism was founded upon his armies, whose pay he augmented one fourth; and that he might

not thereby diminish the treasury, as he had too much done at first, he multiplied the *judicia majestatis*, rendering it still more terrible by the employment of secret informers, (*delatores*,) in order, by confiscations, to augment the wealth of his private treasury (*fiscus*). By confining his cruelty chiefly to the capital, and by a strict superintendence over the governors of provinces, Domitian prevented any such general disorganization of the empire as took place under Nero. His fall confirmed the general truth, that tyrants have little to fear from the people, but much from individuals who may think their lives in danger.

The foreign wars during this reign are rendered more worthy of remark by being the first in which the barbarians attacked the empire with success. Domitian's ridiculous expedition against the Catti, 82, gave the first proof of his boundless vanity; as did the recall of the victorious Agricola, 85, from Britain, of his jealousy. His most important war was that against the Daci, or Getæ, who, under their baave king Dercebal, had attacked the Roman frontiers: this again occasioned another with their neighbors, the Marcomanni, Quadi, and Jazygi, 86–90, which turned out so unfortunate for Rome, that Domitian was obliged to purchase a peace of the Daci by paying them an annual tribute.

23. *Nerva, Jan.* 24, 96.—*Jan.* 27, 98. *His reign the dawn of a happy period.* M. Cocceius Nerva, aged about seventy years, was raised to the throne by the murderers of Domitian; and now, at last, seemed to break forth the dawn of a more happy period for the empire. The preceding reign of terror completely ceased at once; and he endeavored to impart fresh vigor to industry, not only by diminishing the taxes, but also by distributing lands to the poor. The insurrection of the guards certainly cost the murderers of Domitian their lives; but it was at the same time the cause of Nerva's securing the prosperity of the empire after his death, by the adoption of Trajan.

24. *Trajan, Jan.* 24, 98—*Aug.* 11, 117, *the best of the Roman monarchs. Restores the Roman Constitution.* M. Ulpius Trajan, (after his adoption, Nerva Trajan,) a Spaniard by birth, governed the empire from his forty-second to his sixty-second year. He was the first foreigner who ascended the Roman throne, and at the same time the first of their monarchs who was equally great as a ruler, a general, and a man. After completely abolishing the *judicia majestatis*, he made the restoration of the *free Roman constitution*, so far as it was compatible with a monarchical form, his peculiar care. He restored the elective power to the *comitia*, complete liberty of speech to the senate, and to the magistrates their former authority; and yet he exercised the art of ruling to a degree and in a detail which few princes have

equalled. Frugal in his expenses, he was nevertheless splendidly liberal to every useful institution, whether in Rome or the provinces, as well as in the foundation of military roads, public monuments, and schools for the instruction of poor children. By his wars he extended the dominion of Rome beyond its former boundaries; subduing, in his contests with the Daci, their country, and reducing it to a Roman province; as he likewise did, in his wars against the Armenians and Parthians, Armenia, Mesopotamia, and part of Arabia. Why was so great a character disfigured by an ambition of conquest?

The first war against the Daci, in which the shameful tribute was withdrawn and Dercebal reduced to subjection, lasted from 101–103. But as Dercebal again rebelled, the war was renewed in 105, and brought to a close in 106, when Dacia was reduced to a Roman province, and many Roman colonies established therein. The war with the Parthians arose from a dispute respecting the possession of the throne of Armenia, 114–116; but although Rome was victorious, she gained no permanent advantage thereby.

25. *Adrian.* By the contrivances of Plotina, his wife, Trajan was succeeded by his cousin and pupil, whom he is said also to have adopted, P. Ælius Adrian, who reigned from his forty-second to his sixty-third year. He was acknowledged at once by the army of Asia, with which he then was, and the sanction of the senate followed immediately after. He differed from his predecessor in that his chief aim was the preservation of peace; on which account he gave up, (rare moderation!) directly after his accession, the newly conquered provinces of Asia, Armenia, Assyria, and Mesopotamia, and so put an end to the Parthian war. He retained, though with some unwillingness, that of Dacia, because otherwise the Roman colonies would have become exposed. He well made up for his pacific disposition, however, in seeking, by a general and vigorous reform in the internal administration, and by restoring the discipline of the army, to give greater solidity to the empire. For that purpose he visited successively all the provinces of the Roman empire; first the eastern, and afterwards the western; making useful regulations and establishing order wherever he came. He improved the Roman jurisprudence by the introduction of the *edictum perpetuum.* Passionately fond of and well instructed in literature and the fine arts, he gave them his liberal protection, and thus called forth another Augustan age. Upon the whole, his reign was certainly a salutary one for the empire; and for any single acts of injustice of which he may be accused, he fully compensated by his choice of a successor. After having first adopted L. Aurelius Verus, (afterwards Ælius Verus,) who fell a sacrifice to his debaucheries, he next adopted T. Aurelius Anto-

ninus, (afterwards T. Ælius Adrianus Antoninus Pius,) upon condition that he should again adopt M. Aurelius Verus, (afterwards M. Aurelius Antoninus,) and L. Cesonius Commodus, (afterwards L. Verus,) the son of Ælius Verus.

During his reign a great revolt broke out in Judea, under Barcochab, 132–135, occasioned by the introduction of pagan worship into the Roman colony of *Ælia Capitolina* (the ancient Jerusalem).

26. *Antoninus Pius, July* 10, 138—*March* 7, 161. The reign of Antoninus Pius, from his forty-seventh to his seventieth year, was without doubt the happiest period of the Roman empire. He found every thing already in excellent order; and those ministers which Adrian had appointed, he continued in their places. His quiet activity furnishes but little matter for history; and yet he was, perhaps, the most noble character that ever sat upon a throne. Although a prince, his life was that of the most blameless individual; while he administered the affairs of the empire as though they were his own. He honored the senate; and the provinces flourished under him, not only because he kept a watchful eye over the conduct of the governors, but because he made it a maxim of his government to continue in their places all those whose probity he had sufficiently proved. He observed rigid order in the finances, and yet without sparing where it could be of service in the foundation or improvement of useful institutions; as his erection of many buildings, establishment of public teachers with salaries in all the provinces, and other examples fully show. He carried on no war himself; on the contrary, several foreign nations made choice of him to arbitrate their differences. Some rebellions which broke out in Britain and Egypt, and some frontier wars excited by the Germans, the Daci, the Moors, and the Alani, were quelled by his lieutenants.

27. *Marcus Aurelius, March* 7, 161—*March* 17, 180.—*The northern nations begin to press forward.* He was succeeded by Marcus Aurelius Antoninus, the philosopher, (aged 40–59 years,) who immediately associated with himself, under the title of Augustus, L. Verus, (aged 30–40 years, † 169,) to whom he gave his daughter in marriage. Notwithstanding the differences of their character, the most cordial union existed between them during the whole of their common reign; L. Verus, indeed, being almost always absent in the wars, took but a very small share in the government. The reign of M. Aurelius was marked by several great calamities: a dreadful pestilence, a famine, and almost continual wars. Nothing short of a prince like Aurelius, who exhibited to the world the image of wisdom seated on a throne, could have made so much misery tolerable. Soon after his accession, the Catti made an irruption upon the Rhine, and the Parthians in Asia.

L. Verus was sent against them. But the wars on the Danube with the Marcomanni and their allies in Pannonia, and other northern nations, who now began to press forward with great force upon Dacia, were of much greater consequence. They occupied M. Aurelius from the year 167, with but little intermission, to the end of his reign. He succeeded, indeed, in maintaining the boundaries of the empire; but then he was the first who settled any of the barbarians within it, or took them into the Roman service. In the internal administration of affairs he closely followed the steps of his predecessor, except that he was rather too much influenced by his freedmen and family. The only rebellion which broke out against him, was that of Avidius Cassius, his lieutenant in Syria, occasioned by a false report of his death; but it was quelled by the destruction of that general, as soon as the truth was made known.

The war against the Parthians was indeed brought to a successful issue by Verus, the principal cities of the Parthians falling into the hands of the Romans; Verus left them, however, to be carried on by his lieutenants, while he rioted in debaucheries at Antioch. The first war against the Marcomanni, carried on in the beginning and until the death of Verus, by the two emperors together, was highly dangerous for Rome, as many other nations had joined the Marcomanni, particularly the Quadi, Jazygi, and Vandals, and penetrated as far as Aquileia. M. Aurelius ended this war by a glorious peace, 174, as he found it necessary to stop the progress of Cassius's rebellion; in 178, however, the Marcomanni again commenced hostilities, and before their close M. Aurelius died at Sirmium. Contemporary with these wars, yet, as it seems, without any connection with them, were the attacks of other nations upon Dacia, the Bastarnæ, Alani, etc., who poured in from the north, probably pressed forward by the advance of the Goths. *This was the first symptom of the great migration of nations now beginning.*

28. *T. Commodus, March* 17, 180—*Dec.* 31, 192.—*Perennis, Cleander.* By means of adoption the Roman empire had been blessed, during the last eighty years, with a succession of rulers such as have not often fell to the lot of any kingdom. But in T. Commodus, the son of M. Aurelius, (probably the offspring of a gladiator,) who reigned from his nineteenth to his thirty-first year, there ascended the throne a monster of cruelty, insolence and lewdness. At the commencement of his reign he bought a peace of the Marcomanni that he might return to Rome. Being himself unable to support the burden of government, the helm of state was placed in the hands of the stern and cruel Perennis, præfect of the prætorian guard; but who, being murdered by the discontented

soldiers, was succeeded by the freedman Cleander, who put up all for sale, till he fell a sacrifice to his own insatiable avarice, in a revolt of the people caused by their want of provisions. The extravagant propensity of Commodus for the diversions of the amphitheatres, and the combats of wild beasts and gladiators, wherein he himself usually took a part in the character of Hercules, became a chief cause of his dissipation, and thereby of his cruelty; till at last he was killed at the instigation of his concubine Marcia, Lætus the præfect of the prætorian guard, and Electus. The wars on the frontiers during his reign, in Dacia, and especially in Britain, were successfully carried on by his lieutenants, generals who belonged to the school of his father.

29. *State of the Empire at this period.* The disasters under M. Aurelius, and the extravagances of Commodus, had injured the empire, but not enfeebled it. Towards the close of the period of the Antonines it still retained its pristine vigor. If wise regulations, internal peace, moderate taxes, a certain degree of political, and unrestrained civil liberty, are sufficient to form the happiness of a commonwealth, it must have been found in the Roman. What a number of advantages did it possess over every other, simply from its situation! Proofs of it appear on every side. A vigorous population, rich provinces, flourishing and splendid cities, and a lively internal and foreign trade. But the most solid foundation of the happiness of a nation consists in its moral greatness, and this we here seek for in vain. Otherwise the nation would not so easily have suffered itself to be brought under the yoke of Commodus by prætorian cohorts and the legions. But what best shows the strength which the empire still retained, is the opposition it continued to make, for two hundred years longer, to the formidable attacks from without.

SEC. IX—FROM THE DEATH OF COMMODUS TO DIOCLETIAN. A. C. 193–284.

1. *Pertinax, Jan.* 1, *March* 28, 193. The extinction of the race of the Antonines, by the death of Commodus, was attended with convulsions similar to those which took place when the house of Cæsar became extinct at the death of Nero. It is true that P. Helvius Pertinax, aged sixty-seven, præfect of the city, was raised to the throne by the murderers of Commodus; and that he was acknowledged, first by the guards, and afterwards by the senate. But the reform which he was obliged to make at the beginning of his reign in the finances, rendered him so odious to the soldiers and courtiers, that a revolt of the first, excited by Lætus, cost him his life before he had reigned quite

three months. This was the first commencement of that dreadful military despotism which forms the ruling character of this period; and to none did it become so terrible as to those who wished to make it the main support of their absolute power.

The insolence of the prætorian guard had risen very high during the reign of Commodus; but it had never, even in the time of the Antonines, been entirely suppressed. It was only by large donatives that their consent could be purchased, their caprice satisfied, and their good-humor maintained; especially at every new adoption. One of the greatest reproaches to the age of the Antonines is, that those great princes, who seem to have had the means so much in their power, did not free themselves from so annoying a dependence.

2. *Didius Julianus, Septimius Severus, Pescennius Niger, Albinus.* When, upon the death of Pertinax, the rich and profligate M. Didius Julianus, aged fifty-seven, had outbid, to the great scandal of the people, all his competitors for the empire, and purchased it of the prætorian guard, an insurrection of the legions, who were better able to create emperors, very naturally followed. But as the army of Illyria proclaimed their general Septimius Severus, the army of Syria, Pescennius Niger, and the army of Britain, Albinus, nothing less than a series of civil wars could decide who should maintain himself on the throne.

3. *Albinus kills himself, Feb.* 19, 197. Septimius Severus, however, aged 49–66, was the first who got possession of Rome, and after the execution of Didius Julianus, he was acknowledged by the senate. He dismissed, it is true, the old prætorian guard, but immediately chose, from his own army, one four times more numerous in its stead. And after he had provisionally declared Albinus emperor, he marched his army against Pescennius Niger, already master of the East, whom, after several contests near the Issus, he defeated and slew. Nevertheless, having first taken and destroyed the strong city of Byzantium, a war with Albinus soon followed, whom the perfidious Severus had already attempted to remove by assassination. After a bloody defeat near Lyons. Albinus kills himself. These civil wars were followed by hostilities against the Parthians, who had taken the part of Pescennius, and which ended with the plundering of their principal cities. Severus possessed most of the virtues of a soldier; but the insatiable avarice of his minister, Plautianus, the formidable captain of the prætorian guard, robbed the empire even of those advantages which may be enjoyed under a military government, until he was put to death at the instigation of Caracalla. To keep his legions employed, Severus undertook an expedition into Britain, where, after extending the boundaries of the em-

pire, he died at York (*Eboracum*), leaving his son the maxim, "to enrich the soldiers, and hold the rest for nothing."

Agricola had already erected a line of fortresses, probably between the Firth of Clyde and the Firth of Forth. These were changed by Adrian into a wall along the present boundaries of Scotland. Severus again extended the frontiers, re-established the fortresses of Agricola, and afterwards built a wall from sea to sea; his son, however, gave up the conquered country, and the wall of Adrian again became the boundary of the empire.

4. *Caracalla, Feb.* 4, 211—*April* 4, 217.—*Geta murdered, April* 4, 212. The deadly hatred which reigned between the two sons of Severus, M. Aurelius Antoninus Bassianus Caracalla, aged 23–29, and his young step-brother, Geta, aged twenty-one, led to a dreadful catastrophe; for, at their return to Rome, and after a fruitless proposition had been made for a division of the empire, Geta was assassinated in the arms of his mother, Julia Domna, together with all those who were considered as his friends. The restless spirit of Caracalla, however, soon drew him from Rome, and in traversing first the provinces along the Danube, and then those of the East, he ruined them all by his exactions and cruelty, to which he was driven for money to pay his soldiers, and to purchase peace of his enemies on the frontiers. The same necessity led him to grant the right of citizenship to all the provinces, that he might thereby gain the duty of the *vicesima hereditatum et manumissionum* (twentieth upon inheritances and enfranchisements), which he very soon afterwards changed into a tenth (*decima*).

With respect to his foreign wars, his first was against the Catti and Alemanni, among whom he remained a long time, sometimes as a friend, and sometimes as an enemy. But his principal efforts, after having previously ordered a dreadful massacre of the inhabitants of Alexandria, to satisfy his cruel rapacity, were directed against the Parthians; and in his wars against them he was assassinated by Macrinus, the præfect of the prætorian guard.

The præfect or captain of the prætorian guard became, from the time of Severus, the most important officer in the state. Besides the command of the guards, the finances were also under his control, together with an extensive criminal jurisdiction—a natural consequence of the continually increasing despotism.

5. *Macrinus, April* 11, 217—*June* 8, 218. His murderer, M. Opelius Macrinus, aged fifty-three, was recognized as emperor by the soldiers, and forthwith acknowledged by the senate. He immediately created his son, M. Opelius Diadumenus, aged nine years, Cæsar, and gave him the name of Antoninus. He disgracefully terminated the war against

the Parthians by purchasing a peace, and changed the *decima* (tenth) of Caracalla again into the *vicesima* (twentieth). However, while he still remained in Asia, Bassianus Heliogabalus, grand-nephew of Julia Domna, and high priest in the temple of the Sun at Emesa, whom his mother gave out for a son of Caracalla, was proclaimed emperor by the legions, and after a combat with the guards, subsequently to which Macrinus and his son lost their lives, they raised him to the throne.

Mæsa, the sister of Julia Domna, had two daughters, both widows: Soæmis, the eldest, was the mother of Heliogabalus, and Mammæa, the youngest, the mother of Alexander Severus.

6. *Heliogabalus*, *June* 8, 218—*March* 11, 222. Heliogabalus, aged 14–18, who assumed the additional name of M. Aurelius Antoninus, brought with him from Syria the superstitions and voluptuousness of that country. He introduced the worship of his god, Heliogabal, in Rome, and wallowed openly in such brutal and infamous debaucheries, that history can scarcely find a parallel to his dissolute, shameless, and scandalous conduct. How low must the morality of that age have been sunk, in which a boy could so early have ripened into a monster! The debasement of the senate, and of all important offices, which he filled with the degraded companions of his own lusts and vices, was systematically planned by him; and he deserves no credit even for the adoption of his cousin, the virtuous Alexander Severus, as he shortly after endeavored to take away his life, but was himself, for that reason, assassinated by the prætorian guards.

7. *Alexander Severus*, *March* 11, 222—*Aug.*, 235. His young cousin and successor, M. Aurelius Alexander Severus, aged 14–27, who had been carefully educated under the direction of his mother Mammæa, proved one of the best princes in an age and upon a throne where virtues were more dangerous than vices. Under favor of his youth he endeavored to effect a reform, in which he was supported by the co-operation of the guards, who had elevated him to the throne. He restored the authority of the senate, from among whom he chose, with rigid justice, his privy council of state, banishing the creatures of Heliogabalus from their places. The revolution in the Parthian empire, out of which was now formed the new Persian, was of so much importance to Rome, that it obliged Alexander to undertake a war against Artaxerxes, in which he was probably victorious. But while marching in haste to protect the frontiers against the advance of the Germans upon the Rhine, his soldiers, exasperated at the severity of his discipline, and incited by the Thracian Maximin, murdered him in his own tent. His præfect of the prætorian guard, Ulpian, had al-

ready, for the same cause, fallen a victim to this spirit of insubordination, which was not checked even by the immediate presence of the emperor himself.

The revolution in Parthia, whereby a new Persian empire was formed, became a source of almost perpetual war to Rome; Artaxerxes I., and his successors, the Sassanides, claiming to be descendants of the ancient kings of Persia, formed pretensions to the possession of all the Asiatic provinces of the Roman empire.

8. *Maximinus*, *Aug.*, 235—*May*, 238. The death of A. Severus raised military despotism to the highest pitch, as it placed on the throne the half savage C. Julius Maximinus, by birth a Thracian peasant. At first he continued the war against the Germans with great success, repulsing them beyond the Rhine; and resolved, by crossing Pannonia, to carry the war even among the Sarmatians. But his insatiable rapacity, which spared neither the capital nor the provinces, made him hateful to all; and Gordian, proconsul of Africa, in his eightieth year, was, together with his son of the same name, proclaimed Augustus by the people, and immediately acknowledged by the senate. Upon this, Maximinus, eager to take vengeance on the senate, marched directly from Sirmium towards Italy. In the mean time, the legions of the almost defenceless Gordians were defeated in Africa, and themselves slain by Capellianus the governor of Numidia. Notwithstanding this, as the senate could expect no mercy, they chose as co-emperors the præfect of the city, Maximus Pupienus, and Clodius Balbinus, who, in conformity with the wishes of the people, created the young Gordian III., Cæsar. In the meanwhile Maximinus, having besieged Aquileia, and the enterprise proving unsuccessful, was slain by his own troops. Pupienus and Balbinus now seemed in quiet possession of the throne; but the guards, who had already been engaged in a bloody feud with the people, and were not willing to receive an emperor of the senate's choosing, killed them both, and proclaimed as Augustus, Gordian, already created Cæsar.

9. *Gordian III.*, *July*, 238—*Feb.*, 244. *Syrian expedition*, 241–243. The reign of the young M. Antoninus Gordianus lasted from his twelfth to his eighteenth year. He was grandson of the proconsul who had lost his life in Africa, and in the early part of his reign, acquired a degree of firmness from the support of his father-in-law, Misitheus, præfect of the prætorian guard, as well as from the successful expedition which he undertook into Syria against the Persians, who had invaded that province. But after the death of Misitheus, Philip the Arabian, being made præfect of the guards in his stead, found means to gain the

troops over to himself, and, after driving Gordian from the throne, caused him to be assassinated.

10. *Philippus, Feb.*, 244—*Sept.*, 249. The reign of M. Julius Philippus was interrupted by several insurrections, especially in Pannonia; until at length Decius, whom he himself had sent thither to quell the rebellion, was compelled by the troops to assume the diadem. Philip was soon after defeated by him near Verona, where he perished, together with his son of the same name. In this reign the secular games, *ludi sæculares*, were celebrated, one thousand years from the foundation of the city.

11. *The Goths, Sept.*, 249—*Oct.*, 251, 250. *Gallus. Æmilianus, May*, 253. *Valerian. Gallienus*, 259—268 *Thirty tyrants.* Under the reign of his successor, Trajanus Decius, aged fifty, the Goths for the first time forced their way into the Roman empire by crossing the Danube; and although Decius in the beginning opposed them with success, he was at last slain by them in Thrace, together with his son, Cl. Herennius Decius, already created Cæsar. Upon this the army proclaimed C. Trebonianus Gallus emperor, who created his son, Volusian, Cæsar; and having invited Hostilian, the yet remaining son of Decius, with the ostensible purpose of securing his co-operation, he nevertheless soon contrived to get rid of him. He purchased a peace of the Goths; but, despised by his generals, he became involved in a war with his victorious lieutenant, Æmilius Æmilianus, in Mœsia, and was slain, together with his son, by his own army. In three months, however, Æmilianus shared the same fate; Publius Licinius Valerianus, the friend and avenger of Gallus, advancing against him with the legions stationed in Gaul. Both the people and army hoped to see the empire restored under Valerian, already sixty years of age; but, although his generals defended the frontiers against the Germans and Goths, he himself had the misfortune to be defeated and taken prisoner by the superior forces of the Persians. Upon this event his son and associate in the empire, P. Licinius Gallienus, who knew every thing except the art of governing, reigned alone. Under his indolent rule the Roman empire seemed on one hand ready to be split into a number of small states, while on the other it seemed about to fall a prey to the barbarians; for the lieutenants in most of the provinces declared themselves independent of a prince whom they despised, and to which, indeed, they were driven, like Posthumius in Gaul, for their own security. There were nineteen of these; but as many of them named their sons Cæsars, this period has been very improperly distinguished by the name of *the thirty tyrants*, although their intolerable oppressions might well justify

the latter expression. The Persians at the same time were victorious in the East, and the Germans in the West.

The German nations which were now become so formidable to the Roman empire, were: 1. The great confederation of tribes under the name of *Franks*, who spread over Gaul along the whole extent of the Lower Rhine. 2. The allied nations of the Alemanni on the Upper Rhine. 3. The Goths, the most powerful of all, who had formed a monarchy upon the banks of the Lower Danube and the northern coasts of the Black Sea, which soon extended from the Borysthenes to the Don; and who became formidable, not only by their land forces, but also by their naval power, especially after they had captured the peninsula of Crim Tartary (*Chersonesus Taurica*); and by means of their fleets they not only kept the Grecian but likewise the Asiatic provinces in a continual state of alarm.

12. *Claudius*, *March*, 268—*Oct.*, 270. Gallienus losing his life before Milan, in the war against Aureolus, a usurper, had nevertheless recommended M. Aurelius Claudius (aged 45–47) for his successor. The new Augustus re-established in some degree the tottering empire; not only by taking Aureolus prisoner and defeating the Alemanni, but also by a decisive victory gained at Nissa over the Goths, who invaded Mœsia. He died, however, soon after, at Sirmium, of a pestilential disease, naming for his successors Aurelian, a hero like himself, who mounted the throne upon the death of Quintillus the late emperor's brother, who had at first proclaimed himself Augustus, but afterwards died by his own hand.

13. *Aurelian*, *Oct.*, 270—*March*, 275. *Zenobia defeated and made prisoner*, 271–273. During the reign of L. Domitius Aurelianus, which lasted almost five years, those countries which had been partly or entirely lost to the empire were restored. Having first driven back the Goths and the Alemanni, who had advanced as far as Umbria, he undertook his expedition against the celebrated Zenobia, queen of Palmyra, who at that time possessed Syria, Egypt, and part of Asia Minor. These countries he again brought under the dominion of the empire, after having defeated Zenobia and made her prisoner. The western provinces of Gaul, Britain, and Spain, which since the time of Gallienus had been governed by separate rulers, and were now under the dominion of Tetricus, he reduced to their former obedience. Dacia, on the contrary, he willingly abandoned; and as he transported the Roman inhabitants across the Danube into Mœsia, the latter henceforward bore the name of *Dacia Aureliani*. Hated for his severity, which in a warrior so easily degenerates into cruelty, he was assassinated in Illyria at the instigation of his private secretary Mnestheus.

Palmyra in the Syrian desert, enriched by the Indian trade, and one of the most ancient cities in the world, became a Roman colony in the time of Trajan. Odenatus, the husband of Zenobia, had acquired so much celebrity by his victories over the Persians, that Gallienus had even named him Augustus with himself. He was murdered, however. by his cousin Mæonius, 267. Zenobia now took possession of the government for her sons Vabalathus, Herennianus, and Timolaus, without, however, being acknowledged at Rome. After this, in the time of Claudius, she added Egypt to her dominions. Aurelian, having first defeated her near Antioch and Emesa, soon afterward took Palmyra, which, in consequence of a revolt, he destroyed. Even in its ruins Palmyra is still magnificent.

14. *Tacitus, Sept.* 25, 275—*April*, 276. An interregnun of six months followed upon the death of Aurelian, till at length the senate, at the repeated solicitations of the army, ventured to fill up the vacant throne. The object of their choice, however, M. Claudius Tacitus, the worthiest of the senators, was unfortunately seventy-five years old, and perished after a short reign of six months, in an expedition against the Goths. Upon this event the army of Syria raised M. Aurelius Probus to the purple; while Florianus the brother of Tacitus, who had already been acknowledged at Rome, was put to death by his own people.

15. *Probus, April*, 276—*August*, 282. The six years reign of Probus was a warlike one. He defeated the Germans, and forced them beyond the Rhine and Danube; strengthening the frontiers by building a strong wall from the Danube, near Regensburg, to the Rhine. He also obliged the Persians to make peace. Nevertheless, the number of towns which he re-established and peopled with prisoners of war, and the vineyards which he caused his soldiers to plant on the Rhine, are proofs that he had taste and inclination for the arts of peace. This policy, however, would not suit the legions! After he had perished, therefore. by the hands of his soldiers, they proclaimed the præfect of the prætorian guard, M. Aurelius Carus, emperor, who created his two sons Cæsars—men very unlike each other in disposition, M. Aurelius Carinus being one of the greatest reprobates, while M. Aurelius Numerianus was gentle by nature, and had a mind well formed by study. The new emperor, having defeated the Goths, marched against the Persians, but was shortly afterwards killed, it is said, by a flash of lightning. Nor did his son Numerianus long survive him, being murdered by his own father-in-law, Arrius Aper, the prætorian præfect.

16. *Review of the Government during this period.* Although this period gives us a finished picture of a complete military despotism, it is still evident that this was owing to the entire separation of the military

order from the rest of the people, by the introduction of standing armies, and the extinction of all national spirit among the citizens. The legions decided because the people were unarmed. It was, indeed, only among them, situated far from the soft luxuries of the capital, and engaged in almost a continual struggle with the barbarians, that a remnant of the ancient Roman character was still preserved. The nomination of their leaders to the purple became a natural consequence, not only of the uncertainty of the succession, which could not be fixed by mere ordinances, but often of necessity, from their being in the field under the pressure of urgent circumstances. Thus a succession of distinguished generals came to the throne: what authority, indeed, would an emperor at that time have had who was not a general? All durable reform, however, was rendered quite impossible by the quick succession of rulers. Even the best among them could do but very little for the internal administration; as all their energies were required to protect the frontiers, and defend themselves against usurpers, who, with the exception of the formality of being acknowledged by the senate, had claims as well-founded as their own.

17. *Luxury hastens the decline of the Empire.* The decline of the empire also became so much the more rapid, in proportion as, in these days of terror, luxury had increased not only in the splendor and profligate effeminacy of private life, but more particularly in public, to a pitch almost beyond belief. The latter was especially shown in the exhibitions of the amphitheatre and circus; by which not only every new leader, but even every new magistrate, was obliged to purchase the favor of the people. Thus these remnants of a free constitution served only to accelerate the general ruin! What enjoyments, indeed, could be found under the rod of despotism, except those of the grossest sensuality; and to satisfy this, the intellectual amusements of the theatre (mimes and pantomimes), and even those of rhetoric and poetry, were made to contribute.

18. *Progress and effects of the Christian religion.* Yet, during this general decay, the gradual spread of the Christian religion was working a reform altogether of a different nature. Before the end of this period it had opened itself a way into every province, and, notwithstanding the frequent persecutions, had made converts in every rank of society, and was now on the eve of becoming the predominant form of worship. We shall be better able to estimate its value, if we consider it as the vehicle by which civilization made its way among the rude nations that now appeared on the scene, than if we merely consider it as the means of improving the manners and morals of the Roman world. In a political view, it became of the greatest importance, on account of

the hierarchy, the framework of which was now in a great measure constructed among its professors. It was afterwards adopted as a state religion; and although the ancient creed of Rome had formerly been on the same footing, yet it was only calculated for the republic, and not at all for the now existing monarchy. The overthrow of paganism was necessarily attended with some violent convulsions, yet its loss was nothing to be compared with the support which the throne afterwards found in the hierarchy.

The dispersion of the Jews, and especially the persecutions which were renewed from time to time after the reign of Nero (but which only served to kindle enthusiasm), strongly co-operated in spreading the Christian religion. These persecutions were principally called forth against the Christians, on account of their forming themselves into a separate society, which caused them to be regarded as a dangerous sect at Rome, notwithstanding the general toleration granted to every other system of religious belief. Although towards the end of this period, only a very small proportion of the inhabitants of the Roman empire as yet professed the Christian faith, it nevertheless had followers in every province.

SEC. X.—FROM DIOCLETIAN TO THE OVERTHROW OF THE WESTERN EMPIRE. A. C. 284–476.

1. *Diocletian, Sept.* 17, 284—*May* 1, 305. The reign of C. Valerius Diocletian, aged 39–60, proclaimed emperor after the murder of Numerianus, by the troops in Chalcedon, begins a new section in Roman history. To the period of military despotism succeeded the period of partitions. After Diocletian had defeated Carinus, the yet remaining Cæsar, in Upper Mœsia, where he was assassinated, he made M. Valerius Maximianus Herculius, a rough warrior, who had hitherto been his comrade in arms, the sharer of his throne. Herculius now contended with the Alemanni and Burgundians on the banks of the Rhine, while Diocletian himself made head against the Persians. Nevertheless, the two Augusti soon found themselves unable to withstand the barbarians, who were pressing forward on every side, more especially as Carausius had usurped and maintained the title of Cæsar in Britain. Each of them, therefore, created a Cæsar: Diocletian chose C. Galerius; and Maximianus, Flavius Constantius Chlorus, both of whom had distinguished themselves as generals, at that time the only road to advancement. The whole empire was now divided between these four rulers; so that each had certain provinces to govern and defend; without detriment, however, to the unity of the whole, or to the

dependence in which a Cæsar stood as the subordinate assistant and future successor of his Augustus.

In the partition, 292, Diocletian possessed the eastern provinces; Galerius, Thrace, and the countries on the Danube (Illyricum); Maximianus, Italy, Africa, and the islands; and Constantius, the western provinces of Gaul, Spain, Britain, and Mauritania.

2. *Change in Constitution.* This new system could not but have a striking effect upon the spirit of the government. It was now not only in fact, but also in form, entirely in the hands of the rulers. By their continual absence from Rome they became freed from that moral restraint in which the authority of the senate, and the name of the republic, not yet entirely laid aside, had before held them. Diocletian formally assumed the diadem, and, with the ornaments of the East, introduced its luxuries into his court. Thus was laid the foundation of that structure which Constantine the Great had to complete.

3. *The change necessary.* The consequences of this new system became also oppressive to the provinces, inasmuch as they had now to maintain four rulers, with their courts, and as many armies. But however loud might be the complaints of the oppression occasioned thereby, it was, perhaps, the only means of deferring the final overthrow of the whole edifice. In fact, they succeeded not only in defeating the usurpers, Alectus in Britain (who had murdered Carausius in 293), Julian in Africa, and Achilleus in Egypt; but also in defending the frontiers, which, indeed, by the victories of Galerius over the Persians, they extended as far as the Tigris. Did not, however, the gloomy perspective present itself, that among so many rulers, and the undefined relations which existed between the Cæsars and the emperors, the union could not be of long continuance?

4. *Constantius*, 305–307. *Galerius*, 305–313. Diocletian voluntarily abdicated the throne (although the growing power and encroaching disposition of Galerius might perhaps have had some influence), and obliged his colleague Maximianus to do the same. The two Cæsars, Constantius and Galerius, were proclaimed Augusti, and altered the division of the empire, so that the former possessed all the western countries, of which, however, he freely ceded Italy and Africa to Galerius, who had all the remaining provinces. The latter, during the same year, created Flavius Severus, Cæsar, and confided to him the government of Italy and Africa; as he did also C. Galerius Maximin, to whom he gave the Asiatic provinces. The administration of the two emperors, however, was very different; Constantius was as much beloved for his mild and disinterested government, as Galerius was hated

for his harshness and prodigality. Constantius died very soon after at York, leaving his son Constantine heir to his dominions, who was immediately proclaimed Augustus by the legions, although Galerius would only acknowledge him as Cæsar.

5. *Constantine the Great, July* 25, 306—*May* 22, 337. Thus Constantine, who afterwards obtained the surname of Great, began to rule, aged 33–64, though at first only over Britain, Spain, and Gaul; nevertheless, after seventeen years of violence and warfare, he suceeeded in opening himself a way to the sole dominion of the empire. The rulers disagreed among themselves; and formidable usurpers started up and rendered war inevitable.

The history of the first seven years of Constantine, 306–313, is very complicated; after that he had only one rival to struggle with, 314–323. At his accession, Galerius, as Augustus, was in possession of all the other provinces; of which, however, he had given to Cæsar Maximin the government of those of Asia, and to Cæsar Severus, now created Augustus, Italy and Africa. The latter, however, rendering himself odious by his oppression, Maxentius, the son of the former emperor, Maximianus, assumed the title of Augustus at Rome (Oct. 28, 306) and associated his father with himself in the government; so that at this time there were six rulers: Galerius, Severus, Constantine, Maximin, and the usurpers Maxentius and his father Maximianus. But in the year 307, Severus, wishing to oppose Maxentius, was abandoned by his own troops, upon which he surrendered himself to Maximianus, who caused him to be executed. In his place Galerius created his friend Licinius Augustus; and Maximin obtained the same dignity from his army in Asia. In the mean time, Maximianus, after having endeavored to supplant his own son in Rome, fled to Constantine, who had crossed over into Gaul and there defeated the Franks, 306; but having made an attempt upon the life of Constantine, who had married his daughter Fausta, that emperor caused him to be put to death, 310. As the excesses of Galerius soon brought him to the grave, 311, there only remained Constantine, Licinius, and Maximin, and the usurper Maxentius. The latter was soon defeated and slain, 312, before the gates of Rome, by Constantine, who thereby became master of Italy and the capital. A war having broken out about the same time between Maximin and Licinius, Maximin was defeated near Adrianople, and then killed himself, 313. The year 314 brought on a war between the two remaining emperors, Constantine and Licinius, which, however, ended the same year in an accommodation, by which Constantine obtained all the countries on the south bank of the Danube, as well as

Thrace and Mœsia Inferior; it broke out again, however, in 322, and was finally terminated by a decisive victory in Bithynia, and the total overthrow of Licinius, whom Constantine put to death, 324.

6. However opposite may be the opinions formed respecting the reign of Constantine the Great, its consequences are perfectly plain. Although he annihilated military despotism, he established in its stead, if not completely, yet in great measure, the despotism of the court, and likewise the power of the hierarchy. He had already during his expedition against Maxentius, decided in favor of the Christian religion; and since he thereby gained a vast number of partisans in all the provinces, and weakened at the same time the power of his co-emperors, or competitors, it was the surest way he could have taken to obtain sole dominion, the great object of his ambition. This change must nevertheless have had very considerable influence on every part of the government, as he found in the previously established hierarchy a powerful support of the throne; and since he, in concert with it, settled what was and what was not the orthodox doctrine, he introduced a spirit of persecution heretofore unknown.

At a period in which religious parties must almost necessarily have become political parties, we can by no means venture to judge of the importance of the sect by the importance of their points of doctrine. The quarrels of the Arians, which arose at this time, gave Constantine, by the council of Nice, 325, the opportunity he wished for, of making good his authority in religious legislation.

7. *Removal of seat of Government.* The removal of the seat of empire from Rome to Constantinople was connected with this change in the form of worship—as a Christian court would have been awkwardly situated in a city still altogether pagan—although the need there was of protecting the frontiers against the Goths and Persians had a considerable share therein. It did, indeed, become the principal means of establishing the despotism of the court; but those who regard it as one of the causes of the decline of the empire, should remember, that for an empire fallen so low as the Roman was at this time, despotism was almost the only support that remained.

The various partitions of the empire from the time of Diocletian, had led the way to this change of the capital; because a natural result of that system was, that the emperors and Cæsars, when not with the army as they usually were, would reside in different cities. The seat of Diocletian's government was at Nicomedia; of Maximian's, at Milan; even Constantine himself remained but very little at Rome. In these new residences they felt themselves unfettered; and therefore, although the Roman senate existed till after the time of Constantine, its authority must have fallen of itself from the time of Diocletian.

8. *Consequence of removal of Government.* We ought not, therefore, to wonder that the consequence of this removal was so complete a change in the whole form of the government, that after a short time it seemed to be altogether a different state. A partition of the empire was made, which, though it might in part have been founded on those which had previously existed, was yet so different, that it not only changed the ancient divisions of the provinces, but completely altered their mode of government. The court, with the exception of polygamy, assumed entirely the form of an eastern court. A revolution also had taken place in the military system, by the complete separation of the civil and military authorities, which the prætorian præfects had hitherto possessed, but who now became merely civil governors.

Division of Empire. According to the new division, the whole empire was divided into four *præfectures*, each of which had its *dioceses*, and each diocese its *provinces*. The præfectures were: I. The eastern (*præfectura Orientis*); it contained five dioceses; 1. *Orientis;* 2. *Ægypti;* 3. *Asiæ;* 4. *Ponti;* 5. *Thraciæ;* forming altogether forty-eight provinces, and comprising all the countries of Asia and Egypt, together with the frontier countries of Libya and Thrace. II. *Præfectura Illyrici*, containing two dioceses; 1. *Macedoniæ;* 2. *Daciæ;* forming eleven provinces, and comprising Mœsia, Macedon, Greece, and Crete. III. *Præfectura Italiæ*, containing three dioceses; 1. *Italiæ;* 2. *Illyrici;* 3. *Africæ;* forming twenty-nine provinces, and comprising Italy, the countries on the south of the Danube, as far as the boundaries of Mœsia; the islands of Sicily, Sardinia, and Corsica, and the African provinces of the Syrtis. IV. *Præfectura Galliarum*, containing three dioceses; 1. *Galliæ;* 2. *Hispaniæ;* 3. *Britanniæ;* forming altogether twenty-eight provinces, and comprising Spain and the Balearian islands, Gaul, Helvetia, and Britain. Each of these præfectures was under a *præfectus prætorio* (prætorian præfect), but who was merely a civil governor, and had under him *vicarios*, in the dioceses, as well as the *rectores provinciarum*, of various ranks and titles. They were named *proconsules præsides*, etc. Besides these, Rome and Constantinople, not being included in any of the four præfectures, had each its præfect.

Organization of Courts. As principal officers of state and the court, (*s. cubiculi,*) we now for the first time meet with the *præpositus s. cubiculi*, (grand-chamberlain,) under whom were all the *comites palatii* and *cubicularii*, in four divisions; these, at a later period, were frequently eunuchs of great influence; the *magister officiorum* (chancellor, minister of the interior); the *comes sacrarum largitiorum* (minister of the finances); the *quæstor* (the organ of the emperors in legislation; minister of justice and secretary of state); the *comes rei principis* (minister of the crown-treasury) [privy-purse]; the two *comites domesticorum*, (commander of the household guards,) each of whom had his corps (*scholas*) under him. The number of the state officers and courtiers was continually increasing. If the good of a commonwealth consisted in forms, ranks, and titles, the Roman empire must at this time have been truly happy!

Military Department. At the head of the troops were the *magistri peditum* (masters of the infantry) and the *magistri equitum*, (masters of the horse,) under the *magister utriusque militæ* (general in chief of the whole army). Their subordinate commanders were called *comites* and *duces.* Constantine considerably reduced the army. In the arrangement of the troops he also made great alterations; these, however, were but of slight consequence compared with that which was produced by admitting into the service a continually increasing number of barbarians.

9. *Taxes.* It would naturally be expected that these great changes should lead to others in the system of taxation. New taxes, or old ones revived, were added to those already existing, and became by the manner in which they were collected, doubly oppressive. We shall particularly notice, *a.* The annual land-tax (*indictio*). *b.* The tax upon trade (*aurum lustrale*). *c.* The free gift, (*don. gratuit.*,) now grown into an obligatory tax (*aurum coronarium*). To these we must add the municipal expenses, which fell entirely upon the citizens, and especially upon the civic officers, (*decuriones*,) places which must have been generally held by the rich, as Constantine had in great measure appropriated the wealth of the cities to the endowment of churches, and the support of the clergy.

a. The land-tax, or *indiction*, which if not first introduced by Constantine, was entirely regulated under him, was collected after an exact register, or public valuation, of all the landed estates. Its amount was yearly fixed and prescribed by the emperor, (*indicebatur*,) and levied by the rectors of provinces and the decurions; an arbitrary standard (*caput*) being taken as the rate of assessment.

As this register was probably revived every fifteen years, it gave rise to the *cycle of indications* of fifteen years, which became the common era, beginning from September 1, 312. In this manner the tax included all those who were possessed of property. *b.* The tax on commerce, which was levied on almost every kind of trade. It was collected every four years, whence the *aurum lustrale*. *c.* The *aurum coronarium* grew out of the custom which obtained of presenting the emperors with golden crowns on particular occasions, the value of which was at last exacted in money. Every considerable city was obliged to pay it.

10. *Spread of the Christian religion.* The rapid spread of the Christian religion, the promulgation of which was enforced as a duty upon all its professors, was now accelerated by the endeavors of the court. Constantine forbade sacrifices, and shut up the temples; and the violent zeal of his successors unfortunately soon turned them into ruins.

11. *Constantine, Constantius, and Constans.* The three Cæsars and sons of Constantine the Great, Constantine, 337–340; Constantius, 337–361; and Constans, 337–350; had been carefully educated, and yet resembled one another as much in their vices as they did in their names. They indeed divided the empire again upon the death of their father; but were so eager after territory, which neither of them was qualified to govern, that a series of wars followed for the next twelve years, till at last Constantius was left master of the whole; and by the murder of most of his relations secured the throne to himself.

In the partition of the empire Constantine obtained the *præfectura Galliarum*, Constans the *præfectura Italiæ et Illyrici*, and Constantius the *præfectura Orientis.* But as Constantine desired to add Italy and Africa to his portion, he attacked Constans, and thereby lost his life, so that Constans came into the possession of the western countries. In consequence, however, of his wretched misgovernment, Magnentius, a general, proclaimed himself emperor in Gaul, and Constans was slain in endeavoring to escape, 350. A war with Constantius, who was then occupied in the East, became inevitable, and broke out 351. The usurper was defeated first at Mursa in Pannonia, then retreating into Gaul he was again defeated, 353; upon which he slew himself, together with his family.

12. *Constantius alone.* As Constantius, however—sunk in effeminacy and debauchery, and surrounded and governed by eunuchs—was unable to sustain the weight of government alone, he took his cousin Constantius Gallus, hitherto a state prisoner, and whose father he had formerly slain, to his assistance, created him Cæsar, and sent him into the East against the Parthians. But his excessive arrogance, which was fomented by his wife Constantina, rendered him so dangerous that Constantius recalled him, and caused him, upon his return, to be put to death in Istria. His younger brother Fl. Julian, from whom the suspicious Constantius believed he had nothing to fear, was promoted in his place, created Cæsar, and sent to defend the frontiers on the Rhine. Although Julian passed suddenly from study to warfare, he not only

fought against the Germans with success, but also made a deep inroad into their country. In the mean time Constantius, after his generals had been beaten by the Persians, who wished to reconquer the provinces they had ceded, was preparing an expedition against them in person, and with that view endeavored gradually to withdraw the troops of Julian, in consequence of which the latter, suspecting his design, was induced to accept the diadem presented by his soldiers. While marching, however, along the Danube against Constantius, he received information of that prince's death in Asia.

13. *Julian*, *March*, 360—*June* 25, 363. Fl. Julian, (the apostate,) who reigned from his twenty-ninth to his thirty-second year, was the last and most highly-gifted prince of the house of Constantine. Instructed by misfortunes and study, he yet had some faults, though certainly free from great vices. He began with reforming the luxury of the court. His abjuration of the religion now become dominant, and which he wished to annihilate by degrees, was an error in policy, which he must have discovered to his cost had his reign been prolonged. Wishing, however, to terminate the war against the Persians, he penetrated as far as the Tigris, where he lost his life in an engagement, after a reign of three years.

14. *Jovian*, *June* 25, 363—*Feb.* 24, 364. *Valentinian and Valens.* Fl. Jovianus, now thirty-three years of age, was immediately raised to the purple by the army. He concluded a peace with the Persians, by which he restored them all the territory that had been conquered from them since the year 297. After a short reign of eight months he was carried off by a sudden disorder; and the army proclaimed Fl. Valentinian at Nice in his stead. Valentinian almost immediately associated his brother Valens with himself in the government, and divided the empire by giving him the *præfectura Orientis*, and retaining the rest for himself.

15. *Valentinian*, *Feb.* 26, 364—*Nov.* 17, 375. The reign of Valentinian I. in the West, who, in the year 367, created his son Gratian Augustus with himself, is distinguished by the system of toleration which he followed with regard to the affairs of religion, though in other respects a cruel prince. Nearly the whole of his reign was taken up in almost continual struggles with the German nations, who had recovered from the losses they had suffered under Julian. His first efforts were directed against the Franks, the Saxons, and the Alemanni on the Rhine; and afterwards against the Quadi and other nations on the Danube; where he died of apoplexy at Guntz in Hungary.

16. *Valens*, 364–378. In the mean time his brother Valens (aged 38–52 years) had to contend with a powerful insurrection which had

broken out in the East. A certain Procopius had instigated the people to this, by taking advantage of the discontent occasioned by the oppression of Valens, who, having adopted the opinion of the Arians, was more disliked in the East than his brother was in the West. His war against the Persians ended with a truce. But the most important event that happened during his reign, was the entrance of the Huns into Europe, which took place towards its close. This, in its turn, gave rise to the great popular migration, by which the Roman empire in the West may properly be said to have been overthrown. The immediate consequence was the admission of the greater part of the Visigoths into the Roman empire, and this occasioned a war which cost Valens his life.

The Huns, a nomad people of Asia, belonged to the great Mongolian race. Having penetrated to the Don, 373, they subdued the Goths upon that river as far as the Theiss. The Goths, divided into Ostrogoths and Visigoths, were separated from one another by the Dnieper. The former, driven from their country, fell upon the Visigoths, in consequence of which the emperor Valens was requested by the latter to grant them admission into the Roman empire, and with the exception of the Vandals, who had been seated in Pannonia from the time of Constantine, they were the first barbarian nation that had been settled within the boundaries of the empire. The scandalous oppression of the Roman governor, however, drove them into rebellion; and as Valens marched against them, he was defeated near Adrianople and lost his life, 378.

17. *Gratian*, 375–383, *and Valentinian II.*, 375–392. During these events, Gratian (aged 16–24 years) succeeded his father Valentinian I. in the West, and immediately associated his brother, Valentinian II. (aged 5–21 years) with himself in the empire; giving him, though under his own superintendence, the *præfectura Italiæ et Illyrici.* Gratian set forward to the assistance of his uncle Valens against the Goths, but receiving on his march an account of his defeat and death, and fearing the East might fall a prey to the Goths, he raised Theodosius, a Spaniard, who had already distinguished himself as a warrior, to the purple, and gave him the *præfectura Orientis et Illyrici.*

18. *Revolt of Maximus*, 383. *Eugenius.* The indolent reign of Gratian led to the rebellion of Maximus, a commander in Britain, who, crossing into Gaul, was so strongly supported by the defection of the Gallic legions, that Gratian was obliged to seek safety in flight. He was, however, overtaken and put to death at Lyons. By this event, Maximus found himself in possession of all the *præfectura Galliarum;* and by promising Theodosius not to interfere with the young Valentinian II. in Italy, he prevailed upon him to acknowledge him emperor. But having broken his promise by the invasion of Italy, he was defeated

and made prisoner by Theodosius in Pannonia, and soon after executed. Upon this Valentinian II., a youth of whom great hopes were entertained, became again master of all the West. But, unfortunately, he was murdered by the offended Arbogast, his *magister militum;* who, thereupon, raised to the throne his own friend Eugenius, *magister officiorum.* Theodosius, however, so far from acknowledging, declared war against him and made him prisoner. He himself thus became master of the whole empire, but died in the following year.

19. *Theodosius the Great, Jan.* 19, 369—*Jan.* 17, 395. The vigorous reign of Theodosius in the East, from his thirty-fourth to his fiftieth year, was not less devoted to politics than to religion. The dexterity with which he at first broke the power of the victorious Goths (though they still preserved their quarters in the provinces on the Danube) procured him considerable influence, which the strength and activity of his character enabled him easily to maintain. The blind zeal, however, with which he persecuted Arianism, now the prevailing creed in the East, and restored the orthodox belief, as well as the persecutions which he directed against the pagans, and the destruction of their temples, occasioned the most dreadful convulsions. His efforts to preserve the boundaries of the empire, not a province of which was lost before his death, required an increase of taxes; and however oppressive this might be, we cannot impute it to the ruler as a crime. In an empire so enfeebled in itself, and which, nevertheless, had powerful foes on every side to contend with, it followed that every active reign would be oppressive. Yet never before had the internal depopulation of the empire made it necessary to take so many barbarians into Roman pay, as under this reign; whence naturally followed a change in the arms and tactics of the Roman armies.

20. *Final division of the Roman Empire. Arcadius*, 395–408. *Honorius*, 385–423. Theodosius left two sons, between whom the empire was divided. Both parts, however, were certainly considered as forming but one empire—an opinion which afterwards prevailed, and even till late in the middle ages had important consequences—yet never since this period have they been reunited under one ruler. The Eastern empire, comprising the *præfectura Orientis et Illyrici*, was allotted to the eldest son, Arcadius, (aged 18–31,) under the guardianship of Rufinus the Gaul. The Western, or the *præfectura Galliarum et Italiæ*, to the younger, Honorius, aged 11–39, under the guardianship of the Vandal Stilico.

21. *Alaric king of the Visigoths.* The Western empire, to the history of which we shall now confine ourselves, suffered such violent shocks during the reign of Honorius, as made its approaching fall plainly

visible. The intrigues of Stilico to procure himself the government of the whole empire, opened a way for the Goths into its interior, just at a time when they were doubly formidable, fortune having given them a leader greatly superior to any they had hitherto had. Alaric king of the Visigoths established himself and his people in the Roman empire, became master of Rome, and mounted the throne: it was the mere effect of chance that he did not overthrow it altogether.

Both Honorius and Arcadius, especially the latter, belonged to that class of men who never come to years of maturity; their favorites and ministers therefore governed according to their own inclination. Stilico, who made Honorius his son-in-law, was not deficient, indeed, in abilities for governing; and his endeavor to obtain the management of the whole empire, arose, perhaps, from the conviction that it was necessary he should have it. He could not, however, gain his object by intrigue; for after the murder of Rufinus, 395, he found a still more powerful opponent in the eunuch Eutropios, his successor in the East. Under the regency of Stilico, Gaul, in consequence of its troops being withdrawn to oppose Alaric, 400, was inundated by German tribes—by Vandals, Alani, and Suevi—who from thence penetrated even into Spain. Nevertheless, he preserved Italy from their attacks by the victory which he gained, 403, over Alaric at Verona; and again over Radagaisus, 405, who had advanced with other German hordes as far as Florence. But Stilico, having entered into a secret alliance with Alaric, for the purpose of wresting eastern Illyrica from the empire of the East, was overreached by the intrigues of the new favorite Olympius, whose cabal knew how to take advantage of the weakness of Honorius, and of the jealousy of the Roman and foreign soldiers. Stilico was accused of aspiring to the throne, and was executed August 23, 408. Rome lost in him the only general that was left to defend her. Alaric invaded Italy the same year, 408, and the besieged Rome was obliged to purchase peace; the conditions, however, not being fulfilled, he was again, 409, before Rome, became master of the city, and created Attalus, the præfect of the city, emperor instead of Honorius, who had shut himself up in Ravenna. In 410 he assumed the diadem; and, making himself master of the city by force, gave it up to be plundered by his troops. Soon afterwards, while projecting the capture of Sicily and Africa, he died in Lower Italy. His brother-in-law and successor, Adolphus, together with his Goths, left Italy, now completely exhausted, 412, went into Gaul, and from thence proceeding into Spain, founded there the empire of the Visigoths: he carried with him, however, Placidia the sister of Honorius, either as prisoner or as hostage, and married her in Gaul. During these events a usurper arose in Britain and Gaul named Constantine, 407: he was vanquished, and put to death, 411, by Constantius, one of Honorius's generals. This latter prince not only gave Constantius his sister Placidia, who had become a widow and was restored in 417, in marriage, but also named him Augustus in 421. He died, however, a few months after, so that Placidia henceforward had a considerable share in the government. She went, nevertheless, 423, to Constantinople, where she remained until the death of Honorius.

22. *Valentinian III.* 425–455. In this manner was a great part of Spain and part of Gaul cut off from the Roman empire during the reign of Honorius. After his death the secretary John usurped the government, but was defeated by the Eastern emperor Theodosius II. The nephew of Honorius, Valentinian III., a minor, (aged 6–36,) was then raised to the throne, under the guardian care of his mother Placidia (450). Under his miserable reign the Western empire was stripped of almost all her provinces with the exception of Italy. Yet the government of his mother, and afterwards his own incapacity, were as much the cause as the stormy migration of barbarous tribes, which now convulsed all Europe.

Britain had been voluntarily left by the Romans since 427. In Africa, the governor Boniface having been driven into rebellion by the intrigues of the Roman general Ætius, who possessed the ear of Placidia, invited the Vandals from Spain, under the command of Genseric, to come to his assistance. The latter then obtained possession of the country, 429–439; indeed, even as early as 435, Valentinian was obliged to make a formal cession of it to them. Valentinian's wife Eudoxia, a Grecian princess, was purchased by the cession of western Illyricum (Pannonia, Dalmatia, and Noricum); so that of all the countries south of the Danube there now only remained those which belonged to the præfecture of Italy, Rhætia and Vindelicia. On the southeast of Gaul was formed, 435, the kingdom of the Burgundians, which, besides the southeast part of France, comprised also Switzerland and Savoy. The southwest was under the dominion of the Visigoths. There remained only the territory north of the Loire which still submitted to the Roman governors; the last of whom, Syagrius, survived the fall of the empire itself; holding out till the year 486, when he was defeated near Soissons by Clodovicus, or Clovis, king of the Franks.

23. *The Huns. Attila.* But while the Western empire seemed thus of itself almost to fall to pieces, another impetuous rush of nations took place, which threatened the whole of western Europe. The victorious hordes of Huns who now occupied the territory formerly the seat of the Goths, between the Don and the Theiss, and even as far as the Volga, had united themselves since the year 444, under one common

chief, Attila; who, by this union and his own superior talents as a warrior and ruler, became the most powerful prince of his time. The Eastern empire having bought a peace by paying him a yearly tribute, he fell with a mighty army upon the Western provinces. The united forces, however, of the Romans under Ætius and the Visigoths, obliged him near Chalons (*in campis Catalaunicis*) to retreat. Nevertheless, the following year he again invaded Italy, where he had a secret understanding with the licentious Honoria, Valentinian's sister. The cause of his second retreat, which was soon followed by his death, is unknown. The miserable Valentinian soon after deprived the Roman empire of its best general, being led by his suspicions to put Ætius to death. He himself, however, was soon doomed to undergo the punishment of his debaucheries, being murdered in a conspiracy formed by Petronius Maximus, whose wife he had dishonored, and some friends of Ætius, whom he had executed.

24. The twenty years which intervened between the assassination of Valentinian, and the final destruction of the Roman empire in the West, was nearly one continued series of intestine revolutions. No less than nine sovereigns rapidly succeeded one another. These changes, indeed, were but of little importance in this troublesome period, compared to the terror with which Genseric king of the Vandals filled the Roman empire: he by his naval power having become master of the Mediterranean and Sicily, could ravage the coasts of the defenceless Italy at his pleasure, and even capture Rome itself. While in Italy, the German Ricimer, general of the foreign troops in Roman pay, permitted a series of emperors to reign in his name. It would have been his lot to put an end to this series of Augusti, but for mere accident, which reserved that glory for his son and successor, Odoacer, four years after his father's death.

After the death of Valentinian, Maximus was proclaimed emperor; but as he wished to compel Eudoxia, Valentinian's widow, to marry him, she called over Genseric from Africa, who took and pillaged Rome, and Maximus perished after a reign of three months, 455. He was succeeded by M. Avitus, who ascended the throne at Arles; and he again was soon deposed by Ricimer, 456, who, just before, had defeated the fleet of the Vandals. Ricimer now placed upon the throne, first Julianus Majorianus, April 1, 457; but he having distinguished himself in the wars against the Vandals, 461, was set aside, and Libius Severus put in his place, who, however, died in 465, probably of poison. His death was followed by an interregnum of two years, during which Ricimer ruled, though without the title of emperor. At length the patrician Anthemius, then at Constantinople, (where they never gave up their pretensions to the right of naming or confirming the sovereigns of the West,) was, though not without the consent of the powerful Ricimer, named emperor of the West, April 12, 467, by the emperor Leo. But differences having arisen between him and Ricimer, the latter retired to Milan, 469, and commenced a war, in which he took and pillaged Rome, and Anthemius was slain. Ricimer himself followed soon after, Aug. 18, 472. Upon this, Anicius Olybrius, son-in-law of Valentinian III., was proclaimed Augustus, but dying in three months, Oct., 472, Glycerius assumed the purple at Ravenna, without, however, being acknowledged at Constantinople, where they in preference named Julius Nepos Augustus. The latter, in 474, having expelled Glycerius, became also in his turn expelled by his own general Orestes, 475, who gave the diadem to his son Romulus Momyllus, who, as the last in the succession of Augusti, acquired the surname of Augustulus. In 476, however, Odoacer, the leader of the Germans in the Roman pay at Rome, sent him, after the execution of Orestes, into captivity, and allowed him a pension. Odoacer now remained master of Italy till the year 492, when the Ostrogoths, under their king Theodoric, founded there a new empire.

25. Thus fell the Roman empire of the West, while that of the East, pressed on every side, and in a situation almost similar, endured a thousand years, notwithstanding its intestine broils, which would alone have sufficed to destroy any other, and the hosts of barbarians who attacked it during the middle ages. The impregnable situation of its capital, which usually decides the fate of such kingdoms, joined to its despotism, which is not unfrequently the main support of a kingdom in its decline, can alone, in some measure, explain a phenomenon which has no equal in the history of the world.

NOTE.—This chapter is compiled principally from "Heeren, Niebuhr, and Arnold."

MODERN HISTORY.

CHAPTER I.

FEUDAL SYSTEM.

SECTION I.

1. *What are the two revolutions, according to Dr. Robertson, which have exercised the greatest influence on Europe?* The rise and formation of the Roman Empire, and the decline and downfall of the same.

2. *Why is the latter so important to Modern Europe?* Because out of the ruins of the Roman Empire sprang the civilized nations of modern times.

3. *Condition of the Roman Empire, about the time it was overrun?* Government, a military despotism—soldiers often sold the diadem—hence they became corrupted and effeminate—no match for the barbarians in war—in the interior, the worst government prevailed—civil wars were constantly raging—middle classes almost entirely disappeared—two extremes only left, large landholders and miserable rabble—one man would sometimes own for 30 miles around him (Sis. De. and Down. 40).

4. *How then came the empire to endure so long?* Its immense size enabled it to hold together—magnitude of empire creates painful vitality—government of a town could not desolate the town to same extent, that government of a large empire might the empire—some Roman cities of magnitude entirely destroyed by the emperors.

5. *Irruption of the barbarians?* They came from Germany, Swe-

den, Denmark, Poland, Russia, Tartary, and the west of China—for some time, no impression made on the Roman Empire, but at last it lost province after province, until the whole western portion was overrun and settled by barbarians.

6. *Condition of barbarians?* Huns and Tartars were of course nomadic, and those of Europe seem to have been in a sort of mixed state, half agricultural, half shepherd—a situation that gave rise to frequent migrations—they enjoyed great liberty, but of a licentious character, *e. g.*, Clovis and the Vase, chief powerful in war, but not in peace, and often elective.

7. *How came these barbarians to produce so radical a change in manners, customs, laws, and even language of the Romans?* 1st, from causes above explained, the Roman Empire completely exhausted, before its territorial integrity was destroyed. 2d, barbarians came down with wives and children, and consequently carried on an exterminating war to make way for themselves.

8. *Account generally given of the origin of the feudal system?* That it was a defensive system—that the barbarians, finding themselves liable to attack as soon as settled, adopted *deliberately* this system, to guard against fresh swarms—that the king or general of the expedition, divided the conquered country among his superior officers, upon condition of rendering military service, when called on—and these in turn by *subinfeudation* parcelled out their lands among their inferiors on similar conditions—thus, feudal system was as much military as civil—farmer always begirt by his sword, and ready to march at summons of superior.

9. *How came those barbarians, with so much freedom, to tolerate these burthens?* No other service than military required, and barbarians never consider that a burthen.

10. *What condition of the fief at first, and through what stages did it pass?* At first, held by vassal during good behavior, *i. e.* as long as military service was rendered—as vassal would be faithful, soon became an estate for life—then by one more step became hereditary.

11. *Where did the power ultimately lodge?* With the aristocracy; king very little more than a feudal lord.

12. *State of Europe under this system?* At first, supposed a good defence against new swarms of barbarians coming from great Northern Hive—but when lands became hereditary, and all power got into hands of barons, private wars were frequent, because government was too weak to prevent them. All Europe then fell into disorder and confusion, which caused it to plunge deeper and deeper in barbarism till it reached the *Nadir*, about the 10th century—no great expeditions were under-

taken, because barons were more interested in their private, than national wars. Supposed that Europe might easily have been overrun by a powerful nation, but luckily all were in same divided condition.

13. *How came the laws of primogeniture and entails to be engrafted on feudal system?* Entail prevented the alienation of landed property, and the law of primogeniture prevented that subdivision, which would have weakened families too much in those periods of disorder, when individuals were obliged to protect themselves in consequence of feebleness of government—thought best to give all to one, and let him protect the family. Hence, wherever government is weak, and dissensions frequent, it is urged that such expedients will be resorted to for promoting strength of families.

Errors of preceding account.

14. *Mention some causes which have misled British historians on this subject.* The feudal system was introduced into England by William the Conqueror, at once, in its perfect form; hence English writers have too often supposed that barbarians deliberately adopted same system in conquered countries; when in fact it was the slow growth of 600 years on the continent. From seeing the system uniform about the 10th century, they concluded it had always been so—from seeing some fiefs run through the several stages of tenure, *for good behaviour*, *for life*, *and forever*, they concluded all had—therefore at first all were supposed to be for good behavior, when in fact every kind of tenure existed from the very beginning, and it was by the action of various causes, running through a period of 600 years, that the whole was moulded into a uniform system.

15. *Necessary to point out condition of Germans before they overran Roman Empire Tacitus' account?* As before observed, in some agricultural state, great freedom, but licentious—power depended more on personal energy and talent than on property—crown would generally go to the son of king, if able to govern, if not, he would be set aside—tribes were small—sometimes made formidable by confederations. It was the ambition and strength of every chief to be surrounded by young men of promise, to whom presents were made of arms, horses, &c., and in turn fidelity was expected. Barbaric feasts were often given, at which all these companions were present, and they indulged in gluttony and drunkenness; their god was a god of drunkenness—the chief summoned the tribe to arms—sometimes, however, the freemen of the tribe would meet and force the chief to lead them to battle—in all important matters they met in assembly and decided the question by numbers—

the spoils of war enabled the chief to make his presents of arms, horses, &c. to the deserving—feasts, banquets, and presents, together with the spoils of war, constituted the soldiers' pay.

16. *Different tenures by which lands were holden after the conquest of the barbarians?* 1st, allodial; 2d, feudal; 3d, tributary. 1st. Those possessors who owned the fee simple without any other obligation than mere fidelity to the state—name supposed to be derived from *loos*, *sors*, or lot, because the lands were distributed by lot—Franks supposed to have divided principally upon this plan—land would not be given to each soldier, but to chief men in the army, and they would still keep their companions about them, and maintain them as in Germany. 2d. Feudal, when lands were divided on feudal principles, but not so systematically as some have supposed. 3d. Tributary, when the tenant was bound to pay a tribute for the land which he held—when barbarians settled in provinces of the Roman Empire, finding the natives much better farmers than themselves, frequently allowed them to remain on their lands upon the payment of a certain tribute or rent, *e. g.* Lombards exacted third part of the produce from the natives—these farmers called Coloni. When Burgundians settled, each one was quartered on one of the natives, under gentle name of *guest*, but he took largest portion of the produce (H. M. A. 64).

17. *Show the influence produced upon the relation between chief and his tribe by settlement in Roman empire?* In Germany tie was personal —every chief delighted to have a numerous retinue, which he feasted, rewarded and kept about his person. When they settled in Roman provinces *land* became the main article with which the chief rewarded his followers, instead of giving arms, horses, &c., as had been done in Germany—the *personal liaison* of the German forest was then gradually changed into the *real* one of the feudal system—at first all was chaos—all the elements in conflict—the chiefs liked still to have companions about their persons; and yet when lands were given, they had tendency to disperse their companions, and then there were all kinds of tenures, allodial, feudal, and tributary, and all kinds of persons, as slaves, freemen, vassals, and Coloni. It is the presence of every element here which has caused so many different theories on this subject, all of which are partially true.

18. *How came the feudal tenure at length to prevail?* In first place, the allodial lands much more divided, and the possessors not united, hence allodialists not a match for great feudal possessors—again, feebleness of government, and disorder and rapine of society, made it necessary for the small possessors to become dependent on some powerful lord in order that they might be protected, hence the conversion of allodial

into feudal tenures, which was nearly completed through Europe by the 10th century.

19. *Rise of the nobility in Europe?* Two theories; 1st, when province was conquered, the conquerors became the aristocracy, and the conquered the subjects. 2d, that it arose from landed possession. No doubt but conquerors had great privileges at first, as manifested by the difference in *Weregild*, a composition for homicide. But these differences gradually wore away, while the importance of landed possessions became every day greater. In a few generations the Romans and barbarians were blended (Guizot, 212. H. M. A. 69). The quality of feudal possessor had a tendency to become hereditary, while that of *free Frank* or *free Burgundian* was soon lost. Another circumstance which had a strong tendency to build up the aristocracy, was the fact that, in absence of commerce and manufactures, land was almost the only kind of property, and the few who owned it could not easily alienate it, even if disposed, there was nothing to spend it on, except retainers—this circumstance kept property in hands of few, till aristocratic privilege was confirmed.

20. *Assemblies or councils in the feudal kingdoms, and their gradual disuse on the continent?* Germans in their forest assembled their councils, on all great occasions, for double purpose of illustrating the chief, and for deliberation on state matters. When they conquered Roman provinces, the chiefs would naturally at first, for some reasons, assemble their councils—but then, the feudal system would gradually work a change—the division of lands separated widely the principal men, and made each great possessor establish his own little court, and neglect that of the monarch—this produced a system of *insulation* upon the great lords—again, the spirit of individual independence made the great possessor averse to meeting in council when he was placed under the control of the majority, and where his voice was no more potent than that of an inferior possessor—requisitions, too, were sometimes made on the aristocracy through the agency of these councils, by the monarch. Add to this, that the roads and public highways were wretched, and we have the reasons of the almost entire disuse of national councils on the continent.

21. *Character of relation between members of a feudal aristocracy?* An assemblage of individual, isolated landed possessors—each one setting up for himself, a complete spirit of *individuality* prevailed, different from Roman senate, or a house of lords. In the two latter, the voice of the majority prevailed—in the former, each one feeling strong enough to act alone, all union was dissolved, and continental Europe was split into hundreds of principalities.

22. *Effect of this on the continental aristocracies?* Never did any case better illustrate manner, in which societies sometimes overlook *remote* interests, whilst attending to *immediate.* The continental barons were so powerful, that they considered themselves, individually, a match for the king, and, therefore, would not form any union which might impair their individual liberties—hence, when king was finally backed by the power of the new element, the *cities*, he became an overmatch for the disunited nobles, and conquered them in detail. In England, nobles were, from the time of William the Conqueror, too weak for *individual independence*, they united in council, and hence, one potent cause of the liberty of England. Union of the aristocracy of France in great national council might have enabled them to withstand the kings.

23. *Condition of regal power?* Aristocracy grew in power to completion of 10th century, when the power of kings was almost extinct—the regal power, however, was still preserved, and nations prevented from dissolution into mere feudal principalities by three things; 1st, the name and recollection of what the kings had been; 2d, by their great landed possessions, making them greatest of the lords. These possessions in France, greatly augmented by the usurpation of the mayors of the palace, and of Hugh Capet, who added their private possessions to the crown lands; 3d, the organization of the clergy kept up national spirit, and was, in fact, the most energetic body at the downfall of the Roman Empire.

24. *Condition of the people?* Wretched, no trade, no manufactures, no occupation independent of the land, thrown into state of abject dependence on the landholders, constant tendency to degenerate into mere serfs.

25. *Slaves?* Existed in great numbers—this the condition of many of the old Roman citizens who had been spared by the barbarians—again, slave trade existed in all its activity, *e. g.* Venetians supplied Saracens; a slave was valued at about four oxen.

SEC. II.—LITERATURE OF FEUDAL AGES.

Period of about 600 years after subversion of Roman Empire is called the *dark ages*, because of the universal ignorance of the times.

1. *Influence of Roman emperors on literature?* Most of immediate successors of Augustus were a disgrace to humanity, and of course could not be expected to encourage learning, and after the army got into the habit of bestowing imperial purple, illiterate barbarians were often placed on the throne—such men could never patronize learning, and the influence of military government is especially *anti-literary.*

2. *What effect was produced by the subversion of the Western Em-*

pire by the barbarians? This destroyed almost all the remaining literature of the Romans—barbarians were exclusively illiterate. Theodoric, one of the first kings of Italy, and a great chieftain, could not write his name.

3. *What effect was produced by the gradual change of the Latin to the modern languages of French, Spanish, and Italian?* This change gradually shut out from the world the old Roman literature, and as there was, as yet, nothing to compensate for this in the new languages —for a time it added to the general darkness.

4. *Extension of the Latin Language over the western portion of the Roman Empire?* It is well known that the Latin triumphed in all the west except in England, and was even there spoken by the higher classes. All the edicts of the government, laws, &c., were in this language, all aspirants bound to study it. Preaching of the gospel, too, had tendency to diffuse it.

5. *Effect of mere extension on the purity of the language?* Would evidently have a tendency to corrupt it. For, although a civilized nation will give more words to a language in its admixture with a barbarous nation than its proportioned number of inhabitants would indicate, yet the latter will always exert some influence (V. M. A. V. 1. 9).

6. *Intrinsic difficulties of the language which caused a change before irruption of barbarians?* Construction of this language excessively difficult even to natives—Varro says many books were written upon the declension of nouns and conjugation of verbs. Cæsar wrote two books on the analogy and relation of words. Pliny wrote a treatise on doubtful modes of expression—not to wonder that grammar was difficult, and the Roman youth were taught it carefully—*Præcepta latinè loquendi puerilis doctrina tradit.* Besides, there was great difficulty in *orthography.* The grammarians contended for rule and etymology; others, and Augustus was of this class, spelt as they pronounced (V. 51). The great complexity of terminations gave rise to frequent use of preposition to supply place of termination (72). Augustus even adopted often this innovation for the sake of perspicuity.

7. *Influence of the irruption of barbarians?* They adopted language of the conquered—when two people mix the one with most *ideas* will give the most *words.* But complexity of Latin terminations would soon give rise to the use of prepositions instead of terminations; *e. g.* Donabo *ad conjux.* Donatio *de omnia bona.* In præsentia *de judices* (V. 72). Again, difficulty about gender, would lead to a *barbarous* sort of uniformity, *e. g.* in Pope Zachariah's time, baptism, in the north of Europe celebrated in *nomine de patria, et filia, et spiritua sancta* (68). Italy, of course, would be last to undergo these changes, *e. g.* when

Charlemagne came to Rome, people huzzaed him in good Latin. Vivat Carolus, Augustus, Imperator. At this time *pure Latin* had disappeared from France and Spain. The Latin language was defective in regard to the article—barbarians used the pronoun *ille* instead, whence by contraction we have the *le* and *la* of the French, and the *il* and *lo* and *la*, of the Italians. Again, the Latin verb is very complex in its conjugation, hence the use of the auxiliary verbs, (V. 93.) for the same reason, that prepositions were used instead of terminations in the declension of nouns.

The difference between the spelling and pronunciation would soon lead to great corruption, this commenced even under Augustus. With ignorant, constant tendency to drop the unpronounced letters, *e. g.*, *nolege* for *knowledge*, *Gloster* for *Gloucester*, &c. In same way, constant tendency among barbarians to drop letters and syllables of Latin words, *e. g.*, *Domnus* for *Dominus*, in St. Ambrose's time, and, in some places, it was contracted down to *Dom*, *Don*, *Dueno*, (75) so *populus* became *poplus* and *poplo*. Barbarians did not know the distinction of grammarians between *ubi* and *quo*, they used *ubi* in both senses, it was pronounced *oubi*, was contracted to *oub*, and then to *où*, which is French. Whilst Latin words were changing, barbarian words were Latinised, *e. g.* German word *war-herr*, became *guerra*, and then *guerre*, which is French for *war*. In same way, we have *battalia*, *battaille*, French, and *battle*, English. Thus, about the 9th century, the Latin in Spain and France had undergone an almost entire change, and the modern Italian was beginning to be formed. Languages had become chaotic, and required the reforming hand of time, to establish their rules, *e. g.* the oath of Louis the German, in 842, "*pro deo amur*, *et pro christian poplo et nostro commun salvament*, *&c.*" "For the love of God, and for the christian people and for our common safety, &c." In this oath, and in that of the French people, we observe that juxtaposition, and not terminations and articles, points out the regulation of words, *e. g. pro deo amur*, same thing often occurs in modern French, *e. g. Fete-Dieu*, *Hotel-Dieu*. In these two documents some pure Latin words, *e. g. donat*, *jurat*, *conservat*, *&c.* (79).

8. *General depression of literature during the dark ages?* It almost exceeds belief. In the best schools, the *Trivium* and *Quadrivium* only were taught; 1st contained grammar, logic, and rhetoric; 2d, arithmetic, geometry, music, and astronomy. But scanty as this catalogue is, apt to give an exaggerated idea, *e. g.* arithmetic of Cassiodorus, the minister of Theodoric, is a few definitions with some superstitious absurdities on the virtues of certain numbers, without a single one of the common rules—it occupies a little more than two folio pages. His ge-

ometry equally contemptible, only a few definitions and axioms. His grammar and rhetoric no better. His logic is best, and extends to 16 pages (H. L. 2, 3). For many centuries, rare for a layman to know how to sign his name. Charters, till seals were introduced, signed with the mark of a cross. Hence to *sign* originally meant to make the *signum crucis*, and not to write one's name. Greatest monarchs could not write, e. g. Charlemagne, and at much later period, Frederic Barbarossa, greatest monarch of his age, could not read. Du Guesclin, the greatest general of his age, could neither read nor write. Nor could John, king of Bohemia, even in the middle of the 14th century. Very few men of any learning, and they were confined to the church—ignorance of clergy even standing theme of reproach at all the councils, *e. g.* one in Rome 992, asserted not a clergyman of letters in Rome—not one priest of 1000 in Spain in time of Charlemagne, could write a letter of salutation to another. In England, Alfred could not recollect a single priest south of the Thames, (most civilized part of England,) who understood the ordinary prayers, or could translate Latin into his mother tongue. During this age of ignorance, contracts made verbally for want of notaries capable of drawing them up. (H. M. A. 459.) General ignorance greatly increased by growing scarcity of books produced by conquest of Alexandria by the Saracens in beginning of 7th century. This stopped the importation of Egyptian papyrus into Europe, which was the most common and cheapest writing material—afterwards obliged to use parchment, much dearer. Hence monks so often erased classic works to make way for their own miserable legends and absurdities. Hence, books were so dear, none but rich men could purchase them, *e. g.* Countess of Anjou, after the invention of paper, paid 200 sheep, 5 quarters of wheat, and as much rye and millet, for a copy of the Homilies of Haiman (Rob. P. and J. note R). Even so late as 1471, when Louis 11th borrowed from faculty of medicine at Paris the works of Rasis, Arabian physician, he deposited a considerable quantity of plate, besides getting a wealthy nobleman to join him in a bond for the return of the books. Art of making paper from rags was introduced in the 11th century.

9. *Circumstances which preserved the Latin language and Latin literature, during the dark ages?* Hallam thinks the Latin language, upon which revival of literature depended, would have been lost but for three circumstances. 1st, the supremacy of the Pope; 2d, the establishment of monasteries; 3d, use of Latin liturgy, and the Latin Bible, all of which we now condemn. 1st, the papal supremacy rendered it necessary to cultivate some common language in which head of the church could correspond with all its members through Christendom—

Latin was that language. 2d, not only did the idle monks have rather more leisure to become learned than other men, but their monasteries became the safest depositories for books, and thus many classic works were preserved. Luckily, too, St. Benedict, whose order was most numerous, enjoined among other rules, that the Benedictines should read, copy and collect books. Perhaps this rule, coupled with great dearness of parchment, may explain the introduction of the *cursive* or *running hand* instead of the use of capital letters, and also the *minute* writing of the monks, which at later period degenerated into mere trifling, *e. g.* Homer's Iliad, copied on parchment that might be crammed into a nut shell, and Peter Bales, calligraphist under Elizabeth, wrote out the whole Bible on very thin leaves, which were put into an English walnut no bigger than a hen's egg. (D. I. C. L. V. 1, 371.) There is now in imperial library of Vienna, a specimen of this minute writing, a piece of parchment 8 inches by 6 contains Pentateuch, book of Ruth, Ecclesiasticus and the Canticles in Latin, Esther in Syriac, and Deuteronomy in French. 3d, the liturgy and the Bible were both in Latin, and consequently priests were obliged to study Latin to read these, although we condemn this practice of preserving the Scriptures and liturgy only in a dead language, not to imagine the sole object was to conceal them from the vulgar—superstitious veneration for ancient customs had its effect. For similar reason, the Egyptians or Jacobites performed service in Coptic—Nestorians in Syriac—Abyssinians in old Ethiopic, and the prayers of the Mahommedans are to this day offered in Arabic (Wad. 297). Still this custom was one for which the church was culpable, as tending to keep the people in ignorance. Thus three circumstances, each of which we now condemn, constituted, according to Hallam, the bridge which brought the Latin language over the *chasm* of the dark ages.

10. *When did Europe reach her lowest point of depression?* Hume and Robertson fix on the 10th century. This is probably true as to England, and perhaps Italy, but Hallam and Guizot fix on the 7th, as the Nadir of the human mind in France and Germany, and its movement in advance began under Charlemagne in the next century. In Germany the 10th century was one of considerable enlightenment compared with preceding (H. L. E. 3). One reason perhaps of historians fixing on 10th century as that of greatest depression may be the confusion and alarm existing in Europe towards conclusion of that century about destruction of world, founded on a prophecy drawn from the 2d and 3d verses of the 20th chapter of the Apocalypse, that Satan would be let loose to deceive the nations, and that fire would come down from heaven after a little while to devour him. As the end of the century approached, a universal panic spread through Christendom. The pen

of historian stopped. Charters are to be found in all countries about this time beginning with these words, "*Appropinquante fine mundi*," "as the end of the world is approaching." Donations were made to churches, and monasteries—enemies were reconciled—prisoners loosed—slaves set free—ordinary motives of action were suspended—passions lulled—cultivation of the soil was neglected—mankind stood like condemned criminals, counting the hours that were left. About this time not to wonder that an eclipse of the sun should have dispersed the whole army of Otho the Great (Sis. 468, Wad. 261). But for some doubts as to chronology, and the force of habit which triumphs over irregular impression, the prophecy would hence come near realizing itself by stopping cultivation, and putting an end to the ordinary occupation of society.

SEC. III.—MANNERS, CUSTOMS, LAWS, &c. OF THE FEUDAL AGES.

In order to be able to form a proper estimate of the feudal possessor, we must do what M. Guizot has done (L. 4, C. D. H. M.). Must look into the feudal mansion or chateau, to the family of the owner, and ascertain in first place the effect which his mere *physical* condition exerts on his *moral.*

1. *Physical condition of the feudal proprietor?* Aimed to establish his castle on some elevated isolated spot, which could be rendered strong and impregnable—at his table appeared his wife, his children, and small number of free men, not yet landholders, attached to his person, and who lived on his hospitality. These the only inmates of his dwelling, around the castle were the serfs, the coloni, and tenants, who cultivated the lands of the possessor. In the midst of this inferior population, was the humble church, in which the same preacher officiated, who acted as chaplain of the castle.

2. *Effect of physical condition on the character of the feudal possessor?* First marked effect is to make him a man of prodigious importance in his own estimation, and that of those who surround him—he has that sentiment of *personality*, of individual liberty, which the barbarian had in the forest. But he has much more, he feels his importance as landholder—he is the chief of the family and the master of those who surround him—he feels an immense superiority, and a superiority of a very peculiar character. When compared with Roman patrician, found that the latter was chief and priest of the family, master of slaves, &c. He was besides member of the senate, and a subject of most powerful nation on earth—though he had individual importance, yet not like that of feudal possessor—his character of citizen, of member of a corporation, prevailed over his mere individual character. His political character and his honors came from the state—he was but an

element of the mighty system around him, a small part of a great whole. But the possessor of a great fief was purely individual, all his power within himself, though perhaps holding nominally of the king. He was no member of a senate or corporation, all his importance centred in himself—he expected nothing from without. Thus, with no equal around him, with no superior above him, for in the decay of regal power, the king was but a great lord—in his sphere, his will was law—he was restrained by no external power—he was the centre and the soul of the baronial government—in fine, feudal lord must have been the *proudest being on earth.*

3. *Influence of the family of the castle on the feudal lord, and of the female character?* There being no social intercourse between the laborers on the land and the small family of the lord, consequence was, the latter were entirely dependent on themselves for social pleasures, and, however brutal the lord might be—when war and the chase was over he was thrown upon his family. His wife and children would thus become more essential to him—hence one powerful cause for elevation of female character.

4. Compare the condition of feudal lord, with that of the patriarch of the Old Testament, and the chief of a Scottish clan. Patriarch lived in common with a numerous tribe of descendants, relations and slaves—he was engaged in same occupations, had similar interests with the rest. Woman not elevated, her condition rather servile—men not thrown upon a small family for domestic happiness—lived too much in common for the elevation of the fair sex, which requires home and a fireside. In the other family system—the *clan*, some marked differences—true between chief of clan, and followers, more diversity of condition than in patriarchal state—all do not follow same occupations, but then they are supposed to come from a common origin—have a common name—common traditions, community of interests, which produce a moral tie and a sort of equality unknown to the feudal lord and the society around the castle—this state moreover not so favorable to female importance as the feudal system.

5. *Effects of the lord's condition on his notions of property?* Calculated to give him high ideas of his rights in this respect—all disputes turned on questions about landed property. The lord lived in his castle and defended his property till it seemed part of himself—it is this sacredness of property—this notion of *meum et tuum* caused by the feudal system, that lies at the bottom of those obstinate struggles made by the English barons against usurpation of kings.

6. *Relation between lord and the laborers and tenants?* M. Guizot thinks it one of unmixed hatred—not so at first, when dependence

was complete, relation was one of kindness and harmony. But where this tie began to be severed, and the serfs and coloni to gain their liberty, then came on the period of hatred, such as manifested itself by Wat Tyler's insurrection in England, and by that of the peasants of Germany, in Luther's time. Same thing observable about negro slavery, where it is complete, relation one of kindness, but when the law interposes and inspires negro with notions of freedom, then there is insolence on one side and revenge and cruelty on the other, *e. g.* British government decreed that negroes of Demarara should not be whipped without regular sentence of magistrate, and soon Lord Stanley complained that there never had been so many lashes given in Demarara, as since the passage of the law.

7. *Influence of the priest?* At first the chaplain of the palace and the priest of the village church were united in same person, became distinct afterwards. Priest in great majority of cases too much afraid of the lord to act with independence. But still, auricular confession and discharge of common religious duties would give him great influence both in and out of the castle.

8. *Relation between feudal possessors?* Tenures on which fiefs were held produced a deep moral effect. Obligation to protect on one side, to render military service on the other—hence immense importance of fidelity to obligations—whole system turned on this. Only two guarantees, the mere moral obligation resulting from the nature of the contract, and the sword—hence perhaps those peculiar notions of fidelity to engagements and loyalty to superiors, so much more characteristic of the feudal ages than the mere state of civilization would indicate.

9. *Right of private war, and its consequences?* Wherever government is too weak to restrain and punish, individuals will act for themselves—hence right of private war in feudal ages. Barons relied on themselves and not on government for protection—hence all Europe exhibited one scene of confusion owing to the constant wars between barons. Force was the principal guarantee, *e. g.*, in *Magna Charta*, barons stipulate that if King John violates their privileges, they may enter sword in hand on the royal demesnes, and seize sufficient plunder to indemnify for the outrage, taking care not to injure the king, his wife, or children, and when the indemnity is thus forcibly obtained, the baron is to return to his allegiance. It was constancy of private war which rendered allodial property insecure, and forced its possessors throughout Europe to convert into feudal for sake of protection. The church endeavored to check these wars, and the occasional proclamation of the *truce of God* was one of its expedients. Monarchs too, labored to the same end, but none except Charlemagne succeeded—old barons

of the feudal ages clung to this right as we would to the *habeas corpus* privilege, or the trial by jury.

10. *Administration of justice?* Has passed through three stages in modern Europe, the popular, aristocratic and regal. Barbarians of Germany as jealous of these rights as of any others—hence division into *decades* of families, each decade had its own magistrate, called *tithing man* among the Anglo-Saxons, and *decanus* among the Franks and the Lombards. Next above, came the *centenarians* or *hundredary*, judging over 100 families (H. M. A. 107).

11. For similar reasons, county courts and a sort of jury trials were established in England. These tribunals all of a popular character. But with rise of feudal system the great barons gradually usurped judicial powers, till baronial courts superseded all others. This baronial jurisdiction was in turn superseded by the regal tribunals when kings became more powerful, and laws were made and enforced more regularly.

12. *Different modes of trial?* Barons of feudal ages understood use of the sword better than law—hence, instead of unravelling the intricacies of law, they adopted a short method of determining guilt or innocence. The superstition and ignorance of the times led them to believe that God would always interfere to save the innocent, and confound the guilty—hence various modes of appealing to judgment of God, such as by cross, boiling water, ploughshares, corsned, &c., *e. g.*, when bishop of Paris and abbot of St. Denis carried their dispute about patronage of monastery before Pepin the Short, latter confused by the opposite claims decreed the *judicium crucis* as mode of trial—each chose his man—two champions crossed their arms and held them out in form of cross, and the case was adjudged in favor of abbot, because his man held his arms longest without letting them fall. Earl Godwin is said to have met with his death from trial by the corsned. Something like the last still practised among the Siamese, who give certain consecrated purgative pills, and he who retains them longest, gains the cause. Trial by the *bleeding corpse* was very common, especially in England. Person accused, made to touch body, if blood gushed out guilty. (Cu. of Lit. V. 1, 221.) Difficult to see how persons accused, could escape under some of the trials, *e. g.*, handling hot iron—a mode of proof to which Charlemagne was very partial. (H. 463.) Has been said that Emma, wife of Edward the Confessor, proved her innocence, not by treading between 9 red hot ploughshares, as Blackstone supposes, but on them. Similar anecdote related of Cunegunda, wife of Emperor Henry II. Probably the clergy, before whom these trials took place, had some sort of legerdemain by which the usual consequences might be averted.

13. *Trial by combat?* But of all different modes of trial by judg-

ment of God, that by judicial combat became most fashionable, because most accordant with martial spirit of the age. Noblemen fought on horseback with all the usual arms of attack and defence—the plebeian on foot with club and target—if the accused gained victory, he was innocent, if beaten, guilty. Women and ecclesiastics appeared by champions, *e. g.*, Rebecca in Ivanhoe is vindicated by Wilfred of Ivanhoe, who appears as her champion. Celebrated question whether the sons of a father who died before the grandfather should be permitted to share the grandfather's estate with the uncles, was decided by this mode of trial, and as the champion of the nephews was victorious, it settled the law in their favor. In the 11th century contest between two rival liturgies in Spain was decided in same way. A pair of knights in complete armor fought and decided which was the orthodox one. Even when a cause was tried in court, condemned party could challenge each one of the judges, and if he conquered in one day all of them, he was acquitted, and the court condemned, or he might call first judge who decided against him to the field, and if he conquered, sentence was reversed, though the court was not impeached. In the same way, witnesses might be challenged and convicted of falsehood by this sort of martial logic. (H. 110.)

14. *Testimony?* Not to suppose the barons of middle ages acquainted with all the modern science of the law of evidence. In many cases testimony was weighed according to the wealth of individuals who gave it, *e. g.*, testimony of a man valued at 120 shillings counterbalanced that of 6 ceorls, valued each at 20 shillings—again the general proneness to perjury, together with ignorance of the judges, was cause of the curious practice of obliging persons to bring into court *compurgators*, men who knew nothing of the facts, but who swore that they believed the individual for whom they appeared had told the truth. These were sometimes multiplied to 300 and were generally 12, or some multiple of 12.

15. *Punishment for crimes—pecuniary compensation?* Throughout all the barbaric codes, we find the principle of pecuniary compensation for crime to prevail. The life of every man had a value affixed to it, which was called his *weregild*, *e. g.*, king's weregild in England was 30,000 thrismas, about £1300, prince's 15,000 thrismas, bishop's 8000, sheriff's 4000, a thane's or clergyman 2000, a ceorl's 266. By the laws of Kent the archbishop's head was higher than that of the king. (H. E. V. 1, 139.) On the continent, the same principle prevailed with great variety as to the amount, *e. g.*, among the Francs Saliens and Ripuiares, an antrustion, or nobleman in *truste regia*, valued at 606 solidi or shillings. Among the Francs Saliens, same character killed in his house

by armed band, valued at three-fold price, or 1800 solidi. A freeman in general among the Germans valued at 160 solidi. A man of middle class was valued among Burgundians at 100 solidi—among the same, slave, if a *skilful workman*, valued at 150 solidi, freedman of the church among Germans at 80. A slave used for body service among Burgundians at 55, serfs of the church, and of the king among Germans, and the tributary Romans among the Francs Saliens, at 45, hogminder among the Burgundians was at 30, and a slave among Bavarians, 20. (G. Essay 20.) Other offences, besides homicide, punished in this way, *e. g.*, among Anglo-Saxons, a wound of one inch under hair valued at one shilling, but in face at two shillings—ear was valued at 30 shillings its loss always been considered great disgrace. Adultery subjected offender to a fine, and to buy injured man another wife. (H. E. p. 140.) Various principles determined a man's weregild, usefulness or scarcity of class to which killed belonged, whether barbarian or Roman, whether noble or not, the mode of killing, &c., all had their influence.

16. *Circumstances which gave rise to the principle of pecuniary composition in all the barbaric codes?* As the governments of Europe were very feeble, they were unable to execute severer punishments. Such kings as Alfred and Charlemagne, would sometimes enforce more rigid laws, but generally it was impossible. Individuals trusted to themselves or their immediate superiors and not to government for protection—hence private wars and private revenge, this right recognized and even sometimes encouraged by the government, *e. g.*, by Salic law any man by declaration might exempt himself from his family quarrels, but then not considered as belonging to the family, and deprived of right of succession for his cowardice. Pecuniary composition, first step in advance, to check this tendency to individual strife. Hence not peculiar to Germanic nations, we find it among Greeks at siege of Troy, *e. g.*, Nestor's speech to Achilles in 9th Iliad. It prevailed among Irish when a man's value was called his *erie*. It prevailed too among the Jews (H. V. 1, 140).

17. *Field sports of the feudal ages?* Hunting and hawking two great amusements in peace—a knight rarely left his house without a falcon on his wrist and greyhound by his side, *e. g.* Harold thus represented in the old tapestry of Bayeux. Tombs of ladies often with falcon on them, for women joined in falconry. Clergy indulged in these sports—councils endeavored to prevent them, but of no avail. In 774 monastery of St. Denis, which had been interdicted these sports, got back privilege from Charlemagne, on ground that fresh meat was good for sick monks, and the skins to bind books with. Alexander III. by a letter to clergy of Berkshire, dispenses with their keeping the archdeacon in dogs and hawks during his visitation. An archbishop of York

in 1321 had a train of two hundred persons, and hunted with pack of hounds from parish to parish. (H. M. A. 470.)

18. *Forest laws?* Intended to protect game—existed in all feudal countries—grew out of excessive love for field sports—penalties very severe, *e. g.* under Norman kings till time of *Magna Charta* killing *stag or wild boar* punished with death. French code less severe, but even Henry IV. made it pain of death to chase deer often in royal parks.

19. *State of agriculture?* Very low. 1st. Small portion of land cultivated, owing to large amount kept in forest for the sake of hunting. 2d. Most of lands in hands of aristocracy, who took more pleasure in war and hunting than agriculture. Great feudal possessor would beautify and cultivate small part around the castle but neglect the rest.

20. *Trade and commerce?* Excessively oppressed. No great manufactory for several centuries in all Europe. Rich men kept artisans among their slaves to do all their work. Even kings in 9th century had their clothes made by women on the farms. Tools of tradesmen very rude and cheap, *e. g.* at Colchester in 1296 and 1301 carpenter's stock valued at 1 shilling, and consisted of only 5 tools. Other tradesmen in proportion, except tanner, whose stock was valued at £9 7*s.* 10*d.* Latter greatest trade of times, owing to the clothing being made of skins. (H. M. A. 491.) There was scarcely any commerce, for all the highways were infested with robbers, and the water with pirates. Even greatest nobles joined in robbery, *e. g.* Harold son of Godwin, when wrecked on coast of Ponthieu, imprisoned by lord, *according to custom of the country.* Throughout Germany great lords were robbers. For these reasons movable property but little regarded, and hence cities were small and miserable, for they had no trade or manufactures.

21. *Houses?* Nobles lived in circular towers of thick walls, with no light for lower rooms except from loop-holes and from opening above. Houses of common people of very inferior character, covered with straw, and so open that wind whistled through them; hence the invention of *lantern*, ascribed to reign of Alfred, so important. Hangings in houses of the more wealthy supplied place of wainscoting. *Chimneys* not introduced commonly till middle of 14th century—before that time smoke went out at an aperture in centre of the building; and windows, though known early, were not much in use before 14th century—they were of great price and not considered part of the freehold, *e. g.* as late as time of Elizabeth, when Earl of Northumberland left Alnwick Castle, windows were taken out and carried with him. (H. M. A. 491.)

22. *Furniture?* Very scanty. Not more than two or three beds in best houses—a change of straw every night was considered great luxury. In inventory of goods belonging to Contarini, a rich Venetian

trader, as late as 1481, there were 10 beds, glass windows *movable*—no chairs or looking-glasses—Skepton Castle in England, century after, not equal to this; although residence of the great Earl of Cumberland not more than seven or eight beds, and no chairs, glasses or carpets. Silver plate very rare—£94 worth of plate in John Port's house in 1524 reckoned very great. Man and his wife, and sometimes whole family, ate off the same plate. In romance of Perceforest told of a feast where 800 knights had a lady each eating off his plate—drank out of a common bowl—no wooden-handled knives, nor more than one or two drinking cups to a family. There were no wax or tallow candles in Italy even as late as time of Frederic II.—servants held a torch to eat supper by. (H. M. A. 486.)

23. *Food and drink?* A mixture of vegetable and animal food—swine principal flesh—fish and eels much eaten, particularly the last, eels frequently included in the rent of land, *e. g.* Monks of Ramsey made a yearly present of 4000 eels to those of Peterborough. We read of two places purchased where 16000 eels could annually be caught, and they were valued at £21 per annum. Liquors were ale, cider, mead and wine. In the feudal ages, as will always be the case with semi-barbarians, who have a great deal of idle time, they indulged at their feasts in gluttony and drunkenness.

24. *Money?* During the middle ages, in consequence of the private wars, rapine and confusion, the mines of Europe not worked; and consequently, although the wealth to be circulated was small, yet the circulating medium was still smaller in proportion; hence the great value of money during those ages. As society became more settled, even before the discovery of the mines of South America, money gradually fell in value. Hallam thinks it was about 24 or 25 times more valuable in time of Henry III. and Ed. I. than now. In time of Hen. VI. 16 times more valuable, and in commencement of 16th century about 12 times.

25. *Mode of estimating relative values of money at different ages?* No method complete, inasmuch as there is no perfect standard of value. *Necessaries* from century to century vary least, and therefore form the best practical standard, *e. g.* in time of H. 3, and E. 1, bushel of wheat sold generally for 6 pence, and barley and oats in proportion. A sheep was sold well at 1 shilling, and an ox at 10 or 12. Hallam says a multiple of 30 will bring meat into present English prices, and a multiple of 18 or 20 is required for wheat, so that the average will make money twenty-five-fold more valuable then than now. (H. M. A. 498.)

26. *Comparison between estates of middle ages and of present time?* After allowing for change in money estates in England now will be

found larger than formerly, *e. g.*, £10 or £20 per annum large estate for a gentleman under H. III., and a knight who possessed £150 per annum extremely wealthy. Sir John Fortescue speaks of £5 per annum as a fair living for a yeoman. When Sir William Drury, one of the richest men in Suffolk, bequeathed 50 marks to each of his daughters, which was considered fine legacy, the amount was not more than 4 or £500 now—supposed liberality of this bequest marks two facts, 1st, that daughters were generally not well provided for; 2d, that but few men had ready money. As late as 1514 whole expense of a student at Oxford only £5, about £60 now. A curious entry in church warden's account of St. Margaret, Westminster, for 1476, gives some idea of lawyers' fees "also paid to Roger Fylpot, learned in the law, for his counsel, giving 3*s.* 8*d.* with 4*d.* for his dinner"—multiple of 15 will bring it to present prices. Northumberland household book for 1512 rates earl's family at 166 persons, masters and servants; he had an average of 57 guests each day. Meat, drink and fuel, to each one per diem rated at 2*d.* 2*f.*—£1000 whole expense per annum of housekeeping—wheat was 8*d.* 2*f.* per bushel. Most exact account was kept of the quantity and quality of meat consumed—contains even the orders for mustard, of which 166 pounds were consumed per annum.

27. *Who had greatest command over the necessaries and comforts of life, the laborer of the middle ages or of the present times?* Hallam decides in favor of the former, *e. g.*, in the 14th century harvest man had 4*d.* a day, common laborer under H. VI. earned 3*d.* per diem. By act of parliament in 1350, wages of reapers put at 3*d.* a day, without diet; in 1444 at 5*d.* Yearly wages of a chief *hind* or shepherd at £1 4*s.*, those of common servant in husbandry at 18*s.* 4*d.* with meat and drink. Now with these wages laborer could purchase more bread and meat than now. (H. M. A. 500.) This however not decisive, for although he could buy more food, he could get less of other things—manufactures were dear then, cheap now—he got more food and less comfort.

28. Remarks on usual mode of estimating relative value of money in different ages. A comparison of the prices of the necessaries of life forms perhaps the best criterion; but that is not entirely correct, because, with the progress of population and capital in any given country the price of necessaries becomes dearer and dearer, from the necessity of resorting to inferior lands, *e. g.*, wheat and meat are much higher in England than in Poland; and in our country much higher in Massachusetts than in Indiana and Illinois. Yet the values of money in these places cannot be fixed in the inverse ratios of these prices. So likewise England of 11th and 12th century is to England of the present day

something like Poland to England now—hence Hallam has, I think, rather overrated the value of money in former times, not remembering that corn was formerly *absolutely* cheaper than now, owing to the sparseness of population and the great quantity of land in proportion to capital and labor to work it.

29. *Summary of evils and advantages of feudal system?* Destroyed national governments—produced private wars—was period of anarchy and confusion and individual oppression. But deep and dark as was barbarism of those ages, some compensating advantages—favorable to energy and greatness of individual character—hence a period of brilliant history, a period of great events and great men ; chivalry, the crusades, the rise of modern languages, of modern literature, and modern manners, illustrate it. Even the oppression not without its antidote—oppressor and oppressed close together—it was a collection of individual despotisms—not one great despotism where all are reduced to a common level—king had his great vassals, and these in turn had theirs. The spirit of liberty was kept alive in the aristocracy, and by them communicated to the *subvassals*, thus the whole mass was leavened. Downfall of Roman empire not to be regretted, it exercised a crushing influence which repressed individual exertion—tide of civilization was rapidly ebbing under its action. Fortunate for Europe that barbarians could not erect a great empire. Feudal system destroyed *centralization* and broke Europe into a number of political elements, which slowly coalesced into the civilized kingdoms of modern times. Without this change the principle of *immobility* might have reigned in Europe as in Asia. It was this system which first gave notion of sacredness of property, *e. g.*, look in old law books, and see accurate limitations of services of vassalage—the reciprocity of obligation between lord and vassal, consent of all required to general measures, and the administration of justice by one's peers. Again, after downfall of Roman empire, society sank into revolting vices, most prominent were falsehood, treachery, and ingratitude. "Feudal spirit purged off the lees of this corruption," violation of faith utterly at war with essence of a feudal tenure. Feudal law books breathe throughout a spirit of honorable obligation. In the reciprocal services of lord and vassal ample scope for magnanimous energy, and the exercise of the kindliest feelings of our nature—from this relation sprang that sentiment of personal reverence and attachment towards the sovereign, called *loyalty*, distinguished both from stupid devotion of eastern slaves, and the abstract respect of citizens of a republic for chief magistrate—this feeling has had its day, it was the conservative principle of society, and was to feudal monarchies as valuable as patriotism in republics. (H. M. A. 124.)

Out of the feudal system too arose the institution of chivalry and the elevation of the female sex, which has made modern manners and civilization totally different from those of the ancient world.

CHAPTER II.

CHIVALRY.

1. *Importance of chivalry?* Had powerful agency in the formation of modern manners and civilization—it is connected with our tales of romance, and interwoven with our early poetry. Besides, had the effect of remedying somewhat disorders of the times, and hastening the flood-tide of civilization.

2. *What seems to have been the presiding spirit in the institution of chivalry?* Spirit of honor. Three spirits, according to Hallam, have reigned at different times, spirit of *liberty*, of *religion*, and of *honor*, *e. g.*, 1st, in Grecian and Roman republics; 2d, in many of eastern nations, and in Europe during period of reformation, and 100 years after it; 3d, during the time of chivalry. (H. M. A. 509.)

3. *Origin of chivalry?* 1st. Theory on this subject, that the institution was regularly formed for a special object, that Europe had fallen into great disorder—governments were unable to protect—hence the weak everywhere fell a prey to the strong, that the order of chivalry was established to remedy these disorders, *parcere subjectis et debellare superbos*, to succor the oppressed and humble the proud, was the motto of the order; hence women, being the most defenceless portion of society, became the peculiar objects of protection, and as faithlessness was cause of much disorder, knights were to be peculiarly observant of plighted faith. 2d. Theory of Guizot and his school, that chivalry was not regular institution at first, that it gradually grew out of the custom mentioned by Tacitus among the Germans, of using certain ceremonies when the youth were admitted to bear arms; *e. g.*, in full assembly of tribe one of the chiefs, or the father of the young man, presented to him his armor, his sword and lance, and thus made him a warrior and a member of the republic; that in process of time the imagination and the spirit of religion would gradually invent new ceremonies, and the disorders of the times would give to it the character of a regular institution, supplying in some measure the defects of government.

4. *Influence of feudal system on the German custom mentioned*

by Tacitus? When barbarians settled in Roman empire the division of lands would naturally disperse the members of the conquering tribes, but two circumstances would retain a large number about the persons of the great feudal lord; 1st, the officers of his little court; 2d, education of the sons of the inferior vassals. 1st. Just after settlement of barbarians we see great chiefs having about person officers similar to those of Roman emperor, *e. g.*, constable, maréchal, chamberlain, cupbearer, &c. In Germanic empire each of the electors had some one of these offices about the emperor, *e. g.*, count palatine of the Rhine was *grand maréchal*, marquis of Brandenburg, *grand chamberlain*, king of Bohemia, *cupbearer*, &c., and three archbishops were *arch-chancellors*. (Pfister, T. 5. 18.) All these offices at the little *baronial courts* were held upon feudal tenures precisely like the lands, except that they did not so often become hereditary, and we find beside the great offices of constable, chamberlain, &c., there were *pages*, *varlets*, and *squires*—of the latter many kinds, *e. g.*, squire of the body, of the hall, of the stable, and even the *carving squires*. These offices of course had tendency to keep a number of persons about lord's person. 2dly. The inferior vassals soon adopted the practice of sending their sons to be brought up at the court of the castle—several reasons gave rise to this. Great lord richer and more powerful than smaller possessors who held of him—hence latter proud to send their sons to be in attendance on former, that they might live in higher sphere—one way too of often attaching the lord to his vassal. Besides, we like to be where there is most to interest and to engage our attention, and where there is most movement and excitement—the court of the great lord presented such a theatre, *e. g.*, Froissart's account of the Earl of Foix, and his castle, "all honor ther was found, all manner of tidynges of every realme and country ther might be herde, four out of every countre there was resort, for the valyantnesse of this erle." (Sir W. S. 129.) On other hand, great lord liked to have many of his vassals' sons under his eye, where he might train them to fidelity and attachment, and know their dispositions, and hold them somewhat as hostages. (G. H. G. T. 4. 187.) Thus from the two causes mentioned the interior of the lord's castle was peopled; and as the old German custom of conferring arms and initiating into military service by public ceremony was not discontinued, a few more ceremonies being added, it gradually turned to the process of knighting; and the education and training of the knight sprang out of the custom of sending sons of vassals to the castle to be brought up by the lord. This is Guizot's account of chivalry.

5. *Characteristics of chivalry in its most perfect form?* Love of

arms, romantic spirit of adventure, courtesy of manners, the point of honor, and devoted and respectful attention to the female sex.

6. *Different stages through which the candidate for knighthood passed before he was knighted?* 1st, He was from 7 to 14 called page, varlet, or damoiseau; 2d, from 14 to 21 escuyer, esquire or squire; 3dly, at 21 was knighted.

7. *Education and duties of the page?* At early age, generally from 7 to 12, youth was sent to some celebrated knight to be educated in his castle—he was at this stage to learn modesty, obedience, and address in arms—he learnt to manage the horse, to use the bow and the sword—he wore a hood instead of helmet, and tilted against the quintaine to learn the use of the lance. His services sometimes menial though they did not degrade. Attended his master in the chase, blew the horn, was ordered up to despatch the deer when at bay—he waited on the master and mistress, attended them in their journeys and visits, waited on the table, &c., *e. g.*, celebrated Chevalier Bayard attended bishop of Grenoble as page on a visit to duke of Savoy, and waited on him at table. Page taught to reverence knighthood—first impression made on his mind amid the ladies of the court was that of love, gallantry, honor, bravery, and religion—to this end early taught to select some lady as his mistress—to her he displayed all his gallantry, told all his secrets, made her judge of all his actions, sought her counsel in all emergencies, and received smallest gifts and cherished them as most valuable objects on earth. Romantic love of the knight often traced back to the page, *e. g.*, in romance of "*The Golden Thread*" the daughter of the count gives page Leofried a single thread of gold tissue. Youth represented as opening wound in his bosom and depositing the gift as near the heart as possible. (Sir W. S. Art. Chiv. Enc. B. 127.)

8. *Squire?* Name traced to *escu*, shield, because carried the shield of the knight. Squire both valet-de-chambre and groom. In first capacity dressed and undressed the knight, received and waited on guests, cut the meat at table, prepared the great hall for the dance, &c. In words of Chaucer,

> "Curteis he was, lowly and servisable,
> And carf before his fader at the table."

Squire was encouraged besides to add mental accomplishments, to enliven by his conversation, to understand chess, drafts, &c., to be skilled in music and poetry, *e. g.*, Chaucer's squire besides "singing and fluting all the day,"

> ——"Could songs make, and well indite,
> Just, and eke dance, and well pourtray and write." (128.)

As groom trained the horses and kept the armor of the knight burnished. He was now taught use of arms more perfectly, all the difficult feats of horsemanship, to scale walls, climb ladders, keep watch, and do all things serviceable in war.

9. *Services of squire in war?* Carried helmet and shield of knight on a march, and led his war horse, kept all the knight's armor in order, kept near him in battle, supplied him with fresh horse, took possession of his prisoners, came to the rescue when overpowered, &c., *e. g.*, Lord Audley led the van of Black Prince's army at the battle of Poictiers, attended by four squires, who bore him from the press when wounded, and stanched and dressed his wounds. When Black Prince gave Lord A. 500 marks of yearly revenue for his services, it was immediately consigned to the four faithful squires for their services, and the lords *witnessed* the verbal assignment. (129.)

10. *Independent squires?* Some squires never passed into knights, but remained attached to some knight, or became entirely independent, *e. g.*, four squires of Lord Audley were never knighted. Squire never permitted to wear *gold* spurs—reason for so many remaining in this state was great expense of knighthood.

11. *Knight?* At age of 21, if no impediment, the squire might be knighted. Two occasions on which this generally took place; 1st, on field of battle, either before or after the battle, when the motive was either to stimulate or reward; 2d, in time of peace, generally on some festive occasion. Ceremony on field of battle short. Novice armed at all points, but without helmet, sword and spurs, came before the general or prince who knighted him, kneeling down, while two persons acting as sponsors put on his gilded spurs and belted on his sword, then received the *accolade* from the one who dubbed him, consisting of slight blow with flat part of sword on the neck,* with the formula, "I dub thee knight, in the name of God and St. Michael, (or in the name of the Father, Son, and Holy Ghost). Be faithful, bold and fortunate." Then if battle was about to be fought he was bound to *win his spurs*, *e. g.*, at battle of Crecy Edward III. refused to send succors to Black Prince until he should hear he was wounded, or dismounted, being determined to give him opportunity to *win his spurs*. At siege of Thoulouse (1159) Henry II. of England made 30 knights at once, among whom was Malcolm IV., king of Scotland (131). In time of peace at *cour pleniere*, when all the crown

* Ceremony of striking with the sword has been supposed to have originated from one of three causes. 1st. Roman method of manumitting slaves with the *slap of liberty*. 2d. Denoted this to be the last affront which the knight was to receive unavenged. 3d. Was a warning and an emblem of difficulties and dangers to which he would be exposed.

vassals were present, or on occasions of festivity from marriage, birth, baptism, &c., particularly in royal family, knighthood generally conferred with much more ceremony, most of which was religious. Candidates watched their arms all night in church or chapel, preparing themselves by *vigil, fast and prayer*—then divested of brown frock, dress of squire, underwent ablution as emblem of purification of heart, then attired in rich garb of knight, went in solemn procession to church, high mass was said, confession made, and sometimes a discourse was heard on duties of chivalry—novice then advanced to altar, when accolade was received, sword often belted on by churchmen of highest dignity and spurs often buckled on by ladies of quality, then took oath to be faithful to *God, his king, and the ladies*, mounted his horse and performed some curvets in presence of assembly, brandishing his lance, &c.

12. *Who had privilege of conferring knighthood?* All knights, of course most distinguished preferred, *e. g.* Francis I. chose *Chevalier* Bayard to knight him, and latter so pleased with honor that he vowed never to use the sword with which he knighted Francis except against Turks, Moors, or Saracens. As knighthood became more and more important, privilege of knighting gradually restricted to monarchs and princes. (131.)

13. *Suppose knight disgraced himself?* He was formally *un*knighted by a terrible process—mounted on a scaffold, his spurs were cut off close to his heels by a cook's cleaver—his armor was broken before his eyes—his shield and armorial bearings were tied to a horse's tail, and tail of his own horse cut off close to the rump—Herald at arms pronounced him disgraced—funeral service was chanted over him, and a priest pronounced against him maledictions of 108th Psalm— a basin of hot water was poured on his head, and then he was pulled down from scaffold by a rope around his neck, put on hand-barrow, rolled to church, dressed in grave-clothes, and the prayers of the dead chanted over him! (Chat. T. 6. 172.)

14. *Armor of the knight and mode of fighting?* Under dress a close jacket of chamois leather, over which was mail shirt of rings of steel fitted into each other, a suit of plate armor over the mail shirt, and legs and arms were defended by similar means. Sword, lance, and a battle-axe at the saddle bow with a dagger for close quarters, were the offensive arms. Management of lance and horse the great requisites for success, to strike the foeman between the four limbs, as it was called, upon helmet, or full on chest, with point of lance, and at full speed, perfect practice—to miss him, or break lance athwart the body, without striking with point, awkward failure—to strike adversary under the girdle, or to aim at the horse, was a foul act. As knight was cover-

ed in his armor, to distinguish himself wore above his coat of mail a surcoat with his arms emblazoned on it, or they were painted on a shield borne in front of him—each knight too shouted his own war cry, consisting generally of the name of some favorite saint, (St. George, St. Michael, St. James, and St. Martin, most favored.) joined with that of his own family, and all his followers echoed the cry, *e. g.*, Ed. III. in battle before Calais cried out "ha! St. George, ha! St. Edward," for every blow. In battle knights most formidable when mounted and charging in squadron, knights forming front rank, squires the rear rank, horses large and strong, and trained to move at full speed upon adversary without flinching—armed *en barbe*, *i. e.*, iron mask on horse's face, a breast-plate for his front, and armor for the croup—knights' horses generally stallions, considered *unknightly* to be mounted on a mare. In consequence of this armor, until rise of Swiss infantry, cavalry was most efficient part of every army, and was called the *battle* by way of distinction.

15. *Privileges and rank of the knight?* He belonged to a rank which associated him with kings and princes upon terms of equality—took precedence in war and council, and was addressed by the title of *messire* in French and *sir* in English, and his wife by that of *madame* and *dame*. He had the privilege of serving always on horseback. *Chivalry* derived from *chevalier*, a horseman, which in turn comes from old word *caballarius*—a knight was by virtue of knighthood held qualified to command any number of men under a thousand—chief privilege was that knights formed a distinct class of nobility through Europe—knight "a citizen of universal chivalry" and entitled to its privileges in all countries. It was the privileges of knighthood which gave to *vavassors* or inferior gentry a standing which in some measure compensated for want of land, and Hallam thinks had a tendency to save the poor nobility from sinking into mass of common people. (H. M. A. 518.)

16. *Sports of chivalry?* Tilts and tournaments which could only be held by distinguished knight or prince, who sent heralds through neighboring kingdoms to invite all whose knighthood was unstained—knights here jousted with one another, and used either the blunted or sharp lance, if latter, death would often be the consequence. When stranger knight approached field signified his arrival by horn or trumpet—his squire sent before with armorial bearings, spear, helmet, and his *lambrekins*, or favors from his mistress—judges then met him, to whom he gave his name, helmet, arms, armorial bearings, &c., with proofs of his descent, all for registry, and for some days before tournament his shield hung in conspicuous place; two reasons, 1st, for con-

venience of challenge, 2nd, that knight might be known, and if he was disgraced might be driven off the field.

17. *Tournament of Inglebert?* Held near Calais—three knights, Bouçicant, Reynold de Roy, and St. Py, or Saimpi, gave it—knights came from all quarters, particularly from England. Before lodgings of each of three knights who gave the tournament were hung two shields, one *of war*, the other *of peace*, they were *pitted* against the field and held themselves ready to accept any challenge. Sir John Holland, earl of Huntingdon, sent his squire to touch the *war target* of Sir Bouçicant —this a challenge to fight with deadly weapons, accordingly Sir Bouçicant came forth armed *cap-a-pie*, eyed each other a moment, then drove full speed at one another; Sir B. drove his lance so furiously as to pierce the shield of Sir John, but slipped along his arm without injury, both passed and galloped to end of the lists—this much praised. Second time hit each other slightly, and horses refused to complete the third; Sir John wished to tilt on, and returned to his place, expecting Sir B. to call for his lance, but he did not. Sir J. then sent his squire to touch *war target* of the Lord de Saimpi—they couched their lances and drove at each other, but horses crossed each other and Sir J. was unhelmed in consequence—this was blamed. His squires rehelmed him and they returned to the encounter—they met and struck each other so violently in middle of their shields that they would have been unhorsed, had they not held on with their legs. After slight refreshment returned again, and struck on their helmets so hard that sparks of fire came forth—this tilting much praised. After this Sir J. wished to break another lance in honor of his lady, but it was refused him, as he had already broken six with so much skill and courage. The other jousts were performed with equal spirit. Sir Peter Courtney, Sir J. Russel, Sir Peter Sherborne, Sir Wm. Clifton, &c., sustaining honor of England against chivalry of France. (Sir W. S. 134.)

18. *Bravery and feats of the knights?* Particular talents predominant at particular epochs, *e. g.*, eloquence in Greece, military skill in Rome, craft and diplomacy in modern Italy—during feudal ages bravery and individual prowess in most demand, and as Europe was in anarchy and suffered from disorders consequent on feebleness of government, chivalry was gradually formed into an institution, and a part of the knight's business was to succor the oppressed everywhere, and in some sort to remedy the defects of government; this would have done mischief under a regular, efficient government, but in feudal times was an advantage. Everywhere oppressors to punish and evil customs to abolish, and thus the knights of the middle ages were like Hercules, These-

us, Iolaus, &c., of the heroic ages of Greece, performing feats of prowess and justice everywhere.

19. *Gallantry?* As chivalry professed to protect the weak, the fair sex, the weaker half of the human race, soon fell under its peculiar protection; hence one cause of devotion of knight to the sex; but this devotion was gradually prepared as we have seen by the condition of the family of feudal lord in his castle, and was aided by the intermixture of the Moors and the northern nations, which resulted from the two great invasions of the *north* and the *south* striking against each other in Sicily, Italy, Spain, and Gaul, between 700 and 753. Sentiment and fidelity of German character, added to the gallantry and romantic spirit of the Moor, formed the basis of chivalry, soon to be enveloped in the forms of Christianity. The exalted opinion of woman came principally from the Germans—among them great restraint imposed on the licentiousness of youth, hence more disposition to venerate woman, they considered that there was something divine in her character (*inesse quin etiam sanctum aliquid et providum putant.*) In the mythology of Edda and the poems of the Scaldes, among Scandinavians, even the *sun* was made feminine—the brilliant *Sunna.* Pecuniary fines by which the person of woman was guarded, however whimsical, indicate sacredness of her character; *e. g.*, any one cutting off the hair of a young lady was fined 62 sous of gold, for pressing her hand or her forefinger, if a lady of quality, the fine was 15 sous, for pressing any portion of arm from elbow to hand the fine was 30 sous, 35 for pressing arm above elbow, and 45 for daring to press *her bosom* (*si mamillam strinxerit.*) On other hand, the Moors too professed great respect for women, *e g.*, in the poems of *Antar*, compiled under Khaliffe Haroun Al-Raschid, Antar loves the beautiful Ibla, and, like the knight, submits his love to many proofs, performs many adventures, and displays a prowess for his *lady love* worthy of Roland. In these poems all the pastoral manners are preserved with spirit of chivalry, *e. g.*, women drink the milk of the camel, and Antar feeds his flocks, &c. Saladin had all the spirit of a knight, as brave and less cruel than Richard, and it is well known that the amours, the tournaments and combats of Cordova and Grenada reminded the spectator of the chivalry of Europe. (Chateau. T. 6. 162.)

20. *Knight errantry and the follies of chivalry?* It is not to be wondered at, that romantic love of adventure and devotion to sex should soon lead on to many extravagances. A mistress was selected by the knight, all his actions in honor of her—he sometimes went forth determined to perform feats worthy of her, and, to propagate her beauty, her portrait, any device of hers, any gift, even most trifling, was regarded

with utmost reverence—he challenged in her name—commanders exhorted in name of mistress, and the knight when performing brilliant feat often heard to say, "*Oh, si ma dame me voyait!*" "Oh, if my mistress could but see me now!" Sometimes made vows of whimsical character, *e. g.*, in the wars of Ed. III. a company of knights covered one eye each, and vowed not to uncover it until they had performed something worthy of mistress—at the storming of Calais they were relieved from their vows. English and French knights fought at Poictiers and Verneuil as at tournaments, bearing over their armor scarfs and devices as the livery of their mistresses, and asserting their paramount beauty in challenges to enemy. At Cherbourg the armies stood still while a knight challenged to single combat the most amorous of his adversaries, and the general battle did not begin till one killed the other—slightest favor sometimes enough to make the knight go forth as a knight errant till he made himself worthy of the favor, *e. g.*, Joan, queen of Naples, gave her hand to Galeazzo of Mantua, for purpose of opening a ball; soon as dance was done, kneeled down before Joan, and made a solemn vow to wander through the world, till he could subdue two valiant knights, and present them as prisoners at her royal feet. Accordingly, after visiting various scenes of war returned with his two prisoners, who were graciously accepted by the queen and set free without ransom. For this Brantome extols her while he condemns Canons of St. Peter's church who accepted a captive knight under similar circumstances as they would have done a wild beast for the *menagerie.* In time of peace knights went from court to court, from tournament to tournament, challenging in names of their mistresses and proclaiming their transcendent beauty, and conqueror according to this martial logic established the superior beauty of his lady love; nor were ladies at all times opposed to these undertakings, they sometimes enjoined them as a mode of getting rid of troublesome suitors, *e. g.*, in Fableau of Three Knights and the Shift, lady proposes to her three lovers successively to enter unarmed into the melee of a tournament with one of her shifts only for a covering—one accepted, fought, and was victorious. Next day husband of the lady gave a great entertainment, when the knight sent back shift with a request that she should wear it at her banquet all besmeared with blood over her other dress—lady did not hesitate to comply. Sometimes the patience of knight was exhausted by these hard conditions, *e. g.*, at German court a lady purposely let her glove fall into inclosure where two fierce lions were, and commanded her lover as a knight to bring it to her, he leaped over, threw his cloak at the animals as they sprang at him, got back safe with the glove, and renounced her love for ever. Generally, however, lady really intended the knight's honor as well as her own, by prescribing these feats, and hence lady in love often imposed them, *e. g.*, in wars between Ed. I. and Scotland, English in possession of the Castle of Douglas had been often cut to pieces by Sir J. Douglas, who sallied forth from the mountains of Cairntable—at length a lady offered her hand to the lover who would *hold* the Castle of Douglas for a year and a day—he whom she really loved undertook the task, with her request. After he had remained some months she was satisfied, and sent to him to return, but Sir J. Douglas had sent him word that he would take the castle before Palm Sunday—knight felt in honor bound to stay till Palm Sunday—Sir J. stormed castle on eve of Palm Sunday, and the knight was slain, and the letter of the lady found in his pocket. (Sir W. S. 123.)

21. *Advantages of chivalry?* Remedied in some sort the disorders of the time by the succor given to oppressed—but must not forget that great evil might sometimes result; as the knight was an efficient soldier he often became venal, and hired his services to the prince who paid highest—hence usurpers, tyrants, rebels, often found support in the *knights bachelors*, nicknamed sometimes the "*landless resolutes*," whom any adventurer might collect for food and money. Four especial virtues which Hallam supposes to have arisen from chivalry; 1st, *loyalty;* 2d, *courtesy;* 3d, *liberality;* 4th, *justice.* 1st, he defines, according to *original* sense, fidelity to engagements—breach of faith unpardonable—*false*, *perjured*, *disloyal*, the most disgraceful epithets for knight. This institution, 1st, originated practice of discharging the captive knight on his *parole d'honneur*—this virtue of great benefit in an age of perjury and falsehood; 2d, *courtesy*, refinement of good breeding and humanity of the heart—rule to be humane after the battle was over. In the wars between Ed. III. and France this courtesy carried to greatest extent. When noble prisoners were taken they were treated in most princely and kind manner; *e. g.*, after battle of Poictiers King John, who was taken prisoner by the Black Prince, was treated as a king, and waited on by the Black Prince himself. After entertainment English and Gascon knights asked their prisoners what ransom they could pay without straitening themselves, and each prisoner's ransom was fixed at his own assessment. From chivalry is derived the great humanity of modern warfare as contrasted with ancient. 3d, *Liberality*, a liberal open heart was one of the requisites of chivalry, including of course the virtue of hospitality—every castle open to the wandering knight. 4th, *Justice*—by this is meant quick sense of right and wrong, and a determination in knight to take side of former. It was their duty to attack robbers, to break up strong holds of iniquity, &c. &c., though not always done as before stated. And although this led to adventures, of which

the feats of Don Quixote can scarcely be considered as caricature—upon the whole beneficial in age of anarchy and confusion.

22. *Character of virtues of chivalry?* Individual honor the soul of chivalry—most of its virtues *independent;* knights acted not for society or for country, but for individual fame and renown, and from abstract notion of justice, this character of *individuality* observed even in day of battle, when knights were continually breaking the ranks to perform feats of prowess—knight cared more for his mistress than his country—more for his own glory in battle than for the fate of the army to which he belonged—hence the great energy of those times—hence the great men and the great achievements of the crusades were almost as much the result of chivalry as of religion—character of Achilles as drawn by Homer well illustrates in some particulars that of the knight. He loved his own honor and fame more than the cause of Greece—hence insult from Agamemnon makes him retire from field—no calamity can draw him out, till *his friend* Patroclus falls by Hector's arm, then his honor prompts him to avenge his death, he goes to the field for Patroclus' sake, not to relieve the sinking cause of the Greeks, Hector is a totally different character, has less *individuality* and more *patriotism.* Sharon Turner has drawn a parallel between Achilles and Richard *Cœur-de-Lion*, in which resemblance is made very strong. (H. M. A. 510.)

23. *Disadvantage of chivalry?* 1st, although it refined and gave a degree of sentimentality to love unknown to ancient world, yet had tendency to produce dissoluteness. Lady's heart not of stuff stern enough to resist always constant devotion backed by renown for courtesy and valor. This dissoluteness is seen in all the works of fiction in those ages, *e. g.*, in Romance of Round Table, in the Tales of Chaucer, and Boccaccio, in Bandello's Novels, &c. (W. S. 124.) 2d, another disadvantage was that it produced too great a thirst for military fame—a passion too strong in those ages without the additional stimulus of chivalry. 3d, widened the separation between the different classes of society, and confirmed aristocratic spirit of high birth, *e. g.*, at taking of Calais Edward could display utmost generosity to Eustace de Ribaumont while he treated common citizens with cruelty. Said that a poor knight importuned Henry, count of Champagne, for money enough to marry his two daughters. Arthault de Nogent, a rich burgess, tried to rid the count of the importunity by telling the knight that the Count H. had no money left in consequence of his former liberality, whereupon count turned around and told the burgess he did not speak truth, and immediately told the knight he might have the burgess until he ransomed himself, which in the end cost Arthault £500. Strange to say, Joinville praises the liberality of this act, and shows thereby how little

was thought of persons who could not boast of birth. (H. M. A. 516.)

24. *Orders of knighthood?* 3. 1st, *knights bachelors*, those who had all the honors of knighthood irrespective of property—these generally the knights errant, and soldiers who most freely engaged in wars of Europe. 2d, *knights banneret*, distinguishing characteristics, possession of a certain estate, and the ability to bring a certain number of lances into the field, usually about 50—his banner was square and carried by the squire at point of the lance; whereas the pendant of knight bachelor was pointed, and when made a banneret, point was cut off so as to make it square, *e. g.*, before battle of Navarette Black Prince made Sir John Chandos knight banneret by merely taking his banner and cutting off the point. 3dly, *knights baronet*—here the honor descended by inheritance—this order arose as chivalry was on the wane, and was at war with the original idea of the institution.

25. *Fraternities and honorary associations of knights?* Besides the three great orders above-mentioned, there were fraternities formed for particular purposes, *e. g.*, three great orders of knights, Hospitallers, of the Templars, and the Teutonic knights of north—former for defence of the Holy land, latter to propagate Christianity among Saxons—these managed by commanders called *grand masters*, and formed sort of military republic. It was Teutonic knights who laid foundation of the kingdom of Prussia. Monarchs too got into habit of establishing certain associations, like the Round Table of King Arthur, and the Paladins of Charlemagne, *e. g.*, Ed. III. revived Round Table, and offered free passage to all knight who might be disposed to attend splendid jousts to be held at Windsor Castle on the occasion—the festival was to be annual, but Philip de Valois became jealous, and forbade his subjects to attend, and at same time got up an *opposition* Round Table in France—the consequence was that Edward's festival lost much of its brilliancy, and this induced him to establish celebrated *order of the garter*, with the motto, "*Honi soit qui mal y pense*," in allusion to Philip's conduct towards the festival of the Round Table. Twenty-six only of most honorable and distinguished knights of England and Gascony were admitted into this order; of course it was an object of ambition among the great to be admitted into this order.

26. *Causes of decline of chivalry?* 1st, *increase of number of knights;* 2d, *invention of gunpowder;* 3d, *institution of standing armies;* 4th, *civil wars in England, and the wars between Huguenots and Catholics in France;* 5th, *rise of commerce and manufactures, together with a general change in the manners of Europe.* 1st, As knights were found to be most valuable soldiers, kings soon perceived

great advantage of having many of them in their armies, they accordingly conferred the honor too freely, and often even with compulsion —hence with increase of numbers the honor diminished, and as knighthood was very expensive, many chose rather to dispense with the honor, than incur the expense—this produced necessity of using compulsion—hence we find instances of proclamations made to the sheriffs to summon certain persons to be knighted, we see fines imposed for not being knighted, and persons begging for respite, &c., *e. g.*, in 19th H. III. proclamation made to the sheriffs that all who held one night's fee or more of the king in chief should take arms and get themselves knighted. In same reign we find one Roger de Sumery forfeiting certain estates because he did not come to be begirt with belt of knighthood. In reign of Ed. III John de Drokensford paid £10 for a respite from knighthood for three years, &c. &c. (Sir. G. S. 392.) Kings and princes who wished to have distinguished knights about them were often obliged to give them a pension to enable them to support the dignity, *e. g.*, Ed. III. gave to John Atte Lee, a knight, £40 per annum, *in auxilium status sui manutenendi*, and to Sir Nele Loring and his heirs for ever, for same purpose, £20. Richard II. gave annuity of 40 marks to Sir John Walsh for same reason. In household expenses of Thomas, Earl of Leicester, for year 1313, we have 70 pieces of blue cloth, and 100 pieces of green silk, for his knights, and 28 pieces of the former for squires, besides divers other articles, and a charge of £633 15*s.* 5*d.* as fees to earls, barons, knights and squires. (388.) 2d. *Invention of gunpowder*—this made the bullet penetrate through all the knight's panoply, and soon rendered his *complete harness* more cumbrous than useful—it was accordingly gradually laid aside, and the arms changed, and with armor knight soon discontinued those practises so essential to chivalry, and lost the habits of a knight—a weak man with a musket was made equal to strong one, and individual prowess in use of arms became matter of secondary importance. Again gunpowder made war more scientific, and rendered exact discipline in armies more necessary, it made the fate of battles to depend on the movements of masses, and not on the feats of individuals; hence it destroyed the *individuality* which was the soul of knighthood; the knights could no longer break the ranks to display their prowess, they formed but a part of that *great machine*, a modern army, and their importance was sunk, and their glory confounded with the *general merit* of the army. 3d. *The institution of standing armies*—after the invention of gunpowder it was soon found that infantry were more efficient than cavalry, hence the gradual disuse and degradation of the latter; moreover, as war had become more scientific mercenary troops who made a profession of war, although individually the most degraded of mankind, were found more efficient than the feudal militia and squadrons of knights not kept regularly in the field—hence monarchs soon relied on standing armies, rather than the individual prowess and skill of knights. 4th. *Wars between houses of York and Lancaster in England, and between the Huguenots and Catholics in France*—these wars so bitter and rancorous as to be totally inconsistent with the *courtesy, fair play, and gentleness* proper to chivalry, *e. g.*, in wars between Edward III. and the French, village dance would scarcely be suspended when two hostile armies were in sight—they would fight most bravely, and the wounded of both armies would often be sent to the same village, but civil wars of England and France were carried on by murdering, burning, and plundering—the execution of prisoners on both sides, and that rancor which allows no plea of mercy, were fatal to finer parts of chivalry in France and England. (Sir W. S. 142.) But again, these wars not only degraded chivalry, but they destroyed the nobility, from which the ranks of chivalry were recruited; hence we find a comparatively new *noblesse* springing into existence under the Tudors, much less renowned for spirit of chivalry than the old nobility which had been destroyed in the wars of the *Roses.* 5th. *Rise of commerce and manufactures, with a general change in the manners of Europe.* By rise of commerce and manufactures new trades and occupations were established, new channels of industry were opened, a new field was presented for energy and enterprise, war ceased to be the only object of exertion, and as governments became more energetic private wars ceased—a change gradually took place in the manners of Europe, military talent ceased to be the *only* talent which could command applause—the revival of letters hastened the change. Abelard, Petrarch and Dante could command by their learning and poetry as much applause as the bravest knights. As manners and mode of thinking changed, the spirit of chivalry gradually wore out, and the institution became subject of ridicule, till Cervantes at length "laughed it out of the world."

27. *Fate of chivalry in Italy?* In Italy the democracies of the cities early became triumphant, and as chivalry was based on birth and aristocracy, the governments of Italy were unfavorable to its growth, hence it never attained to same importance as in France, Spain and England. Moreover the peculiar political divisions of Italy soon produced a degree of cunning, hypocrisy, treachery, &c., totally at war with spirit of chivalry. Assassinations were frequent and sometimes applauded by the historians, *e. g.*, Brantome in stories of the detestable murders of the Baron des Vitaux calls them bold and brave revenges; and when Cesar Borgia murdered his guests at dinner, historian seems to consider it as a *clever piece of treachery.* Duels in Italy not fought

in the lists and before judges, but in lonely and sequestered spots—every effort made to take advantage, *e. g.*, Quelus says to Antragues when about to fight, "Thou hast both a sword and dagger, and I have only a sword;" "The more thy folly," was the reply, "to leave thy dagger at home; we came to fight, not to adjust weapons." They fought, and Quelus was killed, for want of the dagger in the left hand to parry the strokes of his adversary. The challenged, as with us, had right of naming the conditions of the fight, and Brantome praises ingenuity of a small man challenged by a large Gascon, and who selected *gorget* so constructed that large man could not look down so as to aim his blows. Another had two swords made so brittle that unless used with great caution, and in a manner which he had practised every day, they would break to pieces. No wonder that Catharine de Medecis, brought up in such a school, should have trained her maids of honor as courtesans, and made the manners of court of France hardly equal in decency to those of a well-regulated *bagnio.* (E. B. 143.)

28. *Impressions which chivalry has left on modern Europe?* 1st. The character of the *modern gentleman* has been formed in great measure by this institution—cavaliers of Charles I. were the legitimate offspring of Edward's knights. 2d. It has elevated greatly the *fair sex*, and made woman a most important element in the progress of civilization. It is this institution which has given to the passion of love a degree of *sentiment* unknown to the ancient world. In all the love scenes of antiquity we have very little more than the mere carnal passion of the lovers, but chivalry has imparted to the passion a degree of refined sentiment which has elevated woman, whilst it has softened and polished our rougher sex. 3d. It has mitigated the *laws of war*, and may be considered as in part cause of that mildness and courtesy which modern nations display towards their prisoners. 4th. Sensitiveness on the point of honor and the modern practice of duelling may be considered as springing in great measure from chivalry. 5th. Lastly, modern manners and modern politeness have been in a great measure the result of this institution. Thus, although chivalry may be looked to, in language of Sir Walter Scott, "as a beautiful and fantastic piece of frost work which has dissolved in the beams of the sun; though we look in vain for the pillars, the vaults, the cornices, and the fretted ornaments of the transitory fabric, we cannot but be sensible that its dissolution has left on the soil valuable tokens of its former existence." (144.)

CHAPTER III.

RELIGIONS COMPARED—RISE OF CHRISTIANITY.

SECTION I.

NECESSARY to trace the rise and progress of Christian religion before proceeding farther with history of Europe—subject of vast importance, whether its beauty and simplicity, its grandeur and its truth, be considered, or whether we consider that it is religion of all the most civilized portion of modern world—that it has overthrown the idolatries of polytheism, that it is *our* religion and that of our forefathers. In order to appreciate properly this religion, well to take a rapid glance at most prominent creeds which have existed.

1. *Pythagorean cosmogony?* Pythagoras, and after him Plato, contended that three causes were necessary to formation of universe. 1st. An *intelligent cause*, whose existence is proved by the order, harmony and design in universe. But intelligent cause cannot produce *something* out of *nothing*, *ex nihilo nil fit*, *de nihilo nihil*, *in nihilum*, *nil posse reverti;* hence they said there must have been an *original matter*, a *prima materia*, out of which all things were fashioned, this was the second or *material cause.* Ovid, in his Metamorphoses, has described the original chaos which was the *materia prima* of the Pythagoreans.

> Ante mare et tellus, et quod tegit omnia cœlum
> Unus erat toto naturæ vultus in orbe,
> Quem dixere chaos, rudis indigestaque moles
> Nec quicquam, nisi pondus iners, conjestaque eodem
> Non bene junctarum discordia semina rerum
> Nullus adhuc mundo prebebat lumina Titan
> Nec nova crescendo reparabat cornua Phebe
> Nec circumfuso pendebat in aere tellus
> Ponderibus librata suis; nec brachia longo
> Margine terrarum porrexerat Amphitrite, &c.

Then proceeds to describe formation of all things by Deity out of this original chaos:

> Sic ubi dispositam quisquis fuit ille deorum
> Congeriem secuit, sectamque redigit in membra.

But Pythagoreans went still farther, they not only contended for a material cause, but thirdly, for what may be termed a *modellary cause*, said Deity must not only have matter to work on, but must have the *model* or *pattern* according to which it was to be executed, just as the tailor must have his measure and the brickmaker his moulds—these *models* or *exemplars* must have existed from all eternity, and were perfect, and the reason why the various objects in creation were not created as perfect in form as their archetypes or models, was that the *rigidity and inflexibility* of the original matter prevented even the Deity from accomplishing it. Thus, according to this system, evil sprang from *matter*, and as every thing in nature had its archetype or model much more perfect than the thing itself, therefore Plato, in his philosophy, bade you turn from the actual world and its imperfect works to the world of abstractions and models; he sent you to the closet instead of into the world to study nature—this doctrine had great influence on the sect called Gnostics—it was at the bottom of that theory which mortifies the flesh to purify the mind—it led to monachism, to penances, &c.

2. *Persian religion?* This religion already explained (Vol. 1. 87.) accounted for origin of evil by supposition of two principles or divinities, Ormuzd and Ahriman, former *good principle*, latter *evil*—one originator of all good, the other of all evil—constant conflict between the two—souls of men first unembodied spirits, Ormuzd clothed them in flesh to carry on war against Ahriman; besides, Ormuzd creates an immense number of *good genii* or *spirits;* Ahriman of evil ones—thus Ormuzd would make world perfect, but Ahriman mars his works. Persian and Pythagorean systems met and mixed at the great commercial depôt of Egypt, Alexandria, and produced powerful influence on Christianity, principally through sect of *Gnostics*. Even evangelists in making mention of *demons and evil spirits*, are supposed by some merely to have indulged in language which the general belief of the east had rendered current.

3. *Polytheism?* Most elegant and at same time most *material* of the superstitions of antiquity—before described. (Vol. 1. 49.) But all the gods together were not omnipotent, and rewards and punishments were rather expected in this world than in another—gods themselves had all the foibles and vices of man. Hence this religion left unsupplied nature's great demand for a staff on which to lean when this world affords none—it was unfavorable to morality.

4. *Jewish religion?* Precursor of ours. Abraham and his descendants chosen by God as the depositary of his true religion. Most all religions and ancient systems of laws have been traced to a divine source, *e. g.*, Menes pretended in Egypt to be instructed by Mercury, Cadmus at Thebes by the Oracle, Minos in Crete by Jupiter, Lycurgus by Apollo, and Numa at Rome by Egeria. But divine source of Jewish religion was proved by miracles—law given by God himself from Mount

Sinai in voice of thunder, heard by the whole people—Deity condescended to be the king of this people—Moses did not employ religion to support civil institutions, but the latter were made entirely subservient to former—worship of true God *fundamental law* of his institutions—as God was king of Hebrews a defection from God was considered high treason and punished with death—all kinds of idolatry punished in same manner—a man was obliged to give up his dearest friend if caught in these practices, and even the stranger was punished in same way, if he worshipped while among Israelites any but true God. (J. H. C. 32, 35.) Great object to keep pure true religion amid idolatry of world—hence Jewish people kept separate and distinct, and had little intercourse with the heathen—their rites and ceremonies, particularly that of *circumcision*, were repulsive—their religion seemed to rest of the world *national, austere* and *unsocial*. Cicero speaks of it as a superstition unsuited to dignity of Roman Empire.

5. *One peculiarity of Jewish religion which seems to establish its divine origin independently of miracles?* Only religion of ancient world which preserved unchanged, simple and sublime, worship of *one single God*, and amid the tendencies always existing towards *materialism* and *idolatry*, in an ignorant world, it steadily proscribed worship of divinity under any *material forms*.

6. *Birth of our Saviour?* Jewish doctrine of fall of man and origin of evil, together with necessity for a Saviour to redeem a fallen world well known. The prophecies in the Old Testament point distinctly to his advent—his coming was expected, but it was supposed he would be a universal sovereign—the Jews were anxiously expecting such a deliverer, (*egressum e Judea rerum potiturum*,) hence the murder of the children at Bethlehem by order of King Herod. He was born at Bethlehem in Judea in the reign of Augustus Cesar, and the last year of King Herod's reign in Jerusalem.

7. *Condition of Jerusalem at period of his birth?* Conquered by Pompey about 60 years before—made afterwards a Roman province, governed sometimes by a king, *e. g.*, Herod, sometimes by a procurator, *e. g.*, Pontius Pilate. City of Jerusalem constantly torn to pieces by factions, which the whole power of the provincial governors could not always restrain. Twelve years after birth of Christ Judea and Samaria were united to great Roman province of Syria under Prefect Quirinus, and Coponius was made procurator of Judea, whose successor was Pontius Pilate in the year 26. (421–3.)

8. *John the Baptist and the ministry and death of our Saviour?* In year 29, 15th of reign of Tiberius, and 3d of the procuratorship of Pilate, John the *Baptist* made his public appearance, preparing minds

of people for reception of Messiah, and about six months afterwards baptized Jesus in the river Jordan, and pointed him out to the people as the promised Messiah. After undergoing assaults of Satan in wilderness, Jesus entered on his ministry—after a time he drew around him twelve young men from the lower orders, whom he prepared by example and instruction for carrying on what he began. He traversed the country from one extremity to the other, visiting also the Samaritans and the Gentiles, on coast of Tyre and Sidon, during which time he taught the people the sublime truths of his religion, worked miracles, and made disciples. At length he was betrayed by one of his own disciples, Judas Iscariot, delivered up to the Jews, accused of exciting sedition, brought before Pontius Pilate, condemned and crucified as a malefactor, it is generally supposed in the 34th year of his age, and the 18th of the reign of Tiberius.

9. *Contemporary notices of Christ?* Correspondence of Christ with Abgarus, Toparch of Edessa, and two descriptions of last scenes of his life, the *Acta Pilati* and *Evangelium Nicodemi*, as also pretended *likenesses* of him and letter of Lentulus to Roman senate, describing his person, are all spurious beyond a doubt. Passage in which Josephus speaks of Jesus thought to be genuine, although interpolated. "Now there was about this time Jesus, a wise man, if it be lawful to call him a man, for he was a doer of wonderful works, a teacher of such men as receive the truth with pleasure. He drew over to him both many of the Jews and many of the Gentiles. He was the Christ." (J. 426.) Arguments for genuineness of above are, 1st, agreement of all MSS. since time of Eusebius; 2d, Christians too numerous to have been passed over by Josephus; 3d, Josephus not only mentions John the Baptist, but also death of James, calling him brother of Christ. Against it, 1st, silence of all the fathers before Eusebius, whilst Origen designates Josephus as not believing in Jesus as *the Christ;* 2d, the passage interrupts the connection; 3d, reads as if written by a Christian; 4th, other Jewish historian, Justus Tiberiensis, did not mention Christ. Supposed the passage was interpolated from Eusebius. (Geis. V. 1. 43.)

10. *Preaching of the Gospel and spread of Christian religion?* Fifty days after the resurrection, on the day of Pentecost, (Whitsuntide,) when there was a great festival at Jerusalem, the Apostle Peter, inspired by the Holy Ghost, preached the *new gospel* sermon, in which he unfolded the Christian scheme of salvation, and enforced necessity of repentance, baptism, &c., 3000 were added to the church on that day. (Acts. ii.) On same day apostles received gift of tongues and power of working miracles, and went forth on their mission to preach the Gospel and disciple nations. Until day of Pentecost even disciples them-

selves knew not complete character of Saviour. Before his death they could not throw off Jewish prejudice that he would be temporal prince and the deliverer and restorer of Jewish nation, and even after his resurrection, they put the question to him in a body, "Lord, wilt thou at this time restore again the kingdom to Israel?" (Acts i. 6.) Progress of Christian religion was rapid. In 300 years it mounted the throne of the Cæsars, overthrew the polytheism of Romans, and was made the religion of whole empire by Constantine the Great.

11. *Argument drawn from the circumstances under which Christian religion was spread over the world in favor of truth of the Christian scheme?* All the false religions of the world which have eventually succeeded have commenced in periods of darkness, and grown through ages of ignorance, till their sway was established, *e. g.*, religions of Menu, of Zoroaster, and of Mahomet; so likewise the polytheism of Greece and Rome, &c. But Christianity started forth from Jerusalem in the reign of Augustus, the most enlightened epoch in ancient world, it was ushered forth in the full blaze of all the learning and civilization of the age, in a quarter of the world at that time remarkable for subtlety of intellect and the searching scrutiny of investigation—it boldly advanced to Athens and to Rome, the great luminaries of the ancient world, and has finally triumphed over every obstacle. Could a false religion have accomplished such a triumph? But as Deity works by ordinary means as well as supernatural, *miraculous* triumph of Christianity does not preclude an investigation of those worldly causes which aided in the spread of our religion.

SEC. II.—CAUSES OF RAPID PROGRESS OF CHRISTIANITY.

1. *Causes of success of Christian religion?* Gibbon enumerates five. 1st, *Its zeal derived from Jewish religion, but purified of all its narrowness and unsociability;* 2d, *Doctrine of a future life clearly explained in New Testament;* 3d, *Miraculous powers of primitive church;* 4th, *Pure and austere morals of Christians;* 5th, *Union and discipline of Christian church and establishment of church government.*

2. *First cause explained?* Zeal of Christian far beyond that of polytheist. In polytheism, strictly speaking, no creed, no fixed principles—gods themselves hostile to one another. Difference between monotheists and polytheists; like difference between a well ordered regular army and an undisciplined *polyglott* militia force. Among the Christians each man worshipped the same God, acknowledged the same Saviour, practised the same forms, and expected same salvation. Hence a united zeal and a common faith. But among polytheists worshippers

of one set of gods hostile to those of another set, *e. g.*, in 20th book of Iliad, Minerva, Juno, Neptune, &c., on one side, Apollo, Mars, Venus, Diana, &c., on other. From similar causes religion of the Greeks more social and tolerant of other religions than that of Christian, *e. g.*, said Tiberius proposed to place statue of Christ in Pantheon—indignantly rejected by Christians. Augustus gave orders to make sacrifices for his prosperity in temple at Jerusalem—meanest Jew would have been regarded with abhorrence who should have paid same compliment to the Jupiter in Capitol. Josephus says Caligula gave orders to have his statue placed in temple at Jerusalem. All Jerusalem would have flowed in blood before this would have been permitted. At first mention of this idolatrous proposal said that King Agrippa fainted away. Neither violence of Antiochus, nor the arts of Herod and the example of other nations, could ever persuade Jews to associate elegant mythology of Greece with the institutions of Moses. Christian had all this zeal of the old Jew without same narrow spirit of exclusiveness. But again, skepticism had long entered into Pagan world, philosophers had begun to discern clearly unity of Godhead, and absurdity of polytheism Cicero and Cæsar were probably skeptics—tendency decidedly to doubt and disbelief—this a melancholy state for mass of mankind—Christianity came at decisive moment, inspiring new zeal, whilst that of polytheism was worn out. Hence one cause of its success.

3. *Same advantages on side of polytheism in its conflict with Christianity?* Polytheism was highly *material.* The forms of the gods were in the temples and public places. The arts of painter and sculptor scattered the emblems of this religion every where, all ceremonies and festivals of Pagan world were associated with it. It is a law of our nature that the affections should quickly entwine themselves about material objects, which then gradually become interwoven with all our feelings and emotions; hence an effect which a conviction of the mind cannot always remove. Hence Dr. Johnson affirmed that a conversion from the Catholic religion to the Protestant was much less likely to be permanent than the reverse, because so many material forms and ceremonies connected with former, all constantly reviving old associations, feelings and affections, which often prove too strong for mere convictions of reason. Again, if in polytheism there was no creed, no union, no universal church—if there was want of omnipotence in heavenly hierarchy and consequent distrust as to power of gods, yet the devotee was for that very cause more *familiar* with them, he approached them more freely, and considered himself more on a footing of equality with them. They possessed his affections and feelings more completely. This principle may be illustrated from our own religion, *e. g.*, Christ who became Man

for sins of world, is regarded with more affection and feeling than God. Upon same principle constant tendency to worship of saints and Virgin Mary during dark ages. These could be approached more familiarly and confidently than the infinite majesty of the Almighty—this principle of course would operate against desertion of polytheism.

4. *Second cause of progress of Christianity explained?* The doctrine of a future state and immortality of the soul was only darkly and mysteriously shadowed out in the religions of antiquity. The Hades of Homer and the Elysium of Virgil are gloomy and unsatisfactory, particularly the former. Agency of gods supposed to be employed more in this world than hereafter, hence the prayers to Jupiter, Apollo, &c., were almost always for *temporal happiness.* Even in Old Testament, doctrine of a hereafter not clear and explicit, *e. g.*, among Jews, two sects, Pharisees and Sadducees ; former believed in future rewards and punishments, latter not. But in New Gospel, this doctrine traced with pencil of light, all doubt is dispelled. Hence a new and powerful motive which animated the courage of Christian—hence disregard of things of this world and the heroism with which he died the martyr.

5. *Doctrine of the millennium, and its supposed influence?* The belief in approaching end of the world, and doctrine of millennium are supposed by Gibbon to have had great effect in spreading Christianity. (301.) These expectations were countenanced by 24th chapter of St. Matthew, and 1st Epistle of St. Paul to Thessalonians. The millennium connected with second coming of Christ. World created in six days, therefore, according to tradition ascribed to prophet Elijah, it would continue 6000 years, then would come joyful Sabbath 1000 years, when Christ, and triumphant bands of saints and elect who had escaped death, or been revived, would reign on earth till general resurrection. Early Christians calculating from the Septuagint, believed 6000 years almost elapsed. This cause, Gibbon supposed, produced a sort of panic in the world, and drove many into pale of church. He has probably exaggerated its effects. Whitby on Millennium has proved that it was never generally believed in by the church, that Origen first brought it into general notice by attacking it, and Origen says, that the few who held it, did so with such secrecy, that it had not yet come to the ears of the heathen. (W. 40.)

6. *Third cause explained?* The apostles and disciples, for a short period after the death of Saviour, were endowed with miraculous powers, they possessed the gift of tongues, &c. Not necessary to dwell on these powers as a means of spreading Gospel. The gift of tongues enabled them to preach in all countries, and power of working miracles would demonstrate the truth of their mission, and convert to their faith most

skeptical of beholders. Period during which this power was possessed by primitive church not defined, could not have lasted long.

7. *Fourth cause explained?* That the primitive Christians were distinguished for virtue, and strict morality, there can be no doubt. Pliny, the younger, was governor of Pontus and Bithynia 18 months, during persecutions of Trajan, and was ordered by emperor to ascertain true character of Christians. In letter to Trajan, (107,) he thus speaks of them, "They bind themselves by an oath, not to the commission of any wickedness, but not to be guilty of any theft, or robbery, or adultery—never to falsify their word, nor to deny a pledge committed to them, when called upon to return it." (W. 10 and 28.) Bardesanes, learned Christian of Mesopotamia in time of Marcus Antoninus, thus speaks of the Christians: "In Parthia they do not indulge in polygamy, though they be Parthians—nor do they marry their own daughters in Persia, though Persians. Among the Bactrians and Gauls, they do not commit adultery; but wheresoever they are, they rise above the civil laws and customs of the country." The virtue of charity was corner stone of Christian edifice. Every church provided for its indigent members. Chastity, and continence too, were virtues which eminently distinguished the early Christians amid the general corruption of the times. Their worship was extremely simple, without temples, or altars, or images. Assembled in private houses; and in time of persecution in remote and unfrequented places, and sometimes in night, brought with them voluntary offerings for the Lord's Supper and the Agape, or love-feast connected with it. All over was given to the poor and the clergy, for whose support there was likewise a monthly contribution. (Geis. 103.) Besides the fact that the Gospel inculcates a system of high morality, early Christians had strong temporal motives for practice of virtue, they were a new sect rapidly rising into notice, the eye of the magistrate was upon them, they were accused of receiving into their society some of the most wicked of men, who professed conversion and repentance, hence, the necessity for the most rigid and circumspect conduct. The early Christians form, in point of morality, striking contrast with the Jews at the time Titus destroyed city, of whom Josephus says no city had ever suffered so severely, nor had there ever been on earth so abandoned a race of men as those who then possessed Jerusalem, and he admits that their abominable excesses compelled Titus to destroy the city. (J. H. C. 482.)

8. *Explanation of fifth cause?* Christians became in process of time united under energetic church government, which gave to them union and energy which they would not have possessed under a looser organization. But for the character of church government it is probable that

schisms in church would have weakened it to such an extent that Christian religion might not have survived the irruption of barbarians; as it was, church had so much energy that it *conquered* and proselyted the barbarians as fast as they settled in the empire. Again, as offices in church became more and more important, more persons would enter it, either through motives of ambition or to be connected with a body which had so much life and energy amid the general decay of the rest of Roman world. But if this latter reason augmented the number and power of the church it became source of corruption, as will soon be seen.

9. *Recapitulation?* First cause gave valor and fortitude, three next supplied the Christians with arms, fifth gave them union and discipline. (G. 353.)

10. *Two circumstances which aided in the spread of the Christian religion?* 1st, The excellent roads which traversed the empire and produced facility of intercourse. 2d, Great extent of the empire with only two languages spoken, the *Latin* throughout the western portion, and the *Greek* through the eastern.

11. *Different systems of church government at present day?* 1st, The *Catholic system.* Whole church regarded as one body, called the *Universal Catholic Church.* St. Peter considered as the first pope or head of this church, and the popes who have followed are his successors. Power of the church resided principally in the pope and councils, and is binding over whole catholic denomination. 2d. *Episcopal system.* According to this there are three distinct orders in the ministry, *bishops*, *priests* and *deacons.* Bishops *alone* have right to ordain and confirm by imposition of hands, they have chief administration in diocese, and chief administration of spiritual discipline, besides having all the powers of the inferior grades. Bishops supposed to be the successors of the *apostles.* 2d order, *priests*, formerly called presbyters or elders, have authority from ordaining bishop to preach, to baptize, to consecrate Lord's Supper, and to offer up the public prayers of the church. These supposed by some to be successors of the *seventy disciples.* 3d. All these duties, except consecrating Eucharist, with bishop's permission, may be exercised by the *deacons*, who form third and lowest order in episcopal church. 3d. *Presbyterian system.* According to which there is no distinction of rank among ministers, but perfect *parity*, whether bishops or presbyters.* Besides these three distinct forms of church government, there is every variety of modifications resulting from the

* Any one wishing to see the arguments *for* and *against* the episcopal system of government stated in most masterly manner, will do well to read the Controversy between Bishop Onderdonk and Dr. Barnes—the former of the episcopal, the latter of the presbyterian church.

more or less power of the laity in conjunction with the clergy, from the greater or less independence of the different churches, &c. Besides, there are many who contend that the subject of church government was not settled by Christ or his apostles, that the whole subject was purposely left open, and that the form may be adapted to the varying circumstances of the denomination to which it is applied.

SEC. III.—RISE AND PROGRESS OF PAPAL POWER.

The above one of the most important and intricate subjects connected with church history. Seems, however, to be an admitted fact that papal power sprang from church government.

1. *Church government during the life of Christ and immediately after his crucifixion?* During his life he was of course the Head, and church being small required very little government. Immediately after his death Mosheim and Gibbon think the government was democratical, and the several churches independent, except so far as bound to each other by ties of faith and charity—most amiable harmony reigned among the members—this evidenced by the *agape*, or love feast, which followed the taking of the sacrament, to which all were indiscriminately admitted—by the names of *brethren* and *sisters* with which they saluted each other, and the regular provision made for the support of the needy, &c. Some supposed that there was community of goods too in the first era of the church.

2. *Bishops, presbyters and deacons?* But, however democratic the church might have been in the beginning, soon found necessary to establish more regular discipline. Public functions were intrusted to ministers, called *bishops* and *presbyters*—terms used at first indiscriminately—latter however rather expressive of age, wisdom, gravity, &c., former of power and inspection over faith, manners, &c., of Christians. (G. 331. Mos. 38. Wad. 21.) In first government of church at Jerusalem, not the elders only, but whole church, were associated with the apostles. During the lifetime of the apostles their character and standing would naturally make them the directors of the churches with which they were connected, and of those which they founded. The word *deacon* (Διακονος) means minister. At first confined principally to ministry on table at communion, attendance on the poor—all contributions for charity passed through their hands. Sometimes permitted to read the Gospel, and even to preach and explain it, *e. g.*, Stephen, a mere deacon, disputed publicly on Christian truth with great wisdom and force, and even performed miracles among people, (W. 22.) whatever might have been the quality at first among the ministers, public deliberation requires a president of the assembly, and

there is almost always some one in every Christian congregation to whom all are disposed to look for advice and direction in consequence of his piety, talent, justice, &c. Hence early Christians soon got into habit of choosing one of their wisest and most holy men to preside at their deliberations and execute duties of ecclesiastical governor, &c. This president or governor of the congregation was called bishop, and hence this term, at first confounded with presbyter, began to be distinct, and to imply the highest officer or president of each church ; still primitive bishops considered only first among equals, and honorable ministers of a free people—when episcopal chair became vacant, new president chosen among presbyters by suffrage of whole congregation.

3. *Schisms in the church?* Schism arose in the church immediately after death of Christ, but as the church was small, and the object of persecution, however much the members differed, they stood together against paganism. First important heresy was concerning the old Jewish dispensation. *Nazarenes* adhered to all the Mosaic rites and ceremonies, not supposing the old dispensation abolished; admitted, however, the divine nature of Christ, though not perhaps to same extent as we do. The *Ebionites* seem to have been a sect of Nazarenes, limiting still farther divinity of Christ, or even denying it altogether. Dr. Semler thinks this last sect was origin of *unitarianism*, " the child of Judaism misunderstood, and of Christianity imperfectly received." (Art. Enc. R. K.) The sect of the *Gnostics* embraces so many varieties that it is impossible to specify their tenets—derived from Greek word (Γνῶσις) knowledge. Mixed a great deal of philosophy, particularly of eastern philosophy, with their doctrines. Gibbon, in speaking of Gnostics, considers that portion of them opposed to Nazarenes, and accordingly describes them as not only not observing Jewish rites and ceremonies, but as pronouncing against the whole Jewish dispensation—opposed to pleasures of sense, therefore arraigned polygamy of patriarchs, gallantries of David, and seraglio of Solomon—said the cruelties practised in conquest of Canaan unbecoming a benevolent God—Mosaic account of creation and fall of man, the rib of Adam, the garden of Eden, the forbidden fruit, the speaking serpent, &c., they regarded with derision. Fundamental doctrine—that the Christ whom they adored, first and brightest emanation of divinity, came to rescue mankind from sin, and reveal new system of *truth*. (G. 283.) Besides the specimen of gnosticism given by Gibbon, there were various other doctrines which were propagated by these Gnostic sects—they mixed eastern philosophy, the Persian and the Christian religion all in one compound. They admitted with Pythagoreans that matter was source of evil—hence they totally denied the *humanity* of the Saviour, because every thing *corporeal* they considered as

essentially *evil*—they admitted the two principles of Persian religion, and many of them considered God of the Jews the evil principle and Christ the good, or the brightest emanation of the good principle—they farther adopted the tenets of Persian religion in regard to demons and to good and evil spirits, and in process of time the heathen gods even were admitted to exist, but ranked among demons, &c. The origin of this world generally attributed to evil principle. Alexandria, the great commercial depot of Egypt, was the point of confluence for these gnostical heresies. Most of the Gnostics were austere and rigid in their mode of life—they recommended abstinence and mortification of the flesh, (the material part,) to purify the mind, (the spiritual part.) But the greatest controversy in the church was raised at a later period about the character of Christ. Arius was the originator of what is called *Arian doctrine;* said the Son could not be *co-eternal* with the Father, the thing that is begotten must be *posterior* to that which begets—that Christ was besides produced by Almighty from nothing: He farther disputed *consubstantiality* of Christ, held that he was not of same *substance* with Father, but supported the doctrine of *similar* substances—former expressed by Greek word ('Ομουσιος,) and doctrine called *Homousian ;* the latter by the word ('Ομουισιος,) the doctrine called Homouisian. This controversy settled by great council of Nice, called by Constantine in first part of 4th century in favor of *Homousians.* With regard to nature of Christ one sect called *Monophysites*, who contended that divine and human nature of Christ were so blended into *one*, as to form but one nature; while the *Monothelites* maintained that Jesus Christ whilst existing in the flesh had but *one will.* Besides schisms above-mentioned, disputes were raised about the nature of *original sin* and *fall of man*—the Pelagian controversy was on this point. Disputes, too, of most bitter character, arose about *free will*, *free agency*, *predestination*, &c., &c. This was great subject of controversy in time of St. Augustin.

4. *Effect of these schisms?* At first did not produce much discord among Christians, but as polytheism gave way, and Christian church became more numerous, these sects became more and more intolerant, until one of two results seemed inevitable, either the church must be weakened and finally overthrown by the dissensions of sects, or a church government must arise adequate to the amicable settlement of controverted points—hence the origin of councils, and one powerful cause of the advance of episcopal power terminating in papal supremacy.

5. *Councils and their influence on progress of episcopal power?* At first churches, as we have seen, were independent, bound to each other only by ties of faith and charity; hence at first there was very little necessity for councils or synods; but in process of time, as the churches

increased in number, and schism began to arise, became important to unite churches into a sort of federative system to give them strength and to suppress heresy; hence the institution of *synods* or *councils*. These church confederacies followed the division of Roman empire into *provinces*. A provincial synod would be composed of delegates from all the churches in the province. Bishops of the several churches would naturally be principal members in these councils, president of the council might at first be selected for talent, piety and qualification, but in a very short time the bishop of the metropolis of the province would have the most weighty claims to this office by virtue of the city which he represented, and thus arose the superiority of the *metropolitan bishop*. Before conclusion of 1st century, four bishops in this manner seemed to take precedence of all others. Those of Rome, Alexandria, Antioch and Jerusalem, and after the time of Constantine, Constantinople was added to the number. It was found necessary, in process of time, to summon occasionally what were called *œcumenical* or general councils, to decide upon the question of universal interests, *e. g.*, first council of this kind was held at Nice in 325, and decided against the Arian doctrine; another at Ephesus condemned the Nestorian heresy; another at Chalcedon, the Eutychian, &c., &c. In these great councils at first bishop most distinguished for piety, learning, &c., would preside, *e. g.*, Hosius, bishop of Cordova in Spain, presided at the first œcumenical council of Nice, but afterwards the claims of the aspirants would depend, as in the case of the provincial synods, more on the dignity of city represented, than the character of the man.

6. *Influence of city of Rome on the claims of the bishop of Rome to supremacy?* It was easy to foresee, that in this contest for precedence among the bishops, the Roman see would carry the day. In the first place, Rome had once been mistress of the world, and, until time of Constantine, was first city in the whole empire—it was belief of Christians, that the first Roman church was founded by the two apostles, Peter and Paul, the former of whom was considered as foundation stone in the Christian church. Another circumstance powerfully contributing to the precedency of the bishop of Rome, was the fact that Rome, although often pillaged by barbarians, was the only great city of the west which never long remained in their hands after subversion of empire, it preserved more of the Roman population, character, manners, &c., than any other city—the consequence was, that the old Roman population, from every quarter, turned their eyes to this city—it became the centre of the recollections and associations, the image of all that remained of the Roman world—it was a name dear and popular to the Romans, and

we must remember, that the cause of religion was principally in their hands. (G. T. 3, 63.)

7. *Rise of the patriarchal power, and its subsequent decay in the west?* As the union of the churches in a province gave rise to the superior power of the metropolitan bishop, so in some countries, particularly in the east, a union of the provinces gave rise to the patriarch or primate, who had sort of patriarchal superintending power over several provinces; *e. g.*, patriarchs of Antioch, Jerusalem, Alexandria and Constantinople, bore same relation to the metropolitans of provinces, that these bore to the bishops. The same sort of distinction was tried in western portion of the empire, but with different success. Bishop of Rome soon became a patriarch. In Spain, metropolitan of Toledo, in England of Canterbury. In Gaul and Germany, the archbishops of Arles, of Lyons, of Bourges, and of Vienna, all attempted to seize powers in their respective countries—but all, except the bishop of Rome, failed, because, first, after conquest of the barbarians, there was not union enough among the parts of these several countries to impart nationality to them in a civil point of view—hence the difficulty of constituting a well cemented national church. Second, the metropolitans and bishops in each country would naturally oppose the rise of the patriarchs who claimed a controlling power over them. Third, the bishop of Rome would oppose them. We have seen the vast moral influence which the city of Rome produced in favor of its bishop. As his power increased he naturally desired to put down all rivals—hence we see his constant opposition to the patriarchs of west. In France he artfully contrived to shift the primacy from one metropolitan to another, so as to prevent a permanent institution, *e. g.*, he favored at one time the claims of Lyons, then of Arles, then of Sens, &c., until the claim was finally given up by all of them.

8. *Decay of metropolitan power in the west?* Produced by same causes which operated against the patriarchs. 1st. After conquests of barbarians, metes and boundaries of the provinces were broken up, importance of cities changed, metropolitan of a *ruined* city would lose his power. 2d. While this cause was operating, the bishops in the church were aiming for a power similar to that which the aristocracy were everywhere seizing under the civil governments, they were throwing off the power of the metropolitans or archbishops. 3d. Whilst the metropolitans were thus attacked from below by the bishops, who were all aiming at independence, they were attacked from above by the papal power, or the bishop of Rome, who, with an increase of power, naturally wished to break the organization of national churches, that he might

meet less resistance in extending his own power, and who wished too, to get these metropolitans out of the way, that he might usurp the power which they lost. From the 6th to the 8th century, this revolution in church was going on, and finally consummated. (G. T. 2, 25.)

9. *Effect of the decay of patriarchal and metropolitan power in the west on the growth of papal authority?* When the bishop of Rome acquired patriarchal power over south of Italy, and three chief Mediterranean islands—it so happened that none of the ten provinces forming this patriarchate had any metropolitan, hence the bishop of Rome exercised metropolitical powers as well as the patriarchal throughout his whole patriarchate, such as consecration of bishops, convocation of synods, decision of appeals, &c. Thus, although his patriarchate was small, the union of two sets of powers gave him advantages which no other patriarch possessed. As soon then as downfall of western patriarchs and metropolitans enabled him to extend his patriarchal power from country to country, with each extension of the patriarchate, he claimed to exercise same double set of functions he did in south of Italy, *e. g.*, first encroachment of this kind in province of Illyricum, when annexed to his patriarchate at end of 4th century—he claimed the privilege of consecrating all the bishops, which was a metropolitical and not patriarchal power. In middle of 6th century we find him consecrating archbishops of Milan. So likewise the popes began to exercise appellate jurisdiction in regard to decisions of provincial synods and contests among the bishops, &c.

10. *Effect on the power of bishops?* Although the papal power was thus aggrandizing itself, its progress was slow, and as the metropolitan and patriarchal authority of the church fell into decay, the bishops acquired power *at first* faster than the pope; hence Voltaire says 9th century was the *age of the bishops*, and the 10th, 11th, and 12th, *of the popes.* Hence the first pretensions of the church to superiority over the temporal power came from the bishops, *e, g.*, as early as 682, at 12th council of Toledo in Spain, bishops deposed Vamba king of the Visigoths in favor of Ervigius. In 842 at Aix-la-Chapelle the bishops and priests deposed Lothaire at the instance of his two brothers, Charles *the Bald*, and Louis of Bavaria, (W. 245, H. M. A. 269;) and up to end of 9th century the most flagrant acts of usurpation arose from the *national clergy*, not from popes. About 880 when Hincmar, archbishop of Rheims, heard that pope was coming into France to excommunicate the bishops, he exclaimed, *Si excommunicaturus venerit, excommunicatus abibit.* (G. Lect. 6. 32.)

11. *Circumstances favorable to the popes in their contests with the bishops and sovereigns?* In this struggle, pope had same advantages,

which the kings at a subsequent period had when struggling against their nobles. Bishops not united, jealous of one another; in their quarrels the weaker would appeal to the pope. Same thing happened to temporal princes—defeated party always ready to accept the pope's aid. Hence the pope, by being umpire, soon attained to great power. Again feudal age was one of great violence and oppression, hence the oppressed everywhere were disposed to rally around the papal throne—the man in the *mire* is always first to implore the aid of Hercules. Besides, the popes were often on the side of justice and humanity, and hence their widespread popularity with the *people* of Europe/ Instances illustrative of foregoing remarks. Lothaire, of whom we have spoken, towards conclusion of 9th century divorced his wife, to marry his concubine, wife appealed to pope Nicholas against the decision of three councils, pope excommunicated king, and was supported by people, and the justice of the case. (W. 246.) Rothadus, bishop of Soissons, was deposed by two councils held under Hincmar in 862. Rothadus appealed to Rome, pope Nicholas annulled the sentence, and reinstated the bishop. In this case, the prosecution of Rothadus was unjust, hence the pope, although usurping, was supported by king, and the people. (W. 251.) In the celebrated case of King John, of England, Innocent could never have succeeded, if it had not been for Philip Augustus of France, who was ready to execute the pope's sentence. (W. 345.) Yet, this same Philip had seen, but a few years before, his own kingdom laid under an interdict, because he divorced his Danish wife, Isemburga, the day after the nuptials, (343,) and the pope triumphed over them. If ever king was formed capable of resisting papal power, it was Edward I., yet he was very ready to acknowledge pope's power to annul an obligation, when he wished to get rid of an oath, he had taken to observe the statute against arbitrary taxation. When Pepin, the mayor of the palace, under Childeric, king of France, wished to dethrone the monarch, and take his place, he sent to pope Zachariah to know whether the man who was king *de facto*, or he who had the mere name, was entitled to the office; the pope saw the drift of this question, and decided in favor of Pepin, one of the greatest men of the age, and who he knew would soon be king, and who, as we shall see, ever afterwards became firm supporter of the papal power. If we look at the daring usurpations of Gregory VII., we shall be at no loss to perceive the causes of his success. Germany was the great empire of Europe, its monarch was elective, a struggle was arising between the emperors and the great princes—former wanted to convert empire into hereditary monarchy, and to destroy the power of the princes—latter, of course, were resolved to defend their privileges and liberties. Emperors were rapidly succeeding, when Henry IV., a minor, was made emperor—during his minority, the war broke out—when he came to majority, he developed an unprincipled, violent, and vacillating character. Gregory was on the papal throne at this important crisis; he, of course, became involved with Henry, and whenever he would depose him, or hurl his thunder at him, there were the great princes, particularly the Duke of Saxony, ready to execute his sentence, and some *anti-king* ready to occupy the throne, &c. It was in fact, Gregory who preserved elective feature in the German monarchy, upheld the power of the German princes, and secured the liberties of Germany against the emperors, whilst elevating papal above temporal power. (Pfif. T. 3, 397.) Thus were the popes, by artfully playing off the power of one sovereign, or one bishop, against another, by sometimes espousing the just and popular side, by exercising some contested power when a great prince might stand in need of it, enabled finally to usurp a degree of power, which made them for a time the most formidable potentates of Europe.

12. *False decretals of Isidore?* In the commencement of 9th century, between 820 and 849, appeared what are now called the *false decretals of Isidore.* These purported to be rescripts or decrees of the early bishops of Rome. They denied the power of the metropolitans, and established the appellate jurisdiction of the popes; although now known to be false, they were then universally allowed to be genuine, and gave a sort of *legal sanction* to all the usurpations of the popes up to that time. The bishops generally favored these decretals, because they helped to overthrow the power of the metropolitans. (H. M. A. 273, G. T. 3, 82.)

13. *Donations of Pepin and Charlemagne to the see of Rome?* Some time after the subversion of the Roman empire, the emperors of the east conquered the southern portion of Italy, which was generally governed by an officer called the Exarch of Ravenna—to this exarchate was attached the see of Rome. In north of Italy, the Lombards had early established a powerful kingdom, and in the time of Pepin, it had become so powerful under Aistulphus, as to triumph over the Greeks, and to obtain possession of exarchate of Ravenna. In this emergency, Stephen, the pope of Rome, called on Pepin, then king of France, who was much indebted to pope Zachariah for his crown, to come into Italy and aid the pope against Aistulphus. He did so, took the exarchate of Ravenna from the king of the Lombards, and bestowed it on the pope of Rome—hence the pope's temporal power—this gift was afterwards renewed and confirmed by Charlemagne, when he conquered the Lombards. (M. V. J. 195.) Under Charlemagne and his successors, it is probable that the *eminent* or *high domain* of the pope's

territory was still vested in the kings of France. But when the Carlovingian dynasty was broken up, and the popes threw themselves under the protection of the German emperors, then they acquired the *full* title to the Italian possessions. Thus did the popes become temporal, as well as spiritual monarchs.

14. *Excommunication and interdict?* These were the two great weapons of the church, by which its authority was made so terrible. The first confined in its consequences to the offenders alone; second extended to subjects when princes were the offenders. In height of papal power the excommunicated were looked on with abhorrence, and shunned by their servants, friends, and even families, as if infested with leprosy. Only two faithful attendants remained with Robert, king of France, when excommunicated, and even these threw all the meats which he left at table into the fire, as if polluted. (H. M. A. 276.) Those who had intercourse with excommunicated were deemed worthy of what was called *lesser excommunication.* The body of the excommunicated was deprived of right of burial, &c. Besides these religious consequences, severe civil penalties were frequently added, *e. g.*, by common law excommunicated person could not be witness, or bring an action, and might be imprisoned until his absolution, &c., &c. When excommunication failed in case of a prince, then church had recourse to the higher measure of *interdict*—this was awful. When a county or kingdom was laid under an interdict, gloom and sadness pervaded the land—churches were closed, bells silent, dead unburied, no rite performed but those of baptism and extreme unction. It was by a sentence of this kind that Innocent III. triumphed over John of England, and made Philip Augustus take back his divorced wife; which last Hallam considers the proudest triumph of papal power. (288.) In these interdicts the subjects were almost always released from all allegiance to their prince.

15. *Origin of these punishments, and cause of their greater severity in the western than the eastern church?* Every religious society must of course have the privilege of excluding from its body unworthy members, and this was the origin of excommunication. To all the devout, of course, excommunicated would be objects of aversion, but not for that reason robbed of privileges of citizens or rights of humanity. Nor would princes and kings be robbed of their crowns. Mosheim (194) attributes the hideous aspect of these punishments at a later date, to conquest of the barbarians. When barbarous nations were converted to Christianity, those ignorant proselytes confounded excommunication among Christians with that practised by priests in their own pagan system. Cæsar thus speaks of excommunication among the Druids: "This punishment is most grievous. Those upon whom it falls

are reckoned among the impious and the wicked—they are deserted by all—their approach and conversation are shunned as if contaminating, justice is denied them, and no honor is paid to them." No one can fail to see here the origin of that infernal power which dissolved all the dearest ties of life, and made sentence of excommunication so much more horrid in the west than in the east. This same pagan superstition had no slight influence on papal power, for these barbarians, when converted to Christianity, looked upon bishop of Rome as successor of their *chief druid* or high priest. And as this druid, under the darkness of paganism, had boundless authority, so the barbarians were disposed to transfer it to chief bishop in the Christian church, and make him their great *arch-druid*. Pope, of course, not only assumed these new powers with eagerness, but was willing to give to spiritual punishment all the terrors which belonged to it in a barbarian world.

16. *Celibacy of the clergy, and its influence on the church?* Many of the early Christians, upon the principle of mortifying the flesh, had led a life of complete celibacy, but it was long time before it became the rule of church, that priest should remain single. Pope and higher clergy supported this doctrine, because it favored power of church. Cyrus the Great preferred *eunuchs* as a body-guard, because more they were separated from, and despised by, the world, the more faithful they would be to him. So the church, by cutting off her members from the charities of domestic life, secures their entire affection to her cause, and renders them, like veteran soldiers, independent of all feeling, but fidelity to their commander. Guizot doubts whether the church was benefited by celibacy—he supposes it prevented the introduction of the hereditary principle into the offices of the church, and consequently prevented the popes from acquiring that power they would have gotten, could they have kept it by descent in their families.

17. *Arguments by which the doctrine of celibacy is supported in catholic church?* Two kinds, 1st, from Scripture, 2d, upon principles of morality and expediency. 1st, St. Paul—this *old bachelor* is the great advocate of celibacy, *e. g.*, in Epistle to Timothy, says, "keep thyself chaste." Again, 1 Cor. 7th ch. 7, 8, 9, 27, 28, 32, 33, 34, same sentiment. He tells unmarried men and widows that it is good for them to abide as he does—that he that is married careth for the things of the world, how he may please his wife, and also the married woman how she may please her husband, &c. Again, catholics contend that St. John in 14th ch. Rev. inculcates same sentiment, when he speaks of the voice of harpers harping with their harps, and singing as it were a new song before the throne, and no man could learn that song but the 144,000 which were redeemed from the earth. These are they *which*

were not defiled with women; for they are virgins—these are they which follow the Lamb wheresoever he goeth, &c. Hence the catholics contend that although celibacy is not positively enjoined upon the priesthood, yet it is recommended; and hence the catholic rule not a *command* of the Gospel, but a mere *rule*, annulled at any time by the church. But, 2d, catholics contend that motives of expediency and humanity require celibacy in clergy—an unmarried clergy will be more devoted to their congregations, they have no dread of plagues and infectious diseases on account of their families—they stand by their *flocks* in the hour of sickness and distress, when a married clergy would fly with their families to places of security. The *sisters of charity* illustrate the same principle—no such nurses in the world as those maiden sisters in the catholic church, devoted to deeds of charity and humanity. For same reason it is that those who are uncourteously called *old maids*, fill so important a station in the affairs of this world—they are moved by the spirit of philanthropy—they are restless and active in the affairs of the society to which they belong—they form benevolent and charitable associations—they constitute the 10th *legion* of the Christian church—they are kind and serviceable too in the families to which they are attached, and there is many an individual who owes the deepest debt of gratitude for the kindness and exertions of some maiden aunt. But in spite of all the arguments which may be urged in favor of celibacy among clergy, there is no doubt but that it led to deepest profligacy and corruption of morals among the priests—half the legislation of the church is about the specks and blemishes of this *virgin priesthood*. Again, I agree with Mr. Campbell that there is a class of feelings which no gentleman of single life can thoroughly comprehend. They can only be studied in the bosom of a family. The domestic affections and relations must be learned experimentally, and he who presides over a Christian congregation should have them in all their force and purity. (Debate with Purcell, 203.)

18. *Two circumstances favorable to the growth of the power of the church?* 1st, Clergy had more learning than any other class of men, and consequently were in position to assume that power which superior knowledge will always give. 2d. The difficulty of testing religious projects by any fixed standard. If temporal prince get up a mere temporal project, all will soon be able to judge of its propriety by his success or failure; not so in religion—here the human mind is baffled. A temporal failure may be claimed as a spiritual success, and hence it often happens that whether the scheme succeed or fail, in a temporal point of view, it adds equally to power of the church, *e. g.*, if the crusades succeeded, it was an evidence of the will of God; if they failed,

those who were prematurely cut off had but a quicker entrance into paradise. Again, had Thomas à Becket triumphed over Henry, the church would have reaped the benefit; but he was defeated and murdered, and it was found that Becket *dead* had more power to injure Henry II. than Becket *alive*, and degrading penance of the monarch at his tomb proved the fact, and hence the church seemed to stand like Protagoras in the *conclusion* of the celebrated *syllogism* against Enathius. "Therefore, whether I gain or lose the cause, I shall obtain the reward." (H. L. 141.)

19. *Arguments drawn from the Bible in favor of the papal supremacy?* Not to suppose that catholics have not been able to bring strong texts in their favor. The two verses on which the claims of the pope principally rest are the 18th and 19th of 16th ch. of Matth. "And I say unto thee that thou art Peter, and upon this rock I will build my church: and the gates of hell shall not prevail against it. And, I will give unto thee the keys of the kingdom of heaven: and whatsoever thou shalt bind on earth, shall be bound in heaven; and whatsoever thou shalt loose on earth, shall be loosed in heaven." Again, in the 15th, 16th and 17th verses of 21st ch. of John, three times the Saviour says to Peter after asking whether he loved him, *Feed my lambs—feed my sheep.* These texts are supposed to show that Peter was made first pope, or head of the church, that the keys were delivered to him with power of absolution from sin, &c.; and the catholics allege that there has been an unbroken line of successors to St. Peter down to the present time. Protestants answer the argument from Bible by saying that the pronoun "*this*" before "*rock*" refers not to Peter, as the catholics suppose, but to a great *truth* which Peter had just uttered to Saviour, when he said "Thou art Christ, the Son of the living God," this was the *rock* and not Peter, upon which the church was founded. But does not the name of Peter, which signifies *rock* in Greek, favor the catholic interpretation? To this, the protestant says, our Saviour's metaphors are often drawn from objects before him, *e. g.*, on sea of Galilee, he says to the fishermen, "Follow me, and I will make you *fishers of men.*" To Samaritan woman at the well, he says, "Whoever shall drink of *this water*, shall thirst again, but whoever drinks of *the water* that I shall give him, &c.," while looking at sacrifice of a sheep in the temple, he says, "*My sheep hear my voice*, and they follow me." When on Mount Olivet among the vines, he says, "I am the *true vine*, and my Father is the *vine-dresser.*" So it is said, the name of Peter merely suggested the metaphor on which the Roman bishop has built his tremendous claims to spiritual power. (C. 83.) With regard to the keys of the church, that is supposed to relate to the first gospel sermon which Peter was chosen to preach on

the first Pentecostian morn, when he explained the new gospel, and threw open the doors of the church to the Jew and the Gentile. (85.) But even supposing these metaphors could not be otherwise explained, it would appear absurd, upon a doubtful figure of speech, to erect such a fabric of power as the pope once claimed. A president of the United States with such doubtful claims, would meet with few adherents.

20. *Arguments from Bible in favor of catholic church, and its claims to infallibility?* The catholic believes his church infallible, and therefore he interprets the Scriptures according to its dictates, and judges not for himself—his arguments are drawn from three last verses of 28th chapter of Matthew, where Christ sends his disciples forth to teach all nations, saying, "and lo, I am with you *always*, even unto the *end of the world;*" same power given in Matthew, 18th chapter, 18th verse, and, in the 17th verse, he says, "And, if he shall neglect to hear them, (the witnesses,) tell it unto the *church;* but, if he neglect to *hear the church*, let him be unto thee as a heathen man and a publican." Moreover, the apostle's creed says, "I believe in the *holy catholic church.*" Independently however of the Bible, catholic maintains that the church will be split into schisms, and end in weakness and anarchy, if each man left to interpret for himself.

21. *Arguments from Bible in favor of authority of pope over temporal princes?* 1st, All the churches of all nations must be subjected to one head. 10 John, 16 verse: "And other sheep I have which are not of this fold; them also I must bring, and they shall hear my voice; and there shall be *one fold* and *one shepherd.*" Thus as there is *one God*, *one faith*, *one baptism*, so there must be *one church* with *one head.* By Romans 13th, ch. 1, all power is shown to come from God; and by 1 Cor. 2d ch., 15, the spiritual power is placed above the temporal. "But he that is *spiritual judgeth* all things, yet he himself is *judged of no man.*" Catholics claimed too as applying to papal power the 10th verse of 1st ch. Jer., "See, I have this day set thee over the nations and over the kingdoms, to root out and to pull down, and to destroy and to throw down, to build and to plant." A similar interpretation has been given to 8th and 9th verses of 2nd Psalm. Upon these texts Boniface VIII., in the famous bull called *Unam Sanctam*, came to monstrous conclusion, "that it is absolutely essential to the salvation of *every human being*, that he be *subject unto the Roman pontiff!*" (W. 347.)

22. *Revenues and wealth of the church?* First three centuries church supported by the voluntary oblations of faithful, made once a week or month. As early as Diocletian church had small portion of landed property which was confiscated by him. Constantine was first emperor,

who gave to church full power to acquire and hold all kinds of property. From this time forward, in spite of all spoliations, we find the wealth of church constantly enlarging, particularly after conquest of barbarians, till in 12th century half land of Europe was owned by the church. (W. 224, 232.) A great accession of wealth took place at conclusion of 10th century, when general belief of approaching end of world caused many to make their peace with God, by giving all they had to the church. This wealth fell into the hands of the clergy, the monasteries and the popes, and, for some time, the wealth of the head was but fairly proportionate to that of the members of the church. But in later times, we shall see that the pope became avaricious, and began to plunder the churches, and this was, in fact, main cause of the reformation.

23. *Some advantages which have resulted to the world from the strength and unity of the catholic church?* 1st, Control of church prevented the feebleness and anarchy which would have resulted from schism, if each had been left to interpret the Bible for himself. 2nd, Union and power of the church gave vigor and energy to the Christians, which enabled them to resist and convert the barbarians, and to form the link between the old and new empires. 3d, Unity and discipline of church bound Europe together during the feudal anarchy. 4th, Preserved the languages and learning of ancient world, (see *ante*, page 10;) and although the church played the *tyrant*, yet its *councils* afforded a theatre for intellectual and oratorical display, which compensated in some measure for the loss of the popular assemblies of Greece and Rome. 5th, In some measure exercised a remedial influence against the disorders and vices of times—every place of worship was an asylum, *e. g.*, one of the miseries of Stephen's miserable reign, that soldiers had learned to disregard rights of sanctuary. Again, when council of Clermont proclaimed the *truce of God*, from *sunset* on Wednesday, to *sunrise* on Monday, in every week, on pain of excommunication, how grateful must the peaceable and oppressed have felt towards that power, under whose protection they slept four nights in the week in security. This same power was exercised in the disputes among princes and bishops, and the oppressed and weak of every rank turned in the hour of distress to the papal throne for relief. 6th, The catholic church was the great conservative power of Christendom. Mahomedanism has twice made an onset on Europe, and in its first attack, at least, it would have succeeded, had not the Roman church roused the discordant elements of Europe into action and energy equal to the danger. (S. B. C ch. 10.) 7th, With all its faults and vices, the church was the most democratic institution in Europe before the rise of the cities. Its offices were thrown open to all—the man of low birth could aspire to the papal

throne, *e. g.*, Gregory VII., whose spiritual thunder made every potentate of Europe tremble, supposed to have been the son of a carpenter. Again, for a long time the elections were popular, and exhibited all the turbulence of our own democratic elections, *e. g.*, in 374, when Auxentius, bishop of Milan, died, people and clergy called together in cathedral to elect a successor—two parties, the Arian and the orthodox. Violence of parties produced utmost noise and confusion in assembly—a young man, one of emperor's governors, happened to be in Milan at the time, went into cathedral to assist in stopping the uproar, his voice was melodious —his person captivating—audience found out his name, and one cried out, let us name Ambrose our bishop—multitude instantly infected with spirit, cried out that he should be bishop, and thus was the celebrated St. Ambrose elected. (G. 1, 112.) In consequence of all these advantages of the church, we perceive at once that it was an institution which the disorders of the time called for, and hence we are not to wonder at the deep-rooted popularity of papal power, with the lower orders of Europe; this was one of the secrets of its success—the popes with all their tyranny the most democratic potentates of Europe, and consequently their hold was strong on popular affection; something sublime in spiritual power which governed without physical force, and overawed the mightiest monarchs by a menace or a censure. (W. 232, 361.)

24. *Reason why the eastern church never obtained the same power that the western did?* The bishops or patriarchs of Constantinople for a long time contested the supremacy with the bishops of Rome; but in addition to circumstances already mentioned, which made in favor of Rome, the fact that Constantinople was the residence of an emperor, and his court, placed the church under the shade of the civil power—the patriarch never could rise to a level with an emperor, and it was fortunate for the growth of papal power that the schism with regard to *image worship* for ever separated the eastern and western churches in the 9th century.

SEC. IV.—MONACHISM AND ITS INFLUENCE ON THE CHURCH.

The monasteries of Europe have exercised an influence on the church government similar to that produced by the rise of the cities on the civil government: necessary therefore to trace out the rise and progress of these singular institutions.

1. *Effect of physical causes on the gregariousness of our species?* A cold climate, with few spontaneous productions, prevents solitary life. Men must work for their living, and a common fire gathers the family together. But in mild climate, with clear atmosphere and little rain, where spontaneous productions are abundant, men have more dis-

position to separate and live solitary lives—hence, in Egypt and the east, there has in all times been more hermits than in the west, *e. g.*, Pliny speaks of extraordinary race on borders of Dead Sea, whom he calls the *associates of palm trees*, and who were supposed to have lived in that wild condition for thousands of years. The Therapeutæ or Essenes inhabited the deserts of Egypt and Syria as early as the time of our Saviour, and had dwelt there, no doubt, long before—these practised the austerities of hermits, although not Christians.

2. *Motives which led many Christians of the east to solitary life?* 1st, Influence of climate. 2d, The persecution of the emperors, particularly of Decius. 3d, The belief that every mortification of the flesh added to the purity of the spirit, induced many to lead a life of self denial and rigid discipline.

3. *Influence of eastern philosophy and Persian religion?* Have already seen that in philosophy of Pythagoras and Plato, matter was considered as cause of evil; and in Persian religion two principles, the good and the bad, were supposed to be in conflict everywhere. Under the action of these two systems, the Gnostics had early commenced the practice of fasting and penance by way of raising the spiritual man above the natural, the good principle above the evil. This philosophy acting on the Egyptian character, under all the influence of the climate and government, induced many Christians to leave the society of men, with its comforts and pleasures, to fly into solitude, the true mansion of virtue, where the soul could rise above its terrestrial prison to the contemplation of divine truths. (M. 1, 65.)

4. *Two grounds on which the whole system of penances has been justified?* 1st, that it produces humility and self-command; man under the infliction of pain, learns to endure evil with patience. He who habitually refrains from gratification of his appetites has a self-command which the sensualist never enjoys. The Almighty, himself, takes this method to humble and to chasten, *e. g.*, Job. And some optimists have regarded the whole catalogue of diseases and calamities "which flesh is heir to" as necessary to man upon this principle. A second ground upon which this system is supported, though not often avowed, is, that the Deity has all the passions of man, among which is that of revenge; that when the sinner has offended his God, there is no better way of atoning for it than by penance, upon the same principle that we punish those who injure us. The first ground may be defended on philosophical principles, unless when penance is carried to an extreme. A proper curbing of our appetites and mortification of the flesh may give the mind more freedom of action, but pushed too far, it becomes the cause of sub-

jection of mind to body, *e. g.*, man smarting always under the influence of lash, would never think of any thing, and what man is so much under corporeal influences as a *half starved dyspeptic?* All these causes however, whether good or bad, operated on the Christians of Egypt and the east, and drove them into the solitary lives of hermits. "He who abideth in solitude," said St. Anthony, "is free from the threefold warfare of hearing, speaking and seeing."

5. *Extravagances of the original monks?* After the remarks already made, not to wonder at the extravagances of early monks, *e. g.*, St. Pior walked while eating, because he did not consider that time ought to be set apart for it. St. Pachomius sat on a stone in the middle of his cell, and never laid down, because it would be too comfortable. Beradat enveloped himself in a sack of skins with only holes for his mouth and nose. Eufraxia, female saint, was in convent of 130 nuns, not one of whom ever washed her feet, and a bath was an abomination with them. Linen was too great luxury, hence used flannel, which would soon produce tormenting vermin. St. Macarius (for all these madmen were saints,) one day killed a gnat, struck with remorse, exposed himself for months to all insects in a marsh, till, according to Sosomen, his skin was so hard that his beard could not get through. But St. Simeon was the most ingenious of all fanatics, he built a column near Antioch, and lived on its summit—this aerial saint was so much admired that he even rebuked the emperor, Theodosius, with impunity—he was called St. Simeon Stylites. (L. Q. 22.) The Boscoi or grazing monks, seemed to propose to unite the soul to divinity, by degrading body to a level with beasts. In short, extravagances incredible, if they were not well authenticated; some shut themselves in cells so low and narrow, that they could neither stand nor lie down in comfort, some lived among the tombs, or dwelt with wild beasts in their dens. Men and women sometimes lived promiscuously in the deserts, exposed to sun and rain with scarcely any covering. These holy persons, not contented with a life of mere chastity, sometimes aspired to higher merit. Men and women lay together that they might triumph over temptation. But Mr. Gibbon tells us insulted nature sometimes vindicated her rights, and these over-meritorious saints too often brought scandal into the church. As superstition has advanced from east to west, generally has lost much of its grossness, *e. g.*, mythology of Egypt less grotesque than that of Hindostan, but more so than that of Greece. So these holy ascetics of the east were not often imitated in the west to the full extent, we sometimes, however, hear of cases equally as ridiculous, *e. g.*, St. Senoch near Tours, had himself bricked up between four walls to the arms, so that he could

not move bottom part of body, lived in this way several years, admiration of all the country; so Wulfilaich, a barbarian near Treves, built a pillar and lived on it, like St. Simeon, exposed to all weather. (G. T. 2, 62.)

6. *Establishment of monasteries?* Guizot points out four degrees of monastic life. 1st, Ascetics (from Ασκησις), which signifies exercise, these not separate from society, but pious enthusiasts who practised every mortification of flesh, particularly chastity. 2d, Hermits or anchorites, who fled from society into the woods and deserts. But as these fugitives from society became more and more renowned, there was a disposition to cluster around some one most distinguished, and thus a number of hermits would live near together in huts, where they could imitate one another in religious and ascetic exercises; they thus began to form a sort of community, and now received the name of monks. The pious St. Anthony supposed to have been the first to form such a society. Next stage was very natural, instead of living in huts, one great building would be erected, they would be gathered under a common roof, and lead same life; this, the 4th stage—these called cenobites, though the more generic name of monk, was still applied. As monachism advanced west, it principally assumed this last form, the coldness of climate, the genius of the people, &c., were all unfavorable to solitary life. (G. T. 2, 48.)

7. *Their government?* Until time of St. Benedict, different rules prevailed in government of monasteries, *e. g.*, the rule of St. Basil, of St. Augustine. At last the rule of St. Benedict was given, and, like Aaron's rod, swallowed up all the others; according to this, every ten monks under a dean or decurion (*decanus*), and all the monks in a monastery were under an abbot—the election of these officers was popular—the brethren chose the abbot, and the abbot was requested to consult the brethren on all great subjects, but when once his decision was made, passive obedience was enjoined on all the monks. At first these monasteries were placed under the jurisdiction of the bishops, hence the hostility which early sprang up between them and the bishops—hence, Cassian says, it was advice of fathers to the monks to fly from women and bishops; the former disturbed the purity, and the latter were disposed to tyrannize over them. (G. 66.) It was in consequence of this, that the monasteries, from beginning, threw themselves into the papal arms aginst the bishops, and were to pope, what the cities were to the kings in struggle against the aristocracy.

8. *Monks admitted into the body of the clergy?* At first monks did not belong to clergy, no particular rights and privileges; but in proportion as they increased and attracted attention of world, they were gradually admitted—sometimes they purchased from the bishops certain

privileges. One of first was to have service in monastery instead of going to parish church—to this end a priest was sent to them—soon they got the privilege of selecting their priest from the monks, then of commissioning a certain number to go out into world to preach. Thus did the monasteries gradually arrive at independence and power (G. II. 91), which was secured to many of them by charters granted by bishops.

9. *Exercises of the monks?* One of the most important regulations of St. Benedict was that which required the monks to labor. The saying of the apostle that "every man shall receive his reward according to *his labor*" was fortunately a favorite text with early monks. (W. 366.) Hence Europe much indebted to Benedictines; they have often swarmed out upon uncultivated districts, and thus became the drainers and agricultural improvers of Europe. (G. II. 72.) Of course a large portion of the day was devoted to religious exercises, to prayer, psalm-singing, chanting, &c. Besides they were required to read, or to be read to, and to copy manuscripts, and thus were many valuable books multiplied, and perhaps saved to us by monks. Schools were generally attached to the larger monasteries, in which were taught grammar, rhetoric, mathematics and theology.

10. *Corruptions and reforms among monks?* Incident to all institutions that demand too much of human nature, to experience great vicissitudes—case with monasteries. Extreme self-denial and sanctity of monks would raise reputation of monastery, it would get rich by its own labor, and the oblations of pious—monks became lazy, luxurious, and profligate, until odium would be thrown on them, then some reformer would start forth and adopt the rigid system, *e. g.*, in this manner arose the Dominicans and Franciscans.

11. *Psalm-singing, diet punishment, and penance in the monasteries?* According to rule of St. Benedict labor and religious exercises were well mingled, but the monks of more austere character diminished labor and increased religious service—became particularly enthusiastic in chanting and psalm-singing, till in some monasteries, as Fosbrook says, the best man was looked on as a *barrel organ* set to psalm tunes, and this was carried to such excess in some places that they established the *Laus Perennis*, an infinite series of psalmody, continued by relays of monks day and night, for ever and ever, without coming to amen! Not to wonder when psalm-singing was in such high repute, that the monks should soon get up some marvellous tales about St. Benedict, founder of the order; it was asserted that he sung psalms in his *mother's womb*, and at his birth he came *singing* into the world. A great improvement was made in church music about middle of 9th century by

introduction of the *organ*. As to food, no one was exempt from kitchen service—this service performed by monks in rotation by weeks—dinner among Benedictines was at noon, supper in evening; except on fast days, when dinner was only meal, and taken at *nones*, or 3 o'clock—two dishes were allowed, *cocta duo pulmentaria*, one of pulse, other of herbs, third of fruit sometimes—pound of bread per diem allowed to each person—flesh of four-footed animals prohibited except to sick monks—Benedict allowed a small quantity of wine to each one. For light offences culprit condemned to eat *alone*, at such time, and in such quantity as Abbot chose—for greater faults suspended from oratory and the table, and no one was to hold communion with him. If no amendment, flogged severely, and finally, if still incorrigible, driven from monastery. Repentance and contrition might entitle him to entry again, but after third expulsion gate closed on him *for ever*. In discipline of monastery most convenient penance was inflicted by lash. St. Dominic trained in a most rigid monastery, that of Santa Croce de Fonte Avellana, seemed to think a sinner might be flogged into a saint, as old Parr once thought a dunce might be into a scholar.

12. *Curious valuation of stripes?* Not only did the monks flog one another as means of obtaining favor of heaven, but there was actual value attached to stripes; they were sometimes taken by the score, and the price, as it were, handed over to the treasury of good works for the benefit of those who were deficient. A point of faith in the church that every *mortal sin* deprives sinner of grace of God, and makes him liable to eternal punishment, repentance restores grace, and commutes for temporal punishment what might have been eternal—not known how long a mortal sin would be punished in purgatory; the popes had power, however, to absolve from whole or a part. Now it seems monks of Fonte Avellana had determined that 30 psalms sung, with an accompaniment of 100 stripes to each psalm, making 3000, was a set off for *one year of purgatory*. By a fantastic species of arithmetic 3000 lashes were valued £4. The whole psalter with 15,000 lashes was a set off for five years, and 20 psalters with 300,000 lashes entered in book of recording angel as receipt in full for 100 *years of purgatory!* This scale seems to have been sanctioned by popes. (L. Q. 22, 80.) According to legend of St. Dominic the *cuirassier*, (so named from wearing an iron cuirass always next the skin,) no man was ever so ambitious of laying up this kind of treasure in heaven—he worked *by the piece*—he tasked himself ordinarily at 10 psalters and 30,000 lashes a day, at which rate he could redeem 3,650 years of purgatory per annum. In addition to this, in lent he petitioned superiors for supplementary task of 100 years, at which time his day's work was 2½ psalters and 34,500 stripes. But all

this did not satisfy ambitious Dominic—during another lent he petitioned for 1000 years instead of 100 of extra duty, and Damiano says, during these 40 days, he sung 200 psalters, and inflicted 60,000,000 stripes!!! Well might Yepes say of this saint, "I neither know how his head should have been capable of repeating so many psalms, nor how his arms should have had strength to give him so many blows, nor how his flesh could have endured so inhuman a battery." But with Dominic, according to the legend, increase of appetite grew by what it fed on, until, in *jocky phrase*, he flogged himself *against time.* He commenced one evening singing and flogging, and in 24 hours went 12 times through the psalter, and had begun 13th, and gone to *beati quorum* in 32d psalm, taking 183,100 lashes, equal to 61 years, 12 days, and 33 minutes of purgatory!! Now as old Dominic had never sinned but once, and that was in consenting to receive as a present a *furred robe*, he stood creditor to immense amount in the angel's books, but as no good works are lost, all that was over and above enough to redeem him from purgatory went to great *sinking fund* of holy catholic church. This tale was told to pope Alexander II., in a letter from Pietro Damiano, a *saint* and *cardinal*, of his *own personal knowledge.* A protestant might ask how Dominic counted the stripes while singing the psalms, and also what became of his *cuirass* all the time, for it has well been said, if he kept it on he might have laid on as lustily as Sancho on the trees, and still kept whole skin.

13. *Changes in monastic orders?* Have already observed that monks generally commenced rigid—got wealthy, lazy and luxurious—then reform became necessary—hence the monastic revolutions. 1st. Rule of St. Benedict of Nursia prevailed over all others—then the Benedictines got rich and relaxed, when the order was again revived in all rigor by Benedict of Aniane. Again the system soon relaxed till about year 900; reformed order of Cluni was established under a rigid system of *poverty*, *industry* and *piety*, which soon ran the ordinary monastic career, terminating in wealth, indolence, luxury and vice. It was this order which produced the celebrated Hildebrand (Gregory VII.) and his disciple, Urban II., who preached up the first crusade. When this order declined, then arose the Cistercians, who flourished until 13th century, when condition of Europe produced the *mendicant orders.*

14. *Mendicant orders?* About conclusion of 12th century, many heresies were creeping into the church—Albigenses were becoming numerous, and preaching up reformation, and more were the deformities in the church, the more powerful became schismatics; the old monastic orders were worn out, too rich and lazy and vicious to undertake reform—the mendicant orders arose to supply this defect. St. Dominic,

founder of most distinguished of these, the Dominicans—these monks were poor, rigid and travelling preachers, they went into streets and highways to exhort the people. (S. B. C. 194.) Men who live austere lives, and mortify the flesh, have rarely compassion on others—these monks were sent through Europe to scent out heresies, and punish the heretics, they became the genuine *blood-hounds* of the catholic church. Whether St. Dominic was the founder of the Inquisition, may be doubtful; his order certainly was. It is supposed that to this order was principally owing the extirpation of the Albigenses and the staving off the reformation, which had already commenced, for 300 years. (W. 405, H. 291.) Another order of mendicants was established by St. Francis, called Franciscans. This saint was famous in consequence of the most extraordinary piece of deception which was ever practised on the credulity of mankind—he carried about him always the stigmata of five wounds, which Christ received at his crucifixion—whilst in profound sleep, Christ descended in form of an angel, and pierced his hands, feet and side, which wonnds he always exhibited to an admiring world. The great importance of the stigmata was founded on a text, Galatians, vi., 17. "From henceforth let no man trouble me—for I bear in my body the marks of the Lord Jesus." It was thus St. Francis was made like to Christ in all things. Said this tale about St. Francis raised the jealousy of the Dominicans, who, to make their saint equal to St. Francis, said that Virgin Mary adopted Dominic for her son, and suckled him at her breast; and they even pretended that the honor of the stigmata had been conferred on him, but, through modesty and humility, kept it a secret. (L. 2, 87.) Useless to observe that these two powerful orders were on the side of the pope, and constituted a sort of pretorian guard to papal supremacy.

15. *Nuns and nunneries?* Virgins making profession of religious chastity, and dedicated to cause of Christ, mentioned by early fathers—female recluses collected into communities, probably coeval with monasteries—St. Syncletica, contemporary of St. Anthony, considered the founder of nunneries—Marcella, noble Roman lady, first introduced them into west—rules for government similar to those of monasteries. While St. Benedict was giving *the rule* to monasteries, said his sister Scholastica was forming one for nuns—they lived on common funds, used common dormitory, table and wardrobe, just as the monks—were exercised in temperance, fasting, &c., and manual labor, such as needle work and distaff. At first nuns might withdraw and get married; then council of Chalcedon made such liable to excommunication, but with right of absolution after suitable penance—finally, in 407, Innocent I. closed the outlet of penance against all who had taken the *vow and the*

veil; the ceremony of consecration and imposition of the veil generally performed by a bishop.* The age at which females might take the veil was left to discretion of bishop, but 25 was considered the earliest age at which so important act ought to be performed.

16. *Advantages of monachism?* Great institutions, no matter how vicious, will be found, on examination, generally to be deeply founded in wants of the ages in which they arise—remark eminently applicable to monachism. 1st, Monks gave to Christians a vigor and an aspect which enabled them to convert the barbarians as fast as they conquered Roman empire. It was the monks and the imposing forms and ceremonies of the catholic church, which latter were designedly made as *material* and gorgeous as possible by an artful priesthood, that operated most powerfully on the imaginations of the ignorant barbarians. 2d, Earliest monks lived by labor of their hands—the arts flourished under their mechanical labors—architecture, particularly church building, was improved by them—drained marshes, cut down forests, improved waste districts—their serfs were the best in Europe, and their estates in turbulent times the best managed. 3d, Moral and social advantages were great—they performed the duty of hospitality, supplied the place of taverns, dispensed charity, and thus supplied in some sort the place of our *poor laws*—supplied farther the place of hospitals, and discharged duties of nursing and attending to sick, particularly the nuns, *e. g.*, nuns called Ursulines ministered to the sick, relieved the poor, consoled the miserable, and prayed with the penitent (W. 401.); thus these holy sisters performed purest duties in whole circle of benevolence. 4th, In process of time schools and academies were attached to manasteries, and thus they aided cause of education. It was the monks too who generally gave us the chronicles of their times, and rude and clumsy as they were, it is from them principally we draw our history of the *mediæval ages.* Moreover, monasteries were the means of saving many of the classics, by affording safe depository, or by the monks transcribing them. 5th. Monasteries formed the asylum for those, who, in language of Scripture, were *weary and heavy laden,* and wished to retire from the world. This one of their greatest advantages in an age of violence, confusion, and ruthless tyranny. The poor and the humble could fly from cares and sorrows of the world to these institutions. Even the great made them their retreats; queens when divorced or widowed, and princesses who had lost their establishments, could retire to them with dignity and comfort; kings and princes dethroned, on repenting of their crimes, could pass their days in peace and penitence within their walls.

* Consecrating words were these, *aspice, filia, et intuere.*

The last days of Charles V. were spent in the monastery of Estremadura in Spain. Moreover equally serviceable as recipients for the restless eccentric spirits of the times, whose peculiar character the church could turn to good account, and prevent them from mischief by the strong government of the institution. (L. 2. 75.) They supplied the place of our madhouses; enthusiasts, fanatics, and madmen flocked to them, where their humors could be indulged if not hurtful, and where they met with sympathy and kindness. If they chose to torment themselves, were provided with assortment of *whips* and *cilices*, if they wished to preach, were sent to travel, and if aspired to martyrdom, were shipped off as missionaries among Moors, gentiles and savages (88); and thus even madmen found their proper places, and were turned to advantage of church. The want of monastic retreats has frequently been felt by protestants, and many attempts to introduce them have been made, particularly for women, *e. g.*, Ferrar establishment at Little Gidding. Mary Astel started a scheme of kind under William III., and even Lady Masham entertained similar plan in 1700. In 1815 Lady Isabella King, aided by Dowager Duchess of Buccleuch, Lady Carysfoot, Lady Anson, Lady Willoughby, and Lady Clanbrock, originated a similar plan—the queen subscribed £300, with annuity of £100 more, princess Charlotte £50, &c. This plan I believe partially succeeded (L. 2. 96); but generally these schemes have failed, because of aversion to popery. But must never forget with these advantages two miserable doctrines have been left to modern Europe by monks. 1st. The doctrine of *passive obedience*, far beyond any thing inculcated in ancient world. (G. II. 74.) 2d. That falsehoods may be told for pious purposes. Hence the marvellous legends of the saints, and the lying character of their chronicles; and hence too the frequent alterations and interpolations of the fathers to suit their particular purposes. (83.) Besides, these institutions had effect of withdrawing some of best men from society and their families, and left the common mass of human vice more unmixed. (H. 467.)

SEC. V.—SAINTS, VIRGIN MARY, RELICS, PILGRIMAGES, CRUSADES.

1. *Worship of saints and images?* Natural to revere the memory of the dead when they have been distinguished on earth—hence in all ages there has been tendency to hero worship. On same principle, saints were first revered, then looked to as powerful intercessors with Christ, and finally worshipped. Images were at first kept and revered as mere *emblems*, till finally the sign was taken for the thing signified, and the image itself was worshipped.

2. *Virgin Mary.* Whilst monastic orders contended about relative

merits of deified saints, all joined in adoration to the Virgin—she was soon elevated to highest rank in mythology of Roman church—she was traced in types throughout Old Testament—she was tree of life; the ladder which Jacob had seen leading from heaven to earth; the ever burning bush; the ark of the covenant; the rod which brought forth buds and blossoms; the fleece upon which alone the dew of heaven descended. Before all creatures and all ages, she was conceived in the Eternal Mind, &c. Hence prayers were addressed to her as our life and hope, our advocate and mediatrix who was to reconcile us to her Son—the Pantheon which Agrippa had dedicated to Jupiter and all the gods, was by the pope, who converted it into a church, inscribed to the blessed virgin and all the saints. (B. C. 178.)

3. *Relics?* When saints were worshipped, not to be wondered at that virtue was imputed to every thing belonging to them, *e. g.*, their bodies, apparel, instruments of suffering, &c. We naturally cherish every memorial of those whom we love—hence vast importance of relics in catholic church—they were considered as essential part of church furniture. To this day relics are preserved and occasionally exhibited in the catholic churches, such as skulls, bones, teeth, hair, apparel, &c. Churches vied with each other in these exhibitions. Instruments of the crucifixion were shown, spear and cross, the crown of thorns,* the clothes he was wrapped in in infancy, the manger, the vessels in which he converted water into wine at the marriage feast, the bread which he broke at last supper, his vesture for which lots were cast. Impudence and credulity went still farther, portions of the burning bush, of the manna, of Moses' rod, of Samson's honeycomb, of Tobit's fish, of the blessed Virgin's milk, and of our Saviour's blood, was exhibited. Every traveller who visits Italy is made familiar with the legend of Loretto, where the house in which the Virgin lived, in Nazareth, is still shown, as having been carried there by four angels. He is told the story of its arrival, how it had been set down twice upon the way, and how it was known to be the genuine house, &c. (178.) At one time offerings to an immense amount were contained in this house.

4. *Pilgrimages?* When saints were worshipped, and relics regarded as holy, not to wonder at frequent pilgrimages to the shrines of the saints. The place that has been the theatre of any remarkable event is

* Crown of thorns had been preserved at Constantinople; necessities of government forced it to pawn the crown to city of Venice; not being redeemed it was purchased at great price by Louis IX; and on its way to Paris, the royal family, with king at their head, came out to meet and receive it with all due honors—the king and his brother, with bare feet and no other dress than a shirt, took it on their shoulders and deposited it in the cathedral.

always visited with peculiar emotions, *e. g.*, such places as Rome, Athens, Babylon, &c., and such battle fields as Cannæ, Pharsalia, Marengo, Waterloo, &c. The imagination invests the spot with the character of those men or events which have illustrated it. For similar reason, Christian made his pilgrimage to the tombs of his saints. He felt a holy enthusiasm in treading on the ground which had witnessed their labors, their piety, and perhaps their martyrdom. He gathered with care the legends of the tomb which a pious superstition propagated, and eagerly preserved every relic which time and search of others had spared. Thus motives for pilgrimage founded on best feelings of human nature, and it seems to be order of Providence that a continual intermixture of mankind should take place, and that the human mind should not be left without a principle to effect it. Sometimes carried on by the migratory instinct; sometimes by spirit of conquest; but during the mediæval ages it was effected through the spirit of pilgrimage, which sent thousands to Jerusalem, to Rome, and to Mecca, who imported into their various countries the seeds of knowledge and civilization found in these celebrated cities. (B. 5, 418.)

5. *To Jerusalem?* What country so well fitted to call forth the devout adoration of the Christian as Palestine, the country of our Saviour? What city so holy as Jerusalem, which witnessed so many of his labors and his death? Could the Holy Land be swept clean of its mummeries and superstitions, the thoughts and emotions to be experienced there would be worth a pilgrimage. Hence the rage for pilgrimages to Jerusalem; and this received a powerful stimulus towards conclusion of 10th century, under opinion of approaching end of the world. This pilgrimage gradually became exalted into a spiritual duty, and was often prescribed to the wealthy as a means of absolution from sin.

6. *Treatment which the Christians met with?* Up to conclusion nearly of 11th century Palestine was in hands of Saracens, who, although infidels, yet soon saw advantages to their country resulting from these pilgrimages, and their own practice of making a pilgrimage to Mecca, might have produced spirit of toleration towards Christian. Hence on payment of small tribute caliphs allowed Christians to visit in peace and security the tomb of our Saviour, and the citizens about the spot supplied them with as many relics as their utmost superstition demanded. But about 1076 Palestine was torn from Arabian dynasty by the Turks or Turkomans, a rude and barbarous people—Christians were treated more harshly—all Christendom was roused by tales of Moslem oppression and impiety.

7. *Peter the Hermit and the councils of Placentia and Clermont?* This the man who had the honor to fire the train that threw all Europe

into commotion, and led to the crusades, the most stupendous monument of human folly, which has ever been produced by a fanatical superstition operating on an ignorant world. Peter born at Amiens in France, small stature, keen eye, vehement speech, of respectable family, had served in war under count of Thoulouse—married, wife old and ugly—retired into a monastery, there his imagination powerfully affected—had dreams and visions, finally determined upon the fashionable pilgrimage to Jerusalem, was harshly treated by the Turks—returned to Europe by way of Constantinople, where had an interview with Greek emperor, who represented his empire as liable to be overthrown by the Turks, unless Christians should send aid—then he passed to Rome and threw himself, a most *accomplished fanatic*, before Urban II., laid before him the wrongs and oppressions suffered by the devout in the Holy Land; remonstrated against sacrilege of suffering the infidel longer to trample upon such sacred ground. Pope caught the enthusiasm, sent Peter through Christendom to preach up a crusade, whilst he called the great council of Placentia, at which there were 200 bishops, 3000 clergy, and 30,000 laity, besides ambassadors from the Greek emperor. The business of the crusades not being determined here, another council was called at Clermont, and when the pope had recommended a general armament against the east, the mighty multitude shouted *Deus vult! God wills it!* which was taken as a motto for the crusaders' standard. Thus was this great undertaking resolved on.

8. *Arguments by which crusades were justified?* Two were urged—1st. That Constantinople, the capital of the eastern empire, was in danger of being conquered by the infidels, and then that all Europe might be overrun—necessary to anticipate the blow by carrying war into Asia. 2d. Argument that Holy Land was the rightful inheritance of Christian, because the Saviour of the world had died there; that Christendom should not suffer its pollution by the footsteps of the infidel.

9. *Real motives which operated on the crusaders?* Two kinds, spiritual and temporal. 1st. Spiritual—have already explained doctrine of penance, year of penance valued at 3000 lashes. Rule of the church that this might be commuted for money at £4. Many sinners vastly in arrears, some for 300 years, with consequently 900,000 lashes due, or £1200. Pope proclaimed a plenary indulgence to all those who should join in the crusades. Cold philosophy of modern times can scarcely appreciate the effect of this on a sinful yet a believing world. At voice of pastor, the robber, the incendiary, the homicide, &c., arose by thousands to expiate their sins by this holy war—to purchase an entrance into paradise by an enterprise which it would have been *pen-*

ance indeed not to have engaged in. The imaginations of men too were excited; dreams and visions were mistaken for realities, and miracles were everywhere wrought and believed in, which stimulated into madness the fanatical zeal of the times. 2d. Temporal motives. Religion powerful when coincides with the natural inclinations of mankind —crusades gratified reigning passions of the age, love of arms, and romantic spirit of adventure—the ambition of Europe too was aroused by tales of Asiatic countries—Palestine was regarded as land flowing with milk and honey, possessing mines and treasures of gold and diamond, palaces of marble and jasper, and odoriferous groves of cinnamon and frankincense. Each warrior was anticipating an establishment in this earthly paradise—noblemen were to be princes, and princes were to be kings, whilst the meanest soldier expected unbounded wealth from the rich spoil of Asiatic armies and countries. Besides all this the crusades furnished the means of escape to multitude from feudal and ecclesiastic tyranny; the serf could now escape from the glebe, the wearied monk from the monastery, the debtor from the creditor, and the outlaw and malefactor from justice; for Ducange tells us that the privileges of the *cruce signati* were freedom from debt, from usury, from secular justice, &c. (G. 11. 22.) All these causes were quickened in their operation by the contagious influence of example, which the most circumspect philosophy is often unable to withstand. The old and infirm, and even many women in disguise, were swept on by this irresistible impulse.

10. *Departure and failure of the first division of the crusaders?* Departure was fixed by council of Clermont for 15th August, 1096; but such the enthusiasm, that first division was ready in March. A disorderly band of about 60,000, among whom were many women, gathered around Peter the Hermit; and thus he who preached the crusade, without a single qualification, suddenly saw himself changed into a general, with Walter the Moneyless for his lieutenant. After these followed the *monk* Godeshal, with 15,000 or 20,000 German peasants; and in the rear followed on a disorderly multitude of 200,000 of the refuse of Europe, with a goose and a goat carried in front of them: and these formed the first division of crusaders. Such was the ignorance of this disorderly band, that they had scarcely gotten out of their neighborhood before they began to ask, at the approach of every great city, if *that was Jerusalem?* This lawless army pillaged and murdered the Jews in the cities on the Moselle and the Rhine. In their march through Bulgaria and Hungary they provoked by their conduct the revenge of the natives; and before Peter reached Constantinople he had lost two-thirds of his army. Here Emperor Alexius persuaded them to remain; but fired with zeal, they crossed the Bosphorus, marched against the Turks, and the last remnant

of this disorderly multitude was slaughtered in the plain of Nice, without taking a single city from the infidel. Peter the Hermit had given the command, after reaching Constantinople, which he did not quit till second division came up, to Walter the Moneyless, who bravely perished with his army.

11. *Second division—conquest of Jerusalem?* Consisted of the orderly soldiers computed at 700,000. None of the great monarchs engaged in first crusade; for William Rufus was too much occupied at home, Philip I., of France, was too much a sensualist to leave his pleasures, Henry IV., of Germany, was engaged in a quarrel with the great princes of the empire, and with the pope. Kings of Spain were at war with the Moors, and monarchs of Scotland, Denmark, Sweden and Poland had not yet mixed in the politics of the south. Crusaders were commanded by princes of second order, though of great renown. Godfrey of Bouillon, first in rank, accomplished leader, had fought against pope, under Henry IV.; had pierced the breast of Rodolph, *anti*-emperor, with his own lance; was first, too, to ascend the walls of Rome when taken by troops of Henry IV.; fell sick—felt remorse at fighting against pope—made a vow to lead an army to Holy Land, &c. Associated with Godfrey in the command were Hugh, count of Vermaudois, Robert, duke of Normandy, brother of Willam Rufus, Robert, count of Flanders, Stephen, count of Chartres, of Blois and of Troyes: these had command of the northern troops. Raymond, count of Thoulouse, commanded the troops from south of France; and the celebrated Bohemand and Tancred commanded the Italian and Sicilian troops. This vast armament, which Anna Commena says seemed to uptear the whole of Europe, to precipitate it on the east, took the route by Constantinople, through Asia Minor, Syria, &c. After a series of follies, sufferings, and crimes, perhaps never surpassed in the history of human madness, the victory of Doryleum, followed by the capture of Antioch, opened the road to Jerusalem, and on Good Friday, 1099, 20,000 of the crusaders out of more than a million who had left Europe, with Godfrey at their head, stormed the city of Jerusalem, planted the banner of the cross on Mount Calvary, and, amid shouts of *Deus vult!* inhumanly masssacred, without distinction, thousands of the inhabitants and garrison of the city. Godfrey was made king: and thus was a Latin kingdom established in Holy Land, at the expense of almost all the chivalry of Europe.

12. *Subsequent crusades?* About fifty years after this, loss of Edessa once more roused Europe. St. Bernard, the holy abbot of the monastery of St. Clairvaux, preached up this second crusade. Two greatest monarchs in Europe headed it—Louis VII. of France and Conrad III.

of Germany. Here again Europe lost its flower and chivalry under such a series of disasters, that even the holy Bernard was compelled to have recourse to the most contemptible of sophisms to justify his failing prophecies to the people. Forty years after this failure, Saladin the Great gained the battle of Tiberias, and soon after took Jerusalem from Christians, 88 years after its capture by Godfrey—this produced third crusade, distinguished by adventures of the Lion-hearted Richard of England, and by presence of Philip Augustus of France. 4th crusade, 3 years afterwards, under auspices of pope Celestine III.; this consisted principally of Germans; 5th and 6th under auspices of Innocent III. Lastly, the two crusades of Louis IX. followed by romantic adventures of Ed. I. of England, closed the long series of these mad expeditions, after a period of near 200 years. In year 1299, two centuries after conquest of Jerusalem by Godfrey, last fragment of Christian rule was swept away from Palestine by the victorious Moslems.

13. *Causes which kept up the crusades for so long a period?* The original impulse was fanaticism, which of course would gradually wear out; but then a Latin kingdom was established in Palestine, and feudal policy adopted. This created a thousand ties with all Europe, whose honor was now concerned to support this new kingdom. Again, the latter crusaders went by water, and they attacked the rich countries of the Barbary coast and Egypt, and thus plunder as well as religion was a stimulating cause, *e. g.*, Louis IX. turned his arms against Tunis, and with all his religion, doubted whether he was not as politic as pious. (W. 461.)

14. *Beneficial effects generally attributed to the crusades?* Threefold. 1st, On manners, arts, literature, &c.; 2d, on real property; 3d, on commerce. 1st, In their journey to Holy Land first crusaders went through Constantinople; there found the relics of ancient magnificence, arts, literature, &c., far beyond any thing in west. Immediately after this journey find more splendor in courts, more pomp in ceremonies, more taste in pleasures, and greater variety of manufactures. All the ancient classics too, particularly the Greek, were preserved at Constantinople. Many of the armaments to Holy Land went by sea. The vessels were generally fitted out at Venice, Genoa, Pisa, &c., the rich cities of Italy. Crusades assembled in those cities before departure from Europe, and as they were far above rest of Europe in wealth and civilization, supposed they imparted some of their advantages to the crusaders. Again crusades were gotten up by all Europe—greatest undertaking in modern world; had tendency to destroy mere local character and prejudice, and give to mind that general enlargement springing from travel, and the view of different manners, customs, religion, laws, &c.; hence we find

last crusades more tolerant towards Mahometans, with more freedom from prejudice, than the first. (G. Lect. 8. 20.) But intellect of Europe received a powerful impulse in another manner. Crusades operated on the imagination; they were the greatest adventures of the age. Miracles were supposed to be wrought, saints were engaged, &c., in the cause of these holy warriors—tales were told, and most exaggerated fictions were written. Now, although these lying legends would be productive of infinite mischief in an age of civilization and learning, their effect was rather beneficial in age of ignorance, when human mind was in state of torpor, any thing which could rouse it into action would be beneficial. Intellect of Europe like pool of Bethesda, it required to be roused—to be shaken into action, and crusades produced that effect. 2d. Princes who joined in crusades, obliged to sell their property to get money. None of great monarchs engaged in first crusade—they became therefore principal purchasers. Moreover many noblemen without heirs perished in these wars, and their estates escheated to the crown—thus power of kings was strengthened, while that of aristocracy was weakened, and the consequent energy of the regal power became favorable to order and peace, and thus promoted civilization. It is true, however, that a large portion of these lands were sold to higher clergy and to monasteries, thus strengthening church as much as kings. The kings however, besides purchasing lands, were often enabled during absence of powerful vassals, to extend their possessions by force, and thus add to their power. (Rob. 3, 21 and 198.) Kings gained by crusades in another manner: these wars had a tendency to sweep down all local barriers, and to produce a centralizing effect throughout Europe. Armaments on so grand a scale soon obliterate mere feudal distinctions, and produce a *spirit of nationality.* In commencement of these wars, *nations* scarcely existed; at the conclusion had considerable consistency—change in language of historians marks this transition. 3d. Great cities in Italy received a great impulse by building ships and furnishing provisions and military stores to crusaders, particularly Venice, Genoa, and Pisa. Moreover, these cities traded with countries conquered by crusaders in Africa and Asia. Constantinople was conquered by crusaders, and for 50 years a Latin kingdom was established there—the Venetians opened a great trade with this city. From all these causes wealth flowed rapidly into Italian cities, and revival of commerce and manufactures first took place in Italy. Contended that although this was effected in great measure at expense of rest of Europe, yet was necessary that lodgment of civilization and wealth should be made, no matter at *what cost*, at a few points first, and then that these would gradually arouse rest of Europe. Crusades operated too in favor of freedom of cities in every part of Europe; for they came at time when struggle was going on between cities and aristocracy, and latter sold them charters and privileges, and lands to get money for the crusades, and thus guarantied their freedom.

15. *General remark on the foregoing?* Most historians consider crusades upon the whole as beneficial from effects just described; conclusion does not follow. Because Europe improved during the two centuries of crusades, and some advantages can be pointed out, does not follow that she might not have improved more *without* them. Civilization would have flowed in other channels. Some general remarks will render this probable. Irruption of barbarians has generally been main cause of spread of barbarianism—generally found in Europe, that freedom from barbarian invasion, with any thing like tolerable government, would quickly lead on to improvement, *e. g.*, up to reign of Charlemagne, Europe was constantly disturbed by the northern invaders or by the Saracens. Great power of Charlemagne rolled tide of conquest back on the north, and drove off Saracens from south—he gave comparative repose to Europe—hence rapid improvement during his long reign. But when his empire was enfeebled by division, northern barbarians again got in motion; they were called Danes, in England. Normans on the continent, besides the Hungarians, broke loose on the north-east, and the Saracens on the south—all together threw Europe once more into alarm and confusion. Civilization began to ebb in countries most exposed to this 2d irruption. This inundation spent its force about conclusion of 10th century, and Europe was beginning gradually to rally from its effects, when crusades were gotten up. Now no doubt but the two succeeding centuries would have been ages of great improvement *without* the crusades.

16. *Evils of the crusades?* 1st. Europe lost an immense amount of her wealth, and some of her best population—whole number of persons perished more than 2,000,000. 2d. To the crusades we must attribute the spirit of persecuting whole societies, and even nations *en masse*, *e. g.*, wars against the Albigenses different from any persecutions before known. Crusade taught church to assault, with military force, whole sects and districts, to slaughter by wholesale, instead of in detail. 3d. Crusades introduced practice of plenary indulgence, a practice which operated as a license for every crime, and, in the end, led on to sale of indulgences, which produced the abuses that caused the Reformation. 4th. The crusades generated every corruption and vice among the crusaders. We are told women were involved with the men, and the priest with the warrior, in equal and indiscriminate profligacy—cities of Palestine became sinks of iniquity; the returning pilgrim could scarce have

improved Europe, in morals at least. 5th. They increased enormously pontifical and priestly power, already too great. Merely uniting all Christendom in one great religious enterprise of itself must have increased immensely the power of the pope and the church. But besides this, many in leaving their houses, under the fear of being killed, or the hope of procuring suitable establishments in the east, either sold their lands to the churches or monasteries, or gave them for purpose of making their peace with God, before their departure. Thus a great accession of wealth to the church arose from the crusades. (M. V. I. 255, W. 463.) Has generally been supposed that during the period of crusades, pope proclaimed truce of God, and threatened with excommunication those who should break it, and thus greater tranquillity reigned in Europe. But in those turbulent times, such a proclamation would soon lose its effect, and as the most chivalrous and high-minded princes were frequently drawn off by these holy wars, the more unprincipled, who were left behind, would seize the opportunity to aggrandize themselves at the expense of the absent. 6th. Another evil of crusades were the epidemical frenzies which they generated, breaking out into tumults, which Hallam denominates *enthusiastic risings.*

17. *Enthusiastic risings?* First occurrence of the kind in time of Philip Augustus. Monarch had disbanded some mercenaries, who began to pillage and ravage. One Durand, under inspiration of Virgin, headed populace against them—his followers called *Brethren of the White Caps,* from linen covering of the head—after gaining victory over the plunderers, endeavored to prevent lords from receiving dues from their vassals; this drew against them combination of princes, which soon destroyed them. During captivity of St. Louis, in Egypt, great ferment broke out in Flanders and spread over great part of France. An impostor pretended to be commissioned by Virgin to preach a crusade, not to *rich* and *noble,* whom he styled the rejected of God, but to the *poor.* His followers called *Pastoureaux,* from simplicity of shepherd life. In short time this band swelled to 100,000, banner displayed a *cross and a lamb*—leader assumed a priestly character, preached, absolved, and annulled marriages. At Amiens, Bourges, Orleans and Paris, received as a prophet, even the Regent Blanche was led away by him. His great theme, reproach of clergy for idleness and corruption—in some towns massacred the clergy, and pillaged monasteries. Soon government was roused against them, and most of them were put to the sword. Seventy years afterwards this same party broke out again and massacred great many Jews. About 1260, another of these risings took place—a great multitude of every rank, age and sex marching two and two along the streets and roads, mingled groans and dolorous hymns,

with the sound of leathern scourges upon their naked backs—hence called Flagellants—their career began at Perugia, spread over Italy, penetrated far into Germany and Poland, and then died away. In the month of August, 1399, a description of persons, called Bianchi, from their white linen vestments, appeared all over Italy, passing from city to city, crying out *misericordia!* with faces covered and bent towards ground, and carrying a crucifix before them—their constant song was *stabat mater dolorosa.* This epidemic lasted three months—Muratori ascribes great reformation of manners to it. But, judging from government of France, which prohibited the covering of face, because it gave opportunity to commit crime without detection, and from an act under Henry IV. of England, forbidding any one "under pain of forfeiting all his worth, to receive the new sect in *white clothes pretending to great sanctity*," we may conclude that these fanatics were eminently mischievous. Such was madness of crusading spirit at one time, that in 1211, a multitude of 90,000, chiefly *children*, and led on by a *child*, set out for Holy Land—came principally from Germany, reached Genoa, found the sea in their way, then dispersed in various directions, 30,000 went to Marseilles, where part were murdered, part starved, and rest sold to Saracens! (H. 463.)

CHAPTER IV.

CITIES—GROWTH AND DECAY OF THEIR POWER.

The growth of the power of the cities a subject of immense importance in the history of modern Europe. They form the democratic element in the governments of mediæval ages; it was by their influence that the aristocracy of Europe was conquered, and the power of the kings established.

1. *Character of the history of the cities?* Extremely obscure and defective. 1st, Few in the cities capable of writing history at all. 2d, Progress of cities at first slow and imperceptible, and it was their wish to conceal from great barons the progress they were making.

2. *Condition of the cities after downfall of the Roman empire?* Have already seen establishment of feudal system, which produced the fortified castles of the barons, and caused the cities to be deserted by the great. Moreover, after this time commerce and manufactures were prostrated, and without these impossible to build large and rich cities.

Inhabitants of cities poor and miserable, and subject to all the oppression of times, therefore generally obliged to throw themselves under protection of some powerful baron in their neighborhood.

3. *First step taken by the cities?* Procured privilege of building walls. Germans and Scythians had great aversion to walled towns, and when they conquered cities of Roman empire generally razed the walls. Soon however saw themselves liable to attack from fresh swarms of barbarians, therefore permitted the cities to fortify themselves. It was generally by charter from king or prince that this was allowed. (S. J. R. V. 1. 369—370.)

4. *Italian cities and their early importance?* Cities in Italy never sank as low as those to the north, because, 1st, No great monarchy was formed in Italy, nor was feudal system ever so completely established there as in rest of Europe, hence the municipal government of many of the cities which prevailed under Roman empire was never entirely lost. 2d, The wars between the emperors of Germany and the Italian princes caused both parties, but particulary the emperors, to court the favor of the cities, by granting freedom and privileges to them. 3d, A series of causes, but particularly the crusades, gave an impulse to the commerce and manufactures of the Italian cities, which made them far more wealthy than any others in west of Europe. Hence many Italian cities quickly aspired to govern themselves, and became independent republics.

5. *Form of government in the Italian cities?* During the reign of the Emperor Otho I., most of the free Italian cities adopted a form of government modelled after that of Rome. Two consuls elected by the suffrages of the people united judicial and executive powers—headed the armies of the city when called into field—they convoked the councils and the popular assemblies. Generally two councils, one called the council of *credenza, of confidence* or *secret council*, to advise about matters which were not brought before the magistrates generally—it took charge too of finance, watched over consuls, and the foreign politics. There was another council, generally of 100, called *great council*, or council of the people. This the senate that prepared business for the popular assembly, which was convened on the public square by ringing the great town bell. This assembly was considered supreme, although in most of the cities no matter could come before them which had not been sanctioned by both council of *credenza* and the senate. Although this form of government prevailed under Otho the Great, yet in process of time every variety was adopted, and the cities were the scenes of constant revolutions.

6. *Rise and progress of the cities in the rest of Europe?* Guizot points out three sources of the power of the cities in Europe generally.

1st, In some of the cities old municipal government under Romans had never entirely disappeared—this case with many in south of France, *e. g.*, Perigueux, Bourges, Marseilles, Arles, Nismes, Paris, &c. When the general movement in favor of cities took place in 11th and 12th centuries, these would have great advantages in struggle for power, because of their municipal government (T. 5, 135); *e. g.*, Marseilles in beginning of 12th century equipped powerful navies, and shared in wars of Genoa and Pisa against Saracens of Sardinia. (H. M. A. 116.) 2dly, When barbarians settled in Roman empire reversed the order of things; the great chiefs instead of living in cities as in Roman empire, lived on their lands in castles; hence power left *cities* and passed to *country*. But powerful lord, with his numerous dependents, had numerous wants best supplied by city population—hence agglomerations on feudal lands, which in many cases became considerable towns after the rise of commerce and manufactures. As these cities arose, lord soon discovered it to be his interest to make them flourish, because more wealthy the more money he could get from them, and the more soldiers they could furnish for his wars; hence the privileges and charters so frequently granted to the cities by the nobles. The soldiers from the cities were commanded in the field by the city *preachers*. (G. T. 5. 141.) By these privileges, accorded voluntarily to cities, it was never intended to make them independent of their feudal superiors, although it frequently led to this result; but charters were sometimes voluntarily granted, giving perfect freedom to the cities under peculiar circumstances, *e. g.*, during crusades many bought charters because of the necessities of barons at this time. Again, great devotion of cities to kings or princes, sometimes produced some voluntary grants, *e. g.*, city of Worms in contest between Emperor H. IV. and the pope and princes of Germany, took side of former; hence the municipal and military privileges bestowed on it by Henry. (Pfister T. 3. 332–3.) Third source of power and freedom was by conquest. A great struggle took place almost all over Europe in 11th and 12th centuries between the cities and the aristocracy and the kings. Success various—if barons succeeded, they ruined cities or deprived them of privileges; if cities succeeded, the treaty of peace secured them a charter and independence. In this struggle kings and the cities generally united, for as latter were in dread of the barons they soon leagued with regal power to crush their immediate superiors. Although this was general result, yet we find both parties occasionally invoking regal aid, and thus kings gained greatly when made umpire between the belligerent parties. These three causes, we must always remember, were stimulated in their action by the rise of commerce and manufactures, which occurred first in Italy, and afterwards through greater portion of

Europe, during 11th and 12th centuries; without the wealth which these produced cities never could have gained strength to throw off the feudal domination. Another circumstance powerfully contributing to prosperity of cities was, that they formed the asylum for refugee slaves; if a slave remained *a year and a day* without being claimed by his master he was entitled in most countries to his freedom. Besides slaves the lesser nobility frequently took up residence in towns, and thus added to respectability of population, while they brought great accession of wealth. In Italy the cities absorbed in many cases the whole of the neighboring noblesse.

7. *Government?* Marked difference between cities preserving old Roman municipal government and those of recent origin. Government of former decidedly aristocratic, that of latter highly democratic. At downfall of Roman empire chief power in city was a senate called *curia*, members of which were called *curiales;* these comprehended certain number of families inscribed on a register called *album curiæ*—number not great. The curia had the exclusive privilege of supplying by their own votes all vacancies in their body, and as soon as a new family was thus elected, it was inscribed on *album curiæ*. Government of other cities much more democratic. Most all imitated Romans, but their senate was an elective body chosen by whole body of people, and remained in office but short time. All other magistrates chosen on same democratic principle, and such rapid rotation in office, that in some cities did not remain more than a month or two in office, and in many were chosen promiscuously from whole population by lot. Of course these governments would be liable to constant mutation. Wherever the aristocratic form prevailed there would quickly arise a democratic party, which would overthrow the aristocracy at first favorable crisis, and *vice versa*. (G. 199, 202.)

8. *Condition of Europe at the time the power of cities was at its height?* When we survey rise and progress of nations of modern Europe, find a state of things to which no parallel in ancient world or in eastern nations. At subversion of Roman empire every principle and element of government seemed to be at work in the new compound, and not one has ever completely triumphed. In eastern nations religion and monarchy have been triumphant for ages past, and the *immobility* of society and government has been result. In Greece and Rome there was rarely more than one principle uppermost at a time—no coexisting development of different elements of power. But in feudal kingdoms all the elements were in conflict at once, and no one has permanently triumphed, *e. g.*, when Germanic nations came on the empire they brought with them the monarchical, aristocratic, and democratic elements—they

had kings, chiefs, and popular assemblies. When empire was conquered Christian religion became a new element. In the struggle for supremacy among these, 1st, aristocracy took the lead and kept it till 10th century. Church was next most powerful, and had nearly triumphed in 11th and 12th centuries. But rule of celibacy created constant vacancies, and forced it to recruit its members from without its body; hence priests could never become a distinct caste as in Asiatic countries; hence no *virgin priesthood* has ever been enabled to establish complete and permanent power. All theocratic despotisms have been established by a *married priesthood.* Church contained a large admixture of democratic element, its officers were elective, and filled from all ranks of society—kings were little more during this period than great feudal lords—still power not entirely lost; the name, the binding influence of the national churches, the necessity for a sort of appellate power above the aristocracy, &c., all had effect of preventing total destruction of regal authority—during this first period of mediæval history the democratic principle was the most feeble, and was principally kept alive by the church. Very little property except land, and that was all possessed by church and aristocracy; hence no means of building up a democratic party until commerce and manufactures began to flourish. Rise of cities brought this element into full action throughout Europe during 11th and 12th centuries—cities essentially the democratic party—condition of Europe singular during this epoch—all was still local and on a small scale except papal power—cities were free but did not feel common interest, and therefore not united—aristocracy, in same condition. Power of crown was beginning to advance, though still small. In this state of things it was evidently interest of the cities, as also of the aristocracy, to unite together and form a league capable of maintaining their power.

9. *Circumstances which checked the growth of the power of cities, and finally destroyed their political independence?* 1st. Whenever these cities grew up within powerful kingdoms, the regal power was sure to triumph over them in the end—cities could withstand the nobles, but not the kings, *e. g.*, city of Amiens obtained by force a charter and a guaranty from the court of Amiens, but when county of Amiens was united to crown of France, Amiens could no longer resist so powerful a superior, and soon lost its independence—only one way of resisting—*by league*, as the Lombard cities did Frederic Barbarossa. But a confederation is most difficult and complex of all systems of government—requires great intelligence among people when attempted among democracies—it requires frequent sacrifice of local to general interests, of individual passion and prejudice to enlarged public considerations. More-

over, even if confederation be successfully formed, easy for a single concentrated power, like the monarchy, to break its force by sowing dissensions among members, and turning them one against the other, or by buying off a portion by bribes. Hence great confederation among cities rarely attempted. If ever there was case which called for it, it was that of Albigenses in south of France. By union might have defeated crusades against them. But this was impossible. The great cities in which they resided, Beaucaire, Montpellier, Carcassone, Toulouse, &c., never could form a league; each fought singly, and on its own account alone, and they were all subdued one after the other. In Italy cities enjoyed a better fortune—no great sovereign here, German Emperor had footing, it is true, but was far off, and too much engaged at home. Hence cities and aristocracy fought the battle more undisturbed by extraneous influences than in rest of Europe, and the former won the victory, and absorbed the nobility into their bodies—hence the success of the Italian republics. Similar circumstances, too, favored the formation of the Swiss republics, and upon similar principles, with some modifications, may be explained the rise of the Dutch republics. Second cause for downfall of cities somewhat similar to first; in struggles with nobles, both parties frequently called in kings either to arbitrate or to guaranty the charters or treaties of peace. This gave pretext to monarchs to interfere, and consequently kings often took the lion's share. Moreover, cities hard pressed by the barons frequently threw themselves into the kings' arms, and thus lost political independence. Cannot better illustrate operation of this and succeeding cause, than by history of city of Laon in France. At commencement of 12th century, this commune gained its freedom by conquest from bishop, who was the superior, and who confirmed it by charter. In 1191, the bishop of Laon bribed Philip Augustus by transfer of large feudal territory, to abolish the charter. In next year, the city offered still more than bishop had done, and the charter was re-established by Philip, who at same time held on to lands given by the bishop. It then remained a commune more than 100 years, when Philip-le-Bel again abolished it (1294) at solicitation of bishop upon plea of disorders, murders, profanations, &c., among the population. Very short time afterwards again established, with restriction of king, *quamdiu nobis placeat*, because bishop took side of Boniface VIII., in his quarrel with king—then Boniface issued a bull annulling the charter, which Philip burned. Finally, after many similar vicissitudes, the bishop, Albert de Roye, by great bribe to Philip de Valois, carried his point; the charter was for ever abolished in 1331. (227.) A third cause for decay of city power was character of government. These little democracies extremely turbulent; property miserably protected.

Generally two parties, the aristocratic and plebeian. The richer classes would be regarded with jealousy by lower, and would be considered sort of aristocracy. Nobles, too, who became citizens of towns often regarded with jealousy—hence in this *town chaos* not to wonder at faction, misrule, and constant and violent changes, *e. g.*, in 1041, a gentleman struck one of the lower class in Milan with his cane. Immediately a nobleman named Lauzone, who wished to ride into power on popular favor, headed the people, made an attack on the palaces and houses of the nobility. Many bloody skirmishes took place in streets, but nobility finally overthrown—their houses and castles demolished—were driven from city; then rallied their country dependents, and besieged town for some years, which made Lauzone and popular party call in the German emperor, &c. (S. J. R., V. 1, 397.) Effect of this kind of government was that many cities threw themselves into arms of kings to secure tranquillity, which was impossible under city government, *e. g.*, Meulan, in 1320, thus surrendered its charter to Philip-le-Bon, and Soissons, in 1325, to Charles-le-Bel. (T. 5, 230–1.) Again, dissensions in city would cause the people to yield finally to any form of government which would heal dissension and give repose. Thus most of Italian cities yielded to aristocratic rule, *e. g.*, Florence to the family of Medici, Venice to an oligarchy headed by a doge, &c. But when the city was near enough to a great monarch, one party would almost always call in foreign force, as in case of Milan just mentioned. As power of kings was thus advancing, they at last made general regulations, binding on all cities in their kingdoms, *e. g.*, Louis IX. and Philip-le-Bel, in France, first to make these general regulations. Thus did the cities which were so independent at one time as to coin money, send and receive ambassadors, declare war, make laws, &c., gradually lose their separate political powers, during the 13th and 14th centuries, and with their fall and that of the aristocracy, the monarchs enlarged their power, until all these elements, unless under peculiar circumstances, were moulded into the great nations of Europe, under monarchical governments.

10. *Influence exercised over Europe by the cities during the period of their independence?* First, the effect on character of their own people most wonderful, although governments factious, turbulent, &c., and property badly protected, yet they awakened genius and stimulated energies of the people, and this compensated in some measure for misrule. At time when Florence was most turbulent democracy on earth, when rotation in office was so rapid as to require tri-monthly elections, and spirit of democracy was pushed so far as to determine by lot, in many cases, the fortunate candidates, yet are we told by Machiavel, that this

city, with only 80,000 souls, contained more great men within its walls, than all Europe north of the Alps. It was in these *volcanic* democracies that the literature of the modern world first arose. Their poets, philosophers, historians, painters, sculptors, &c., were far ahead of rest of Europe. And, strange as it may seem, Italy never possessed more wealth than during this period. No country in Europe has so many magnificent churches, palaces and public monuments—emphatically called *monumental land.* And, in spite of proscriptions and mobs and revolutions, the citizens of those cities were the wealthiest, their arts and manufactures were far ahead of rest of Europe, and credit of the cities far better than that of great monarchies, *e. g.*, while France and England borrowed money with difficulty at 40 per cent per annum, Venice and Pisa could get it from 5 to 10. These effects are in part due to the fortunate position of Italy, for carrying on commerce of Europe with the east, before discovery of passage round Cape of Good Hope. But only in part, small democracies if not overawed by neighboring great powers very favorable to development of energy and character, stimulus of government is applied to all, and energy thus awakened sometimes more than compensates for badness of government. Upon these principles alone can we account for character of Grecian democracies. Governments of the Italian republics were most complete despotisms on earth—they were not limited by law, or constitution, or any other checks—but then they were despotisms of people over themselves. Each one who bore oppression to-day, knew that it would be his turn to oppress to-morrow. There were movement and action throughout whole of these little commonwealths, all was life and bustle within, every man felt his importance and called forth all his energies. In great consolidated despotisms the principle of immobility and inaction reigns, and although such governments are *noiseless* in their oppression, yet history shows us every thing stationary under their action, *e. g.*, empires of Asia. But the great effect of these communes on the continent, was to form an equipoise to feudal aristocracy, and by means already explained to establish the power of kings over different countries, and thus by setting up a great central authority in each nation, contests and private wars of the barons were prevented by energy of government. Thus looking at Europe from 11th to 14th century, during which period these communes ran their career, we find a wonderful change—in 11th century, all was *local*, nothing *national.* Europe was one great scene of feudal dissension and private wars. At the close, governments began to assume a more *national* aspect, and kings were exercising powers to which were before strangers. With the increase of regal power, administration of justice became more regular, and the king's courts began to prevail over those of the barons. The trial by combat began to be disused in proportion as courts became more respectable and faithful in administration of justice.

But one of the most important effects of cities was the aid which they furnished in the emancipation of serfs of Europe. The rise of commerce and manufactures gave so great an impulse to cities that they furnished at once an immense demand for labor ; hence they could absorb all the emancipated and refugee slaves into their bodies. The example of Europe has often been urged in favor of emancipation of our negroes—but cases totally different. 1st, Their slaves were white, therefore refugee slave in a city could soon throw off all badges of former condition, and mix with free men ; not so here, *color* is a badge which cannot be thrown off. No legislation in our country can conquer the antipathy to an intermixture of the two colors—the philanthropist may call it a prejudice, but the *white* woman in this country who shall conquer it, and consent to marry a *black* man must be corrupt at heart before she can do it. 2d, We have no such recipient for emancipated slaves as were furnished by the cities—such a combination of circumstances may never occur again in the world's history. After a prostration for ages, the rapid rise of commerce and manufactures breathed life into the cities, and made them grow in wealth faster than they could be filled up by population, hence all kinds of labor could be supported in them. Moreover cities were constantly engaged in wars with the feudal barons, and of course would use every means to deprive them of their slaves—a state of things which can never occur in this country—for local wars between cities and barons were much more favorable for dissolving the tie between master and slave, than international wars. 3d. Our southern climate and southern productions, will ever make slaves in the south the best labor which can be used, *e. g.*, no instance of the successful cultivation of sugar except by slave labor. The sugar and cotton districts of China, the most densely populated country on earth, are cultivated by slaves; but in the north, slavery disappears, because free labor is cheaper. Again, another most efficacious means of liberating serfs in Europe was this—most of them were attached to soil, and considered part of the freehold—*adscripti glebæ*. Now, in process of time, proprietors got into habit of giving up land to them, and charging them with a certain amount of the products. In Italy and south of Europe, one-half was paid the landlord. (*Metayer system.*) Easy to see that this system might soon lead on to independence and even wealth among the serfs. (J. R. 12, 364.) Such a result can never take place with regard to our blacks.

Another effect of the cities was to make industry and attention to business more respectable than they had ever been. The leading families were generally those that became wealthy by commerce or manufactures, and the greatest of them in Florence, Venice, Genoa, Bologna, Lucca, &c.; in midst of all their political cares frequently Genoa, Bologna, Lucca, furnished chiefs of mercantile houses. The city aristocracies were generally built on mercantile wealth, *e. g.*, that of the Medici in Florence. Idleness even in higher ranks was rather disgraceful. (S. J. R. V. 12, 46.) Philip Strozzi, brother-in-law of Leo X., the father of Marshal Strozzi and of the grand Prior of Capua, and who was regarded as one of the first citizens of all Italy, remained till his death the active head of a banking house; had seven sons, and brought every one up to business and industry, although his fortune was immense. (Sis. V. 16, 223.)

With regard to influence on morals we must beware of judging too much by mere appearances. There is nothing secret in a little democracy, all is open and noisy—hence the vices of the people become notorious, and strike the imagination. Whereas in a monarchy or an oligarchy all may be secret and noiseless, when in fact there may be more vice and corruption. But after making every allowance cannot deny that democracies give full scope for development of both virtue and vice upon a grand scale. All here depending on individual energy and exertion, every principle and feeling and passion of the head and the heart will be called into action. Generally supposed that the miserable system of hypocrisy, cunning, diplomacy, treachery, &c., for which modern Italy has been remarkable, was growth of little democracies. Many of these vices are necessary product of small states, jealous of one another. Hence little republics not entirely free from them, *e. g.*, democracies of Greece. But these vices in Italy arose from the aristocracies, and little princes operated on by fear of the great monarchies of Spain, France, and Germany. Republics act with too much publicity and notoriety to be very remarkable for these vices, which require secrecy, silence and dispatch, *e. g.*, no commonwealth could invite its enemies to dinner and have them all treacherously murdered during the repast; but a little prince like Cesar Borgia might. Little democracies perfectly independent as those of Italy were at first, and not overawed by neighboring powers, may act towards each with all the candor and fairness of large states, but the moment they are overawed, they are forced to substitute cunning and diplomacy for force and fair dealing. The early wars of Italian republics were far from being cruel, and their diplomacy was not deceitful. But when princes and aristocracies were everywhere introduced into Italy, and the great northern powers began to interfere, then the political school of Italy became a disgrace to Europe.

Another vice sometimes attributed to these little democracies of Italy was the corruption of the women, and the growth of the wretched custom of each married lady having her *cicisbeo* or *cavealiare servente.* This again is a vice of aristocracies and not of republics, and Sismondi tells us (V. 16, 221.) it was introduced by the Spaniards, who, on conquering greater part of Italy established entails and the primogenitory right; and, moreover, substituted what was called *a noble leisure* or life of laziness and inaction among the higher classes, for the one of industry and energy which had characterized the republics. As Castilian pride conferred all upon the eldest son he alone could marry, others were doomed to celibacy and dependence. Hence, as a sort of compensation, the younger sons were allowed to seek the secondary honors of the *cicisbeo*, and two of the most corrupting and ridiculous laws of etiquette were soon imposed on fashionable world, 1st, that no married lady could appear in public without an attendant; 2d, no husband could be that attendant on his wife without making himself ridiculous! Now although Italians contend that this practice was often harmless, yet we can easily divine the great corruption to which it might give rise. But although this miserable system was not growth of republics, may not the general licentiousness of manners be traced to them? Certainly not. This not the vice of republics, too much equality. If a man loves a woman no excuse in a democracy for not marrying her; but in a society with ranks and titles and exclusive privileges a bar is interposed to matrimonial union between the classes, but none to the feelings of the heart. The nobleman of birth and fortune will never marry the female beneath him, but he may love her, and his rank and fortune will be the means that will enable him to corrupt her heart. Again, in such a society marriage is a matter of convenience and policy, and not of love; hence infidelity of both parties to the marriage bed. Licentiousness of manners in Italy was one of the after-growths, and not indigenous to the democratic system.

11. *Some reflections on downfall of Italian republics?* Italy different from other nations. As we advance towards our time most nations improve in wealth, learning, and greatness of character. Not so with Italy. Compare 14th and 15th centuries with 17th and 18th. At former period, all bustle and life and greatness; in latter, to use strong language of Sismondi, Italy appears struck by the hand of death. The poet tells us with historic truth that the citizens of the present day

"Creep
Crouching and crab-like through their sapping streets."

In contrast with their ancestors of the democratic ages:

"As the slime
The dull green ooze of the receding deep,
Is with the dashing of the spring-tide foam,
That drives the sailor shipless to his home."

This great revolution supervening, contrary to the march of civilization every where else, has been effected by change in government. Capital mistake committed by the republics was, that as they conquered other cities and territory, did not admit the new conquests to equal rights and privileges with themselves. The conquering city became therefore in regard to the whole, a close oligarchy, *e. g.*, at end of 15th century Pisa, Pistoia, Prato, Arezzo, Cortone, Volterra, were all subject to Florence, who excluded them from all share in government, and thus was committed in Italy the great error of the Grecian democracies. Effect of this easily traced; great secret of strength of little democracies lies in intense patriotism of its citizens, caused by identifying themselves with the state, from the share they take in the government. Sismondi tells us, that a duke of Milan would at any time have caused an insurrection by imposing in war, half the burthen on his subjects, which the Senate of Florence could easily impose on the Florentines, for, after all, matter of little consequence to the Milanese, whether he obliged a Visconti or a Sforza, a Frenchman or a German. Obedience to some master was his lot. But with the Florentine the question was, whether he should *obey* or be *obeyed*. Now, when a city extended its conquests, without admitting conquered party to any share in government, the latter would feel no more loyalty towards the ruling city than to a monarch or an aristocracy, and of course would be ready to revolt on all favorable occasions. Thus did the conquest of the cities deaden everywhere the feeling of patriotism, and introduce a principle of weakness, dissension, and resistance, among the Italian republics. By erecting government alone upon the narrow basis of the conquering city, it stood as tottering as a pyramid on its lesser end, and this remark is particularly striking. We find in all the dominant cities themselves, before the conclusion of the 15th century, the democracy giving place to an aristocracy, so that but few families of the whole population administered the government, *e. g.*, not more than 2 or 3000 citizens admitted to any share in Venetian government, embracing several millions of subjects—from 4 to 5000 in Genoa. In Florence, Sienna and Lucca, altogether from 5 to 6000,

&c. (S. J. R. V. 12, 17.) So that in all Italy, close of 15th century about 16 or 18,000 citizens out of 18,000,000 enjoyed all the rights of citizenship, while on the 14th, about 80,000 did, and in the 13th, the *golden age* of the republics, about 1,800,000, or the 10th of the population. These simple statistics will explain how the spring of enterprise and industry was deadened with the decay of patriotism. A province ruled despotically by a distant power, soon loses its wealth, energy and character—few districts can stand blighting effects of heavy taxation, without any compensation in disbursements, and no country more sadly illustrates this principle than Italy. But effect greater still on individual character than wealth. There was no *independent* city in Italy, no matter how small and even poor, that did not have its great men, its own literature, often its own great university, &c. No city, no matter how large and rich, that did not fail to produce these as soon as subjected to another, *e. g.*, Pisa was a leading republic in her prosperity, and was illustrated by great men, a flourishing literature and beautiful monuments; from moment of her subjection to Florence, she was struck with the hand of death—not one great man, great philosopher, or great monument arose here afterwards. Even the little cities of Monte-Feltro, Urbin, Rimini, Pesarro, &c., insignificant in size, far surpassed her, and numbered each some great men or distinguished philosophers in their walls. In all the Duchy of Milan, only single city of Milan was illustrated. Pavia, Parma, and Placentia, subject cities, produced nothing of distinction. While Ferrara and Mantua with no more population, but with independent governments, exhibited all the lustre of the arts, of poetry, and of science. But Neapolitan kingdom most striking illustration of same principle. In this beautiful kingdom, comprehending one-third of Italian population, favored beyond every other portion by climate and soil, less exposed to ravages of war than any other state, we look in vain beyond her great capital for that life, and energy, and greatness that belonged to the independent commonwealths. Not all the patronage of King Alphonso, with the aid of the *savans* of his court, could raise the character of even the greatest of the provincial cities. No man of talent ever opened a school even in any of the populous and well situated towns of Apulia or Calabria (J. R. V. 12. 32); and to this day they have scarcely emerged from barbarism. When causes above described had prepared Italy for subjection, about conclusion of 15th century, her wealth attracted the more barbarous, but powerful nations, beyond the Alps, and the French, the Swiss, the Spaniards, and the Germans, henceforth made this garden of Europe the theatre of their bloody wars, and soon completed the ruin and degradation of the once noble character of the Italian. Under the rule of the foreigner there has been less bustle and excitement in Italy than in the palmy days of her republics, and a superficial observer might conclude that she was happier during the 17th than the 13th and 14th centuries. But the appearance is wholly deceptive—because suffering is silent and not a matter of historic notice, does not follow that it may not be intense. What silent suffering for example must the *cicisbeo* have introduced—he must have destroyed the peace of families throughout Italy—the husband no longer looked on his wife as faithful companion, associated with his whole existence—a counsellor to him in his doubts, a support to him in his adversity, and a comforter in despair. He was not sure that the children who bore his name were his, neither loved by them nor his wife, incommoded constantly by the presence of her gallant—he must have been a stranger to the sweet and tender feelings of father and husband. He was thus driven to seek pleasures without, which can only be permanently enjoyed in bosom of a family. Well may we conclude with the historian of Italian republics, that the people who first introduced this custom into Italy were criminals against the cause of humanity. The great fabric of society can only be kept in due repose and harmony by a strict observance of those exclusive rights conferred by the two great institutions, the pillars of the social edifice, marriage and property.

12. *Could the fate of the Italian republics have been averted?* Had circumstances favored the consolidation of the Italian states into one great transalpine monarchy, it might have sustained its independence against foreign powers, but its history would probably have been less brilliant—it would have been like Spain. At commencement of wars which destroyed liberties of Italy, Spain, which had formerly been divided into almost as many little states as Italy, had still five independent monarchies, Castile, Aragon, Navarre, Portugal and Grenada. Charles V. first reduced them to one consolidated monarchy, and with loss of liberty they soon lost every thing else that was valuable. Agriculture, manufactures, commerce, immediately declined, and by far most brilliant period of Spanish history was before union. (J. R. V. 12, 8.) In same manner a monarchy in Italy might have built up one splendid capital. But wealth and energy and greatness would have deserted provinces. One great university might have been established in the capital which would have exercised an influence in learning similar to that of monarchy, but they would all have disappeared from the provinces, where, as under the republics, hardly a city which did not have some great university or flourishing school. The only hope then for Italy was to have established a federative system of republics, which, like that of United States, could have given union to whole against a

foreign foe, and might at same time have left to each republic an amount of power adequate to prevent the blighting influence of consolidation. But this system too complex and difficult to be put in successful operation at so early a period.

CHAPTER V.

REVIVAL OF LITERATURE.

1. *Four causes of the revival of literature?* 1st, Institution of universities. 2d, Cultivation of modern languages, multiplication of books, and extension of art of writing. 3d, Study of law, particularly the civil or Roman law. 4th, The revival of ancient literature. (H. L. V. 1. 9.)

2. *Rise of universities?* Have already seen literature almost expire after conquest of barbarians. After rise of monasteries schools were often attached to them. When nations became a little more settled, and theology began to assume a more scholastic and metaphysical character, then universities were established. University of Paris one of first and most noted—like Oxford, cannot be positively traced to origin, although like Oxford usually ascribed to a great man, Charlemagne. Remigius first we know of to read lectures at Paris about 900. Next two centuries history obscure; in 1100 find William of Champeaux teaching logic and philosophy with great credit. A disciple of his still more famous, Peter Abelard, gave by his lectures wonderful reputation to university. When retired to his monastery of Paraclete immense number of pupils still gathered around him. Fame of Paris rapidly advanced; students from all nations flocked there till they became more numerous than the citizens. Before 1169 students seemed to have been divided into *nations*, and in last year of 12th century received its earliest charter from Philip Augustus, making it a corporation, free from the rule of bishops and aristocracy, and capable of governing itself. (H. M. A. 524.) Faculty of arts divided into four nations; those of France, Picardy, Normandy and England—these had distinct suffrages, and when united, outnumbered three higher faculties of theology, law and medicine. In 1169 H. II. offered to refer the dispute with Becket to the provinces of the school of Paris, such was its renown at that time. Oxford in 13th century was next to Paris. Generally traced to Alfred, though without sufficient authority. Frequented during time of Edward the Confessor; then follows an interval of more than a century

during which its continuance is not spoken of, but which may be inferred from fact that in Stephen's reign, Vacarius, a foreigner, read lectures there on civil law, which he probably would not have done had there been no great seminary there. In reigns of Henry II. and Richard I. Oxford became a flourishing university, and as early as 1201 had 3000 students. Earliest charters granted by King John. University of Bologna ranked next in dignity, and, judging from date of its incorporation, was older than that of Paris or Oxford. After resurrection of Roman jurisprudence in the 12th century, it became greatest law school in Europe, and its charter of incorporation was granted by Frederic Barbarossa as early as 1158. Earliest authentic mention of university of Cambridge occurs in Mathew Paris, 1209. John caused three clerks of Oxford to be hanged on suspicion of murder, and all the students left, some for Reading, some for Oxford, to carry on their studies—hence inferred it had a school of great note. It was incorporated in 1231 under Henry III. Early history of universities noted for struggles with municipal authorities, and the bishops, in which they were sometimes aggressors and conquerors—they are to be regarded as new powers developed in Christendom of very peculiar character. After a period of incorporation they became extremely flourishing—13th century the *golden age* of universities—almost only seats of learning—students resorted to them from all Europe—numbers enormous, *e. g.*, Oxford said to have had 30,000 students in time of Henry III. ; Paris 25,000 as late even as Ch. VII. ; Bologna 10,000. During this century universities were greatly multiplied ; those of Padua and Naples arose under patronage of Frederic II., those of Toulouse and Montpellier arose in France, and Salamanca in Spain. Prague earliest of German universities, founded in 1350. Hussite schism produced a secession of the Saxon students, and gave rise to university of Leipsic, &c. Universities had generally celebrity each for some peculiar department of learning, *e. g.*, Paris famous for scholastic theology, Bologna, Orleans and Bourges for law, Montpellier for medicine, &c. Each country found it advantageous to encourage foreigners as much as possible ; hence free passports generally given to students coming from abroad to the universities. Where students were so numerous of course subjected to a regular police under college government. Occasional disorders, *e. g.*, told that when there were 30,000 at Oxford, "a company of *varlets*, pretending to be students, shuffled themselves in, and did act much villany in the university by thieving, whoring, quarrelling," &c. By special laws made to prevent stealing, may infer that this vice, almost unknown to modern universities, was not so rare formerly.

3. *Causes of this sudden mania for college studies?* The restora-

tion of civil, and formation of the canon law, were eminently calculated to give an impulse to colleges, a large proportion of students in all the universities studied law alone. But chief attraction was new *scholastic philosophy.* Speculations on the mysterious questions of metaphysics and theology exceedingly fascinating to human mind just wakened up from state of inaction. About middle of 11th century Roscelin, a professor of logic, revived the old question of the Grecian schools about the *reality* of universal ideas, which he denied. This got up the great dispute which so long agitated Europe about realism and nominalism, which kindled the spirit of metaphysical discussion, kept alive in England by Langfranc and Anselm, successive archbishops of Canterbury; and in next century Abelard and Peter Lombard completed scholastic system of philosophizing—this taught in all universities by professed scholars—hence one great attraction of those seminaries. (H. 526.)

4. *Scholastic philosophy and theology?* Two ways of treating theological subjects in middle ages. 1st, By reference to scripture authority alone, illustrated by the ingenuity of the disputants or the decisions of the church. 2d, By reference to the writings and opinions of the fathers, upon the ground of their great piety, and the fact of their coming so soon after death of Christ as to be best judges of his deeds and doctrines. These comprehended *positive theology. Scholastic theology* arose afterwards, and was a third method. According to this method, orthodox system of the church assumed as true, but arranged and demonstrated according to the rules of Aristotelian dialectics, and sometimes on premises furnished by metaphysics alone. Scholastic philosophy distinguished from this only by being more exclusively metaphysical. This philosophy generally traced back to 9th century, age of celebrated Scotus Erigena; but produced little influence till time of Roscelin, a little before 1100. There were many mysteries and difficulties in the Christian scheme well calculated to call in the aid of metaphysics and dialectics, at a time when human mind was just beginning to act with new energy, *e. g.*, nature of *Trinity*, of *incarnation*, of *angels*, reconciliation of *evil* with *omnipotence* and *benevolence* of God, *free will*, *grace*, *faith*, *wine and bread in eucharist whether flesh and blood*, &c. There were besides thousands of questions about the *conception*, about *Virgin Mary*, about *spirit*, *demons*, &c., &c. The works of Aristotle, translated from the Arabian, with the commentary of Averroes, became the great authority of the schoolmen, and his whole system of logic imperfectly comprehended was introduced to explain the mysteries of theology. Well might the logic of Aristotle, when applied to the mysteries of religion, beget a sort of mongrel science which has sometimes been called *quidlibet per quodlibet ars probandi*—

the questions were sometimes called *questiones quodlibeticæ*, and the scholastics, *quodlibetarians*. (J. V. 1. 87.) The Dominicans and Franciscans were particularly addicted to this scholastic theology—former produced perhaps the greatest disputant of all the schoolmen, Thomas Aquinas; latter produced his great rival, Duns Scotus. Thomas Aquinas wrote the *Summa Totius Theologiæ*, 1250 pages folio. Articles alone exemplify nature of scholastic theology—168 on love, 358 on angels, 200 on soul, 85 on demons, 151 on intellect, 134 on law, 3 on the catamenia, 237 on sins, and 17 on virginity! Such was his acquaintance with *angelography* that he was called *angelical doctor*, and D'Israeli says you might have supposed from his writings that he was an old experienced angel himself. (V. 1. 91.) *E. g.*, he treats of the substance, orders, offices, natures, habits, &c. of the angels, some of his conclusions most singular, *e. g.*, angel composed of action and potentiality—more superior he is, the less his potentiality. Every angel differs from another angel in species; angels have not naturally a body, they may assume bodies, but they do not want to assume bodies. The velocity of motion of angel not according to quantity of strength, but will—the motion of the illumination of an angel is threefold, circular, straight and oblique, &c., &c. This same doctor gravely debated whether Christ was an Hermaphrodite? whether there are excrements in paradise? whether pious at resurrection will rise with their bowels? &c. And yet Erasmus considered Aquinas as the greatest man of the schools, and it was his work, *Secunda Secundæ*, which was first book of morals read by Sir Thomas More; fact is, as Fontenelle says, "there is pure gold in the impure mass of scholastic philosophy." Amid all the nonsense of the schoolmen there was occasionally sound philosophy.

5. *Advantages and disadvantages?* Advantages are that it produced ability in management of doctrinal metaphysics, great subtlety of thought, and sagacity in development and distinction of ideas, together with great intellectual efforts, &c. (T. 222.) Ill effects, dissemination of a minute and puerile spirit of speculation, a total forgetfulness of practical common sense—total neglect of the accurate sciences. Experiment, history, and study of language neglected, &c., &c.; hence no advance made by them in real science. John of Salisbury says of the Parisian dialecticians, after many years absence he found them just where he had left them, urging and parrying the same arguments, and after 300 years same remark applicable; had not untied a single knot, nor added one valuable truth to philosophy. (H. 528.) Most agitating subject discussed by schoolmen was that of *nominalism* and *realism*, whether a general term applies to something *real*, independent of the species or individuals, or whether it is a mere name, *e. g.*, whether we

could form the idea of an *ass* prior to, or independently of, individual asses? On this question Aquinas and Duns Scotus took side of realism. Roscelin and Abelard, and afterwards, in 14th century, Occam took side of nominalism. Famous Louis XI. espoused at first side of nominalists, Pope John XXIII. of realists; but pope triumphed over king and made him in latter part of his reign persecute the nominalists. (J. V. 2. 39.) This question remarkable as being one of the few purely philosophical questions which have produced the shedding of torrents of blood.

6. *Second cause for the revival of literature?* Have already seen how the Latin language was gradually changed to the modern. Period of transition exceedingly unfavorable to literature. M. Raynouard asserts that there has been no great work in any language till it had definite forms of expression according to time, number and person, *i. e.*, till its grammar was formed. (H. L. 20.) Besides, in Europe, while the corrupt Latin language was spoken the pure was neglected, but when Latin became a dead language, after formation of the modern languages, then it was studied in all its purity. Thus did it happen in middle ages after formation of modern languages there were two literatures, or, as Villeman calls it, two civilizations in presence of each other totally distinct, one the civilization of reminiscence and of study, which arose from studying ancient authors, another the growth of the castle and feudal life and feudal court, the former belonged to antiquity, the latter was indigenous to the moderns. (T. 1. 98.) The first of modern languages to produce a literature of any notoriety was the *Provençal*, spoken in south of France.

7. *Provençal literature—Troubadours?* This literature was of gay light character, generally in verse and songs; and the poets were called *troubadours.* Must look to condition of south of France to understand character of the troubadours and their poetry, whilst north of France was divided into number of warlike provinces, always at war with themselves or northern barbarians. In the south the little kingdom of Arles, afterwards known by name of Provence, enjoyed, comparative repose and good government. In Provence there were many little princes who in time of peace had very little to do except to hawk and hunt, to make verses and sing them, and to discuss little questions learnedly, like question discussed by La Harpe: whether Orosmane was most miserable while believing in Zaire's infidelity, or when he discovered her innocence after he had killed her. This gay literature was stimulated by the gay courts of counts of Provence and Barcelona, the latter of whom was neighboring to Spain and the Moors, where literature was as far advanced as anywhere in Europe. A troubadour was sometimes a gentleman with a castle and lands and vassals, like Bertram de Born, who

had 1000 subjects. Sometimes a sovereign prince, like William, count of Poictiers and duke of Aquitaine, who was first of the troubadours—sometimes he was an obscure vassal or attendant in the castle like Bernard de Ventadour, the son of a baker, at the court of count of Ventadour. As the knight had his squire so the troubadour generally had his juggler or mountebank, who sang his verses and recited little romances and tales of chivalry, and when they were tired of verses, songs, &c. then he performed his legerdemain feats—if the attendant learned to make verses which pleased princes and celebrated beauties, and made himself master of Provençal learning, then he might become troubadour, and when honor of knighthood was conferred he was then *full* troubadour sometimes troubadour degraded to condition of juggler for doing something unbecoming, *e. g.*, Gaucelm Faidit losing all his property at dice was degraded to mountebank. (V. 1. 114.) Subjects were principally love, chivalry, war, particularly tales and adventures of the crusaders; these poems were short, and often retained in memory alone—many could not write. Troubadour, like a knight, often wandered from court to court, making and singing his songs, *e. g.*, Bernard de Ventadour lived in court of the Count de Ventadour till count suspected an intrigue with his wife—then went to court of Eleanor of Guienne, who first married Louis VII. of France, then Henry II. of England, was great favorite of Eleanor, of whom he says,

"J'ecris pour elle; et elle sait lire."

He quitted Eleanor when she went to England, then he passed to court of Raymond, count of Toulouse, and after this life of singing and court favor he went into a monastery and ended his days. In poetry of troubadours we meet with nothing profound and great, but then we find in them the great features of the times. In addition to causes above given for origin of this literature, the Arabian or eastern literature is supposed to have had great influence. Saracens conquered Spain and invaded southern districts of Europe. For a long time were far more civilized and learned than Europeans, *e. g.*, in 9th and 10th centuries, when no arts, no civilization among Christians, Seville, Toledo, Grenada, were filled with sumptuous palaces. (144.) The number of Moorish authors in Spain upon philosophy, poetry, eloquence, and the arts was very great. Hence impossible but that much must have been communicated to Europe. Many inventions we know came through Arabians, *e. g.*, paper, compass, gunpowder, &c. (146.) Some of caliphs of Arabian empire great patrons of learning, *e. g.*, Haroun Al-Raschid and his son Al-Mamoum. Schools and academies were endowed, of which those of Bagdad and Cufa were famous. (141.) They had their grammarians.

professors, commentators, lexicographers, &c. without number, when even the court of Charlemagne could boast of nothing equal. Some suppose Arabians authors of the system of universities unknown to ancients. The Moors with all their civilization passed into Spain. Hence when the schools of Christian countries were inferior those of Spain were flourishing, and Christians often attended the Arabian schools, *e. g.*, Gerbert after studying in monastery of Aurillac, went to the great Arabian school of Toledo, where he studied mathematics, astrology and magic, under Arabian doctors, then returned to France, became preceptor to sons of Hugh Capet, and bishop of Rheims, then passed into service of emperor of Germany, who made him bishop of Ravenna, then pope of Rome (Sylvestre 2d); thus was pope turned out from an Arabian school! (146.) Not only however did the Moors thus produce influence on Europe by their schools, but they exerted powerful influence on south of France. The Provençals and Catalonians were in constant communication with them. The Provençal knights visited courts of the counts of Saragossa, and Arabian knights say the chroniclers visited courts of Christian princes, and some of them, like the troubadours, were both poets and warriors, and often these poets sang alternately in Arabian and Provençal language. Arabian poems were amorous, passionate, warlike, brief, like those of troubadours. The rhyme too was used extensively in Arabian poetry, and was no doubt one cause of its introduction into modern European languages. The Provençal literature flourished till the war against the Albigenses, which produced on it an influence similar to the war of roses in England on chivalry. These wars put an end to the gayety, light-heartedness and tranquillity which had produced the songs of the troubadours. The Provençal poetry was imitated through Europe. Abelard was the first to sound it on banks of the Seine. Richard *Cœur-de-Lion* was a poet of this order, &c., &c. In north of France it became monotonous and commonplace, too much about the spring, and the "everlasting nightingale." The *minne-singers* or lyric poets of Germany were of the character of the troubadours—love their peculiar theme, as name imports.

8. *Romance language and literature?* As late as 7th and 8th century, songs in north of France written in Latin, *e. g.*, great victory of Clotaire II. celebrated in camp by Latin song—these songs were all in rhyme. At Paris the capital of the north, all the preaching was in Latin. (V. V. 1, 233.) After formation of the Romance, or French language, it was a long time before it possessed any thing like a literature, *e. g.* such men as Abelard and St. Bernard spoke and wrote in Latin. Their letters were in Latin, and it is even supposed that all Abelard's love songs were in Latin. (243.) The Normans, strange as it may ap-

pear, were first to give reputation and character to the Romance, or modern French. It is known that for a long time these barbarians were the terror and scourge of Europe—at last conquered one of the most beautiful provinces in France (Normandy) under Rollo, the Dane. In mixing with the French they gradually came to speak French with but little modification from their own language, and it was by these hardy conquering Normans that the language quickly spread in every direction. Well known that England was conquered by William of Normandy, who used every means within his power to introduce the French language. He commanded it to be used in all legal proceedings, in the market and at court. If a man could not speak French, William would not permit him to retain office, *e. g.*, in 1093 Wistan, a bishop and statesman of first order, was driven from king's council because he could not speak French—*quasi homo idiota quia linguam Gallicam non noverat.* All the acts of British parliament were in French to end of 15th century; and among the old rules of Oxford University. one forbids students to converse in any other language than French or Latin. (V. V. 2, 215.) In same way when Normans conquered Calabria and Sicily they introduced French language into all south of Italy; and when Henry was elected king of Naples, he refused the throne because could not speak French, *quæ maxime necessaria esset in curia.* Thus did conquest of Normans spread the French over England, Sicily and Naples; and their policy caused them to propagate it as a badge of their power. French in those countries became a sort of learned or superior language, spoken by the higher classes, and consequently acquired a reputation which it did not have even in France. This high character given to French gradually overcame the aversion which the literati had to writing in it, and was no doubt one principal cause of the literature which soon began to appear in the Romance language. (234.)

9. *Romances and works of fiction?* This kind of writing first successfully cultivated in Romance or French language. Villeman points out three fruitful sources of this romantic chivalric fiction. 1st, Influence of Charlemagne and his court. 2d. The adventures of the Normans. 3d. The influence of the Cid in Spain. 1st. Under Charlemagne every thing to rouse the imagination, his great enterprises, his march across the Alps to Rome, his mysterious coronation, his wars against Saxons and the Moors, his magnificence, his fêtes, his tournaments, his splendid court at Aix-la-Chapelle that dazzled barbarous world, his person so majestic, &c., all conspired to rouse the imagination and lead on to writing of romance. Hence most ancient romance said to be "Legende du voyage de Charlemagne," by Turpin, in which Roland figures so conspicuously. 2d. Influence of Normans already

partially explained, most adventurous people of their day, had ravaged the coasts of Baltic and Mediterranean, had traversed Russia, gone to Constantinople, had been precursors of crusades, 40 of them had visited Holy Land, had protected pilgrims, had joined in the rescue of Salerno from Saracens, besides all this they conquered England south of Italy, and Guiscard conquered Greece and threatened Constantinople. Each little adventurer among this people was a Charlemagne unto himself. Imagination roused by these adventures, consequence of which was a prodigious progeny of romances and fictions similar to that of *The Knights of the Round Table.* 3d. A third class of romances arose from the character of the Cid in Spain. He flourished at conclusion of 11th century—most distinguished at siege of Toledo, against Moors, where single combats were fought every day between chiefs of two armies. In these wars diversity of manners, costumes, armor, &c., between men of the north and the south; the concourse of Christians from all Europe to serve under banner of the Cid; this great man himself, whose life was full of glory, of adventure and peril, and above all his noble generosity gave an impulse to the imagination of Europe, which developed itself in popular songs and tales of romance. (253.) In the Cid we admire grandeur of his character more than that of events —we are struck with heroism struggling within the narrow limits of Spain. In the romances of this class you perceive mixture of Arabian and Spanish life. Love more important than ambition, and partakes of all the passion and jealous delicacy of eastern nations. In romances springing from Norman adventures we have long expeditions, great conquests, few knights who do not become kings, few squires even who do not acquire territory, an island for example (a domain so coveted by Sancho). It is the spirit of adventure, but selfish, which by battle and carnage arrives at something sure and profitable. In romances of school of Charlemagne there is ambition depicted, but less sweeping and grasping—every body does not aim at highest station—first place already filled by the great monarch—no one disputes it—the peers of his court know their places, and, however fond of adventure and fight, it is not for lucre and advancement; none, says Villeman, arrive at great fortune, except Ogier the Dane, who marries a fairy and becomes immortal. These three classes of romance have been pronounced three supplements to history of those times—they give the great character of the age although marvellous. Great number of fictions produced likewise by crusades, which were the greatest events of their age.

10. *Italian language and its literature?* Italy last of old Roman countries to acquire an independent language. Nearly end of 12th century before most searching scholars can find even a few lines of mo-

dern Italian. Hence literature altogether Latin till late period. Dante and Petrarch morning stars of modern literature; they formed and polished their language. *Divine comedy* of Dante commenced before his exile from Florence in 1304—superior to Petrarch in depth of thought, but latter produced more effect on language and literature of his country. He formed the Italian school of poetry—did not invent the sonnet, but made it fashionable for so many ages. (H. L. 33.)

11. *English language and its literature?* Anglo-Saxon language was formed, when Norman conquest again produced confusion. Impossible to fix period when French and Anglo-Saxon were fused into English. Anglo-Saxon vastly predominant—higher classes spoke French, but great mass of people stuck to their native tongue. Old Saxon words gave place very slowly to new compound, *e. g.*, Saxon Chronicle, continued to death of Stephen in 1154, in Saxon, only few French words on the latter pages. First specimen extant of modern English is proclamation of Henry III. to people of Huntingdonshire in 1258. Another early specimen, with fewer obsolete words, is song in honor of battle of Lewes in 1264. English was seldom written and hardly employed till middle of 14th century. Earliest English prose work Sir John Mandeville's Travels, (1356,) Wickliffe's translation of Bible, great work, (1383,) Trevisa's version of the Polychronicon of Higden, (1385,) Astrolobe of Chaucer, (1392.) Trevisa says when he wrote (1385) even gentlemen had much left off practice of having their children taught French, and names John Cornwall, the schoolmaster, who soon after 1350 introduced great innovation of making boys translate Latin into English. The man who beyond all others assisted in the formation of our language and literature was Geoffrey Chaucer. No English poet of middle ages can compare with him, in fact no one in Europe out of Italy. Gower, his contemporary, stood high, though far inferior to Chaucer. (H. L. 36, 37.)

12. *Languages and literature of Europe at beginning of 14th century?* Seven European languages formed before that epoch, three in Spain, and the French, Italian, German and English. Italian was most polished and had greatest writers; French had largest number and variety. English, in consequence of Norman conquest, was latest in its formation, and did not acquire a literature of importance before the time of Chaucer and Wickliffe. (39.)

13. *Extension of art of writing, and multiplication of books?* Have already seen unfavorable influence produced by Saracens taking Alexandria in 7th century—stopped importation of papyrus into Europe—parchment too dear for several centuries—art of writing practised by very few—laymen could very rarely write—autograph signatures not

found till late period. Philip the Bold mounted the throne 1272; could not write, though all his successors could—writing more common towards conclusion of 13th century. Out of eight witnesses to testament in 1277, five could write their names—at beginning of century, historian says, not one could probably have done it. There are endorsements on English deeds as well as signatures by laymen as early as time of E. II. Earliest penmanship extant, of a lady in England, is a letter of Sir John Pelham's wife to her husband in 1399, highly ungrammatical. (H. L. 41.) The art of writing gradually extended as paper began to be used instead of parchment—period of invention of paper uncertain. Paper from cotton, *charta bombicyna*, made long before that from linen rags—supposed to be first invented in the east—called *charta Damascena* by the Greeks, because they procured it from manufactories of Damascus—hence used by the Saracens in Spain long before rest of Europe. Dr. Robertson fixes on 11th century as period of invention, and seems to infer that it was generally introduced at once for purposes of writing, and was cause of rapid multiplication of books. Not so. Very gradually introduced and not generally used in Europe till about close of 14th century. Its great influence was felt in 15th century and not before. (46.) First paper used was as thick as pasteboard.

14. *Third cause of progress of learning?* Study of law. Popular opinion endorsed by Dr. Robertson, that copy of Justinian's Pandects now in Laurentian library at Florence, was accidentally found at Amalfi, after capture of that city by Roger, king of Sicily, in 1135, and was brought to Pisa, and became means of reviving study of law in Italy and rest of Europe. But although an important copy of the Pandects might have been discovered at Amalfi, yet it is certain that the knowledge of the civil law had not been lost, and the Pandects have been proved to be subject of legal study before siege of Amalfi. The increasing appetite for study of law arose in a great measure from the democratic character of little Italian states, where liberty and law were more talked about than in any other part of Europe. Doctors of the law frequently made podestâ or criminal judges in little republics, because of their law knowledge. Irnerius first to give lectures on law at Bologna early in 12th century, commenced too practice of making notes on his law books called *glosses;* these glosses at first interlinear, then marginal; at first mere explanations of obscure passages, then became running commentaries. Irnerius followed by a swarm of glossers, *e. g.*, Martinus, Gasias, Bulgarus, Placentinus, &c. These glosses so increased, that early in 13th century were collected by Accursius of Florence—called *corpus juris glossatum.* This made epoch in law, substituted glosses for lectures—authority for research—authority of

glosses became undisputed, and were finally considered of more value than the text, and this too in spite of the verbal trifling and strange ignorance displayed by many of the glossers, which had often subjected them to ridicule, *e. g.*, explanation of *etsi* by *quamvis*, or *admodum* by *valde.* They derived name of *Tiber* from *Tiberius* (emperor). Supposed that Ulpian and Justinian lived before Christ, that Papinian was put to death by Marc Antony. They interpreted *pontifex* by *papa* or *episcopus*, &c. (H. L. 56.) But although such ignorance subjected them occasionally to ridicule, still the glossers were of great service, they studied their texts closely, although they sometimes showed ignorance of history. In 13th century a sort of scholastic jurisprudence was introduced, making a mongrel science of logic and law just as had been done in case of scholastic theology. Bartolus and Baldus most distinguished of new school. Great school of Bologna sent out all the early glossers. In 14th century it began to decline as each nation began to encourage its own law schools. Revival of Roman law gave impulse to modern literature by diffusing generally through Christendom a system of laws, with all their imperfections, greatly superior to the learning and civilization of that age.

15. *Study of law in England?* In accordance with an article of Magna Charta, all the chief courts of justice were established at Westminster. This brought together professors of municipal law who had before been dispersed over kingdom and formed them into aggregate body. Between clergy and civil officers there had long been a contest; former wished to introduce civil or Roman law, and together with ecclesiastical to make it supersede the municipal or common law. As clergy had control over universities they excluded professors of common law from them. These assembled generally at Westminster, where all the chief courts were holden and formed a sort of university. They began by purchasing certain houses and lands (afterwards called *inns of court and chancery*) between Westminster, the place of holding king's courts, and city of London, for advantage of ready access to one, and plenty of provisions in the other—here they fell into collegiate order, performed their exercises, read lectures, &c. After some time crown took them under protection. H. III. issued a proclamation forbidding teaching law anywhere in metropolis except by these bodies. He formed the members of each *inn* or *lodging-house* into a corporation, and established rules for their regulation—they then began to confer rank on their students by granting two degrees, that of barrister and sergeant, answering to bachelor and doctor of laws in the universities. In the inns of chancery younger or freshmen students were placed, learning, says Sir J. Fortescue, the originals, and, as it were, the elements of the law.

After passing through these they went to the higher inns, the inns of court, where the higher studies of law were completed. Fortescue says during his time (1461) there were about 2000 students at these inns, almost entirely *filii nobilium*, gentlemen born. Comparatively few studied for purpose of practice of law, but for mere accomplishment. Number diminished as it gradually ceased to be customary to learn law by way of accomplishment; and Coke says under Elizabeth the number of students diminished to 1000, and is now still less. These corporations had a great deal of property bestowed on them from time to time so as to become rich, *e. g.*, James I. by letters patent bestowed the premises, of the Middle and Inner Temple, in perpetuity for the reception and education of the professors and students of law. Gray's Inn was given by H. VIII., Lincoln Inn by Queen Elizabeth, &c. (W. B. H. 64.)

16. *Fourth cause of progress of modern literature?* Revival of the ancient. Have seen the gradual disuse of pure Latin as it was gradually changing to modern languages of Europe, and its study could not be revived till it became dead language. Eichhorn fixes on latter part of 10th century as period of revival of classic taste—considerable improvement in the 11th. In the 12th, particularly first half, improvement more rapid, though Latin used was still a little barbarous. Most distinguished writers, Abelard, Eloisa, Bernard of Clairvaux, Saxo Grammaticus, William of Malmesbury, Peter of Blois. (H. L. 58.) Heeren says 13th was unfruitful of ancient literature, except in Italy. This age was one of too much action for the study of a dead language. The men at head of affairs were more distinguished than the scholars. In this century two of the greatest popes appeared, Innocent III. and Gregory IX.—former got up the bloody crusade against the Albigenses. In France age distinguished by three most active kings, Philip Augustus, Saint Louis, Philip-le-Bel. In Spain we have Ferdinand III. and Alphonso X. In Germany we have the 1st and 2d Frederic, two of the greatest men of their age. In England the very meanness of John and weakness of H. III. gave rise to most agitating events. And in Italy 13th century was period of independence and power of cities, and most bitter wars between Guelfs and Ghibelins. (V. T. 322.) 13th century an age of action, not of literature. Heeren and Meiners say relaxation of morals in the monasteries, and the swarms of mendicant friars filling Europe with stupid superstitions, together with too exclusive study of scholastic divinity in the universities, had a very unfavorable influence on learning of this age. (H. L. 60.) The 14th century not beyond the 13th except in Italy. Looking at 13th and 14th centuries north of the Alps, in Europe, they seemed to have been stationary, or even retrograde, in regard to classic learning, and even general litera-

ture. Hence Hallam says it is not correct to speak of the dawn and twilight of learning, and he farther considers those two centuries as proving there is not necessarily an advance in learning and science in Europe, that even in this quarter of the globe there are frequent halts in the march of the human mind. This stagnant condition of literature applies only to north of Europe. In Italy 14th an age of great progress—age of Petrarch and Boccacio—former real restorer of polite letters. He studied the pure Latin, relished beauties of Cicero and Virgil. Such became his love of classic studies that he almost deified classic writers. (H. L. 63.) So much in love with them that he even wrote letters to them almost as loving as his sonnets to Laura. (V. T. 3. 25.) Ho was prouder of his Latin poem called Africa than of all his sonnets and odes which have made his name immortal. It was Petrarch who began first to study Greek, who collected most assiduously all the ancient books he could find, and who impressed upon Italy what may be called a classic mania. And as students began to study ancient authors, every advance would show their vast superiority over the writers of that age—hence the wonderful industry displayed in finding classic books—an industry to which we are indebted for many an ancient work, *e. g.*, to Poggio Bracciolini, who lived and hunted for books through first half of 15th century, we owe eight orations of Cicero, a complete Quinctillian, Columella, part of Lucretius, three books of Valerius Flaccus, Silius Italicus, Ammianus Marcellinus, Tertullian, and 12 comedies of Plautus, besides some less important works. (H. L. 66.)

16. *Causes of rise of this sudden mania for classic studies?* Italians identified themselves more with ancient Romans than any other people in Europe—lived in the country of the genuine Romans. Their governments were mostly democratic, with close imitation in many cases of early Roman government; fall of house of Swabia released them from foreign yoke, and gave prouder sense of their importance. Italy besides is a land of classic monuments with classic inscriptions. The Italian cities too had become wealthy and more luxurious after middle of 13th century, and their governments had given greater impulse to human mind than anywhere else in Europe. Copying of books had become a regular trade—50 persons lived by copying, in Milan, about year 1300. At Bologna it was regular business at fixed prices. Painting too, in this classic land, had revived in the works of Giotto and his followers. Under all these circumstances, Italy only wanted some great man of classic enthusiasm to rouse the public mind—Petrarch was that man, and his friend Rienzi, in the wild revolution which he produced at Rome, in his attempt to revive old Roman republican government, but exemplified in politics that enthusiasm for antiquity which

Petrarch exhibited in literature. These were kindred spirits, and represented true character of their age in Italy. (H. L. 81.) Although Petrarch commenced study of Greek, was not so successful as in Latin. In one of his letters to Homer he tells him there were only ten persons in all Italy who knew how to value him, five at Florence, one at Bologna, two in Verona, one in Mantua, one in Perugia, and not one in Rome. (H. L. 76.) Greek literature not revived till 15th century, or at least very late in 14th. Crusades supposed to have had some effect, though less than generally imagined. Main cause was war between the Greeks and Turks. As danger grew greater to Greek empire, the scholars began to desert and went westwardly with their books and their knowledge, where they could have more repose, *e. g.*, in 1430 Thessalonica fell into hands of Turks, and Theodore Gaza, learned Greek of that city, fled to Italy, became rector of university of Ferrara. Many others fled in like manner, and became teachers of their language and literature; and the fall of Constantinople about middle of 15th century completed the dispersion of literary Greeks through Europe, and contributed powerfully to revival of the language and literature.

18. *Effect of revival of ancient literature?* Many, among whom is Kant, suppose revival of classical literature was pernicious; that it was not in unison with the condition of modern world; that literature ought always to be expression of the character of the age; that it turned the mind of Europe in a false direction, and produced contempt for the native languages and native literature. On other hand, more forcibly urged that learning of ancient world far surpassed that of modern at the time of its revival; that accordingly it became a new power, a mighty stimulus in the advance of the human mind; that it was proper to cultivate it with ardor until the European had raised himself to the intellectual level of the ancients; then alone could the scaffolding be thrown aside; that the very mania which spread through Europe in the 15th century in favor of classic literature proves that the great minds of that age felt that it was immeasurably superior to the modern; hence, if unfavorable to the exercise of original genius, it more than atoned for this by the useful knowledge which it imparted; and, although not entirely adapted to the mediæval ages, yet true science and knowledge will always contain a great deal which is common to all nations and ages.

CHAPTER VI.

PROGRESS OF REGAL AUTHORITY—STANDING ARMIES—BALANCE OF POWER.

1. *Contrast in condition of Europe in* 11*th and* 12*th centuries, and in* 17*th and* 18*th?* From 5th to 12th all the elements of government seem to have existed in the societies of Europe without coalescing into any thing like a national centralized government. We find kings, aristocracy, clergy, commonalty, &c., but no national government—no *nation*. We have a multitude of individual powers, of local institutions —no true nationality. But all is changed in 17th and 18th centuries. In language of Guizot, only two grand figures appear on the stage of Europe, *the government* and *the people*. We have homogeneous governments every where acting over large masses of people, and the people again reacting upon the government. It is this reciprocal action which constitutes internal history of modern European nations—the nobility, the clergy, the commonalty. All those distinct classes, those special and individual powers, that divided Europe in 10th and 12th centuries into a thousand little local governments, have undergone a total transformation—they have all been absorbed and melted down, as it were, into the great powers, the government and the people, *e. g.*, suppose with M. Guizot that a citizen of one of the communes of Europe in 12th or 13th century could now arise in the same city, what a wonderful change—would see no ramparts, no citadel, no town militia, no special defence, no town elections and democratic assemblies—he would soon find that the importance of the city had been merged in that of the nation—war and peace, navies and armies, treaties and battles with neighboring barons, no longer themes for debates when the town bell rings—he would see that centralization had prevailed, and that great national government had enveloped all local powers, (T. 5,) and yet he could not understand the meaning of *nation*, nor M. Seyes' question, "what is the *tiers etat?*" nor his answer to it, "it is the French nation *minus* the nobility and the clergy." So likewise a baron of the 10th or 11th century, suddenly appearing in France before the revolution of '89, could not have comprehended his new position. His court, his obedient vassals, his wars, his individuality, his complete independence, would all have disappeared. He would have found himself involved too in the great government, the mere glittering satellite about the monarch, now

the centre of the system—his fief gone and its inhabitants forming but small portion of that to him incomprehensible something called *a nation*.

2. *First events favorable to progress of regal power and centralization?* Have already seen influence of clergy and national churches. Crusades next great operating cause. 1st, By their *universality*. Great *European* expeditions, nothing similar before. It was European civilization at war with the Asiatic, the Christian religion with the Mahomedan. 2d, Not only European but *national*—in each country all classes join in them. 3d, Moral influence great—crusaders saw other lands, laws, institutions, &c., got rid of local prejudices, and became morally prepared for something like nationality in government. Have already explained influence in breaking up the fiefs and enlarging the royal demesnes, in building up the cities, and thus producing a democracy. Again have seen the influence of cities; did not league together, each one set up for complete independence; in wars with the barons often called in the king, whose supervising controlling power became gradually acknowledged.

3. *Advantages of royal power in this conflict with local and individual powers?* Precisely same advantage which the pope had in contest with bishops. As soon as circumstances elevated monarch above aristocracy he could play off one local power against another, could interfere in their affairs under various pretexts, and enjoy advantage of concentrated force over disunited and often hostile forces. Again during the feudal ages constant tendency to confusion, anarchy and oppression. There must have been great demand for some power which could restrain and give peace—a power that should have a sort of appellate jurisdiction—a power to which the weak and oppressed could everywhere turn for succor and support. Pope at first that power, then the kings, *e. g.*, in France monarchy first began to develope under Louis le Gros in 12th century—disorders great—clashing among local powers incessant—Louis an able man and powerful lord—called on at one time to repress gross injustice, at another to quiet the tumults in a neighboring district, at another to settle a dispute between two little belligerents, &c.,—thus becoming gradually a sort of conservator of the peace, a common arbiter, a general redresser of wrong. Thus for first time royalty in France under Louis le Gros, aided by his able minister, Suger, begins to stand forth a new power, undefined and confusedly acknowledged—still a power. (G. 9, 31.)

4. *Attempts at union of local powers—deliberative bodies?* As royal power began to develope, only means of preserving local powers was to unite them. This might have been done by deliberative bodies. When barbarians settled in Roman empire they were accustomed to

meet often in council. If then the aristocracy of the feudal system had formed a sort of deliberative body in which the will of each could have been subjected to that of whole, they might have formed a united power sufficient to preserve their independence, as the house of lords actually has done in England. But on continent aristocracies almost every where so powerful that each set up for complete independence. When cities arose they acted in same manner, and when afterwards power of kings was developed these local governments were destroyed for want of union. A mixed organization was attempted which should represent all these different powers, *e. g.*, States General in France, Cortes in Spain and in Portugal, Diet in Germany and Parliament in England. These bodies represented the nobility, the clergy and the commons. These attempts likewise failed almost every where except in England. As to states general and the cortes, they met but rarely, and therefore, M. Guizot says, were mere *accidents*—not a regular organization—not a systematic means of governing. In Germany system partially succeeded. Much more of local powers remaining there than in any other continental nation. Their emperor until a late period was elective. For a long time the struggle was to convert empire into hereditary monarchy, and to destroy power of the great princes. But union among latter with the aid of the papal power preserved their independence. Parliament of England, as will be explained, succeeded. General causes for failure of these mixed deliberative bodies were too little knowledge, too little civilization, every thing too local, too special, too prejudiced, no great general interest or common opinions capable of triumphing over local interests and prejudices. (G. 10, 36.)

5. *Character of the 15th and 16th centuries in regard to royal power and progress of consolidation?* During 14th all efforts at union and organization of local powers seem to have failed. Thus prepared the 15th exhibits every where tendency to consolidation—events of this century tend to creation of general interests and general ideas—all the elements of society conspire to same result without intending it. Thus 15th prepared public mind for consolidated government, and in 16th century work was accomplished.

6. *Influence of wars between England and France during latter part of 14th and first half of 15th century on progress of royal power?* In those long wars between England and France, during which latter was almost conquered, a national spirit formed in both countries. All classes in each nation were united, and patriotism the result, *e. g.*, Joan d'Arc, the maid of Orleans, illustrates influence of these wars—her enthusiasm patriotic—not result of a *local* but *national* feeling—she did not fight for Orleans and its territory, but for France and her king.

Before reign of house of Valois feudal character prevailed in France—*French nation*, *French patriotism*, did not exist—all was local and special—wars of this house with England united all classes, and greatly contributed to form French nation. Again, great change effected in government. Look at Charles VI. and even first part of reign of Charles VII., and then to last part of Charles VII., when wars were ended—difference immense. It was during these wars that French became convinced that feudal militia could not oppose English troops, who were much more like regulars, hence Charles VII. permitted to keep on foot a standing army of 16,000 infantry and 9,000 cavalry—first standing army of modern Europe. Charles VII. first monarch to levy an extraordinary subsidy without concurrence of states general—likewise prevailed on his subjects to render certain taxes perpetual which before were occasional. Thus getting both a standing army and a revenue—the sword and the purse—he became the most absolute prince in the latter part of his reign that had ever sat on the French throne. As the royal power advanced so did the administration of justice extend itself and become more national. Five new parliaments* were instituted in a short time, and these superseded the old baronial courts.

7. *Influence of union and extension of French territory?* After death of Henry V. of England and the appearance of Joan d'Arc in France, latter nation successful against English, who are beaten out from almost whole of France except Calais. Thus English provinces, Normandy, Touraine, Poitou, Santonge, &c.; were added to France, and gave immense weight to the crown. Under reign of Louis XI. ten more provinces were united, Roussillon, Cerdagne, Burgundy, Franche-Comté, Picardy, Artois, Provence, Maine, Anjou and Perché. Under Charles VIII. and Louis XII., Brittany, by successive marriage of Ann with both kings, was permanently annexed to France. (G. 11, 10.) Thus did France become physically consolidated.

8. *Louis XI.—influence of his character and policy?* Character of Louis complex—suited to the times—subtile, unfeeling, cruel—great object to break down power of his nobles—sows dissensions among them—his maxim *divide et impera*—fills offices of government with men taken from lowest and most despised functions in life—nobles treated with mortifying neglect—their privileges violated—tried by his judges, who had no right, and often condemned to death, and thus thousands perished by hands of common executioner—augmented the standing army of his father by addition of 6000 troops hired from Swiss republics—augmented his revenue by taxation without concurrence of

* Parliaments of France were courts of justice, and not deliberative bodies.

states general, and even if he called this body together he possessed the art of managing and corrupting them—first taught fatal art of attacking public liberty by corrupting its source—he bribed at the elections, and if he failed there he bribed or overawed the members so as to make them subservient to his policy. Thus he almost completed work of consolidation by breaking down power of his nobles, and acquiring a larger army and larger revenue than any other French monarch, *e. g.*, Charles VII. levied taxes to amount of 1,800,000 francs, and had an army of 16,000 infantry and 9000 cavalry; Louis raised 4,700,000 francs annually by taxes, and augmented his army to 25,000 foot and 15,000 horse. (R. V. 3, 81.) But the political tactics of Louis worked a wonderful change in the diplomacy of courts, and had tendency to elevate the intellectual above the physical. Before his time feudal governments had but one way of getting on, that was by force, by *material means;* but he set a new machinery in motion—he used cunning and diplomacy, the Italian politics instead of feudal, and although his tactics were those of the liar and the hypocrite, yet were they intellectual rather than material. Forms a perfect contrast with his celebrated rival, Charles the Bold. Latter represents ancient mode of governing—knows no other means than force—in every difficulty appeals to the sword—has no patience—will not wait for tardy results of management and diplomacy. While Louis never resorts to force if he can avoid it—manages men by his arts—balances interests—his institutions all remain as before, so far as external appearance is concerned, but he makes them work differently by his secret management, by the corrupting tactics of his power. Thus was it a great advance to give up the constant resort to force and to make a trial of intellectual means although of a dishonest and disgraceful character. When this became general, experience soon taught that honesty and plain dealing were really the best policy. So that soon a still more important change took place in diplomacy, by substituting more justice for egotism, openness and truth for falsehood and duplicity.

9. *Circumstances favorable to consolidation in Spain?* In 15th century Grenada, the kingdom of Moors in Spain, was overthrown by Ferdinand—thus ended the long struggle between Moors and Christians. This, together with marriage of Ferdinand, king of Aragon, with Isabella, queen of Castile, united three most important kingdoms of the peninsula under one monarch. That monarch, with fewer vices, had much of the character of Louis XI.—substituted management and diplomacy for force, and by such means contributed still farther to consolidation.

10. *In Germany?* Here events of 15th century likewise favorable

to imperial power. In 1538 house of Austria restored to imperial throne, and towards conclusion of same century Maximilian arrived at a degree of power possessed by none of his predecessors. By marriage with Mary, daughter of Charles the Bold and heiress of all his possessions, he annexed an immense territory to his hereditary Austrian dominions—thus gave a decided preponderance to the Austrian family in the German confederation, which enabled him to give centralization to government. Like Charles VII. he introduced a standing army in his hereditary possessions. Like Louis XI. he introduced the mail, &c., and it was during his reign that the empire became prepared for the great rôle which it subsequently played in the politics of Europe under Charles V.

11. *In England?* Here, as will be explained, the establishment of parliament gave a degree of nationality at very early period, which no other country possessed. Yet events of 15th century gave in England as every where else a violent tendency in government towards consolidation. Long wars with France produced same effects in England as in France. Henry V. most successful of all English kings on continent—was so popular that parliament voted him a large revenue during his life—an act unprecedented. Wars with France followed by civil wars of houses of York and Lancaster—effects in favor of centralization: 1st. These wars between two parties supporting rival kings—not local and feudal, but national. 2d. Many aristocratic families were destroyed by these wars, the estates of many more were confiscated, and when Henry VII. mounted throne his aristocracy no longer able to oppose him. Hence reign of two first Tudors considered transition period in the British government. Henry, like Ferdinand and Louis of France, was highly politic, substituting caution and cunning for force—watched by the powerful faction of Yorkists, was obliged to proceed more cautiously than Louis of France. As power of nobles declined, afraid to take all to himself, but suffered it to go to the house of commons. Hence one additional cause of more perfect balance of English government—people gained while the aristocracy lost. Whereas, in France, king took all that his nobility lost, and consequently soon became absolute. Under Henry VIII. suppression of monasteries and confiscation of their property furnished king with such ample means as to supersede a resort to parliament for money. Hence this king one of most absolute in British history, and his parliaments were so subservient that he used them as convenient instruments to execute his tyranny. This ultimately favorable to liberty, for while Henry VIII. called on them to execute all kinds of tyranny because of their subserviency, he undesignedly established precedents in favor of their right to act in all such

cases, and when afterwards the temper of these bodies was changed, and they began again to take the side of liberty, no reign furnished so many precedents in favor of their claims as that of H. VIII.

12. *In Italy?* Here royalty was not established except in south. Still we see same general tendency to consolidation. In 15th century all the republics fall—even when name preserved the power passes into hands of one or two families—Lombard republics change into the Duchy of Milan, Florence in 1434 passes under the sway of the Medici, in 1464 Genoa becomes subject to Milan, &c.; shortly afterwards great northern powers set up their pretensions to different portions of Italy, particularly to Milan and Naples, which led on to successive invasions from these more barbarous countries, that made Italy for so long a period the battle ground of Europe.

13. *Summary?* Thus, to whatever part of Europe we turn, we behold ancient elements and forms of society undergoing change—local powers disappearing under the action of centralization. There is something exceedingly melancholy in contemplating the overthrow of the old feudal and municipal liberties of Europe—the revolution caused torrents of blood to be spilt—the aristocracy and the cities fought long and hard for their independence. But principle of consolidation prevailed. Europe wanted more repose and security than baronial and city governments could afford, and the rapid increase of regal power, consolidating all the elements of society into a sort of homogeneous whole, alone could satisfy this want.

14. *Change in the military system of Europe?* Invention of gunpowder, next to printing, perhaps, most important invention of modern times. In using ancient arms personal skill and prowess of great value—fate of battles determined in great measure by it. Invention of gunpowder produced wonderful change—placed men more on footing of equality—little man with a musket equal to big one—defensive armor of little avail against bullets—all this unfavorable to feudal mode of governing—destroyed that personal distinction resulting from skill and strength. Invention of powder placed at first the art of attack above that of defence, and introduction of artillery tended to sweep down all local powers, and to mould heterogeneous forces into a homogeneous compound. Baron's castle could resist arrows, javelins, and even battering engines, but not cannon balls. Again, fire-arms have made success of modern battles to depend more on the discipline of armies, and the skilfulness of their evolutions, than on the mere bravery of soldiers and skill in using weapons. War is a science now. Hence standing armies kept constantly in the field found to be infinitely superior to militia. Monarchs soon found that the feudal troops, remaining only

forty days in the field, would not answer—began to hire soldiers, who were much more efficacious than feudal militia—this one of the secrets of success of English against the French in 15th century—their armies were kept longer in the field, and more of the troops were mercenary than in France. As soon as influence of gunpowder was felt, cavalry service began to decline, and the superiority of infantry to be developed. This was another circumstance unfavorable to feudal system of government. Monarchs preferred low-bred mercenary soldier to the knight on horseback with all his prowess and his honor. Hence introduction of standing armies.

15. *Standing armies?* Even before invention of gunpowder all history proves that standing armies could bear down every other kind of force. Philip, king of Macedon, first among Greeks to institute a standing army—conquered the militias of the Grecian republics, and in hands of his son Alexander overthrew still more numerous and undisciplined forces of Persia. In wars between Rome and Carthage, fate of two countries determined principally by standing armies. Army led into Italy by Hannibal a standing army, formed under Amilcar and Asdrubal in Spain. Battles of Trebia, Thrasymene and Cannæ were won by this army against the armies of Rome, which were then militia—for during the long peace Roman armies had been disbanded. As Hannibal's army wasted, he was obliged to recruit it in Italy, while Roman army became more and more disciplined from day to day. When Scipio went into Africa things were reversed—his army was a standing army, and Hannibal's a militia force, hence gains battle of Zama. From this time forward Romans kept up standing armies, hence their conquest of world. In their wars against the east the standing army of Macedon made some resistance—it cost Rome two wars and three bloody battles to conquer that little kingdom. But militias of Greece, of Syria and Egypt made a feeble resistance. The Scythian and Tartar militia, which Mithridates drew from the north of Euxine and Caspian seas, were much more formidable, because more like standing armies; and for same reason Parthian and German militias always made respectable resistance. Under the emperors soldiers became corrupt and effeminate, the civil character prevailed over the military, and the armies degenerated again into militia—vastly inferior to the militia of Germany and Scythia, hence overthrow of Western Empire. It is these standing armies that have every where triumphed over liberty—it was a standing army with which Julius Cæsar overthrew the commonwealth—it was a standing army by which Cromwell turned the parliament out of doors and made himself dictator. During the feudal ages of Europe every prince relied on feudal militia, hence all countries in

same condition, but moment any one prince obtained a regular standing army after the invention of gunpowder, it might easily have been foreseen from history of the world that he would endanger the liberties of Europe, unless others would follow his example. France was first nation to establish such an army, and she soon forced all the continental nations to follow her example or lose their liberties. These armies, although the result in the first place of centralizing tendency of the 15th century, enabled the monarchs to complete work of consolidation, to quiet interior dissension, and to act externally with more vigor. Hence after this century wars of Europe are carried on upon a more gigantic scale—exterior relations become as important, or even more so, than the interior—the age of negotiation and diplomacy, of alliance and political balancing arrived. Up to this period history of each nation separate and insulated—afterwards so close a connection that Robertson says, from time of Charles V. of Germany, he who writes the history of one or two great nations in Europe, must write that of all the rest.

16. *Invasion of Naples by Charles VIII. of France,* (1494) *political equilibrium?* One of the first events in modern Europe, which proved the superiority of a standing army and forced the great nations to attend to *balance of power* was invasion of Italy by Charles VIII. of France. This monarch weak but ambitious, with a revenue and army at his command, was anxious to achieve something great. Ludovico Sforza wished to depose his own nephew, Duke of Milan—he feared a combination of Italian powers against him, therefore persuaded Charles to march into Italy and seize the crown of Naples as heir to the house of Anjou. Charles readily came into the projèt—put in motion 20,000 regulars—militia and mercenaries of Italy unable to contend with them. Florence, Pisa and Rome opened their gates at the approach of this army—all Italy was panic struck. One king of Naples died of fright, say historians—another abdicated, and a third fled, and Charles took possession of Naples, after marching through Italy with all the rapidity of a mere military promenade. (R. 3, v. 89.) Italians finding that they were not equal to contest with Charles, immediately commenced negotiations with great powers to form an alliance to drive him out of Italy. While Charles wasted his time in festivals at Naples, they formed league among the Italians, supported by two of greatest monarchs in Europe, Ferdinand of Spain and Maximilian of Germany, both alarmed at progress of the French. An army of 30,000 men was quickly brought into field. French broke through and made their escape, and thus were they driven from Italy as fast as they had conquered it, by an alliance formed by Italian diplomacy. In this expedition was developed in eminent degree the irresistible superiority of a standing army against

militia troops, and all the nations of Europe henceforth began to abandon the feudal military for the regular army, and to rely on infantry trained after the Swiss manner rather than cavalry. This expedition too first taught the expense of one of those regular military invasions, and led on to more exorbitant taxation throughout Europe. Money, which Charles provided, gave out before he reached Italy, and was obliged to borrow of the Genoese at enormous rate of 42 per cent. per annum. All monarchs of Europe made similar blunders about this time in their financial calculations. Ministers of finance henceforth became most important counsellors. It was study of finance forced on monarchs by expenses of their wars, which first originated the great science of political economy. This invasion too seems to have furnished first instance for successful formation of one of those alliances, by which balance of power is preserved in Europe. Venice, Germany, and Spain, all united to drive Charles out of Italy. These alliances were not formed during feudal ages, for monarchs had not sufficient power and military force to form them, and the aristocracy, in whom the power rested, were more interested in private wars than in attending to political equilibrium of Europe. Soon after league against Charles followed that of Cambray against Venice (1508)—then holy league headed by Pope Julius II. against Louis XII. of France. During reign of Charles V. of Germany every court in Europe was the scene of these negotiations; for the immense dominion of Charles nearly destroyed balance of power in Europe.

17. *Influence of international relations and negotiations on regal power?* From the 15th century these external relations become more numerous and important, and form in fact the great subject of history. The popes, the Venetians, the emperors, the kings of France, Spain, England, &c., watch each other, negotiate alliances and treaties, and endeavor by all means to preserve political equilibrium among themselves. Now although these external relations were in first place the result of increase of regal power, they in turn powerfully augmented it, for management of all these new relations fell into hands of the kings. They often demand secrecy and dispatch, therefore unfit for deliberative bodies—people are not sufficiently interested in them, therefore apt to surrender them to the cabinets of kings—moreover were too ignorant of details to interfere with effect, *e. g.*, as late as James I. parliament of England insisted on war against France, and voted £70,000 when nothing less than £900,000 would answer to begin it with—even such were the miscalculations of bodies unacquainted with financial matters. When spirit of liberty began to spread, that portion of royal prerogative, which claims management of external relations, was last to be

attacked. People exceedingly timid against this branch of kingly power, *e. g.*, look to history of England in 16th and 17th centuries, in reigns of Elizabeth, James I., Charles I., and we see it opposing greatest obstacles to English liberty. Monarchs constantly claim plenary powers over all external relations—over peace and war and all commercial intercourse. Even to time of American revolution colonists were disposed to make difference between right of mother country to lay a direct tax and to levy one equally burthensome on commerce. This same principle has had an effect even on our own legislature, and perhaps exerted no slight influence in favor of the tariff. Concentration of these new powers in hands of kings after 15th century gave them the more power, as these relations became for three centuries most important affairs of Europe.

CHAPTER VII.

REFORMATION—IMMEDIATE CAUSES.

SECTION I.

Perhaps the most important event of modern times is that usually denominated the *reformation;* whilst it was itself the result in a great measure of the progress of civilization and knowledge, it became in turn a most powerfully operating cause on their onward march, and has produced more important results than any other revolution which has occurred since the downfall of the Roman empire. Shall commence first with the immediate cause and then proceed to the more general.

1. *Sale of indulgences?* Have already seen that catholic church was in habit of imposing penance on offenders, which were considered as satisfactions for offences. Whenever a part of the penance was remitted called an *indulgence.* Those who depart this life indebted for sins not atoned for by penance, must suffer in another life in purgatory. Indulgences may extend to purgatory, and church may for certain considerations exempt from whole or part of punishment. Argument for indulgences, that the death of Christ constituted fund of merit sufficient to save the human race—Bull of Clement VI. asserted that one drop of his blood on Mount Calvary was sufficient. Besides this, however, if one man falls short in good works, another may do more than enough for his salvation. Now the infinite merits of Christ, added to works of supererogation of saints, constitute inexhaustible treasure, the keys of which have been given to St. Peter and his successors, the popes. Upon

this treasure the pope and the church can draw to any amount, transferring to any man for money a portion of this superabundant merit, which may exempt him or any one now in purgatory, on whose behalf he feels an interest, from the pains of purgatory.* *Plenary* indulgences seem not to have been introduced till time of crusades. (W. 466.) First granted by Pope Urban to the crusaders; then granted to those who hired a soldier to go; finally given to those who gave money for accomplishing any pious work enjoined by pope, *e. g.*, Julius II. bestowed indulgences on all who contributed towards building St. Peter's church at Rome, and Leo's grants were based on same pretence. When once the popes had gotten into practice of selling them, it became a means of taxing all Christendom, and consequently there was every temptation to abuse a practice which so enriched the see of Rome; hence it was an evil complained of every where even before the appearance of Luther. The agents who were employed to sell them practised every device to insure success, their assertions to modern years would appear impious and revolting, *e. g.*, Tetzel boasted of saving more souls from hell than St. Peter had converted; that the cross erected by indulgences was as efficacious as that of Christ; that the purchase of indulgence would expiate the most horrible sin, even a violation of mother of God, if such sin were possible—for 12 pence, he would exclaim, you may redeem the soul of your father out of purgatory, and are you so ungrateful as not to rescue him from torment? the moment your money tinkles in the chest your father's soul mounts up from purgatory, &c. Not to wonder then that sale of indulgences should have been the immediate exciting cause of reformation. It was against this abuse that Luther first distinguished himself.

2. *Luther—goes against indulgences, and then against the whole*

* The following is translation of the form of the indulgence used by Tetzel in Saxony. "May our Lord Jesus Christ have mercy upon thee and absolve thee by the merits of his most holy passion. And I, by his authority, and of his blessed apostles, Peter and Paul, and of the most holy pope, granted and committed to me in these parts, do absolve thee from all ecclesiastical censures, in whatever manner they have been incurred, and then from all thy sins, transgressions and excesses, how enormous soever they may be, even from such as are reserved for the cognizance of the holy see; and as far as the keys of the holy church extend, I remit to you all punishment which you deserve in purgatory on their account, and I restore you to the holy sacraments of the church, to the unity of the faithful, and to that innocence and purity which you possessed at baptism; so that when you die the gates of punishment shall be shut and the gates of the paradise of delight shall be opened; and if you shall not die at present, this grace shall remain in full force, when you are at the point of death. In the name of the Father and of the Son and of the Holy Ghost." (R. v. 4, 71.)

papal power? Martin Luther, born of poor parents, at Eisleben in Saxony, (1483,) received a good education, commencing at schools of Magdeburg and Eisenach, and completing it at Erfurt, where he studied the philosophy of nominalists and took master's degree at 20 years of age; commenced study of law with a view to that profession, but a severe illness and death of a friend by his side from lightning, together with influence of a melancholic temperament, made him, contrary to his father's wishes, enter an Augustinian monastery—soon became distinguished for powers of disputation—found a Latin Bible in library—studied it most thoroughly—began to see the futility of scholastic theology which he learned at college—discarded authority of Aristotle, and betook himself almost exclusively to Bible and the writings of St. Augustin—became great favorite of Staupitz, vicar general of Augustinian order—was recommended by him to Frederic, elector of Saxony, to fill the chair of philosophy (1508) in the university of Wittemburg, (a new and *pet* institution of the elector;) after a while promoted to the most important chair, that of theology—had the degree of doctor conferred on him. In 1516 wrote a dissertation against doctrine of *merit of good works*, at time when the great Swiss reformer, Zwingle, was preaching at Einsiedlin. Such his life when he began to preach and write against indulgences. (1517.) As ordinary revenues of Leo X. did not suffice for his own extravagance and completion of church of St. Peter, issued a bull proclaiming plenary indulgence for building this church. Albert, archbishop of Mentz and Magdeburg, was commissioner general for sale of indulgences throughout his diocese, including that part of Saxony in which was Wittemburg—employed John Tetzel his agent of Dominican order. Saxon princes had prohibited sale of indulgences in their dominions, nevertheless Tetzel came to every gate of Wittemburg urging the sale in most impudent and impious manner. On the eve of All Saints, when a great concourse was expected at Wittemburg to visit the fine collection of relics in cathedral, Luther published his 95 *theses* or propositions against indulgences, accompanied with usual challenge, that he was ready to defend them against all the doctors; moreover preached against them in great church of Wittemburg. In this move was supported by Augustinian friars, and gave no alarm to church, and there was great difference of opinion even in church on indulgences. Pope too had but little religion, if any; was of noble family of Medici, and felt no alarm. Thought Augustinians were jealous of Dominicans because sale of indulgences had been trusted to latter—hence, when Prierio called his attention to 95 theses, replied that brother Martin was a man of talent, and that whole dispute was nothing but squabble among the friars. Character of Luther quieted all fears; a devout catholic, going to Rome some years before, as soon as came in sight fell on his knees, raised his hands to heaven, and said, "*I salute thee, holy Rome.*" (Pfister 7, 33.) And on present occasion wrote to pope and archbishop of Mentz—to former says, "wherefore, most holy father, my life and death are in your hands. Call or recall me, approve or condemn me, as you please. I shall acknowledge your voice as the voice of Christ, who presides and speaks in your person." (Ling. 6, 80.) Luther however was a man of violent temper, and the Dominicans, together with John Eckius of Ingolstadt, one of the most famous theologians and dialecticians of his day, soon urged him into extremes, and made him appear great champion against indulgences and papal power. His theses, too, rapidly spread through Germany, began to operate on popular mind. Pope at last summoned him to Rome, to submit his doctrines to the inquisitor general, Silvestro Prieirias; but from intercession of the elector, pope agreed to have Luther interrogated at Augsburg instead of Rome. For this purpose Cardinal Cajetan, a Dominican, was sent: received Luther with respect, tried argument at first; produced no effect, for he adhered to papal decrees, and opinions of schoolmen, whilst Luther appealed to Bible alone. Cajetan then commanded him to recant; Luther refused, professing still a reverence for the pope. Said of Cajetan afterwards that he was no more fitted for a discussion of the subject than an ass to play upon a harp. (Pf. 7, 34.) Leo sent forth a bull confirming right to grant indulgences and threatening excommunication to all who should oppose them, but did not name Luther, who immediately had bull printed with a severe commentary, and then, on 28th November, appealed from the pope to a general council, as the university of Paris had done on another question; the elector was pressed to send Luther to Rome or banish him. Would do neither—always warm friend of Luther. Had interest of his new university very much at heart, and knew that Luther and Melancthon were the brightest ornaments. Pope determined once more to try Luther. Selected John Miltitz, better acquainted with German character and interests; had interview with Luther, so well pleased that he embraced him at table. Luther agreed to be silent if other party would, and wrote a letter to pope that would not retract, but assured his holiness he never had an idea of overthrowing power of church or of pope, above which there is but one other power, that of Christ. But opposite party could not keep silence. John Eckius challenged Carlostadt to a public debate, and requested Luther to be present. Duke George of Saxony designated Leipsic for the debate. Luther was present, carrying with him his young friend, Philip Schwarzerd de Pforzheim, to whom Reuchlin, a relation, had given more euphonious Greek name of Melancthon. Melancthon was at that time professor of Greek in university of Wittemburg, a man of great mildness and learning, and a reformer. Debate was held. Great point sustained by Luther and his party was that Bible explained itself and needed not interpretation of the fathers. It was in discussion of this branch of subject that Luther for first time began to call in question papal power. Both parties of course claimed victory. Death of Emperor Maximilian year before very favorable to Luther. Vicariate of that part of Germany fell into the hands of the elector, his friend. Moreover, political world agitated by great question of election of new emperor. Leo himself more interested in this question than the theological one, and did not wish to do any thing to offend Frederic, who had great weight in the electoral world; therefore was reluctant to issue bull of excommunication against Luther. Meantime the doctrines of Luther spread with immense rapidity. All Germany was in a blaze; his doctrine was the popular doctrine. Whilst Luther was succeeding in Germany, another reformer appeared in Switzerland, commencing about same time, Zuinglius or Zwingle. Doubtful even whether he was not little in advance of Luther. Luther became bolder and bolder, one investigation led to another, till he was ready to pull down the whole papal fabric, parts of which are so closely united, *e. g.*, indulgences produced inquiry into true cause of our justification and acceptance with God; that by degrees led him to see inutility of penances, pilgrimages, and reliance on saints; that led to consider abuses of auricular confession, and to call in question existence of purgatory; so many errors led him to investigate character of clergy; wealth, celibacy, monastic vows, were considered as so many sources of corruption. But one step more to call in question papal power. Did it as soon as bull of excommunication came, which Leo was induced to issue on 15th June, 1520, after hearing from all quarters that Luther was becoming incorrigible heretic, commanded at same time all Luther's writings to be burnt. Luther now came out against the whole papal scheme, wrote a piece on the Babylonish captivity, pronounced the pope the Antichrist foretold in Scripture; and, as they burned his writings, was at last provoked to assemble a crowd of professors, students, &c., before the gate of Wittemburg, and burnt on a sort of funeral pile the *canon law* and the *pope's bull*, exclaiming "as thou hast afflicted the bosom of our Lord, so may the eternal fire afflict and consume thee." (Pf. 7, 49.) The affair had now come to crisis, breach complete. Germany more excited than ever, celebrated Ulric Von Hutten, greatest wit and satirist of the day, came out for reformation, and openly attacked the pope and clergy with his withering satires.

A new scheme was now fallen on. Newly elected emperor, Ch. V., too much indebted to elector to wish to proceed harshly against Luther; therefore summoned him to appear before Diet of Worms, and gave him a safe conduct; wrote superscription with his own hand, "*To our honorable, dear and fervent doctor, Martin Luther.*" (March 6, 1521.) Diets had occasionally interfered in affairs of church; Diet was urged to condemn Luther unheard, Charles opposed. Luther counselled not to trust himself at Worms, lest might share fate of Jerome and Huss at council of Constance, replied that he would enter Worms in spite of al the powers of hell, for Christ still lived. As he passed to Worms a crowd pressed on him to see a man who had put all thunder of Vatican at defiance. Day of his arrival, (17th April, 1521,) called before Diet, appeared in gown of a monk, lean and pale from care, fatigue and sickness, on the journey; emperor eyed him closely, was disappointed in his looks, said that he was not the man that would ever seduce *him* from the faith of his fathers. After certain interrogatories, before an immense crowd within, and without pressing against windows, Luther rose, and with calm mien, pronounced his discourse; begged pardon in advance if he should be wanting in respect either in word or action, for that he had been reared in silence of cloister at a distance from courts. When he had finished, emperor requested, as he did not understand German well, that Luther would repeat his discourse in Latin, which he did in low tone, for he was oppressed with fatigue, and covered with perspiration. His manner was mild, till Eckius interrupted him and demanded a categoric and precise answer, when he answered that he would give one without *horns* or *teeth;* that he could not retract unless convinced by the testimony of the Bible, or clear arguments, for he neither believed in popes nor councils, since it was manifest they were often deceived, and contradicted each other. As a conscientious man he was bound to conform to the divine command.

Thus spoke the poor monk before the greatest body of princes in Europe, with the greatest monarch at their head. Never did enemies of Luther commit greater blunder than to consent to his appearing before the Diet. The assembly was august, the occasion agitating, the sympathies of Germany were with him, and no circumstance could possibly have produced so rapid a spread of his principles as this exhibition before the Diet; he was listened to with deepest attention; his house was crowded with visitors; the first noblemen were anxious to see and know him, and he was even a greater *lion* in Worms than Charles himself. Emperor was pressed to violate safe conduct given to Luther, and to bring him to trial, as John Huss was at Constance; but would not violate his honor; told Luther (26th April) that his passport should last him for 21 days more. Luther immediately left Worms, went to Hesse, when he sent his passport with his thanks to the emperor; passed on to Meiningen, where he was during the night taken from carriage by two noblemen, disguised, placed on horseback, and carried by winding ways to castle of Wartburg, where he remained for some time concealed from world—all this planned by his patron, the elector. Three days afterwards emperor published the *Decree of Worms*, calling Luther a hardened heretic twice excommunicated, and proscribing him and all his adherents, and ordering magistrates to hand over the culpable to justice, that their estates might be confiscated and themselves burned. (P. 63.) Although decree was in favor of catholic, result was for protestant. The violence of the decree and the disappearance of Luther operated on the sympathies and imaginations of the people, and gave that publicity and notoriety necessary for the success of reformation. Luther in mean time was not idle, wrote incessantly against his opponents, and commenced his great work, translation of Bible, while confined to the castle which he called his *isle of Patmos.*

3. *Circumstances immediately favorable to reformation after the edict of Worms?* 1st. Emperor was absent from Germany for several years, in consequence of troubles in Spain and war with France. 2d. The constitution of Germanic empire was favorable. Emperor left a regency to govern in his stead, with no definite directions as to special mode of executing the decree—fell of course into hands of the princes, many of whom were already for reformation. Such were the difficulties in the execution that it was agreed in diet at Spires, in 1526, that each prince should be left to regulate religious matters in such manner as to be able to give an account to God and the emperor, until call of a general council—hence non-execution of decree. 3d. During the absence of Charles, Luther completed large portion of his translation of Bible, and gave it as fast as finished to the people, and during same time Melancthon drew up his *Hypotyposes Theologicæ*, a manual of Christian doctrine. This in beautiful Latin, and calculated to operate on the intelligent public, whilst Luther's German Bible operated on all.

4. *Unfavorable circumstances?* 1st. Schism among the reformers themselves, particularly in regard to the eucharist, which will soon be explained. 2d. An insurrection of the peasants took place, accompanied, as those insurrections always are, with great horrors. Although notorious that this was result of oppression, and although Luther condemned the excesses, yet it was attributed to spread of reformation, and the latter made to bear all the odium. 3d. A sort of crazy, wild sect arose at Munster, calling themselves *Anabaptists*, because of rejection of infant baptism. These soon expelled catholics and Lutherans from city—pillaged churches and convents, adopting all the time as watch-

word the exhortation to repent addressed by John the Baptist to the multitudes around him in wilderness of Judæa. John de Mattheison, chief prophet, established community of goods, and burnt all books except Bible. John of Leyden, his successor, had been journeyman tailor and a *rogue*—commissioned 12 princes as representatives of 12 tribes of Israel to mount the thrones of Europe—practised polygamy—made Munster, which he called New Jerusalem, a type of the old, by encouraging every vice and enormity—sent missionaries to preach his fanatical doctrines, which spread with great rapidity through north of Germany and Netherlands. All this injurious to Luther and reformation, 1st, Because one reformation or innovation is apt to be confounded with another. 2d. It was believed that Luther's antinomian doctrines—his ascribing too much to mere *faith* and too little to *good works*, led on to these excesses of the anabaptists, who imagined it to be possible to be at same time a *Christian* and a *knave*—to have a justifying faith without good works. Bossuet has charged with great power this consequence on Luther's creed, and Hallam has recently countenanced the charge. For Defence of Luther see E. R. No. 138.

5. *Protestants—confession of Augsburg—Smalcaldic league—success of the reformation?* Charles at last having settled matters with foreign princes, particularly with the pope of Rome, and having more leisure to arrange affairs of Germany, commenced in earnest the settlement of religious disputes—called a diet at Spires (1529)—resolution of former diet, that each prince should manage ecclesiastical affairs till calling of a council, revoked, and instead decreed that every change in doctrine, discipline or worship of Catholic church should be unlawful till meeting of council, which it was well known pope would not call. Against this decree five princes, the Elector of Saxony, the Margrave of Brandenburg, the Landgrave of Hesse, the Prince of Anhalt and the Duke of Lunenburg, met on 25th April, 1529, and drew up a solemn *protest*, and on same day fourteen towns of empire joined them, and Philip of Hesse and the Elector of Saxony had it printed. This protest caused name of *protestants* to be give to reformers. It contained the fundamental declaration that religious belief could not be controlled by human power, and that the Bible alone should furnish a standard for belief, thus protesting against the catholic mode of interpreting the Scriptures. (P. 159.) A copy of this protest was sent to the emperor, who was not at the diet. Meantime protestants began to prepare for worst—a league was desirable of all the protestants—unfortunate dispute about the eucharist divided protestant church. When Luther left catholic church did not entirely give up the catholic doctrine of *transubstantiation*, or of the *real presence* of the body of Christ in

the eucharist, but adopted doctrine of *consubstantiation*, *i. e.*, that these are *real* bread and wine, and at same time *real* flesh and blood of Christ became united with them—as in hot iron there is iron and heat. (H. C. H. V. 1, 24.) Zwingle and Æcolampadius on contrary contended for what we do, that the expression is Scripture is metaphorical, and that bread in sacrament is neither Christ's flesh, as catholic supposes, nor united with that flesh, as Luther contended, but a mere emblem. Philip, Landgrave of Hesse, ardent reformer, anxious to settle this difference, that German and Swiss reformers might unite against the gathering storm, prevailed on parties to meet and discuss the subject. They met—Luther was put against Œcolampadius, Melancthon against Zwingle—this done on principle of placing violent man against a mild one. Result as might have been foreseen—both sides more confirmed in their belief—the breach widened between parties.

When the Emperor Charles arrived at Augsburg, as protestants knew their *protest* had met with unfavorable reception, they determined to draw up a confession of their faith and present it to emperor. Mild Melancthon, best draftsman of all the protestants, and resembling in character James Madison of this country, drew up the paper with infinite skill. It contained Luther's notions about the eucharist. Emperor in diet on 25th June, 1530, gave audience to protestants. Dr. Boyer read the paper, being occupied from 4 until 6 o'clock, with a voice so loud and sonorous that all heard and were delighted. Even emperor was deeply impressed by it, and after sleepless night is said to have declared for Luther's notion of *consubstantiation*. Campeggio, however, the papal legate, soon satisfied him and made him hostile to the whole of what was afterwards called *Confession of Augsburg*. A committee of *impartial* men, at head of whom was the violent Dr. Eckius, appointed to examine the document—wrote what was called the *refutation*. Protestants procured with difficulty a copy of this under condition that they would neither attempt an *answer* to it, or *publish* either of the documents. Four towns, Strasburg, Constance, Memmingen and Lindau, imbued with the Zwinglean doctrine, sent in a confession of faith, (*Confessio Tetrapolitana*,) which was treated like the Augsburg Confession. Zwingle prepared and sent to emperor a separate confession for himself, which was not noticed, and even Melancthon, when he heard of the manner in which the German doctrines were spoken of, said that Zwingle *had become a fool*. Although orders were given not to publish Confession of Augsburg, it soon appeared in every language of Europe, and produced great effect on popular mind. As Charles seemed preparing for the extirpation of protestantism, the protestant princes at length formed the celebrated league at Smalcald, headed by

Elector of Saxony and Landgrave of Hesse, in which they united against their enemies. Henceforth, to the peace of Westphalia, for more than 100 years, the politics of Europe turned upon this great religious question—it was a constant struggle between the catholic and protestant religions—all local or mere national matters were merged in this great question. The contest at last finished by the two religions dividing Europe nearly equally between them.

SEC. II.—REMOTE AND GENERAL CAUSES.

6. *General causes?* Of two kinds, moral and physical. The moral enumerated by Dr. Robertson are: 1st. Long schism in church, to which may be added the secession to Avignon. 2d. Peculiar character of the popes immediately preceding reformation. 3d. Immoral lives of the clergy generally. 4th. Wealth and exactions of church and venality of court of Rome. 5th. Revival of learning and invention of printing press.

7. *First moral cause?* Towards conclusion of 14th century, (1378,) college of cardinals at Rome elected Urban VI. under circumstances of popular intimidation, which led to belief that his election was not fair; besides he proved to be a man of very harsh temper, and what the clergy of Rome disliked still more, a great enemy to all abuses—he announced his determination to reform them, commencing with the college of cardinals. (W. 513.) This more honest than politic. All the cardinals, except the four Italian, retired with pope's permission to Anagni, to spend the summer months, where they declared Urban's election null and void—then went to Fundi in Naples—wrote to each of four Italian cardinals to join them, and gave each one secret intimations that he would be elected. The four at once fell into snare, joined their brethren at Fundi, and when all were assembled college elected Robert, cardinal of Geneva, pope, under name of Clement VII. (20th Sept. 1378.) His election supported by France, Scotland, Cyprus, Savoy, Geneva and many of the German princes. All rest of Europe adhered to Urban VI.—thus commencement of schism. From this time for near 40 years constantly two and sometimes three popes roaming about Europe, fawning on princes whom they wished to gain, extorting money from friendly countries, hurling their thunder at one another, each denying infallibility of other, &c., &c. Thus papal authority was weakened and brought into contempt, and popes began to lose reverence and respect of Christendom. The continuance of the schism too gave rise to the assembling of councils, which endeavored to settle the disputes and determine the true pope. These councils claimed a jurisdiction above the

popes themselves, and this another cause which had tendency to degrade the papacy. With regard to what is generally called the secession to Avignon, that took place in 1305. Clement V. left Italy and resided in France, principally at Avignon, and was imitated by his successors till 1376, a period of 70 years. (W. 478.) During this period the pope could not but be under French influence, hence other nations lost respect for the head of the church—this was everywhere called the *Babylonish captivity.*

8. *Second cause?* Six popes came after Pius II., 1404, filling up a large portion of 15th century and a considerable part of 16th, whose character had great influence in bringing on reformation: 1st. Paul II. sold benefices to highest bidder—simony intolerable during his reign—he was proud and fond of luxury. 2d. Sixtus IV., so odious that at day of his death people thanked God for their deliverance from a man, in whose composition there was no love or benevolence, whose avarice was unprincipled, and who was fond of pompous fêtes, &c. He too sold benefices in most scandalous manner. 3d. Innocent VIII. still worse—with him everybody, even the assassin, could expiate his guilt by money. His treasurer used to say, "God does not wish the death of a sinner; let him pay for his sins and live." He is first who provided out of papal treasure for his illegitimate issue. 4th. But of all the men who ever sat on papal throne, perhaps Alexander VI. was greatest monster of iniquity. He was father of John and Cæsar Borgia, the latter of whom was the most treacherous, villanous character of his age, and yet he was made cardinal, and then general in chief of the papal armies—to John the duchy of Benevento was given. It was this pope who divorced his daughter Lucretia from her first husband, and gave her to Alexander Pezarro, and on the wedding night appeared in company with his *concubine*, Julia Bella, by his side. At age of 60 lived with this same daughter, Lucretia, in such a manner as to produce suspicions of most odious character. All historians concur in representing public life of this pope and his sons as a tissue of revolting avarice, perfidy and cruelty; and their private life as detestable, luxurious and voluptuous to an extent before unheard of. He died at last from accidentally swallowing poison, which his own son had mixed for Cardinal Corneto. (Pf. 6, 434.) 5th. Julius II. was energetic, but at same time an ambitious, violent pontiff—the politician with him predominated over the priest—he was constantly involving his dominions in war, and by mixing too much in European strife, he lost respect and reverence of Christendom—a monarch loses all veneration for the pope against whom he is obliged to wage war. He has been accused besides of being addicted to drunkenness and voluptuousness. 6th. Leo X., a younger

son of the celebrated Lorenzo de Medicis—educated like a prince—surrounded papal throne with all that pomp and luxury for which his family was remarkable—at his coronation mounted on a splendid Turkish horse—he went to chase, of which he was passionately fond, with young and rich cardinals by his side, who accompanied him to banquets and theatres—table always provided with rarest and most exquisite dainties—played at cards and betted high, throwing down his gold pieces in most pompous manner before spectators—very much addicted to his pleasures, some of most depraved character—exceedingly prodigal, and bestowed offices of church in most careless manner, without reference to piety of individual. Supposed by many to have been atheist. Many of these popes, particularly last, were patrons of the arts. (P. 6, 432.)

9. *Third cause?* Complaints were loud against immorality of whole body of clergy—ecclesiastical discipline, says Bossuet, was relaxed, and disorders and abuses had penetrated even to the altar, which filled the virtuous with mortification. (W. 696.) Rule of celibacy soon covered the church with scandal.

> Naturam expellas furca tamen usque,
> Tamen usque recurret

was but too well exemplified by clergy—had concubines, with whom lived in most open and shameful manner. Monks and nuns even had become profligate in extreme, *e. g.*, Gerson, chanceller of university of Paris, and one of greatest men of his time, in sermon before council of Rheims, in 1408, called the monks the Pharisees of his age, and of the nunneries he said, I do not call them sanctuaries of God, but the execrable temples of Venus, "*lascivorum et impudicorum juvenum ad libidines explendas, receptacula. Ut idem hodie sit puellam velare, quod ad publice scortandum exponere.*" Earliest ministers of Gospel were devout, humble, charitable. As wealth increased piety diminished—clergy became luxurious, ambitious, and insolent; poverty was disgraceful, and economy a vice; avarice became their great and crowning sin; as revenue of each was too little for his avarice, became fashion to seize that of others; to pillage, to assault, and oppress inferiors. (W. 549.) In the early ages of church we have seen that its offices were thrown open to all, but for more than century before reformation it had become fashionable for younger sons of noble families to assume religious character solely for purpose of obtaining rich offices of the church, in which they might indulge themselves in all the vices that wealth and luxury engender; hence additional reason for growing corruption of church. The immoral lives of the clergy produced a loud call for reform within the body of the church long before time of Luther, and furnished him with some of his most powerful arguments and illustrations. Scandal in church was aggravated by facility of obtaining pardon. Have seen in early ages of feudal system that the principle of pecuniary composition pervaded all the codes of law in Europe, same principle introduced into church, and continued there long after it had ceased elsewhere, *e. g.*, deacon guilty of murder, absolved for 20 crowns; bishop for 300 livres—any clergyman might violate vow of chastity, under most aggravating circumstances, for 100, &c.

10. *Fourth cause?* During first portion of feudal ages spiritual power was the object aimed at by the clergy and the popes; but with advance of time accumulation of wealth became the object. In ambition of early popes there was something noble and even sublime, in that of the latter all was mean and degrading.

The Gregories and even the Innocents would have bent Europe under the spiritual power to gratify a principle of grasping ambition, the Johns and Bonifaces would have done it to gratify a principle of avarice. Gregory VII. would have stripped a king of his crown and a bishop of his mitre that he might reduce Europe to one great spiritual despotism, with pope of Rome at its head. Boniface IX. or John XXII. would have done it that he might sell the throne and the benefice to the highest bidders. The rapacity and avarice of the popes were greatly augmented during removal of papal court to Avignon. Whilst pope was at Rome his temporal dominions, although not always submissive, could furnish a revenue; but at Avignon that revenue could be but rarely collected, and those dominions were often in state of revolt, and there was need for money to enable him to keep them in subjection. Thus papal court, which had become one of most luxurious and profligate in Europe, had recourse to every device to draw from Christendom the money which its profligacy and its exigencies demanded.

11. *Modes of exaction?* Have already examined the shameful abuse of sale of indulgences, which was immediate cause of reformation—connected with this was the abuse of the jubilee. At first jubilee was every 100 years, then every 50, and then every 33; last period being the probable duration of the life of Christ. In the year of jubilee pilgrims from all quarters were invited to Rome to obtain by this pilgrimage and their oblations in the papal capital a plenary indulgence, *e. g.*, Boniface IX. proclaimed jubilee year after his election—thousands flocked to Rome for pardon of sins, and their offerings brought immense sums into papal treasury. Boniface, however, not satisfied with offerings of the pilgrims alone, sent out agents to sell plenary indulgences to all who could not make the pilgrimage, at same price which it would have cost to come to Rome. When these *indulgence-mongers* arrived

29

in city, put their flags out at windows emblazoned with arms of pope and keys of the church. Boniface so greedy of money which these jubilees yielded that he permitted other towns, *e. g.*, Cologne and Magdeburg to hold them, he sharing with them the profits. (W. 518.) *Annates*, or first fruits, was another mode of drawing large amounts into papal treasury; arose from presents which in early ages a bishop at his consecration, or a priest at his ordination, paid to officiating prelate; abolished by Gregory Great, but soon grew up again and was gradually rated at *year's income.* When pope of Rome usurped metropolitical powers, that of ordination fell into his hands, and with it these first fruits, or *annates.* The first fruits of smaller benefices were for long time left to bishops and archbishops, till Clement V. reserved *all* for his own use, and John XXII. followed his example. Not only did the popes take the annates, but by system of reservation often no appointment would be made to the vacant benefice, and thus the diocese would be without its pastor, whilst the revenues would be taken by the pope. Again, the tax of tenths and first fruits was frequently laid on Christendom for particular purposes, *e. g.*, for crusades or other pious objects. Besides these, many other modes of exaction might be practised from time to time. Following mentioned as sources of papal exactions in England. 1st, Peter's pence for support of English pilgrims at Rome. 2d, King John's census of 1000 marks per annum; this paid till 1366, when parliament declared it illegal. 3d, Annates or first fruits and revenues of vacant benefices. (W. 493.) The *centum gravamina*, or 100 griefs, a sort of *standing dish* before German diet, included following abuses: payments for dispensations and absolutions; sums of money drawn by indulgences; appeals to Rome; reservations, commendums, annates; exemptions of ecclesiastics from legal punishments; excommunications and unlawful interdicts; secular causes tried before ecclesiastical tribunals; great expenses in consecrating churches and cemeteries; pecuniary penance; fees for sacraments, burials, &c. (W. 719.)

12. *Effect of these exactions?* Sums drawn by various methods from all parts of Christendom had become a grievous burthen; princes as well as subjects were sending forth loud complaints. The cloud of mystery which had so long hung over the chair of St. Peter, filling nations with awe, had been dispersed by the avarice of later popes, and in its place was seen all the nakedness of human turpitude—prejudice in favor of papal power was rapidly on the wane, the charm of public opinion was dissolving—disaffection was rapidly spreading through the church itself, ecclesiastical property every where was burthened for the benefit of the pope. As long as the scheme of papal aggrandizement enriched every portion of the church, so long did the church remain

united, but from the hour that the head began to plunder the members a spirit of discontent and rebellion arose among the latter. This cause has operated in church precisely as in civil governments. It has been on the *monetary principle* that great battle of liberty has been fought every where. When cities became wealthy they rebelled against the exactions of barons—aristocracy and people of England resisted crown most firmly whenever it endeavored to plunder them, the revolutions of England and France and the United States have all been brought about by similar causes, resistance against arbitrary exactions, and investigation will show that the reformation forms no exception to the general rule. The lofty pretensions of the early pontiffs, supported by deep religious enthusiasm—the magnanimous audacity of the Gregories and even the Innocents—that settled ecclesiastical fanaticism, which dazzled the reason, were applauded by the church, and pardoned by the world. But the sordid motives and settled avarice of later popes produced resistance among nations and deepest discontent among the clergy. In the church, as every where else, it has been found that the *pocket nerve* is really the most sensitive.

13. *Fifth cause?* We have already given an account of the revival of literature and its effect on the human mind. Had of course a favorable influence on reformation; spread of knowledge produced a spirit of inquiry and investigation; men began to think for themselves, prejudices of past ages gave way; catholic system built on decrees of popes and councils during ages of ignorance, could not expect to pass unscathed. Erasmus truly said the world was weary of the ancient theology, with its useless questions and vain subtleties. The people were thirsting for the doctrine of the Gospel, men of learning were throwing off the shackles of human authority, and holding up to derision the absurdities of the old system, *e. g.*, Erasmus, the most learned man of his age, was scarcely inferior to Luther in bringing on the reformation. By his wit, his sarcasm, and his learning, he had already shaken the very pillars of the church. The monks excited his unsparing ridicule. In his *Encomium Moriæ*, or Praise of Folly, addressed to Sir Thomas More, (1511,) uses most poignant satire against all professions of men, even princes and peers, but particularly against mendicant orders of monks. Higher clergy and nobles were amused with his wit, and seemed not to observe, says Dorphius, that he was fitting asses' ears to their heads. Eighteen hundred copies of this were printed and speedily sold. (H. L. 230.) And by such writings as these did Erasmus prepare the way for Luther. Hence said to have *laid* the egg which Luther *hatched*—true his fear of the stake, for he con-

fessed he had no love for martyrdom, made him halt, and even write against Luther; still deserves the name of reformer. When asked by the elector of Saxony, just after Luther had declared against the pope and called him Antichrist, what he thought of Luther's doctrines, answered, Luther had made two great mistakes in attacking the *tiara* of the popes and the *bellies* of the monks. Erasmus was one of those men who outrun the world in thought, and lag behind in action. In the heat and struggle of the reformation his conduct was rather discreditable.

Revival of ancient literature in particular had great influence in hastening reformation. 1st, Ancient literature greatly superior to modern at that time—these studies called *humane*, because supposed to be the most elevated in which the human understanding could be engaged, and to lead on to perfection of *humanity*—students called *humanists.* (P. 6. 440.) Revival of dead languages led to a more critical study of the Bible and the fathers. But the enthusiasm of the classic school in favor of ancient learning implied something more than admiration of writings of ancients; it included admiration for whole structure of society, its laws, institutions and freedom; it was this that roused Rienzi to rebellion in Rome, and stimulated researches of Petrarch; it was this veneration for antiquity and its institutions which animated the whole body of humanists during the 15th century; hence hostility between clergy and the classic school. The latter would interpret Bible for themselves, they were for system of free inquiry and investigation, for freedom of thought. Constantly shackled by the authority of popes and princes, they sighed for the freedom of the ancient republics, they were prepared for revolution. (G. 11. 32.) At moment when this enthusiasm for ancient learning and institutions was so intense, the taking of Constantinople by the Turks added a new impulse—Greek refugees scattered over Europe—carried with them books and manuscripts, established schools, &c. Invention of printing press between 1436 and 1452, hastened the reformation—spread knowledge with rapidity unknown before. Before this time books were written in Latin principally, but as reformation advanced people became so much interested in the contest that the writers began to throw aside the Latin and write in their native tongues. So well were the doctrines of the reformers suited to popular taste, that large editions of their works were printed and sold at once, while the writings of their antagonists were such a drug in the book market, that the printers, who were then the booksellers, would not undertake the printing unless paid in advance. But besides the causes above mentioned the great events of the age preceding the reformation had a tendency to rouse the human intellect from its slumber, to break up the prejudices belonging to the past, and thus to lead on to a revolution in religion and morals, as well as in physics and politics. 15th century age of voyages, enterprises, discoveries, inventions, &c. of grandest character. It is the age of Portuguese expeditions along coast of Africa, of discovery of Cape of Good Hope by Vasco de Gama; of discovery of America by Columbus; of the wonderful extension of commerce, &c. Men were thus roused from their old modes of acting and thinking, and prepared for revolution every where.

14. *Physical causes of reformation?* All the physical causes which operated against the feudal system favored the reformation. Rise of commerce and manufactures produced an independent class everywhere, which naturally supported reformation. Progress of arts and manufactures too enabled the great dignitaries of the church, like the other nobility of Europe, to spend their estates on luxuries, and thus weaken themselves as a body. Again, the clergy, like other great landholders, found it to their interest to make long leases to their tenants—this gradually produced independence and wealth among the latter, and diminished the importance of the former. Lastly, as the reformation advanced, great wealth of the catholic held out, no doubt, in many countries strong temptations to princes and the people to embrace protestantism, that they might appropriate or confiscate church property, *e. g.*, the property of the monasteries seized by Henry VIII. in England gave to the crown an immense revenue, and enabled the monarch by his grants to form a new aristocracy.

15. *Necessity for reformation—different attempts before Luther?* Easy to see that all the above causes conspiring together made some sort of a reformation absolutely necessary—hence Luther may be looked on as the individual who set fire to the train already prepared for combustion, and the reformation must sooner or later have taken place if he had never existed. Before his day there had been three kinds of efforts at reformation, and though they all failed, they served to mark the necessity for change and the onward progress of events. First, efforts were made by the church itself. Second, by princes. Third, by the people.

16. *Efforts of the church?* We have seen during long schism that general councils were convened for purpose of terminating schism. These councils claimed power above the popes, right of deposing them, &c. Besides this they proceeded to investigate grievances in church—called loudly on pope for his plan of reform—particularly clamorous against avarice and exactions of the popes. This scheme of internal reformation failed. 1st. Popes hated councils as the Stuarts did parliaments, and therefore would not call them together, or did every thing to

defeat reformation when they were convened. 2d. A great many of the more dissolute clergy feared the effects of reformation, and joined the popes to uphold existing abuses. 3d. Those œcumenical councils were too large, too heterogeneous, assembled from too many countries, ever to grow into orderly deliberative bodies. But although this scheme failed as a system, had an effect in hastening reformation. Some of the greatest divines of the age, like Gerson of Paris, came out warmly for reformation of abuses, and thus gave impulse to the spirit of discontent.

17. *Efforts of princes and nations?* As abuses of church advanced, monarchs from time to time made efforts at reform, *e. g.*, in France, in 14th century, celebrated *pragmatic sanction* was proclaimed at Bourges, and made a law of France. This suppressed most of the abuses and took away from popes the annates, the right to consecrate bishops, &c. This law was soon introduced into Germany by the diet of Mayence. But in 1448 the diet gave it up in consequence of treaty with Nicholas V., and in 1516 Francis I. substituted for it a *concordat* agreed upon with Leo X. Thus the effort made by princes likewise failed, although it left the most lasting effects.

18. *Popular efforts?* What might have been the effect of two former modes of reform if they had succeeded, impossible now to say; but they were evidently only means which had any chance to stave off more violent popular reforms. Have seen the effort of the Albigenses and their melancholy fate—this was a popular reform. John Wickliffe, in England, made another attempt, but this was premature, and the Lollards were finally suppressed. These were but preludes to more violent reform of John Huss and Jerome, commenced in 1404 in Bohemia. Huss and Jerome were summoned before council of Constance, whither they repaired with safe conduct of the emperor, which was violated—they were condemned by council and burnt at stake. But their doctrines spread through Bohemia, produced a most bloody civil war, and although emperor finally triumphed, still the impression was left on the popular mind. This reform a perfect contrast with that attempted by the councils composed of the ecclesiastical aristocracy—the latter was cautious, embarrassed and timid—former was violent and passionate—the one maintained the perfection and inviolability of the system, whilst it acknowledged manifold abuses—the other proceeded from abuses to the system itself, and aimed at nothing less than radical change. (G. II. 30.) Thus it is clear that the reformation of Luther was not an *accident*—a result of his personal character—it was one of the great wants of the times—Luther merely gave expression to the feelings of the age.

SEC. III.—EFFECTS OF REFORMATION.

18. *Reformation succeeds in some countries and fails in others—causes?* 1st. Ceteris paribus, authority of Rome could be maintained better in countries near than remote—hence Italian states kept to the faith. 2d. All other things being equal, countries farthest advanced in commerce and manufactures would be first to throw off the papal yoke—hence we see why independent towns of Germany, the Dutch provinces, ten provinces of the Netherlands, England, &c., should early declare for protestantism. The commercial ports of France too were protestant, but checked by power of the crown. 3d. Have seen that small states are favorable to democracy—same principle which would lead a people to throw off the rule of a monarch would produce resistance to papal usurpations—hence reformation made great progress in Swiss Cantons, and was of democratic character, being of presbyterian order. (M. E. G. 2, 435.)

The preservation of catholicism in seven of the Swiss cantons, particularly in Schwitz, Uri and Underwald, three of the smallest and most democratic, may seem to controvert the above, bnt easily explained: 1st. These cantons were small, poor and mountainous, hence papal exactions never reached them—too insignificant. 2d. Catholic religion had assumed the form amongst them suitable to their republican habits. 3d. To a mountainous people material forms and ceremonies are more important than to others—hence catholic religion more suitable in this respect. 4th. In this country remembrance of great men and great events connected with catholic religion, *e. g.*, a chapel was the monument generally erected on field of battle—who has not heard of chapel of William Tell?—thus a species of idolatry, a national fanaticism produced a mixture of worship of liberty with that of religion.

19. *Reformation in England?* People of England prepared for reformation, but course which it ran modified by power of the crown. Henry VIII., something of a dialectician, undertook to write against Luther—obtained from Leo title of *defender of the faith* Luther handled him very roughly, admitted his language to be good, but called him a *fool and an ass, a blasphemer and a liar*. (Ling. 6, 80.) All this well calculated to keep Henry in the faith—but fell in love with Anne Boleyn, and wanted to divorce his wife, Catharine of Arragon, aunt of Charles V.—pope would not grant a divorce. Henry consulted universities and divorced Catharine without pope's consent, and married Anne Boleyn. She was favorable to protestants—Henry took middle course, broke with pope, declared himself head of church, and persecuted both parties. From this time each party hoped to gain him, hence both bore

with his persecutions and his tyrannies. His son Edward was a protestant, but reigned a very short time. Mary was a bigoted catholic, and persecuted with demoniac fury. Her sister, Queen Elizabeth, was protestant. During her long and energetic reign she established protestant episcopal church—she was fond of show and magnificence, hence she would not permit all the forms and ceremonies of catholic church to be abolished—she preserved the gown, surplice, &c. Towards the conclusion of her reign there were two kinds of persecution—she persecuted both those who went too far and those who did not go far enough—the presbyterians and the catholics. By thus attempting to stop the reformation before it went too far, the non-conforming party were made to go farther than they otherwise would—hence the puritanical character of the presbyterians, and hence one cause which assisted in bringing Charles I. to the block.

20. *Intellectual effects of reformation?* Reformation favorable to development of intellect. Catholic religion substituted the decrees of popes and councils for the judgment of individuals. Reformation proceeded on the principle of free inquiry, that each one should read the Scriptures and judge for himself. Roman church said *submit yourselves to authority without examination*—protestant says *examine and submit yourselves only to conviction.* In dispute between catholic and protestant at Prague, former said to the latter, "all that we require of you can be summed up in one word—*crede, believe*"—to which protestant answered, "and all that we require of you can be summed up in one word likewise—*proba, prove*"—need scarcely say that the protestant principle is more favorable to exercise of mind and discovery of truth. Protestant universities for same reason have been generally far superior to the catholic. Catholic professors too much under influence of authority to give full play to the intellectual faculties—they make excellent teachers of mere elementary knowledge, but not of the profounder sciences. Villars says there is more real knowledge in one single university, like Gottingen, Halle or Jena, than in the eight Spanish universities of San Jago de Compostella, Alcala, Orihuela, &c. In these last they teach what must, *with* or *without* the consent of reason, be believed—the *decretals* are given as infallible oracles, whereas in the protestant seminaries no oracle is acknowledged but reason and well supported facts. (V. 143.) Chateaubriand says, the protestant cultivates the reason most, the catholic the imagination. Greatest philosophers of modern times have been protestants.

21. *Moral effects?* It was the immorality of the catholic church which gave a most powerful weapon of attack to Luther and the reformers. Not only were protestants more moral than catholics had

been, but the latter were forced by the presence of an opposing religion to change their mode of life, *to reform* likewise. Mr. Hallam seems to be under impression that there is something in catholic system, which keeps the balance in point of morality tolerably even when compared with protestant. Villars maintains that the facts are against him—most vicious populations in Europe are the Italians, Spaniards, Portuguese, &c., all catholic. Said more crimes are committed by catholics than protestants, *e. g.*, Cit. Rebman, president of special tribunal at Mayence, in account of the four dèpartments of the Rhine, says that number of malefactors in the catholic and protestant cantons is as 6 to 4. At Augsburg containing a mixture of two religions, of 946 malefactors, in ten years, only 184 protestants. Howard the philanthropist, observed that prisons of Italy were incessantly crowded. At Venice had seen 300 or 400 prisoners in the principal prison—at Naples 980 in the succursal prison alone, (Vicaria,) whilst prisons at Berne were almost empty, in those of Lausanne there was not one, and at Schaffhausen only three.

22. *Economical effects?* In catholic countries too many holidays, too much exaction, oppression of various descriptions, hence prosperity not so great as in protestant countries, enjoying more liberty and more security, *e. g.*: Observe miserable state of agriculture in beautiful provinces of Naples, Rome, Spain and Portugal, then look to its flourishing condition amid the cold and comparatively unfertile fields of Scotland, England and Holland—contrast immense. Germany and Switzerland illustrate this subject most strikingly, because traveller is constantly passing from catholic to a protestant district—mud cottage covered with thatch, fields badly kept, wretched, rude peasants and beggars, betoken the catholic country—neat houses, well cultivated fields, energetic enterprise, mark the influence of the protestant religion; *e. g.*, compare fertile plains of Soleure with less favored soil of Argori, the rocky sterile land of the Pays de Vaud with the magnificent Italian Switzerland or the well sheltered Valois, the territory of Neufchatel with fruitful fields of Abbe of St. Gall; and in little states of this monkish prince, compare that portion which follows Roman worship with that still smaller portion, which under protection of Zurich and Berne has adhered to reform, and it will every where appear that activity and knowledge of man rise superior to the liberalities of prodigal nature. Agriculture carried to such perfection in Berne that even English farmers have adopted its improvements—they are the authors of the system of irrigation considered of so much importance by farmers. (V. 140.)

23. *Political effects?* Infused new life into Europe—a universal and deep interest agitated all nations and developed their powers—

former revolutions exercised men's *arms*, this their *heads*—the great mass of people interested—political equilibrium influenced by religion, *e. g.*, from 1520 to 1556 Charles V. and Francis I. two great actors—former headed catholic party—France, Turkey and protestant princes of the north were the balancing power. Bonaparte says Francis was but a *pigmy great man*, for it was as clear as light that Charles must have been the head of catholic party; and therefore that Francis ought to have taken the protestant side openly and avowedly; whereas he acted with indecision, and professed always to favor the catholic cause. From 1556 to 1603, Spain and England are the two great powers. Former heads catholic interest, latter protestant. Lower Countries revolt from Spain and gain their liberty. Naval operations as important as the land during this period. From 1603 to 1648 great war between emperor and protestant princes. In 1630 Sweden appeared on theatre with Gustavus Adolphus at her head. This war terminated by peace of Westphalia, (1648,) and afterwards religion ceased to be the exciting cause in national quarrels. (V. 112.)

24. *Reaction in favor of the catholic religion?* By the middle of 16th century, it seems that protestantism had conquered much the largest portion of Europe. A letter written from Rome, by Tiepolo, envoy from Venice about the middle of 16th century, says that England, Scotland, Denmark, Norway, Sweden, and all the northern nations are estranged from papal see. Germany is almost entirely lost; Bohemia and Poland to a great degree infected; the Lower Countries so thoroughly corrupted that the Duke of Alva can scarce restore them; France is full of confusion, so that nothing remains to the pontiff in a secure state except Spain and Italy, with a few islands, and those parts of Dalmatia and Greece possessed by your serene highness. Such the report of a sagacious Venetian to the signory of Venice. (L. Q. No. 116, 206.) Cannot doubt then that at this time much larger portion of Europe was protestant than now. Two causes favorable to reaction. First, dissensions, schisms, and excesses of protestants. Second, institution of order of Jesuits, and their activity.

25. *First cause of this reaction?* In hour of victory, the protestants began to divide and to split up into sects; having no controlling head, they were much more liable to this than the catholics, *e. g.*, have already seen the enmity between Luther and Zwingle about the Eucharist, in very commencement of reformation; we have seen startling dogmas of the anabaptists at Munster, and insurrection of German peasants. Again, reformation included two classes, as far apart as poles in practice: 1st, calm, rational men, content to emancipate themselves from papal superstition, without insisting upon rigid definition of those articles of belief

beyond human comprehension. These were for leaving each one to judge for himself in these matters; this, in fact, true theory of reformation. 2d class, those more severe and dogmatic, offering a creed as definite and peremptory as that of the catholic, with requisition of minute observances as severe as that of the papal church, and proscribing all mankind who resisted their internal scheme of unity as dogmatically as the Vatican did those who revolted from its despotism. Melancholy to see the reformers who commenced the reformation upon principle of freedom of inquiry, and liberty of thought, as soon as the victory was won, turning around and practising on those very principles which they condemned in the catholic; the protestants persecuted wherever they had the power, *e. g.*, John Calvin had Servetus burnt at the stake; Cranmer had a woman, Joan Boucher, and a Dutchman, executed because of their religious opinions. The princess Mary petitioned her brother, Edward VI., to allow her to exercise her religion at home, and although Charles V. several times interceded in her behalf, Edward would not agree to connive at what he called idolatry. (H. C. H., V. 1. 131.) It is for this reason Guizot says the reformation did not understand itself, and thus laid itself open to the powerful attack of the *Eagle of Meaux*, (Bossuet.) This division into sects disposed to persecute one another, produced dissension and consequent weakness in the reformed church, and was one cause which produced reaction.

26. *Second cause?* Ignatius Loyola, founder of the order of Jesuits, was cotemporary of Luther. He saw that catholic religion wanted more action and energy in contest with the protestant—therefore founded order of Jesuits. Besides the three vows of *poverty*, *chastity*, *and monastic obedience*, the Jesuits took a fourth, *implicit obedience to the pope*. Thus the Jesuits became at once the *standing army* of the catholic church. Their discipline totally different from other monastic orders; in solitude of cloister the monk worked out his salvation by acts of mortification and piety; he was dead to world. Not so Jesuit; he was to form himself for *action*. He was chosen soldier for the work of God. He scrupled at no means for holy purposes. He was to study the dispositions of kings and princes, to insinuate himself into their confidence, and sway their councils. He was to instruct himself in science, and get possession of the schools and universities, that he might influence the youthful mind. He was to be ready for missions to foreign countries. He was to be governed implicitly by a chief, called the general of the order. Consequence of this was, that Jesuits infused new life and vigor into catholic party. Distinguished above all other societies by one thing—*rigid method*. Every thing calculated—every thing had its object. Such a union of wisdom with indefatigable zeal, of study

and persuasiveness with pomp and the spirit of caste, of universal propagandism with unity of the main principle, never existed before or since. They were laborious and imaginative; worldly-wise, yet full of enthusiasm; above personal interest, each assisting the progress of the other. No wonder that they produced a powerful reaction, especially when we consider that at this moment the protestant republic was in all its parts rent by fierce and hostile factions.

Pontificate of Sextus V. period of great crisis in papal history; turning point in imperilled fortunes of catholic system. Catholic religion was evidently now gaining on protestant, and continued to do so until Jesuitism in turn began to spend its force—until the cry of nations was raised against its enormous doctrines, and loose and pliant morals. The thirty years' war was last general effort of two contending systems. The peace of Westphalia (1648), silenced strife of religion as well as of arms. Both parties content to rest upon present possessions; in both aggressive power was worn out. Strong impulse of protestantism had subsided, and Roman catholic reaction had expired: the torpor of death seemed to succeed to these last most violent and exhausting struggles. Henceforward *religion* ceased to be the most conspicuous figure on the political theatre. New subjects and new topics engage the attention of cabinets, and the political spring of European politics is moved by a different power.

27. *Has the protestant religion any cause to fear a reconquest by the catholic?* Past history would lead us to answer in the negative. Five centuries have now elapsed, during each of which, in spite of all the efforts of the Mendicants and the Jesuits, the Roman see has been rather on the decline. Silently receding from their claims to temporal power, the popes have scarcely been able to preserve their capital, amid the concussions of modern times. The revival of catholic institutions, such as they were in former ages, must ever be impossible; such an event would be at war with the spirit and genius of the age—with the onward march of civilization. "A calm comprehensive study (says Mr. Hallam) of ecclesiastical history, not in such scraps and fragments as the ordinary partisans of an ephemeral literature obtrude upon us, is perhaps the best antidote to extravagant apprehensions. Those who know what Rome has once been are best able to appreciate what she is; those who have seen the thunderbolt in the hands of the Gregories and the Innocents, will hardly be intimidated at the sallies of decrepitude, the impotent dart of Priam amid the crackling ruins of Troy."

CHAPTER VIII.

FORMATION OF ENGLISH CONSTITUTION.

SEC. I.—ANGLO-SAXON PERIOD.

THE formation of the British constitution is perhaps the most beautiful political phenomenon of modern times, and particularly interesting to the American student, as our own institutions are the result of English civilization. As the British constitution is an anomaly among modern governments, totally different from any thing which we observe on continent, necessary to treat it separately.

1. *Establishment of the Saxons in England—conquest of Danes?* Saxons belonged to those races of barbarians who overran Roman empire. As they invaded England by sea, they could not deluge it with large armies like those that overran Roman empire—conquests smaller at each invasion in England than on continent—hence the formation of one little kingdom after another until they reached the number of seven. (*Heptarchy.*) All these finally united under one monarch, (Egbert.) About conclusion of 8th century Scandinavia poured forth a race of pirates under the name of Danes, who, with their little sea kings, met with various fortune in England, till Canute the Dane was seated on English throne. This invasion of Danes produced but little influence on the general history of England, because of same character with the Saxons—they early embraced Christian religion—adopted manners of the Saxons—and, besides, the people had soon an opportunity of returning to ancient stock of kings, &c.

2. *Regal government of Anglo-Saxon period?* They had kings, and the hereditary principle only partially prevailed. If eldest son was grown and fit to rule, his title was acknowledged, if not, set aside for a more energetic member of royal family, *e. g.*, Alfred himself excluded the progeny of his elder brother from throne, and his will bases his title on triple foundation; 1st, will of his father; 2d, compact of Ethelred, his brother; and 3d, *consent of West Saxon nobility.* In like manner sons of Edmund I. were postponed to their uncle Edred, but preferred afterwards to Edred's issue.

3. *Judicial system?* Here democratic principle prevailed as among the northern barbarians generally. England seems to have been divided somewhat on the old Jewish plan. Under Mosaic institutions decimal division prevailed—there were rulers of thousands, of hundreds, and of

tens. A Jewish synagogue was placed under 10 elders, &c. (Mil. V. 1, 174.) Thus, too, England divided into counties or shires, and these into hundreds and tens, with their respective officers, the alderman or earl, the centennarius and decennarius, or tithing men, all probably at first elected by the people of the respective divisions. In the division of tens, each of the ten families became a sort of security for the good behavior of all the rest—this called *frank pledge.* Doubtful whether the tithing had any judicial authority, if not, the tithing man was a sort of petty constable—there was a court belonging to the hundred, but the most important court was that of the county; in this court most important business of county transacted—met monthly—bishop and earl, or his officer, the sheriff, presided. Trial by jury supposed to be referable to Anglo-Saxon period. Strongest proof in the case of monastery of Ramsey. A controversy about lands between that society and a certain nobleman was brought into county court—when each party was heard, it was *referred* by the court to 36 *thanes* equally chosen by both parties. By referring to instances of compurgation and of supposed jury trial, find a constant preference here, as on the continent, given to the number 12, or some multiple of it.

4. *Wittenagemotte?* This a derivation from the councils held in the German forests. When Saxons conquered England each chief still retained the custom of governing with consent and advice of a sort of national assembly called in England *Wittenagemotte*—meaning, a meeting of *the wise* or *knowing men.* Prelates, earls, a large though unascertainable part of the *thanes* or inferior nobility, (the *gentry*,) composed this body. A freeman not noble raised to rank of *thane* by acquiring certain portion of land, by making three voyages at sea or by receiving holy orders. (J. M. 40.) If this was aristocratic body, it was very open at first, as all could enter who acquired certain amount of land, &c. When England however was united under one monarch and one Wittenagemotte, all could not attend who had a right—hence reason why Athelstan sent commissioners to hold *shire gemotes* or county meetings, where they proclaimed the laws made by the king and his council, which being sworn to at these *folk motes*, became binding on the whole nation. (41.) Anglo-Saxon kings showed strong desire to confirm all their acts by Wittenagemotte and the county meetings.

5. *Progress of the aristocratic principle in Anglo-Saxon institutions?* In England, as on the continent, every thing seemed tending, though not with same rapidity, towards aristocracy. Division into tens and hundreds was fast obliterating—county courts met less frequently, only twice a year—frank pledge was wearing out and became a sort of nullity. Wittenagemotte, which formerly comprehended all the *wise*

men, or as in German forest, all the freemen who bore arms became first an assembly of *thanes* or landholders—then in process of time *thanes* were divided into the *greater* or royal thanes and the *inferior* —former alone attended in council, and even these were beginning to withdraw from Wittenagemotte, for same reason that continental barons withdrew from their deliberative bodies, because they were become individually so powerful as to be impatient of restraint imposed by king and council—disposed to retire each into his own domains, and set up an independent government of his own—hence from middle of 10th century Wittenagemotte almost disappears from Anglo-Saxon history. (G. 379.) The growth of the aristocracy, too, was among the Anglo-Saxons undermining the power of the kings precisely as on the continent, *e. g.*, Count Godwin, Siward, duke of Northumberland, Leofric, duke of Mercia, and many others, became formidable rivals to the throne, and finally Harold usurping the crown over Edgar Atheling was very like to usurpation of Hugh Capet in France.

6. *Was feudal system established among Anglo-Saxons?* This has been a contested point. As society advanced in England there was no doubt a tendency towards the growth of feudal tenures as on the continent, *e. g.*, numbers of freemen lived under the protection of the great nobles, who in many cases exercised a jurisdiction which seemed to be inherent in the domain, as on the continent. Here then was undoubtedly a feudal relation. But then the insular character of England which shielded her from invasions, the smallness of the kingdom which had a tendency to prevent both the ruin of kingly power and the growth of such formidable baronies as existed on the continent, all had a tendency to prevent, before the invasion of William the Conqueror, such a complete system of feudality as existed on continent. Although among the Anglo-Saxons the aristocratic principle was advancing, yet the democratic was still much more active here than on the continent.

7. *Conquest of the Normans—establishment of feudal system?* Well known that after the death of Edward the Confessor, two great competitors for throne, Harold, an English noble of great possessions and power, and William, Duke of Normandy—latter raised a great army, composed of his own nobility, together with great portion of the chivalry of Europe, who flocked to his standard to engage in what was considered greatest enterprise of the age. Besides these he carried a large force of hired troops. He completely defeated the English army under Harold, at Hastings, and the prize was crown of England.

SEC. II.—EFFECT OF NORMAN CONQUEST—PROGRESS OF BRITISH GOVERNMENT TO GRANTING OF MAGNA CHARTA.

1. *Feudal system established in England?* William established feudal system in England in all its perfection at once.

2. *Condition of the conquered and the conquerors?* Must never forget that the Anglo-Saxons, although conquered, were a very powerful people, equal in civilization to their conquerors, and hating them with a most fervent hatred. There was not so great a *subject people* in all Europe, for we must remember, that even the Anglo-Saxon nobility was now confounded, through the oppression of the conqueror, with the people, and must have greatly elevated their spirit and character. In this respect conquest of England by William totally different from the conquests of barbarians in Roman empire—in latter province so completely exhausted before conquest, that the conquered people may be said to have exercised scarcely any influence on the conquerors. Not so in England—here the subject party were nearly as great and powerful as dominant. Hence the constant dread which the latter had of the former: hence too the cruel treatment of the Anglo-Saxons, &c., &c., by the conqueror.

3. *Great power of the Norman kings, and union among the Anglo-Norman aristocracy?* Authority of William in England was more complete than that of any other monarch of Europe in his domains. 1st, William himself was one of the ablest kings and greatest generals of the age. 2dly, He had conquered England at head of finest army in Europe, a large portion of which consisted of mercenary Brabançons devoted to his will; and, 3dly, The great crown vassals were disposed to acquiesce in his power for two reasons. First, they held estates in England and likewise in Normandy, therefore they did not wish the two countries severed, which might cause confiscation of their property in one or other, and they felt that the union of the two under one government must depend upon the power of crown. 2d, They were afraid of Anglo-Saxons, who had been recently conquered. Hence we find barons during William's time constantly united among themselves, and rallying around the king, in order the better to prevent the terrible insurrections of the Anglo-Saxons. It was for this reason that while we behold on continent each nation gradually splitting up into a number of independent local powers, in England the aristocracy never set up for this *individual* independence, but remained *united* for the sake of security. What could the barons of William have done if each one had been entirely independent and isolated? The native English would soon have conquered them in detail. Whereas, by union, by making

common cause with each other, they were enabled to maintain their government.

4. *General consequence of this relation between the Norman government and the native English?* Paradoxical as it may appear, the liberties of the English people are due to the despotic character of the British government after the Norman conquest, and to the energy and the power still inherent in the conquered English. For the latter circumstance produced, as we have seen, a union between the king and his aristocracy, existing nowhere else in Europe. But in process of time, as the differences between the English and the Normans began to wear away, and the fear of popular insurrections subsided, the compressing force, which brought the king and his aristocracy so closely and harmoniously in union, was removed, and immediately, as was to be expected, hostility arose between these two orders in the government. The aristocracy being the weaker party, was forced not only to remain *united* among themselves to resist the crown influence, but were compelled to form a *union* with the subject party—*the people*, whom we have before shown, were from particular causes the most respectable and potent populace in all Europe; hence the rise as we shall soon see of the house of commons. Thus we shall see England in her progress exhibit a totally different phenomenon from any thing we see on the continent—we shall find the aristocracy constantly uniting with the people against the king, and the interests of the people regularly provided for in all the charters, whereas on the continent the aristocracy act for themselves alone, and there is scarcely seen, except in the cities, any such orders of society as *the people.* The chain of sequence may thus briefly be pointed out. 1st. The dread of insurrection united the nobles and king, and gave to the latter a preponderating influence. 2d. The great power and oppression of the king in process of time produced resistance from his nobles and kept them united, hence a *house of lords.* 3d. The latter being the weaker party called in *the people*—hence the *house of commons.*

5. *Great council or parliament of the first Norman kings?* Had different names, *e. g.*, *Curia regis*, *concilium*, *magnum concilium*, *commune concilium*, *&c.* Have already seen that German chiefs in their forests called their councils not only for purposes of state business, but to illustrate the chief, by the presence of the great men of his tribe, and after settlement in Roman empire these councils were discontinued gradually from various causes. This custom, however, was kept up by William in England—three times in the year, the Saxon chronicle says, the council was assembled, during the passover at Winchester, at Westminster in Whitsuntide, and at Gloucester at Christmas. On these oc-

casions, we are told that all the great men of England were present—these great men probably comprehended all the nobles and higher clergy who held of the king—*tenants in chief*—who in William's reign were 600 in number, and were denominated *barons*. On these three occasions the king wore his crown and appeared in state, and the meetings of his barons were called as much for the purpose of gratifying the vanity of the monarch by adding to his pomp and magnificence as for business.

Powers of this assembly undefined—they were occupied about all subjects, legislation, war, religion, taxation, &c. Although, however, these subjects were treated of by the council, yet we find on a thousand occasions the king acting in arbitrary manner as if there was no such power as that of a council in existence, *e. g.*, he made laws, often raised taxes, ousted his barons, &c., without consulting his council. Thus we see two great and substantial powers in presence of each other—the king and his barons at first coalescing and harmonizing for fear of the Anglo-Saxons—although these powers were very indistinct.

6. *Three kings with bad titles of William the Conqueror—effect of it?* Favorable to liberty. William Rufus, Henry I. and Stephen, were all usurpers. Such monarchs anxious to have their titles confirmed—courted the barons, courted too the popular favor.

7. *Charters?* The first and most natural guarantee of liberty is the *charter* in which every thing is clearly defined. Soon as English aristocracy began to claim certain rights against the crown, it sought to confirm by obtaining charters from the kings. (401.) First charter spoken of is that which William granted to his new subjects, the Anglo-Saxons, wherein he fixed the character of his own government, and made certain promises to the conquered, particularly the enjoyment of the laws of Edward the Confessor, for till granting of Magna Charta, the English who had always looked back with longing to the Anglo-Saxon period, considered these laws of Edward the Confessor as the most gracious boon which could be conferred on them.

Henry I. on mounting the throne found himself in a very embarrassing situation: he had usurped over his elder brother, Robert Duke of Normandy, and the separation of the two countries would of course be resisted by those barons who owned property in both. Robert invades England, (1101)—he had a powerful party there—Henry was in great danger—convokes his council in London—heaps reproaches on his brother for his temper, brutality and pride, says that he looked on the nobles as a band of drunkards and gluttons, whom he would trample under foot, that he, Henry, on contrary, was a mild and pacific king, and would carefully preserve the ancient liberties of his people—a charter was granted—most complete of all those which preceded Magna Charta —enumerates the grievances of preceding reigns, and promises redress —renews the laws of Edward the Confessor—pardons the murders which had been committed, and promises to extend no farther the royal forests. (405.) This charter was granted for the purpose of securing a popularity with both barons and people, that would enable Henry I. to overthrow Robert, and may be considered a sort of foundation charter which was a model for all the rest.

Stephen was a usurper, and like Henry, we find him obliged to grant charters to maintain his power, *e. g.*, grants one to his barons, and another to the clergy, in which he makes the fairest promises.

Henry II. had a good title, and was an able prince he granted a fifth charter, containing the usual promises. His power was greatly increased by marrying Eleanor, the divorced wife of Louis VII. of France, who added Guienne and Poictiers to the crown domains. Henry was most of his time on the continent—his feudal militia did not answer for these foreign wars—he used Brabançons; to pay them, he was obliged to levy taxes—the *scutage* was his chief resource—it was the amount which the vassal paid in case he did not attend the lord to war—it was very partial before time of Henry II., being altogether voluntary on part of the vassal, but became then a general contribution, the money being required instead of service. By these means Henry was fast dispensing with the presence of his barons, and the meetings of the councils were becoming less and less frequent—a few such monarchs as Henry II. coming one after the other, and the liberties of England would have been irreparably lost.

Richard I., successor of Henry, was only one except Wm. Rufus of all Norman princes who granted no charter, nor did he experience any resistance from his barons, for 1st, his father by his long and able reign had firmly established the kingly power, and 2d, Richard himself was one of those men who completely personify the character of the age in which they live—the people admired him, his person, his strength, his chivalry, his taste, his passions, his very vices, &c., all contributed to his popularity. When they were raising money in England to ransom him, all parties gladly contributed, nobles, clergy and people.

8. *John?* To Richard, fortunately for England, succeeded one of those kings, who by their vices and tyranny seem born to make men assert their rights. John was insolent, cowardly, mean, scarce on the throne before barons began to unite against him—when called together at Oxford, unanimously determined not to follow in France, if he would not promise to restore their privileges and respect their rights—in spite of this refusal, he engages in the war, was foiled every where by Philip

Augustus—in midst of the shame caused by his failure in France, killed his own nephew, Arthur, and with all the odium of his situation still endeavors to play the tyrant—carried about with him hired bullies to settle cases between himself and barons by judicial combat—his exactions became worse and worse—he imposed a new scutage, and debauched on all occasions both wives and daughters of his nobles. In midst of this tyranny barons once more refuse to follow him to the continent—did not yet rebel openly, but united more closely every day, and began to separate themselves from the royal cause—John, as if not contented with opposition of his nobles, gets into a quarrel with the pope and clergy, and is excommunicated by Innocent III., and his kingdom handed over to Philip Augustus. John obliged to humble himself before the pope, accepts his crown from Pandulf, the pope's legate, and thus disgraced himself in the eyes of the world.

Reconciled to the pope, John soon commenced again his tyranny over both his barons and his clergy—a necessity for union between these interests becomes evident. In August (1213), when John assembled his barons and higher clergy at London to obtain some aid from them. The archbishop of Canterbury, Stephen Langton, engages them to hold a *secret meeting* on 25th August for the purpose of forming their plans against John. At this meeting, he produces the charter of Henry I., barons received with applause, and decided to exact its confirmation of John. After another meeting was kept secret from John, they met on 6th January (1215), in arms at London, and there required of the king a renewal of the charter of Henry I., and also of the laws of Edward the Confessor. John taken by surprise asks for time—at last when told that he must confirm the charter of Henry I., he told them they had better demand his crown, and refused to confirm—consequence was that on 5th May, barons met with their troops at Wallingford, renounced their allegiance to John, elected Fitz-Walter their general. On the 24th May, they took possession of London, and John retired to Oldham, in the county of Surrey, with but seven attendants. In this distress forced to come to a conference with the barons, which was held on the plain of Runnymede, on the 13th June (1215), when the *great charter* (*Magna Charta*) was granted. This justly esteemed the bulwark of English liberties.

SEC. III.—FROM THE GRANTING OF MAGNA CHARTA TO THE CALLING OF THE BURGESSES TO PARLIAMENT BY THE EARL OF LEICESTER.

1. *Provisions of Magna Charta?* Embraced all the orders of society, the clergy, the aristocracy, and the people. John had before

granted charter to the clergy, and Magna Charta confirmed all the immunities and privileges before granted. It defined the main feudal rights and relations and confirmed or extended them. But essential clauses of Magna Charta are those protecting personal liberty and property—speedy and equal justice was promised to all—trial by jury was established—from this time forward the courts awarded the *habeas corpus* privilege to all, and it was ordained that justice shall neither be sold, denied, nor delayed.

2. *Remarks on Magna Charta?* 1st. The success of the barons against John proves that weak and tyrannical princes are rather favorable to liberty. 2d. Magna Charta is very peculiar from embracing all orders of society. It has become fashionable, says Hallam, to depreciate this great instrument because it was obtained by the aristocracy, and therefore is supposed to have inured to the benefit of a few selfish barons alone, but this a great mistake, its peculiar beauty on contrary is the equal distribution of civil rights to all classes of freemen. (H. 341.) And here we observe a marked difference between England and all the continental nations. *People* of England are an important substantial element of society, too powerful to be neglected. The barons too and the people are found to be united, which was the case nowhere else—leading barons in England all popular favorites, *e. g.*, no individuals more popular with monkish annalists, who speak the language of the populace, than Simon earl of Leicester, Thomas earl of Lancaster, and Thomas duke of Gloucester, all leading barons and great opposers of the royal power. (H. 432.)

The clergy, too, are found cordially united with these two orders against the king. Thus does it curiously happen that, while on the continent the first move for liberty was every where *against* the aristocracy and the clergy, in England, on the contrary, these two orders have been the first to fight the battle of popular rights. Upon Stephen Langton, archbishop of Canterbury, the head of the English church, and William, earl of Pembroke, one of the most distinguished of the aristocracy, must rest the chief glory of the Magna Charta. The reason of this peculiarity too, has been pointed out—particular causes made the Norman kings the preponderating power in the government, and consequently it was necessary for all the other forces in the nation to coalesce in order to oppose them—whereas, on the continent, the kings at the corresponding period were comparatively powerless, whilst the aristocracy and the clergy were the preponderating power.

A third remark is on importance of Magna Charta. A new soul infused from this time in British nation—her liberties before in abeyance now tangible possession. Until this time the rally was around the *laws of Edward the Confessor*, but afterwards *Magna Charta* becomes the true pole star of English liberty. Pass from the history of Roger de Hovedon, under the 2d Henry, to that of Matthew Paris, under the 3d, and we shall be struck with the mighty change wrought by Magna Charta. Sir E. Cook reckons 32 instances of solemn ratification of this great instrument.

3. *Guaranty to the faithful observance of Magna Charta?* Sounds curiously enough to a modern ear that the only guaranty to this important charter was that of *force*—the *right of resistance.* Twenty-five barons were chosen as conservators of the compact. If the king violated any article, any four might demand reparation, if refused, it was carried before the rest, who might do justice by levying war on the king, the charter containing the provision that in such case the 25 barons with all the commons of the land "shall distrain and annoy us by every means in their power, that is, by seizing our castles, lands, and possessions, and every other mode, till the wrong shall be repaired to their satisfaction; saving our person and our queen and children. And when it is repaired they shall obey us as before." Curious, says Hallam, to see common law of distress upon so grand a scale, and capture of king's castle treated as analogous to impounding neighbor's horse for breaking fence. (431.)

This guaranty of force seems to have been the principal one known to mediæval ages; we find it admitted, though carefully regulated, even among the laws of St. Louis in France, *e. g.*, if a lord called on his vassal to march against the king, the vassal was first to ascertain from the king whether he had refused the lord justice; if he had, then the vassal was to go with the lord against the sovereign. (G. 442.) And this remedy was frequently resorted to, *e. g.*, William, earl of Pembroke, whom we have mentioned above, invaded the king's (Henry III.) domains, sword in hand, to obtain satisfaction, and when called to account by the king he told monarch that justice had been denied him; that he was therefore absolved from all homage and at liberty to employ force. And he told him further that it would not be for his (the king's) honor that he should submit to injustice; nor did Henry deny this right, however he may have supposed the earl to have misapplied it. (H. 431.)

4. *Henry III. and the new guaranties?* Son of John, and worthy of his sire—faithless, weak, and presumptuous—mounted the throne before majority—obliged to confirm Magna Charta five times during his long reign. In consequence of his treachery in the violation of the Magna Charta at every new ratification, some new expedient would be devised as a guaranty for the observance of this instrument, *e. g.*, 13th May, 1253, they decreed that sentence of excommunication should be passed on all those that violated the royal charters; and the prelates

who were present threw burning torches on the ground, exclaiming, "May all those who incur this sentence be thus extinguished in hell;" and the king who was present responded, "God is my witness that I will not violate any of those things, as I am a man, a Christian, a knight and a crowned and consecrated king." But kings' consciences have always been very pliant, and moreover the pope of Rome could easily absolve from the obligation of an oath, consequently, on 14th March, 1264, the barons obtained a still more efficacious guaranty of the king—they forced him to ordain that twice during the year at the festival of Easter and of St. Michael—the charters should be read in all the county courts in presence of all the people, and that the sheriffs, the judges, the bailiffs, both of the king and the nobles should be there to swear to observe them, and that the citizens should not obey any magistrate who had not taken this oath. Finally, in 1267, a statute was passed declaring that writs granted to apprehend the violator of the charters should not be charged for by the courts of justice or the royal officers. (423.)

5. *The new guaranties show the importance of the English people?* The object of reading the charters twice a year in the county courts, was to make them known to the whole people of England, to teach them to look to the charters as the basis of their liberties. This custom too marks the importance of the *English people.* Barons would not have been so careful to make them acquainted with these charters but for kind feelings existing between them, and the fact that great power resided in their body; and the union between people and aristocracy was necessary to resist the crown. (424.)

6. *Edward I.?* Was successor of Henry III. an able monarch. In first part of his reign but little contest between him and his barons. All tired of civil war—hence some years before he was called on to ratify the charters. Circumstances favorable to popular rights in his reign were the wars he carried on with Scotland and France—he wanted money, and the parliament would not give it to him without confirmation of the charters. Hence, when he ceased to rule, in 1307, Magna Charta had been so often confirmed, and under such different circumstances, as to be regarded as a sort of fixed constitutional law of the realm.

7. *Inadequacy of force as a guaranty for constitutional rights?* Evident that right of insurrection is a very inadequate sanction. 1st, Levying of war produces the most lamentable consequences, and therefore subject party would submit to great oppression before they would have recourse to so disastrous a remedy. 2d, The oppressing party being the government, and therefore the *organized* party, is too apt to prevail in the contest. 3d, There is a *vis inertiæ* in every large body

which disposes it to persevere in present order of things, until it is overcome by powerful impulse. Now if the *vis inertiæ reipublicæ* is on the side of the king and *against* the people, liberty can never be secure. This is the case where our remedy is *resistance.* If the king commits an act of tyranny, you are obliged to overcome the *vis inertiæ* of the people before you can apply your remedy. But although this remedy was so inadequate, yet we are not to admire less the constancy and wisdom of the barons in their struggles against the crown—they were men of good heads and firm hearts—they fought and got their charters—they made their kings swear to maintain them—they had them read in the county courts—and if violated anew, they were ready always to renew the struggle and to devise some new check on the monarch.

8. *Formation of parliament only effective guaranty of the liberties of England.* To the individual of the present day, who looks back over the long line of British history, it is but too manifest that the only permanent security to English liberty has been furnished by the gradual development of the parliament with its controlling powers. So soon as the powers of this body were acknowledged by both people and king, it became necessary to secure the action of parliament before the king could oppress; consequently the *vis inertiæ* was now in favor of liberty. Necessary therefore to explain the gradual formation of this deliberative assembly, which is one of the interesting phenomena of modern history.

9. *Parliament of England before the knights of shires sat in it?* Have already seen that William the Conqueror generally assembled his great barons (*tenants in capite*) in council three times per annum for three purposes: 1st, as counsellors of the king in regard to state matters, they being considered as representatives of various portions of England in which their lands lay, and knowing the interests and wants of those districts; 2d, by their means the laws could be best promulgated through England; and 3dly, for the purpose of illustrating the throne; the last perhaps as operative on the monarch as either of the others. All these barons seemed to have been first on a footing of equality, and although not always punctual in attendance, they were all summoned, and in the same manner. In process of time a distinction grew up among them—they became divided into barons—*primæ et secundæ dignitatis*—of first and second dignity. This probably arose from the division of some fiefs, and consequent variety in their size, some being much larger than others, and it may have been in part owing to the fact whether the fief was an ancient one or newly created—latter, *ceteris paribus*, being less respectable than the former. (H. 357.) Whatever it was which produced this difference, we soon find them to be summoned

differently, *e. g.*, barons of *first dignity* have a *special writ* directed to them from the king, whilst the others are summoned *en masse* by writs directed to the sheriffs. This difference is recognized in Magna Charta. By-and-by, as the number of the crown vassals increased, they became too numerous to meet in council; many would therefore absent themselves, especially as it was often considered a greater burthen than advantage to attend. This process continued till the grand council came to be composed almost entirely of barons *primæ dignitatis;* and as the inferior barons dropped off they merged into general population of counties, and became the principal county officers, and gave rise to the system of *county representation* in parliament.

10. *Knights of the shire or county representatives?* The origin of system of county representation in British parliament involved in some obscurity. In proportion as lesser barons separated from king's council, they merged into county population and united with the *freeholders* in attending to the business of the county. Great mass of these freeholders were the vassals of the great lords, and the remainder might consist of a few allodial proprietors of sufficient property to be admitted among the vassals. (447.) Here then were the elements about to grow into that important class, the yeomanry of England, being, 1st, vassals of the nobles, some of them with as large property as the barons themselves; 2d, the lesser barons; and 3d, allodialists with large property. This order could not in a country like England remain long without its weight in the government, and that could only be exercised by *representation.* As early as time of William the Conqueror, 12 men were summoned from each county for the purpose of informing the monarch of the laws, customs, conditions, &c. of the country; and the laws and customs reported by these representatives were sanctioned by the king. Sir Matthew Hale says this was "as sufficient and effectual a parliament as ever was held in England." (B. 359.) But it had no other power except that of merely reporting on the usages of the realm, they being assembled merely to give the king information, and to promulgate his decrees; and the case is besides a solitary one followed by no permanent result. We find no other instance of county representation till 15th of John, (1214,) when the king, finding that the great barons had deserted him, convoked an assembly general at Oxford, and directs the sheriffs to have 4 knights returned from each county—not known in this case whether they were to be elected by the county, or merely returned by the sheriff at his discretion, just as he would empannel a jury. The object of John in this case was to summon the knights as a sort of check upon his barons, but they united firmly with the barons.

During whole reign of Henry III. struggle between king and barons was continued, and we find more and more effort with each party to favor the counties. In 1225 Henry III. ordered the sheriffs of 8 counties to have *elected* in each of their county courts 4 knights, to repair to Lincoln, where his council was assembled, for the purpose of urging their complaints against the sheriffs, and the sheriffs were ordered to come likewise to defend themselves. (452.) In this case the representatives of the 8 counties were not constituent branch of the legislature, but a sort of envoys sent from the counties to treat with the king. During this reign we find that subsidies granted in parliament were assessed, not as before by the justices upon their circuit, but by *knights* freely chosen in the county courts. In 1254, when Henry was in want of money, he summoned a parliament at London, and he directed writs to the sheriffs to have elected in each county court *two knights*, who should be considered as *acting for all and each in the county—vice omnium et singulorum eorundem.* Here a most distinct recognition of the *principle of representation* in the very writ of the king.

With regard to the electors some suppose they were only the tenants in chief who had ceased to go to the council; others, that they were all the freeholders without regard to tenure. Mr. Hallam embraces the latter opinion, and thinks that the electors were nearly the same as at present. Others suppose they were elected in the county courts.

11. *Causes which led to establishment of a commission of 25 barons to govern the kingdom conjointly with the king?* Henry III, in addition to his being a weak and faithless king, and therefore highly unpopular from this cause, entered with the pope into the silly project of placing his 2d son, Edmund, on the throne of Sicily, and in the vain attempt he contracted an enormous debt, to the most exacting of all creditors, the pope of Rome. As the pope pressed the king, the king pressed his parliaments for the money; and the barons, who were disgusted with his conduct, took these opportunities to tie up the hands of the monarch. Henry had already ratified *Magna Charta* five times, and he would break it as soon as sworn to—the resort to force was not desirable, the barons therefore attempted a reform which would give effectual guaranty. In 1255 they demanded that the grand *justiciary*, the *chancellor*, and the *treasurer*, should each be chosen by the common council of the realm. They said if this much was not granted they could never succeed in binding their *Proteus* of a king. King rejected demand. Council called again in a few months—object of the king to get money. He had not convened all according to requisition of *Magna Charta.* Barons refused an answer or a subsidy unless all their peers were present. Again in 1257 grand council assembled at London. So many

people were present that city could scarce contain them. King called for money for his Sicilian enterprise, but barons refused.

In 1258 obliged to convene them again, for it had become settled principle that money could not be raised without them. When king met them he found them all in their armor, with swords by their sides, and when asked if he was to be made prisoner by them, Roger Bigod told him no; but that he must discharge the foreigners from his councils; that he must reform the government according to their plan, and make the pope abate somewhat of his exorbitant demands. (457.) And in meantime that a commission of 24 should be appointed to reform the government; that 12 of king's councillors, with 12 others chosen by the barons, should compose this commission, and report to a parliament to be holden at Oxford. King obliged to sanction all.

Parliament met 11th June, 1258. This body the first that was *officially* called *parliament*—a name which adhered to it ever afterwards. The acts of this parliament known by name of *Provisions of Oxford*. In these the charters were confirmed—the barons were to elect the judges, chancellor, treasurer, &c.—ordained that parliament shall meet 3 times a year—4 knights were to be appointed in each county to report upon the grievances and misdemeanors of king's officers in the county. (460.) Finally it was determined that the *commission* of 24 *barons* should continue with all power necessary to reform abuses, and to make in the name of the king such regulations as the times called for. No wonder that the king at later period, when again in possession of his full prerogative, should have called this the *parliamentum insanum;* for here was already a revolution in the government.

12. *Character and consequences of this regency?* Soon found that instead of dividing power with king it usurped the whole and left him a mere pageant in the government. At the head of this commission was Simon Montford, earl of Leicester, a bold and dexterous baron, who soon began to aim at nothing less than kingly power—a man who hated, and was hated by, the king, in consequence of a quarrel between them. Was soon found that as this commission usurped on the king, so the earl of Leicester was fast acquiring by his popular arts the complete control of the regency; its acts became more and more odious and oppressive, many of the barons and counties became disgusted; a reaction commenced; a deputation of the knights waited on the king to take the government in his own hands; king gets the pope's absolution; summons a parliament at Westminster, and agrees to leave the whole matter in dispute to the arbitration of St. Louis of France. St. Louis decides that *Provisions of Oxford* shall be annulled—that king shall appoint all his officers—admits strangers to enter his council—general

amnesty and confirmation of charters only things favorable to liberty in the arbitration.

13. *Civil war and its consequences?* This award of Louis generally praised as impartial—not considered so in England—civil war the consequence—Leicester heads the malcontent party—victory at Lewes puts Henry and his son Prince Edward in his possession, and makes him ruler of the kingdom—forgets that a *coalition* of barons had won this victory—imagines it was all for his benefit—tells the barons who came to demand their share of the ransom money, that they ought to be satisfied that he had saved their lives and property for them. (466.) Freeholders of the counties had for some time been disaffected to his government. This haughty demeanor now disgusted a large portion of the barons, and a counter revolution was rapidly preparing, when Leicester endeavored to support his power by calling a new order into existence.

SEC. IV.—FROM THE SUMMONING OF THE CITY AND BOROUGH REPRESENTATIVES TO THE COMPLETE FORMATION OF PARLIAMENT INTO TWO BRANCHES, THE COMMONS AND LORDS.

1. *Burgesses summoned to parliament?* Became necessary to call a parliament—Leicester wished to break down the authority of great barons, and seat his own power on more popular basis. Composition of the parliament of 1264 explains his views—he issued writs to 120 of the clergy, many not *immediate* vassals of the kings—he aimed at being popular with the clergy—issued writs to *only twenty-three barons;* all that he feared or suspected were left out—sheriffs were directed to have two knights elected from each county—finally letters were addressed to the citizens of London, York, Lincoln and the Cinque Ports, Dover, Sandwich, Romney, Hastings and Heathe, and some of principal towns and boroughs of England, commanding them to *elect two burgesses each*, and send them to parliament, and this seems to be first undoubted representation of the cities in parliament, and as it was the origin of the *House of Commons* is particularly interesting. County representation was altogether on feudal principles—grew out of feudal principle that *all* the immediate vassals of the crown had right of exemption from burdens of a pecuniary character, unless consented to by them—they had the right of sitting in king's court and taking part in his government. Now, when the *lesser barons* became too poor and numerous to go in person, they dropped off, entered the county population and sent representatives along with others, hence this branch was considered *feudal* and not *popular* like the burgesses.

2. *General circumstances which prepared the cities for representation and influence in the government?* It was the increase of com-

merce and manufactures which gradually breathed life into the cities, and prepared them to be an element in government. Under Anglo-Saxon kings cities were flourishing—Norman conquest prostrated them again for a season, *e. g.*, York dwindled from 1607 houses to 967—Oxford from 721 to 243—Chester from 482 to 282, &c. When they recovered, however, increased faster in England than on the continent, for the power of the crown was enough to protect them from the exactions of the great barons, and from wars among themselves. As the cities became more and more wealthy became an object of consideration, and their representation in parliament became a necessary event.

Before this time the kings employed the judges on their circuit to levy contributions on the cities, and in time of first and second Henry the sheriffs generally procured the contributions. (473.)

3. *Course of the burgesses in parliament—overthrow of Leicester's government?* The burgesses were far from furnishing the expected support—they refused the imposts which were required of them, set at liberty their commerce, and in short time the Cinque Ports betook themselves to piracy, which was encouraged by the state of the times. The consequence of all these disorders was, that nobles became disaffected, as also the counties—Prince Edward made his escape, barons rallied around him, gained a complete victory over Leicester at Evesham, and re-established the kingly government.

4. *General remarks on the course of the barons under Henry III.?* Have before stated that weak, tyrannical princes, like John and Henry III., are favorable to the acquisition of liberty by the people—a *succession* of such princes, however, becomes unfavorable, for it is possible for men to conquer their liberties *too fast*, and this actually happened under Henry III. Barons usurped all power by means of the regency of twenty-four, which resulted, as we have seen, in the ascendency of Leicester, who gave such disgust as to bring about a great reaction in the popular mind, and consequently the battle of Evesham restored the monarch with more power than he had before the meeting of celebrated parliament of Oxford. A parliament at Westminster (1265) just after restoration, empowered king to confiscate the property of the rebels. The city of London, the chief support of Leicester, was stript of all its privileges, and a great number of persons were imprisoned or placed at king's disposal, &c. (477.)

Two first parliaments after that at Westminster seem not to have had either knights or burgesses—king then was for a time left more absolute. Still those events, although they produced reaction, were not entirely useless—deep impression had been made on popular mind—change was necessary, and although Leicester and his party had over-acted, yet the barons had found out the secret that combination made them superior to the king; and Henry, and more important still, Prince Edward, had seen that tyranny would not be borne by the English. Leicester, in spite of all his vices, became a sort of *popular saint*—the monks collected his relics—miracles were performed at his tomb—the people visited it in crowds, and this alone was calculated to teach the king and Prince Edward some moderation.

5. *Final establishment of the city representation in parliament?* It was a great step taken to have brought the knights, the burgesses, and the barons, in presence of each other in parliament, although first experiment was rather unfavorable. The example in a government developing like that of England could not but be followed. The growing necessities of the crown made king use every expedient to get money—the cities were becoming too rich to be exempted from taxation, and it was already become a fixed principle that the king could exact money from no order unless consented to by that order.

Before the death of Henry III. the burgesses *once*, if not twice, are found in parliament. During the reign of Edward I. we see the meetings of the parliaments become much more regular. These bodies admitted by all parties to be a permanently constituent portion of government. Accession of Edward I. favorable to formation of British government—during a succession of weak kings subjects acquire their liberties, and under an energetic one, like Edward, they consolidate the institutions requisite to their preservation. Under such men as John and Henry III. they are apt to upset the balance of the government by wild extremes—an Edward then becomes necessary to temper the reform, to hold it in proper bounds. However such a man may be disposed to act arbitrarily, his capacious mind will be sensible to the symmetry and beauty of regular government, and it will yield to the necessity of temperate reform. Edward I. has deservedly been called the Justinian of England.

Edward was in Holy Land when his father died. (1272.) A parliament was assembled at Westminster under the auspices of archbishop of York to take oath of fidelity to Edward. Matter of general importance, consequently all interests were here; in addition to the barons there were four knights from the shires and four *burgesses from the towns*. When Edward returned (1275) they are again found in the parliament of Westminster, as also in the two next of 1276 and 1278. In January, 1283, king wished men and money for conquest of Scotland. All interests were here represented; one part of the parliament sat at York, the other at Northampton, for the sake of convenience and despatch. In month of June, Scotland was conquered and the king a prisoner—all interests again represented in the parliament. Even the clergy were summoned, for he wanted their money. This body too sat in two different places, the burgesses and clergy at Acton Burnell, the barons and knights at Shrewsbury. The burgesses *alone* passed a statute for the prompt recovery of the debts of merchants, and the barons and knights *alone* had a voice in the disposal of the Scotch king. Thus each part of the parliament acted on its own interests alone.

From 1283 to 1290 there were many parliaments, but although some important laws were made, we find no mention of either knights or burgesses—reason was that knights and burgesses were not supposed to be interested in the business of those parliaments, and therefore not summoned. In 1290 parliament summoned at Westminster; barons and county deputies alone present—reason was that the matter before them was the alienation of fiefs, a subject not supposed to interest the towns. This parliament passed the celebrated statute of *Quia Emptores.* From 1290 to '94 barons alone present, because the business brought before them was about regulating the Scottish succession, in which the towns and counties were not supposed to be concerned.

In 1295 Edward was engaged in war with France, and greatly in want of men and money. Philip le Bel was threatening invasion of England—here all interests were concerned. Hence parliament the fullest that had ever been called. Two assemblies met, one *ecclesiastic*, other *lay*—in former were archbishops, bishops, 67 abbots, the grand masters of 3 religious orders, as also deputies from the chapters and inferior clergy; these deputies were ordered to get instructions from their constituents before they came, in order to be able to act decisively in regard to means for defence of kingdom. This whole body was about 160. (490.) In the lay parliament there were present 49 barons, 2 knights, from each county, and 2 burgesses from each town; and the writs directed the sheriffs to take care that these deputies should get full powers from their constituents, that the business of parliament might be dispatched without delay. One hundred and twenty towns received this summons. The barons and deputies of counties voted one-eleventh of their movables to the king, the burgesses one-seventh, and the clergy, after long struggle, gave one-tenth of their ecclesiastical revenues.

From this time forward parliament was definitively established. We know of its convocation at least 11 times in the 12 last years of Edward I., and almost every time the deputies from the cities and counties were in attendance. The principle that no class could be taxed without its consent was settled. In the parliament (1299) writs were directed to the two chancellors of the universities of Oxford and Cambridge to order them to send 4 or 5 deputies from Oxford, and 2 or 3 from Cambridge, for the king wanted their money as well as their counsel.

6. *Were the cities anxious to be represented?* They were not, for the reason that the main object in summoning their deputies was to *get money*—hence the king was interested in making this representation as extensive as possible; and thus royal interest was at first favorable to growth of that branch, which has since become the effective check on the monarchy. If the exigencies of the government could have been relieved *without supplies*, this order of the government would never have existed. But Edward was engaged in war either with Scotland or France a greater portion of his reign, and consequently could not get on *without money*, and could not get the money *without consent* of the different branches of parliament.

7. *Cities sending burgesses to parliament vary from time to time?* We can now explain why the number of cities sending burgesses should vary. Sheriff seems to have had sort of discretionary power in selecting the cities; we may suppose that as the cities did not wish to incur the expense they might sometimes bribe the sheriff to pass them over, or the sheriff himself might show favoritism, *e. g.*, in 1313 the sheriff of county of Buckingham declared there was no other city but Wycomb fit to elect, although there were 3 others which had already sent deputies twice to parliament. In 1339 sheriff of county of Wilts returned burgesses from only one town and two boroughs, affirming there were no others, although 8 more had been in habit of sending delegates to previous parliaments, &c. (497.)

8. *Who were the city electors?* Varied according to circumstances. In some cities electoral right belonged to the corporation or city authorities, who elected without intervention of citizens; in others, to the freeholders, or what we call *pot boilers.* The king in summoning the cities to elect delegates had nothing to do with the mode of election farther than to direct that they should have full instructions from their constituents so as to be able to act with dispatch. When therefore a writ was directed to city, the election was made according to circumstances, *e. g.*, if a city was held in *fee farm** by a corporation composed of a certain number of individuals, those individuals alone would have the electoral right.

9. *Organization of parliament into two separate houses?* Carte fixes the epoch in 17th year of Edward III. (1344). Parliamentary

* A town was said to be let in *fee farm* when the individual tribute due from the city to the lord or the king, was converted into a perpetual rent from the whole borough. Town then said to be *affirmed* or let in *fee farm* to the burgesses and their successors for ever. (H. 363.)

history fixes it in the 6th of this monarch. Hallam in the 1st (Edward III.) if not the 8th year of Edward II. This diversity occasioned by the various circumstances regarded as evidence of the separation into two houses. Sometimes this organization inferred from county and city deputies being in *same house*—sometimes from discussion *together*—sometimes from *uniting their votes* on the *same questions*, &c. Instead of looking for date precise, best to cite causes which led to it. At first all the barons who alone were in parliament of course sat together. When were distinguished into *first and second dignity*, still all sat together. When the knights of shires came to parliament always sat with the barons, for they were mainly, as we have seen, the deputies of the inferior barons, who had gradually disappeared from parliament.

When the burgesses came they were a new order, not at all *feudal* in character, and were thrown into a body to themselves, which is proved by votes given for subsidies, *e. g.*, in 1275 burgesses *alone* granted to the king a duty on exportation of wool and skins. In 1295 they grant one-seventh of their movables, whilst clergy give one-tenth and barons and knights one-eleventh—here are three distinct bodies. This distinction kept up until parliament of 1333 under Edward III. Barons and knights vote one-fifteenth, the burgesses one-tenth. Here, although the sums granted by the first two classes were same, the registers of parliament say that the knights *sat with the burgesses*, and not with the barons. In 1345 the knights vote two-fifteenths of their movables, the burgesses one, and the barons nothing, because they are to follow him to war. Here then it seems the knights have separated from the barons, although yet distinct from the burgesses. (504.) In 1347 the *commons* without distinction vote two-fifteenths to be raised in two years. This the first undoubted case not only of knights and burgesses *sitting together*, but *voting together*, which soon afterwards became the general custom.

Thus will it be seen, by reference to parliamentary history, that for about first 80 years after the burgesses went to parliament they sat by themselves, whilst the barons and county delegates were united. The county delegates were much more respected than the city, were much oftener called to parliament, because they were strictly *feudal* in character. In all commercial matters the cities were consulted exclusively. When the whole parliament sat in same place, all the parts were generally in the same house—the barons and knights in the *upper* story and the burgesses in the *lower*. Such was the tendency to separation of interests at first, that even the burgesses sometimes divided, those from the royal domain forming a class distinct from the others. Not to wonder then that the high barons and county delegates should separate.

We find the latter alone consulted about the alienation of fiefs, which resulted in the statute, *Quia Emptores Terrarum*, and afterwards their separation became more and more frequent, till at last it became permanent. When this happened there were many reasons for union with the burgesses.

30. *General causes which produced the union of the burgesses and county delegates into one body—the commons?* 1st, They came to parliament by same kind of right—*election*—and consequently both acted not for themselves, but for their constituents. 2d, Their interests were similar. There must have been great community of interest between the county and its towns. 3. The county courts were the centres where the whole county population met to transact business, often the townspeople did their business in that court likewise, and even sometimes held their elections there. Besides this, the county courts had a wonderful influence in wearing away all the aristocratic differences in the county population, because of the equality of rights which all the freeholders possessed in court, and because they here held their consultations, debated their interests, and concerted their measures in common. As the county population became more democratic, it lost its feudal character, and became more assimilated to the cities. 4th, Lastly, the barons formed the king's council and courts, besides sitting in parliament. They would therefore often be convened without the knights—were a sort of permanent branch—always concerned in the exercise of the kingly power. Whereas the knights and burgesses went on the business of their respective constituents alone, and did not meddle with central power farther than as it *immediately* affected their constituents. These were main reasons which brought the burgesses and knights together.

10. *Concurrence of both houses becomes necessary to legislation?* Main object of calling burgesses and even knights was to get money of them, and as different interests would give differently, so they acted apart. But it is in the nature of such bodies when called together to increase gradually the sphere of their action. Not only to determine whether they will give this or that subsidy demanded of them, but to recommend certain things to the king, to make petitions, to call for changes in the laws, &c., &c. Thus their action becomes more and more general, and consequently, while special interests and special actions tended to divide the body into different parts, these general interests and general actions would have a tendency to unite—hence we have seen formation of house of commons by knights and burgesses. Again, if king in passing laws deemed the interests of the commons to be at all concerned, he would naturally consult them—ask their advice,

&c. Or if the commons wanted any laws changed they would petition and press for change, &c. And such monarchs as the Edwards soon saw that it was best to have advice and concurrence of all to their general measures, for then all would be more willing to vote money. Edward III. even consulted his parliaments as to war and peace, in order the *more gracefully* to ask for the supplies. In this manner it became, by degrees, before the end of the long reign of Edward III., a settled practice for both houses to *concur* in the framing of all laws—the commons, who before this reign were rarely mentioned in the enacting clause, were now as rarely omitted—laws were declared to be made at the *request* of the commons and by the assent of the lords and prelates —in fact it is evident from the rolls of parliament, that statutes were almost always founded on *their petition*. (H. 379.) Here then we have the complete formation of the British parliament into *lords* and *commons* with joint concurrence necessary to all legislation.

11. *Beneficial effects of the organization of the British parliament on the liberties of England?* It is manifest that if all the interests in the government had remained *distinct and isolated* parliament could never have had the same beneficial influence—the king would have managed them all with much more ease, and moreover they would have naturally been hostile to each other. Take for example the great question of granting supplies. Suppose the monarch calls for a certain amount, then if each interest votes its own portion separately, each would be concerned to make the others contribute as much as possible—if you could throw a double weight on one or two of them, then the others would have less to bear, *e. g.*, if the cities and counties could be made to contribute more than their share, the clergy and barons would have to pay less than theirs, and *vice versa.* In this the struggle would not be so much to lessen the exactions of the monarch, as to dodge the burthen by throwing it on other shoulders.

Again, if every interest were distinct, an attack on *one* might not be resisted by *another;* and hence the capacity to resist the crown might be lost for want of proper sympathy and union among the different interests, &c. No one interest in the British government could probably have sustained itself *alone and unaided*, through all the vicissitudes of the English history, against the regal power, *e. g.*, the cities without union with the counties could never have produced a body of commons capable of maintaining themselves—they would have shared the fate of the continental cities, but by union with the yeomanry a power was engendered capable of checking effectually every other. Lastly however, it is evident that whilst such would be effects of complete isolation of each interest, if all had been, on contrary, consolidated into one single body, the votes of which had been given *per capita*, then the interest that could command a majority of votes would have always governed the others, *e. g.*, in a house thus composed, suppose the cities and counties by their delegates to outnumber the aristocracy, then on every question of conflict between these two interests the latter would be outnumbered, and of course would become a mere nullity, and *vice versa.* Every student of Roman history has been struck with the exemplification of this remark in the Roman commonwealth, *e. g.*, if a case were tried before the *commitia centuriata*, *property* was every thing and mere *numbers* nothing; if it were brought before the *commitia tributa*, then the thing was reversed, *numbers* were every thing and *property* nothing. Hence the constant struggle between the *patricians* and *plebeians*—each for that tribunal which favored its interests.

. Thus it is seen in British constitution that consolidation stopped exactly where it ought, and that the formation of parliament into two bodies, both necessary for legislation, was best calculated for preservation of liberty. By the necessity for two concurrent majorities for every act of legislation, that hurry and overaction which are the besetting sins of single deliberative bodies, are guarded against; and the danger of one interest overthrowing the other effectually prevented.

12. *General remarks?* 1st. All interests in England were properly represented; hence government reposed on a broad and secure basis. 2d, None but *parliamentary* lords were invested with aristocratic privileges. In France, Spain, Germany, in fine, almost every where except in England, all who are born of noblemen are invested with privileges which make them distinct from the *people.* In England the law has never taken notice of the mere *gentry* or lower nobility, but only of the peerage or parliamentary lords. The younger sons of peers all sunk into the commonalty—there are no exclusive privileges attached to the mere *blood.* This peculiarity in England, whilst it makes the peers much more important as hereditary legislators of the realm, has tendency to destroy much of the odium of aristocracy. No part of British constitution, says Hallam, so admirable as this equality of civil rights. (351.) The British law is no respecter of persons—it screens not the gentleman of ancient lineage from the judgment of an ordinary jury, nor from ignominious punishment—it never did confer those unjust immunities from public burthens which the superior orders arrogated to themselves on the continent, and which was main cause of French revolution. This descent of the unprivileged portion of the English aristocracy into the mass of the commons has kept up a cordial sympathy and harmony between those great interests—it has produced a constant circulation between the two orders—it has formed a connec-

tion, a sort of breakwater between them, which has prevented those violent collisions that have so often resulted in other countries. Need scarcely add that main cause of this beautiful feature is due to the original separation of the barons of the *lesser dignity* from those of the *first*—to their withdrawal from the king's council and entry into the county population, and subsequent institution of county representation.

3d. He who examines the British constitution will see a beautiful exemplification of the virtue of perseverance and the necessity of continued, unwearied vigilance in the defence of liberty—the struggle against the royal prerogative was like that of the waterman against a rapid stream—the slightest relaxation of exertion and the fruit of years of labor would be swept away under weak princes the principal acquisitions were made—under the able ones liberty would be regulated and restrained—the conflict with the 1st and 3d Edwards was a noble one. Just before his death the 1st Edward seemed to have triumphed, and Roger Bigod and Humphrey Bohun, two of the most stout-hearted of the noble band that had battled it with Edward and his father, were in their old age brought upon their knees before the stern monarch. But the feeble successor is scarce upon the throne before the aristocracy have won back all that was lost. The war with France, like a ruinous lawsuit, was entailed upon the English nation by the Edwards—it made the monarchs *call for money*, and their subjects would take the opportunity to *call for liberty*. It has been said that English liberty has been purchased *with blood*, true only in part—much more of it has been actually purchased *with money*. Some of best laws of England, with Magna Charta itself, as confirmed by Henry III., were *literally purchased with money*. In many of the parliaments of Edward III. and Richard II. this *sale of redress* is chaffered for as distinctly as any transaction of bargain and sale between two merchants.

4th. Between the whigs and tories there has been much discussion as to the regal power in the first period of the government, and whether the people usurped on the kings or the kings on the people, history proves the first Norman kings to have been very absolute, and the cause has been explained—the king was looked to as the great fount of power, and it will be seen that the representatives of the people and the barons too always approached him in the language of supplication and petition—they asked for privileges and liberty rather as grants of the royal favor, than as rights to which they were entitled independently of him. The first parliaments were summoned rather for the purpose of granting supplies and furnishing information to the king than for general purposes of legislation. From this beginning, so unpropitious to liberty, the fabric of English freedom rose, step by step, through toil and sacrifice, each generation adding something to the security of the work, until the whole fabric was completed.

13. *Judicial system of England?* In England, as in all feudal countries, there was standing council to assist king in collection of revenue, administration of justice, and dispatch of business, called the king's court, (*curia regis*,) and held in his palace—composed of the great officers, the chief justiciary, (the greatest officer in England after the king, and who at first governed in his absence,) the chancellor, the constable, marshal, chamberlain, steward, and treasurer, and any others appointed by the king. Of this great court a particular branch took cognizance of revenue cases, and although the members were the same, yet as for this purpose they sat in different part of the palace, it was distinguished by special denomination of *exchequer court.* Besides the exchequer, two other branches emanated from the *aula regis*, the court of *common pleas*, and of *king's bench.* The former for the decision of private civil suits, the latter for criminal causes.

14. *Circumstances which caused the division of the aula regis into the exchequer, common pleas, and king's bench?* Aula regis was at first ambulatory—followed the king's person; this inconsistent with deliberation requisite for judges, and incompatible with the interest of parties who were obliged often to follow the court from place to place. With multiplication of laws and growing complexity of legal science, this burthen became more and more oppressive, particularly in cases requiring the presence of numerous witnesses. The necessity for a stationary court was therefore quickly felt.

Again, the great increase of judicial business soon suggested the propriety of a division of judicial labor. There is a marked distinction between *criminal* and *civil actions.* Trial for crime requires dispatch; public safety and public indignation demand often a speedy decision. Criminal too must be arrested and sometimes imprisoned, to prevent escape. All this demands expedition. Lawsuits about property are different—spectators are cool and indifferent—parties may be left in great measure to their discretion in bringing the suit to a close—no necessity to imprison either party. Besides this, the laws pertaining to civil rights are infinitely more numerous and complex than the criminal laws. Thus pleadings are multiplied and delays increased. From these causes the king's bench and the common pleas with separate jurisdiction arose. So great had been the inconvenience of the great ambulatory court, that we find in Magna Charta a special provision in favor of the court of *common pleas*—"*Communia placita non sequantur curiam regis, sed teneantur in aliquo loco certo.*" Upon similar principles may be explained the separation of the exchequer court. As these courts had different jurisdictions, they had separate places for their meetings; they soon came to be composed of separate judges, and had different presidents; the members lost gradually their mere *political* character and assumed exclusively that of the *legal*—a most decided improvement on the old *aula regis*—by turns a council of state and a body of judges.

By this division into the three separate courts, the *chief justiciary*, as he was called, who was the presiding officer in the *aula regis*, lost his power and high character, and it is supposed that the jealousy of the king towards this officer hastened the division. The office of grand justiciary was originally an appendage of that of lord high steward, in all feudal kingdoms the chief officer of the king's household, and next to sovereign in power. Pepin bore this office in France, when he dethroned the Merovingian race of kings.

15. *Great judiciaries of principal feudal kingdoms of Europe analogous in their origin to the English?* The *cour de roy* in France grew out of the national council, and, like the aula regis of England, was at first ambulatory—same inconveniences were felt as in England. To remedy it, Philip le Belle established a stationary branch at Paris, and another at Thoulouse, (1302,) called *parlements*. Other courts of similar nature soon arose in other parts. Difference between the judiciary of England and France was, that in former three great courts at Westminster presided over the whole kingdom, while those of France were separate and distinct. In like manner the *aulic council* in Germany arose out of the *diet* of the empire, and was ambulatory. Feudal forms slowly gave way in this country; hence long time before this court gave off a stationary one. Occurred in time of Maximilian, in establishment of the *imperial chamber* (1496). In Scotland a similar revolution is observed in judicial system to that of England.

16. *French system of jurisprudence not so uniform as that of England?* Separation and independence of the great judicial tribunals in France have produced inconsistent and jarring decisions—hence the diversity of laws and customs in that kingdom. Judicial system of England free from this inconvenience. Great courts at Westminster have jurisdiction over the whole kingdom. Principles of law in every department being decided by same set of judges are reduced to uniform standard. No country in the world where lawyers and judges are so impressed with advantages of uniformity and stability; that a certain rule should be invariably maintained is considered almost as important as that it should be a good one.

Although English system secures uniformity in judgments, by the supremacy of the courts of Westminster, throughout the kingdom, yet have they been able by appointment of certain extraordinary judges, as auxiliaries, to bring justice almost to each man's door. When the king's bench was stationary at Westminster, became necessary to grant special commissions for trying particular crimes in the districts where perpetrated. Seldom happens that a crime can be proved other than by *parol* testimony. Now this method of proof is the most expensive and burthensome, especially where witnesses must travel to a distance—hence the appointment of extraordinary judges under two special commissions, 1st, of *oyer and terminer*, to hear and determine all treasons, felonies, misdemeanors, &c., and that of *jail delivery*, to try every prisoner confined in the several jails of their respective circuits.

As soon as these circuit judges were appointed to facilitate criminal trials, idea was naturally suggested that the same commissioners might expedite the trial of civil suits; with this view the commission of *assize* and that of *nisi prius* were granted to them. By the former they were empowered to take verdict of jury in trial of landed disputes; by the latter to investigate all such matters of fact as were then under dispute in any of the courts of Westminster. Thus, in civil processes, the proofs, averments, and matters of fact, came to be discussed in the county, often in the neighborhood of the place where the dispute was, while the *matter of law* was left to consideration of the great courts at Westminster.

17. *Justices of the peace—magistrates?* When quarrels or fights occurred among individuals, or outrage and violence were likely to be followed by riots and insurrections, timely interposition could not always be expected from the regular courts of justice; it became, therefore, expedient to invest men of character and rank in different parts of the country with power to seize and confine in any emergency disorderly persons, or to demand of them sureties for maintenance of public peace. Hence the appointment of *conservators* or *justices of the peace*, elected at first by the freeholders of the county, afterwards by the king. (H. M. A. 345, 419, M. 2, ch. 7.)

18. *Chancellor of England, and his jurisdiction?* This officer was originally the king's secretary and chaplain, and had sole charge of writing his letters, and afterwards of issuing *writs* in the name of the crown. When the deeds issuing from the crown became numerous, and were often executed for the sake of dispatch by inferior persons, the subscription of the chancellor, and afterwards the affixing of the great seal, of which he had the custody, became necessary. Subscription of *Referendarius*, who was probably the *chancellor*, occurs as far back in Anglo-Saxon period as reign of Ethelbert, first Christian king. In reign of Edward Confessor we meet with a charter subscribed by chancellor

under the very name—"Ego Rembaldus *cancellarius* subscripsi." In this way all important writings issued by king passed through the medium of the chancellor; and before he affixed great seal it became his duty to examine them, and if erroneous or illegal to repeal or cancel them, upon principle that every servant of the crown is responsible for measures executed by him, although emanating from the king. Thus, when Richard II. made certain grants to his favorites, the chancellor refused to seal them, as being too profuse and indiscreet, and Richard was obliged to take the seal and seal them himself. Thus arose the *ordinary* jurisdiction of the chancellor. His *extraordinary* jurisdiction, it is supposed, arose from the necessity of occasionally mitigating the harshness of the common law. In the application of strict law to particular cases it might often occur that the principles of equity would be violated, although letter of the law might be observed; *e. g.*, seal of a bond might be accidentally torn off, or bond itself lost, or the essential witness in a case might be fraudulently kept away, and the strictness of common law might defeat the plaintiff. Such cases as these would naturally be referred by the aggrieved party to the king in council, the fountain of all justice, and he would naturally devolve the burthen of this duty on his chancellor, who thus became the *keeper of his conscience*, and a judge in equity.

After Norman conquest, when the principal judicial business was transacted in the *aula regis*, and the great multiplication of lawsuits demonstrated the hardship of a universal application of the rules of common law, the necessity of relaxation was more and more felt, and numerous exceptions were admitted. As applications for this purpose became frequent, provision was made to facilitate their progress, and thus the office of chancellor was gradually invested with all the attributes of a court of equity, and laws were afterwards made to define and regulate what was at first of fortuitous origin, (M. 2, ch. 7, sec. 4.) Particular limits, however, of this equitable jurisdiction remained for a long time exceedingly indefinite, and were the source of much contention among the lawyers; *e. g.*, Coke was bitterly opposed to it; the character of his mind narrow, contracted and technical, yet exceedingly acute, naturally inclined him to this opposition, and his personal enmity towards Edginton, the keeper of the great seal, inspired him with additional zeal. The kings were generally in favor of this jurisdiction, because the chancellors were their officers and members of their privy councils.

19. *Petty jury?* Among all the Gothic nations the custom of deciding lawsuits by a sort of trial by jury seems to have prevailed. In England this custom prevailed, first, in all the allodial courts of the

county and the *hundred*, and afterwards was introduced into the baron courts, and finally into the king's courts. The same custom, however, was not introduced into the great courts growing out of the national council in any other country except England; *e. g.*, it was not introduced into the *cour de roy* in France, nor into its derivatives, the parliaments. Nor do we find it in the *aulic council* or the *imperial chamber* of Germany. This difference may be accounted for perhaps by the facts, first, that the continental judiciaries were more numerous; 2dly, that they were more governed by the *civil law*, to which juries were unknown; 3d, in England the combination between the aristocracy and commonalty for limiting the royal prerogatives was much more successful than in any other European country, and this mode of trial was pushed up to the courts of Westminster, as being the most favorable to popular rights, and the best guaranty against the corrupting influence of the crown on the judges. (M. E. G. 2, 295 and 300.)

The ancient constitution of juries was different from the present. Now they are the *triers* of the *issue*, and found their verdict on the evidence adduced before them; but the ancient jurors were the *witnesses* themselves, and their verdict was their *own* evidence. Trial by *jury* therefore was only a trial by *witnesses*. They only gave *evidence* of the fact, not *a judgment* on the accusation; *e. g.*, when Alice Perrers, the mistress of Edward III., was tried under Richard II., the jury consisted of 16 knights and esquires, of the late king's household, selected because they had constant opportunities of witnessing the conduct of Perrers. The trial was before a committee of house of lords, and six of the jury were examined *against* the accused. (4 Ling. 139.) When Tresilian tried the insurgents in Wat Tyler's insurrection, he impanelled three juries of 12 each. The first was ordered to present all whom they knew as chiefs of the insurrection, the second gave their opinion on the presentation of the first, and the third gave the verdict of guilty or not guilty. There were no witnesses examined; the juries spoke exclusively from *personal* knowledge. (W. B. H. 64.)

20. *Grand jury?* Administration of justice not only requires a proper decision when case is *presented*, but likewise that the *case* should be *discovered* and brought before the court. In controversies between private individuals, each party is attentive to his own interest, and therefore there is but little danger of such cases being neglected. But in all crimes requiring punishment for the sake of example, there is danger that the public interest will be neglected. No one may choose to take the trouble and odium of being informer or prosecutor; some regulation becomes necessary to secure the public interest. In Greece and Rome,

every body was invited to be prosecutor, and sometimes certain advantages were held out to those who would incur the trouble and odium. This produced the worst effect possible. The prosecutors too often acted from secret motives of revenge and malice or sordid avarice. Hence the detestation which all virtuous men in Greece felt for the whole race of sycophants that swarmed in those little republics. In modern feudal nations, judge himself was originally public prosecutor. This practice mischievous. Same person cannot acquit himself with propriety in twofold character of accuser and judge. Even in speculative debate, we acquire a prejudice in favor of our side in argument, which often prevents our weighing opposite argument fairly. This much stronger in a trial; judge, who hunts up the case for trial, who encourages the witness to depose, who tries to prove all that can be proved, is apt at last to be prejudiced in favor of the prosecution, and his pecuniary interest being on the same side, such trials would become unfavorable to liberty. This soon gave rise to appointment of a procurator or factor, to act in name of sovereign, called *attorney general* in this country and England, and the *king's advocate* in Scotland. But he could only conduct the prosecution; he could do very little in the way of hunting up the cases. This led first to the establishment of *coroners* and their inquests, and finally to the establishment of the *grand jury*, by whose inquisition the judges were authorized to proceed in the trial of public offenders.

This grand jury had two methods of finding the fact, 1st, by *presentment* from personal knowledge, 2d, by *indictment*. The object of preferring indictments to the grand jury was originally to avoid the trouble and expense of fruitless prosecutions, by procuring the approbation of a jury before entering into the prosecution. This last method became in process of time a most important bulwark of liberty. For whilst the necessity of getting the sanction of a grand jury to the prosecution will rarely screen the real criminal, whose trial will always be anxiously pressed, it has on the contrary been the protection of the innocent against those shameless prosecutions undertaken for purpose of serving a political job, or of gratifying malicious passions.

Thus one great benefit arising from interposition of grand jury is not only different, but diametrically opposite to what was originally intended. It was intended to assist the crown in the discovery of crimes, and to multiply prosecutions. But when the monarchs became powerful and their police energetic, one chief object of the grand juries was to guard against abuses of discretionary power in the officers of the crown; for when an innocent man is singled out to be sacrificed, a jury of his fellow citizens will sympathize with him, and regard his case as theirs—they foil the attack by responding to the bill of indictment that it it is *not true.* (M. E. G. v. 2, 302–310.)

SEC. V.—GOVERNMENT OF ENGLAND FROM THE REIGN OF EDWARD III. TO THE ACCESSION OF THE TUDORS, 1377—1485.

Shall now proceed with a rapid sketch of the progress of the British government from the period of its complete formation, under Edward III., to accession of Tudors.

1. *Parliamentary opposition in the latter part of Edward III.'s reign?* This monarch, who was exceedingly able and energetic in last years of his life, formed a foolish attachment to an unprincipled woman, Alice Perrers, who used her great influence in a manner degrading to the king. Duke of Lancaster, too, a younger son, became the favorite of the king, who excited the jealousy of the Black Prince, lest his title might be set aside to make way for the younger brother. Black Prince however was one of the most popular men in the kingdom, and consequently he gave countenance to an opposition party in the parliament. This opposition was led on in House of Commons by Peter de la Mare, a dependent of the earl of March, who had married the sole heiress of the second son of Edward III., and therefore stood before Lancaster, the third son. This opposition was becoming so powerful as to be able to dictate terms to the king, when the death of the Black Prince gave once more an ascendant to the favorites, and Peter de la Mare was thrown into prison. Fortunately, however, Edward died soon after, and the crown devolved on Richard II., son of the Black Prince.

2. *The parliamentary opposition under Edward III. forms an epoch in English history?* It was a new mode of attacking the king and his favorites—it was peaceful and not forcible. It shows the complete organization of the body, and marks the progress of civilization—the law of *force* yielding to the law of *reason* and public opinion. It led the aristocracy to look on the commons as an indispensable auxiliary in opposing the king, and produced proper harmony and dependence among all the departments of the government. There occurred too here, what will generally occur in such monarchies as England, and which is highly favorable to liberty—the heir apparent threw his whole weight into the scale of the opposition. In every government like that of England the two great parties are the *government* and the *opposition.* The latter will always, if possible, secure the support of the heir apparent, and he will be disposed generally to unite with them, for it makes him at once a chief and a leader, whilst adherence to the other retains him

in a state of dependence and pupilage, and subjects him to frequent mortifications.

3. *Reign of Richard II. highly favorable to increase of parliamentary power?* Richard was in his eleventh year, of course incapable of government. The kingdom during the minority was governed by a regency, which can never wield the energetic concentrated power of a monarch. The three uncles of Richard were mutually jealous of each other. Under such a state of things the parliament during the minority naturally became the most important branch in the government, and rapidly advanced in power. When Richard arrived at majority and took the reins of government in his hands, his unstable and vacillating policy afforded to the parliament a fit opportunity to display its newly acquired powers. The character of Richard too was extremely unfavorable to the preservation of regal authority—he was violent in his temper, devoted to favorites and to pleasure, fond of idle show, recklessly extravagant* and treacherous. Occasionally, as towards the insurgents in Smithfield, he displayed great energy and decision of character, but generally he was inert and unenterprising. Under all these circumstances, not to wonder at the energetic parliamentary proceedings of this reign; *e. g.*, chancellor of the king, earl of Suffolk, was impeached—the first instance of the impeachment of a *minister*. Lord Latimer, impeached under Edward III., was only steward of the household. Not contented with the victory over the minister, the parliament appointed a council of eleven lords with three chief officers of the crown to regulate the affairs of the kingdom for one year, and thus, says Mr. Hume, the king was in truth dethroned. When this parliament was dissolved, Richard procured from his judges an opinion, that every act of parliament, particularly the impeachment of ministers, was treasonable, unless permitted by the king. The very next parliament, in spite of all the efforts to corrupt at the elections, impeached both the ministers and the judges.

At last, in 1397, the king succeeded in corruptly modelling his parliament, which became a base instrument of oppression in his hands. It impeached the Duke of Gloucester, king's uncle, and two other noblemen, as traitors, for resistance to Richard nine years before; it formally sanctioned the slavish decision of the judges, voted larger present supplies than had ever been granted before, and settled some portions on the king for life, and then concluded by delegating the whole power of

* In his kitchen alone he had 300 domestics, and daily entertained 6000 persons. When he married Isabella of France he received 200,000 marks as dower, and spent 300,000 on the marriage

parliament to a commission of twelve, six lords and six commoners—thus uniting the whole power of the government in the hands of the king, with a small junta. This increased authority soon led to tyranny and oppression. Duke of Lancaster, who had before been driven out of the kingdom by Richard, was invited by the opposition to redress their grievances—he returned from exile during Richard's absence in Ireland, and Richard, finding on his return that all was hopeless, abdicated. But in spite of this it was deemed proper to depose him formally, and the measure was justified by thirty-three articles of accusation alleged against him. In surveying this reign, we find that, of the three capital points contested during the reign of Edward III.—that money could not be levied, nor laws made without consent of the commons, and that the administration of government was subject to their inspection and control—the first was absolutely decided in their favor, second was admitted in principle, and third was confirmed by frequent exercise. Besides these advances the commons acquired the right of *directing* the application of subsidies, and calling accountants before them; as also that of impeaching the ministers for misconduct—two engines of immense efficiency. (H. M. A. 393.)

4. *Hume's account of this reign unsatisfactory?* Reign of Richard II. is one of the most important in English history, and perhaps the least understood. It evidently, in some important particulars, is strikingly analogous to that of Charles I. Hence Mr. Hume has been biassed in his narration into a direction opposite to that he has generally taken in regard to the earlier kings. To extenuate the conduct of the Stuarts, to whom he was almost culpably partial, he has generally represented the early monarchs as exercising an almost unlimited and arbitrary power. Richard II., however, he speaks of as conducting himself with great moderation, during the period of eight years from the termination of his minority, that is, during very nearly the whole of his actual exercise of power. An impartial survey of this reign, however, must convince every unprejudiced mind, that if the parliament was often carried into unauthorized exercise of power, the oppressions and provocations of the king in a measure justified them; and as to the amiability of Richard's character, there is no doubt but that he committed deeds of the deepest crime; *e. g.*, says Sir J. Mc Intosh, "There are few instances in history of a deadly hatred, hoarded for eleven years by a gay and convivial youth, hidden from the victim by the disguise of smiles and caresses, and at length gratified with more falsehood, more treachery, more inhumanity, a grosser breach of the substance of justice, and a more offensive mockery of its forms, than is exhibited in the murder of the duke of Gloucester." (142.)

5. *Wat Tyler's insurrection?* In 1382, during Richard's reign, occurred famous revolt of the lower classes, so similar to the insurrection of the *Jacquery* in France. This revolt, denominated from its leader, is somewhat difficult to explain, although its proximate cause is manifest. The insurgents were the slaves and villeins of the farms, and the lowest classes in the cities. The insurrection marks one of those periods when old relations are dissolving and new ones forming. The spirit which actuated the cities had crept down into the villeins and slaves, and the very amelioration which had been introduced among them but served to hasten the catastrophe. These commotions were near that particular epoch in the progress of slavery and villanage towards emancipation, when the hope of freedom produces sullenness and insubordination on the one side, and revenge and cruelty on the other. The sudden rise of the cities afforded a recipient for the liberated slave, and at same time an employment, which must have impaired the value of the slave, by rendering him discontented, and facilitating his escape; for a residence of a year and a day in a walled city without apprehension secured his freedom. Let us only for a moment suppose, in every considerable district of our southern country, a populous and powerful town, adverse to the landed interest, rapidly rising in wealth and power, in such need of labor, that even that of the runaway slave was eagerly sought for, and we may form some notion of the condition of Europe during the fourteenth century.* Monarchs had set the example of liberating slaves on the crown lands; *e. .g.*, Louis Hutin by ordinance liberated his, on condition of composition, (1315,) and his son confirmed it (1318.) In 1339 a like commission came from Edward III.; some barons and some monasteries† followed the example, and although these instances of voluntary emancipation were rare, yet they served to influ-

* In 12th R. II. commons complain that villeins fly to cities and boroughs, whence their masters cannot recover them, being hindered by the people, and they pray that the masters may seize their villeins in such places without regard to their franchises. But the king put his *veto* on this measure, and likewise on petition of same parliament that children of villeins might not be put to school, in order to advance them in the church, "and this for the honor of all the freemen of the kingdom." (H. M. A. 540.)

† The church was generally on the side of amelioration in condition of slavery, but it is curious fact, that the villeins upon church lands were among the last emancipated. Enfranchisement by will was among the most frequent, and generally for salvation of the soul; *e. g.*, in will of Seniofred, count of Barcelona, have the following piece of corrupt Latin: "De ipsos servos meos et ancillas illi qui traditi fuerunt faciatis illos liberos, *propter remedium animæ meæ.*" But those he received from his parents he leaves to his brothers; "et alii qui fuerunt de parentorum meorum remaneant ad fratres meos." (91.)

ence the minds of those left in servitude, and to beget a spirit of inquiry.

With the progress of luxury too, the landlords had frequently found it more profitable to demand fixed rents of the villeins, than to exact involuntary labor. The facility with which slaves could make their escape after the rise of the cities must have added a powerful stimulus to the increase of this practice, for when the land was handed over to the villein, and a rent only required of him, he had no farther motive to run away from his master, and he might accumulate property and become independent. But this very step towards freedom generates fresh disturbances between the villein and his master, the former wishing to pay as little as possible, and the latter to exact as much as possible. A new relation begins to exist, new rights spring up, new sources of heart-burnings and jealousies are opened, and the relation between master and villein becomes in fact more complex and inharmonious, infinitely more difficult to adjust, than in a sate of perfect freedom. While then there were so many orders of society, and servitude itself was exhibiting so many phases, not to wonder that even the lowest should begin to ask how they came to be at the bottom of the scale. These speculations found their way into the pulpit; and Froissart tells us that John Ball, a foolish priest of Kent, preached to the peasants, that in the beginning of the world there were no bondmen, all were equal.

> "When Adam delved, and Even span,
> Where was then the gentleman."

Wherefore, he insisted that no one could be bond without doing treason to his lord, as Lucifer did to his God.

Under such circumstances any grievance may excite insurrection. In England an accident kindled the flame: the collector of an obnoxious poll tax levied it with insolence in the house of a tiler of Dartford, and in order to ascertain age of the tiler's beautiful daughter, on which the tax depended, offered an indignity to her, which caused the tiler to knock down the tax-gatherer with a mortal blow. The men of Kent rallied to the support of the tiler. Essex too was already in rebellion, caused by a commissioner who had come to inquire into the causes of the deficient collections in the county. The people of Fobbings refused to answer before him, the judge attempted to punish for contumacy, the rabble came to the rescue, made the judge flee for his life, murdered the jurors and clerks of the commission, and mounted their heads on pikes. These insurgents were headed by a profligate priest, called Jack Straw. A third body of insurgents rose at Gravesend, caused by one Simon Burley, who laid claim to one of the burghers as his absconded slave, and sent him a prisoner to the castle of Rochester. a body of insurgents soon stormed the castle and liberated the captive. The slaves, the villeins, poor people, &c., of Norfolk, Suffolk, Essex, Sussex, and the other eastern counties, rallied at the cry of the men of Kent, to the amount of 60,000, and marched directly to London, and took possession of the town. The terms which they insisted on were abolition of bondage, the liberty of buying and selling in fairs and markets, reduction of all rents to an equal rate, and a general pardon. (Mac. 137.)

6. *Insurrection of the Jacquery in France* (1350)? In France the condition of the peasantry was worse than in England; but still they were infected, from similar causes, with the spirit of liberty. The passiveness and good nature of the peasants had become proverbial, hence the name applied to each one, *Jacques Bon Homme*, *James Good Soul*, from which comes name of *Jacquery*. They were beaten always into compliance when they resisted the exactions of the proprietors of the soil; and this became an object of pleasantry with the higher orders, who used to say, *Jacques Bon Homme* will not give his money unless you beat him, but *Jacques Bon Homme* shall pay up, for he shall be beaten. Hence we can understand the proverb of that epoch. *Oignez vilain il vous poindra, poignez vilain il vous oindra.* (S. H. F. 10, 488.)

The intercourse with the Italian cities, occasioned by the conquest of Naples, by Charles d'Anjou, produced, too, marked effects on the French—it diffused a spirit of liberty among them, particularly the cities; for we must remember that the little Italian republics were then enjoying all their glory and wealth, and it introduced a taste for luxury, which the wealth of the Italians had so long enabled them to enjoy. Whilst the first effect made the peasants more restive and rebellious; the second made the aristocracy more exacting and cruel, in order that they might provide for their increased demands. Hence relation between the proprietor and his villein was every day becoming more and more inharmonious.

Immediate causes of insurrection were the depredations committed by the companies of hired soldiery that infested France, and ruined the villages, and by the heavy exactions which the nobles were obliged to make on their tenants to pay their ransom in wars between Edward III. and France, particularly after the two great battles of Crecy and Poictiers.* Accordingly, we find this tremendous insurrection breaking out

* In France the cultivators of soil, for safety, were forced to live in villages, and go out to work every day, but this union in the village made robbery on a *large*

shortly after the battle of Poictiers, while King John was still a prisoner in England, and the nobles of France were every where inflicting the most cruel tortures on the tenants, to make them pay up money for the purpose of ransom. Wm. Caillet was the leader.

7. *Remarks on these insurrections?* They evidently are of mixed character, though partaking mostly of nature of servile insurrections. The horrors occasioned by both were similar to those of servile insurrections. In England the insurgents pillaged the manors of the lords, demolished the houses, burnt the court rolls, cut off the head of every justice, and lawyer, and juror, whom they caught, swore fealty to the king, but none to the nobles, and opposed all taxes except fifteenths, the old tallages of their ancestors. (Ling. 4, 146.) In France they were armed with pitchforks and clubs, and killed the gentry, burnt castles, and ravished women. In England they were dispersed without much fighting, by a solemn promise of the king, afterwards violated.* In France they were finally routed at Meaux, where the Captal de Buch, and Count de Foix, the two most distinguished knights of England and France, with 60 of their own followers and a few other attendants, sallied forth, and slew or caused to be drowned in the Marne, 7000 of the Jacquery in one day! The result as given in James' novel is historically true; the reason no doubt was the superior armor of the knights, and their greater courage, and superior skill in use of weapons. Like servile insurrections generally, each was of short duration, only for a few weeks; and each attended with the same complete failure—in France with most ruinous effects to the country, in England

scale much more easy. The king quartered his soldiers on them, the proprietors could more easily rob their granaries, and their cattle, and their pretty daughters, than if they had been dispersed through the country, particularly when we remember that the nobles would not permit these villages to be fortified. The lawless companies of soldiers, too, which were every where plundering during the captivity of King John, could get more plunder from these villages than from isolated peasants in the field. Just before the insurrection, this oppression became intolerable. At one time there were seen rushing into Paris, for protection, nearly all the peasants of the Isle of France, with wives, children and goods, and at the same time all the nuns of Poissy and Longchamp, all the monks of Melun and St. Antoine, and all the friars of St. Marcel. (S. H. F. 10. 489.)

* The king revoked his promise after the death of Wat Tyler and the execution of the leaders, in the following bitter and insulting language to the villeins of Essex county. "*Rustici quidem fuistis et estis, in bondagio permanebitis, non ut hactenus, sed incomparabiliter viliori, &c.* (H. 440.) And this revocation was sanctioned by lords and commons in parliament, who added, that such enfranchisement could not be made without their consent, "which they would never give to save themselves from perishing altogether in one day." And *riots* were henceforth made treason by same parliament.

with less injury, because sooner and more peaceably quelled. In England, after insurrection, Judge Tresillian hanged 1500, among whom were Jack Straw and the preacher John Ball. Many of them were hung in chains as a mark of ignominy. In France, when the higher orders were victorious, many villages were burnt up, and sometimes the inhabitants in the houses; *e. g.*, after the battle of Meaux, the town was burnt, and none of the inhabitants who had favored the insurgents were permitted to leave their houses. (S. 531.)

In both countries no great interest would acknowledge any connection with the insurgents. In France, although the king of Navarre and the Dauphin were at war with each other, and the Dauphin's party had suffered intensely by the insurrection, yet did the king of Navarre hang William Caillet, the leader of the insurgents, and several of his attendants, when they came into his camp to ask assistance. They were considered as outlaws, *Hostes humani generis*, whom it was allowable to put to death wherever caught. The spirit of chivalry, then at its height, was totally at war with both the order of society which furnished the insurgents, and their brutal and ruffian-like mode of carrying on wars.

8. *Six kings before the accession of Tudors?* Of the six reigns following Richard II., those of Henry IV., V., and VI., belong to the branch called the *house of Lancaster;* the three next, Edward IV., and V., and Richard III., belong to that other branch called the *house of York.*

9. *Title of the Lancastrians?* Preferable *at first* to that of the house of York, because the former was derived from duke of Lancaster, *third son* of Edward III., while the Yorkists derived their title through the duke of York, *fourth son* of Edward III. But there was another individual, with better title than either, the earl of March, drawing his title from the *second son* of Edward III. As he was only 7 years old, however, at deposition of Richard II., he was turned aside for a more efficient ruler. During civil wars of the *Roses*, the title of Yorkists became the best by intermarriage. The grandfather of Edward IV., Richard, earl of Cambridge, married Anne, sister of the earl of March, who was the true heir. When the earl died the sister was the heir, and of course her title descended to her grandson, Edward IV. (Mil. 2, 327.)

10. *Reign of Henry IV. extremely favorable to the growing power of the parliament?* For his title was bad, and consequently he had to rely on support of parliament, by whose authority he had been preferred to the earl of March. The instinct of self-preservation led him to strengthen the pillar on which his own authority rested. Richard, too,

whom he had deposed, was son of the Black Prince, who was a popular idol; and therefore, under the constant dread of a revulsion in the public feeling, he dared not attempt the same stretch of power, which a popular legitimate monarch might have exercised with impunity. Conscious of the embarrassment of the title by which they held the royal power, the princes of the house of Lancaster, says Mr. Hume, never ventured to impose taxes without the consent of parliament, and thus this valuable principle in the British constitution was firmly settled.

11. *Reign of Henry V.?* Cold and cautious address of Henry IV. could not conciliate the affections of the people. A prince of a different character was required for that purpose. Henry V., says Rapin, was exactly of the temper required by the English people at that time, to dispel the ill humors that had spread through the nation. Excessively gay, and even a little waggish, he possessed nevertheless a respectful deference for parliament and the constitution, and it seems he constantly forbore to encroach on the liberties of the people.* In his wars with France he pushed the national glory to the highest pitch. All hearts were gratified, the nation was proud of him, and he of the nation. Parliament always voted him liberal supplies; and after the splendid victory of Agincourt it voted him a revenue *for life*, more considerable than any that had been given by even the most obsequious parliament of Richard II.

12. *Reign of Henry VI.?* Henry V., after a short and brilliant reign of nine years, was succeeded by his son Henry VI., not quite nine months old. In the long reign of this prince, (39 years,) which Hume calls a perpetual minority, in consequence of his imbecility, the parliament, which had been respected by the apprehensive policy of Henry IV., and by the unsuspecting generosity of his son, enjoyed an ample opportunity of asserting its importance. We accordingly find this body, in beginning of reign of Henry VI., disregarding directions of the deceased monarch, taking on themselves a new arrangement of the government, and moderating with entire liberty the competition of the

* Henry IV. was jealous of his son, and allowed him no share in the government: this it is supposed drove him into low company, so that for some time nothing was talked of but the riotous and extravagant pranks of the prince and his companions. One of them was arraigned before Sir William Gascoign, the chief justice of king's bench, for felony. The prince tried to overawe the judge by his presence, but failing in this, he struck the judge in his face, who instantly ordered his arrest, and sent him to prison, to which the prince at once submitted. The low society into which he was thrown had perhaps its advantage when he came to the throne—it gave him sympathy for the lower order, by whom he was beloved both in England and France, and whom he protected against the oppression of the nobles.

two houses of York and Lancaster. In all these transactions, says Mr. Hume, impossible not to see a more settled authority of parliament than had appeared in any former period of English history. It was in the eighth of Henry VI., that the elective franchise was finally restricted to persons possessing a freehold of annual value of 40 shillings, supposed to have been equivalent to about £30 now.

13. *Wars of the Roses?* These wars were conducted with great cruelty on both sides. Margaret, actuated by a furious spirit, first began a system of extermination, by act of attainder and execution of prisoners, which enormities of course excited retaliation in the opposite party. When she led her northern army, after the battle of Wakefield, towards London, they were guilty of barbarities which had no little effect in turning the popular favor towards the house of York. With regard to the chief strength of the parties, that of the Lancastrians lay in the nobility and the higher orders, whilst that of the Yorkists was in the city of London and the neighboring counties, and among the middling and lower people. (H. M. A. 447.) The marriage of Edward IV. with Lady Elizabeth Gray, who was a mere *commoner*, contributed greatly to this kind feeling of the people, although it exasperated some of the nobles, particularly the powerful earl of Warwick. The attachment of the ladies of London to the king, Comines attributes to this marriage, and says they had no little agency in restoring him to the throne, when he had been driven from it for a few months. (Mil. 2, 342.)

14. *These wars weakened the nobility of England?* Because the nobles were the most gallant in waging them, and many were destroyed by the sword. Many lost their lives on the scaffold, and as Edward IV finally triumphed, and most of the nobility, particularly of the higher order, were on the other side, those who escaped the sword and scaffold in many instances lost their property. That reverence and authority, which antiquity of family alone can give, were thus in a measure lost to the nobles. When they lost their most renowned leaders, and their ranks were to be filled with a set of mere *novi homines*, not to wonder at their degraded condition under the Tudors.

15. *Parliamentary history during these wars, and under the Yorkists?* Have but little insight into the condition of parliament during these wars. No contemporary chroniclers of any value. The meagre rolls of parliament are all we have, being very little more than registers of private bills, or of petitions relating to commerce. Reign of Edward IV., says Mr. Hallam, is first during which no statute was passed for redress of grievances, or maintenance of subjects' liberty. In civil wars, when the two great parties separate, each is disposed to give almost unlimited power to its leader. Nothing but a powerful par-

liamentary opposition can check regal authority, and this you cannot have regularly in civil wars, where each party has its own parliament. The character of Edward, too, was well calculated to lead to popularity, although he was false, cruel and incontinent.* He was gay, affable, courageous, and the handsomest man in England; unfaithful to his wife, yet he honored her, her relations, and the order of society from which she came; but such a hold had he in spite of his irregularities on the affections of his people, that he was restored to the throne in spite of the defection of the powerful Warwick, and Henry VII. was compelled always to treat his memory with respect. His demands on his parliament in latter part of his reign were moderate. Fortescue says, that nearly one-fifth of the whole realm had come to his hands by forfeiture. Edward was first who raised money by *benevolences*, *e. g.*, by *forced loans* levied on wealthy traders. (H. 449.) The short remainder of the period of the house of York, comprehending little more than two years after the death of Edward, was but the crisis of transition to new dynasty of the Tudors. It was filled with the crimes and usurpations of Richard, duke of Gloucester, uncle of Edward V., who within a few months effected the destruction of the young prince and his brother, when he had already taken possession of the throne, under plea that the marriage of their father was void. (Mil. 2, 343.)

SEC. VI.—GOVERNMENT OF ENGLAND UNDER THE HOUSE OF TUDOR. 1485 TO 1600.

1. *Title of Henry VII. defective?* Henry, the earl of Richmond, who conquered Richard III. at Bosworth, and mounted the throne with title of Henry VII., belonged to the Lancastrian party, and was descended from John of Gaunt, by Catherine Swineford, and, therefore, even supposing the defects of illegitimacy removed, he was still not the nearest to the throne of John of Gaunt's descendants, for there were then in Spain descendants of both his first wife, Blanche of Lancaster,

* So much so, according to Rapin, that his whole life was a scene of lust. Had many mistresses—of three of whom he said, one was the merriest, the other the wittiest, and the third the holiest, for she was always in church when not sent for by him. Celebrated Jane Shore, was one of his mistresses. Born of respectable parents, and married to a wealthy man against her inclinations, although her mind was formed for virtue, it could not resist the allurements of the gay and amorous king. Her subsequent reverses, her doing penance in St. Paul's, and miserable death, are well known. Was seen by Sir Thomas More, so late as reign of Henry VIII., poor, decrepit, and shrivelled, with no trace of that splendid beauty that once excited envy and admiration of the court. She is said to have perished of hunger in a ditch, which gave a name to that quarter of London. (W. B. H. 92.)

and his second wife, Constantia of Castile, and there were in England two unfortunate claimants of the house of York, whose titles were both preferable upon the principle of indefeasible succession. This defect was remedied by marriage of Elizabeth, daughter of Edward IV., and a settlement of the crown upon Henry and the heirs of his body, by act of parliament, thus uniting the rival claims of York and Lancaster.

2. *Reign of the Tudors?* Marks a new era in the British government; regal power rose to its height under Henry VIII., and although it somewhat declined before the accession of the Stuarts, yet never was it exerted with more effect during any similar period, than from the accession of Henry VII. to that of James I.

3. *Character of Henry VII.?* The character of Henry well adapted to the *rôle* which he seemed destined to play. He was man of a mean spirit, yet combined with cool and cautious sagacity, and inflexible steadiness. He was brave and active, yet he preferred craft to force. He had infinitely more avarice than ambition. There was never generosity in his purposes, or tenderness in his rigid, unamiable nature. He had displayed affection to no one but his mother. He resembled, in many particulars, Louis XI. of France and Ferdinand of Spain, contemporary monarchs, who seem to have had a similar mission to accomplish in their respective countries. Bacon has aptly denominated these kings the three *Magi* among the princes of their age. Each labored to crush the nobility which had before rivalled the authority of the throne.

4. *Means used by Henry for the aggrandizement of the regal power?* As his title was defective, he was constantly harassed, during the first portion of his reign, by pretenders to the throne, and as the powerful faction of the Yorkists bore him no love, and were ready to rise under every pretext against his power, he was constrained to proceed in the most cautious, covert manner to achieve his purposes. He did often by indirection, that which under other circumstances might have been accomplished directly. Hence Bacon, who inordinately praises this king to James I., as realizing the *beau ideal* of *kingcraft*, has pronounced his laws "deep and not vulgar, not made upon the spur of a particular occasion, but out of providence for the future." To this reign is attributable the revival of the measure adopted under Richard III., called fine and recovery, by which *estates tail* could be alienated.* Whilst this weakened the nobility, by enabling them to squander their estates, the law against their retainers and liveries lessened their consequence. They were farther degraded by a sort of systematic exclu-

* This measure was first devised for a different purpose, but was subsequently used for this.

sion from the important offices of state, and the employment of lawyers and ecclesiastics wholly obsequious to the king's wishes.

Throughout his whole reign he was ever attentive to the accumulation of money. When he made war, it was to get money out of his parliament; when he made peace, it was to get it out of his enemies. During first part of his reign the frequent revolts of portions of his kingdom, furnished a rich harvest of confiscations; in the latter part, when firmly seated on the throne, his courts of justice, under the guidance of the infamous Empson and Dudley, became most intolerable engines of extortion to minister to the king's avarice. Besides these various means, he sold pardons, he sold the offices of his court, he even sold bishoprics, and he made his son Henry marry Catharine of Aragon, the widow of his elder brother Arthur, because he thought it the only means of retaining the rich dower that came by her. By such shameful means as these, and by rigid frugality in his expenses, Henry is said to have amassed in money before his death, £1,800,000, equal to £16, 000,000 of present money, a sum almost incredible.

This great accumulation of money contributed to his political power by rendering him independent of his parliaments. In the last 14 years he called but one, that of 1504. The history of England shows that there is no principle upon which both lords and commons make a stand for liberty with so much obstinacy as the *money principle.* By his exactions, it is true, that Henry had most grievously invaded that principle, but still it was in *detail*, against rich members of the aristocracy. The great mass of the people felt safe and prosperous, and as they were pressed for no general contributions, they heeded not the invasion of individual liberty. Moreover it was the constant policy of Henry to favor the commons against the aristocracy, to make the former the preponderating power in parliament.

5. *Henry VIII.?* Circumstances of his accession extremely favorable. First prince for more than a century with an undisputed title. He was 18 years old—a period of life naturally regarded with indulgence, with hope, and a warm fellow-feeling in its joys. His accession was welcomed by his people, who thought they saw in him perfect contrast to the unamiable character of his father. He was handsome, lively, accomplished and learned. His savage temper had not yet displayed itself, and he inherited none of the avaricious spirit of his father.*

* Following is the flattering description of this prince by a Venetian ambassador, 10 years after his accession. "His majesty is about 29 years of age; as handsome as nature could form him—handsomer by far than the king of France, (Francis I.) He is an excellent musician and composer, an admirable horseman and wrestler, and possesses a good knowledge of French, Latin, and Spanish. Goes three times to

6. *Cruelty and tyranny of his reign?* Had Henry died even as late as twentieth of his reign, his name might have come down to us with all but the praise at least generally bestowed on gayety and enterprise. But the execution of More marks the moment of transition from joviality and parade to a species of capricious actrocity, unparalleled in English history. This singular revolution in his character has been ascribed to the fall of Wolsey, who, with many vices himself, could yet govern the strong passions of his master better than any other minister. In his dying words he predicted his unmanageable character whenever "a sharp enough spur" should strike his passions. Henry is only prince of modern times who carried judicial murder into his bed, and imbrued his hands in the blood of those he had caressed. Perhaps no other monarch since the emancipation of woman from polygamy, says McIntosh, has put to death two wives* on the scaffold, divorced another whom he owned to be faultless after 24 years of wedded friendship, and rejected a fourth, without imputing blame to her, from the first impulse of personal disgust. (238.) His parliaments, too, were servile, to a degree truly disgusting. They permitted him to extort money from his subjects by odious system of benevolences, (forced loans,) and then they gave them to the king and cancelled the bonds. (C. H. 30.) They gave him all moneys that had been deposited in trust, or lent on the national faith, and released him from obligation to pay. In the parliament of 1544, they not only released him from payment of all sums borrowed since 1542, but added the disgraceful provision, that if he had already paid any of them, the party or his heirs should repay his majesty! His parliaments became, too, base and willing instruments for the execution of his most odious and revolting cruelties. All his caprices were obeyed; *e. g.*, succession to the crown was altered at his bidding, first to take it from Mary and give it to Elizabeth, then from Elizabeth to any issue by Jane Seymour, and

mass on hunting days, and five times every other. He is uncommonly fond of the chase, and never engages in it without tiring 8 or 10 horses. He takes great delight in bowling, and it is the pleasantest sight in the world to see him engaged in this sport, with his fair skin covered with a beautifully fine shirt." (Mac. 206.)

* Execution of Anne Boleyn was particularly revolting. She was inhumanly brought to trial after he had spilt the purest blood in England to maintain her honor; after she had produced one child that could lisp his name with tenderness, and when she was just recovering from the languor and paleness of the unrequited pangs of a more sorrowful and fruitless childbirth, a circumstance so well calculated to melt the human heart, but which only steeled his against pity, whilst it deepened his aversion. By the execution of More and Anne, says McIntosh, he bade defiance to compassion, affection and veneration, and approached as nearly to the ideal standard of perfect wickedness as the infirmities of human nature will allow.

lastly he was left to settle it by will. Treasons were multiplied, often of most ridiculous character. It was first treason to *doubt*, and then treason to *maintain*, the validity of his marriage with Anne Boleyn, or the legitimacy of his daughter by her. It was treason for an unchaste woman to marry a king without telling him of her conduct. It was treason to call him a heretic, or even a schismatic.

He was permitted to lay violent hands on the monasteries, and to seize their rich revenues. He set up a creed of his own device in religion, by which he transferred to himself the supremacy hitherto claimed by the pope over the church of England, at the same time that he refused to sanction the reformation; and after setting up this arbitrary standard, brought to the stake all *non-conformists*, both catholics and protestants. We have all read how three persons, convicted of disputing his supremacy, and three deniers of transubstantiation, were drawn on the same hurdle to execution. Lastly, the parliaments filled the measure of their servility by giving to the proclamations of the king all the force of laws. Speakers in parliament fed his vanity by the most fulsome praise; *e. g.*, Cromwell was unable, he believed all men unable, to describe unutterable qualities of the royal mind, the sublime virtues of the royal heart. Rich told him that in wisdom he was equal to Solomon, in strength and courage to Samson, in beauty and address to Absalom; and Audeley declared before his face, that God had anointed him with oil of wisdom above all his prdecessors and all the kings of earth, and had given him that *perfect* knowledge of scripture, by which he had prostrated the Roman Goliath; that *perfect* knowledge of war by which he had gained most brilliant victories; and that *perfect* knowledge of government by which he had secured, for thirty years, his realm in peace and prosperity. (L. 6, 280.) During these harangues, as often as the words "*most sacred majesty*" were repeated, the lords rose, and whole assembly bowed most reverently towards the demi-god on the throne. Henry, the most fallible of men, seems to have become a believer in his own infallibility, and treated as treason every opposition to his most capricious will.

3. *Henry's power not due to circumstances on which absolute princes generally rely?* Military force is the rude instrument by which despotism usually gains its ends; not so under the Tudors. Except the yeomen of the guards, fifty in number, and the servants of the king's household, there was not in time of peace an armed man, on pay, throughout the kingdom. So small was the military force of the Tudors, that the most insignificant insurrections were difficult to suppress; *e. g.*, a rabble of Cornish men, in reign of Henry VII., headed by a blacksmith, marched from Cornwall to suburbs of London without

resistance. The insurrections of 1525, after Wolsey's illegal taxes, those of ten years later date, and those under Edward VI., all gave most serious alarm. (C. H. 63.)

4. *Circumstances favorable to Henry—first, condition and character of the nobility?* Reproach of servility falls not on the English people, but on their natural leaders, the nobles. The house of commons now and then gave signs of independent spirit; the house of lords was always compliant. This was owing to the weak condition in which the wars of the Roses and the subsequent policy of Henry VII., had left the nobility. Their numbers were thinned, their wealth had been confiscated amid the triumphs of contending factions, their spirit was broken, the charm of antiquity was disolved. During the reign of the Tudors, England made rapid advances in commerce and manufactures; habits of luxury were introduced, which dissipated the immense fortunes of the ancient barons. A new and independent class, too, of merchants and manufacturers, living on the fruits of their own industry, was thus introduced into society. A nobleman, instead of that unlimited ascendant which he assumed over those maintained at his board, retained only the moderate influence of a customer over tradesmen. Landed proprietors, too, having a greater demand for money than men, dismissed from their lands those useless hands which were formerly always at their call, and in every stand which was made against the government. By these means the nobles were falling, the commons were rising; a new plan of liberty was commencing. Yet, in interval between fall of the nobles and the rise of the commons, sovereign took advantage of his position, and exercised almost unlimited power. It is true that Henry VIII. enriched his nobles by his profuse grants, particularly after the suppression of the monasteries; but wealth thus acquired was unfavorable to liberty; it produced too much dependence on the power that gave, too much fawning on the hand that fed; it made them favor royal spoliations, that they might fatten on the royal grants. Parliaments then ceased to oppose, because the nobility ceased to lead. The house of commons had hitherto fought its battles against the crown under the lead and stimulus of the house of lords. That stimulus was now withdrawn, the balance of the constitution was destroyed, and the power of parliament was for a season paralyzed.

5. *Second, influence of the Star Chamber?* The energy given to that most oppressive judicial tribunal, the *Star Chamber*, under the Tudors, may be mentioned as one principal cause of their great power. This court consisted of the king, his privy council, some of the judges, and such other persons as the king chose to nominate, and was intended for such criminal actions as were beyond the ordinary tribunals, supply-

ing the deficiency of the common rules of *penal* law, like the chancery in relation to *civil* rights. (M. E. G. 2, 114, 419.) Its name derived from the hall in which it sat." Although this tribunal had sometimes been favorable to justice, yet we can easily see how it could not fail ultimately to become an engine of oppression. As its powers related to matters about which no rule had been established, they necessarily became discretionary and fluctuating. As the officers of this court, too, were the dependents and servants of the crown, removable at pleasure, they naturally became obsequious to his will. They had not, it is true, the power of life and death, but then they could sentence to the pillory, to the prison, to corporal punishment, and above all, they could impose heavy fines, which unfortunately it was their interest to do, because the more they poured into the royal lap, the more they could receive from the royal bounty. This irregular tribunal became, under the Tudors and the Stuarts, a sort of excrescence, whose polluted and cancerous fibres contaminated the whole constitution. When the king exacted benevolences, it was here he punished the refractory. When he wanted to enforce royal proclamations, or to punish those who opposed his measures or sounded the alarm to the people, it was before this tribunal the offender was dragged. It overawed and intimidated the regular courts of justice. The judge who gave an opinion obnoxious to the crown, or the juror who supported an uncomplying verdict, might be summoned before this body, and have his ears nailed to the pillory, and a heavy fine inflicted. Members of parliament themselves were not free from its terrors. This court was finally abolished by long parliament under Charles I., and for this at least it merited the gratitude of posterity. For instances of its oppression, see Ancient History, p. 184.

6. *Third, Henry's policy towards the reformation favorable to his power?* In Henry's reign the protestants were no doubt the weaker party, but they were rapidly increasing, and destined soon to become the majority. There was at first a remarkable apathy among the people of England in regard to religion, and the honors and emoluments of church officers were more cared for than the interests of religion.* Under these circumstances both parties were anxious to secure the king. His weight was sufficient to give the victory to either side. At first he was

* In 1559, when Elizabeth placed the church on the protestant basis, out of 9,400 *beneficed* clergymen, only 15 bishops, 12 archdeacons, 15 heads of colleges, 50 canons, and 80 parochial priests quitted their preferments, rather than change their religion. (W. B. H. 143.) The fiery zeal which characterized the reformation on the continent did not appear among the people of England until the time of the Stuarts, when the Puritans had become so numerous as to wage open war with both catholics and episcopalians.

devout catholic, and had even entered the lists as a disputant against Luther. But pope opposed the divorce of Queen Catharine, and marriage of Anne Boleyn, hence his denial of pope's supremacy. This gave hopes to the reformers, and made them support his government, for they believed his defection would soon be complete. They regarded him as an avenging minister of heaven, by whose giant arm the chain of superstition was sundered:

> "The majestic lord,
> Who broke the bonds of Rome."

The catholics, on the other hand, hoped yet to reclaim him. They feared that resistance would drive him into arms of the reformers. Thus both parties courted him, both humored his caprices, and submitted to his will, and the struggle between the two made him absolute

7. *Fourth, taxes not burthensome under Henry?* Another cause of the power of Henry VIII. was, that he was placed in condition to administer the government without laying heavy general taxes. The vast hoard he inherited from his father, the exactions of the star chamber, forced loans, but above all the spoliations of the monasteries, threw into his hands such large resources as enabled him almost to dispense with regular taxation. The total number of religious houses is stated at 1041, and it is supposed they owned a fifth of the land of England. The revenue suddenly thrown into the king's hands by their suppression was enormous, and might have made the crown for ever independent of the parliament, if Henry VIII. had managed with the strict economy and deep policy which his father, under such circumstances, would have used. But it has been fortunate for the liberties of England, that Henry chose rather to slaughter the prey than to gorge himself with the carcass. He squandered this immense property on his pleasures and his minions; and we are to look to this as the means by which some of the old nobles were enriched, and many of the new ones endowed. A great many of the noble families of England at this day can trace their origin only as far as to this period.

8. *Fifth, people not oppressed under this monarch?* The reign of Henry VIII., although tyrannical, was not unfavorable to the great mass of the commonalty. It was only the high heads that were struck at; the taxes were light, the government energetic, and the people prosperous, and consequently contented; and this, together with the peculiar religious condition of the kingdom, may explain the fact that Henry was not regarded with that detestation which some of his acts deserved. The chroniclers of the times often speak of him with kindness, even after his death.

9. *Remote effects of this reign favorable to liberty?* Strange as it may seem, the very servility of Henry's parliaments proved in the end favorable to British freedom. Because the parliaments were servile, Henry employed them as convenient instruments to execute his will, and these formed precedents in favor of parliamentary powers in after times, when a different spirit had entered into the body ; *e. g.*, if during Henry's reign they could attaint queens and ministers, regulate the church, settle the succession to the crown *according* to the wishes of the monarch, in another reign they could lay claim to these or similar powers *against* the monarch's wishes.

Again, the constitution of England could never have been what it is without many of those changes in property and religion brought about by Henry VIII.; *e. g.*, without the subserviency of parliament the monasteries could not have been suppressed; without the suppression of the monasteries the protestant religion could not have been *legally* established in England. For the mitred abbots and priors, entitled to a seat in the house of peers, joined to the twenty-one spiritual lords in that body, formed a decided majority, and therefore could have stopped any reform unfavorable to their interests. But with the suppression of monasteries the abbots and priors lost their seats in the house of lords, and thus gave the preponderance to the temporal peers.

10. *Parliament under Edward VI. and Mary?* Children of Henry VIII. did not preserve his absolute dominion over parliament. Several instances under Edward, and still more under Mary, where commons rejected bills sent down from house of lords, and, although the majority of peers were always with the throne, yet the minority was respectable and growing. A symptom of the increasing importance of the commons was exhibited in the great efforts made to influence the elections.

11. *Marian persecution and circumstances which secured the acquiescence of the nation?* The persecution of the protestants by Queen Mary forms perhaps the most disgraceful feature in English history. It appears almost unaccountable that a nation which had so recently acquiesced in the establishment of reformed religion, under Edward, should be willing to acknowledge Mary, and even acquiesce in her bigoted persecutions, which brought some of the noblest men of England to the stake. A great deal of this ascribable to the fact that Edward, in his anxiety for protestantism, had named Lady Jane Gray, grand-daughter of Henry's sister, as his successor. Lady Gray had married Gilbert Dudley, son of Duke of Northumberland—offensive to nobles by his pride, and to the people by his cruelty. The general hatred borne to this man drove even the protestants to the support of Mary,

who had made promise to people of Sussex that there should be no change in religion. But, after all, this acquiescence of the nation in persecution must be ascribed in great measure to the indifference and indecision of great mass of English people on religious subjects. Mary, with all her bigotry, never dared, although anxious to do so, to take back her father's grants of church property. The restoration of abbey lands, or the attempt to place England under the control of Philip of Spain, were always firmly met and defeated.

12. *Ultimate effect of this persecution favorable to the protestant cause?* Because it gave the English a perfect horror of the catholic religion, and made an impression on the nation which is visible even to the present times. It was the recollection of this gloomy reign that made the nation rally around Queen Elizabeth and the protestant cause; it was this which inspired the hatred against Spain, and brought out the fleet that conquered the *Invincible Armada;* it was this that brought Mary, queen of Scots, to the block;* it was this which had no little agency in driving James II. from his throne, and which ultimately brought in the Hanoverian dynasty. Dreadful, however, as was the Marian persecution, it is not the worst which has been witnessed in modern Europe. It is computed by Burnet, that during four years of Mary's reign 284 persons were burned at the stake for their religion: a number inconsiderable when compared with the executions in the Netherlands and Spain. In the former, Grotius computes that, from edict of Charles V. to 1588, 100,000 persons had been hanged, beheaded, burned, and buried alive on account of religion. Torquemada, first inquisitor general in Spain, in eighteenth year of his administration, committed to flames more than 10,000 persons. To these must be added more than 90,000 condemned to secondary punishments, infamy, confiscation, perpetual imprisonment, &c. (W. B. H. 133–6.)

13. *Elizabeth?* This great queen, whose reign is one of the longest and most illustrious in British history, seems to have possessed a character in some measure compounded of those of her parents and grandfather. She had a great deal of the hot, fiery, arbitrary temper of her father,† united with the calculating caution and rigid frugality and economy of Henry VII. With this masculine character she united all

* All the great ministers of Queen Elizabeth were anxious for Mary's death; each one trembled for his life if another catholic should mount the throne.

† Her language at all times was sprinkled with oaths, and when enraged, with imprecations and abuses. Nor did she content herself with words alone; she frequently laid hands on those about her; *e. g.*, she collared Hatton, gave a blow on the ear to the earl marshal, and she spat on Sir Matthew ———, with the foppery of whose dress she was offended. (L. 8, 296.)

the womanly traits of her mother, was vain, coquettish, and exceedingly solicitous about her personal charms. Schooled by adversity, and stored with that learning which had been her resource and consolation during the gloomy reign of her sister, Queen Elizabeth preserved, almost without interruption, the domestic tranquillity of her kingdom for nearly half a century, whilst neighboring nations were torn by religious dissension. Almost single handed she maintained the protestant interest against Spain, Austria, and France, and first developed those naval energies of England which have given to that nation empire of the ocean, and which enabled it to uphold the political balance of the world, and to save Europe from that universal dominion, so fearfully threatened by perhaps the greatest military chieftain which the world has ever produced. Her situation was one of extreme difficulty, and ably did she conduct herself in it. She was, it is true, selfish, arrogant, and arbitrary. The fiery temper of her father but too often manifested itself in the daughter, and led to many an execution which stains the character of this reign. But still it is one of the most popular in English annals. Elizabeth knew full well the temper of the British people. She always conciliated public opinion and courted the approbation of her subjects. She was excessively economical, because she knew the reluctance of parliament to grant supplies. She knew when to press the royal prerogative, and when to recede; and it must be said, to the honor of this queen, that no monarch ever retracted with the same grace that Elizabeth did, *e. g.*, in case of the monopolies, which had thrown the house of commons into a violent agitation, perceiving her error, she acknowledged it without hesitation, retracted with such inimitable tact and grace as to make all England ring with her praises. It was by such acts as these she won the confidence and loyalty of her subjects.

14. *Hume's estimate of this reign erroneous?* In his anxiety to palliate the arbitrary conduct of the Stuarts, Hume has gone so far as to compare the government of Elizabeth to the despotism of Turkey. There is no question that she was arbitrary; the court of star chamber, the high commission court and martial* law were all used during her

* The high commission court was in ecclesiastical matters precisely what the star chamber was in criminal; it was a sort of supplemental court, established during religious dissensions, to supply the defects of common law on those subjects, and like the star chamber, it was liable to the grossest abuses. With regard to *martial law*, that is peculiar to no age or country; it has always, in all countries, been proclaimed in times of extraordinary alarm and danger, when more summary remedies are required than those furnished by ordinary civil processes. This, too, is extremely liable to abuse, and there is no question but that Elizabeth often proclaimed this law when there was no necessity for it.

reign for oppression. But yet the government was far from being a despotism. The queen's authority rested greatly on public opinion; her reign was popular. The Tudors committed very tyrannical acts; but in ordinary dealings with the people they could not safely be tyrants. The high heads about the royal persons were exposed to fearful dangers. Buckingham, Cromwell, Surrey, Sudley, Somerset, Suffolk, Norfolk, Percy, Essex, all perished on the scaffold. But, in general, the country gentleman hunted and the merchant traded in peace. The nation was really proud of the high and fiery blood of the Tudors, and indulged them in many excesses; but there was a limit to this. Without military force, they could not dispense with popular support. The Tudors found it as dangerous to oppress their subjects by grievous taxation, as Nero would to have left his prætorians unpaid. Even the proud and obstinate Henry VIII., in attempting to raise a forced loan of unusual amount, was encountered by such firm opposition as forced him to desist. We have already seen how Mary was successfully resisted in her wishes to revoke the grants of the church lands, how Elizabeth had to give up the monopolies, &c. The reign of Elizabeth was essentially popular. She, it is true, raised ship money, and demanded loans, and in this respect Hume considers as tyrannical as Charles I.; but then how different were the circumstances! *e. g.*, when England was threatened with invasion from Spain, Elizabeth asked the city of London to furnish her with fifteen ships and five thousand troops, and what was the reply of the mayor on behalf of the town? Why, they begged that her majesty would allow them to furnish "in sign of their perfect love and loyalty," thirty ships and ten thousand troops. Besides which they loaned her a large amount of money. Nothing like this occurs during the reign of the Stuarts.

15. *Cabinet ministers of Elizabeth—of a new order?* Before time of Elizabeth, ministers of the king were generally warriors or priests: warriors, whose rude courage was neither guided by science, nor softened by humanity: priests, whose learning and abilities were devoted to tyranny and imposture. The Hotspurs, the Nevilles, the Cliffords, rough, illiterate and unreflecting, brought to the council board the fierce imperious temper acquired amid the tumults of war, or in the gloomy repose of the moated castle. On the other side was the calm and subtle prelate, trained in the school to manage words, and in the confessional to manage hearts. Seldom superstitious, but practising on the superstition of others. Selfish, as men naturally become who can form no domestic ties. More attached to his order than his country, and governing with a constant side glance at Rome. In the time of Elizabeth, increase of wealth, progress of knowledge and reformation

of religion, produced a great change. Nobles ceased to be military chieftains, priests ceased to possess a monopoly of learning, and a new order of statesmen arose, corresponding to the new order of society. Queen Elizabeth's ministers were all *laymen*, yet they were men of learning and men of peace. They were not members of the aristocracy, yet they were not low men, such as those whom kings, jealous of their nobility, sometimes raise from forges and cobblers' stalls to the highest stations. They were all *gentlemen* by birth, had all received liberal education, and what is very remarkable, were all educated at same university (Cambridge).* These men were great without being brilliant. They observed closely the signs of the times, and had great practical acquaintance with human nature. They were more remarkable for vigilance and moderation, than for invention and enterprise. They had the more influence over their sovereign, because they knew how to yield when they saw her determined. They dexterously directed the politics of England during the eventful period of her reign, at less cost perhaps than had ever occurred in accomplishment of such results. They humbled the pride of Philip, backed the unconquerable spirit of Coligni, rescued Holland from tyranny, laid the foundation of maritime greatness of England; outwitted the crafty politicians of Italy, and tamed the fierce chieftains of Scotland. These men all possessed of minds well balanced, and passions well regulated; were hurried into no excesses or imprudence; none of them had any taste for martyrdom. Nothing could shake them in the queen's confidence. Their power ended only with their lives. Burleigh was minister 40 years; Sir Nicholas Bacon held the great seal more than 20; Sir Thomas Smith was secretary of state 18 years; Sir Francis Walsingham about as long, and at their death they all enjoyed both the public respect and royal favor. (Mac. 2, 294.) Far different had been the fate of such ministers as Wolsey, Cromwell, Norfolk, Somerset, and Northumberland, and far different, too, was the fate of Essex, Raleigh, and Lord Bacon.

SEC. VII.—FROM ACCESSION OF JAMES I. TO DISSOLUTION OF THE THIRD PARLIAMENT OF CHARLES I.

1. *Increasing wealth of England favorable to the power of house of commons?* Period included between the accession of the house of Tudor and that of the Stuarts is one of great prosperity in England. Manufactures and commerce flourished to a degree before unknown. The discovery of passage to India by Cape of Good Hope, the disco-

* Cambridge, says Macaulay, had the honor of educating those protestant bishops whom Oxford had the honor of burning. Cambridge formed principally the minds of those statesmen who established the protestant religion in north of Europe. (2, 292.)

very of America, and the influx of the precious metals had given a wonderful impulse to the energy and enterprise of the world, particularly to England. Formerly the nations around the Mediterranean and the Baltic were most favorable to commerce; but as soon as the discoveries just mentioned, aided by the use of the mariner's compass, threw the main commerce of Europe on the Atlantic ocean, England, a great island standing in front of Europe, with a fine soil, fine bays and rivers, and one of the most enterprising populations in the world, was naturally among the foremost in carrying on this great commerce which had newly arisen. The reign of the Tudors was upon the whole pacific, and favorable to the rapid accumulation of wealth. The rapid growth of London is an unerring symptom of this fact. It increased so fast as to be considered a public calamity. In 1580, a proclamation was issued, forbidding erection of houses in three miles of London, under penalty of imprisonment, and forfeiture of materials, and this prohibition is often repeated, on account of the too great increase of the city.

When the power of the aristocracy was first overthrown, we have seen that the commons had not power and spirit sufficient to act alone against the crown, but this rapid increase of wealth was fast infusing an irresistible energy into the commons. They were far more formidable, for example, during the latter than the first portion of the reign of Queen Elizabeth. When the third parliament under Charles I. met, in 1628, house of commons is said by some historians to have been thrice as rich as house of lords. (G. 1, 10.) With every increase of wealth among the middle classes, their power and respectability were augmented; and the house of commons, the exponent of this order, became more formidable to the crown.

2. *James I.?* James I. mounted the throne with many advantages. His title was unquestionable; he united the kingdoms of Scotland and England, and thus terminated the long and disastrous struggle between those countries. Although his mother was a catholic, he was brought up a protestant, and hence no violent change was feared in the religious establishment.

3. *Character of James calculated to hasten revolution?* In his person he was extremely awkward and unprepossessing: of middle stature, a little corpulent, slovenly in his clothes, which he wore until ragged, dirty in his habits.* His beard was thin, his tongue too big for his mouth,† which made him roll it out often, and slabber. His

* "His skin vas als softe as tafta sarsnet, wich felt so becausse he neur washt his hands, only rubb'd his fingers' ends slightly vith the vet end of napkin. (Balf.)

† Balfour says his thick tongue made him "drinke wery vncomelie, as if eating his drinke, wich cam out into the cupe in each syde of his mouthe."

eyes were large, and constantly rolling about, sometimes staring one out of countenance. His legs were weak, which gave him a rickety walk, and a propensity to lean on others' shoulders. He had nervous tremblings, was timid and suspicious.* Wore a doublet, quilted *stiletto proof*, and breeches in great plaits immoderately stuffed. He had broad Scotch accent. Much of his time was spent in hunting, playing at golf, carousing at table, laughing at his own conceits, and the buffoonery of his courtiers. Was excessively fond of the cock-pit. His master of the cocks had a salary of £200 per annum, equal to the salaries of the secretaries. (W. B. H. 167—172.)

James was a learned man for the age,† and would have made a good schoolmaster or college tutor. He wrote several books: one on the law of free monarchies, in answer to Cardinal Perron; another on demonology, in which he had the good fortune to discover "why the devil did worke more with ancient women than others." There was nothing on which he more prided himself than his knowledge of *witchcraft and kingcraft.* Henry VII. was his model of a prince, and hence the labored eulogy of Bacon on this monarch. James was of the blood of the Guises; thus, by family connections and habits of his country, was attached to France, and the maxims of absolute monarchy which prevailed in that country. In *theory* he was the greatest despot on earth, in *practice* he was timid and inefficient. Henry IV., of France, called him "captain of arts and clerk of arms;" in England he was, in derision, sometimes called *Queen James* while his predecessor was called *King Elizabeth.* His vanity, therefore, and his ridiculous pretensions only excited contempt or resistance. James was proud of his tyranny, and is one of the very few who attempted to make the world believe he was more of a tyrant than he really was.‡ He claimed to reign by

* He was angry with almost every one that approached him; hence a person once hung a remonstrance around the neck of one of the king's hounds, with this petition; "Dear Cæsar, we beg you to speak with the king on our affair, for he hears you every day, but us never!" (Reau. 1, 458.)

† Hume observes of James I., that "the speaker of the house of commons is usually an eminent man, yet the harangue of his majesty will always be found much superior to that of the speaker, in every parliament during this reign." It must be confessed, however, that his rhetorical flourishes were generally in bad taste before so grave a body; *e. g.*, in his parliament of 1620, he told the house he had "often piped to them, and they had not danced, often wept, but they had not mourned;" but that he entertained better hopes for the future.

‡ Elizabeth always spoke of the affection and loyal sentiments of her subjects; James was always talking about *fear, submission, obedience.* He had a perfect *passion* for making the world think that his subjects were afraid of him, and never was passion less gratified. Beaumont, the French ambassador, in a letter to his court

jure divino right. In a speech made in star chamber, in 1616, said, "It is atheism and blasphemy to dispute what God can do: Good Christians content themselves with his will revealed in his word; so it is presumptuous, and high contempt in a subject to dispute what a king can do, or say that a king cannot do this or that." (C. H. 1, 452.) This ridiculous parallel just equals his blasphemous presumption in dedicating a work to Jesus Christ! Well might the sagacious Sully pronounce him "the *wisest fool* in Europe." Macaulay (2, 61) says, James was one of those kings whom God seems to send for the express purpose of hastening revolutions. He was like the man in a Spanish bull-fight, who goads the animal to fury by shaking a red rag in the air, and now and then throwing a dart, just sharp enough to sting, without serious injury. James was constantly provoking the ill-will or resentment of his subjects or his parliaments. The people were proud of martial glory—he was eternally preaching about the blessings of the peacemaker. The people abhorred court of Spain—he sought the infanta as wife for his son. They asked indulgence for scrupulous conscience—he could tolerate no deviation from uniformity.* They writhed under the yoke of the bishops—he regarded them as the main support of the throne. The people admired the frugality of Elizabeth—he squandered the public treasure on the most profligate favorites. The puritanical tendency of the age demanded at least exterior decency

says, "What must be the situation of a state and of a prince, whom the clergy publicly abuse in the pulpit, whom the actors represent on the stage, whose wife goes to these representations in order to laugh at him, who is defied and despised by his parliament, and universally hated by his people. When he thinks to speak like a king, he proceeds like a tyrant, and when he condescends he becomes vulgar." "I believe that the breaking of a bottle of wine, or any such trifle, affects him more than the ruin of his son-in-law, or the misery of his grand-children." (Reau. 1, 458.)

* On his way to London, to take possession of the throne, the malcontent clergy presented the *Millenary Petition*, which contained, says Hallam, no demand inconsistent with the established hierarchy, or which might not have been granted without inconvenience. The king determined to gratify his vanity by holding a conference with them, at Hampton court. At this meeting he was himself a principal disputant against the puritans; and if, in the exercise of his wit against their champion, Reynolds, he showed himself a very shrewd disputant, as D'Israeli supposes, he certainly manifested but little wisdom as a monarch. He who occupies the judgment seat, forgets the dignity of his office when he descends to the ridicule of one of the parties concerned, and little does he know of human nature, if he expects to correct error by such means. The non-conforming clergy were more discontented than ever, and James not only ordered the bishops to proceed against all non-conformists, but committed ten of the millenary petitioners to prison, after consultation with the star chamber. Such was the beginning of the reign of the "British Solomon," whom D'Israeli has labored to prove a wise man. (Mis. of Lit. v. 3.)

of morals—the king's court was a scene of dissoluteness and extravagance the most disgraceful. There was as much laxity of female virtue as during the reign of Charles II. Young females, driven to necessity by the fashionable ostentation of their parents, were brought to the metropolis as to a market, where they obtained pensions or marriages by their beauty. When Gondomar, the Spanish ambassador, passed to his house, the ladies were at their balconies on the watch to make themselves known to him; and it appears that every one had sold her favors at a dear rate. In Sir Dudley Carlton's (a grave statesman) narration of the adventures of a bridal night, and all the petty sorceries, the romping of the great ladies, who were made shorter by the skirts, we discover the grossest manners and the coarsest taste; but when we find the king going to the bed of the bride in his night gown, to give a *reveille-matin*, and remaining a good time in or upon the bed, we must admit the bride was not more decent than the ladies who publicly solicited the personal notice of Gondomar.

This coarseness of manners of course polluted the language of conversation. Most of the dramatic works of the day are too obscene to be read now, and the domestic language and domestic familiarity of kings, queens, lords and ladies were incredibly gross. The obscene and silly correspondence of James with Buckingham well illustrates this grossness.* Drunkenness was so general as to be imputed to many ladies of the court. In addition to all this, it is remarkable, says D'Israeli, that never was so much blood shed in broils, nor duels so tremendously barbarous fought, as in the pacific reign of James I. (Mis. Lit. 3, 415.)

4. *Charles I.?* This prince had much to recommend him, both in person and mind. Of a comely presence, of a sweet but melancholy aspect; his face was handsome; he was of middle stature, strong, healthy and well-proportioned,† capable of enduring great fatigue, and well skilled in horsemanship and other exercises. (H. 4, 43.) He was reserved, distant, and stately; cold in his address, plain in his discourse.

* In accordance with this vulgarity of language were the curious epithets and nicknames applied by the monarch to even the highest personages in the kingdom; *e. g.*, in an edict on duels, he calls the queen our *dearest bed-fellow*. In his letters, he calls Buckingham *dog Steine;* and Buckingham subscribes himself *your slave* and *dog*, and calls the king *dere dad* and *gossope*. Even the queen, writing to Buckingham to intercede for Raleigh, addresses him, *my kind dog*. The king's nickname for the grave Cecil was *my little beagle*. (J, 2, 412.)

† In his infancy Charles was rather feeble and delicate, and the story has been told that while King James was at Hinchinbrook, on a visit to Sir Oliver Cromwell, Prince Charles and young Oliver, being of the same age, met, played and fought, and that "the shambling and tottering king's son received what ought to have satisfied him for life—*a bloody nose*." The curtain of the future, says Foster, was surely for an instant upraised here.

He was diligent, learned and frugal; maintained the domestic relations with exemplary propriety, and seemed to possess a deep sense of religion. His character formed a most agreeable contrast to that of his father. Sickened of the meanness, the talkative and familiar pedantry, the inert and pusillanimous politics of James I., England looked forward to happiness and liberty under a king whom she could respect. But there were two points in the character of Charles, fatal to him in the actual crisis in which he was placed: he misunderstood the true nature of the kingly office in Great Britain, and he was insincere. Nurtured by his father in the maxims of absolute despotism, at an early age he had visited the court of Spain, where he had been received with great honor. There he saw monarchy in all its splendor, majesty supreme, exacting from attendants a devotedness almost religious. He was afterwards married to Henrietta Maria, daughter of Henry IV. of France; for his vain father had determined that no alliance worthy of the dignity of his throne could be found beyond these two courts. The impression made on the mind of Charles by this union was similar to that he had received in Spain; and the monarchies of Madrid and Paris were eternally floating before his imagination, as true models of the natural and legitimate condition of kings, and, like his father, he always believed that a king of England could not be of lower degree than his equals. Hence, in his struggles with parliament, he looked on them as audacious brigands, who sought to rob him of the birthright of kings. This opinion clung to him throughout, even in his trial, and on the scaffold; he was conscientious, but wofully mistaken; and his example is an awful lesson to royalty to watch the growth of public opinion, and to moderate in time the pretensions of the crown to the standard of the reasonable desires of the subjects. The duplicity and insincerity of Charles were in some measure the result of this misconception about the kingly prerogative. He seems to have considered promises made to his parliaments in the same light in which we regard those extorted by robbers, as not binding on the conscience. He thus lost the confidence of his subjects, who could never believe their liberties secure until they had deprived the king of all power to do harm.

5. *Importance of his reign?* It offers the finest speculations in human nature; it opens a protracted scene of glory and infamy; all that elevates and all that humiliates our kind are seen wrestling together. The French revolution, although in many respects different from the English, may still be regarded as a commentary on it; a commentary, however, at times more important than the text which it elucidates.

6. *Spirit of liberty made rapid advances under James I.?* The pacific reign of James I. contributed rapidly to the progress of England

in the accumulation of wealth in the hands of the middle classes; and, with this rapid augmentation of wealth, the house of commons, the exponent of the middle classes, was becoming more important, and the whole reign of James did little more than train them to conflicts with their sovereign. His pedantry and vanity were constantly challenging them to discussions upon the fundamental principles of monarchy, the most dangerous of all discussions to princes, and his want of resolution and firmness gave them so frequently the victory, that we may safely affirm that, at the accession of Charles, their confidence was greatly augmented, and they had become well trained for the important struggles which awaited them.

7. *The mere spirit of liberty not sufficient of itself to have produced the English rebellion?* Great, however, as was the spirit of liberty among the English, it was not enough of itself to have dethroned the lawful sovereigns of England. That spirit only existed among men of property and intelligence; it had not yet descended to the lower orders. In the time of Richard II., in the wars of the Roses, under the Tudors, &c., the populace of England had generally been on the side of *legitimacy.* The great struggles for liberty had been produced by resistance to pecuniary exactions. Beyond this the English seem not to have been very powerfully operated on by any ardent love of liberty or of abstract right. During the 16th century monarchy every where triumphed on the continent, and ran into consolidation. In England, during the corresponding period under the Tudors, the same result was fearfully threatened. The accession of the house of Stuart occurred at the turning point in the fortunes of England, just as parliament was recovering from its long prostration, and shaking off the inglorious lethargy in which it had so long reposed. Still it is probable, even under the Stuarts, that they would merely have taken their stand, as of old, on the *money principle*, had not a new principle of action come into play, which produced the English revolution, nearly 150 years before the French: that principle was a religious one.

8. *Religious zeal supplied the deficiency?* The first serious attacks on the government were made through the pulpit. Those who made the greatest exertions in favor of their liberties were the puritans, animated with religious zeal. Under Charles I. a universal frenzy seized the nation. It was religious enthusiasm that gave that spirit to the Long Parliament, which enabled them to withstand the formidable exertions of the cavaliers. From whatever cause, says Cromwell, the civil war began, if religion was not the original source of discord, yet God soon brought it to that issue; and he constantly affirmed that,

amidst the strife of battle and the dangers of war, the reward to which he and his followers looked was freedom of conscience. (Al. 1, 47.)

9. *Rise and progress of the puritans?* To explain the zeal and influence of the puritans in the reign of Charles I., necessary to revert to the peculiarity of the reformation in England. Whilst on continent and in Scotland the reformation was generally directed and urged forward by religious men, such as Luther, Zwingle, Calvin and Knox; in England it was commenced and carried on by the government. Elsewhere men of piety and deep religious zeal were the *principals;* in England they were merely *secondary.* On the continent, it has been well observed, worldliness was the tool of zeal; in England zeal was the tool of worldliness. The greatest despot in English history, the murderer of his wives, the man under whose reign it is said 72,000 persons were executed, whose ministers were unprincipled, whose aristocracy was rapacious, and whose parliaments were servile, commenced the reformation. It was continued under his short-lived son, by Somerset, the murderer of his brother, and it was completed by Elizabeth, the murderer of her guest. There were pious men in England, whose names can compare with any that the reformation produced; but they were not men of influence at court. Of those who exerted much influence, Ridley is almost the only one who did not consider it a mere political job. (M. 1, 207.) Cranmer's character has evidently sunk under scrutiny.

In many respects it is well for the church of England that, in an age of exuberant zeal, her founders were mere politicians. To this she owes her moderate articles, her decent ceremonies, and her noble and pathetic liturgy. But, on the other hand, it was this circumstance that made her the servile handmaid of monarchy,* the steady enemy of liberty. Her favorite tenets were the divine right of kings and the duty of passive obedience. She held to them firmly through times of oppression, persecution and licentiousness; and she never swerved from them, until James II., in an evil hour, assailed her dignity and her property. The reformation, cradled in the spirit of free inquiry, was almost

* James I. was flattered by his clergy almost into the belief that he was a demi-god. Archbishop Whitgift, in reference to the Hampton court conference, said he was convinced the Spirit of God spoke through the king. Bishop Bancroft added, I can testify that my heart overflowed with joy, because Almighty God has, in special mercy, given us such a king as there *has not been since the time of Christ!!* In the prayer which Laud composed on the birth of the prince of Wales in 1630, he says, "double his father's graces, O Lord, upon him, *if it be possible.*" Well might old Bishop Williams be scandalized at this "*loathsome divinity,*" as he called it. (Reau. 1, 461, C. H. 2, 52.)

every where favorable to the cause of political liberty, except in England. Here the supremacy of the pope of Rome was thrown off, it is true, but that of the king of England was substituted. The whole church establishment, with its bishops and archbishops, lost none of its powers, its allegiance was merely transferred from the pope to the king. The church felt its dependence on the crown, and supported its power; the crown soon comprehended the benefit it received from the learning and loyalty of its religious ally, and resolved to drive all its subjects into her folds. Hence the severe penal laws by which the church was supported.

In this reformation, as before observed, the people seemed to display a remarkable apathy. But under Edward VI., and in the reign of Elizabeth, a spirit began to develope itself in favor of a more thorough reformation. The government had stopped too soon for the people; they thought they beheld in the church too many of the papal doctrines, rites and ceremonies; they considered that the "Babylonian enchantress had been robbed of her ornaments merely to transfer the full cup of her sorceries to other hands;" they wished less power in the hands of the bishops, and a more simple and pure worship—hence the name of *puritans*. This sect being hostile to the established church, naturally allied itself to the opposition party in the government, and gave to it a strength and zeal which could never have been imparted in that age by the mere abstract love of liberty. Elizabeth saw among the puritans a spirit hostile to her spiritual supremacy, and persecuted them with rigor. But the sect, in spite of all her vigilance, grew rapidly during her long reign. James, although educated a presbyterian in Scotland, became episcopal in England. *No bishops, no king*, was his favorite motto; he persecuted, insulted and laughed at the presbyterians. But his conduct merely trained them to disputation and zeal; and, before his death, their numbers were greatly augmented, and their resolution indomitable. When Charles I. mounted the throne, therefore, this sect had swelled into a formidable party, had allied itself with the cause of freedom generally, and bade fair to trample down the monarch, the church, and the aristocracy.

10. *Character of the puritans under Charles I.?* Was in many respects ridiculous and unamiable. "The ostentatious simplicity of their dress, their sour aspect, their nasal twang, their stiff postures, their long graces, their Hebrew names," and scriptural phrases, their contempt of human learning, and detestation of polite amusements and popular recreations, were indeed fair game for the satirists and dramatists. But in spite of their ridiculous practices, their unamiable austerities, their unpolished manners, we are constrained to admit the charac-

ter a great one. It combined four requisites in an eminent degree, which rarely fail to insure triumph in this world—*zeal*, *perseverance*, *courage*, and *cool judgment* in council. They believed in *predestination*, and of course that they were among that small number called the *elect*. Such men naturally recognize no title to superiority but the favor of heaven; they despised the accomplishments and the dignities of this world. They looked on kings, princes and palaces as contemptible in the sight of the Lord; they, the elect, had the true inheritance; their palaces were houses not made with hands, their diadems were crowns of glory which should never fade; if they were not waited on by crowds of menials, ministering angels watched over them. The puritan was all self-abasement, penitence, gratitude towards God, but, towards man, proud, calm and inflexible. "He prostrated himself in the dust before his Maker, but he set his foot on the neck of his king." He prayed with convulsions, groans and tears. He heard the lyres of angels or the tempting whispers of fiends. But when he appeared in the council chamber, or in the field, these tempestuous workings of the feelings subsided into calm deliberation; the intensity of his feelings on one subject produced calmness on all others. The people who saw nothing of the godly but their uncouth visages, and heard nothing from them but their groans and whining hymns, might laugh at them; but he who encountered them in the hall of debate, or on the field of battle, learned full soon to feel and dread their power. (M. 1, 59.) "Cursed be he who doeth the work of the Lord negligently, and keepeth back his sword from blood," was a favorite exclamation on the day of battle, and in their eternal quotations from the Bible, it may be observed that the sanguinary texts of the Old Testament were preferred to the milder language of the New.

11. *First parliament of Charles I.*, 1625? In the very first meeting of parliament, Charles, as has been said, found that he had been married to a sullen bride. The character of the parliament was wholly changed from what it had been in the days of the Plantagenets. It was no longer the great barons of the house of lords, followed timidly and cautiously by the more humble house of commons, that stood up for the liberties of England against the power of the throne. But it was the house of commons that now took the lead; they were waxing stronger from day to day. James, in derision, sometimes called them the 500 kings; and on one occasion, when he heard that a committee of 12 were about to wait on him, he said with bitter irony, "let 12 armchairs be prepared; I am going to receive 12 kings."

When Charles's first parliament met, neither prince nor people had yet unravelled the principle nor measured the strength of their claims, and, as soon as the session opened, the commons turned their investigations to all branches of the government—foreign and domestic affairs, negotiations, alliances, subsidies, past and to come, religion, popery, &c. The king came to the throne with the nation involved in war with Spain, the charges of which were £700,000 a-year; his debts were £600,000. He asked for money. They granted him two small subsidies, (£145,000.) and when, in his urgent need, he asked for more, they raised the old demand for a redress of grievances. The king was thrown into bad humor, dissolved his parliament, and attempted to raise money by letters under his privy seal; besides which he compounded for knighthood. All persons of £40 or more per annum were forced to receive the honors of knighthood, and of course to pay for them, or for not receiving them; these expedients brought but little money into the treasury. The expedition against Cadiz failed—it was attributed to ignorance of the admiral, and the drunkenness of the troops. The necessities of the king increased, another parliament became necessary.

12. *Second parliament*, 1626? The king took measures to keep some of the more popular orators out. The Earl of Bristol, personal enemy of Buckingham, received no summons to attend among the lords. Sir Edward Coke, Sir Robert Philips, Sir Thomas Wentworth, Sir Francis Seymour and others, named sheriffs, could not be elected. In was hoped the commons, in the absence of these able and ardent champions of liberty, would be more submissive. The king was wofully mistaken. The parliament promised considerable supplies, but withheld them until grievances should be redressed. They boldly resolved to strike at Buckingham, the minister of the throne, the supposed author of all their grievances. He was a handsome, presumptuous, magnificent,* rash and careless courtier. His ambition was unsupported by talents; the gratification of frivolous passions was the sole aim of his intrigues. To seduce a woman, to get rid of a rival, he compromised, with arrogant insensibility, sometimes the king, sometimes the country. He appeared to the people an upstart without glory, an incapable and daring favorite, whose power was an insult and a misfortune

* When he visited France, he entered Paris in "a rich white satin velvet suit, set all over, both suit and clothes, with diamonds, the value whereof is thought to be £80,000, besides a feather made with great diamonds, with sword, girdle, hat-band, and spurs with diamonds." He had 27 other suits, all "rich as invention could frame or art fashion." (Ling. 9, 209.) He had the presumption to make love to Anne of Austria, the young queen of France. Richelieu, who seems to have been jealous of Buckingham, would never let him afterwards visit the French court, to prosecute his amour with the queen, and this is supposed to have furnished the true motive to Buckingham in urging Charles to the imprudent war with France, in which the transcendent genius of Richelieu paled the star of Buckingham.

to the country. Sir Dudley Digges moved the impeachment, and compared Buckingham to a meteor exhaled from putrid matter. The two great lawyers, Glanville and Selden, followed on the same side. Sir John Elliot, with a power of declamation that bore down every thing, closed the prosecution. He described the duke as the canker in the king's treasure, the man that sat on the kingdom's revenues, and exhausted the fountains of supply; the moth of all goodness; a man who could find no parallel in the page of history, except in the profligate Sejanus, described by Tacitus as, *Audax, sui oltegens, in alios criminator, juxta adulator et superbus.*

The king's conduct on this occasion was the beginning of his troubles, and the first of his open attempts to crush the popular party. He said, "if Sir John Elliot compares the duke to Sejanus, he must intend *me* for *Tiberius*." On that day, accordingly, the prologue and epilogue orators, Sir Dudley Digges, who opened the impeachment, and Elliott who closed it, were committed to the tower. (J. 2, 233.) This threw a gloomy sullenness over the commons. Sir Dudley Carlton, formerly ambassador to France, attempted in vain to comfort them, by telling how much better off they were than the people on the continent, with no store of flesh on their backs, like so many ghosts, all skin and bones, with some thin cover to their nakedness, and wearing only wooden shoes on their feet; who could not eat meat or wear clothes, but they must pay the king for it. He bade the house beware lest they should force Charles to "*use new counsels*," which was understood to mean that he would govern arbitrarily, without parliaments. All this but the more roused the spirit of the commons. Those who made threats of what the king would do were forced to apologize. They refused to do business till the prisoners were released, and accordingly they were set at liberty. Urged by this example, the lords demanded the earl of Arundel, confined in the tower, and the king had to comply. (G. 1, 27.) The commons then prepared a remonstrance against the levying of tonnage and poundage, which constituted half the crown revenues, and likewise a petition to remove Buckingham from the king's counsels, whom they classed among the vipers and the pests to their king and commonwealth. The king dissolved them for their impertinence. The remonstrance was circulated every where; the king commanded it to be burnt, and circulated a tame, spiritless declaration. But in such cases the attack is more vigorous always than the defence: the remonstrance produced tenfold the influence that the declaration did.

13. *Exigencies of the crown after dissolution of the second parliament?* Were greater than had ever been known before. The king was obliged to mortgage his lands in Cornwall to the aldermen and

companies of London. A rumor spread that the pension list was to be revoked. The royal distress was so great, that the tables at court were put down, and the courtiers put on board wages. A letter of the times describes "the *funereal supper* at Whitehall, whereat *twenty-three tables were buried*, being from henceforth converted to board wages." Another says, "I see a rich commonwealth, a rich people, and the crown poor." In the mean time, the fatal descent on the isle of Rhe sent home Buckingham discomfited, and spread dismay through the nation. The spirit of insurrection was stalking forth in the metropolis and the country. An army and navy returned unpaid, and sore with defeat. London was scoured by mutinous seaman and soldiers, roving even into the palace of the king. Soldiers without pay form a society without laws. A band of captains rushed into the duke's apartment as he sat at dinner, and when reminded by the duke of the proclamation forbidding soldiers to come to court in troops, on pain of hanging, they replied, whole companies were ready to be hanged with them, that their reputation was lost and honor forfeited, for want of their salary to pay their debts. All these disorders were heightened by the scattering of letters, which was one of the symptoms of the times. Sealed letters, addressed to leading men, were seen hanging on bushes. Anonymous letters were dropped in shops and streets, saying that the day was fast coming when "such a work was to be wrought in England, as never was the like." A groom detected in spreading these papers was brought before the inexorable star chamber, and fined £3,000. In the midst of all these troubles a fresh expedition was planned against Rochelle; a new army was to be raised, and Buckingham, the most hated man in England, swore if there was money in the kingdom it should be had.

14. *Means used by the king to raise money?* Charles was sick of parliaments, and determined to raise money, if possible, without them. The principal means was by forced loans, apportioned among the people according to the rate of the last subsidy. On this occasion, Hampden made his first stand for liberty; he refused to advance his portion of the loan. He was asked his reasons. He answered he could lend as well as others, but feared to draw on him the curse of *Magna Charta.* The privy council sent him a close prisoner to the Gate House. The prisons were every where crowded with these loan recusants, as well as with those who had sinned in the freedom of their opinions. Many were heavily fined for saying they knew no law besides that of parliament to compel men to give away their property. Many of the lower people who refused to lend were impressed for the army and navy. Soldiers were billeted on the people. Crimes of ordinary occurrence were punished by martial law. The seaports and maritime districts

were forced to supply and equip a certain number of armed vessels. This was Charles's first attempt at ship money. London was rated at 20 ships. It was objected that this was more than Elizabeth asked to repel the Invincible Armada; the reply was that the precedents of former times were obedience, not objections. Besides these various expedients, money was raised by a commission issued for compounding with popish recusants.

15. *Doctrine of passive obedience?* Was every where preached by the established clergy. A member of the house, under James I., called the race of divines "spaniels to the court and wolves to the people." (J. 2, 376.) Such divines as Dr. Mainwaring, Sibthorpe, and Dean Bargrave, were constantly hunting for ancient precedents to inculcate passive obedience. The publication of one of Sibthorpe's sermons caused his house to be burnt down. Mainwaring sent to a friend for all the ancient precedents he could find for absolute monarchy; the friend replied, he could help him in nothing, but only to hang him, and that he might be sure of a halter at the next meeting of parliament. The crown demanded this support of the clergy. George Abbot, archbishop of Canterbury, refused to sanction the spread of these sermons in his diocese; he was suspended in his office, and banished from London. The crown lawyers and judges too were active in hunting up precedents on the same side. But there were two lawyers on the popular side, who could never be surpassed in this respect, Selden and old Coke. Their learned industry established the freedom of the subject in the very dust of the records of the Tower.

16. *Meeting of the third parliament*, 1628? The whole policy of the king but served to excite the people. All the illegal expedients failed to supply an adequate public revenue, and in the midst of the king's troubles, news arrived that the great naval armament sent to Rochelle, commanded by Buckingham in person, of 100 sail with 7000 troops, had failed, after losing one-third of the troops. This reverse spread a general mourning and indignation through England. The French navy was triumphant, and the English merchantmen were compelled in many places to remain in port. Sir Robert Cotton, one of the mildest of popular party, was called to the king's council: he spoke with candor, quoting the words of old Burleigh to Elizabeth, "gain their hearts, and you will soon have their arms and purses." He advised a new parliament, the king reluctantly consented, and it was agreed that the duke of Buckingham should move it in council, to render him popular. The king now tried to get the nation into a good humor. The prisons were opened, and men who had been confined for resistance to tyranny came forth, and were received with transport.

Twenty-seven of them were elected members of the new parliament. Among them was Hampden, re-elected burgess for Wendover. In this parliament, besides Hampden, who was fast becoming one of the master-spirits of the times, were the three great lawyers, Coke, Selden, and Glanville—the three bold orators, Pym, Elliott, and Wentworth, afterwards earl of Strafford, an apostate from the popular cause. Besides these were Philips, Hollis, &c., and among them was Oliver Cromwell, in his 29th year, a member for Huntingdon, his native place. It was his first year in parliament. He was introduced by his cousin, John Hampden, to the leading men of the popular party.*

17. *First proceedings—Petition of Rights—Prorogation?* With the exception of some ill-advised threats in the royal message, the first meetings of the prince and his parliament were friendly. A large subsidy was unanimously voted, but not passed into a law. Charles was so overjoyed as to shed tears, and declared that he was again in love with parliaments. But, as usual, this subsidy was to be granted with conditions. An instrument, called the Petition of Rights, drawn by Selden, passed the commons, embracing four principal matters of complaint—the exaction of money without consent of parliament, the commitment of those who refused, the billeting of soldiers on private persons, and the too frequent employment of martial law. Charles tried hard to prevent the passage of this petition. He wished them to rely on his royal word, and have no *law* on the subject. But old Coke said, although he did not distrust the king, yet he could take "his *majesty's word no otherwise than in a parliamentary way;* that is, of a matter agreed on by both houses." Therefore he moved, "that the house of commons, *more marjorum*, should draw a petition *de droit* to his majesty." Charles tried to evade by promising to confirm *Magna Charta* anew; but nothing but a sanction of the Petition of Right, considered as a second Magna Charta, would answer; the insincerity of the king had already been too manifest. The king, after having by his

* The personal appearance of these two cousins must have presented a striking contrast to the groups of liberals among whom they mixed. Hampden, mild, affable, with broad high brow and bright contemplative eyes, a sad, sweet, loving and thoughtful face, breaking often into kind smiles—a finished gentleman. Cromwell, 5 years younger, dressed in a threadbare and torn coat, and greasy hat, a rough, strong-built frame, of five feet 10, the most robust health expressed in every feature, of a rough, warted, gnarled and stern face, a nose so large and red as to be a standing jest, with deep-set piercing eyes, shaded by large bushy eyebrows. His maiden speech was in furious and bad language against the indulgence of a bishop to an obscure preacher, and, as he called him, a rank papist; his voice was sharp and untuneable, and he at once commanded the attention of the house by a sort of mystic and blustering enthusiasm, in spite of his confused and often unintelligible language.

first answer and subsequent threats worked the house up into a perfect tempest,* came forward and gave his full sanction to the bill, and, in return, five subsidies were granted him (£350,000), a large amount in comparison with former grants. Popular gratitude now burst forth in every quarter. Bells were rung, bonfires were kindled, a universal holiday was kept through town and country. But this joy was very short-lived. In spite of the Petition of Right, the king continued to levy tonnage and poundage, *without* consent of parliament. The commons were ready to grant him this revenue, but he must first give up his right to levy it without sanction of law. Charles said he never meant to do this when he signed the Petition of Right. The commons voted a remonstrance on this subject, and likewise another against Buckingham The king lost his patience and prorogued his parliament.

18. *Conduct of Charles during recess of parliament?* Charles circulated 1500 copies of Petition of Right through the kingdom, with his *first evasive answer* appended, instead of the *second*, giving his full sanction: a silly, audacious attempt to deceive, where deception was impossible. Buckingham was assassinated by Felton two months after the prorogation. This circumstance, instead of relieving the nation, seemed to determine Charles again to tyranny. He had lately found it necessary to restrain his clergy in their extravagant preaching in favor of episcopal power and passive obedience. He now promoted Montague, whom the commons had prosecuted, to the bishopric of Chichester, Mainwaring, whom the house of lords had condemned,† was endowed

* Charles had threatened dissolution. Sir John Elliott thought it hard to dissolve before business was transacted, and was proceeding as usual to censure Buckingham. The speaker told him he had orders from the king not to suffer him to proceed. Elliott sat down in sullen silence. Next day old Coke broke the ice, by rising in his place and asserting, "that man (Buckingham) is the grievance of grievances." He said that "the liberties of the commons were impeached," &c. This vehement cry of Coke was followed up, "as when one good hound recovers the scent, the rest come in with full cry." A sudden message from the king absolutely forbade them to asperse his minister, and threatened an immediate dissolution. This message fell like a thunderbolt; it struck terror and alarm among the commons; some were weeping, some expostulating, some prophesying, and some calming the house; some tried to speak, but were too much affected for utterance. Coke was one of these, and when he sat down tears were seen on his aged cheeks. The speaker himself shed tears, and asked leave of absence for half an hour. He returned with orders from the king to adjourn till next day. The interval was awful. A letter writer speaks of that black and doleful Thursday: "What we shall expect this morning (Friday) God of heaven knows; we shall meet timely." The king, however, gave way and signed the petition. (J. 390.)

† He was sentenced to be imprisoned, suspended for three years, fined £1,000, and to make his submission, which he did with tears.

with a rich benefice. Laud, so famous for devotion to powers of church and king, was promoted to see of London. The duty of tonnage and poundage was collected with rigor. The merchants, Chambers,* Rolls and Vassal, refused to pay the duty; their goods were distrained, and on suing writs of replevin were told by the judges the king's right was established, and could not be disputed. Trial by martial law still continued. Charles now tried a new set of political tactics; he attempted to break the opposition by conferring office and favor on some of the parliamentary leaders, Saville, Wentworth, Digges, Noy and Littleton successively deserted the popular party for office under Charles.

19. *Apostacy of Sir Thomas Wentworth?* This talented man, perhaps the most brilliant and bold orator of the opposition, was taken into office after the death of Buckingham. He was made a peer, (Earl of Strafford,) privy councillor, and chief minister, and from this time forward employed all his abilities and perseverance to crush those liberties which he had before so ably defended; and he bore towards his old associates ever afterwards all the deadly hatred of a renegade.

20. *His character?* No one names him, says Macaulay, "without thinking of those harsh, dark features, ennobled by their expression into more than the majesty of an antique Jupiter; of that brow, that eye, that cheek, that lip, where, as in a chronicle, are written the events of many stormy and disastrous years; of that fixed look, so full of severity, of mournful anxiety, of deep thought, of dauntless resolution, which seems at once to forebode and defy a terrible fate, as it lowers on us from the living canvas of Vandyke." This great, brave, bad man entered the house of commons at the same time with Hampden. Both were among the richest and most powerful commoners in the kingdom; both were distinguished by force of character and personal courage. Hampden had most judgment, Wentworth more force and brilliancy of expression. In 1626, both were committed to prison for their bold opposition to regal oppression. (M. 2, 72.)

21. *Second meeting of third parliament—its dissolution?* Charles, surrounded by more able ministers than formerly, encountered the second session of parliament without fear or dread. The commoners met in no very complying humor. They found fault with the toleration of papists, with the relaxation of morals, with the proceedings of the court during the recess. The king asked for tonnage and poundage; Sir John Elliott proposed a new remonstrance against levying it without act of parliament, and when he began to read it, the speaker told

* Chambers was afterwards prosecuted in the star chamber, for saying "merchants were more screwed up and wronged in England than in Turkey," and fined £2,000.

him the king had ordered him not to permit it. It was insisted on. The speaker left the chair; Hollis and Valentine seized and carried him back—Hollis exclaiming, "By God, you shall sit till it shall please the house to depart!" "I will not, I cannot, I dare not," cried the speaker. But he was held fast. The king hearing of the tumult, ordered the gentleman usher to withdraw with the mace, which would have broken up the meeting; but the usher was held, the keys were taken from him. The king sent a second message to dissolve parliament—the doors were all locked inside. Mad with rage, he called the captain of his guards, and ordered him to break open the doors, but the commons in the mean time retired, having first declared the levying of tonnage and poundage illegal, and both the individual who should levy, and him who paid, guilty of high treason. The king dissolved the parliament immediately, calling the refractory vipers. Hollis, Elliott, Coriton, Hobart, Valentine, Selden, Hayman, Long and Stroud were all committed close prisoners to the Tower. Elliott died from the effects of his long confinement.

SEC. VIII.—FROM DISSOLUTION OF THIRD PARLIAMENT TO THE MEETING OF THE LONG PARLIAMENT—1640.

1. *Charles determines to rule without parliament?* Charles was now thoroughly disgusted with parliaments, and resolved to rule without them. This diffused joy through the court. In presence of the commons the courtiers were constrained; they were afraid to push boldly their fortunes or enjoy their credit. The king was care-worn, the queen was intimidated, the intrigues of Whitehall were interrupted, and a gloom thrown over its festivals; now suddenly all became merry as the marriage feast.

2. *Policy of the king?* Whatever may have been the natural disposition of Charles, a close examination of the period of eleven years, from dissolution of parliament in 1629 to its meeting again, 1640, must prove him to have been, in *fact*, one of the most tyrannical princes in British history. He set at open defiance the laws and opinions of the country. He violated without scruple his most solemn promises, particularly that to observe the Petition of Right. Subtle and unprincipled counsellors were ever rummaging among old records for precedents to justify iniquity, for abuses which they could claim as rights of the crown. The servile judges became the tools and accomplices of tyranny, and where the ordinary tribunals could not act, then the extraordinary ones, the *star chamber*, the council of York,* and a number of others, placed

* Instituted by Henry VIII., at York, (1537,) to maintain order in the northern counties. Its jurisdiction was confined at first, but became very extended and very arbitrary under James and Charles.

above the common law, took their place. The positions long disused were now re-established, and others were invented; *e. g.*, the odious monopolies reappeared which had been introduced and abandoned by Elizabeth, recalled and then surrendered by James, and abolished by Charles himself.* Compositions for knighthood were rigorously exacted. The extension of the royal forests, which had so often driven the barons to arms, was so rapid, that the royal forests in Essex were hyperbolically said to include the whole county. The Earl of Southampton was nearly deprived of his whole estate by the enlargement of *New Forest*. The forest of Rockingham alone was increased from six to sixty miles in circumference (G. 1, 73); and the smallest encroachments or trespasses were punished by exorbitant fines; *e. g.*, Lord Salisbury, for offence of this kind, was fined £20,000, Lord Westmoreland £19,000, Sir Christopher Hatton £12,000, Lord Newport £3,000, Sir Lewis Walton £4,000. The severity of judges was made one of the principal sources of revenue; under the slightest pretext the heaviest fines were imposed, striking a terror through the community. Those who dreaded a similar fate often rescued themselves by compounding before trial. When discontent appeared in any of the counties, the native militia was disbanded and other troops sent among them, who were not only kept and quartered on the inhabitants, but were equipped at their expense. Impositions, imprisonments, judgments, rigors, daily increased and were exercised in the most arbitrary manner, on the rich, because there was profit, on the poor, because there was no danger. Fines imposed during this epoch amounted to more than six millions. (G. 1, 74.)

3. *Ship money levied under Charles?* Of all the exactions of the crown none were more noted than the famous *ship money*. Noy, the attorney general, who, like Wentworth, had vehemently supported the popular cause in parliament, and like him, too, had basely deserted his principles for office, must have the credit, in conjunction with Finch, the chief justice, of devising this scheme for raising money, which completed the alienation of the people from the throne. A writ was issued (1634) commanding London and other seaport towns to raise a certain number of ships of a prescribed tonnage and equipage for king's service, and empowering them at same time to assess all the inhabitants. The success of this soon suggested to the court the plan of extending these writs from the seaports to the whole kingdom—thus attempting, in the language of Clarendon, to make this exaction "a spring and magazine that should have no bottom, and for an everlasting supply on all occa-

* These monopolies were granted on almost all articles, for the sake of revenue, such as salt, soap, coals, iron, wine, herrings, butter, rags, hops, &c.

sions." This was a stretch of power which Elizabeth, in her greatest need, had never dared to exercise. And even if precedent could have been found, it was a shameless violation of the Petition of Right, which Charles had solemnly sworn to maintain.

4. *Refusal of Hampden to pay the ship money—trial?* Buckinghamshire, the county of Hampden, was assessed at one ship of 450 tons, estimated at £4,500. Hampden's share of this tax was only 20 shillings, a sum so small for so rich a man, that the sheriff was blamed for fixing it so low. Payment, however, was refused; and Hampden determined to have the cause argued before the judges of the exchequer. He was, of course, condemned by the servile judges.* But the trial roused all England, and gave to the popular party an impulse which made this victory of the crown one of the most efficient means for the ultimate triumph of the people. The protraction of this cause six months, from the opening speech of Hampden's counsel to the final judgment, was of infinite disservice to the king's cause. The powerful arguments of St. John and Holborne sunk deep into the popular mind. Hampden henceforth became the people's idol, and the most noted man in England. His bearing in the trial was such, that even courtiers and crown lawyers spoke respectfully of him. But there was one man who hated him with a bitter hatred—that man who had been his quondam friend, who had bravely set at defiance with him all the terrors of despotism, and with him had suffered all the hardships of imprisonment, in a cause similar to the present—that man was Strafford! The sunshine of royal favor had thrown new light over his mind, and *now*, he thought that such men as Hampden should be "well whipped into their right senses; and if the rod be so used that it smart not, I am the more sorry." Now it must never be forgotten, that the forced loan of 1626, for refusing which Wentworth was imprisoned, was demanded under incomparably greater exigencies than when ship money was levied; at the one time, England was at war with both France and Spain; at the other, at peace with all the world.

5. *Treatment of the puritans—Archbishop Laud?* The policy towards the puritans was in keeping with the civil policy of the government, during the same period, and was in the highest degree impolitic, vexatious and arbitrary. The court of high commission, the great religious tribunal, became daily more severe in its punishments. The complete adoption of the Anglican canons, the minute observance of the liturgy, and all the rites performed in cathedrals, were rigorously

* Two judges, Croke and Hutton, were unqualifiedly for Hampden, three others were in his favor on technical grounds, but against him on the principle, and the other seven were unqualifiedly for the crown. (C. H. 2, 30.)

commanded to all ecclesiastics; all cures were taken from non-conformists. Laud was the principal adviser of the king in these matters. The mean forehead, the pinched features, the piercing eyes of this prelate, mark him out, says Macaulay, as a lower kind of St. Dominic. "When we read his judgments, when we read his report, setting forth that he had sent some separatists to prison, and imploring the royal aid against others, we feel a movement of indignation. We turn to his diary, and are at once as cool as contempt can make us." There we see a chronicle of the man's mind. How his picture fell down, and how fearful he was lest it should be an evil omen; how he dreamed that the Duke of Buckingham came to bed to him, that king James walked past him, that he saw Thomas Flanage in green garments, and the bishop of Worcester wrapped in linen. On the 9th of February, 1627, he dreamed that he had the scurvy, that all his teeth became loose, "there was one especial in my lower jaw, which I could scarcely keep in with my finger, till I had *called for help*;" and this was the man who supervised the church of England, persecuted the puritans, and regulated the religious conscience of the king. Even James had the sagacity to detect his narrow intellect, his violence of temper, his uncompromising, vindictive spirit, and most reluctantly consented to his advancement.

At the very moment when public opinion in England was running with the utmost violence against all the ancient ceremonies of the church, Laud, instead of attempting to conciliate, resolved, with the narrow spirit of a zealot, not only to retain the old, but to introduce new ones. His soul rejoiced in bowings and crossings, and genuflexions. He was, says Burnett, a hot indiscreet man, expending all his energies in pursuit of things beneath the aim of real greatness. When the church was struggling for her very existence, he was contending about the proper position of the altar; when she was at her last gasp, he was fighting for the sign of the cross. A rich and large crucifix, embroidered with gold and silver, in a fair piece of arras, was hung up in his majesty's chapel, over the altar, to which the chaplains were ordered to make their best bow, Laud setting the example. Pictures were set up in the churches, consecrations were used after the Romish manner, and copes were worn at the sacraments. In the consecration of the church Laud used such ridiculous mummeries as made him the most hateful man in England to the puritans. His love of pomp and ceremonies made all believe him fast falling back to catholicism. Like all zealous and narrow-minded men, he imagined that force could easily produce uniformity, and thus, while his practice was every day widening the breach between the puritans and the church of England, he vainly imagined that an energetic exercise of civil authority would soon produce uniformity in religion.

6. *Differences as to observance of the Sabbath?* The English reformers, after abolishing most of the catholic festivals, made very little change in the observance of those retained. *Sundays* were placed on the footing of other holidays; the modern observance of the first day of the week, as a season of rest and devotion, was considered as an ecclesiastical institution, and in no degree more venerable than other festivals, or the season of Lent, which the puritans so much despised. At a very early period, the puritans were disposed to place Sunday on the footing of the Jewish sabbath, and to interdict all worldly business, all recreation and sport. James I., with his accustomed indiscretion, published a declaration to be read in all churches, permitting all lawful recreations on Sunday after service, such as dancing, archery, May games, morris-dances, &c. The cynical temper of the severe puritan revolted at this impious license; May games and morris-dances were hardly tolerable six days in the week—this declaration recommended them on the seventh. This insult on the *precise* clergy was, however, never inflicted under James, by the actual reading in the churches—thanks, pehaps, to Archbishop Abbot; but, under Charles, the violence of Laud delighted in this kind of persecution, and the puritans were shocked every where by this promulgated license to profane the sabbath, and those who refused to read publicly the *Book of Sports*, as it was called, were prosecuted before the high commission court as schismatics. The sabbatarians, of course, attacked with bitterness violators of the sabbath. One of the most serious charges urged in Martin-Mar-Prelate against Bishop Aylmer was, that he played at bowls on Sunday. On the other hand, Laud and his clergy treated the puritans as a set of absurd, rebellious hypocrites, who called themselves saints in the excess of vanity, manifesting their holiness in ridiculous trifles, with broad-brimmed, high-crowned hats, and cropped heads, eternally whining about the *Lord's day*.

7. *Emigration of many puritans?* The more the puritan preachers were persecuted, the more popular they became; the people crowded to hear them preach. The police drove them from the churches; they wandered from town to town, teaching and preaching in taverns, private houses, in the fields and woods. They were taken as chaplains and tutors into rich families. But persecution followed them every where; *e. g.*, Dr. Workman, a minister of Gloucester, maintained that pictures and ornaments in churches were remains of idolatry. He was thrown into prison. The town of Gloucester had granted him a life annuity of £20 a-year; it was recalled, and the mayor and municipal

officers were heavily fined. When liberated from prison, Workman opened a little school; Laud put it down. To earn his daily bread Workman practised as a physician; Laud forbade him the practice. Workman was struck with insanity, and soon died. (G. 1, 83.) Under this gloomy persecution, the puritans left England in great numbers for Holland and the colonies in America. It seldom happened that the vessels were large enough to take as many passengers as were desirous of going. The parties on these occasions assembled on the sea-side, while the vessel was at anchor. There, on the margin of the water, the minister of that part of the congregation which remained, preached a farewell sermon; the one who accompanied the emigrants answered him by another. Long did they pray together, and then embrace each other for the last time; and while one party sailed away, the other returned sorrowfully.

8. *Emigration stopped by order in council?* Several expeditions had taken place without impediment; the obscurity of the fugitives was their protection. But all at once, in 1637, the king perceived that they had become frequent and numerous, that citizens of note were among them, and that they carried away with them considerable wealth. It was thought £12,000,000 had already gone. The spirit of emigration was becoming contagious; the government was odious, and thousands were anxious to leave, impelled by various motives. An order in council forbade emigration. At that very time eight vessels were ready to start, all anchored in the Thames. Pym, Hazlerig, Hampden and Cromwell were among the emigrants. What a mighty difference would it have made, for both *New* and *Old* England, had these four men been suffered to depart! They were forced to remain, and with them remained the evil genius of the house of Stuart.

9. *Punishment of Prynne, Bastwick, Burton and others by the star chamber?* The iniquitous punishments inflicted by the star chamber during this period were of so cruel and revolting a character, as to have no little influence in preparing the English mind for rebellion and revenge. As always happens, the intolerance of one party increased the resistance of the other; hence not to wonder that the attacks on the established church should often pass the bounds of decorum; *e. g.*, in writings of Leighton, Prynne, Burton and Bastwick, the archbishop was called an arch officer of the devil, the bishops satanical lords, ravening wolves, &c. A few of the remarks of Prynne, a puritan lawyer, will well illustrate the spirit of the opposition. In his Histriomastix, written principally against theatres, we read, "Our English shorn and frizzled madams have lost all shame; so many steps in the dance, so many steps towards hell. Those who attend playhouses are no better than devils incarnate; at least like those who hunt, play at cards, wear wigs,

visit fairs, &c., they are in the high road to damnation. And yet their number is so great that it is proposed to build a sixth chapel (theatre) to the devil in London, whereas in Rome, in the time of Nero, there were only three. Church music is nothing else than the lowing of stupid beasts. The choristers bellow out the tenor as if they were oxen, bark the counter point like a pack of hounds, groan out their shapes like bulls, and grunt the bass like a herd of swine." (Reau. 1, 542.) In the index to this work occurs the unfortunate expression, *Women actors, notorious whores.* Six weeks *after* the publication of this book, the queen performed a part in a mask at court. Poor Prynne was dragged before the star chamber, upon charge of comparing the king to Nero, and indirectly calling the queen a whore. He answered that he only inveighed against vices, and mentioned no names, and had no intention to insult the king and queen. He was sentenced to stand twice in the pillory, to be branded in the forehead with S. L. (seditious libeller), to lose both his ears, to pay a fine of £5000, and to suffer perpetual imprisonment. The dogged puritan employed the leisure of a jail in writing a fresh libel on the church. For this, with two other delinquents of the same kind, Burton, a divine, and Bastwick, a physician, he was again dragged before the terrible star chamber, which sentenced them to a fine of £5000 each, to lose their ears,* to stand in the pillory, to be branded on both cheeks, and to perpetual imprisonment.

The most deliberate cruelty was employed in the execution of the sentence. They were put into the pillory at noon, that their faces might be exposed to the burning heat of the sun. Their friends were forbidden to visit them in prison, they were allowed neither books nor writing materials, &c. These individuals, however, bore their punishment with the heroism of martyrs, and commanded the sympathies of England. When the executioner was ordering the crowd away, Burton cried, "Let them remain; they must learn to suffer!" A young man turned pale as he looked at him—"My son," said Burton, "why art thou pale? My heart is not weak, and, if I needed more strength, God would not let me want it." Some one gave Bastwick a bunch of flowers—a bee lighted on it. "See this poor little bee," said he, "even on the pillory, it comes and sips honey from the flowers; and why should I not enjoy the honey of Jesus Christ?" "Christians," said Prynne, "if

* Prynne had been sentenced to lose his ears by the first sentence, but the hangman, through mercy, had not cut them close. The brutal Finch, one of the judges, had his hair turned back, and expressed indignation at seeing that so mnch of them was left. They were now literally *grubbed* out, so that the mercy in the first execution only served to inflict on him a double suffering; and so anxious were they the last time to do the work faithfully, that a part of his cheek was cut off.

we had prized our own liberty, we should not be here; it is for the liberty of you all that we have exposed our own." The air rang with acclamations. A few months afterwards, the same scenes were renewed around Lilburne, who suffered for the same cause. Tied to a cart's tail and whipped through the streets of Westminster, he never ceased to exhort the multitude that followed him. When bound to the pillory, he continued to speak; he was ordered to be silent, but in vain; they stopped his mouth. He then drew tracts from his pockets, and scattered them among the people. His hands were tied; the multitude still gazed on the unsubdued, silent martyr.

But one of the most barefaced, unjust sentences passed by the star chamber was on the venerable Williams, bishop of Lincoln, the man who first patronized Laud, and who was repaid by the blackest ingratitude and malignity. His only crime was that he had in his *possession* a letter from Osbaldiston, the master of Westminster school, stating that "the little vermin, the hedgehog, hocus pocus (Laud), is engaged in a great dispute with the leviathan" (Lord Weston). Although Laud's name was not mentioned in the letter, and Williams had never divulged it, yet it was adjudged that Williams should pay £5000 to the king and £3000 to Archbishop Laud, to make submission, and to be imprisoned at pleasure. Osbaldiston was sentenced to a still heavier fine, to be deprived of all his benefices, to make submission, and be imprisoned; moreover, to stand in the pillory before his school in Dean's-yard, with his ears nailed to it. So sensitive was Laud, that even Armstrong, the king's fool, was banished, because he spoke disrespectfully of him. Allison and Robins were fined £2000, Bastwick £1000, Bowyer £3000, &c., for the same offence.*

10. *Influence of the queen (Henrietta Maria) over Charles—jealousy of the nation?* Whilst the puritans viewed with such horror Archbishop Laud, and the whole body of the bishops, they equally hated the queen, and believed that she exercised an undue influence on the king, particularly in favor of the catholics. She was a catholic herself, stipu-

* Besides taking the established church under its protection, the nobility and the monopolies were likewise especially protected by the government; *e. g.*, Granville was condemned to a fine of £4000, and as much in damages to Lord Suffolk for having called him a base lord. Pettager was fined £2000 for similar offence towards Kingston. David Forbes for opprobrious epithets against Lord Wentworth £5000, and £3000 to Wentworth. A man was fined £5000 for merely sending a challenge to the Earl of Northumberland, &c. Hilliard was fined £5000 for having sold saltpetre, Goodenough £1000 for the same cause. John Overman, and several other soap-boilers together, £13,000 for having deviated from the king's orders in making soap. Sir Anthony Roper was fined £4000 for converting arable land into meadow, &c. but enough of such disgusting details.

lated before marriage for the exercise of her religion, for the support of a number of French attendants at court, &c. At first, she lived inharmoniously with the king. When she landed Charles was somewhat disgusted at her wishing to do penance before marriage. On the other side, she complained that she was not received with sufficient pomp and respect. She fretted at having to sleep in an old state bed of queen Elizabeth. She quarrelled with Buckingham for wishing to force his wife's sister and niece upon her, and with the king because he meddled too much with the details of her household. The king was too grave and serious, and she took no pains to disguise the insipidity and dulness which she felt in England. The queen's little colony of Frenchmen, a set of impertinent meddlers, was the principal cause of these disturbances. The king soon lost all patience, and drove the whole of them, (120 in number,) in spite of the marriage contract, from the kingdom. Henrietta went into hysterics, tore her hair, fell speechless on the floor, then sprang up with loud cries, dashed her head against the windows, &c. She was gradually appeased, became more reasonable, lived better with her husband, became fascinated with the pleasures of reigning, and, being lively and agreeable, soon acquired the entire love of her grave and faithful husband. She went so far as to beg him, in order to honor her, as she said, in the eyes of the people, to consult her on all occasions, and to do nothing without her advice. (Reaum. 1, 467, G. 1, 57.) She became a great meddler in politics, engaged in all the political intrigues, and was supposed to have no little influence in disposing the king to favor the catholics. Certain it is he winked at the domestic exercise of their religion, allowed its professors to pay compositions for recusancy, and connived at their resort to the queen's chapel in Somerset-house, though it was done so openly as to give rise to scandal; and lastly, through the queen's influence, he was induced to receive an accredited agent from the pope—Pauzani. Hence although the queen never liked Laud, she was almost as much hated by the protestants as that obnoxious prelate.

11. *State of religion in Scotland?* It is impossible to say how long the English people would have borne with the tyranny of Charles, if he had not precipitated matters by most unwisely involving himself in war with Scotland. To understand this matter, it is necessary to bear in mind that the reformation in Scotland was wholly different from that in England. In the former country it was a popular reformation, commencing with the people, and mounting up to the aristocracy and the throne. Whereas, in the latter, it began with the throne and descended to the people. The people were almost universally presbyterian—the principles of John Calvin and John Knox were those they

professed. They held as a fundamental maxim the spiritual independence of their church, and of course denied the religious supremacy of the monarch. They despised every thing catholic, and therefore were opposed to most of the forms and ceremonies of the Episcopal church, as savoring too much of popery. They likewise supported the *parity* of the clergy, and opposed with great bitterness the power of the bishops.

12. *Charles attempts to enforce uniformity in the church of Scotland—reading of the new litany and service?* Although Scotland was decidely presbyterian, and had hoped, when James mounted the throne of England, himself a presbyterian before his accession, that he would tolerate, if not establish their religion;* yet did the nation bear with patience its disappointment, and even yielded to some innovations from a native prince, who was always insisting, with his accustomed pedantry, on *one* king, *one* constitution, and *one* form of worship. Before James's plan of uniformity had been fully established, he died. Scotland was always well disposed towards the Stuarts, except on the subject of religion. The Scotch parliament of 1625 voted large sums to Charles, and showed every disposition to support him, but when the same parliament, in 1631, was called to vote on the ordinances of the church, the whole kingdom was thrown into a ferment—the presbyterian spirit was excited to the highest pitch. It was then that Dr. Alexander Leighton recommended the extirpation of all the bishops, and called the queen a Canaanite and an idolatress. For this offence Leighton was dragged before the court, and sentenced to be publicly whipped at Westminster, and set in the pillory, to have one side of his nose slit, one ear cut off and one side of his cheek branded with a hot iron—to have the whole of this terrible process repeated on the other side the next week at Cheapside, and to suffer perpetual imprisonment, besides paying a fine of £10,000. But this cruel punishment of a Scotchman had only the effect in Scotland which the treatment of Prynne and others had in England; it roused the sympathies of the nation.

Charles and Laud, although they perceived the spirit of the Scotch in these matters, vainly imagined that all could be rectified by the interference of authority. Laud, therefore, in conjunction with the bishops of Dumblane and Ross devised a new liturgy for Scotland, and brought it still nearer to the catholic form than the old one. The king, on the 20th December, 1636, caused notice to be given by sound of trumpet

* He had called the church of Scotland "the sincerest kirk of the world," and spoke of the service of England as an "evil said mass." But he was scarcely on the English throne before he discovered that "a Scots presbytery agreed with monarchy as weel as God with the divil!"

that he had approved of it, and the 23d July, 1637, was set apart as the time when it was to be formally introduced into all the churches. All eyes were turned towards the great cathedral church of Edinburgh. On the appointed day the bishop and dean of Edinburgh, with the lords of the council, the judges and the magistrates, proceeded to the cathedral—it was already crowded chiefly by women. The moment the dean commenced the service, the women of all ranks shouted that "the mass was entered, that Baal was in the church;" they upbraided him with the most opprobrious epithets, and even brandished at him the stools on which they sat.* The dean, affrighted, gave his place to the bishop, who had no sooner opened his mouth than his voice was drowned by cries of *fox*, *wolf*, *belly god*, (he was corpulent,) and at last a stool from a strong arm whizzed by his ear, and admonished him to retreat. The magistrates then turned the riotous out, locked the door, and went on with the service. But the windows were soon broken by a shower of stones, accompanied with loud shouts of "*a pope*, *a pope*, *antichrist*, *stane him*, *pull him down!*" And as soon as the bishop made his appearance in the streets, the women caught him and rolled him in the mire. (Ling. 10, 38, Reau. 2, 17.) Every where in Scotland did these discontents manifest themselves, and every where the women were the chief rioters. In Glasgow, William Annan, with three or four ministers, was attacked by a crowd of women, at 9 o'clock at night, who beat him with neaves, staves, and peats, but no stones; they tore his cloak, ruff, and hat, and when he escaped, he was all bloody with wounds, and in great danger of being killed.

13. *Rebellion of the Scotch?* It is not necessary to narrate all the details concerning this effort to establish episcopacy in Scotland. Suffice it to say, that Laud considered the projet a glorious one; Charles was made to think that the first failure was owing entirely to want of energy in the police; that the disorders arose only from the lower classes, from the women principally.† He persisted, therefore, with his usual blundering; things advanced from bad to worse, until the Scotch were driven to the renewal of the memorable national *covenant*, first formed during the progress of the reformation. Within two months

* "Ane godly woman, when sche hard a young man behind sounding forth *amen* to that new composed comedie, quickly turned her about, and after sche had warmed both his cheeks with the weight of her hands, sche thus shot against him the thunderbolt of her zeal: 'False thief, is there na uther pairt of the churche to sing mess in, but thou must sing it at my lugge.'" (Balf.) Baillie, in his narrative of this tumult, differs a little from Balfour; he makes Jenny Geddes, the woman who threw the stool at the dean's head, reproach the dean in the language above cited.

† The puritans, however, every where said that the populace, like Balaam's ass, had spoken first by divine dispensation. (Reau. 2, 19.)

after this instrument was drawn up, almost all Scotland entered into the solemn engagement, with an additional declaration of hostility to the liturgy, the canons, and episcopacy, the original covenant being only opposed to the church of Rome. The government agents, two or three thousand Roman catholics, and the city of Aberdeen, alone refused to join it. Even the higher nobility of Scotland were arrayed against the king, because of their jealousy of the bishops' power. In every Scotch parliament there was a sort of standing committee, called *lords of the articles*, who had the power of originating all measures, nothing being acted on which was not proposed by them. The lords of the articles were 32 in number, and originally chosen by king and parliament together, in some manner which probably gave the principal agency to the nobles. Now, however, eight bishops, entirely dependent on the crown, chose eight noblemen, making sixteen, and these chose sixteen other persons among the deputies of the counties and towns. The high nobility could but see that an election like this made the lords of the articles, and consequently the whole Scotch parliament, dependent on the eight bishops, eight creatures of the crown; hence an additional reason for their union with the covenanters. Charles was astounded by the news from Scotland; his courtiers had deceived him. He resolved to employ force; nothing was ready. The Marquis of Hamilton was sent to cajole and flatter the rebels with hopes: 20,000 covenanters, assembled at Edinburgh for a solemn fast, went out to meet him; 700 priests stood on an eminence on the roadside, and sang psalms as the marquis passed. After several parleys, several journeys from Edinburgh to London by Hamilton, and another instance of duplicity and bad faith on the part of Charles, the covenanters determined at last to stand to their arms.

14. *Meeting of the fourth parliament, April*, 1640? But Charles acted in this crisis with Scotland just as we might expect from his character. After oppressing, threatening, and blustering, he hesitated and failed. "He was," says Macaulay, "bold in the wrong place and timid in the wrong place." He would have shown his wisdom by being *afraid* before the liturgy was read in the cathedral of Edinburgh. He put off his *fear* however till he had reached the Scottish borders with his troops. Then, after a feeble, inglorious campaign, he concluded the pacification of Berwick, and withdrew his army. The terms were not complied with. Each charged the other with foul play. The Scots refused to disarm. The king found difficulty in re-assembling another army. His late expedition had drained the treasury. He could not make up a revenue by his illegal expedients. It was dangerous even to continue them, with Scotland in rebellion,

and England disaffected. Nothing was left but the old resource, the expedient so much abhorred by the Stuarts, the summoning of parliament. And thus were the king, his ministry and church, with the accumulated wrongs and tyranny of eleven years of misrule heaped upon their heads, reluctantly compelled to face this representative of the English people, the faithful mirror of the popular will.

15. *Its proceedings and dissolution?* The parliament was for granting a supply, but not till after redress of grievances. Charles promised them, if they would give him money at first, that they might sit and discuss grievances afterwards, and that he would redress them. The commons knew full well the value of Charles's *royal word*, and although urged by the lords refused to comply. The king then sent word to the commons, if they would vote him 12 subsidies, about £850,000, he would give up the right of levying ship money. The popular leaders asserted that he had asked for more money than was in the kingdom, that a compliance with his request would be an acknowledgment that he had heretofore had the right to levy it; finally, if he had ever possessed the right, he had surrendered it unequivocally in assenting to the petition of right, which had been paid for by 5 subsidies, and which he had most shamelessly violated after having received the equivalent. The king got angry and dissolved parliament. Even the king's own party condemned this step. "No man," says Clarendon, "could imagine what offence the commons had given. The house generally was exceedingly disposed to please the king;" and in another place he says, "it could never be hoped that more sober or dispassionate men would ever meet together in that place, or fewer who brought ill purposes with them." Charles himself, on the very evening of the dissolution, was himself full of regret, and had serious notions on the next day of recalling the mandate, but gave it up as unworthy of a king.

16. *Conduct of Charles after the dissolution?* The king determined once more, if possible, to rule without parliament, and again plunged in the most reckless tyranny. Strafford had just returned from Ireland, and was prostrate with a violent attack of gout, and was threatened with pleurisy. But he had obtained, from the Irish parliament, money, soldiers, and promises, and as soon as he could leave his bed he returned to work with all his vigor. In less than three weeks, by the influence of his example, more than £300,000 were *voluntarily* paid into exchequer, the papists furnishing the greater part of it. But this was not enough, the government renewed all the vexatious modes of raising money, forced loans, ship money,* monopolies, buying on long

* This was exacted with more rigor than ever, and the mayor and sheriff of Lon-

credit, and selling for cash, and even talked of debasing the coin. Necessity, in their eyes, excused every thing; but necessity is never the true limit of tyranny. Charles was vindictive, he renewed his persecution of members of parliament. Sir Henry Bellasis and Sir John Hotton were imprisoned for their speeches; the house and papers of Lord Brook were searched; Mr. Crew was sent to the tower for having refused to give up the petitions he had received during the session as chairman of the committee appointed to examine them; an oath was exacted from the clergy never to consent to any alteration in the government of the church, "ruled as it is at present by archbishops, bishops, deacons, archdeacons, &c." Never had more arrogant language been used; a few Yorkshire gentlemen had refused an arbitrary request; the council wished to prosecute them; "the only prosecution," said Strafford, "is to send for them and put them in irons." He again fell ill, and was at the brink of the grave; but his feeble condition only increased the harshness of his counsels. As soon as he could leave his bed, he departed with the king to take command of the army already assembled on the frontiers of Scotland.

17. *Second expedition against the Scots—its failure?* Shortly after the dissolution of parliament, the Scotch army advanced boldly into England, in all probability upon the advice of Hampden and the popular leaders in England with whom he acted. The second campaign of Charles was more disastrous to his cause than the first. "His soldiers, as soon as they saw the enemy, ran away as English soldiers have never run either before or since." The flight was the effect of disaffection, and not of cowardice. After the late dissolution of parliament, the utmost aversion to aid the king in the Scotch war was manifested in every part of England. In London, placards were posted up denouncing Laud, a furious crowd attacked his palace, and forced him to take refuge at Whitehall. St. Paul's church was forcibly entered by a crowd, crying *no bishops, no high commission!* Recruits for the army could only be raised by violence; to avoid being enrolled, many mutilated themselves, some it is said committed suicide. Those who enlisted without resistance were insulted and treated as cowards; some officers suspected of popery were murdered by their soldiers. When this reluctant army saw the written covenant floating on the Scottish standard, heard the drum summoning the troops to sermon, and beheld at sunrise the whole camp ringing with *psalm singing* and *prayers*,* the soldiers cursed the impious war in which they were

don were prosecuted before the star chamber for slackness in levying it. Strafford said, things would never go right till the aldermen were hanged.

* A presbyterian camp in those days must have been a rare scene: besides the

engaged, and felt that they were fighting against their brethren and their God.

18. *Charles obliged to summon parliament—meeting of the Long Parliament, November* 3, 1640? After the disgraceful flight on the Tyne, Charles fell into deep melancholy; he had risked and lost his last stake—the game of tyranny was up. He had no money and no means to obtain any; mutiny was in his army, whole bands of soldiers deserted together—the people were every where agitated, impatient of his tyranny, and overwhelmed him with petitions and addresses. They looked on the Scots as friends. The Scots too, after their late victories, had spared the counties they invaded; they were prudent in action, humble in speech, and treated all their prisoners with kindness, and constantly asserted that their disposition was pacific. Charles still struggled on for a while; he evaded, he hesitated, he tried every shift rather than meet parliament again. But no shift would answer. He made a truce with the Scots, and called another parliament.

SEC. IX.—FROM THE MEETING OF THE LONG PARLIAMENT TO THE GRAND REBELLION (1640—42).

1. *Long Parliament—character?* The character and proceedings of this parliament are of transcendent importance in English story. Its period has justly been said to be that from which the factions of modern times trace their divergence. It has accordingly been the theme of eulogy and reproach: the synod of inflexible patriots with some, a conclave of traitorous rebels with others. The house was more numerous than had ever before been known at the first meeting of parliament. It had scarcely met before it was found that its temper was greatly changed from what it had been at the last meeting. Clarendon says, that the same men who six months before were observed to be of very moderate tempers, and to wish that gentle remedies might be applied, talked now in another dialect, both of kings and persons. The chief men of the popular party were Pym, Hampden, Denzil, Hollis, Nathaniel Fiennes, St. John, the younger Vane, Selden, Rudyard and

regular psalm singing and prayers in the morning, with two sermons during the day, when not engaged in the drill, the Scotch spent the remainder of their time in devotion. "Had you lent your ear," says Baillie, "and heard in the tents the sound of some singing psalms, some praying, some reading scripture, you would have been refreshed. I found the favor of God shining upon me; and a sweet, meek, humble, yet strong and vehement spirit, leading me all along." And it was precisely this spirit of the puritan, meek before his *God* but violent towards *men*, which made them so formidable in battle, slaying their enemies, as they said, *hip and thigh.*

35

Cromwell.* Falkland and Hyde belonged to the same party, though they were moderates. But Pym and Hampden occupied decidedly the first place. Pym was considered perhaps the greatest speaker, particularly where set speeches were required; his influence was so great that the opposite party called him *King Pym*. Hampden seldom rose till late in the debate. His speaking was of the sort which has been always most effective in parliament, ready, weighty, perspicuous, condensed. His manner always so courteous and gentlemanly, that even the royal party bestowed their commendations on him. His talents for business were as remarkable as his talents for debate. "He was," says Clarendon, "of an industry and vigilance not to be tired out or wearied. When this parliament began, the eyes of all were fixed upon him, as the *patriæ pater*, as the pilot that must steer the vessel through the tempests and rocks which threatened it. And I am persuaded his power and interest at that time were greater to do good or hurt than any man's in the kingdom; for his reputation of honesty was universal, and his affections seemed so publicly guided, that no corrupt or private ends could bias them."

2. *First proceedings?* Almost every member was the bearer of a petition from his county or town, setting forth grievances, and calling for redress, all of which were read, and often commented on by those who presented them. More than 40 committees were appointed to inquire into abuses, and to receive complaints. Day after day, tradesmen and farmers came, on horseback, to state grievances, in the name of their towns or districts; in every quarter the people were encouraged to bring forward their complaints. By these means, in a short time after the opening of parliament, the grievances and opinions of the whole country were made known. Monopolies, ship-money, arbitrary arrests, usurpation of the bishops, proceedings of the courts, &c., were all dragged to light and exposed to the eager and indignant gaze of the nation.

3. *Impeachment and execution of Strafford?* Among all the advisers of the king none were more hated or feared than Strafford. He wished to avoid the coming storm by remaining at the head of the army in Yorkshire, or by repairing to his government in Ireland; but the king could not dispense with his services at court. He promised that a hair of his head should not be touched, and upon this assurance the stern and fearless minister lost not a moment in repairing to the

* He was sent from Cambridge, in spite of a formidable opposition, headed by Cleaveland, the poet, then a tutor of St. John's, only however by one single vote. Oliver Cromwell elected to the Long Parliament by a *single vote!* "That single vote," exclaimed Cleaveland, "hath ruined both church and kingdom." (W. R. 64, 108.)

metropolis. That the popular storm should break over the head of this ill-starred minister was absolutely certain. No man in England, no matter what should be his politics, could be blamed for taking office under his king, and no one taken into office can expect to administer the government without some concession and compromise; but woe to the man who, like Strafford, in accepting office, at once renounces all the cherished principles of his life, and instead of using his place and influence, like Falkland and Hyde, to moderate the harshness of regal power, imbibes at once all the feelings of the despot, and urges with impatience his monarch to deface and destroy that very system, to whose value and beauty his whole previous life has borne testimony. The whole course of Strafford, from the very day he sold himself for office, was in direct opposition to *his former self.* He was indeed the lost archangel, the Satan of the political apostasy, and the motto adopted by him and archbishop Laud was "*thorough.*"

As president of the council of the north, and afterwards as lord lieutenant of Ireland, his conduct was of the most despotic character. It is true that upon the whole he might have benefited Ireland; but he did it at the expense of justice and the constitution, and his personal enmities often dictated his most tyrannical measures. Lord Mountnorris, for an expression which could scarcely be called rash, and which certainly at this day could not be made the basis of a civil action, was, six months after it was uttered, dragged before one of Strafford's tribunals, and sentenced to death. Every thing but death was inflicted; and Mountnorris, it must be remembered, was married to a relative of Strafford's own wife, the lady whom he afterwards, in his defence, spoke of as a saint in heaven. His conduct towards Lord Ely was still more disgusting. That nobleman was thrown into prison to compel him to settle his estate suitably to the wishes of his daughter-in-law, whom there is every reason to believe Strafford had debauched. In spite, however, of all his vices, in spite of all his dangerous projects, Strafford was certainly entitled to the benefit of law. "But if justice, in the whole range of its wide armory, contained one weapon which could pierce him, that weapon his pursuers were bound before God and man to employ."

"If he may
Find mercy in the law, 'tis his: if none,
Let him not seek't of us."

The journals of the lords show that the judges were consulted, and that they unanimously answered that the articles on which the earl was convicted amounted to high treason. This opinion, says Hallam, which is not mentioned by Clarendon and Hume, seems to have cost Strafford his life. It was relied on by some bishops, especially Usher, whom Charles consulted, as to whether he should pass the bill of attainder. (C. H. 2, 146.) Although this opinion of the judges is now generally considered erroneous, it goes very far to justify parliament. It is the opinion of the judges which has been generally brought to sanction the usurpations of Charles. If it be said, that from the very moment that Pym moved the impeachment of Strafford at the bar of the house of lords, and had him arrested, the whole government was affrighted, and the judges were too much alarmed to give a conscientious opinion, it may be answered that they were the same judges that upheld the tyranny of Charles, and besides being operated on by the same kind of influence from the throne, when they upheld its tyranny, they were under the still more dangerous influence of self-interest. The more condemnations, and forfeitures, and fines, the more money would flow into the royal fisc, and the better would the king be enabled to reward the base servility of the judges.

After all, however, the execution of Strafford cannot be fully justified. In his case, as in that of Laud, they were obliged to accumulate many transgressions together, and make them *collectively* high treason, when none *individually* amounted to that offence. As one of the advocates of Laud observed, although one *black rabbit* did not make a *black horse*, yet it was decided that 100 might.

The whole trial of Strafford is one of the most interesting recorded in history. His defence was perfect of its kind. Pym, in answering it, is said to have faltered and failed. Charles, after assuring Strafford that he should not suffer in life, fortune or honor, signed by commission the bill of attainder, an act for which he never forgave himself, and to which he was urged by the threatening aspect of the city mob, by the fears of the queen, who really never liked Strafford, and lastly, it is said, by a message from Strafford himself, who advised the king to sacrifice him.* Every effort, however, was made to save him. Balfour, the lieutenant of the tower, was offered £22,000, and one of Strafford's daughters in marriage to his son, and the king's guaranty of indemnity for his escape, but the stern keeper could not be bribed. Charles then almost begged for his life, or for commutation to perpetual imprisonment, but in vain. Strafford was beheaded 12th May, just six months and one day from that on which Pym carried up his impeachment to the house of lords. The vote on the bill of attainder against Strafford was, in the commons, 204 to 59, and in the house of lords 26 to 19.

* It is said, however, that when he heard the king had yielded, he exclaimed, "Put not your trust in princes."

Among the minority in the house of commons, Selden is almost the only distinguished name. Hyde, Falkland and Colepepper were all for the prosecution, though there is doubt as to whether Hyde voted. Certain it is he did not vote *for* Strafford. In this stroke against Strafford, it is to be observed, that the house acted in one respect with a generosity which the crown had never shown in any case of treason; a bill was immediately passed to relieve his children from the penalties of forfeiture, and corruption of the blood. (C. H. 2, 149.)

4. *Proceedings of parliament during its first session?* Besides the execution of Strafford, Laud was impeached and imprisoned. Others were alarmed: Lord-keeper Finch fled to Holland, Secretary Windebank to France. All whom the king had employed for oppression, from the servile judges down to the sheriffs and custom-house officers, were summoned to answer for their conduct. The church was purged, by expelling many incumbents, and restoring to their livings all such clergymen as had been deprived by the bishops or by the court of high commission for nonconformity. The star chamber, the high commission court, the council of York, were all abolished,* and those unfortunate victims of Laud and Charles, who had been immured in prisons, were now set free, with their cropped ears, slit noses, branded cheeks and foreheads, and lacerated backs, and wherever they passed they called forth the plaudits of an admiring people. Prynne, Burton and Bastwick came to London, on different days, in triumphal procession, attended by hundreds of carriages and thousands of horsemen, amidst multitudes on foot, wearing bay and rosemary in their hats. Their sentences were reversed, and damages to the amount of £5000 were awarded to each against his judges. (M. 2, 82. Ling. 10, 66.) Ship money was abolished; the condemnation of Hampden was proclaimed illegal; tonnage and poundage were abolished, and the forest courts and stannary courts, those relics of feudal oppression, were reformed. But the two most important measures were, that the parliament then sitting should not be prorogued or dissolved without its consent, and that a parliament should be held at least once every three years. Even Lord Clarendon admits that many of these measures were most salutary.

5. *Hostility to the established church—division of the popular*

* It seems strange, indeed, that in none of the previous parliaments had any effort been made to abolish these hateful tribunals, and this must be considered as decisive evidence of the moderation of the popular party, up to the meeting of the Long Parliament. These irregular courts were in fact the main spring of corruption and despotism, and their abolition is the true cause why Charles II., a worse man than Charles I., was nevertheless, with far more obedient subjects, never enabled to tyrannize to the extent that his father did.

party? The tyranny, rashness and folly of Charles's bishops were notorious. As we have seen, they had become so infatuated, as to impose on the clergy the celebrated *et cætera* oath, binding them *never* to attempt any alteration in the government of the church by bishops, deans, archdeacons, *et cætera*. They had in convocation enacted many canons by which the church was to be governed: all these were rescinded by an act not only denying the right of a convocation to bind the clergy, but impeaching the bishops at the same time of a high misdemeanor. But the house was beginning to manifest a spirit not to be contented with mere reformation. There was among the commons what was called the *root and branch* party, for the entire abolition of episcopacy. This party was composed chiefly of presbyterians and other sectaries. This is the party that was aided and stimulated by the Scots and their commissioners, at this time in London. By the instigation of these commissioners, a petition had been gotten up as early as December 11, 1640, with the signatures of 15,000 citizens, and 1,800 ministers, for the abolition of the hierarchy. This petition was favorably received by a majority of the house of commons, although Clarendon and the writers of the times think there were but few at first who were really anxious for a *total* destruction. The king informed parliament that he would never consent to the overthrow of episcopal government. The Scots commissioners, on the other hand, solicited, reasoned, prayed, and preached in favor of the presbyterian kirk. The church allotted for their use was crowded from morning to night. "The knot of the question (said these prayerful men) can only be cut by the axe of prayer." Fasts were solemnly observed by the godly, that "the Lord might join the breath of his nostrils, with the endeavors of weak man, to blow up a wicked and anti-scriptural church."

The spirit of ecclesiastical, rather than civil democracy, was the first sign of the approaching storm that alarmed the Hertfords and Southamptons, the Hydes and Falklands. A bill brought in by Sir Edward Deering, for the utter extirpation of episcopacy, actually passed to a second reading by a majority of 139 to 108. The debate on the petition mentioned above is remarkable as being the first in which the popular party was divided. Digby, Falkland, Selden, and Rudyard opposed it with great vehemence. Many, attached to the venerable church of the reformation, but who had hitherto gone along with the popular party, now halted in their course, when they saw that, for the sins of the bishops, the whole church was threatened with ruin. They feared the puritan bitterness, aggravated as it was by long persecution; they revolted from the indecent devastation committed in churches by the populace, and from the insults which now fell on the conforming ministers. They shuddered, when they saw Robert Harley under powers granted by the commons, taking from the churches all pictures, crosses, and superstitious figures, both inside and outside.*

6. *Rebellion in Ireland—its consequences?* Whilst the anti-episcopal party by its violence were driving from the popular side many of the moderates, who began to fear that the constitution would be overthrown by the intemperate spirit of innovation, an event occurred well calculated to stimulate the zeal of the presbyterians, and to increase the apprehensions of all who were averse to pushing reform into revolution. On the 23d September, 1641, occurred the famous Irish rebellion and massacre, headed by O'Neil, in which the number of protestant victims has been variously stated at from 4,000 to 200,000. The Irish catholics, both leaders and people, every where took up arms, claiming liberty for their worship and their country, calling on the name of the queen, and even of the king, whose pretended commission was exhibited by O'Neil. This cold-blooded massacre spread dismay over the whole of England and Scotland; every protestant thought himself in danger. A furious outcry was raised against popery, all over the kingdom. The king's well known hatred of the puritans, the confidence he had often placed in the papists, the intrigues that he had carried on in Ireland for the last three months to retain strongholds and soldiers in case of need, the queen's constant partiality and imprudent behavior towards the catholics, the forged commission of O'Neil, by many thought to be genuine, the supposed leaning of the episcopal church towards popery, the violent Arminianism of Archbishop Laud, his childish attachment to ceremonies, his superstitious veneration for altars, vestments, and painted windows, his opinions in favor of celibacy, all conspired to excite a strange suspicion, though really unfounded, in the popular mind, that the court was criminally implicated in this horrid rebellion, and accordingly it was found, when the parliament met again in November, after a short recess, that the puritans were more intractable than ever. The commons denounced to the peers 70 catholic lords and gentlemen, as dangerous persons, who ought to be confined in close custody. The queen's confessor was sent to the tower, and the establishment for the service of her chapel dissolved. Pursuivants were appointed with powers to apprehend priests and Jesuits; the king was importuned not to grant pardons or reprieves, and a resolution was passed by both houses of parliament against tolerating the catholic worship, either in Ireland or any other part of the British dominions.

* By the hand of this zealous knight fell the beautiful crosses at Charing and Cheapside, to the lasting regret of all faithful lovers of antiquities and architecture.

7. *Grand remonstrance?* Shortly after the meeting of parliament, Pym, Hampden and St. John drew up what was called the *grand remonstrance*, containing a dark picture of all the grievances under which the nation had labored since the death of James I., of the obstacles surmounted, the perils encountered, and those which still threatened the nation. It was, in fact, a sort of appeal to the people, and especially the presbyterians, inflaming all the passions which the Irish rebellion had kindled. This remonstrance excited one of the most stormy debates which had ever occurred in the house. It lasted for 12 hours. Many who were with the popular party up to this time now went over to the royal side. They saw no good that could possibly result from this measure. Why talk of grievances now, when they had all been redressed? Why such harsh and bitter language towards the king, when he was almost powerless? Why hold out expectations to the sectaries, that ought never to be complied with? In fine, why agitate and alarm, when the country needed repose and tranquillity? The remonstrance was finally carried in full house* about midnight, by the small majority of 159 to 148. Cromwell was most violently in favor of the remonstrance, and whispered to Lord Falkland after its passage, "had the remonstrance been thrown out, I would to-morrow have sold every thing I possess, and have left England for ever, and I know a great many honest folks who would have done the same thing."

As soon as the remonstrance passed, Hampden rose and proposed to have it printed. Hyde pronounced it contrary to usage, illegal and fatal, and said if adopted he should *protest.* Mr. Palmer, another of the moderate liberals, cried out "*I protest*," and immediately "*I protest, I protest*," echoed from every part of the hall. On the other side the utmost indignation was excited. The right of protest had never before been claimed in the house of commons. Pym rose and denounced it as dangerous and illegal; he was overwhelmed with invectives; he persisted, and was answered with threats. The whole house was in confusion. Several times the members had their hands on their swords. At last Hampden rose, with his characteristic mildness and gravity, and, after deploring the occurrence of such humiliating riots, proposed the adjournment of the question till the afternoon; it was then about two in the morning. In the evening session the parties became more tran-

* This I have said on the authority of Hallam, (2, 166.) Others assert that the debate was protracted to so late an hour, that the weak, the old, and the indifferent had left; even Nicholas, one of the king's ministers, left the house before the vote was taken. Sir Benjamin Rudyard said, when the vote was about to be taken, "this will be the verdict of a starving jury." The house generally met at 8 o'clock in the morning, and retired early. (G. 1, 193. W. B. H. 184.)

quil, and the printing was carried, and Palmer, who had been sent to the tower, was immediately released. Hyde, who first protested, was not sent to the tower, because his friends would not give him up.

8. *Reaction in favor of Charles?* The vote on the passage of the remonstrance developes a most important fact; it shows that a great reaction had commenced in favor of the king. On the bill of attainder against Strafford, the vote was 204 to 59, on the remonstrance it was 159 to 148, only 11 majority. It is easy to point out the causes of this reaction. The parliament had triumphed over the king; Strafford, the ablest and most fearless supporter of the throne, had been brought to the block, whilst the king was even begging for his life; the whole government was overawed; the monarch himself appeared humbled and care-worn. Men of moderate principles were satisfied with the political changes which had been achieved; they thought it time to halt. The rancor of the presbyterian party against the church of England, augmented as it had lately been by the catholic rebellion in Ireland, increased the apprehension that reform was fast running into revolution. Hampden saw this reaction in favor of Charles, and feared that it would be the means of losing all that had been gained. The people of England are generous; they always sympathize with the conquered, and consequently their sympathies were now running very strongly in favor of the king, who was regarded as the conquered party. It was to stem this returning tide of loyalty that the remonstrance was gotten up. But it had directly the opposite effect; it appeared like striking an antagonist when flat on his back, a thing which the bystanders in England especially will never permit. Not only did the vote in the house of commons indicate a change which might soon bring the king into a majority, but there were demonstrations of popular feeling in every direction, which clearly indicated the returning loyalty of the people. In his late journey from Edinburgh to London, Charles was received every where with loud acclamations of joy and affection, particularly at York. This spirit of loyalty had even reached London, the stronghold of radicalism. Richard Gurney, a friend of the king, was elected lord mayor, and when Charles returned from Scotland, Gurney prepared a most brilliant reception for him. Multitudes went out on horseback to meet and escort the king to Whitehall. The militia lined the streets, the houses were decorated, the bells were rung, and shouts of "Long live the king! God bless King Charles and Queen Henrietta Maria!" resounded on all sides.

Notwithstanding the fall of the feudal system, its spirit still animated the gentry. They began now to despise those talkative, cavilling citizens whose rigid creed forbade wine, games, and all the pleasures and sports of Old England. At first this class had gone with people against regal tyranny, but now they thought the king had made concessions enough. Many of them came to London armed for the purpose of defending the honor and life of the king, threatened as they said by parliament and the rude mobs of London; they walked the streets proudly, visited the taverns, and went often to Whitehall. They were joined by the young lawyers, students in the temple, patronized by the court, eager to take part in its pleasures. To this restless and presumptuous throng, that began daily to assemble around Whitehall, may be added a less honorable set—a band of bullies, composed principally of officers and soldiers of fortune, tutored in the continental wars, dissolute, servile, and bold, irritated against parliament for disbanding them without pay or employment, and with the people for detesting their loose morals. Thus was formed a sort of court mob, who inveighed bitterly against the commons, laughed at the presbyterians, took obnoxious royalists under their protection, and quarrelled and fought with the London mobs. (G. 1, 195, 200. Beau. 2, 151. M. 1, 226, 2, 87.) The party names of *roundheads* and *cavaliers* were introduced about this time. Captain Hyde, drawing his sword amidst the mob at Westminster, and saying he would crop the ears of those *round-headed* dogs that bawled against the bishops, is said to have fixed the name on the popular party. The apprentices wore their hair cut round and short. (W. B. H. 184.)

9. *Insincerity of Charles—Attempts to arrest six members of parliament—Consequences?* Never did the bad character and the bad luck of the Stuart family more decisively manifest itself than at this juncture of affairs. Had Charles only taken advantage of the returning loyalty of his subjects, without again attempting to be treacherous and tyrannical, there is little doubt but that he might yet have maintained himself. But he once more attempted the old game of treachery and tyranny, and he was undone. The late demonstrations of loyalty raised his hopes; the young cavaliers always around Whitehall raised his courage and presumption. All his old prepossessions in favor of the indefeasible rights and privileges of kings, came back upon him in full force. He gradually assumed a more haughty bearing towards parliament, and a disposition to intimidate. William Balfour, so faithful to the popular cause, was removed from the tower, and Sir Thomas Lunsford, an audacious cavalier, put over it. There occurred about this time some riots and fights, attended with the spilling of blood, between the London mob and the court mob, about the bishops in the house of peers, the bill for whose exclusion was then pending before that body. Twelve bishops considered their lives in danger, and withdrew

from the house of peers, and at the same time sent up a solemn protest in advance against the legality of any measure that should pass them without their concurrence. The commons considered this attempt to stop the wheels of legislation as nothing less than a daring attempt to annihilate parliament. An impeachment of the bishops was immediately sent up to the peers. The upper house admitted the justice of the charge, and immediately committed the twelve bishops to the tower.

Now it was that Charles began to meditate one of *his* strokes of policy, and to execute it too in *his* own way. All of a sudden he seemed again to despair. He made no move in favor of the bishops, said no more of the riots, ceased entirely to complain of the debates. The commons had been indignant that such a man as Lunsford had been set over the tower; the king now consented to remove him, and put Byron in his place. As the number of cavaliers about Whitehall was daily increasing, the commons asked for a guard to protect them. The king did not give the guard, but answered, "*I solemnly promise, on the honor of a king, to preserve you, one and all, from all violence, with as much care as I would take for my own safety and that of my children.*" On that *very day*, Herbert, the attorney general, went to the house of peers and preferred an accusation of high treason against Lord Kimbolton, and five of the most distinguished members of the house of commons, Hampden, Pym, Hollis, Strode, and Hazzlerig. It is difficult to find in English history a more striking instance of tyranny, treachery and folly combined. The attorney general had no right to impeach these men; the house of lords had no right to try them, even if guilty. But the charges against them would equally have involved all the other members of their party, forming still a majority of the house. This was all the work of the king, the queen, and the apostate Digby; they alone were responsible. The new advisers, Hyde, Falkland, and Colepepper, were not even consulted, so much was the monarch determined on this stroke of policy. All three condemned the act, when it occurred, as weak and ruinous.

The result was just what any other man than Charles might have anticipated. The commons refused to surrender their members; the peers had no wish at such a crisis to usurp an unconstitutional jurisdiction, although attempted to be forced on them by the king. The king sent an officer to seal up the lodgings and trunks of the accused. The commons sent their sergeant to break the seals. A parley ensued. The king again endeavored to lull them, by saying that he would give a definitive answer to their petition on the next day, and the house adjourned. In the mean time he determined to try one more stroke of policy. In making the charge before the house of peers, he struck at the institution of juries; in sending an officer to arrest the members, he struck at the privileges of parliament. He resolved now to go in person with an armed escort, and seize the obnoxious members in the house. No one knew this secret but the queen; she babbled it to the Countess of Carlisle, supposed to be Pym's mistress, and the countess managed to convey the intelligence to Pym. The five members, however, kept their seats until Captain Langrish came in, and said that the king was coming with 3 or 400 men, guards, cavaliers, and students. The house counselled the five members to abscond—all obeyed but Strode; and his friend, Walter Earle, at last pushed him out after Charles had gotten into the yard. When the king got to the door he ordered his guard to remain behind; with his nephew alone he traversed the hall, looking particularly as he passed towards the seat of Pym. All the members rose to receive him. He took the speaker's chair, and asked the speaker where the five members were. The speaker told him, in that hall he had no eyes to see, nor tongue to speak, but as the house directed. Charles then said he perceived the birds were flown, protested that he never meant to use force, but to proceed in a fair way; and told the house they must give up the members when they returned. He then left the chair with his hat still in his hand, and, as he withdrew, many members cried out *privilege! privilege!* The baffled monarch, mortified and chagrined at his miserable and ridiculous failure, returned to Whitehall with his company of bravoes, who had been impatiently waiting for the word, cocking their pistols and crying "*fall on.*" He and the queen had built their last hopes on this *coup-de-main.* He kissed Henrietta in the morning when he left her, and promised he would return in an hour the master of his kingdom. The queen had been sitting all the while, with watch in hand, eagerly counting the minutes as they passed. A gloom was now thrown over Whitehall. The ears of the monarch were assailed every where by the cry of *privilege! previlege!* and now and then by the still more alarming shout which the rebellious Israelites of old had thundered in the ears of the hateful Rehoboam, "*to your tents, O Israel!*" All was undone; Hyde, Falkland, and Colepepper, sorrowful, mortified and offended, kept aloof.* The king issued a proclamation to have the gates closed, and that no one should shelter the accused; but, at the moment that he was issuing it, he felt, and all around him felt, how utterly impotent he was to enforce it. Every body knew where the five members were, yet no one dared to touch a hair of their heads.

* The king had before promised these three men, decidedly the most worthy of all his counsellors, that he would take no measures in regard to the House without consulting them. (M. 1, 227.) Thus was he treacherous to friend as well as foe.

10. *Consequences?* The attempt to seize these five members was undoubtedly the real cause of the war. This treacherous tyrannical act destroyed all confidence in the king; it checked at once the returning loyalty of the British people; it demonstrated to the moderate party the bitter truth, that the king of England could never be rendered harmless without making him impotent. To talk of the guaranty of his royal word and his royal promise was worse than ridiculous. From that moment the parliament felt itself compelled to surround the hall with defensive army. The city assumed the appearance of a garrison. From that moment, too, says Clarendon, the carriage of Hampden became fiercer; he now drew the sword and threw away the scabbard, with the significant motto, *vestigia nulla retrorsum.* Up to this time, although firm and decisive, he had nevertheless been one of the most mild and temperate men of his party. He had often calmed the house when lashed into a storm, and given moderate counsels, when his more hot-headed cousin, Oliver Cromwell, would have drawn the sword. When the news of Hampden's danger reached Buckinghamshire, the county of his residence, and the one he represented in parliament, 4000 of the freeholders, each wearing in his hat a copy of the protestation in favor of the privileges of parliament, rode up to London to defend their beloved representative.

11. *The king retires from London?* The king, shut up in Whitehall, forsaken by his best counsellors, was fast becoming an object of contempt in London. He heard that the *five members* were to be brought back, in spite of him, in triumph to Westminster, under an escort of the militia, the people, and even the watermen of the Thames.* Charles could not endure the idea of seeing this triumphal procession under the very windows of his palace. The queen, alternately mad with anger, and trembling with fear, conjured him to leave the city. Royalists and messengers, who had been sent to different parts of the kingdom, made favorable reports, and advised him to leave London, the stronghold of the Roundheads, and repair to some place where his authority would be obeyed. They said the king, away from parliament, would be free, but that the parliament could do nothing without the king; that the king's authority was still acknowledged in far the larger portion of the kingdom. Thus was Charles induced, on the 10th January, 1642, the very evening before the five members were carried back in triumph to the house, to depart from London and the palace of Whitehall, which he was never to re-enter, save on his way to the scaffold.

* His first exclamation on hearing the news was, "What! do these *water-rats* also forsake me?" The circulation of this speech among the watermen soon made those who had hitherto been very loyal, extremely hostile to the king. (G. 1, 220.)

12. *Dispute between the king and parliament about the command of the army—grand rebellion?* It is needless to dwell on details. It was easy to see that the differences between the king and his parliament could not be adjusted, but were rapidly hastening to a crisis. Without noticing minor matters, we at once pass to the great question which was the immediate cause of the civil war. The rebellion in Ireland still continued—an army was to be sent there. Who shall command that army? Who shall command the militia? The king was undoubtedly the constitutional commander of both. But the parliament could not trust him; and insisted on having command of the militia, and ths direction of the Irish war. "No, by God! not for an hour!" exclaimed the king, "You require in that what was never before required of a king; what I would not grant to my wife or my children." "Keep the militia, keep the militia," cried the queen—"that will bring back every thing." Upon this issue the two parties appealed to God and the sword. And on the 23d November, 1642, the king erected the royal standard at Nottingham, with the significant motto, "*Render unto Cesar the things which are Cesar's.*"

SEC. X—FROM THE GRAND REBELLION TO THE REVOLUTION OF 1688.

1. *General remarks on the grand rebellion—histories of that event?* There is no subject which has been debated with more warmth than the question about the right and wrong of the parties in the English rebellion. So intimately is this subject connected with the great and fundamental principles of government, that to this very day it is debated with scarcely diminished zeal between the great political parties, not only in England, but all over the world. In the discussion of this question, the first thing evidently to be attended to is the source from which our information is derived. It has been well observed that the Roundheads labored under the disadvantage of the lion in the fable. Though they were the conquerors, their enemies were the painters. As a party, the Roundheads rather decried and ran down learning; and the consequence was, that *learning took* its revenge by running down them in turn. The best cotemporary book on their side is Mrs. Hutcheson's Memoirs. May's History of the Parliament is good, but is cut short too soon. Ludlow is foolish and violent. Most of the later writers, until a very recent period, who have taken the same side, have had much more zeal than either candor or skill; *e. g.*, Oldmixon and Catherine Macauley. On the other side are the most authoritative and popular works in our language, those of Clarendon and Hume. The former, always able, stately and dignified, makes even his numerous prejudices

and errors appear respectable. The exceedingly fascinating narrative of Hume is known to all; hundreds, perhaps thousands, have formed their opinions exclusively from a perusal of it. He is, however, culpably partial to the Stuarts—so much so, that he has warped the whole tenor of his history to make out the best possible case for them. He hated the liberty of this period, because it allied itself with an austere and canting religion, and has consequently every where, whilst affecting the impartiality of the judge, pleaded the cause of tyranny and the Stuarts with all the dexterity of an advocate. Later writers, such as Millar, Guizot, Hallam, and Macaulay,* have corrected the errors of Hume; but still the deep impressions made on the public mind by this great and popular historian, are far from being yet effaced.

2. *Difference between king and parliament—ministerial responsibility?* In looking to the struggles of Charles with his parliaments, the British government as then administered appears almost *impracticable.* The commons on the one side, with an overwhelming majority against the king, have only to stop the supplies, which they clearly have the right to do, and the government is paralyzed. If, therefore, the king thinks his honor or his vital interests will not allow him to grant their demands, the *regular* supplies being cut off, he is forced to play the tyrant, to recur to all irregular shifts and expedients for raising money. This is the principal cause of the tyranny of Charles from 1629 to 1640. He was undoubtedly a prince of more amiable disposition than many mentioned in British history, and yet few have ever tyrannized to the same extent. Again, this same cause must almost necessarily push reformation into revolution. The more determined the parliament on the one side, the more tyrannical is the king on the other—the parties become exasperated, the breach between them widens, until confidence in each is lost, and there is no common ground of compromise. Any one question may lead to such a result. Take for example the attack on a minister. The commons will do nothing unless the minister is removed; the king thinks his honor is involved in defending him and holding him in office. Parliament is dissolved, and every kind of machinery is put in motion to extort money from the people; but this will only answer for a short time. The regular supplies cannot be dispensed with, parliament must again be called, and the late tyranny of course has made the minister more hateful than ever, and the commons more resolute to do nothing without his removal. Thus the king is constantly aggravated and stimulated to violent efforts, to

* The masterly articles of this writer, in the Edinburgh Review, are perhaps the ablest and most interesting which have ever been written on this subject, and have gone very far to settle the question of right between the two parties.

annihilate the power that plagues him; and that power becomes more distrustful and ferocious with every effort that he makes to overthrow it.

The remedy to all these difficulties is now very clear—it consists in this. The ministry are held responsible for the measures of the king. If there be a clear and decided majority of the two houses of parliament against the government, the king *must* dismiss his ministry, and puts in another that will administer the government on the principles of the opposition. Thus the executive government is kept in harmony with parliament, and there is no such thing now as stopping regular supplies; for there would be no motive in a majority in parliament to do it when the power is in their hands. This salutary change has been brought about in the English government by the revolution of 1688, more clearly defining the rights of kings and parliament, and by the gradual usages which have sprung up since that time, particularly under the two first Georges. These kings were German, totally unacquainted with the English character, and one of them with even the English language; and withal, they and their successors to the present time have been far inferior men to the average of the Plantagenet, the Tudor, or even the Stuart kings.* Under these circumstances every thing has been trusted to their ministers. The king of England has become more and more a mere state pageant. This being the case, that violent conflict which so often occurred between king and parliament, never takes place now. For the king is not now the real governor; the minister is the man, and he goes out of office, as a matter of course, when the majority is clearly against him on great measures. Sir Robert Walpole forms perhaps the last link in the transition period from the old system to the new. He held office for some time, and had recourse to bribery in order to secure a concurrence of the houses. It was perhaps from looking too exclusively to the order of things prevailing under Walpole, that Alexander Hamilton was led to make the famous remark chronicled by Mr. Jefferson. When the elder Adams affirmed that the British government, with equality of representation, and purged of its corruption, would be the most perfect ever devised by the wit of man, Hamilton answered, "Purge it of its corruption, and give to its popular branch equality of representation, and it would become an impracticable government; as it stands it is the most perfect government

* Every cross of the Plantagenets seems to have been productive of injury to the intellect. The Tudor princes were great, but perhaps not equal to the Plantagenets. The cross with the Stuarts produced an evident depreciation of the Tudor stock. And, lastly, the German cross has brought down the stock far beneath the Stuarts. It is perhaps well for England that this degeneracy has occurred; for it has evidently facilitated the important change spoken of in the text.

which ever existed." (J. 4, 450.) But, according to the present plan of administering the government, there is clearly no necessity for bribery to insure its practicability.* This same change explains another thing which would be inexplicable without it. We see at once why no late minister has ever been pursued by the majorities in parliament to the scaffold; it is not necessary now. Buckingham and Strafford could never have held their places under the present system. Public opinion would have displaced them, without recourse to impeachment or the block.

3. *On the character of Charles?* But although, under any circumstances, according to the plan of administering the government in the time of the Stuarts, there must have been collisions of a dangerous character between king and parliament, yet may we fairly assert that Charles was himself to blame for a large portion of the calamities which overtook him. On himself rests a great deal of the responsibility. He was, after making every allowance for the difficult crisis in which his lot was cast, insincere and treacherous to a most disgraceful extent. No one, after a perusal of his history, can justify his double dealings, and violations of royal promises and oaths. He could not be trusted; he had rather too much of the Darnley blood, too much of the Darnley deceit and treachery in his character† to be defended on any set of sound principles. Such men always push their adversaries into extremes, and are the most unfit of all characters to pass safely through a revolutionary crisis. Let us for one moment imagine Charles to have been king of England instead of Elizabeth, when parliament made the grand at-

* There is one respect in which the inequality of representation may have contributed to the practicability of the government. *The rotten borough system* enabled the government to command a greater number of votes in parliament than it could otherwise, owing to the influence that might so easily be exerted in the elections in those districts where there were very few voters. Hence if the government should ever find, in spite of this advantage, a majority against it in the two houses, it would yield at once, because there would be a certainty that the majority in the nation would be much greater than that in parliament. But under a complete equality of representation, a mere majority in parliament would not by any means be so clear a proof of a decided majority in the nation, and therefore ministers would not be so ready to yield. A majority in the American congress against the government is not *decisive* evidence that a majority of the people are against it; but under the rotten borough system of England, a majority in the house of commons was always decisive as to the popular will.

† It was this Darnley cross that seems to have spoiled the blood of the Scottish line. James V., the father of Mary, was a great and noble prince, and seems to have had a presentiment of the result which would follow from the accession of his daughter Mary to the throne, when he made that celebrated exclamation, "By a woman the kingdom came, and by a woman the kingdom will go."

tack on the monopolies. (See ante. p 404.) We can scarcely doubt but that his conduct would have been in perfect contrast with that of Elizabeth ; he would have resisted, evaded, equivocated, promised, have violated his promise, imprisoned members for debate after solemn guaranty of protection, and finally, when forced unequivocally to yield, he would have done it in such a manner as to obtain neither the thanks nor confidence of the people. There has been great sympathy excited in favor of this monarch, in consequence of his exemplary private life. He was a constant and devoted husband, and a pious man, but still all this did not justify his conduct to his parliaments, but only made him to be a ruler after the Italian fashion—"constant at prayers as a priest, heedless of oaths as an atheist."

4. *Principles on which the discussions were conducted?* The English revolution differs from the French most strikingly in one particular. In the latter there was no appeal to precedents by the popular party ; it was at once acknowledged that the past practice of the government was all against the people. The movement was justified, however, on the great and fundamental principle of government, that sovereignty resides, de jure, in the people, and that they have a right to change their government whenever they choose. The French democrats argued the question on the principle of inherent right, and therefore made the past acts and privileges of the monarchy as so many acts and evidences of usurpation and tyranny, all calling aloud for revolution. In England the case was totally different. Both parties professed the utmost reverence for the constitution. The statutes, jurisprudence, traditions, customs, &c., of the realm, were constantly invoked by both parties as the only legitimate judges of the strife. Coke and Selden would have been wholly out of place in the French revolution ; they were indispensable to the English. From the dusty records of the Tower, their indefatigable labors drew forth those precedents and authorities that gave the popular party the ascendency in the argument. In the *petition of right*, for example, drawn by Selden, the commons say to the king, "your subjects have *inherited* this freedom ;" and in the declaration of rights accompanying the petition, they do not pretend to frame a government for themselves, but strive only to secure the religion, laws and liberties, *long possessed*, and lately endangered ; and their prayer is only "that it may be declared and enacted, that all and singular the rights and liberties asserted and declared are the true, ancient, and indubitable rights and liberties of the people of this kingdom." (Al. 1. 49.) Even at the moment when they were clearly transcending all the limits of the ancient constitution, you find them still indulging in the belief that they are justified by the past. Instead of

appealing to the fundamental principles of government, they clung still to the laws, customs, and traditions of *Old England.* And it was on this very account that the advocates of Charles gained decidedly the advantage over the parliamentarians in the great discussion on the *militia bill.* It was on this principle that Turgot remarked "that while England is the country in the world where public freedom has longest subsisted, and political institutions are most the subject of discussion, it is at the same time the one in which innovations are with the most difficulty introduced, and where the most obstinate resistance is made to undoubted improvements. You might alter the whole political frame of government in France, with more facility than you could introduce the most insignificant change into the customs or fashions of England." (Al. 1, 48.) This has indeed been one of the distinguishing characteristics of the British people. Throughout their whole history, during the gloomy period of Norman oppression, it was on the more equal laws of Saxon reigns that they looked back with fond affection. When the barons assembled at Runnymede, it was not an *imaginary* system of government which they established, but the old and consuetudinary laws of Edward the Confessor were only moulded into a new form and put on a firmer basis in *Magna Charta.* The memorable reply of the barons to the proposal of the prelates at Mertoun, *Nolumus leges Angliæ mutare*, has passed into a rule which has preserved the constitution through the convulsions of later times. The principle here alluded to is at once the consequence and the reward of free institutions. Universally it will be found that the attachment of men to the usuages and customs of their forefathers, is greatest where they have had the largest share in the enjoyment of them. The danger of innovation is most to be feared where the exercise of rights have been unknown to the people. The dynasties of the east are of ephemeral duration, but the customs of the Swiss democracies are as immovable as the mountains in which they were cradled. When Uri and Uterwalden were offered fraternization with the French republic, they expressed almost as much horror as Agrippa did when Caligula proposed to set up his statue in the temple at Jerusalem, and with one voice they declined an honor which had seduced so many other states, and begged that they might be permitted to live on under their government and institutions, precisely as William Tell had left them.

5. *Roundheads and cavaliers—influence of property moderates the revolution?* From too exclusive a view of some of the phases exhibited by the French revolution, shallow reasoners have often been induced to think that all these revolutions are agrarian in their character, and consist of an outbreak of the *under stratum* of society against the

upper, the men of *no* property against those who *have* property. But the fact is not so; the great revolutions of modern times have been brought about principally by the agency of the property. It is true that at such times there is a violent tendency to run into agrarianism, but it is not with that intent that the revolution begins. In England there is no doubt but that up to the breaking out of the rebellion a majority of the property was on the side of the parliament; and during the contest it was pretty generally the *unprivileged* against the *privileged* property. The fact is, that in England the lowest classes would have been most probably on the side of the monarchy, but for the influence of religion. The popular party in England was made a preponderating party from the union of two elements, the liberals and the puritans; the former were generally men of property, and interested in its defence; the latter included a great number of men without property. John Hampden is the true exponent of the first class, and perhaps the younger Vane, who came to America in order that he might take the sacrament *without* kneeling at the altar, of the second. It was the religious persecution that threw the οι πολλοι, *the many*, on the side of the parliament; and the usurpations and arbitrary conduct of the government which drove the larger portion of the property in the same direction. But, whilst the popular cause could boast of so much respectability, wealth and numbers, we must at the same time do justice to the other side. Throwing out the horse-boys, gamblers and bravoes, who sometimes formed a sort of royal mob, and confining our attention to the genuine *cavalier*, we find his to be a noble character. Well may an Englishman feel pride in comparing him with the vile instruments used by despots in other lands—with the mutes who crowd their antechambers, or the Janizaries who mount guard at their gates. Well has it been said that the cavaliers were not mere machines dressed in uniforms, caned into skill, intoxicated into valor, defending without love, destroying without hatred. It was not for a treacherous king, or intolerant church, that they fought. They scarcely entered into the merits of the mere political question; but it was for the old banner which had waved in so many battles over the heads of their fathers, and for the altars at which they had received the hands of their brides. They had more of the graces of private life than their adversaries, particularly the puritanical portion of them. They had more profound and polite learning—their manners were more engaging, their tempers more amiable, their tastes more elegant, and their households more cheerful.

The humane and temperate spirit of the English revolution is due to the respectability and wealth of both the parties engaged in the conflict. Property is always opposed to excesses; it countenances no violent innovations; it opposes proscriptions; it supports order and regular government. The armies during the rebellion fought on the humane principles of the laws of modern warfare. Few were taken to the scaffold, either before or after the grand rebellion. The few excesses committed during the belligerent operations were principally found on the king's side and were due mainly to the foreign officers, such as the rough, ill-bred, reckless Count Rupert, who had no sympathy with the people. The parliamentary troops were remarkable for good discipline and perfect subordination. So that we may upon the whole confidently assert, that few revolutions have occurred, in the history of the world, stained with less crime and less excess than the English. The English revolution avoided the curse of these popular movements; it never ran into agrarianism, like the French. In the French revolution property began the work; but as soon as the class possessing the property propelled it through one stage, then the class immediately below them was roused, and considered the one above them as aristocratic. In England very strong symptoms of disorganization, similar to those which occurred in the French revolution, occasionally manifested themselves; but the sober temperate character of the revolution stifled all such developments at their birth; *e. g.*, the burning the records in the Tower was proposed formally in parliament, and a powerful speech from Selden silenced the incendiary. This is a fair parallel to the conduct of Hebert in the French revolution, who directed his satellites towards the greatest library in the world, the *Bibliotheque Nationale*, and was prevented from destroying it only by being persuaded to postpone it for a day or two, when, luckily for the cause of literature, the guillotine intervened and took off his head. Under Cromwell there was a debate on the proposition to dissolve the universities, as fitting to *be taken away for the public use.* The perpetual invectives of the *sans-culottes* of France against *proprietors and property* is well known; we find precisely the same spirit manifesting itself among a very small party in the English revolution; *e. g.*, the parliamentary journal, called the "*Moderate*," in 1649, assumed that "*property* is the original cause of any sin between party and party, as to civil transactions. And, since the tyrant is shaken off, and the government altered *in nomine*, so ought it really to redound to the good of the people *in specie*," &c. That is to say, property ought to be divided or abolished. (J. 2d, Sec. 2. 412.) Thus are we admonished by the English revolution, as well as by the French, of the besetting sin of such movements. The men of no property are apt at last to be excited, and wage war against property and all regular governments.

6. *Roundheads and cavaliers—former beaten at first, victorious at*

last? We have already stated that the roundheads embraced two parties, the *liberals in politics* and the *reformers in religion;* and that they were the more numerous, and, in the aggregate, had more of the wealth than the opposite party. At first the cavaliers seemed to triumph; they were a better organized party, more high-spirited, better skilled in the use of arms, and had more of the habit of command, and, consequently, more self-reliance and decision of character. So prosperous was the king's cause at first, that some of his adherents, like Hyde and Falkland, were afraid that his success would be so complete as to restore him to the throne under circumstances which would make him absolute. The moderates of his party did not wish him to conquer too easily. But a popular party, although weak at first, is apt with any thing like equality in resources, to triumph at last; not that it has more perseverance, for in that it is generally deficient, but if put tegether, it soon comes to display more energy of character. The very chaotic condition of such a party gives hope to all; every man is urging himself forward. Aristocratic birth, and the ancient order of things, does not stand in the way of real merit. The cobbler from his last, or the blacksmith from his anvil, both feel that they have an equal right to the highest offices of the land, if they can only display the talents. In the violent ebullition of the political caldron, the bottom stratum may be thrown to the top. And it seems to be a sort of law of human greatness, that the man who has had energy to rise from the bottom to the top, goes up with an impulse which carries him as far beyond the great men of the aristocracy, as they are usually above the lower orders. Hence perhaps philosophy might easily have foreseen that the master spirit of the times must have arisen on the popular side. It is a remarkable circumstance, that the officers who had studied tactics in the best schools of Europe, under Vere in the Netherlands, and under Gustavus Adolphus in Germany, were not as efficient as English officers who had never seen any thing of war till the rebellion; *e. g.*, Hampden was far better than Essex, and Cromwell than Leslie. And it is a little curious, too, that the most distinguished men were past the middle age. Cromwell was upwards of 40, and Hampden about 50, when they commenced their military career. In France they were always young men who rose the fastest. Perhaps this difference may be attributed in some sort to the sober, temperate character of the English revolution—resulting from the respectability of the parties, and the influence of property.

7. *Play of political affinities which brought Charles to the block?* The two great parties, the political reformers and the religious reformers, as might have been predicted, quarrelled in the hour of victory.

By 1643 the political reformers had gained all they wished, and the larger portion of the party were more averse to the introduction of the presbyterian religion as the established church, than to retaining a moderate episcopacy. The presbyterians, on the other hand, cared but little for political reform. What they wanted chiefly was to put their church in the place of the episcopal. These two parties agreed in one thing: neither of them wished to get rid of the monarch. The presbyterians wished to retain Charles, but make him introduce the presbyterian religion. The majority of the political reformers wished to retain him, because they thought the revolution had been carried far enough, and were by no means in favor of pure republicanism. As was naturally to be expected from such a state of parties, two others quickly arose, and, by a coalition, triumphed. As the parliament began to triumph, the presbyterians began to act as if their religion was to be the established religion. It was seen from their spirit that they were just as intolerant as the episcopalians had been. They did but act as all religious parties have ever been found to do. In the time of oppression and intolerance, they clamored for freedom of conscience; in the hour of victory they became intolerant. This naturally produced an opposition party, known by the name of the *independents*, who maintained that no *national* church was necessary—that every congregation of true Christians was a church, and should be independent of all others, and be governed by its own laws. These farther maintained the principle of freedom of conscience. Of course other dissenting sects, like the Brownists, Anabaptists, &c., would league with the independents.

Again, while the religious reformers were thus schismatizing, the political reformers were exhibiting a similar scene. The moderate portion, as already stated, forming the great majority, wished to stop the revolution without abolishing the monarchy; another portion, called the republicans, were for establishing a republic upon the ruins of the monarchy. Around this party of course clustered all the utopian dreamers, the levellers and the agrarians. It was this party which was beginning now, for the first time in the British revolution, to utter those powerful words which, whether well or ill understood, have always roused the most energetic passions of the human heart, *equality of rights*, *a just distribution of social wealth*, &c. Hitherto the parties had appealed to the precedents and practice of the government in by-gone times; the party of the republicans however was beginning to appeal to the inherent rights of man. The republicans and the independents of course united against the moderates and the presbyterians, and formed a great, though rather grotesque party, containing philosophers, levellers and fanatics. Among them were Harrington, dreaming of a society of sages; Sydney talking of the liberty of Sparta and Rome; Lilburne of the re-establishment of the old Saxon laws; Harrison of the coming of Christ, &c. The presbyterians predominated in the parliament, but the independents and republicans composed the army under the nominal command of Fairfax, but really controlled and managed by the much abler head of Cromwell.

In the mean time this play of affinities between the parties was singularly well calculated to mislead, and finally ruin, a man of the temperament of Charles. Although a captive, he was soon induced to entertain irrational hopes, from finding that all parties were trying to gain him. The moderates were for retaining him, with some abatement of regal power, and some modifications of the church establishment. The presbyterians were for him, if he would only sanction *their* church. The whole Scottish people were for him, on this ground. Cromwell, who was as subtle, artful and calculating in politics as he was skilful in the field, and who was in some measure the exponent of the army, was disposed to conciliate and flatter the king at first; for he did not yet see clearly his own way to the dictatorship, and, in the event of a restoration, he was anxious to have some claims on the favor of the monarch. Under such circumstances, Charles's usual indecision reappeared. He undertook to coquet with all parties, and would satisfy none. If he had quickly, and in good faith, embraced the offer of the presbyterians, he might perhaps have again been placed on the throne—he would have been backed by parliament and the whole kingdom of Scotland—but the establishment of their church, which was the *sine qua non*, he could never be brought to accept.

The army, of course, soon felt its power, and began to exercise it. After a series of negotiations and altercations between it and the parliament, Colonel Pride's *purge*, as it was called, on the 6th December, 1648, forcibly excluded from parliament the friends of the king, and gave the ascendency in that body to the independents. From this moment the cause of Charles became hopeless, and he was brought to the block on 30th January, 1649.

8. *Protectorate of Oliver Cromwell?* The party which brought Cromwell into power, was evidently a very small minority of the whole British kingdom; but it gained the victory through the agency of the army, which was one of the best that has ever been formed in any country. After the king's execution, the house of lords was abolished; a council of 39 members exercised the executive functions. The whole power of the government was vested in this council, and in this mutilated parliament, called the *rump;* and they depended upon an army of 45,000, under the command of Cromwell. For four years this clumsy

machinery worked with great energy. Cromwell, at the head of the army, subdued Ireland and Scotland, and defeated Charles II. at Worcester. His reputation and power were prodigiously enhanced by these wars, and he terminated the struggle by turning the *rump* out, and assuming the powers of a dictator.

His protectorate constitutes one of the most brilliant periods in British history. Most political convulsions evoke some master spirit to fashion and direct them. Cæsar was produced by the convulsions of the expiring commonwealth. Bonaparte was the giant child of the French revolution, and Cromwell was the natural product of his age. His character exhibits that curious mixture of elements marvellously suited to the times in which his lot was cast. His extraordinary and peculiar talents of subtlety, fanaticism and resolution, enabled him to accomplish the great purposes of his ambition. Knowing the character of the British people, he endeavored to rule by means of parliaments, but he could never succeed. He summoned four of them, and was meditating about a fifth when he died; but they were all too refractory for his impatient spirit, and he could not tolerate them. A people that have been trained, like the English, through successive ages, in all the forms and practices of free government, cannot easily be cheated into quiet submission to arbitrary power, merely by the brilliancy of results —they look to permanent principles rather than particular facts; they look to the future rather than to the present; they regard the average of human nature rather than the man on the throne. In spite of all Cromwell's success, at home and abroad, his government could not rally around it the sound public opinion of the British nation. In spite of the glory and power of England, the people detested the military despotism of the dictator, and sighed for the restoration of their kings and parliaments.

9. *Restoration of the Stuarts?* The death of Cromwell, and the imbecile and unambitious character of his son Richard, at once made way for the restoration. Never was any event more welcome to a people than the return of the Stuarts to the British throne. England had run through all the stages of revolution, anarchy and military despotism, and was now rejoiced that this scene of change and revolution had given place to one of permanence and stability, under a monarch of the ancient line. The revolution had not worked many of those violent changes in property which have ever been found to give the new possessors an unshaken fidelity to the new government. Even the bulk of ecclesiastical property still remained; the colleges still held their estates; the parson still received his tithes. Thus the old constitution of England could without difficulty be re-established; and, of all its

features, none seemed so dear to the people as the monarchical. All accounts represent the nation as in a state of hysterical excitement, of drunken joy, on the return of the monarch. Bonfires blazed, bells jingled; the streets were thronged at night by boon companions, who forced all the passers-by to swallow on their knees brimming glasses to the health of his most sacred majesty, and the damnation of *red-nosed Nol.* Such was England in 1660. (M. 3, 47.)

10. *Reign of Charles II. and James II.?* Never was loyalty so complete; and never were people so sadly requited. Charles had an immense advantage over other princes. He was acquainted with all the vicissitudes of this life, and all diversities of character; he had known restraint, danger, penury and dependence; he had suffered from ingratitude, insolence, and treachery; but he had experienced, too, faithful friendship and heroic attachment. He had seen, if ever man saw, both sides of human nature. But only one side remained in his memory. He had merely learned to distrust his species—to consider integrity in men, and modesty in women, as mere acting. Under his reign, says Macaulay, came those days, never to be recalled without a blush, the days of servitude without loyalty, and sensuality without love, of dwarfish talents and gigantic vices, the paradise of cold hearts and narrow minds, the golden age of the coward, the bigot and the slave. The king sank into viceroy of France, and pocketed, with complacent infamy, her degrading insults and her more degrading gold. The caresses of harlots, and the jests of buffoons, regulated the measures of a government, which had just ability enough to deceive, and just religion enough to persecute. (3, 48, and 1, 55.) Such a bench and such a bar England had never seen. Jones, Scroggs, Jeffries, North, Wright, Sawyer, Williams, Shower, will ever remain, it is to be hoped, the blackest spots on the legal chronicles of England.

But it is impossible to say how much the people of England would have borne, but for the bigotry and folly of James II. Even after the bloody judicial campaign of that sanguinary fiend, Jeffries, no member in the house of commons ventured to whisper the mildest censure on his conduct, and no man, but old Edmund Waller, ventured to attack the cruelty of the military chiefs. It is true there had been reactions against the throne, but whenever they bade fair, as was the case towards the latter part of Charles's reign, to terminate in civil war, so great was the horror of the British people of this result, that they immediately rallied around the monarch, and left the agitators to their fate. But James, besides being a tyrant, was a bigot likewise. He was resolved on the establishment of the Catholic church; and this measure was all that was wanting to set all parties against him. Hitherto the church of England had been the unflinching supporter of the restored house of Stuart, and the doctrine of passive obedience. James seems to have been stupid enough to suppose that they would still advocate their principles, even when they should become martyrs to them; but he was sadly disappointed. The moment he showed an unequivocal design to fill all places with catholics, the church renounced the doctrine of passive obedience, and hoisted the standard of revolt. Even the university of Oxford, the stronghold of toryism, the disgusting supporter of the monarchy, through all its shameless tyranny, enrolled itself now against James. James, as is well known, was driven from his kingdom, and his son-in-law, William, placed on the throne.

11. *Revolution of* 1688? The revolution of 1688, which brought the prince of Orange to the throne, forms in every respect one of the most important epochs in British history. There happened on this occasion a fortunate concurrence of circumstances for fixing the British constitution on a solid basis, such as we rarely witness in the history of nations. In the first place, the late history of England was admirably calculated to prepare the public mind for a temperate policy. The people, in attempting to get rid of the tyranny of the old dynasty, had run through rebellion, regicide, republicanism and anarchy, into a military despotism. This brought on, of course, a violent reaction; the Stuarts were restored by acclamation, and such was the loyal frenzy of the moment, that Charles II. was placed on the throne without the imposition of a single restraint, or the requirement of a single guaranty except the royal promise in the declaration of Breda. Thirty years of most disgraceful and tyrannical misrule had convinced the people of the fatal mistake which they had made in recalling the Stuarts without a guaranty. They had thus tried both extremes, and found neither to answer, and were now admirably prepared for a temperate middle course. Never did human being so admirably suit the wants of a people as William did those of England at this moment. He was stadtholder of Holland, a power just considerable enough to aid him greatly in his descent on England, and yet not large enough to awaken any jealousy or apprehension in a great nation like England. His character too was just such a one as was most suited to the occasion. He was cold, cautious, and taciturn; and, although in fact one of the noblest patriots recorded in history, yet he was a man not to be beloved. He never could become a popular favorite. The people of England never could love him. Although nearly allied to the expelled family, being both nephew and son-in-law to the king, this circumstance had just force enough to keep the people from looking on him *wholly* as an impertinent intruder, without by any means securing to him that hearty loyalty which a much

worse *native* prince might easily have commanded. From these causes, although William was in fact the master spirit of his age, and although he came to the British throne by one of those revolutions which ordinarily throw immense power into the hands of the successful aspirants, yet he could never venture during his reign on any very great stretch of power. It was impossible for him to carry the people with him.

William, and his successors too, had the strongest motive which princes can possibly have for the maintenance of the constitution of 1688, which forms to this day the basis of the British government. As it was the people, through the parliament, that made *him* king, he nor his successors could deny the doctrine of the inherent sovereignty of the people, without annulling their own title. A war on popular rights and parliamentary guaranties, was a war against themselves; and even if the temptations of power were well calculated to make them sometimes forget the principles on which their own authority had been erected; yet the intrigues and efforts of the exiled family for sixty years, seconded by a powerful party in England, admonished them ever and anon of their danger, and taught them to look to the rock on which all their strength was planted.

CHAPTER IX.

FRENCH REVOLUTION.

SEC. I.—TO THE MEETING OF THE STATES GENERAL.

It has been well observed, that the Revolution of France is one of the great eras of social order. The period of its accomplishment constitutes one of the grandest epochs in the history of man. Never before appeared, on the great political theatre, such actors, such virtue, such vice. Never were there such comminglement and chaos of all that was great and mean. Never before had Europe seen such armies in the field, nor such Generals to lead them to battle. Never, perhaps, did national convulsion ever before exert such deep and widespread influence over the nations of the earth. Whole empires swung from their moorings. The world for a season was madly intoxicated with *liberty.* The history of this great event is one of the most mournfully interesting and deeply instructive lessons, that can be gathered from the records of the past. This great event has, of course, called forth many historians, but we must be permitted candidly to say, that we do not know of a single English historian, except Carlyle, who has done justice to it. Sir Walter Scott and Alison have both failed to come up to the requisitions of the subject. Alison, after ably stating a long list of grievances, which led to the revolution, most inconsequentially concludes that it was wholly unjustifiable, and was the work of the mere spirit of innovation. Able and accurate generally in his details, he has most signally failed in the linking together of cause and effect. He is for ever telling how this little event, or that little accident, would have stopped the revolution, and he is far, very far, from penetrating the true motives of the principal actors in that great drama. Whatever may be the facts, he never fails to make the revolution, from beginning to end, one great unmixed crime. Unquestionably, as far as we have been enabled to judge from our own reading, Mignet and Thiers are greatly superior to all others who have ever attempted a regular history of the French revolution. Mignet has given the most condensed, most philosophical and beautiful narrative of the progress of events; whilst Thiers, belonging to the same school and entertaining similar views, has given us one of the most copious and expanded which has yet been published, and without making any effort at philosophizing, he enables us, perhaps, to gather the philosophy of the revolution more accurately from his work, than any other historian. He has narrated every thing in its proper place, and at the proper time. He has every where given us the close connection between the military and civil affairs, and shown how they influenced each other. Mr. Alison, after the fashion of the English school, has a great passion for grouping similar subjects together, and treating of them apart in separate chapters. One chapter treats of civil matters, another of military, a third philosophizes on them, etc. This plan answers well in most historical compositions, but will not do on the subject of the French revolution. Here, events of every variety are so interlocked and intertwisted with each other, that it is impossible to get a clear idea of causation, without presenting the whole *tableaux* at once to the eye. It will not do to give fifty pages on the 20*th June*, the 10*th August*, and the *September massacres*, and then fifty more on military affairs; but it is necessary to blend the two series together, for they, in point of fact, reciprocally produced each other, and cannot be appreciated unless exhibited in the closest connection. Carlyle's work, in spite of his miserably affected style, is perhaps the ablest view of the French revolution which has ever been published in England. It must be regarded as entirely of the dramatic order. He reproduces the very scenes of the revolution, and makes us feel with the spirit and motives of the actors. His work is exceedingly profound, and requires a thorough knowledge of the facts and incidents of revolutionary history, to be able to appreciate it. We have been led to bestow much reflection on this portion of French history, and have no hesitation in saying, that we know of no work of the kind which bears a closer scrutiny than Carlyle's. But without extending this critique, farther, we propose to give in the following pages a brief compendious view of the French revolution. We do it the more willingly, because, however inadequate we may be to the task, we cannot but hope that the richness and variety of the subject will in some measure compensate for our defects; and we do not know of a single compendium which has ever appeared in this country or England, that has exhibited a just philosophical view of the whole series of events. The fact is, until very recently, intelligent men both in England and in this country, have had most crude and indefinite notions about the French revolution. Its horrors have, of course, produced a deep impression on their minds, and not studying the whole series of causation with accurate attention, they have gotten into the habit of indulging in a sort of wholesale judgment, entirely unwarranted by the facts. Who, for example, that had ever read any tolerably fair history of the French revolution, could believe it possible that a writer of the ability, learning and research into national character of Chenevix, could possibly have drawn the following picture of the *National Convention:* "If something worse than the worst man that ever existed were conceived, and that being multiplied by the number of conventionalists, and all their bad propensities increased by the mad audacity which association gives to vice, it would present but a feeble picture of this body." (V. 1, 238.)

1. *Difference between the career of the Government of England and that of France?* We have already seen that the great difference between European civilization and that of Asia is, that the former has never fallen under the reign of an exclusive principle. The different elements of government have combined with and modified each other,—they have been obliged to come to a compromise and subsist together, without a perfect annihilation of any one. England has hitherto been, in this respect, to Europe, what Europe is to the rest of the world. There, the civil and religious orders, monarchy, aristocracy, democracy, local and central institutions, have all grown up and thriven together. No ancient element has ever entirely perished,—no new element has ever entirely gained the ascendency. On the Continent, and in France particularly, the march of civilization has been less complex, and the different elements have not developed themselves so much *abreast*, as *successively*. No one, it is true, has ever been entirely annihilated, but then, every element, every system, has had its turn. During the preva-

lence of Feudalism, for example, how much greater was the power of the feudal lords in France than in England, and how contemptible was the power of the French kings and French democracy, in comparison with those of England afterwards. When the democracies of the cities came into play, they for a season displayed a preponderating force on the Continent, which they never acquired in England. Many of the cities on the Continent attained the stations of independent powers. No city in England ever became independent. Again—whilst we have seen monarchy in France, during the fifteenth and sixteenth centuries, gradually increase in force till all the other elements seemed almost to have vanished, in England, although there was a simultaneous monarchical development, yet even in the proudest days of the Tudors, the democratic element was alive and on the advance. The aristocratic was on the decline, in an enfeebled condition, but it always maintained its station, and was never entirely driven from the field. Lastly, in England we have seen, during the struggles for liberty under the Stuarts, that the ancient constitution, the ancient customs and laws, were never lost sight of. No one of the elements of power was decreed, except for a short time, to be entirely unlawful; and in the settlement of the government on its permanent basis in 1688, all the great forces, religion, monarchy, aristocracy and democracy, negotiated and compromised their pretensions and interests; and thus was formed the present British constitution, a complex but harmonious whole, in which all the elements of power meet and blend, and subsist in full and fair proportions to each other. Very different has been the correspondent revolution in France.

2. *Monarchical power in France culminated during the reign of Louis XIV.* We have seen, during the fifteenth and sixteenth centuries, the gradual rise of monarchical power, until it became the all-absorbing element,—we have seen that there was no check in the legislative department, because the States General of France never became a regular power in the government, as Parliament did in England. These meetings are extremely rare; as Guizot says, they are but accidents in French history. Hence, as the power slipped from the aristocracy and the cities, it centered in the monarchy; and the reign of Louis XIV. is, by common consent, fixed as the period when this monarchic power attained its greatest development. In the first place, never did man tread in the shoes of royalty with such surpassing effect as Louis; never did king better understand what king James called *king-craft*. He was, indeed, the first of kingly actors, and had consummate skill in all the stage tricks of royalty. He came into actual possession of power at a very favorable juncture. France had become tho-

roughly disgusted with the miserable factions and civil wars which had distracted the kingdom during the minority of Louis,—she was nauseated with the sordid foreign priest who had so long ruled the queen-regent, and never did one man die so opportunely for another, as Mazarine for Louis. He came into possession of his power, at the moment when the nation ardently longed for an energetic monarch, who would silence all court intrigue and court factions. He found himself at the head of the most warlike nobility in Europe, with a set of most accomplished generals at the head of the finest troops in the world, which he might increase at pleasure. He had, besides, the greatest engineers, the greatest statesmen, and the greatest negotiators in Europe, with the largest, richest, most central and compact kingdom.

3. *Reign of Louis XIV.* With such a monarch and such materials, it required but little wisdom to foresee that the peace of Europe must be interrupted for a long period. The brilliant wars of the first portion of Louis's reign, are but too well known. France was intoxicated with military glory. The king was regarded as the representative of the concentrated honor and glory of the nation. Every true Frenchman submitted, without murmur, to the *absolutism* of the *grande monarque*,—it was necessary to make France victorious. There was more of generosity and patriotism than of meanness and servility, in this sentiment of loyalty. While the wars of Louis continued so brilliant and successful, every Frenchman bore his burthens without a murmur; he felt like an individual in a crowded theatre, who regards not the heat and pressure, while his mind is absorbed by the splendor of the representation. Every one felt compensated by his share in the national glory, and was proud of the pomp and magnificence of the monarch, because he represented the nation. In the intoxication of the national vanity, the people every where exclaimed, "*Earth hath no nation like the French, no nation a city like Paris, nor a king like Louis.*" (S. 1, 23.) At such a period as this, we might well expect a complete *Anglophobia* in France. Accordingly, we find the checks and balances of the British constitution, the perfect horror of Frenchmen,—they were looked on as impeding national glory. The French proverb ran—

"Le roi d'Angleterre
Est le roi d'enfer."

"*The king of England is the king of hell.*"

But the ambition of Louis XIV. and the success of his arms, at last roused all Europe to a sense of their common danger. From the moment that William III. drew the British government into the *Anti-Gallican* alliance, the career of Louis was checked. His last wars were every where disastrous, and had it not been for a sudden cabinet revolution at St. James, caused by feminine caprice, Marlborough and Eugene would, perhaps, have marched to Paris in the ensuing campaign.

4. *Its effects.* From this reign dates the decline of monarchy in France. The complete power of Louis over all the resources of the kingdom, and his inordinate ambition, led him into the most ruinously extravagant wars, and to the most profuse and lavish expenditures at home, until France was completely exhausted during his long reign. It is true she preserved her loyalty to the end; but a deep gloom fell upon the whole kingdom in his latter days, which portended evil and difficulty to his successors.

5. *Reign of Louis XV.* The very absolutism of monarchy under Louis XIV., was obviously calculated to hasten its ruin. The central power having nearly absorbed every other, was left without institutions to support itself. Wherever despotic power has become permanent, it rests on institutions, sometimes on the division of society into castes, sometimes on a system of religious institutions. Nothing of this kind existed in France. All institutions were rendered powerless by the centralization of the monarchy. There was no breakwater left to moderate the action of the monarchy on the people, or the reaction of the people on the monarchy. This absolute power in the hands of the monarch, can never fail to produce the most disgusting corruption, sooner or later. Accordingly, in the reign of Louis XV., we find France, for nearly two generations, ruled by men who had all the vices, without any of the virtues of Louis XIV. They had not even his stage tricks,—they did not give themselves the trouble to *humbug* the people,—they exhibited their tyranny and corruption in all its naked, disgusting deformity, without any of that strange enchantment which the *grande monarque* had thrown around them. We may with truth borrow the strong expression of Carlyle, and pronounce the government, during nearly the whole of Louis XV., a miserable *strumpetocracy.* Since the period of the Roman Emperors, profligacy had never been conducted in so open and undisguised a manner. Louis XV. asserted that he could prove by facts not to be doubted, that from his earliest youth, there had been no young female in France, possessed of extraordinary personal charms, that had not either directly or indirectly been offered to him; and that he had met with only one perfectly virtuous female in his whole reign. Her name was Noë. He used every effort to seduce her for four years, but all in vain, amid such universal

corruption. When we seek for the characters who governed the nation, we are obliged to search the antechambers of the Duke de Choiseul, or the boudoirs of Madame Pompadour or Du Barri.* Besides this profligacy in the court, there was ruinous extravagance in the finances,† schism in the church, faction in the parliaments, and abroad, the French were beaten and humbled every where by land and sea, on the Elbe and on the Rhine, in Asia and America. Well might we imagine

* Frederick the Great divided the reign of Louis XV. into three parts. The first was that of Madame de Chateauroux, the second that of Madame de Pompadour, and the third that of Madame Du Barri,—which he designated *Petticoat No.* 1, *Petticoat No.* 2, *and Petticoat No.* 3. Madame Du Barri tells us, that the king was once made very angry in meeting with a letter of a refugee Frenchman from the court of Berlin, stating that his Prussian Majesty, correcting a wrong date of one of his Ministers, cried out, "My dear sir, the thing was not done under the reign of *Petticoat No.* 1, but at the beginning of that of *Petticoat No.* 2." (Mem. 1, 326.) Before concluding this note, it is proper to observe, that in an absolute monarchy, like that of France antecedent to the revolution, the mistresses of the king often, in some measure, supplied the place of a deliberative body, and became often the means of effecting changes in the government. The king being the fount of all power, if he falls into the hands of one party, the resource of the other party often is to rally around the mistress, and by her influence to operate on the king. Thus, after the death of Madame Pompadour, the Duc de Choiseul and his party, who wielded the power of the throne, were of course extremely anxious to perpetuate their power. Hence their great solicitude to give the king a mistress from among themselves. The Duchess de Grammont, the Duke's sister, was so anxious to become the acknowledged favorite, that she is said to have disgusted even Louis himself. Madame Du Barri was the lucky candidate. She was from the lower orders. She was not, like Pompadour, a politician, and yet she as effectually overthrew the Choiseul ministry, as if she had been endowed with all the genius of Richelieu. Being from the lower orders, the Choiseul party naturally hated her,—that hatred provoked her anger. The opposition party immediately rallied around her. The breach widened, and the strife between the parties soon waxed so warm, that it was necessary for the king either to give up his minister, or to give up his mistress, and hence the fall of the Choiseul ministry. The Countess Du Barri, in this instance, performed precisely the same function that would now be performed by the Chambers of France, in case there should be, for any length of time, a dead majority against the ministry. The Choiseul ministry was *put in* by Pompadour, and was *put out* by Du Barri.

† As one instance of most profligate extravagance, we need barely mention that Louis XV. had built, during his reign, a most costly structure, called the *Parc Aux-Cerfs*, a receptacle for girls of all ages, from 12 to 18, who were considered as particularly beautiful. These creatures were generally decoyed, or bought, early in youth, from their relatives, and were trained in the *Parc Aux-Cerfs*, to administer at the proper time to the king's pleasures. There were governors and governesses to this most abominable establishment, and thousands were annually lavished upon them. The cost of this establishment has been estimated at 4 or 5,000,000 livres per annum, and amounted to more than £6,000,000, during the thirty-four years of its existence under Louis XV.

it impossible for French loyalty to survive a period like this,—it was an apt prelude to the revolution which brought his successor to the block.

6. *Louis XVI.* Necker says this monarch possessed qualities suitable for a balanced government like that of England, which would have relieved him from burdensome responsibility, and supported him in his well-directed wishes. In his actual situation he displayed patriotic intentions, which encouraged innovation, accompanied by a feebleness of will, which kept him in a state of constant vacillation amid the conflicting impulses that acted on him. It was this feebleness of will, and infirmity of purpose, that finally destroyed the confidence of the people in the rectitude of his intentions. His conduct often wore the appearance of treachery, when in fact it was nothing but irresolution of purpose. His character was well calculated to develope a revolutionary crisis, not to prepare one; it was favorable to the consummation of a revolution, not for sowing the seeds of one.

7. *Causes of the Revolution.* There is great truth in the exclamation of Robespierre, that "the people will as soon revolt without oppression, as the ocean will heave in billows without the wind." Every great convulsive movement, like that of the French revolution, betokens some deeply-seated grievances,—some universally operating causes,—which alone can lash the public mind into a general political frenzy. Without doubt the manifold evils flowing from the vicious organization of the government, may be considered as the principal causes of the revolution. Changes took place in the social system, wholly at war with the political. It became necessary either to roll back the tide of civilization or else to fit the government, by timely changes, to the constant revolutions which were taking place in the several organizations. France was outgrowing the old government as a boy does his old clothes. She was no longer fitted for the institutions of feudalism, and change or revolution became absolutely necessary.

8. *Organization of the Government.* We have already stated that in France during the age of feudalism, the barons were, *individually*, so powerful, that they never felt the necessity of combination. Each one was powerful enough to set up for independence, and was too proud and too jealous of all authority, to endeavor to form themselves in a united body, where the voice of a majority should rule. Hence, the French nobility never formed themselves into a regular deliberative body, like the House of Lords in England. We have further seen, that it was this very circumstance that caused the overthrow of the aristocracy in France, whilst in England it never lost its position in the government. When the monarchy fully developed itself in France, the aristocracy fell, because there had been no habit of combination among its members.

They were conquered in detail, and by their own disunion. Had they been formed into a compact and organized body, like the House of Lords in England, they would probably have maintained their place in the constitution. Their fall was, in truth, the result of their *individual* power. But as the aristocracy fell, and the power all concentrated in the monarch, a new rôle devolved on the former. The monarch employed them every where as the agents of his government,—they filled the offices around the throne, executed all the missions, and commanded the armies;—and when we reflect on the power and energy of the monarchy, these privileges were of immense importance, and compensated to the aristocracy, in some measure, for the loss of their rank as an independent order in the government; particularly when we remember, that their great private landed estates were left to them. So that even in the time of Louis XVI., the nobles and the clergy still possessed two-thirds of the land, and the whole of it was exempted from taxation, under the miserable sophism, that the aristocracy fought, and the clergy prayed, for the nation, and it was therefore the duty of the remainder to pay the taxes. The king, of course, was now regarded as the cause and fountain of all power, and the aristocracy became, consequently, in the process of time, as remarkable for all the graces and elegances of the polished and loyal courtier, as they before had been for the rudeness and roughness of individual independence.

9. *Judiciary—Parliaments.* As regards judicial power, we have already seen that the system of France was not one concatenated system, like that of England, but each province had its own separate tribunal, called a *parliament*, each independent of the other. Of course the most important of all these would be the parliament of Paris,—the metropolitan parliament. Strange to say, the members of these judicial bodies bought their places of the crown in the first instance, and then the office became hereditary in the family of the grantee, which he or his heir could sell at will to another. Monstrous as this anomaly appears, in the judicial system of France, it is the true secret of the spirit and resistance of those bodies, amidst the general servility which prevailed in all the other branches of the government. A man who had purchased a seat in a parliament felt immediately towards it as one does towards his private property. Having thus obtained a sort of indefeasible right, he became more independent of the monarch. Hence we find, during the wars of the Fronde, that the parliament of Paris was generally opposed to Mazarine and the court, and during the reign of Louis XV., and part of that of Louis XVI., the parliaments, particularly that of Paris, were very much disposed to resist. It had always been the custom of the monarchs to have their laws and edicts registered in

the parliament of Paris. In process of time, this parliament claimed the privilege of deciding whether they would register or not. A refusal became a practical *veto* to the law. To overcome this obstinacy, the kings were often obliged to hold a *bed of justice*, and force the registry, or else to punish the refractory members by *lettres-de-cachet*,* which banished them for a time from the city. As regards the members of this court, they were almost universally of the noble families, and consequently even the judiciary formed no exception to the general rule in France, of bestowing all the important offices and trusts of the kingdom exclusively on the nobles and clergy. Nevertheless, this was the body around which the people of France were generally disposed to rally, until the meeting of the States General, because it was the only department of the government which dared to resist the throne.

10. *The People—the Tiers Etat.* So far we have been considering the government and its members. Let us turn to the people. The people in France never had attained to the political importance they did in England. Whilst in England we find them the objects of special mention and special provision in *Magna Charta*, in France, at a corresponding epoch, they are never mentioned. When the cities rose to importance, the people *of the towns* enjoyed political power for a short period, but even then the great mass of the country people were unknown to history; they were scarcely above the condition of absolute

* These *lettres-de-cachet* were among the greatest grievances of the government. If an individual became obnoxious, the government had only to send a lettre-de cachet to the police office, and have him removed from his residence to any place, or prison, designated in the letter. The courtiers and mistresses of the king employed this expedient on all occasions, to get rid of rivals, both in court intrigue and in love matters. Madame du Barri tells us, that Madame Pompadour once discovered that the king was very much in love with a beautiful girl, who bore a surprising resemblance to her brother, one of the king's valets, and that this girl was in the habit of dressing in her brother's clothes and going into the king's bed-chamber, and had so engaged his affections, as to be on the eve of supplanting herself. As soon as Madame de Pompadour found it out, she had two lettres-de-cachet issued, one against the brother, the other against the sister, and they were both hurried off to prison. Just seventeen years and five months afterwards, Madame du Barri being told the anecdote, felt all a woman's curiosity to find out what had become of the parties, when she found, to her astonishment, that the brother had died in prison after ten years confinement, and that the woman, having been forgotten at court, was actually in prison at that time. An order for her release was immediately issued, and Madame du Barri, who saw her, says her appearance was shocking,—not a single trace of beauty left, her countenance pale and emaciated, with all the wrinkles of premature old age, was sad and dejected even to idiocy. When this horrible neglect was mentioned to Louis XV., he excused himself by saying that he could not, consistently with his professed regard for Madame Pompadour, interfere *at the time* in the execution of her vengeance, and that the thing was forgotten afterwards.

slavery, and when the monarchical power worked the great change in the government, during the fifteenth and sixteenth centuries, the people were as yet wholly unprepared and unfitted to occupy any position in the government, and thus did they continue completely unorganized and unrepresented, down to the meeting of the States General in 1789. But whilst they were thus condemned to political insignificance, the advance of civilization was rapidly working a change in their condition which made a revolution almost indispensable. The progress of agriculture, manufactures, commerce, and all the industrial arts, had caused a great accumulation of property among the people. As they became more wealthy they were better educated and became more intellectual. They thus acquired the two great elements of power, which had been completely wanting to them during the feudal ages, wealth and talents. The third great element, *numbers*, had always been on their side, but rendered wholly inefficient in consequence of the want of the other two. If any order in society have property and talents, they immediately become restless until they can get a share in the government, for the principal action of all government is on property, and the owner of property does not like to see it touched, except by his consent. Even if government were just, yet, if perfectly irresponsible, at the same time, the property holder will grumble at his burthens. Aristides himself will become suspected, if he have alone the double power of laying the tribute and disbursing the proceeds. Besides this, the offices and trusts of government afford the fairest opportunities for the display of all the energies of the mind; they are, therefore, the stations most ardently desired by honorable ambition. Systematic exclusion, except as to the privileged orders, is extremely odious. It is a systematic insult to the merit of all the unprivileged classes.

11. *Theory of the French Revolution.* We are now prepared to understand the whole theory of the French Revolution. All the political power was in the hands of kings, nobles and clergy, and as long as the people had neither wealth nor talent, the government was stable. The political power was united with the elements that can always maintain it. But when the great middle class of France acquired wealth and talent, they naturally wished for their share of political power. Of course they would be resisted. The age, however, in which the people might be expected to succeed, would be that in which the physical power of the *tiers etat*, resulting from numbers, wealth and talent, should so far exceed that of the privileged orders as to counterbalance all the advantages resulting from organization and the actual possession of the government. When the wealth and talent of the subject classes had risen to an equality with those of the privileged, well might the

great but eccentric philosopher of France exclaim, "The age of revolution is at hand." The grand explosion may come sooner or later, according to the application of stimuli, but that is only a question of time, and generally of short time too. For, in the history of government, when the train is already, the match is rarely withheld long.

From this exposition of the theory of the French Revolution, it will be seen how absurd are the views of those who look on that movement as being at war with the rights of property from the very beginning. It was, in fact, the increasing wealth and talents of the *tiers etat*, infinitely more than their numbers, that produced it. In the beginning it was truly an insurrection of the *unprivileged* against the *privileged* property, and not a war of those who *have*, against those who *have not*, as has been too often represented.

12. *Most aggravating abuses of the French Government.* The people were not only systematically excluded from all important offices, but the burthens of taxation were thrown on them principally, while the higher orders were almost entirely exempted. The clergy and nobles had two-thirds of all the land in France, yet their lands were entirely exempt from tax, and, we must remember, in a great landed nation like France, the land tax is always the most important. Taxes, however, were not only heavy upon the people, but they were unequally distributed among those who bore them, and were particularly offensive to farmers. More than half of the produce of the taxed lands were taken for the government. The taxes on consumption were laid without any regard whatever to equality, and varied in all the provinces, being light or heavy in many cases according to the favoritism or hatred of the government. All these evils were greatly embittered, not only by a sense of their crying injustice, but by the arrogant demeanor of the privileged towards the unprivileged classes. The distinction of nobility and of base born in France was carried to a most provoking extent. The pride and insolence of the old aristocracy were intolerable. Every one with them was either *noble* or *roturier*. They would recognize no middling class, no *tiers etat*. They were literally spell-bound by the charm of caste, the veriest slaves to conventional etiquette. They could never be brought even to tolerate those who bought patents of nobility. These latter were called *Parvenus*, and were cordially despised by the old nobles.* The feudal rights still left to the nobles were exceedingly harassing to the people. The forest laws were not

* It was this intolerable arrogance and haughty demeanor of the old nobility, towards all the rest of the nation, which produced the cry in the revolution rather for *equality* than for *liberty*. Hence the title of *Egalité*, given to the Duke d'Orleans for espousing the popular side.

only tyrannical, but injurious to agriculture. Game, of the most destructive kind, such as wild boars and herds of deer, were permitted to go at large through whole districts called *capitaineries*, without any inclosures to protect the crops. The annual damage done by them in the four parishes of Mouceaux, were estimated at more than thirty-six thousand dollars. (A. I. 73.) Sometimes hoeing and weeding were prohibited, lest the young partridges should be killed,—mowing, lest the eggs should be broke,—taking away the stubble, lest the birds should be deprived of shelter,—manuring, with night soil, lest their flavor should be injured, &c., &c. The *corvées*, or obligation to work on the roads, was not only a heavy burthen on the laborers of the country, but sometimes road-making was executed in a most oppressive manner.

In filling up one valley in Lorraine, no less than three hundred were reduced to beggary. The administration of justice, too, was, to the last degree, partial, venal, and infamous. Fortune, liberal presents, court favor, the smiles of a handsome wife, &c., often influenced the decisions. We must never forget, however, in spite of the manifold defects, that the parliaments were the most independent bodies in the kingdom, and that of Paris had no little agency in hastening on the revolution. It is useless to proceed farther with the enumeration of abuses. They are of too much notoriety to need specification.

13. *Increasing knowledge of the people, philosophy, spirit of inquiry, freedom of abstract investigation.*

Whilst these aggravating evils existed in the government, the general progress of civilization was diffusing through France a spirit of inquiry and a freedom of investigation which was dispelling the gloom of centuries, as with the enchanter's wand. Not a question, in religion, jurisprudence, legislation, finance, or social polity, escaped the searching scrutiny of literature and philosophy. For a long period the Academy of France, which had been formed by the wily Richelieu, and placed under the patronage of the crown, united the literature of France into a focus which supported, whilst it illustrated the throne. The greater nobles soon caught this ardor of patronage from the sovereign, and as the latter pensioned and supported the principal literary characters of his reign, the former granted shelter and support to others, who were lodged in their houses, fed at their tables and admitted to their society, not as equals, but upon such terms, as great artists and musicians would be received, giving knowledge and amusement for hospitality and support.* Unfortunately, even in literature as elsewhere, *fawn-*

* We can now, perhaps, explain the secret of the brilliant conversational talent of the best society in France, at the commencement of the revolution. It was owing,

ing follows patronage, and during the greater part of the reign of Louis XIV. literature was sycophantic. The writers of the day covered with adulation and flattery those who fed them, and the monarch exercised a power over the literary public no less despotic than over the political, e. g. he persecuted the Seminary of Port Royal, of which Paschal was head; he made poor Racine die of grief; he exiled Fenelon, and opposed the honors which they wished to confer on La Fontaine. (De S. I. 21.) But no matter how sickly and unmanly a literature, thus fostered, may be at first, it is very apt to right itself at last. The spirit of philosophy is like Ahmed on the enchanted steed, when once aroused and put in motion, no power can restrain it. Even in the latter part of Louis XIV'the reign, it was beginning to assume a bolder and purer aspect. It was directed towards the two great subjects which ever have and ever will engage the attention of mankind, government and religion. Writers discussed these subjects as *connoisseurs* and theorists, not as practical statesmen. As long as they did not make any application to the French Government, so long were they tolerated, and their beautiful theories were embraced and advocated by the nobles. These abstract opinions became fashionable in the higher circles, even sooner than among the people. Men of rank "assumed," says Sir Walter Scott, "the tone of philosophers, as they would have done that of Arcadian shepherds at a masquerade, but without any more thoughts of sacrificing their own rank and immunities in the one case, than of actually driving their flock a-field in the other." (I. 33.)* The king and the aristocracy for a long time felt too secure in the actual possession of

in a great measure, to the manner and condition on which the literary class were patronized. The literary man strove not only to obtain the greatest amount of knowledge, but cultivated, at the same time, his powers of address and conversational talent, that he might render himself agreeable and instructive to his patron. There was a tacit contract in all such cases, to wit: patronage and support on the one side, for instruction and amusement on the other, and the philosopher could not comply with his part of the contract without cultivating, to the highest degree, his conversational talent.

* When Benjamin Franklin and Silas Deane went to France, to obtain the aid of the French Government, it is supposed that the eagerness to see Franklin and to form his acquaintance, had no little influence with the aristocracy, even in favor of the American cause. A lively French writer says, "with much good sense, Franklin, at first, kept aloof from the crowd with which he was besieged, and this reserve only still farther excited French curiosity. 'Pardon me,' was the answer of the kind-hearted old plenipotentiary, 'but until the independence of my country is recognized, I cannot accept your kindness or friendly invitations; reasons of the greatest importance restrict me to a life of privacy until then.' 'But the Princess of ——, the Duchess of ——, the Marchioness ——, are all looking for the happiness of seeing you.' 'Acknowledge my country free, and I will submit to be led whitherso-

power to fear the practial tendencies of mere theoretical principles and abstract discussions. They could applaud the ingenious arguments and eloquent tirades against ranks and distinctions, and in favor of primeval equality and savage independence. All the dreams of Rousseau on the Social Contract, had their admirers among the aristocracy as well as among the people. Even when Raynal proclaimed to the nations of the earth, that they could only be free and happy when they had overthrown every throne and every altar, no alarm was taken. Such doctrines as these were merely regarded as abstract, never to be seriously applied to the government of France. A direct attack on the *monarch* would have been instantly followed by a place in the Bastile. But general disquisitions or general assertions were considered as harmless.

14. *Action of literature and philosophy on the French and English revolutions compared.* We are now prepared to explain that extraordinary difference between the agency of philosophy on the French and English revolutions. In England, owing to the mixed form of government, the constant existence of a great deliberative body and the representation of the democracy in that body, the development of a new theory of government, or the inculcation of new dogmas, in morals or religion, will quickly assume a practical bearing. They instantly make their appearance in the House of Commons and strive to impress themselves on the British government. They thus fall into the hands of practical statesmen, who, however they may be fascinated with the new theory, are, nevertheless, forced, at the same time, to keep their eyes on

ever you think proper.' 'Assuredly, we must do so, since your society is to be obtained upon no other terms.' And the most lively solicitations were made to the King and the Compte de Maurepas on the subject." The nobility generally took a very warm interest in his behalf. There were very few who, like the old Marechale de Mirepoix, ever stopped to apply republican principles to France. The Countess Du Barri tells us, that when she one day boasted to Madame Mirepoix of Franklin's visit to her, and of his charming conversation on republicanism,—"All that sounds very well," said the old Marechale, "but, for my own part, I am a stanch royalist. A Republic! Why, my dear Countess, what would become of us under a form of government where no Court existed, and where no one could distribute the treasures of the state among his friends and mistresses? Really, the very idea savors of famine and starvation." "But consider,' says Du Barri, "the charm of being wholly free, as the Americans now are." "Nonsense! For heaven's sake consider the baneful effects of such a system. What would become of such as you and I, were it to become prevalent in France? Just imagine what a change; no more gay and elegant courtiers; but the reins of government held by the coarse, rude hands of a vulgar set, who would never have the soul to bestow one liberal pension, and from whose clammy fingers not a sous could be extracted. For my own part, I never hear of insurgents but it puts me in a rage, and, for that reason, I have never been to see Franklin." (V. IV. 105.)

the old machine. They proceed to alter and repair with the utmost caution. They may put in a cog here and a pin there, but they have too much veneration and confidence in the old machinery, ever to substitute it entirely by any thing that is new and untried. Thus do philosophy and government, in England, act and re-act on each other. While the spirit of philosophy has quickened and developed the reforms of the government, the government, on the other hand, has clipped the wings of philosophy and shorn it of its fancies and its vagaries. It has brought it down from the clouds into the regions of real life and practical experience. In France, however, before the revolution, the case was widely different. The philosophers and encyclopædists published their theories and principles without daring to apply them specifically to the French government. Their investigations, consequently, became eminently *utopian.* Every principle was pushed out to its greatest extent,—the speculation of the philosopher was not hampered at each step by the difficulty of practical application. These abstract speculations were like theoretic mechanics, who sit in their closets and contemplate diagrams and figures, representing levers, pulleys, &c., with all the accuracy of mathematic precision, and never reflect that, in applying them to practice, it is necessary to allow for *friction and resistance.* When, therefore, the French revolution came, and the evils of government were at last to be corrected, unfortunately for France, there was nothing but this utopian philosophy to shed light on the path of the revolution. When the power of the old government had passed away, and the nation was suddenly called on to construct a new one, then did French philosophy, which had hitherto been standing aloof from the actual government in all the nakedness of metaphysic speculation, suddenly descend into the political arena, exhibiting her abstract theories and utopian systems, as models for practical statesmen. Carlyle speaks of the national assembly as "twelve hundred individuals, with *the gospel of Jean Jacques Rousseau* in their pockets, congregating in the name of twenty-five millions, with full assurance of faith to make the constitution." (II. 60.) Unhappily, too, there was but little in the bygone history of the government for the eye of patriotism to rest on. Few were the Frenchmen who could exclaim, in regard to their institutions, like the English patriots, *nolumus leges angliæ mutare.* They had no idea of *welding* and *mortising* a few of the new principles into the old system, but were disposed to tear down too much of the old fabric, in order that they might rear up a new one after the most approved models. Hence, the constant and glaring violation by the national assembly of that conservative maxim of Erasmus, so applicable to all changes in government, "*festina lente.*"

15. *American Revolution.* In speaking of the events which exercised an important bearing on the French Revolution, we must not forget to mention the Declaration of Independence by the thirteen British North American Colonies, and their subsequent revolutionary struggle of seven years. This struggle commenced at the time that the parliaments of Paris were resisting the monarchical power in France,—at the time when the spirit of inquiry was fast liberating the ideas of the age. It was, in part, at least, the application and realization of those principles of government, so fraught with hope and interest, which the philosophers, particularly those of France, were so enthusiastically propagating. The assistance lent by France to the Americans, in their struggle with Great Britain, caused the French, of course, to take a deeper and closer interest in our struggle and our government. The characters, too, which our revolution produced, had a most wonderful influence on France. What people could fail to have confidence in principles and institutions which had produced Washington, Franklin, Jefferson, Adams, and we may almost say La Fayette. When Franklin was at the Court of Versailles, he became the rage in France. A perfect mania existed to see and converse with him, and to obtain these coveted advantages, all ranks and classes contended with the most violent eagerness. His open and ingenuous character won over all hearts to his cause, and none, we are told, who had the gratification of listening to the persuasive eloquence of this highly gifted man, hesitated for one moment, to wish well to the American cause. His very dress had its influence. Let us listen, for a moment, to the testimony of one of the most beautiful, most gay and dissolute women of the French court:—"He was a man advanced in years, tall, and his hair quite white. He wore neither powder nor sword, and was dressed in a broad, square cut, brown coat, without any kind of ornament, square-toed shoes, tied with large bows, a dark colored waistcoat, a broad round hat, turned up at the sides; in his hand he held a thick ivory-headed walking stick; and, although this costume neither partook of the foppery of our *petits maitres*, nor the heavy grandeur of our financiers, its very simplicity, charmed and heightened as it was by the pleasing and graceful manner of the wearer, induced a comparison between the talented man, who now appeared before us, and our own statesmen, by no means to the credit of the latter."

16. *Causes which led to the convocation of the States General.* The meeting of the States General, 5th May, 1789, is universally considered as the commencement of the revolution. The immediate cause of the convocation was the embarrassed condition of the government, caused by the impossibility of raising a revenue adequate to the na-

tional exigencies. The ruinously long and expensive wars of Louis XIV.,—the disgraceful wars of Louis XV., with the still more disgraceful administration and disbursement of revenue,—the expensive wars of Louis XVI., in behalf of the American Revolution, had all contributed to swell the debt and the burthens of France to an intolerable height.* Ministers had pursued the ruinous system of borrowing money to satisfy the demands of the government. This system, however, only put off the evil day to make it come at last with an aggravated pressure. Capitalists soon saw the game that was playing, and distrusted the government. The more the minister borrowed, the more ruinous were the terms on which his loans were made. Besides, the parliaments often refused to register the edicts for loans or for additional taxes. Beds of justice would be held and the registry would be enforced, or the refractory members would be banished. The people, of course, supported the parliament. This struggle became warm, and threatened a revolution. Colonne at last saw that it was impossible to continue the system of increasing taxes on the people, or of borrowing from the capitalists. The people could not and would not bear any more, the capitalists would not lend, the parliaments would not register. Under these circumstances he determined to call together the notables, or representatives of the privileged classes, and to ask them to make up the deficit by taxing themselves. But they merely examined into the finances, saw the alarming condition of the country, threw the whole blame on the minister, and refused to tax themselves. Cardinal de Brienne, who headed the opposition to Colonne, in the assembly of the notables, was then put at the head of the ministry, under the vain belief that the refusal of the notables to tax themselves arose from their hostility to Colonne. The notables, however, still refused to raise the requisite supplies. The minister then tried the old system of taxing the people and negotiating loans. The parliament refused to register. He then

* The court of Louis XVI., in point of morals, stood greatly higher than that of Louis XV. But there was one vice, that of gambling, carried to a much more disgraceful extent by the former than the latter, and Marie Antoinette, the queen, is principally responsible for introducing the fashion. We are told that the court became, at last, one vast gulf of ruinous play, where money, jewels, estates, were staked and sold. Married and single alike shared in this gambling fury, and Paris looked with horror on the amusements of Versailles. Necker, at length, told the king of the ruinous state in which it would involve the finances, and implored him to put a stop to the practice. The king replied—"Tis merely the fancy of a female under the queen's circumstances (she was pregnant), and will cease after her delivery." "Then the delivery of her majesty will be that of the nation also," rejoined Necker. But, unhappily, the delivery and recovery too of the queen came, without stopping this most ruinous of vices. (Mem. D. IV. 126.)

tried the bold expedient of stripping the parliament of all political right, and introducing a new body in its stead, the *cours pleniere*, filled with the creatures of the court.

The *cours pleniere* was detested by the people,—its decisions were everywhere resisted,—anarchy was rapidly rising in the land,—the king was obliged to yield. The deficit in the finances augmented, —the interest on the national debt was unpaid, and a national bankruptcy was threatened;—some new expedient must be tried, or all would be lost. The convocation of the States General was talked of, and immediately all parties demanded it, as the great panacea to cure the disorders of the state, and Necker, one of the most popular financiers in the kingdom, was called to the head of the ministry. The parliament of Paris was in favor of the States General, because its continual opposition to the government had, at last, made it friendly to any power that bade fair successfully to resist the king, and it believed, moreover, that its own power and importance would be enhanced by the measure. The nobility acquiesced under the impression that they would have, in this body, the same ascendency which they had generally possessed in more feudal times, that it might be the means of regaining their long lost political power. The king, in the goodness of his heart, hoped it might be the means of raising the requisite supplies, and restoring tranquillity. The States General were convoked, and the 5th May, 1789, fixed as the period of their meeting. Thus, says Thiers, the first authorities of the state exhibited the singular spectacle of usurpers disputing the possession of an object, before the face of the rightful owner, and, at last, calling upon him to act as judge between them.

17. *Meeting of the States General. Dispute about orders. Comparison with former bodies of that name.* In the States General, the three orders of the kingdom were represented—the nobles, the clergy, and *tiers etat*. It was provided, that the latter should have as many representatives as both the others combined, and this was the only point fixed on before the meeting. As soon as they assembled and proceeded to the verification of their powers, the question came up, whether they should sit together in one chamber and vote per capita, or whether they should form three separate bodies, each with a negative on the proceedings of the other. As is well known, the representatives of the *tiers etat* at last determined, 17th June, 1789, to form themselves into a National Assembly, and proceeded to business. They were joined at first only by a portion of the nobles and clergy. Thus, did the *tiers etat* suddenly, from political insignificance, rise into political omnipotence. The baptism day of democracy, and the extreme unction day of feudalism had come. (C. I. 135.) How had the times changed since the last meeting of the States General

in 1614! How much had the prospects of the *tiers etat* brightened! In 1614, in the language of Abbe Seyes, *it was nothing*,—in 1789 it had become *every thing*. It is interesting to recur, for a moment, to some particulars concerning the meeting of 1614. The speaker of the *tiers etat* was then obliged to address the king on his knees, while those of the clergy and nobility addressed him standing. When the speaker of *tiers etat*, M. de Mesme, addressing the nobles and clergy in behalf of his order, ventured to declare France to be the common mother of all, and that the three estates were three brothers, nursed at the same bosom, of which the *tiers etat* was the youngest, Baron de Senecci, in the name of the nobility, rebuked him, and told him *tiers etat* had no right to fraternity, *being neither of the same blood, nor of equal virtue*. They sat in different bodies. The clergy required permission to collect tithes on all fruit and corn,—to be freed from excise duties and the expense of repairing the roads. The nobility demanded all the principal offices of state for themselves, and that the plebeians (*roturiers*) should be forbidden the use of guns, pistols, and even dogs, unless houghed to prevent their indulging in the chase. They required augmentation of seignorial duties to the proprietors of the fiefs,—that all pensions to the *tiers etat* should be suppressed,—that they should wear a different dress from that of noble families, &c., (De S. F. R. I. 94,) and they finally made the *tiers etat* pay all the expenses of the meeting, for themselves and the other two orders likewise. No wonder, then, that the higher nobility and clergy, in 1789, should so energetically have exclaimed, "Give us 1614, and our last States General; these are our masters, these are our models."*

SEC. II.—FROM THE MEETING OF THE STATES GENERAL TO THE MEETING OF THE LEGISLATIVE ASSEMBLY.

1. *Composition of the National Assembly—Coté Droit—Coté Gauche—Centre.* From the important rôle which was played by this body, its composition has become a subject of considerable interest. The whole body was one thousand one hundred and twenty-eight,—of which the clergy were two hundred and ninety-three,—the nobles two

* We are not to suppose that the meeting of 1614, was a true type of all former meetings. On the contrary, the States General held at Blois, in 1576, were almost as different, in composition and form of proceeding, from that of 1614, as from their predecessors under King John and Louis XII. The fact is, no meeting of the three orders had been arranged on clear principles. None had led to permanent results. Hence, the authority of precedent was nearly as much on one side as the other;—it was indecisive.

hundred and seventy, and *tiers etat* five hundred and sixty-five. In the *tiers etat* there were no less than two hundred and seventy-nine lawyers. Burke, who looked on the whole train of provincial lawyers in France, as but little better than mere pettifoggers, fomenters of petty war and village vexations, says, "from the moment that I read a list of their names, I foresaw distinctly, and very nearly as it happened, all that was to follow."* He believed such a body to be necessarily litigious, and that they would of course make, to use his own phrase, "*a litigious constitution.*" Burke complains heavily that there was not a sufficient representation of the landed interest. The reason is obvious,—it could not be otherwise, because the nobility of France formed almost exclusively the landed interest, leaving the lawyers, physicians, merchants, men of letters, tradesmen and farmers, of which the representation of the *tiers etat* was composed, the true exponents of the great middle class.

The members, in a French deliberative assembly, always take their seats according to their politics. In the National Assembly the royal party, opposed to all innovation, sat on the extreme right, and were called the *coté droit.* Those who were considered moderates, or undecided, occupied the centre seats, and were called the *centre.* The democrats occupied the extreme left, and were called the *coté gauche.* Alison gives us the following table to show the composition of the three parties:

Coté Droit—Royalists.

Archbishops and Bishops,	39
Abbots and Canons,	25
Curates,	10
Nobles,	180
Magistrates,	10
Lawyers,	18
Farmers,	40
Total,	322

* Mr. Burke, however, when it suited his purpose could be highly complimentary to lawyers. In his speech on American affairs, 1775, he speaks of them as that profession which teaches men to "augur misgovernment at a distance, and snuff the approach of tyranny in every tainted breeze." He has certainly underrated the lawyers of the National Assembly. In England, owing to the organization of the courts, all the great forensic talent is concentrated in London. It was not so in France. There were twelve or thirteen parliaments, entirely distinct from each other, in as many provinces. Each of these had its own body of lawyers, customs &c., and in many

Centre—Undecided and Moderates.

Clergy,	140
Nobles,	20
Magistrates,	9
Lawyers,	101
Tiers Etat,	210
Total,	480

Coté Gauche Democrats.

Prince of the blood,	1
Lawyers,	160
Curates,	80
Gentilshommes,	55
Merchants, Farmers, &c.	30
Total,	326

By the above table, it will be seen, that the nobles and clergy were not unanimous. The lower class, of both orders, ranged themselves with the *centre* and *coté gauche*. More than one half the clergy belonged to the *centre* and *coté gauche.* The three hundred and twenty-six democrats belonging to the *coté gauche*, Alison has thus designated, rather because of their politics, as afterwards developed, than from any open avowal in the national assembly, in favor of dethroning the monarch. During the whole session of that body, there was no avowed party for the abolition of monarchy and the establishment of a pure republic. No measure, more radical than the establishment of a *constitutional monarchy*, with Louis XVI. at the head of it, was seriously attempted. As to the divisions on the scheme of government to be adopted, there was —1st. The party that wished to introduce the constitution of Great Britain. This was the scheme advocated in the assembly by Mounier, Lally Tollendal, Clermont Tonnere, and, out of the assembly, by Necker

of the Provinces, the bar rivalled that of Paris. The Thourêts and Chapaliers of Rouen and Rennes, acquired as great an ascendant in the National Assembly as the Targets and Camuses of the Parisian bar. The separate organization of the courts in France had the same effect, in preventing the concentration of foreign talent in Paris, that the division into States, of our confederacy has, in preventing the concentration of all political talent in Washington.

and the ministry. These were, afterwards, sometimes called the *monarchiens*. But the great majority of the national assembly were resolved on a more radical change. They were determined, says Scott, like Media, to fling into their renovating kettle, every joint and member of the old constitution, in order to its perfect renovation. La Fayette without, at the head of the National Guards, and Barnave within the assembly, were at the head of the most moderate portion of this party. The other, and more democratic wing, contained, in *embryo*, the two great parties of the Girondists and the Jacobins, who were at heart favorable to the abolition of monarchy and the introduction of a purely republican government.

2. *Clubs.* We are now prepared to explain the origin and influence of the Clubs. In times of excitement and revolution, men naturally swarm out into clubs. These assemblages, as Carlyle says, are the sure symptom of social unrest. The nation was eager for reform, and the majority in the national assembly did not always advance with dispatch sufficient to suit the eager wishes of the most ardent. Hence the resort to all those means without, that could both stimulate the assembly to action, and could insure it support in any position it should take. Duport, formerly a member of the Paris parliament, a man of ardent temperament, and who had known, in his former struggles with the throne, the great advantage of popular support, seems to have been the first to conceive and execute the famous confederation of clubs, (Mig. 1, 109,) by which all France was to be agitated and kept constantly at fever heat. The extreme *coté gauche*, who could not bring out their plans in the national assembly, of course resorted to the clubs, where they enjoyed perfect license. Of all the clubs, none attained such power and infamous notoriety as that of the Jacobins. It was the offspring of the Breton club, first established at Versailles, and afterwards removed to Paris. It there leased the hall of the Jacobin's convent, from which its name comes. Here met, at first, all the principal popular deputies. Barnave, the Lameths, as well as Robespierre, Danton, etc., were constant attendants. No less than three hundred affiliated clubs, over the whole length and breadth of France, were soon formed in close connection with this great mother society.

But this club could not satisfy all,—hence, it soon threw off, as Carlyle expresses it, two dissatisfied swarms, one to the right and the other to the left. One party thought the Jacobins lukewarm,—they seceded and formed the *Club of the Cordeliers*,—"*a hotter club*:" it was Danton's element. Another party "thought the Jacobins scalding hot,"—they flew off to the right,—became the *Club of* 1789,—friends of the monarchic constitution. This club was subsequently called, from the place of their meeting, the *Club of the Feuillans.* La Fayette first organized it, in concert with Baily and other moderate men, to counteract the Jacobins, who, he saw, were pushing forward the revolution too fast and too far. The remedy proved powerless. An assemblage of cool, cautious heads, could not attract the multitude like the clubs of the Jacobins, where all the popular passions were allowed full scope; and hence, in the progress of the revolution, the Jacobin club, like Aaron's rod, swallowed up all the rest.

3. *National Assembly deficient in business habits and parliamentary tact.* It is not to be wondered at, that the people of France, who had been so long under an absolute monarchy, without any great deliberative council, should, when the revolution commenced, have been totally devoid of the business habits and parliamentary skill so requisite for the success of all deliberative bodies. Even in their elections for members to the national assembly, this defect was glaringly manifest. The liberal institutions of England and the United States, train the people in the forms and habits requisite for the transaction of public business. In county meetings, town meetings, caucuses, etc., we become early accustomed to the working of parliamentary machinery on a small scale. Presidents, committees, secretaries, reports, debates, parliamentary laws and usages, are familiar to us all from our infancy. The genius of our institutions trains us in all these forms, and the value of this training cannot be too highly appreciated. The French were totally deficient in all such experience, and hence one reason for the clumsy and mob-like manner with which business was done in the national assembly. The members were, at first, totally unacquainted with the forms of proceeding or the tactics of debate. As many as a hundred members were sometimes on their feet at once. There was no rule in making motions. The spectators' gallery was allowed to applaud and hiss, and their president was appointed once a fortnight. Although there were three hundred and seventy-four lawyers in the assembly, Dumont tells us that the only orators who possessed any talent for improvisation were Maury, Clermont Tonnere, Barnave and Thouret; and that Barnave was, in fact, the only man who could extemporise an entire speech of any length.* Mirabeau, one of the greatest orators, if not

* There is no kind of practice which sooner trains to extempore debating, than *stump* speaking between rival candidates. Hence, perhaps, one reason for a greater proportion of good extempore debaters in this country, in proportion to the general talent of the nation, than in any other country in the world. It is to be remarked, however, in regard to the French, that although they were very deficient in this respect in the commencement of the revolution, they rapidly improved up to the period of the reign of terror. Robespierre, who was at first an indifferent debater,

the very greatest, of modern times, could not. Most of his best passages are short, rapid and electrical, flashing out from between trains of argumentation laboriously prepared, like lightning through clouds. Many of the set speeches were written and read. The extempore debating consisted of short, vehement speeches, delivered with all the energy of passion. The national assembly, the legislative assembly, and the convention, were much more like mobs than either a British parliament or an American congress, and hence they were much more under the influence of oratory. In an American congress, it very rarely happens that a speech changes a single vote. In the national assembly, and afterwards in convention, we find such orators as Mirabeau and Vergniaud frequently carrying the body by overwhelming majorities, against measures which had just been adopted almost by acclamation.

4. *Mirabeau.* There have been men in particular ages, who might be considered as concentrating within themselves all their country's character,—who represented, at the same time, both the good and evil traits. Themistocles was the very impersonation of all the virtues and vices of Athens, in his day. That moral *antithesis*, Alcibiades, was a still more remarkable compound of the manifold virtues, vices, foibles, etc., of this same Athens, at a later and more degenerate period. In looking over France during the session of the national assembly, we shall find the celebrated Mirabeau, without doubt, to be the *type-Frenchman* of that epoch; and if Louis XIV. could say, in his day, *I am the nation*, Mirabeau could say, in his latter days, with more truth, *I am the national assembly.* This extraordinary man had been born among the nobility, and been maltreated. He had experienced every kind of tyranny from his very birth,—that of his own father, of the government and of the tribunals. He was thus trained to despise the government and the upper class of French society. His travels, observations and immense reading, had taught him much, and his memory retained it. He had seen all manner of men, from drill sergeants to prime ministers, from his inmates of the jails of Pontarlier to princes and kings. He had made himself notorious by his dissolute manners and his quarrels. Thiers speaks of him as frightful with ugliness and genius; yet no man had more *amours*, or was so successful in them.* His character was so

became at last, by constant practice in the Jacobin club and in the convention, both a ready and forcible speaker.

* His power in this respect is represented as bordering on the miraculous. The Countess Du Barri tells us that she received an anonymous letter, directly after her introduction to Mirabeau, informing her that he had wagered with four friends that he would, without the slightest effort on his part, make her desperately in love with him. She was amused, and thus forewarned and forearmed, resolved, with every caution, to fight him with his own weapons. Yet, in the very first interview in

low at the meeting of the States General that there was a murmur in the assembly when he first entered to take his seat. But no sooner did this eccentric man appear in the tribune, than his power became manifest. He was immeasurably superior to every mind with which he came into contact in the assembly. He had, in fact, no second,—it was *Eclipse first, and the rest nowhere.* From the member that was hardly tolerated, he soon became the member that was gazed on by every eye and courted by every order. Proud of his high qualities, jesting over his vices, by turns haughty and supple, he won some by his flattery, awed others by his sarcasms, and led all in his train by the extraordinary influence of his oratory. Of the Abbe Maury, the leader of the *coté droit*, he used to say, "when he is on the right side, we debate; when he is on the wrong, I crush him." His sarcasm, irony, originality, were so great, that every body was afraid of him in the tribune. The aristocracy at last, not being able to meet him in debate, made an effort to get rid of him by duel. Many sent him challenges, but he always refused, merely noting down their names in his pocket-book.* It

which he spoke of love, she says, "how shall I be able to make myself understood, when I confess that all these wise resolutions melted into air, and I fell as completely into his snares as he could have wished me. Alas! often when listening to his overpowering eloquence, I have raised my eyes to his coarse and deeply-scarred physiognomy, the words of Isabel have recurred to my recollection, and I have fully comprehended her comparison of the bird attracted spite of itself, by the wily fascination of the serpent. None, indeed, but those who have seen and heard this wonderful man when he particularly aimed at pleasing, can form the least notion of his power of captivation. Never did lover express himself with so burning a passion, (in his love letters.) It seemed as if each line had been traced by a pen dipped in the fiery lava of a volcano." (4, 225,) But, with all his power of pleosing, he was exceedingly unprincipled in love matters, being as treacherous as he was seductive.

* His answer was nearly the same to all,—"Monsieur, you are put upon my list, but I warn you that it is long, and I grant no preferences." (C. 402.) During the first period of the revolution, duels, as we might suppose, were very frequent. In this sort of rencounter, the higher orders have, perhaps, generally the advantage. They have more of that kind of conventional courage exacted by the laws of chivalry, and generally they are better skilled in the use of weapons. Hence, perhaps, their eagerness in France, to kill off their opponents, and the settled conviction among the people that this was a regular system to get rid of all their distinguished men. From this cause, public opinion began to condemn the practice, and when young Barnave fought Casalès, the great leader of the royalists, and made the best shot, the Jacobins censured him for accepting the challenge, although they were evidently proud of his superiority to his antagonist. When Charles Lameth was challenged by a hot-headed young man of Artois, he refused. When he appeared next day in the corridors of the assembly chamber, he met with the grossest insults and taunts of cowardice. Lameth said to Lantree, a hunchback, who had insulted him, "Monsieur, if you were a man to be fought with!"—"I am one," cries the young Duke de Castries. The

is not fair, said he, in regard to one of his opponents, to expose a man of talent like me, against a blockhead like him. What is very extraordinary in such a country as France, this conduct did not bring him into contempt, or even cause his courage to be doubted. There was something so martial in his mind, so bold in his manner, that no one could impute cowardice to him. He made partisans every where,—among the people, in the assembly, in the very court,—and to crown the measure of his greatness, as soon as he learned the secret of his power, and saw the career that was opened to him, he suddenly became one of the hardest working men who have ever appeared on the stage of action. If I had not lived with him, says Dumont, I should never have known what a man can make of one day. A day for this man was more than a week or a month is for others. The mass of things he guided on together, was prodigious; from the scheming to the executing not a moment was lost. The fact is, that he at last, tough as was his physical frame, overworked himself, and died from fever generated by his excessive labors.

Seyes.—But whilst Mirabeau represented the whole national assembly, and all France, in his single self, there was another being of great notoriety in the assembly, who may be looked on as a sort of living embodiment of French philosophy and French political science. This was the Abbe Seyes, a light, thin man. Although cold in his manners, he was yet wiry, elastic, and passionate enough in his philosophic abstractions. He was the great system builder of the revolution,—the ready draftsman of constitutions, which came forth as complete from his prolific brain, as Minerva from the head of Jove. "Politics is a science," said he one day to Dumont, "I think I have perfected." While Mirabeau was the great man of the tribune, Seyes became the great man in the committees. He was exceedingly intolerant towards all other systems but his own, and his plans were stated with great philosophic precision, and when produced, he could not bear to have the philosophic beauty of the whole impaired, by what he considered awkward amend-

parties went instantly to the Bois de Boulogne, and Lameth was badly wounded and confined some time to his bed. The populace became deeply excited,—they rushed to the Castries hotel, and broke and destroyed every thing within it, just thirty-six hours after the duel, with the cry, "he shall be hanged that steals a nail," and when Lafayette arrived on the spot with the national guards, he found this *plebeian Court of Cassation,* as Camille Desmoulins punningly called it, had done its work, and they exhibited themselves to the General with their vests unbuttoned, their pockets all turned inside out. "Sack and just ravage, but not plunder," was their confident but impudent motto. From this day the practice of duelling began to be unpopular, and the nobles were obliged to renounce this Bobadilian mode of stopping the revolution.

ments and ugly deformities. He was the father of many of those philosophic maxims and aphorisms, so current in his day, which seemed to condense into a nut-shell the whole philosophy of government; *e. g.*, in drafting the first constitution, he was opposed to two chambers and to the royal veto, and his short formula was, that the nation *wills*, the king *executes*. Hence the absurdity of a double organ to give expression to that will, or of the right of the royal *veto* to defeat it.

6. *Difficulties of the French Revolution—Paris Mobs—Scarcity of Provisions?* After the description of the composition of the national assembly, and mention of the two most distinguished men in that body, we will now proceed to give an account of the progress that was made in the great work of the revolution; and in order to this, we must be well acquainted with the position of affairs during this epoch. First, then, the king, court, higher nobility, etc., would naturally oppose every thing that portended thorough revolution. Even after acquiescence in reform, they would naturally seize with avidity every opportunity to regain the ground they had lost. The means on which they would rely, in case they could not command the majority in the national assembly, would be the military. They would meditate a *coup-de-main*. How would the popular party naturally meet such a threatened stroke of policy? They had no army at first, and were without organization. One expedient was, if possible, to gain the military,—to bring it over to the popular side. This was often done in the first period of the revolution, and without this defection of the military, it may be doubted whether the revolution could have been achieved as completely as it was. But, of course, it would not do to rely exclusively on the defection of the military,—it rarely happens that the troops of royalty are ever so penetrated with the spirit of the times, as to turn against the hand that feeds and pays them. The next expedient was, to rouse the nation to bring the public opinion, and if need be, the unorganized popular masses, to bear against the government. Hence, the hundreds of affiliated clubs scattered through France, with the constant injunction from the great Paris mother, to agitate! *agitate!* In case force were needed, of course the Paris mob, within thirteen miles of Versailles, where the court and assembly were, would be the first to rise. Dangerous as it is, at all times and under all circumstances, to encourage such assistance, the revolutionary party felt themselves constrained to do it. Now, it most unfortunately happened, that the Paris mob, one of the worst in the world under the most favorable circumstances, was rendered particularly ferocious by the scarcity of provisions. On 13th July, 1788, just before harvest, there was one of the most destructive hail-storms in France, that had ever been witnessed. For sixty leagues

around Paris, the ruin was almost total. This was followed by one of the coldest winters on record. Hence, the Paris population had been, during the winter of 1788–89, in both a starving and freezing condition. The government made efforts to insure a regular supply of provisions, but its efforts could not keep pace with the immense mass of indigence, which was swelled by the confluence of dissolute and abandoned characters from every part of France. These wretches assembled around the throne, like the sea-birds around a wreck,—the harbingers of death to the sinking mariner. When the assembly met, this lowest and most ignorant stratum of society seemed to entertain the notion, that reform in government would give both freedom and bread; hence the simultaneous cry for the *Constitution and for bread.* "Imagine," says Carlyle, "that the *millennium* were struggling on the threshold, and yet not so much as groceries could be had—*owing to traitors.* With what impetus would a man strike traitors in that case." The indigent and starving condition of one-half of the Paris populace, was the principal cause of the savage cruelty so often displayed by the Paris mobs during the revolution.

7. *Illustrated by the 14th July, and 5th and 6th October*, 1789. If we now turn to the two greatest outbreaks which occurred during the session of the national assembly, we shall see a perfect exemplification of the truth of the above remarks. We have already seen, at the opening of the States General, the first great cause of angry dissension was, whether they should sit in three orders, or in one body. The nobility wanted three, on the principle of precedent and conservatism; the *tiers etat* contended for one, on the principle of its being absolutely necessary for any reform whatever. The last proposition was carried, and the king yielded; but the court and nobility, though acquiescing, were never satisfied. In an evil hour, the vacillating Louis gave heed to the secret counsels of the uncompromising royalists around the throne. He agreed to try a bold stroke. Regiment after regiment was seen arriving, till fifteen, mostly foreign, were in the environs of the capital, with old Marshal de Broglie, commander-in-chief, and Baron de Besenval in command of those about Paris. The exultations of the courtiers already began to reveal the danger,* when suddenly, on the 11th July, Necker, then the most popular man in France, and the prime minister, was secretly dismissed, together with two of his colleagues, and the most offensive royalists placed in their stead. The moment this news arrived in Paris, the city was thrown into commotion. The na-

* The Countess Du Barri says that the Duke de Cossé told her, on the 13th July, "All will be well ere this time to-morrow night; the national assembly will be purged of those unquiet spirits which at present agitate it. (4, 298.)

tional assembly beseeched the king to dismiss the troops and establish a civic guard. The king, contrary to his character, returned a cold, dry answer, alleging that Paris was unable to govern itself. The commandants of the troops had received orders to advance in the night, between the 14th and 15th. Paris was to be attacked on seven points, the Palais Royal surrounded, the assembly dissolved, etc. (Th. 1, 66.) But the Paris mob was too quick and too strong for the royal troops.* The celebrated 14th July, when the Bastile was stormed and demolished, and some obnoxious individuals were put to death by the fury of the mob, is too well known for description here. The king dismissed the new ministry, and recalled Necker with most pressing dispatch. His journey back from Basle was a triumphal march. The citizens of the towns through which he passed, pulled his carriage. The Parisians were intoxicated when he was again seen in their midst; and Madame de Stael declares, that the day he entered Paris was the last day of her *pure happiness* on this earth. Thus triumphed the people, in this first great outbreak of popular violence. "M. Necker," says Burke, "was recalled, like Pompey, to his misfortune, and like Marius he sat down on ruins." But, in spite of the assassinations on this day, it was at first hailed with joy throughout France and the world. Madame de Stael calls it a day of grandeur. "The minds of the people," she says, "were exalted, but as yet there was nothing but purity in their souls." The movement was national,—all France participated in it; and the emotion of a whole nation is always founded on true and natural feeling. It was the 14th July which caused Bailly to be elected Mayor of Paris, and Lafayette commandant of the *civic militia*, called the national guard.† Thus do we find this great movement of the Parisian populace, as it were sanctioned and endorsed even by the moderate party of the revolution, and the fatal precedent established of placing the cause of freedom under the protection of mobs. It is true that this day caused the more perfect organization of the civic militia, or national guards, and led to the appointment of Lafayette as their commandant; but these guards themselves had too much of the spirit of the populace, to be an adequate check to their excesses.

* The result proved that the troops were infected with the popular enthusiasm. With the exception of two German regiments, that drew their sabres in the gardens of the Tuileries, scarcely any of the regiments could be made to act against the populace.

† There was, in the hall of the Hotel de Ville, where the election took place, a bust of Lafayette, presented to the city of Paris by the United States. Maureau de St. Mery pointed to it with his finger. A general cry in the hall instantly proclaimed the Marquis de Lafayette commandant. (T. 1, 72.)

After the 14th July, the royal party being for the time conquered, the business of reform was pushed rapidly forward in the assembly. The court became excessively anxious to retire beyond the influence of the Parisian mob; the latter, of course, wished to bring the court more under its influence. Hence, while the royal party began to plot and scheme for the removal of the king and court to Metz, where they could escape the terror of Paris mobs, communicate with the emigrants, place themselves under the protection of the army of Bouillé, declare the national assembly rebels, and at once, if need be, bring on a civil war for the recovery of lost privileges; the patriots, on the contrary, wished the court and assembly to be at once translated to Paris. They considered Versailles even, as too much under kingly and aristocratic influence; they considered that the cause of the revolution would be constantly jeoparded by the *coup-de-mains* which the monarch would strike from time to time. Hence the cry that was raised, of *the king and the national assembly to Paris!* The debates upon the *veto* particularly, exasperated both parties; and although they compromised by the adoption of the *suspensive veto*, yet the rumor soon ran that the court was meditating again some bold stroke of policy. Under pretext of providing against Paris movements, the body guards at Versailles were doubled, new troops were summoned, the regiment of Flanders arrived. At the Luxemburg, at the Palais Royal, at the Champs Elysées, new faces, new uniforms, and new cockades were seen in numbers. The enemies of the revolution once more were in high spirits. The flight of the king to Metz, and the dissolution of the national assembly, were hourly expected. On 1st October, the body guards gave a dinner to the officers of the garrison at Versailles, and the celebrated song, "*O Richard! O mon Roi! l'universe t'abandonne,*" was sung. White or black cockades only were distributed, the national tri-color cockade was trodden under foot,—the health of the king and queen was drunk with rapturous applause, and with drawn swords,—that of the nation neglected. To crown the heinous character of this scene, so revolting to patriotic sensibilities, Marie Antoinette, "with a woman's vehemence, not with a sovereign's foresight," entered the festive hall in the midst of the carousing, with the king at her side and the dauphin in her arms. She walked around the tables, bowing as she passed. Of course, her appearance filled the company with enthusiasm, and loyal bursts of applause gladdened the royal hearts. The next day a nearly similar scene took place, at a breakfast given by the life guards. The queen here expressed her delight with the dinner of Thursday. She was eagerly listened to, because less reserved than the king. Every word she uttered was repeated. The populace, already agitated by the discussions on the *veto*, irritated by the black cockades, annoyed by the continual patrols, and suffering from the most pinching hunger, were at once thrown into the most violent commotions by the festive scenes of the 2d and 3d Oct. On the 4th (Sunday), all Paris was more deeply agitated than ever. The patrols of Lafayette were on the alert, but they were beginning to be unpopular; the sentiment of the caricature, "*le patrollatisme chassant le patriotisme*," was beginning to take hold of the popular mind, and the general opinion of the Parisians seemed to be, that another bold stroke, like that of 14th July, had become necessary.

Meanwhile, on Monday, whilst the male portion of the Parisian population seemed somewhat in awe of Lafayette's patrols, in one of the guard-houses of the quarter St. Eustache, a young woman seized a drum, commenced beating it, and calling on the women to avenge themselves. Immediately, says Camille Desmoulins, the female insurrectionary force became like a British naval force,—there was a universal press of women. These poor creatures, if they could not comprehend the politics of the times, felt at least all the misery of an empty pantry, and their constant cry was *bread! bread!* They had no fear of patrols or of national guards. Gallant Frenchmen, commanded by such a specimen of genuine chivalry as Lafayette, could, of course, never be brought to fire on women. These women first went to the bakers' shops, and as bread was scarce, they rushed on to the Hotel de Ville, to complain to the *commune*. They broke in and sounded the tocsin. A citizen named Maillard, a man who had become noted in the capture of the Bastille, undertook to draw them off from the Hotel de Ville. He seized a drum and drew them after him, under pretext of leading them to Versailles. This amazonian host, armed with bludgeons, broomsticks, muskets and cutlasses, marched, with Maillard at their head, to the Champs Elysées. There he found they were resolved to execute the project which he had put into their heads, of marching instantly to Versailles, and laying their complaints before the king and national assembly, and he was forced to be their leader. All the concession he could obtain from them was, that they should disarm, and appear before the national assembly as petitioners, and not as furies with arms in their hands. Never was such a mob led by man, as Maillard led out from Paris to Versailles on the 5th October, 1789. Some hours after their departure, Lafayette assembled the national guard and marched after them. The *ludicro-tragic* scenes enacted at Versailles on the 5th and 6th October, are known to all. How this amazonian mob entered the hall of the national assembly,—how poor Mounier was obliged to go with a deputation of twelve of them to wait on the king, to ask for the adoption of the constitution on behalf of the national assembly, while the women asked *for bread*,—how the palace of the king was attacked next morning, the Swiss guards murdered, and their heads stuck on pikes and paraded in front of the host on their return to Paris,—how the king and the queen were forced to join in the procession, etc. This outbreak, like that of 14th July, was successful, and the king and the national assembly removed from Versailles to Paris, and were henceforth placed under the immediate action of Paris mobs. From this day forward, the king was very little more than a close prisoner in his palace at the Tuileries.

8. *Emigration from France—its effects?* Immediately after the scenes of the 14th July, the nobles began to emigrate. The Polignacs, the favorites of the queen, Compte d'Artois, brother of the king, the prince of Conde, etc., were among the first. After the 6th October appearances were still more gloomy, and the emigrating fever became so general, that the roads leading to the Rhine were crowded with elegant equipages of the nobility. They did not sell their estates even before going, but abandoned them, under the vain hope that they would soon regain them, sword in hand. The two principal points of reunion for the emigrating nobles, were Coblentz on the Rhine and Turin in Italy. By thus withdrawing from France, the nobles left the opposing party in complete possession of the power. Had they remained, it is true, they would have been in danger of their lives—but with every excess of the revolutionary ardor the reaction would have been proportionably great, and the weight of the nobles on all such occasions would have been of the utmost importance to the moderate party, if they could only have consented to act in good faith. There are in politics as in morals, certain inflexible duties, and the first of all is, never to abandon our country in a crisis, and scarcely under any conceivable circumstances should we call in a foreign foe to settle intestine divisions. By leaving the kingdom and taking up arms against France, the nobles stimulated the revolutionary ardor, afforded a justificative cause for the confiscation of their estates, and thus furnished the basis on which the Jacobinical government afterwards were enabled to issue that flood of assignats, with which more than one million of men were kept under arms, and France became an overmatch for the rest of Europe combined. As for the aid which the nobles furnished to the coalition against France, it was contemptible through the whole war, and their morals, too, were as dissolute in exile as their military efforts were inefficient. The example of emigration, first set by the nobles, did not stop with their order; but as soon as a political party was conquered, the leading men immediately took to flight like the nobles. Thus, as the revolution ad-

vanced, the heroes of to-day became the emigrants of to-morrow. And at Coblentz, which has been called an extra-national Versailles, the nobles endeavored most ridiculously to keep up all the distinctions which had formerly been observed at Versailles, and pertinaciously to frown down all the unfortunate exiles who had favored at all the progress of the revolution.

9. *Dissolution of the National Assembly?* The national assembly dissolved itself on 30th September, '91, after having passed the bill of rights, the constitution, and several hundred statutes, by which the orders of nobility were abolished, all titles suppressed, the church stripped of its immense possessions, most of the feudal abuses eradicated, and the power of the king circumscribed within the narrowest bounds.

10. *General remarks on the progress of the Revolution from the meeting to the dissolution of the States General.—Fusilade of the Champs de Mars.—Adoption of the Constitution?* In order to form a correct notion of the character of the national assembly, we must understand a striking difference between the French revolution and those which occur in such countries as ours, or even in Great Britain, where the people are in possession of great political power and activity. In France there had been an absolute monarchy; the people entirely deprived of political power, had no political action. They slumbered in their chains. The more enlightened and wealthier classes were the first to awake and assert their rights. The awakening was progressive; ambition too was progressive, and kept spreading to the lower classes till the whole mass was in motion. Very soon satisfied with their progress, the higher classes wished to stop the revolution, but they could no longer do so,—they were pushed onwards by the classes behind them. Those who stopped, even if in the very last rank *but one*, when they opposed the *last*, were to it an aristocracy, and were stigmatized with the name. The mere tradesman was called aristocrat by the artisan and hated as such. (Th. 1. 196.) The national assembly, in spite of all the denunciations of Burke, and the assertions of his more shallow disciples, represented the enlightened classes which first awoke in France and cried out against power, and the extent to which the assembly pushed reform, marked the extreme limits to which those classes were willing to go. Let us illustrate by the career of parties and their leaders in the national assembly. During the first period of its session, Necker, the minister, was perhaps the most popular man in France, as evidenced by the scenes of 14th July; but all the reform he wanted was a financial one, with a constitution like that of England. In a very short time the action of the assembly passed beyond the point of Necker's wishes, and his popularity gradually died away. His great

organ, Lally Tollendal, was among the first of the members to set the example of secession from the assembly,—Lafayette and his party were more thorough than Necker,—they were for the bill of rights and a constitution with a bicameral legislature, similar to that of the congress of the United States. In a short time, however, the action of the assembly passed the point of Lafayette's wishes, particularly in regard to the bicameral feature in his plan of government.

Let us now look to the individual, who, beyond all question, was the most perfect type of the assembly. We find in the commencement, Mirabeau exerting all his powers to stimulate the national assembly to accomplish its destinies, battling with all his might against the moderates as long as the revolution seemed lagging back, but in his latter days we as often find him fighting *against* as *for* reform. The revolution then had evidently advanced up to the limits which he had prescribed, and was threatening to pass them. Thus he was against taking away the *veto power* of the king, against the law against the emigrants, in favor of energetic police and the establishment of better order in the capital, etc., etc. It has been said that he was bought up by the court, and that henceforward, if he had lived, his services would have been devoted to the royal cause—that he had made his bargain with the king there is little cause to doubt—and that he would consent to receive both money and court favor, we may easily believe, from the general looseness of his moral character. But still, this *bargain* with royalty laid little or no restraint upon his wishes—it was rather the effect of his *conservatism*, than his conservatism the effect of the *bargain*. Mirabeau, with all his violence of character, with all his hatred of nobility and of royalty, with all his ardent desire to evoke the mighty power of the French people, did not nevertheless wish to see the revolution advance to the pitch that would put the power into the hands of the *bottom stratum* of society. He was a man of birth and splendid intellect; he did not, therefore, wish to reform on the *Jack Cade* principle of bringing all to an exact level. He had contracted hatred for the nobility, who had maltreated him and driven him from their ranks; still he had no idea of taking refuge in the bosom of the lowest class, with which he had no sympathy. He was vain of his birth, in spite of his hatred of the nobility, and could not help showing it even in the days of his most revolutionary ardor, *e. g.*, could never speak of the day of St. Bartholomew without saying, "Admiral de Coligny, who, by the way, was a relation of my family." (D. S. 1. 152.) The death of Mirabeau has been considered a great calamity to France. It is supposed, had he lived, his extraordinary powers might have been sufficient to have held back the revolution, and to have established the constitution on a moderate and permanent basis. If any man could have achieved this great function, it would have been Mirabeau. But certainly he could not have accomplished it if the legislative bodies had continued to hold their sessions in Paris, and the war with Europe had broken out. At the period of his death, the people of France, and of Paris particularly, were ahead of the assembly in revolutionary ardor, and soon the assembly and Mirabeau, its great representative, would have become unpopular.

The action of the national assembly in the latter period of its session was decidedly conservative after the king was brought back from Varennes. Both the clubs of the Jacobins and Cordeliers were for dethroning him at once. Numberless addresses were written to this effect, among which was one by Thos. Paine, distinguished in the American revolution. He alleged France had been tranquil during the king's absence, and consequently did not require a king to govern it—that his flight was an implied abdication—that Louis ought to be dethroned—that all history was full of the crimes of kings, etc., etc. (T. 1. 188.) On 16th July the subject was brought up in national assembly, and after a warm debate, Robespierre, Buxot and Petion *against*, and Duport, Barnave and Salles *in favor* of, the king, it was decided that the journey to Varennes was not culpable, that the king was inviolable and should not be dethroned.*

Meanwhile the Jacobin club had framed a petition for deposing the king as a perfidious traitor to his oaths. This petition was carried on the day after to the Champs de Mars, where every friend might sign it on his country's altar. There was a tremendous concourse in the Champs de Mars, Girondists and Jacobins were both there. As the decree in favor of the king, however, had already passed the assembly, Bailly and Lafayette determined to disperse the assemblage in the Champs de Mars as riotous. Lafayette at first ordered the guard to fire in the air, but the mob not dispersing, he sent a volley amongst them, which killed many and soon dispersed the rest. This bold act of Bailly and Lafayette, although denounced by the Jacobins, was fully sustained in the national assembly, and in spite of their increasing unpopularity, the factions were ended by their energy, and Robespierre, particulary, was so much alarmed, that he hid himself for some days. The constitution was then adopted, and but for the royalists, who threw every thing into confusion by their ridiculous protests and uncompromising course, it would have been made much more favorable to royalty than it was, for several important modifications had been agreed upon

* When these resolutions passed, Robespierre rose and protested against them in the name of humanity.

among the leaders, and would certainly have passed, but for the absurd conduct of the *coté droit*. (T. 1. 191.) Thus, in spite of the many denunciations which have been pronounced against the national assembly, when all its acts are fairly reviewed, we are constrained, taking its whole course together, to pronounce it a fair representative of that middle class in France, possessing wealth, intelligence and prudence, and wishing well to order and the laws. Mirabeau, whilst he lived, was the organ of this body, and after his death, perhaps young Barnave. Lafayette was its military chief, and the national guard its military force. Upon the whole, then, we may safely pronounce the national assembly, with all its faults, to have deserved well of France. It was neither agrarian nor disorganizing in its wishes. Sir James McIntosh, who wrote his *Vindiciæ Gallicæ* in April, 1791, says, "*no commercial house of importance has failed in France since the revolution.* Commerce, which shrinks from the breath of civil confusion, has resisted this tempest, and a mighty revolution has been accomplished with less commercial derangement, than could arise from the bankruptcy of a second-rate house in London or Amsterdam. The manufacturers of Lyons, the merchants of Bordeaux and Marseilles, are silent amid the lamentations of the Abbe Maury, M. Calonne and Mr. Burke. Happy is that people whose commerce flourishes in *ledgers*, while it is bewailed in orations; and remains untouched in *calculation*, while it expires in the pictures of eloquence." This simple fact is worth a thousand arguments, and constitutes a high eulogy on the French revolution through its first stage. But, unfortunately, this first period constitutes only the first act in a drama, which we shall find growing more deeply and darkly criminal as it advances.

11. *French Society and Manners during the Session of the National Assembly.* Madame de Stael tells us that French society was never so brilliant and serious as during the first three or four years of the revolution, reckoning from 1788 to the end of 1791. Political power was still in the hands of the better classes—all the vigor of liberty and all the grace of former politeness were united in the same persons. Never was more brilliant conversational talent displayed than during this period. The highest questions to which social order can give rise, were the fruitful themes. In France, the social discussions on politics were softened by the influence of the ladies, who, in that country, always take the lead in conversation at their houses, and enliven it with the kindest and most lively pleasantry. Party spirit caused, it is true, divisions in society; but every one lived with those of his own side. At court, the two battalions of good company, one faithful to the old order of things, the other to the new, drew up on opposite sides, and

did not approach each other. Madame de Stael says, she sometimes tried a mixture of the two parties at her dinners; but she found political differences too serious to admit often of this kind of amalgamation. The liberty of the press was not suspended a single day during the session of the national assembly. The newspapers abounded in the most lively witticisms on the most important matters; it was the history of the world converted into daily gossip. Every thing was then in opposition —interests, sentiments and manner of thinking; but so long as scaffolds were not erected, the use of speech and the press proved an acceptable mediator between the parties. It was the last time that the talents of the French showed themselves in all their splendor—it was the last, and in some respects, the first time that the society of Paris could convey an idea of that communication of superior minds with each other, the noblest enjoyment of which human nature is capable. Those who lived at that time admitted that they never witnessed, in any country, so much animation or so much intelligence. When Madame D'Arblay (the celebrated Miss Burney) met with the emigrants of a later period, (the constitutionalists) at Norbury, among whom were De Stael, Talleyrand, Norbonne, etc., although she had lived in intimacy with Johnson and Windham, with Mrs. Montague and Mrs. Thrale, yet she was forced to confess that she had never heard conversation before. The most animated eloquence, the keenest observation, the most sparkling wit, the most courtly grace, were all united to charm her with the splendid little *coterie* at Juniper Hall.

SEC. III.—FROM THE MEETING OF THE LEGISLATIVE ASSEMBLY TO THE MEETING OF THE NATIONAL CONVENTION.

1. *Organization of the new government under the Constitution of* 1791—*meeting of the Legislative Assembly.* With the close of the first national assembly, we may consider the *first act* of the revolution as completed. France had now a new constitution, and a most interesting experiment was immediately to be tried, as to the working of the new machinery of government. According to the constitution, the first biennial parliament met on the 1st October, 1791, called the *Legislative Assembly.* This assembly remained in session not quite one year, and the history of France during this period constitutes the *second act* of the revolution.

2. *Composition of the Legislative Assembly.* The national assembly, in a paroxysm of Roman patriotism, excluded all its own members, by a self-denying ordinance, from seats in the legislative assembly. In such a country as France, this was particularly unfortunate. Where the forms of public business were so little understood, it would have

been a great advantage to have had in the second assembly a number of those who had acquired experience in the first. Moreover, those who had framed the new constitution, might naturally be regarded as the best fitted to start it into operation, and faithfully to superintend its movements. There was no ministerial or royal influence exerted at the elections, and the right of suffrage being almost universal, the political complexion of the legislative assembly marked the state of public opinion in France. Not one single advocate of the *old order* of things appeared in the assembly. The *coté droit* of the national assembly had disappeared entirely. The *constitutionalists*, or the advocates of the present constitutional monarchy, who formed the *coté gauche* in the national assembly, now sat on the right in the legislative, and formed its *coté droit*. This, from having been the reforming party in the national assembly, was now the conservative in the legislative. The *coté gauche* was composed of those who were at heart republicans,—who wished to form a government without a monarch. It contained two elements, which harmonized as long as they formed an opposition party in the government, but became afterwards the two great antagonistical parties in the national convention; these were the *Gironde* and the *Mountain*, —the former so called, because the most talented men of the party were the deputies of *La Gironde*. This section of the *coté gauche* were for a republic, but for a virtuous one only. They were of the genuine Plutarch school,—they longed for a government that should display all the severe virtues and manners of the old Roman republic. Vergniaud was the greatest orator of this party; Brissot the greatest manager. But, besides these, there were many others of high character, such as Gaudet, Gensenné, Isnard, etc. Condorcét was its writer and philosopher, and was to the legislative assembly what Seyes had been to the national. The other section of the *coté gauche* were republicans of a more violent and unprincipled character than the Girondists; they were called the *Mountain*, because they sat on the highest seats of the hall. These were the Jacobins, whom we shall find finally triumphing and introducing the reign of terror; for the present, however, they acted with the Girondists. Besides the *coté droit* and *coté gauche*, there was a *centre*, or neutral party, sometimes voting with *the right*, sometimes with *the left side*. In such a crisis as France then presented, this party was looked upon as rather cowardly and contemptible, and received the ignominious title of *Ventre* (*belly*).

3. *Difficulties of the new government—found to be impracticable.* Although the members of the legislative assembly swore fidelity to the constitution, yet some appalling difficulties quickly developed themselves, and the government proved to be impracticable. It was clearly

seen that the new order of things in France was at war with the old order of things in Europe. The two systems could not march together. The sovereigns of Europe were every day assuming a more hostile attitude towards France, and their *declaration* from Pilnitz had already admonished the French that they would make common cause against the revolution. The emigrated nobles, with their adherents, were forming camps on the borders of France, and were openly urging the sovereigns of Europe to join them in putting down the revolution. The clergy, the other great portion of the privileged orders, had not emigrated as extensively as the nobles, but they were equally suspected and believed to be hostile to the new order of things. What was to be done? The assembly passed laws confiscating the estates of the emigrants, if they should not return before the 1st January, and declaring them outlaws. It passed another, requiring the clergy to take the civic oath, under heavy disabilities and penalties. The king, with all his pliancy of temper, could not sanction these two unpalatable decrees,—hence *Veto No.* 1 and *Veto No.* 2. This firmness of the king produced a tremendous outburst of public feeling. It was impossible to confide in him. Every one felt that he must, in heart, wish well to the emigrants and the allied powers,—that it was impossible that he could ever faithfully administer the government,*—that the system could not possibly advance, with a hostile executive constantly arresting its action. The king and queen were nicknamed *Monsieur and Madame Veto*, and the ministry, composed principally of constitutionalists, became so unpopular, that the king determined to dissolve it, and to appoint a ministry of Girondists, to give satisfaction to the dominant party in the assembly. The new ministry was called the *sans culotic ministry*. Its two chief members were Roland and Dumouriez. Roland, the minister of the interior, with his wife to aid him, (for she was infinitely his superior,) was the true type of the Gironde party. He was deeply impressed with the simplicity of Roman republicanism, and the first time he

* The constitutional party, true friends of the king, had cause, too, to complain of the duplicity of the court. On the 8th October, Lafayette, in imitation of the national assembly, resigned the command of the national guard. He was the constitutional candidate for the mayoralty of Paris,—Petion that of the Girondist, and although against the monarchy, was supported by the court party, because the queen disliked Lafayette, who, she said, would become *mayor of the palace*, if he was ever elected mayor of Paris; but Petion, the republican, she considered as too great a fool to become the dangerous head of a party. Thus proving that her only object was to confuse and embarrass the revolution, and that she was really the friend of neither of the great parties. Petion was elected by the immense majority of nearly 4000 votes, and thus, in a great degree, by the agency of the court, the national guard and the city of Paris were placed under the command of the republicans.

presented himself at court, he wore strings in his shoes instead of silver buckles, and a round citizen's hat instead of the etiquetical *chapeau.* The master of ceremonies was horror-struck at his appearance, and refused for some time to admit him. Dumouriez, the minister of foreign affairs, was an able, supple, but rather unprincipled politician, willing to espouse any party that could promote his fortunes. As soon as he entered the cabinet, he put on the red cap of the Jacobins. The queen was excessively dejected at this cabinet revolution, and could not conceal her violent antipathy to the new aspect of affairs.

On the 20th April, 1792, war was declared against Prussia and Austria. Rochambeau, La Fayette and Luckner, appointed commanders under the former ministry, still retained their command. The French were unsuccessful in their first military movements. La Fayette threw the blame on the plan of movements dictated by the minister, Dumouriez; the minister threw it on the generals, who were constitutionalists. The Jacobins attributed all to treachery; they asserted that opponents of the revolution raised the cry in the army of *sauve qui peut*, which caused the disgraceful defeat and flight of the soldiers, and they denounced with bitterness a supposed Austrian committee which governed the king. Something must be done, and done quickly. The assembly determined to meet the crisis with the boldest measures. It disbanded the royal guard,—passed a decree of exile against the refractory priests, and another decree for the establishment of a camp of 20,000 men in the neighborhood of Paris, taken from all the departments. This army was intended as a *corps de reserve*, and for the defence of Paris in case of sudden invasion. The *right side* opposed vehemently these measures, because they regarded the camp in the neighborhood of Paris as an establishment to supersede the national guard and to prostrate the throne. They were against the banishment of the priests, because they regarded it as an act of proscription, which ought to be resisted at once; otherwise no class that should become obnoxious to the government, could be safe in France. The king, with all his infirmity of purpose, was nevertheless obstinate on these two questions. Roland addressed to him a letter, written by his wife, advising him to come forth the true king of the French,—to head the revolution in serious earnest, and to win back the confidence of his subjects, by sanctioning the two late decrees of the assembly, and dismissing all the priests from his service who had not taken the civic oath. Instead of the compliance which Roland had vainly expected, the ministry was dissolved and a brace of *vetoes* put upon the decrees. A new ministry was taken from the constitutionalists. The fact is, the king had assumed new courage, for the court confidently believed that the allies would soon be in Paris. The agitation in the clubs became tremendous—a crisis was rapidly approaching—the Girondists and the Jacobins were now firmly convinced that the constitution of 1791 was a total failure, that no government could work well with a king at the head of it. The constitutional party had fallen into a most impotent minority. La Fayette, opposed to any farther progress in revolution, imprudently wrote to the assembly, on 16th June, denouncing the Jacobin clubs and demanding their suppression, at the same time urging the necessity of adhering to a *constitutional throne;* and all this he pressed in his own name and that of his army. From this moment La Fayette lost his popularity, and was denounced bitterly in the assembly for aspiring to be the Cromwell of France.

4. *Means used to overcome the king—Scenes in Paris on the* 20*th June and* 10*th August*, 1792. The republicans seeing the Roland ministry dissolved on the 13th June, their two important decrees stifled by the veto, and La Fayette lecturing the assembly and denouncing the Jacobin clubs, determined to try the influence, once more, of a Paris mob. The plan was arranged among Jacobins and Girondists. On the 20th June, an immense multitude assembled to celebrate the anniversary of the Tennis court oath. This assemblage, about eight thousand, marched to the hall of the assembly and insisted upon presenting a petition. In spite of the violent protests of the *right side*, their extraordinary demand was complied with. Vergniaud, the great orator of the Girondists, advocated their claims. Their audacious petition was then heard. It stated that the people were ready—that a bold stroke was necessary to carry into execution article second of the bill of rights, which sanctioned *resistance to oppression.* They called on the minority in the assembly to cease polluting the land with their presence, and to go at once to Coblentz and join the aristocrats; finally, they demanded an inquiry into the causes of the evils of the times, and the annihilation of the executive power, if that should be the cause. The president of the assembly, after promising vigilance and recommending obedience to the laws, granted them, in the name of the assembly, permission to file off before it. The doors were then thrown open, and the mob, amounting, by this time, to thirty thousand, passed through the hall. Ragged silk breeches were held up in the air, with shouts of *vivent les sans culottes*, and a *calf's heart* was stuck upon a pike, with the horrid inscription, *heart of an aristocrat.* But this produced such indignation that it was immediately taken down. The mob now rolled on to the garden of the Tuileries. The king had the gates thrown open. The mob poured in, shouting under the windows of the palace, *down with the veto!* the *sans culottes* forever! It afterwards rushed into the palace, broke open

the closed doors, and penetrated into the room in which the king and his friends were assembled, crying, *no veto! no priests! no aristocrats! the camp near Paris!* Legendre, a butcher, then stepped up and demanded the sanction of the decrees. "This is neither the place nor the time," replied the king, with firmness; "I will do all that the constitution requires." The mob were rather pleased by the king's firmness, and cried *vive la nation!* "Yes," resumed Louis, "*vive la nation!* I am its best friend." "Prove it then," said one of the mob, holding him a red Jacobin cap at the point of a pike—the king instantly put the cap on his head, which produced a burst of applause. The king was oppressed with heat and thirst; a half drunken fellow, who had brought with him a bottle and glass, stepped up to him and offered him drink. He drank without hesitation, amidst still louder applauses. Meanwhile, the queen had not been able to join her husband, but stood behind the council table with some grenadiers. Her little daughter was weeping by her side—her son, the dauphin, was frightened at first, but soon recovered from his terror, and became quite diverted with the scene passing around him. One of the mob handed a red cap to the little boy, and the queen immediately put it on his head; which Santerre took off when he perceived it, saying, "the boy is stifling." Meanwhile, a deputation came from the assembly to restore order, and afterwards the Mayor Petion came up, who was accused of coming too late. He told the king to fear nothing, he was in the midst of his people. Louis, taking the hand of a grenadier, laid it on his heart, saying, "feel whether it beats quicker than usual;" this noble answer was warmly applauded. Petion then addressed the mob from an arm chair; and Santerre and his rabble retired in a peaceable manner at about seven in the evening. The king, queen, and their children then met in tears for the first time since the mob had broken into the palace. The red cap was still on Louis's head—he had forgotten it; he instantly threw it off with great indignation. At this moment fresh deputies came to learn the condition of things. The queen showed them the broken furniture and shattered doors. Merlin de Thionville wept—the queen remarked it. Merlin answered, "I weep over the misfortunes of a beautiful, tender-hearted woman and mother of a family; but do not mistake, there is not one of my tears for *the king* or *the queen*—I hate kings and queens."

Thus terminated the disgraceful scenes of the 20th June. All France was indignant,—a powerful reaction in favor of the king was the consequence. The Gironde party in the assembly were mortified. When Vergniaud was called on for his testimony and opinion in regard to the scenes of that day, he shrunk from the call and remained silent.

When Lafayette heard of these scenes in his camp, he determined to go to Paris and execute some bold measure. On the 28th June he was admitted to the bar of the assembly. He told them that his army was exasperated at the scenes of the 20th June—demanded the prosecution of the instigators of the late mob—the suppression of the Jacobins, and the enforcement of due respect to the constituted authorities. When he finished, he sat down among the *coté droit.* Hersaint, a deputy, cried out that his proper place was on the petitioner's bench. Lafayette removed to that bench. Guadet asked if the enemy were conquered and the country delivered, that Lafayette should be in Paris; and proposed to ask the war minister whether he had given him leave of absence from the camp. He repaired to the palace, was coldly and even insolently received there by the king, queen, and courtiers; the queen could never conquer her prejudices against him, although he was the only man in France who could, by possibility, save the throne and the constitution; and, beyond all question, he was the most honest and most trustful. This noble man, who was truly worthy of the pure school of Washington, in which he had imbibed his stern political principles, was nevertheless determined, if possible, to do something to save the king and stop the onward progress of the revolution. He tried to rally a sufficient number of the national guard to assist him in his schemes; but when he came to the place of rendezvous, he found but few willing to join him. His life was in danger every moment he delayed in Paris; he therefore repaired again to the army. Thus did the visit of Lafayette to Paris, prove a total failure in regard to its great purpose; the revolution was too far ahead to be arrested by a single arm, particularly when that arm was palsied by the senseless prejudices of the court. His schemes, too, for conducting the king and family to a place of safety, were resisted by the court, because, their hope of a rescue by the allies had been strengthening every day since the 20th June; and they wished, in case of re-establishment in power, to be perfectly unshackled by any debt of gratitude towards the constitutionalists.

The popular reaction in favor of the king soon spent its force. All thinking respectable men condemned the scenes of the 20th June; but they were not, on that account, willing to see the king restored to all his former power, and the whole work of the revolution annihilated by foreign bayonets. The Jacobins and the Girondists soon rallied—the sentiment was becoming universal, that the safety of the nation required the dethronement of the king. The allies, of course, became more exasperated than ever after the 20th June. The Duke of Brunswick was commander-in-chief of their army, composed of seventy thousand Prussians and sixty-eight thousand Austrians. He pushed his army across the Rhine, at Coblentz, into France; and directed his movements boldly towards Paris, and in the mean time he published his celebrated manifesto, dated 25th July; in which he declared that he should march to Paris to put an end to anarchy and the attacks upon the throne and the altar, and restore the king to safety and all his rights; and he stated that he held the constituted authorities responsible for all the disorders that should break out before his arrival, and admonished Paris and other cities of France to behave with propriety, under the penalty of prompt barbarous military execution. All France was roused by this impudent manifesto. The solemn warning was pronounced by the legislative assembly, that "*the country is in danger!*" The speedy dethronement of the king was considered absolutely necessary to the cause of the revolution. But the legislative assembly could not be brought to pronounce sentence of dethronement, and rejected the motion of impeachment against Lafayette for his visit to Paris, by a large majority. Once more the discontented determined to try the virtue of a mob. The 20th June had been gotten up to intimidate the king and force him into compliance; it had failed to do so. He was still firm in adhering to his vetoes. A bolder measure was now projected, principally under the auspices of Danton, who was the Mirabeau of the lower orders. An insurrection was organized for 10th August. Accordingly, on that day the mob assembled—stormed the palace of the king—butchered the brave Swiss guards, and drove the king and royal family to take refuge in the hall of the assembly.

5. *Dethronement of the King—Call of a Convention.* After the 10th August, the *commune* of Paris, which now commanded the forces of the metropolis, and had become more powerful than the assembly itself, insisted on the dethronement of the king. At length, Vergniaud proposed three measures, which were instantly and unanimously adopted.—1st. To convoke a national convention.—2d. To dismiss the present ministry.—3d. To suspend the power of the king till the meeting of the convention. The Roland ministry were recalled—the celebrated decrees which had been vetoed were ordered to be executed, etc.; and the 23d September, 1792, was the day fixed for the meeting of the national convention. Poor Louis and his family were transferred to the prison of the temple, from which he never departed until he was led to the scaffold.

6. *Lafayette flies from France—Reflections on his conduct.*—When the news of the 10th August reached Lafayette, he resolved to make one effort more to save the constitution—he determined to appeal to the army under his immediate command, consisting of about thirty

thousand men; but his army, although in many particulars devoted to him, could not be brought to act against their country—his scheme of resistance failed—all the officers of the second grade, such as Dumouriez, Custine, Biron, Kellermann, Labourdonnaie, were in favor of the late movements at Paris. Lafayette's power and popularity were now entirely gone, and he was forced to flee from his country. The Austrians seized him as he was endeavoring to make his escape to the United States, and, contrary to all the principles of national law, confined him in the prisons of Madgeburg and Olmutz, under the most rigid treatment, for four years.

Thus ended the career of Lafayette in the French revolution. He assisted most earnestly in pushing the revolution forward in the beginning. He was the ardent friend of the constitutional government established by the first national assembly, though opposed to some of its provisions. He believed the cause of liberty in France depended on the preservation of that government. He thought France could not bear a pure republic; hence, all his exertions were used to save the king and arrest the farther progress of the revolution—his failure was signal. His plan, perhaps, in the then condition of France, was impracticable. It had come to this, either the allies and the emigrants would triumph and totally efface all the work of the revolution, or the revolution must advance till republican and Jacobinical ardor had evoked the whole power and energy of the kingdom, to push back the forces of the allies. A middle course, with a constitutional government, headed by an executive, at heart opposed to the whole system which he headed, and disposed, whenever he could do it without danger, to embarrass it by his vetoes, was utterly impracticable,*—it had not

* In this country we are now the better enabled to judge of the difficulties of France under the constitutional government, because we have lately seen a vice-president, without the support of any party, become suddenly president, by the demise of the incumbent, with opinions upon some of the leading questions of the day wholly at war with those of the dominant party in both houses of Congress; and the fact that this president, unsupported by a party, merely appearing as a *constitutional part* in the government, has been enabled to use his *veto* with the utmost freedom, and to defeat the most cherished schemes of most triumphant majorities in the two houses of Congress, led on by one of the master spirits of the age, is, perhaps, the most satisfactory proof that could be given of the strength of our institutions, and the capacity of the people for self-government. To get the idea of the situation of France, we have only to imagine, in addition to this, the United States at war with all the world—the bosom friends of this executive its most violent enemies, and the executive, in his heart, wishing well to their cause, and cordially disposed to co-operate faithfully with no branch of the government; and withal, the country unable to get rid of him by any other means than revolution.

the strength and energy requisite to meet allied Europe. Lafayette, in this emergency, looked too exclusively, perhaps, to the horrors of revolution, without regarding sufficiently the evils of a forced restoration at that juncture of affairs. His character, likewise, was too mild and moderate, and genius too limited, for the *rôle* he was disposed to play. Carlyle calls him *Grandison Cromwell.* But, however unfortunate he may have been, no one can reproach him with dishonesty,—he was one of the noblest spirits of the age; and every American may feel justly proud of his conduct, for he had been trained in the school of Washington, and in the armies of America; and if there was one single man in the French revolution, who planted himself immovably on principle, and looked alone to what he considered his country's welfare, that man was Lafayette.

7. *Commune of Paris after the* 10*th August.* We have hitherto omitted to say any thing of the commune of Paris; but as it became the leading power in France after the 10th August, we shall now give some account of its character and bearing on the revolution. The first national assembly divided France into eighty-three departments, entirely irrespective of the old political divisions; and each one of these departments was divided into sections, and each section into cantons. Each department had a sort of local administrative government of its own, the members of which were elected by the people of the department. Each *district* was organized as the department, but on a smaller scale. The canton was a mere electoral division, in which those who had the right of suffrage* cast their votes. At the same time that the country was divided into departments and sections, the organization of the town governments was fixed on a similar basis, and the officers every where made eligible by the people. (Mig. 1, 140.) It was this *departmental*, *communal* and *sectional* organization of France, which powerfully contributed to the rapid ramification and descent of the revolutionary spirit through all the classes of society, from top to bottom of the social fabric. Now, it may at once be seen, that of all these local administrations, that of Paris must, under all circumstances, have infinitely surpassed the rest in importance. But when we consider further, the powerful influence exerted by the Paris mobs, we can at once appreciate the importance of the *mayor*, *and commune or town council of Paris.* Up to the 10th August, the commune may be regarded

* The qualification fixed by the national assembly was very low. An annual contribution to the state of the value of three days' labor, conferred the right of suffrage. But even this low qualification was removed by the legislative assembly, and *universal suffrage* prevailed when the delegates to the national convention were elected.

as a respectable body; but when the assembly, on the 8th, acquitted Lafayette, and on the 9th refused to dethrone the king, then the forty-eight sections* of Paris declared themselves in a state of insurrection, —they elected each three delegates, and sent them with plenipotentiary powers to the Hotel de Ville. There these one hundred and forty-four delegates of the sections turned out the old commune, and installed themselves in their stead. This was a genuine *sans culottic* body, composed of such men as Hueguenin, Chaumette, Billaud Varennes, Fabre d'Eglantine, etc. They instantly sent for Mandat, the commander of the national guard at Paris, accused him of a wish to fire on the citizens, broke him on the spot, and ordered him to prison. The multitude, however, saved all further trouble, by murdering him as soon as he came out of the town hall, and the notorious Santerre was put in his place. From this day, we may regard the commune as the genuine representative council of *Parisian sans-culottism*,—as the very senate of *Pandemonium*. Its power, too, owing to the influence of the Paris mobs, which were now under its control and direction, was vastly augmented. In fact, from the 10th August to the meeting of the national convention, it was the true governing power of France,—it almost entirely superseded the legislative assembly, which was regarded on all hands as a mere floating piece of wreck of the constitutional government, doomed to annihilation the moment the convention should meet. The assembly, it is true, made some little show of power, and issued proclamations calling the citizens to their duty, but it was instantly insulted by the most threatening, bullying messages from the ferocious *commune*. One member of the commune said to the assembly, "I come to announce, that at midnight the *tocsin* will be sounded and the *generale* will be beaten. The people will be avenged,—they will do themselves justice." Another said, "If before two or three hours, the tribunal* is not appointed, and ready for action, all Paris will be in commotion. These threats usually succeeded. The commune was in constant session, armed with loaded pistols, attending to all the business of the country, such as enrolling, provisioning, judging, corresponding, etc. We hear of as many as ninety-eight decrees from it in one day. It sent its agents, too, over all France, agitating and urging to arms,—speaking in town-houses, market-places, highways and byways; and here we may remark, that

* Except one.

† This was the beginning of the celebrated *revolutionary tribunal*. It was first established on 17th August, 1792, to try the conspirators of the 10th August. Danton was its projector, and was, at a later period, himself condemned by it, in the most infamous manner, under the direction of that most infamous of all attorney-generals, Fouquier Tinville.

however darkly criminal the Jacobinical government of France may have been through all its stages and ramifications, it was, nevertheless, the most hard-working, energetic, decisive government, of which history gives any account. It carved out more business for itself, than any other government was ever known to do, and executed it with more resolution and dispatch. Armies were formed in a hurry, trained in a hurry, and beat the enemy in a hurry; legislative and communal decrees were sent forth in a hurry, judicial tribunals decided in a hurry, and men were shot, drowned and guillotined in a hurry.

8. *September Massacres.* We shall now give an account of the massacre of the prisoners in Paris, which commenced on Sunday, the 2d September, 1792, and continued till the Thursday following. This has ever been considered as one of the darkest and most revolting tragedies which the annals of the world exhibit, and its history, as Carlyle says, has always been written in *hysterics.* For the sake of humanity, it becomes us faithfully to portray the causes which led to it, for we shall find, even amid these horrid and disgusting scenes, some mitigating circumstances, and shall derive some consolation from the fact, that even the most degraded classes, plunged in ignorance and want, are nevertheless not capable of performing such black deeds, but under a delusion which the dispassionate judgment of cold philosophy can now scarcely appreciate. The commune of Paris* may be considered as reponsible for these horrors, but Danton has the credit of being the chief instigator. It was the misfortune of the French revolution, that in proportion as it advanced, whole classes which at first favored it became hostile. The nobles in the first instance set the example of emigration, which was afterwards followed by the *moderates*, when the revolution ran beyond their notions of propriety. Thus, after 14th July and 6th October, 1789, the nobles and clergy emigrated, but after 20th June and 10th August, 1792, the constitutionalists began to emigrate in great numbers likewise. At a later period, when the Jacobins triumphed

* Or rather its *committee of surveillance*, at the head of which was the ferocious Marat, with such colleagues as Collot D'Herbois, Billaud Varennes, Panis, Sergent, Tallien, etc. It is believed the September massacres were arranged between Danton and this committee. The chief instigator, on the part of the committee, being Marat, whose only remedy for the disorder of the times, from his first appearance in the revolution till he was stabbed by Charlotte Corday, was *murder! murder!* He had a perfect *monomania* on this subject,—believed nothing could be done without murdering the aristocrats. "Give me," said he, "two hundred Neapolitans, armed with daggers, and bearing on the left arm a muff by way of buckler; with them I will traverse France and produce a revolution." He once proposed to the assembly to make the aristocrats wear white ribbon on the arm, and that it should be lawful to kill them whenever three were found together.

in the convention, we shall find the Girondists running away in like manner. Now this constant emigration had two most injurious effects, —first, it left the party in power a clear sweep, by the removal of all opposition,—secondly, it rendered all those of the unsuccessful party who did not emigrate, *suspected;* hence one principal cause of the deep and thorough conviction throughout the whole French revolution in the minds of the populace, that they were beset on all sides by traitors,—that those who ran were plotting with those who remained. This is the key note which we find the leaders of the lower classes, such as Danton, Marat, Robespierre, etc., always sounding. We have already mentioned the severe decrees passed by the assembly against the emigrants and the clergy. After the proclamation of Brunswick and the 10th August, the prisons, particularly those of Paris, were filled with suspected persons. Whilst these internal difficulties and suspicions were thickening, foreign affairs, after the 10th August, were every day becoming more and more appalling. The emigrants and allies were, of course, exasperated to the last degree by the scenes of the 10th August. They were seriously determined to execute the threats of the proclamation. The armies of the French, in a most miserable condition since the flight of Lafayette, were not yet organized by Dumouriez. All was confusion. In this state of things, the Duke of Brunswick pushed forward towards Paris, invested Langwi on the 20th August, bombarded it on the 21st, and took it on the 24th; on the 30th he sat down before Verdun. All France was in consternation; Verdun once taken, there was nothing to stop his march on Paris. The executive council, composed of the ministers, deliberated on the means of safety. Some were for waiting to fight the enemy under the walls of Paris,—some for leaving Paris to its fate, and retreating to Saumur. Then it was that Danton* made that celebrated speech, so replete with dark threats. He said the 10th August had divided France into two parties, one of royalists, the other of republicans,—that the republicans alone could be relied on, and they were in a minority,—that the royalists were in heart with the enemy, and would do all they could to make Brunswick succeed,—that thus beset by foreign and internal foes, it was necessary to disconcert the plots of traitors, as well as arrest the progress of the enemy. My advice is, said he, *to strike terror into the royalists.* The ministry disconcerted him by its silence; he then arranged matters with the *commune.* It was determined to disarm and apprehend all suspicious persons; to effect this, the plan of domiciliary visits was conceived and executed in the most frightful manner. The barriers of the city were closed for forty-

* He was minister of justice.

eight hours, from the evening of the 29th. Guard-ships were stationed on the river to prevent escape. The streets were to be cleared and illuminated by ten o'clock at night, and all persons to be at their houses to receive the visits of the police, whose arrival at each door was announced by a tap of the drum. During these forty-eight hours of domiciliary visits, the prisons of Paris so rapidly filled, that it is supposed they had nearly 15,000 prisoners in them.

On the 1st of September, a rumor reached Paris that Verdun was taken, and that Brunswick in three days would be in the city. The commune, at the instance of Danton, immediately issued orders for the assemblage of the citizens next day in the Champs de Mars, and concerted its plans. It was now evident that something terrible was in preparation. The next day was Sunday, the 2d September,—the whole city was in motion. Profound terror pervaded the prisons; even the jailers were frightened. The king and queen, in the Temple, anxiously asked what was the matter. The prisoners' dinners were served up *two hours* sooner than usual, and without any knives,—they earnestly asked the jailers what this meant. At length, at 2 o'clock, the *generale* beat, the tocsin sounded, and the alarm guns were fired. Twenty-four priests, apprehended on account of refusal to take the oath, were, about three o'clock, conveyed to the prison of the Abbaye, in six different carriages. As the first coach drove up in the court-yard of the Abbaye, Maillard (who formerly headed the women on 5th Oct.) was present with his rabble; they fell immediately on the priests, and murdered them one after another until the whole were dispatched, with the solitary exception of the Abbe Sicard, who was saved almost by a miracle. At this moment, Billaud Varennes, whom Bonaparte always considered the greatest villain of the revolution, came up and encouraged the murderers: "Good people," said he, "you sacrifice your enemies; you do your duty." Billaud was a member of the commune, and the only one of the organizers of this horrid massacre who dared to show his face and defend it. From the Abbaye they rushed to the Carmelites, where they butchered two hundred more priests. After this, Maillard went in to the committee of the section of the *quatre nations*, and asked for wine *for the brave laborers who were delivering the nation from its enemies.* The committee shuddered, and granted them twenty-four quarts. The wine was poured out on tables surrounded by the corpses of the murdered. After it was drunk, Maillard, pointing again to the prison where the first twenty-four priests had been murdered, cried with a fiendish shriek, "*to the Abbaye!*" The Abbaye was then entered, and the murder of the prisoners commenced; but suddenly it was proposed to establish something like a judicial tribunal. Maillard was instantly elected president. His formula for condemnation was, "*let the prisoner be taken to La Force*," when he would be instantly carried out and murdered by the ruffians. At *La Force*, the *Châtelet*, the *Conciergerie*, like courts were formed, and similar horrid cant formulæ adopted. For one hundred hours, these murders were continued. The very sabres grew dull, and required sharpening. The murderers refreshed themselves from time to time by drinking from wine jugs, and eating in their shirt sleeves, and with their hands all reeking with blood, the victuals which were brought to them, sometimes by their own wives, who said their husbands *were at work at the Abbaye*, or any other one of the prisons where they happened to be murdering at the time. At length the murders ceased on Thursday, when, in fact, but few of the unhappy prisoners remained. The estimate of the number of victims varies between 6 and 12,000.* (T. 1, 367.)

Amid this carnage, however, some victims were spared, and what is very strange, to the inconceivable joy of the mob. A young man, claimed by one of the sections, on being acquitted, was immediately embraced and borne in triumph off the ground in the bloody arms of the executioners. The venerable Sombreul was condemned; his daughter perceived him from the prison, rushed into his arms, and piteously besought mercy. One of the ruffians stepped up with a pot full of blood, saying, "*drink, drink the blood of the aristocrats!*" She drank, and her father was spared. Old Casotte was saved in like manner by his daughter, and without drinking the blood. M. de Journiac, when acquitted, was borne off in the arms of two of the ruffians. When they carried him clear of the mob, he offered them money—they refused to take it, and only asked leave to embrace him. Another was carried home by the executioners, who begged to be allowed to witness the meeting with his family, after which they hastily returned to the carnage. What may appear exceedingly strange is, that many of the murderers came and deposited with scrupulous honesty, on the bureau of the committee of the Abbaye, the blood-stained jewels found upon the prisoners.

It may naturally be asked whether, during the progress of this dreadful tragedy, no effort was made to arrest it? The assembly did issue decree after decree, demanding of the commune the state of Paris, to which the latter answered it was doing all it could to preserve tran-

* Before the carnage had ceased, the prisoners, who kept an observer at the window to find out the best mode of receiving death, discovered that those who stretched out their hands had the hardest fate, because they were longer in dying. They therefore advised one another to put their hands behind, and receive the sabre and cutlass strokes unresistingly on the head.

quillity.* But the assembly never once thought of going in a body, and placing themselves courageously between the butchers and the victims. It only sent a deputation, at the head of which was old Dussaulx, the translator of Juvenal,† which, after blundering about, returned, saying, "It was dark, and they could not see well what was going on." The fact is, the assembly had become perfectly impotent in Paris, ever since the 20th August. Santerre, the commandant of the national guard, pretended to do something, but excused his inefficiency by saying the national guard would not act. Petion, the mayor, went to the prisons, and generally stopped the murders whilst present, but the moment his back was turned, they commenced again. The virtuous Roland made every exertion in his power, but all in vain. What makes this whole tragedy the more astonishing is, that it was perpetrated by not more than three hundred persons. All the circumstances, when taken together, show that the Parisian population were laboring under the dreadful delusion, that the prisoners were plotting with the enemy, and in the unprotected condition of Paris, their murder had become absolutely necessary.

At this distant day, we can scarcely appreciate the influence of the panic which prevailed in Paris at the approach of the Duke of Brunswick. We see now too clearly the position of things, to make proper allowance for delusions. We forget how, at such a crisis, the apprehensions of the people can torture the most innocent and frivolous accidents into proofs of guilt "strong as holy writ." Witness the *war of conspiracies* carried on by contending factions in the reign of Charles II. How boldly were such charges fabricated, how easily believed, and how difficultly unravelled. To this very day, it is doubtful how far Queen Mary was an accomplice in Babington's conspiracy,—what was the real connection between Charles I. and the Catholic insurgents of Ireland. It took more than a century to unravel completely the Rye House plot, and to discover exactly the extent to which Russell and Sydney were implicated. (M. 95.) But all such instances as these sink into utter

* This was false. That miserable wretch, Billaud Varennes, was encouraging, in the name of the *commune*, throughout the whole time, the murderers of the prisoners, and promised them twenty-four livres apiece. After the massacre, the committee of *surveillance* actually addressed a circular to the other cities of France, calling on them to murder their prisoners in like manner.

† Dussaulx was very proud of his translation, and was in the habit of announcing himself, even in addressing the people, as the *translator of Juvenal*. When, therefore, he had made this customary announcement on one occasion, one of the mob cried out, "*Juvenal!* who the devil is Juvenal? one of your *cursed aristocrats! To the Lanterne!*" As may well be imagined, Dussaulx soon stopped talking of Juvenal.

insignificance by comparison with the great Parisian panic of September, 1792, caused by the approach of Brunswick, who had promised *military execution* to the city of Paris, and was about to make his word good at the head of more than 100,000 troops, joined by an army of infuriated emigrants, eager to liberate the king, the aristocracy and the priests, confined in the prisons of France.

9. *From the September massacres to the meeting of the National Convention.* The legislative assembly became more impotent than ever, and as the convention was soon to meet, all parties began to look to that quarter for an adjustment of difficulties. In the mean time, Dumouriez, by bold generalship, threw himself into the Argonne, arrested the progress of Brunswick, and for the time being saved France from foreign invasion. The commune of Paris, too, during this period, whilst it may be considered as the chief governing power of France, was securing to itself immense funds, by sequestrating the effects of the unfortunate persons murdered in the prisons of Paris, and on the roads to Versailles, of which it refused ever after to give any account. It sold, too, on its own responsibility, the furniture of the great mansions, to which seals had been affixed ever since the departure of the owners. It seized the money in the hands of Septeul, the treasurer of the civil list, also the plate of the churches, the rich movables of the emigrants; and, lastly, it drew considerable sums from the public exchequer, under various pretences. The robbery of the *Garde Meuble*, containing the most valuable of those effects which contributed to the splendor of the throne, has likewise been charged to the commune of Paris. (T. 1, 385–6.) Thus did the infamously notorious town hall add the meanness of robbery and theft to the catalogue of its other crimes; and prove itself to be the true representative of the *worst part* of the worst mob of the worst rabble in all France.

SEC IV.—FROM THE MEETING OF THE NATIONAL CONVENTION TO THE FALL OF ROBESPIERRE.

1. *Meeting of the National Convention—its composition.* This body met on the 20th September, 1793. All eyes were turned on it—it was hoped that the forty days confusion and crime, since the 10th August, would turn out but an *accident* of the revolution—that all things would be made to work well under a body fresh from the people, and representing the true wishes of the whole nation. A warm interest was every where taken in the elections. The Jacobin clubs made great efforts throughout all France; but in spite of their exertions, the Girondists triumphed in the elections.

The September massacres, as might have been expected, produced a tremendous reaction throughout all France, and wherever the news was received in time to influence the elections, it operated against the Jacobins. In Paris, however, the violent faction completely succeeded, and a bare list of its delegation is sufficient to prove, that upon Paris, not on France, rests the greatest sins of the French revolution. The two Robespierres, Danton, Marat, Collot d'Herbois, Billaud Varennes, Panis, Sergent, Legendre, David the painter,* Camille Des Moulins, Fabre d'Eglantine, Manuel, Duke d'Orleans (*Egalité*), Old Dussaulx, Freron, and a few obscure individuals, completed that famous delegation, containing but one single *moderate man* in the whole number.† It was a true exponent of the *chaos of the city*, containing several mercantile men, several lawyers, a butcher, an engraver, a painter, three or four writers, and an abdicated prince. (387.)

As soon as the convention assembled, as was to be expected, a new formation of parties was discernible. The constitutionalists, who formed the *coté droit* in the national assembly, disappeared in the convention, just as the nobles and clergy who formed the *coté droit* in the first national assembly, disappeared in the legislative. The Girondists and Jacobins, who had worked together as long as there was a king upon the throne, now separated for ever, the former taking the *coté droit*, the latter the *coté gauche*, in the hall. The former contained almost all the most brilliant men who had distinguished themselves in the legislative assembly, such as Vergniaud, Guadet, Gensenné, Condorcet, etc., besides many others. This party was the most numerous, the most eloquent and the most talented in the convention. It was a brave party too—a respectable party—a conscientious party, seriously determined to check the horrors of the revolution, and to make it truly respectable in the eyes of the world. Besides these two parties, there was in the convention, a middle party, constituting the *centre*, composed of the moderates, the undecided, and the timid. Although the Girondists were the most numerous party, the *centre* could occasionally give the triumph to the Jacobins, by a union with the *coté gauche*. It is to be observed, that in revolution, the *centre*, or middle party, is scarcely ever much respected; because, although a portion of the party is always highly honorable, and occupy their position from conscientious conviction; yet, another portion of it always consists of trimmers and cowards, who are governed by their hopes and their fears. Moreover, the mid-

* This hideously ugly man, was more remarkable for his cruelty even, than for his genius. His cant phrase was, "*let us grind a little more of the red*," in allusion to his art.

† Dussaulx.

dle party loses the great influence of the press, and it cannot agitate through clubs with the same efficiency that the two extreme parties can.

2. *Test Questions—Tactics of the Parties.* A series of questions quickly came before the convention, which, at once, drew the line of distinction between the parties. All agreed with perfect unanimity, to the abolition of monarchy. But on almost all other questions, the two wings voted against each other. The Girondists were for punishing the authors of the September massacres. The Jacobins defended them. The Girondists knew that most of the excesses of the revolution came from the Parisian mobs; they, therefore, wished to destroy the influence of Paris. The Jacobins wished to increase it. The Girondists wished to remove the convention to some smaller city, where their deliberations would be free. The Jacobins were opposed to it. The Girondists wished to establish a departmental army, taken equally from all the eighty-three departments, to be at the command of the convention, and to supersede the national guard, which had disgraced the country ever since Santerre had been its commandant. The Jacobins resisted this measure too, and made the boldest assertions in regard to the views and intentions of the Girondists. They accused them of a wish to ruin Paris—to move the seat of government into the south, that they might give up the whole north to the enemy. They charged them with being *federalists*, wishing to make a weak federative government like that of the United States, instead of a great consolidated republic, with Paris its capital. Of course, on all these leading questions, the sympathies and wishes of all the Parisian authorities were on the side of the Jacobins.

3. *Fall of the Girondists—Causes—2d June.* Without entering into details, we can easily point out the general course of events which produced the overthrow of the Girondists, and left the Jacobins in complete possession of the convention. In the struggles between the two parties, the Jacobins looked always to the Paris authorities and Paris mobs for support. Their policy was to intimidate their opponents. On the other hand, the Girondists looked to France—to the *whole country*, and threatened, in case of the murder of any of its members, by the Paris mobs, that the city would be annihilated by the rest of France.* Whilst this struggle was going on between the parties in the convention, a turn took place in military affairs, which enabled the Jacobins to triumph. After the beheading of the king, on the 21st January, 1793, nearly all Europe, disgusted with the horrors of the

* "*Paris will be erased from the list of cities,*" said Isnard.

French revolution, joined the coalition against France. England, now for the first time, entered the lists, throwing her immense weight on the side of the allies. The whole circuit of France was begirt by enemies. Never was country in a more appalling condition. Disunion within,—all Europe rushing on her from without! La Vendee in a state of revolt, with a brave army in the field, commanded by brave officers; displaying a zeal—a perseverance and endurance in the royal cause, which have never been surpassed. To crown this series of calamities, Dumouriez became disgusted with the government—lost the great battle of Neer Winden, and afterwards attempted to gain the army and establish a constitutional monarchy. He failed just as Lafayette did after the 10th August, and was forced to take refuge among the allies; leaving the military affairs of France in the most deplorable condition. Here, then, was another cause for a Parisian panic—for crimination and recrimination, between the two great parties in the convention. Although the Girondists had never claimed Dumouriez as one of their party, the Jacobins insisted that he was. They said the whole government was infested with traitors—that the party of the Girondists must be overthrown, or the enemy would soon be in the capital. A Paris insurrection was at length organized by the Jacobins; the convention was surrounded on the 2d June, and the arrest of the twenty-two leading Girondists in the convention peremptorily demanded.* This bold stroke annihilated the Girondists. Henceforth the Jacobins had complete possession of the convention; and filled all the departments of the army and government with their party, and the prisons with their enemies. From this period, the guillotine became more ac-

* France had now reached the point when the imprisonment of a man of distinction, was the almost certain precursor of his execution. These imprisoned Girondists, to the number of twenty-one, were all condemned to death by the *revolutionary tribunal,* at midnight, on the 30th October, 1793. Their last night, says Thiers, was sublime. Vergniaud had poison, but threw it away that he might die with his friends. They took a last meal together, at which they were, by turns, merry, serious, and eloquent. They all joined in singing hymns to France and liberty. On their way to the scaffold, next day, they sang the *Marseilles hymn;* and on alighting from their carts, they embraced one another, shouting *Vive la République!* and then died with a heroism which does honor to humanity; the guillotine dispatched them all in thirty-one minutes. Such was the end of those noble and courageous citizens, combining youth, beauty, virtue, talents; they fell a sacrifice to their generous Utopian principles. The mere recapitulation of their names and ages has something extremely touching. Brissot, Guardien and Lasouree were 39; Vergniaud, Gensenné and Lehardéy were 35; Mainvielle and Ducos, 28; Boyer Fonfrède and Duchattel, 27; Duperrét, 46; Carra, 50; Valzé and Lacase, 42; Dupratt, 33; Sillery, 57; Fauchet, 49; Listerpt Beauvais, 43; Boileau, 41; Attiboul. 40; and Viget, 36. (T. 2, 351.)

tive than ever; and realizing the celebrated exclamation of Vergniaud, that *the revolution, like Saturn, was devouring its own offspring.* From this time the right side was reduced to silence. In fact, regular debating almost entirely ceased in the convention, but commenced with renovated vigor in the Jacobin clubs.

4. *Revolt occasioned by the 2d June.* When the news of the fall of the Girondists was spread through France, it produced the utmost indignation; and in a very short time, at least two-thirds of the whole nation were in a state of revolt—and, for a season, the triumph of the allies and the restoration of the Bourbons, seemed absolutely certain. During this period, Charlotte Corday went to Paris and assassinated Marat. This assassination increased greatly the confusion of the times, and happening as it did, made Marat (the most bloodthirsty man of the revolution,) an object of enthusiasm with the mob. His name was, for a time, invoked by the Jacobins in all public places, his bust was put up in all the Jacobin clubs; and the convention, which was now entirely Jacobin, voted him the honors of the Pantheon.

5. *Quelled.* This insurrection, so threatening at first, was soon quelled, with the exception of La Vendée and a few other points. In the first place, the Jacobins acted with the utmost decision and energy, while the insurgents were disunited and doubtful. In the second place, the Jacobins gave, very promptly, a new constitution* to the people of France, as democratic as was ever proclaimed over so large a nation; and they sent it forth to the people with a decree, calling on the insurgents to return to their allegiance, and giving them only three days of grace. This afforded a favorable opportunity to the revolted republicans to return. They had, by this time, began to see that they were working entirely for royalists. When two parties revolt against government, that which is the most thorough, is apt to run away with the whole benefit of the revolt; thus the Girondists saw they could not successfully oppose the Jacobin government, without joining the royalists and the allies. They began to reproach themselves for compromising their country, by a culpable diversion. They began to feel that it was criminal to discuss whether they ought to be revolutionists, such as Petion and Vergniaud, or such as Danton and Robespierre, at a moment when all Europe was in arms against France. It became but too evident, that all opposition to the revolution would turn to the advantage of the enemies of liberty—that it would be the agents of the old court—the retainers of the old clergy, and the partisans of absolute power, who

* Herault Sechelles, the handsomest man in France, was the author of this constitution. He was to the Jacobins, what Seyes was to the constitutionalists, and Condorcet to the Girondists, the ready draftsman of their plans.

would reap all the advantages. Hence, by the last of July, France, with the exception of La Vendée and a few royalist cities, was once more united against Europe.

6. *Difficulties of the Jacobin Government Assignats.* Although the greater portion of the revolted had returned to their allegiance, still the condition of France was extremely critical; she was invaded on all sides at once—in the north—on the Rhine—the Alps, and at the Pyrenees. There was the cankering sore of La Vendée in the west—an obstinate sedition at Marseilles—secret treason at Toulon, and open resistance and siege at Lyons. But the difficulties stopped not here—corn was dear—provisions scarce—the poor people every where, and particularly in Paris, on the verge of starvation. The productions of the country had not diminished during the revolution; but they were not properly distributed, owing to the miserable condition of the monetary system, caused by the issue of assignats. We must here make a few remarks on this subject. When the property of the emigrants was confiscated, it was soon found that it could not be advantageously sold; first, there was constant apprehension that the Bourbons would be restored, and that the emigrants would regain their lands,—hence the caution of capitalists; second, throwing so much land into the market in absence of any other cause of depression, would of itself, at once depress the price to a mere nominal value. The scheme was consequently devised of issuing *assignats*, on the faith of the public lands. This scheme, as might have been anticipated, was soon converted into a great government bank, the public lands constituting the capital.

The value of these issues would, of course, depend on two circumstances; first, the ratio of the *supply* to the *demand* for currency; and secondly, on public confidence. As they were the only means of defraying the expenses of the revolutionary government, their issues were, of course, rapidly advancing with the increasing exertions of the government; and consequently, rapidly depreciating. Again, whenever the affairs of France wore a gloomy aspect, the assignats fell from loss of confidence; because they depended on the faith and resources of the *revolutionary government*, which would be annihilated, in case the allies succeeded. Hence, a cause of accumulated difficulty with any fresh disaster. Before the 2d June the depreciation was considerable; from that event to August, the progression downwards was alarmingly rapid—one silver franc, at the latter period, being worth six paper ones. The convention had decreed, that no one, under heavy penalties, should make a difference between paper and silver. This did not hinder the depreciation. Creditors were now rapidly paid off their debts in paper money, with only one-sixth. These had to bear their losses in silence

But another effect was produced; corn and all kinds of provisions rapidly rose in price—for, of course, every seller expected to be paid in paper. This rise in price produced a tremendous outburst from the indigent classes, against the whole class of corn-mongers, the forestallers and regraters, etc. They began to demand that these men should be sent to the guillotine. This cry, of course, produced its inevitable effect; the corn was kept back, and this again produced starvation and more violent indignation. Such was the condition of France in the critical period succeeding the scenes of 31st May and 2d June. Let us now see how the Jacobin government acquitted itself under such appalling difficulties.

7. *Means used by the Government to meet the crisis* The month of August, 1793, was the epoch of those grand decrees which set all France in motion, all resources in activity, and which terminated this last and most terrible crisis of the revolution entirely to its advantage. First, as we have seen, came the adoption of the new constitution, which, however, was immediately suspended. Representatives from all France, were invited to meet at Paris, and celebrate the anniversary of 10th August,—to carry back from this focal point of Jacobinism, a revolutionary ardor which might stir up the whole nation. Then came the decree for a *levy en masse*, stating, "the young men shall go forth to fight; the married men shall forge the arms and transport the supplies; the women shall make tents and clothes, and attend on the hospitals; the children shall make lint out of the rags; the old men shall cause themselves to be carried to public places, to excite the courage of the warriors, to preach hatred of kings and love of the republic." All unmarried men from 18 to 25 composed the first levy (*first requisition*). The generation between 25 and 30 constituted the *second requisition*, —those between 30 and 60 the third. When the first levy would suffice, it alone was called into the field; in some places, however, all were called out. In a short time there were fourteen armies in the field, amounting to one million two hundred thousand soldiers! Whilst they were thus levying immense armies by generations, there were corresponding requisitions made every where for provisions. The army commissioners pressed horses and beasts of burthen for public service. Muskets were given to the generation that marched, fowling pieces and pikes to those that remained. Armories were erected every where; but the principal one was at Paris, with its forges in the garden of the Luxemburg, and its boring machinery on the banks of the Seine. All the gunsmiths, as well as the watchmakers and clockmakers, were put in requisition. These extraordinary means were to be used till the product should be, at Paris alone, one thousand muskets per day. Saltpetre

being scarce, the chemists were set to work; and all cellars and damp places were entered and dug up, that the mould might be lixiviated when it contained saltpetre. Thus, France was converted into a camp and a great work-shop. And here, we may remark, that the foundation was laid of that military system, which made the finest armies and generals which the world has ever seen. Carnot, who presided over the military department in the committee of public safety, proclaimed to France, that merit alone would entitle to preferment. All offices in the army were consequently thrown open to all, and when a free competition was thus granted to twenty-five million, Carnot contended, that France would produce a number of great generals, almost as far exceeding that of other nations, as the whole population of France exceeded the privileged orders in those countries; and events seemed to justify this calculation. The number, superiority and skill of the French generals, in a short time, became manifest to the whole world, and appeared almost miraculous. The very soldiers of the army exhibited a degree of intelligence, enthusiasm, tact, and courage, which seemed almost to realize the wild assertion of the enthusiastic, hot-headed Jacobin,—who exclaimed in debate, that France had *three million generals!**

But, to return to our subject, while such enormous preparations were making to repel the foreign foe, the internal enemies were not neglected. The famous law against *suspected* persons was passed. The prisons were rapidly filled under this terrible decree. In Paris, and all towns, it required that every house door should have the names of the inmates legibly printed on it, not more than five feet from the ground. Every citizen was to be ready to produce his *carte de civisme*, signed by the president of his section, whenever called for. With every advance of the revolution the *suspected*, of course, rapidly augmented. Before the 10th August, 1792, the prisoners were almost entirely of the nobility and clergy; after that event, to the 2d June, we find them nobility, clergy and *constitutionalists*,—and from the 2d June, and particularly after the August decrees, the great class of *moderate republi-*

* Bonaparte, during his first Italian campaign, in a letter to the Directory, speaking of his soldiers, says, "They jest with danger and laugh at death; and if any thing can equal their intrepidity, it is the gayety with which, singing alternately songs of love and patriotism, they accomplish the most severe forced marches. When they arrive at their *bivouac*, it is not to take their repose, as might be expected, but to tell each his story of the battle of the day, and produce his plan for that of to-morrow; and many of them think with great correctness on military subjects. The other day, I was inspecting a demi-brigade, and as it filed past me, a common chasseur approached my horse and said, General, you ought to do so and so. Hold your peace, you rogue! I replied; but the manœuvre which he recommended was the very same which I had privately resolved to carry into execution."

cans furnished its quota, and the guillotine was made to work with most frightful dispatch.

The execution of these extraordinary measures could not be otherwise than extraordinary. Local authorities could not be relied on; their zeal did not always respond to the Jacobinical ardor of the capital,—hence the appointment of commissioners by the convention, to go into the armies to stimulate the generals, and to go into the provinces and towns to kindle up the zeal and ardor of the citizens, and superintend the raising of the levies.

With these military plans, the convention, with equal boldness of decision, passed their financial decrees. The public debt was in the utmost disorder, and stock-jobbing had reached a most ruinous height. There were many different kinds of debts, such as those contracted under the *old monarchy*, those under the *constitutional monarchy*, and at different times under the *republic*, and they were all fluctuating in value, and selling at different prices in the market. Generally, the *old monarchy* bonds sold best, for the *republic* had recognized them, and consequently, if it should be continued, they would be equal to the other debts, but if the Bourbons should be restored the *republican* bonds might be repudiated. For a similar reason, the *constitutional monarchy* bonds were rather preferred to the republican, because more likely to be recognized in case the repblic were overthrown. Cambon, the great financial genius of the Jacobins, quickly remedied these evils by *republicanizing* the whole national debt; that is to say, a decree was passed calling in all the bonds, old and new, under the penalty of forfeiture, and cancelling and burning them, after issuing their equivalents in a new republican scrip, all of which bore the same date. After this there was no *preferred* national debt in the market. The scrip was all of precisely the same character,—it was all *republican*,—all placed on the same basis; and this measure had a most powerful influence in rallying all state creditors around the government; for with every successs of the new government the public funds would rise, and nothing but disaster could be expected by the fund-holders from a restoration. But the most extraordinary task that was ever undertaken by man, was the serious effort of the Jacobin government to remedy by decrees all the evils flowing out of a rapidly depreciating paper currency.

8. *The Maximum.*—Never, perhaps, since the foundation of the world, did the wisdom of man attempt so seriously to supplant the laws of trade, and to render the whole economical mechanism of society dependent on legislative edicts, as from the overthrow of the Girondists to the establishment of the directory; and certainly never, in the history of the world, was there a set of men at the head of government, less

scrupulous in the use of means, no matter how violent, to attain their ends. This whole subject most beautifully, but mournfully, illustrates the danger of substituting the wisdom of man for the self-sustaining laws of trade. We can only designate prominent points, without entering into details.

As we have already said the assignats were constantly depreciating, and, of course, there was quickly a difference in the value of a paper and a metal franc. Then came the decree saying there should be no difference. This caused the metals to disappear, but of course could not appreciate the paper. All prices rose, because all sellers expected to be paid in paper. Then came the clamor against forestallers and monopolizers, who would not sell as cheaply as formerly. The poor were every where crying out for cheap bread, and starving for the want of it. Then came the law of the *maximum*, imposing a price on corn beyond which it should not be sold; the immediate effect of which was, that the farmers held back their corn, and would not sell it at all at the unremunerating maximum fixed by the government. This produced, of course, still more frightful want and distress among the indigent classes; hence a still more infuriated cry from the starving thousands, of *sans culottes*, against the hard-hearted farmers and corn-dealers, who would not bring their corn to market. Then came that still more formidable decree, making it criminal to hold back the corn when ready for market, and those odious inquisitorial visits to search for it on every farmer's premises. These regulations, at a time when heads were struck off without remorse, were obeyed for a season, and partially removed the distress; but it was soon seen that the next resource of the farmer was to quit farming, and go to something else. This was followed by a decree to make it criminal to desert the lands.

But whilst the convention was thus regulating corn in all its details, other articles were rising with every depreciation of assignats, and consequently a clamor was rising against the venders. The corn producers and corn sellers considered it, too, but a matter of justice, to put a maximum on other commodities as well as corn, and consequently joined in the clamor. Then came the decrees regulating the prices of most every article of common use, such as soap, candles, sugar, etc.; each had its maximum, and in every case greatly below its cost of production. This, of course, produced a disposition to transfer capital from the most hardly favored to the most mildly treated occupations, or to send it out of the country to be invested abroad. Good foreign stocks, particularly, would be eagerly sought for, but every evasion only called for a fresh sanguinary decree to put a stop to it. The law every where *tried to head* the cupidity of individuals. No one, who has not well considered the working of that complex economical mechanism, by which the distribution of commodities is so beautifully made with such unerring precision to all the members of a large empire, under the simple influence of the laws of trade and the pursuit of individual interest, can form any idea of the prodigious amount of business which the Jacobin government carved out for itself by its system of maxima. What a net-work of prying, odious despotism, must it have spread over the whole realm! How many thousands of police officers did it require to drag the offenders to light; and what hard-hearted cruelty to execute the punishment. What a struggle must it have engendered between the hopes of selfishness and the fear of punishment,—between the sly, calculating cunning of the property holders, and the keen-scented sagacity of the inquisitorial police officer. In the mean time, it was making France, but particularly Paris, one enormous pauper establishment. It was teaching the poor every where, that provisions must be reduced to their capacity to purchase.

The fact is, the revolution had now run through all the higher grades of society down to the bottom stratum. This lowest grade had always looked on revolution as a something that would not only bring political change, but would give them a plenty of happiness and plenty of food. The poor expected Elysium, and the Jacobins seriously attempted to give it to them. Hence, we easily discern another powerful cause of the rapidly increasing horrors, as the revolution advanced. Under the most favorable circumstances, revolutions disturb the regular operations of the laws of trade; there is not always a proper adjustment of supply to demand; products are not well distributed when made,—hence greater distress among the lowest people. But, in France, this lowest grade expected plenty,—the demagogues had told them such would be the effects of revolution. Then the cry was gotten up, we have traitors who prevent this result; these traitors must be dispatched; they are the true cause of the high price of corn, and the starving of the people. Thus, in the first stage of the revolution, the nobles, the priests, and the king, were accused of doing all the mischief; with another advance, the constitutionalists were added to the number, and called aristocrats; when the government became a pure republic, then the Girondists were added,—and we shall soon see, under the Jacobins, that one section of the party charged the distress on another; all the time, the most indigent, particularly in Paris, were taught to believe that the revolution had never gotten far enough, as long as there was any suffering among the people.* The maxima, and the serious effort made to provision the

* The operation of this cause on the revolution was so well understood, that one

great city of Paris,* together with the tax law,† may be considered as the last term of the revolutionary series. There was no point beyond this to which the revolution could go. This period coincides with the reign of terror; and under the directory, when the reaction was very powerful, the whole system was repealed,—and thus terminated this herculean but most absurd project, for superseding the laws of trade, and feeding the idle and the indigent. Holy writ has proclaimed that the poor will be always amongst us. Judicious laws may alleviate, but can never eradicate pauperism. He who, in revolutionary times, stimulates the poor to excesses, under the promise that revolution will remove all indigence and want, must be either an ignorant fanatic, or an unprincipled demagogue; and it is such miserable delusions as these, that caused the revolution of France but too literally to realize the prediction of Rousseau, that, "*when the people shall have nothing more to eat, they will eat the rich.*"

9. *Committee of Public Safety.* After giving an account of the prodigious exertions of the Jacobinical government, it is now proper to

of the most ardent revolutionists once forgot himself in a letter, and said, "*tout va bien ici, le pain manque.*" "All goes well here, bread is scarce."

* The city of Paris was actually for some time put on allowance, and only a certain amount of bread and meat allowed to each citizen. In the winter of 1793–4, each citizen was reduced to half a pound of meat per diem, and the daily allowance of Paris was 75 oxen, 15,000 pounds veal and mutton, and 200 hogs. In the winter of 1795, the quantity of bread to each individual was reduced to one pound per diem, except to laborers, who were entitled to one and a half pounds. Small as this allowance was, it was soon found necessary to reduce it still farther, and for several weeks each citizen's ration was only *two ounces* of black and coarse bread a day, and this pittance could only be obtained by first procuring tickets from the committees of government, and afterwards waiting at the doors of the bakers, from 11 o'clock at night, often till 7 in the morning, during the rigor of an arctic winter. The horrors of the scarcity during this year were increased by the rigor of the winter, which was more intense than any known in Europe for one hundred years. It was during this celebrated winter (1794–95) that Pichegru conquered Holland, owing to the freezing of the rivers and the canals, which enabled him to march his army over the whole country without any impediment. It was during this campaign that vessels were actually taken by cavalry, so thick was the ice in the ports.

† The principle was, as Camille Desmoulins expressed it, "while the *sans culottes* fight, the *monsieurs* must pay,"—hence the *impôts progressive*, or ascending taxes. Incomes were exempt to 1000 francs per annum to each individual of a family; all above 1000, were taxed one-tenth; when the income of the individual passed 10,000 francs, then the whole of the excess was demanded by the government *as a loan.* This was the celebrated *voluntary* loan which, it was supposed, would bring 1,000-000,000 francs into the treasury, and raise the value of assignats, by diminishing the amount in circulation. Thus do we see, according to the Jacobinical tax law of 1793, all incomes exempt up to 1000 francs,—above that point, as Carlyle expresses it, you *bleed freely*,—but when you get to 10,000, you bleed gushing!

examine a little into the machinery by which these tremendous effects were produced. As soon as the king was dethroned and a pure republic established, there was only one great acknowledged power left in France,—*the national convention.* The Girondists, for a short time, were triumphant in this body ; they were an extremely patriotic and respectable party, and ardently wished for a virtuous republic. During their reign, whilst the convention was adjudged politically omnipotent, the old system of acting by ministers was still kept up, and the celebrated Roland ministry, composed of Girondists, were considered as a sort of executive, responsible, however, to the convention. But the overthrow of the Girondists involved the overthrow of their ministry, and as energetic action became necessary, the convention fell on the plan of appointing committees to do the executive business, responsible, of course, to their body. These committees, although considered as mere supervisory bodies, in a very short time absorbed all the powers of the government. In the first place, it was impossible for so numerous a body as the convention to attend to the manifold duties of the government. Secondly, ever since the fall of the Girondists the convention had become terror-stricken, and was disposed to follow the lead of the most daring spirits, without even discussing subjects. The numerous arrests which had taken place in the convention, destroyed at once the freedom of debate, and gave rise to the more secret out-of-door influence of the committees. Of all the committees that of *public safety* (*salut public*) was the most important, and soon became, in fact, the dominant power of France. The ministers henceforth were its mere creatures, and considered as very little more than clerks in their respective departments. It was this committee which, in fact, appointed the generals, judges, juries, etc.—which sent its commissioners throughout all France to supervise and report to them. It was this committee that struck down the opposing factions, initiated all laws, had complete command, over all *persons*, by the law against the *suspected*,—over all lives, by the *revolutionary tribunal*,—over all *property*, by means of the *requisitions* and the *maximum*,—and over every member of the convention, by the *decrees of arrest*, which could so easily be obtained from a panic-stricken body. It was through the agency of this celebrated committee that Robespierre both acquired and lost the dictatorship ; and although the principal names* on this committee, during the reign of terror, are sufficient to sicken the heart of the philanthropist, yet all

* Robespierre, St. Just, Cauthon, Collot D'Herbois, Billaud Varennes, Barrère, were on this committee. Collot D'Herbois, who always supported the most cruel measures, used to say, "that the body politic becomes more healthy, the more it *perspires*."

must agree that never was there a more hard-working, energetic body of men at the head of any government. They distributed the duties among themselves, and worked with an energy and earnestness worthy of better men. One of the most distinguished on this committee was the celebrated Carnot, who presided with such wonderful success over the war department. Humanity is forced to regret that the name of this great, I had like to have added virtuous, man is found appended to all the sanguinary decrees and horrid proscriptions of the committee of public safety, during the reign of terror. His excuse was, that it was absolutely necessary to sign these decrees without examination. With such an enormous mass of business, the members of the committee could only discharge the public business on the principle of the division of labor and mutual confidence.

10. *Decline of Danton's influence—Increase of Robespierre's.*—After the fall of the Girondists, on the 2d June, the government was left ertirely in the hands of the Jacobins, amongst whom dissensions quickly arose, as might have easily been foreseen. Up to this period, Danton may be regarded as perhaps the master-spirit of the Jacobins,—it was his daring and his eloquence that had infused courage at every critical and decisive moment. He had hitherto gone all lengths, and devised the boldest and most violent means; but the time had now come, when even this daring spirit should be denounced for *moderatisme*,—for lagging too far behind the revolution. Although Danton has many of the very worst sins of the revolution to answer for,—although dissipated, loose, perhaps corrupt, yet he was far from being one of the worst; in many respects, he had even an elevated character. He regarded the revolution as a great game, in which heads were stakes; when he won, he took them—had he lost, he would have been ready for the sacrifice. He was not blood-thirsty like Marat,—he had not personal hatreds like Robespierre. Under other circumstances, he might have been regarded as what the world would call a *fine, generous-hearted fellow.* He was a warm friend, and whilst he could plan the slaughter of multitudes, as he did on the 10th August and 2d September, 1792, he was extremely accessible to pity towards individuals.* What he did, he really considered necessary. He had no personal antipathies, and conse-

* One great difference between the cruelty of Danton and Robespierre was, that the former slaughtered by *wholesale*, the latter in *detail*,—the former used mobs and cannon, the latter used decrees, revolutionary tribunals, and the guillotine. The cruelty of the former spent itself in a few bold strokes,—daring *coups-de-main*,—which he justified on the plea of political necessity. The cruelty of the latter assumed the form of system,—pretended to work under the sanction of law,—permeated all the ramifications of society, and struck at the heads of individuals rather than of masses.

quently but few personal enemies. He was fond of his pleasures, devoted to his wife, and loved good dinners and good wines; and it was supposed, as the revolution advanced, that he became too greedy for money to spend on his private pleasures. His honesty and integrity began to be doubted, and he became rather indolent after the 2d June. He did not attend the Jacobin clubs so often. He was beginning to incur the censure of not relishing the company of his old *sans-culottic* friends,—"Danton left me," said a Jacobin in the tribunal, "to go and *shake hands with a General!*" Besides all this, Danton was accused of *moderatisme*. It was said that he barely acquiesced in the fall of the Girondists,—that he did not consider them as traitors, as accomplices of Pitt, etc.—that he positively disapproved of the *violent* scenes of the 2d June, and particularly of the conduct of Henriott, the commandant of the national guard; and that he was the warm personal friend of Dumouriez, and did not believe him to be a traitor.

Whilst Danton, hitherto the great man of his party, was thus sinking in their estimation, another was rapidly supplanting him,—this was Robespierre. It is to be remarked, that in violent revolutions like that of France, statesmen run their career within extremely short periods.* Robespierre had the advantage of not being so prominent as Danton, in the first stages of the revolution. He developed himself more gradually. In the first national assembly, he was looked on as an enthusiast, but was a poor speaker, and his influence inconsiderable. The celebrated fusilade of the Champs de Mars under the orders of Lafayette, caused him to skulk and hide for several days in a most dastardly manner. With such a nation as the French, this would have been fatal to his popularity, if his fame had been so bright at the time as to have attracted the public scrutiny. As the revolution advanced, Robespierre played his part with a skill admirably adapted to the times and the party with which he was connected. He had never, like Danton, shown affection for any proscribed individual, although he was very vain—dressed with scrupulous neatness;† whilst the more shabby costume

* From May 1789, to July, 1794, when Robespierre fell, a period of little more than five years, we have no less than five distinct sets of statesmen, who rose, flourished for a day, and were cut down. The Constitutionalists, the Girondists, the Dantonists, the Hebertists, and the terrorists of Robespierre.

† He was particular about having his linen very fine and very white. The woman who took care of it was frequently scolded on this account. He had his frills plaited with extreme neatness: he wore waistcoats of delicate colors—pink, light blue, chamois, elegantly embroidered; and we must remember, as Carlyle says, that waistcoats, in those days, *were waistcoats*,—they came down low enough to cover the hips! The dressing of his hair occupied much of his time, and he was very difficult about the cut and color of his coat. He had two watches, wore several costly rings

was the boast and badge of the Jacobins; and had his room hung round with looking-glasses, busts and pictures of himself,—on which he was forever gazing with more than a woman's vanity. Yet, all this seemed not to give offence to his *sans-culottic* friends. His character, his bearing and demeanor in other respects, obtained for him the reputation of *incorruptible.* One capital feature in the character of Robespierre, was his entire freedom from avarice, or the love of money. "He was a fanatic, a monster," said Napoleon; "but he was incorruptible, and incapable of robbing, from a desire of enriching himself. It was truly astonishing to see those fanatics, who, bathed up to the elbows in blood, would not for the world, have taken a piece of money or a watch from the victims they were butchering. At the very time when Robespierre and Marat were committing those massacres, if Pitt had offered them two millions of money, they would have refused it with indignation." Robespierre never associated with any general, financier, or deputy,—hence, he was regarded as the *people's friend.* He indulged in no pleasures during the revolution; he lived obscurely and cheaply, at a poor cabinet-maker's in the Rue St. Honorè, and kept up an entirely unknown connection with his eldest daughter. Thus did he acquire the character of being austere, reserved, upright, and was reputed to be one of the most incorruptible patriots of the revolution. He won the entire confidence of the people,—he was assiduous and laborious when he became a member of the committee of public safety, and he was constant in his attendance at the Jacobin club. His character, his position, his assiduity, enabled him to scold even his crusty Jacobins; whilst Danton, who always became indolent and negligent the moment any great crisis was past, absented himself so frequently from the club, that when he appeared, he was obliged to excuse himself, and protest that he was still a patriot, etc.

11. *Hebertists—Their Atheism—Their excesses in Paris.* Whilst Danton and his party were supposed to be lagging *behind* the revolution, there was another party that seemed to be running *ahead* of it—these were the *Hebertists.* We have already seen the immense influence exercised by the commune of Paris, during the latter period of the legislative assembly. Whilst the Girondists were in the ascendant in the national convention, the commune and the Jacobins labored together for their extermination; which was effected, as we have seen, on the 2d June. From June to November, 1793, the committee of public safety gradually

on his fingers, and had a valuable collection of snuff-boxes. His elegant appearance formed a singular contrast with the studied squalidness of the Jacobins. The populace would have insulted a stranger who should have dressed with such care; but in its favorite Robespierre, this was considered as perfectly republican. (M. P. F. 3, 51.)

became the most powerful body in France. But, violent and intemperate as was this committee, the commune of Paris and the Hebertists were diposed to go greatly beyond it. The policy recommended by this party may be considered as representing the last term in the revolutionary series. They pushed the democratic principle to the extreme of licentiousness and *mobocracy*. Anarchy and atheism were the symbols of the party. It is to be remarked, that each political party which arose in France, during the progress of the revolution, was characterized by its religious, no less than by its political opinions,—thus the refractory and nonjuring clergy belonged to the old regimé, and represented their opinions. The constitutional clergy were Jansenists. Philosophical deism, with the worship of one God alone, was the creed of Robespierre, the committee of public safety, and of most of the Jacobins. The atheistical materialism of the society of Holbach, with the *worship of reason and nature*, was the religion of the commune and the Hebertists. Chaumette and Hebert were the political chiefs of this latter party.* Ronsin, the commandant of the revolutionary army, was its general—the atheist and madman, Anacharsis Clootz, the self-styled *representative and orator of the human race*, was its apostle. The club of the Cordeliers was its head-quarters,—the lowest rabble of Paris and other cities constituted its popular support, and the *Père Duchesne*, the most calumnious, the most violent and obscene of all the newspapers published during these terrible times, was its organ, edited by Hebert, the greatest of scoundrels. The excesses of this party have, perhaps, thrown more odium on the French revolution, than those of any other, particularly its *anti-religious* excesses. It was, for a season, all powerful in Paris, when the commune and rabble supported it. During this period, it prevailed on Gobel, the bishop of Paris, and the other clergy of the city, to renounce Christianity; and substitute the *worship of reason* for that of Christ. The churches were shut up or transformed into *temples of reason*, and the most scandalous scenes were enacted in the most public manner. Every tenth day a revolutionary leader ascended the pulpit, and preached atheism to the bewildered audience. Marat and Lepellettier† were deified—the instrument of death was sanctified under the title of *holy guillotine*. The inscription "*death is an eternal sleep*," was placed on the public cemeteries. Pache, Hebert and Chaumette, the leaders of the commune, publicly expressed their determination to dethrone the king of Heaven as well as the kings of the earth. The comedian, Monart, carried disgusting blasphemy to its utmost height, when he exclaimed,

* Marat was the undoubted head as long as he lived. But then the party was not entirely developed in all its hideous deformity.

† A Jacobin who had been assassinated.

"God, if you exist, avenge your injured name! I bid you defiance! you remain silent—you dare not launch your thunders! Who, after this, will believe in your existence!" The first festival of reason was held with pomp on 10th November, 1793. In Paris, it was attended by all the sections and constituted authorities. A young and beautiful, but immodest woman, the wife of Momoro, the printer, represented the goddess of reason. She was dressed in a white drapery; a mantle of azure blue hung from her shoulders; her flowing hair was covered with the cap of liberty. She sat upon an antique seat entwined with ivy, and borne by four citizens. Young girls, dressed in white and crowned with roses, preceded and followed the goddess,—then came the busts of Lepellettier and Marat. Speeches were delivered, and hymns sung in the temple of reason. After which they proceeded to the national convention; where Chaumette announced the fall of fanaticism, and the establishment of the only true worship, that of *liberty and reason.* The goddess of reason then descended from her throne, and went up to the president of the convention, who gave her the fraternal kiss, amid universal bravoes and shouts of "*the Republic forever! Reason forever! down with Fanaticism!*"

Never had power overthrown, with greater violence, the habits of a people. All lives were threatened, all fortunes were decimated, the standard of exchanges was arbitrarily fixed, the ceremonies of religion were abolished, the pulpits were deserted, baptisms ceased, the burial service was discontinued, the sick received no communion, the dying no consolation, the village bells were silent, and Sunday was obliterated. The names of weights and measures were changed,* and the names of months and days were altered; and a new calendar, with a *new style* for the computation of time, was introduced.†

* The new system of weights and measures, one of the results of the audacious spirit of innovation, was most admirable. The idea was conceived of taking for the unit of weight and for the unit of measure, natural and unvariable quantities. Thus, distilled water was taken for the unit of weights, and a part of the meridian for the unit of measure. These units, multiplied or divided by ten, *ad infinitum,* formed the beautiful decimal system of the French, which surpasses all others.

† They made the year and the new era commence with the 22d day of September, 1792,—a day which, by a fortunate coincidence, was that of the institution of the republic, and of the autumnal equinox. The decimal system was observed in all the divisions, except as to the months; here nature commanded a deviation from the decimal computation. The year was divided into twelve months, each of thirty days. The three fall months, commencing on 22d September, were named Vendemaire, Brumaire, Frimaire; the three winter months were called Nivose, Pluviose, Ventose; the three spring months were Germinal, Floreal, Prairial; and the three summer months were Messidor, Thermidor, Fructidor. Each month was divided into three portions, of ten days each, called *decades;* the tenth day of each decade

12. *Overthrow of the Hebertists and the Dantonists—Reign of Terror.* After having thus described the position and policy of Danton and his party, and the excesses of the Hebertists, we will briefly explain the manner in which both those parties were overthrown by Robespierre and the committee of public safety. After the fall of the Girondists, Danton and his party being the *moderates*, and wishing, therefore, to hold back the revolution, and keep it from running into farther excesses, became, of course, most directly and violently opposed to the commune of Paris, and the Hebertists, who were the *ultra* revolutionists, and whom we have just seen running into every extravagance, both political and anti-religious. The celebrated journal, the *Old Cordelier*, edited by Camille Desmoulins, perhaps the most powerful and witty journalist which those celebrated times produced, was the organ of the Dantonists; and was violently opposed to the *Père Duchesne*, the organ of the Hebertists.*

Whilst these two parties were thus violently denouncing each other, Robespierre, who had become the decided leader in the committee of public safety, was determined to render the committee omnipotent in France,

was a day of rest, making only three to the month. The days were named according to their succession, Primidi, Duodi, Tridi, Quartidi, Quintidi, Sextidi, Septidi, Octidi, Nonidi, Decadi. The day was divided according to the decimal system, into ten parts or hours, these again into ten others, etc.; and new dials were ordered, to put into practice this new method of computing time. As each month had only thirty days, five *complementary* days were required to make out the year of three hundred and sixty-five days,—these were all inserted at the end of the year, between Fructidor and Vendemaire, and were called *sans-culotides.* They were set apart for holidays and national festivals,—the first was for the festival of *genius*,—the second, of *labor*,—the third, of *noble actions*,—the fourth, of *rewards*,—and the fifth, of *opinion*. This last festival was perfectly characteristic of the French; it was a political *carnival* of twenty-four hours, during which, people should be allowed to say and write what they pleased with impunity, concerning every public man. Every leap year, of course, brought a sixth *sans-culotide*, which was called the *Festival of the Revolution.*

* In speaking of the *Père Duchesne*, Camille exclaims, "Knowest thou not, Hebert, that when the tyrants of Europe wish to make their slaves believe that France is covered with darkness and barbarism—that this Paris, so extolled for its attic wit and its taste, is peopled with Vandals; knowest thou not, wretch, that it is scraps of thy paper which they insert in their Gazettes? As if the people were as ignorant as thou wouldst make Pitt believe; as if they could not be talked to but in so coarse a language; as if that were the language of the convention and the committee of public safety; as if thy obscenities were those of the nation; as if a sewer of Paris were the Seine." On the other hand, the *Père Duchesne* does not hesitate to call Camille *a party intriguer, a scoundrel fit for the guillotine, a conspirator who wishes the prisons to be opened in order to make a new Vendée with them, a knave in the pay of Pitt, a long-eared ass, etc., etc.*

and consequently it became his interest to put down the Hebertists, who were jealous of its power, and were pushing the revolution into the wildest anarchy, which would, eventually, have thrown all the powers of government into the hands of the communes and rabbles of the cities, particularly of Paris. Besides this motive, which operated on Robespierre, we can scarcely doubt that he was actuated by a religious one likewise. He was violently opposed to the atheism of the Hebertists. He was, perhaps, as vain of his *philosophical deism*, and of his speeches and reports on the existence of the *supreme being*, as of any acts of his life. His enthusiasm upon this subject, almost amounted to *monomania.* He became so inflated with his importance in this respect, that he at last got up a festival in honor of the supreme being, and he himself was honored with the office of high priest on the occasion. Besides the political and selfish motive, then, we must suppose that Robespierre was governed by a religious one likewise. Be that, however, as it may,—he formed, for a time, a closer union with the Dantonists, and openly denounced the Hebertists. In the month of March, 1794, nineteen of the leaders of the Hebertists were arrested and guillotined as athiests and traitors, who were hired by Pitt and foreigners, to push the revolution into such excesses as would disgust the world with the French government. This victory of Robespierre announced that the progress of the revolution had stopped; for it was the first time since its commencement, that the most forward party had failed to triumph. Whilst running down, however, this party of the *ultra*-revolutionists, Robespierre began to incur the odium of being himself a *moderate;* and he became fearful of compromising his own popularity and power. He therefore resolved, most meanly, to run the revolution over the only man and the only party in France, who stood between him and absolute power. Accordingly, just six days after the execution of the Hebertists, he denounced Danton and his party before the convention. The leaders were arrested, and after an infamous trial, conducted by the infamous Fauquier Tinville, they were guillotined on the 5th of April, 1794.*

Thus did Robespierre strike down, with relentless cruelty, both those who went *beyond* and those who fell *behind* him in their revolutionary ardor. The Dantonists were the last defenders of humanity and moderation. The Girondists had wished to prevent the reign of terror, —the Dantonists to stop it. All had now perished. After them, no voice was heard for some time against the dictatorship of terror. It

* Here again, we find something touching in the mere ages of those who were guillotined. Danton was only 34; Camille Desmoulins was 33; Bazire was 29; Herault Sechelles and Philippeaux were 34, etc. Thus talents, courage, patriotism, youth, were all again included in this new holocaust, as in that of the Girondists.

struck its silent and reiterated blows from one end of France to the other. After the fall of the Girondists, a reign of terror had commenced. But, after the fall of Danton, for about four months which elapsed, till the fall of Robespierre, we have a reign of terror far more dreadful than any which had preceded it.* Every citizen of France felt alarm. It was impossible to say who was safe. Formerly, the guillotine was only dreaded by those who lagged *behind* the revolution. But the committee of public safety had destroyed both those who had too much zeal and those who had too little. Men knew not what principles to profess,—what doctrines to advocate, to save their lives. There seemed to be but one resource left to all public men, and that was, to sing the praises of Robespierre† and the committee of public safety. There was but one policy to pursue, and that was, to adopt with eagerness, all the measures recommended by these infamous men, and execute with frightful dispatch their terrible decrees. During this period, Robespierre had around him a kind of court, composed of a few men, but mostly of women, who paid him the most delicate attentions. They were constantly eulogizing his virtue, his eloquence, his genius.

* A simple tabular exposé of the monthly returns of prisoners guillotined in Paris, from the fall of the Girondists on 2d June, 1793, to the fall of Robespierre, in July, 1794, will show the terrible progressive increase of victims during the four last months.

1793—	June,	14	
	July,	13	
	August,	5	
	September,	16	
	October,	60,	including Brissot and the Girondists.
	November,	53	
	December,	73	
1794—	January,	83	
	February,	75	
	March,	123,	including Hebertists.
	April,	263,	including Dantonists.
	May,	324	
	June,	672	
	July,	835,	exclusive of Robespierre and his accomplices.

† And yet it was sometimes dangerous to praise him, when it operated on his fears. Thus, when the Journal de la Montaigne and the Moniteur asserted of a speech of his, that "it was a master-piece which was not susceptible of analysis, because every word was equivalent to a sentence, every sentence to a page," etc. He accused these two journals of praising him inordinately,—that they might ruin him with the people by producing the appearance of his being all-powerful. Both journals were obliged to retract what had been said, to apologize for praising him, by assurances that their intentions were pure.

They called him a divine, a superhuman mortal. As the committee of public safety had now usurped all the powers of government, Robespierre, who was the acknowledged leader of the committee, was universally regarded as the dictator of France. It was customary to say, *Robespierre wills it*,—not the *committee wills it.* The agents of power constantly named Robespierre in their operations. The victims imputed to him all their sufferings, and the inmates of the prisons recognized him alone as their oppressor. Foreigners called the French soldiers *Robespierre's soldiers.* Whilst Robespierre was thus dazzling all eyes by his influence, he seemed to have planted his power on a firm basis. The lower classes, who had hitherto advocated the onward progress of the revolution, seemed now to consider him the very impersonation of the revolution, and sustained him for a time as the representative of their doctrines and interests. The armed force of Paris, commanded by his creature, Henriott, was at his disposal. He was all-powerful at the Jacobin club, which he had purified at his pleasure. All the important places were occupied by his creatures. He formed the revolutionary tribunal and the new commune of Paris to suit his ambition, by making Payan *procureur general* in the place of Chaumette, and Fleuriott *the mayor* of Paris in the stead of Pache. Whilst Robespierre was thus securing, as he supposed, a firm basis for his government, the committee met the difficulties of its position with an energy, an assiduity, a determination, which have rarely been equalled in the history of the world. It not only attended to the weighty political and military concerns of the country, but it shrank not, at the same time, from that immensity of labor which the *maxima* and the unwise tampering with the laws of trade had imposed upon it. It boldly reformed the whole system of agriculture, changed all the legislation of farming for the purpose of dividing the tillage of lands, introducing new rotation of crops, artificial meadows, and the rearing of cattle. It instituted botanic gardens, naturalized exotic plants, formed nurseries of trees, had courses of lectures opened on farming. It ordered the general draining of marshes, invited the architects to furnish plans for rebuilding villages and for changing the opera house into a covered arena, where the people might assemble in winter. Thus did it execute every thing at once, with an industry which no government has ever surpassed. In this respect, the extreme of democracy is very analogous to the extreme of monarchy. Take, for example, the Prussian government under Frederick the Great. When all power was concentrated in him, all the officers of the government were mere agents. His secretaries were little more than clerks. His extraordinary ability, industry, and distrust, made him inspect every thing, arrange every thing, order every thing, down to the very dishes on which he dined, and the prices that should be paid for them.

13. *Fall of Robespierre—End of the Reign of Terror.* We shall now proceed briefly to explain the manner in which this most extraordinary government was overthrown. In the first place, then, we may remark, that a government like this, based on terror, must soon become absolutely insupportable. All the prisons had rapidly filled with both high and low, male and female,—all upon whom the suspicions of the committee, and their thousands of spies and emissaries, had fallen,—and were exhibiting in their interior scenes of squalid misery, worse than any thing which had occurred during the revolution.* The work

* The history of the prisons during the reign of terror, forms by no means the least interesting, or even the least instructive, portion of revolutionary history. After the fall of the Girondists, and the passage of the celebrated law against the *suspected,* the prisons began to be filled, not only with royalists and priests, but with republicans likewise. The best society of France was to be found in them. At first they were all thrown in them *pell-mell,*—time, however, soon brought more order and more indulgence. The prisoners paid all the expenses of their detention. They were permitted to have communication with their friends and relatives, who furnished them with beds, and such comforts as the prison-houses would allow. At this period, the gardens of the Luxemburg every day presented a scene as interesting as it was melancholy. Married women from various quarters, crowded together around the prisons, in the hope of seeing their husbands at the windows. No weather could banish them from the gardens. Afterwards this consolation was denied the prisoners,—their intercourse with friends and relatives was stopped. From that moment the prisoners, doomed to associate exclusively with one another, became bound to each other by much closer ties than before; and never, perhaps, in the history of the world, did the interior of prison-houses exhibit such splendid society, such scenes, such amusements, as those of Paris did. Little coteries were quickly formed. Each sought intimates of corresponding character and taste. Certain rules were established among themselves,—the domestic duties were divided and performed in turn by each. A subscription was opened for the expenses of lodging and board, and thus the rich contributed for the poor. Household affairs all arranged, the inmates of the different rooms assembled in the common halls, where groups would form around a table, a stove, or a fire-place. Some employed themselves in writing, some in reading, others in conversation. Poets recited their verses, musicians gave concerts. The ladies indulged in dress and in coquetry,—formed ties of friendship and of love, and enacted all the scenes of fashionable life, till the very day that the guillotine put an end to them,—singular example of French character, of its thoughtlessness, its gayety, its aptitude to pleasure. The inmates of a hotel do not manifest so much curiosity about the daily arrivals, as the prisoners did about the new comers that were pouring into the prisons. When Danton and his party were sent to prison, the anxiety to see this noted character, to talk with him, to condole with him, was excessive. So, likewise, when the Hebertists were incarcerated, there was great curiosity to see these greatest monsters of the revolution, and, at the same time, pleasure was taken in making them feel their meanness.

of death, too, advanced with such frightful rapidity, that the revolutionary tribunal could not condemn fast enough for the wishes of the government. They were at last obliged to overleap all the forms and ceremonies of judicial process,—to invent modes of trial by which numbers might be accused together, and condemned without a hearing. A trial of one by one could not feed the guillotine fast enough, which was destroying during the last days of Robespierre, at the rate of sixty or a hundred per diem; and, at the time of his fall, arrangements were making for executing one hundred and fifty. Such accumulated horrors were fast annihilating all the charities and intercourse of life. Men became suspicious of those they loved most dearly. Every one assumed the coarsest dress and most squalid appearance. Every family assembled together early at night,—"with fearful looks they gazed around the room, fearful that the very walls might harbor traitors. The sound

All, except Rousin, were as cowardly as they had been cruel. One of the prisoners stepped up to Chaumette, called him philosopher Anaxagoras, and began to run the verb *suspect* through its passive variations, "*I am suspected—thou art suspected,—he is suspected—we are suspected,*" etc. Chaumette skulked away from this new kind of torment, and never made his appearance afterwards at the prisoners' levees.

Even the Conciergerie, adjoining the Palace of Justice, and containing the prisoners destined for the revolutionary tribunal, who never had more than five or six days to live, had likewise its peculiar amusements. It was in this prison that the Girondists made extempore, and performed, singular and terrible dramas, of which their own destiny and the revolution was the subject. It was at midnight, when all the jailers had retired to rest, that they commenced these doleful amusements. One which they devised deserves particular mention. They personated the judge and jury of the revolutionary tribunal, and the famous prosecutor, Fauquier Tinville. Two, placed face to face, represented the accuser and the accused. The accused was, of course, condemned. Extended immediately on a bedstead, turned upside down, he underwent the semblance of guillotining, even to its minutest details. After many executions of this kind, Fauquier Tinville himself was accused, condemned and guillotined. After a while he was represented as returning from hell, covered with a sheet, and describing the torments which he was enduring there; then, after foretelling the destiny of all the judges of the revolutionary tribunal, he seized them with hideous shrieks, and dragged them all down with him to the infernal regions. It was thus, said Riouffe, that we sported with death, and told the truth in our prophetic diversions, amid spies and executioners. (T. 2, 344.) It is very strange that, during these terrible times, the prisoners did not generally lose their patriotism or their confidence in the final triumph of republican principles. They manifested constantly, with the exception of a few royalists, excessive joy at every triumph of the revolutionary armies. The prisons were constantly resounding with the shouts of *Vive la Republique*, and with patriotic songs. Even when the wretched Hebert and Momoro, just before going to the guillotine, bewailed their fate and said that liberty was undone, Rousin, one of their party, exclaimed, "Liberty undone! because a few paltry fellows are about to perish! Liberty is immortal. Our enemies will fall in their turn, and liberty will survive them all."

of a foot, the stroke of a hammer, a voice in the street, froze all hearts with horror." In such times, the suspicion of one involves a whole family. When Cecile Renault was found with a sharp knife in her bundle, inquiring for Robespierre, no less than fifty-four of her relations and friends, amongst whom were her father and mother, were hunted down and brought to the scaffold with her. The very affections of the heart became evidence of guilt. The mother dared not weep over her son, or the wife over her husband.* It was a crime sometimes to look sad, at others to look joyful. I repeat it, then, that the reign of terror had become too intolerable for humanity to bear. France had become sick of the loathsome tyranny. Symptoms alarming to Robespierre began to be exhibited,—the populace no longer flocked as formerly to witness the operations of the guillotine. The shop-keepers in the streets through which the carts passed every day, shut up their shops. This sign of pity alarmed Robespierre, and the guillotine was removed from place to place to prevent this negative sort of sympathy from being observed. In the mean time, death was descending among the lower orders, —the horrors of the revolution were invading every rank. We find, during this period, on the list of the revolutionary tribunal, tailors, shoemakers, hairdressers, butchers, farmers, and publicans. Of course, Robespierre being the leader in the committee of public safety, was made responsible for all these evils. He became in the eyes of the French the very impersonation of the system of terror. It was impossible, therefore, long to protract his odious dictatorship. Humanity revolted at it, and despair itself would soon have found some bold arm to strike down the tyrant.

But whilst the system of terror was thus preparing the downfall of Robespierre, a schism sprang up in the committee of public safety, which greatly facilitated this result. There were, after the execution of Herault Sechelles, only eleven members in the committee. Of these, two, Jean Bon St. André and Prieur de la Marne, were absent on missions; Carnot was exclusively occupied with the war department; Prieur de Cote d'Or and Robert Lindet, with provisioning. These were called *examiners*,—they took no part either in politics or in rivalries. The other six members were, Robespierre, St. Just,† Cauthon,

* The beautiful wife of Camille Desmoulins was guillotined because she manifested too much grief at the death of her husband.

† St. Just, whilst he may without doubt be considered as one of the most terrible men of the revolution, is, at the same time, one of the most interesting. He really had a faith in what he was doing,—his convictions were as profound as his acts were cruel. He had no hypocrisy, like Robespierre,—no meanness and baseness, like Collot d'Herbois or Billaud Varennes. He had a large, fixed, penetrating eye, with

Collet d'Herbois, Billaud Varennes, and Barrère. The three first had early leagued together and formed a sort of triumvirate, who had great contempt for the three last. Barrère was, in their estimation, but a weak and pusillanimous creature, — a contemptible trimmer; Collot d'Herbois, a club declaimer, and Billaud Varennes, a weak, gloomy, envious man. These last three became excessively jealous and envious of the pretensions and haughty bearing of the other three, who were called the members *of the high hand.* They accordingly began to intrigue against Robespierre, who was called *Pisistratus.* In another very important committee, that of *general security*, (*sureté generale*,) Amar, Vadier, Vouland, Jagot, Louis of the Bas Rhin, were all jealous of the tyranny of the committee of *public safety*, and disposed to resist it. We must here observe, that this division and opposition in the committees, were not the result of difference of principle and policy, but was a mere rivalry of pride and power. The men in the committees who were most active in the overthrow of Robespierre, were among the most cruel and most violent men of the revolution.

large features, and strong, melancholy expression. He had long black hair, with a wholly bilious temperament, and although he had a most enthusiastic soul, his manners were cold. Simple and austere in his habits, he pushed forward without hesitation to the accomplishment of his designs, and he was in politics what a Jesuit is in religion. So confident was he of the goodness of his system, that it justified in his eyes every thing necessary to establish it. Although he was only twenty-five years old, he was most indefatigable in the committee; and when sent on missions to the army, no man could undergo more fatigue, and no one in the hour of battle would risk his life more than he did, and merely for the purpose of encouraging both soldiers and generals. St. Just had early been drawn towards Robespierre by his supposed incorruptibility. Robespierre saw the strength of his character, and took pains to secure his friendship. In the estimation of St. Just, all that Robespierre asserted about his intentions and the government was true. He really believed that Robespierre was laboring to establish a pure and virtuous republic, after the manner of the ancients. Sovereignty of the people, magistrates without pride, citizens without vices, simplicity of manners, in one word, the *reign of virtue*, were the professions of Robespierre,—they were really believed in by St. Just. The fanatics in the English revolution did not more confidently and conscientiously look forward to the second coming of Christ, and the reign of the saints on earth, than St. Just did to the ultimate reign of virtue in the French republic; and in proportion to his desire, so did he become more fierce and uncompromising in the enforcement of a system of terror, for the purpose of attaining this glorious result. When Robespierre defended the system of terror in the name of virtue and morality, he was a hypocrite, —but St. Just was in earnest. He was the very incarnation of the metaphysical, abstract spirit of democracy, and hence he was the most terrible of all the actors in the reign of terror, because he never relented and never felt remorse. Like the Israelite of old, he slew his enemy *hip and thigh*, and really believed that he was hastening on to the reign of virtue,—such was his political fanaticism. He was the *type-Frenchman of the reign of terror school.*

The first case which occurred of successfully resisting the wishes of Robespierre, was that of Catharine Theot, a crazy old woman, who called herself the *mother of God*, and prophesied the speedy coming of *the Messiah*. Dom Gerle, who had been formerly a companion of Robespierre, was one of her prophets, and it was whispered that Robespierre was to be her Messiah. These fanatics were brought before the committee of *general security*, and sent to prison, in spite of Robespierre, who wished to protect them. Nothing ever threw more ridicule on this odious tyrant, than this old woman; and the manner of her condemnation was excessively galling to his vanity. He soon saw that his influence was declining in the committee of *public safety*,—questions were frequently carried against his wishes. He became irritáble, peevish and fretful. He had been spoiled by his career of success, and lost his customary prudence and dissimulation. He at last had the vanity to think, that by ceasing to attend the meetings of the committee, his absence would throw every thing into confusion. He was mistaken. The committee only became the more hostile to him; and the period of his secession happening to correspond with the most brilliant success of the French armies, under Pichegru, Jourdan, Moreau and Hoche, his enemies in the committee gained all the credit of the splendid victories won by these generals, by far the most skilful which the revolution had yet produced. There was but one expedient now left to Robespierre, and that was to denounce his enemies in and out of the committees, and bring them all to the guillotine. The effort was made, —and the 9th Thermidor (27th July, 1794,) witnessed the overthrow of the dictator, who was hurried off to the guillotine with St. Just, Couthon, and some others of his accomplices; and thus terminated the reign of terror. At the head of the coalition which overthrew Robespierre, was Tallien; and the party were called *Thermidorians*, from the month in which they triumphed.

SEC. V.—FROM THE OVERTHROW OF ROBESPIERRE TO THE ESTABLISHMENT OF THE CONSULAR GOVERNMENT.

1. *Reaction—Establishment of the Directorial Government.* The 9th Thermidor was the first day of the revolution on which the *attacking* party was conquered. This fact was a most important sign; it showed that the revolution had not only run as far as it could go, but that it was now recoiling. The fall of Robespierre indicated a decided reaction. From this day, we find the revolution retracing its steps one by one,—we find generally, in the struggles between parties, *moderatism* prevailing over *ultraism*, till at last a new form of government, with a new constitution, was established in 1795, called the *directorial govern-*

ment. In this retrograde movement of the revolution, we find the party of the moderates sometimes visiting on the Jacobins a few of the horrors which they had inflicted on their adversaries. As the Jacobins condemned by the revolutionary tribunal, so the Thermidorians condemned by a military commission. In the South of France, the September massacres were in many instances repeated, particularly where the royalists were suddenly thrown into the ascendant. At Lyons, at Aix, at Tarascon, at Marseilles, the Jacobin prisoners were murdered. Companies were formed at Lyons, who scoured the country and killed the violent Jacobins, wherever they could meet them, without any form of trial farther than to say, *Voila un Matavon.* As the spring of the revolution uncoiled itself, all parties began to feel the necessity for the establishment of a new and better balanced government. Old Seyes, who had kept perfectly quiet in the convention during its stormy existence, once more aroused himself from his long torpor, and with new zeal and fresh experience set to work at his *old vocation of constitution making.* His reappearance in politics was a most interesting symptom in the times, and although his plan was so altered and amended that he would not agree *to father* the constitution, yet does this new government, emanating in part from the prolific brain of the old Abbé, the celebrated architect of the first constitution adopted by the national assembly, mark most definitively the point to which the revolution had recoiled. It is only necessary to allude to the principal features in the *directorial government*, to be convinced of the truth of this remark. The legislature was *bicameral*, being composed of—first, the *council of five hundred*, having exclusively the right of proposing laws, *one-third* to be renewed every year, and each member to be at least thirty year's of age; second, the *council of ancients*, composed of two hundred and fifty members, of at least forty years of age, all either widowers or married, having the sanction of the laws, to be renewed also by *one-third* annually. The *executive* was composed of a directory of five members,—to decide by a majority,—and was renewable annually by *one-fifth.* The directory had a responsible ministry.

2. *State of Society—Manners, etc.* We have already given a sketch of the brilliant society of France, during the session of the national assembly; we have described it as possessing all the polish and elegance which a court and aristocracy could impart, combined with all that vigor of intellect and energy of thought which democracy, reform and agitating events alone can generate. After the overthrow of the constitutional government, the dethronement of the king and the emigration of the nobles, the society of Paris lost somewhat of its polish and elegance; but still, during the ascendency of the Girondists, it

may be pronounced of the first order. The assemblages at Madame Roland's were extremely brilliant in point of intellect and conversational power. Madame Roland herself was a most extraordinary woman in this respect, and could not have failed to impart a high character to any circle in which she moved, even if composed of much less brilliant men than the Girondists.

After the overthrow of the Girondists, the Jacobinical government soon destroyed the character of French society. The reign of terror introduced distrust into the social circle, and the ascendency of *sans-culottism* introduced bad dressing, bad manners, and rough, vulgar conversation. Society during this period was thrown into chaos, utterly devoid of all polish and refinement.

After the overthrow of Robespierre, we find French society again emerging from chaos, under the auspices of Madame Tallien, who was one of the most beautiful and admired ladies of Paris, and her drawing-room was the most brilliant and most frequented. Her parties exhibited a perfect picture of the times. By birth and two marriages, she was connected with both the old and new regime. She was in prison at the time of Robespierre's fall, and had no little agency in stimulating Tallien to the decisive part he took against the tyrant. She felt indignation, therefore, against the system of terror, as well from resentment as goodness of heart. She wished to make Tallien play the part of peace-maker,—of repairer of the evils of the revolution. She drew around her those who had contributed, with her husband, to the 9th Thermidor,—she won them by her graces, and endeavored to produce harmony amongst them, for it was an extremely heterogeneous party. She was surrounded by graceful and accomplished women, who assisted in this scheme, among whom was the celebrated widow, Josephine Beauharnois, who had been in prison with her, and afterwards married Bonaparte. At Madame Tallien's parties, there were present simple, enthusiastic and plainly-dressed republicans. In the most amicable manner, they were sometimes rallied on their dress, manners, and the severity of their principles, but at the same time were caressed and flattered. They were placed at table by men more elegantly attired, and of more polished manners and less rigid principles. It was in this way that society was brought back from that extreme point of fanaticism and coarseness, to some degree of polish and elegance. The violent revolutionists, however, kept aloof from these drawing-rooms, and denounced the Thermidorians for obliterating republican manners and republican principles. As the revolutionary spring, however, relaxed itself, and the violent Jacobins, such as Fouquier Tinville, Carrier, Lebon, Billaud Varennes, Collot d'Herbois, etc., who had disgraced human nature, had been either guillotined or banished, the society of Paris plunged into the amusements of the winter, with a zeal and relish proportioned to the restraints under which it had been suffering. The women strove to dress with taste and elegance. The theatres were once more opened, and became quite the rage. Balls were attended with eagerness, where both gentlemen and ladies seemed to spite by their pleasures, dress and tastes, those sanguinary terrorists who were accused of wishing to stifle all civilization. The most singular of all these balls, and which, whilst it shows the violence of the reaction, illustrates most happily the French character, for it never could have been gotten up in any other country,—was the *ball of the victims*,—to which no person was permitted to go who had not lost some near relative by the guillotine, and had not crape on his arm.

Madame de Stäel took advantage of the times, to return once more to her beloved Paris, in company with her husband, the ambassador of Sweden. She threw open her drawing-rooms for the purpose of displaying her brilliant talents. Foreigners of distinction, all the ambassadors, literary men of most renown, assembled at her house. It was no longer Madame Tallien's drawing-room, but Madame de Stäel's, which attracted exclusive attention. And by this standard, might be measured the change which French society had undergone in the last six months. But whilst manners were thus regaining their former polish and elegance, primary schools, colleges, lyceums, universities, were again organized,—the arts were patronized, and the revolution seemed reverting to its true mission, that of promoting the arts, industry, knowledge and civilization.

3. *Difficulties of the Directorial Government—Overthrown by Bonaparte.* As soon as the system of terror was overthrown, and the revolution commenced its retrograde movement, the convention, which once more became the ruling power, had two sets of enemies to contend with. The violent revolutionists opposed to the reaction, and the *violent reactionists* (*reactionaires*), if we may use the expression, who wished to hasten the government back to monarchy. In Paris, the former party was very numerous, owing to the rabble and the hunger which prevailed there, and to the influence of the commune. The Thermidorians were obliged to meet the Paris mobs by what was called the *Jeunesse Dorée*, or *gilded youth*,—consisting of fashionable young men, armed in a particular manner,—who constituted a sort of Thermidorian or conventional mob,—who were, at all times, ready to encounter the Parisians in street fights. But whilst the convention combated with earnestness, the *ultra-revolutionists*, it was equally opposed to the *ultra-reactionists*. The great difficulty in the backward movement of the revolution, was to keep the royalists from reaping all the advantage. Examine into the structure of the directorial government, and you will

see that the two extreme parties constituted the evil most difficult to guard against. So fearful were they of too rapid a recoil, that after the constitution was framed, the convention adopted a decree that two-thirds of the first legislature should consist of members of the convention; and when they elected the first five directors, care was taken that every one should be a *regicide*. When the vote was taken on the adoption of the directorial constitution, with the decree of the convention, entitling its own body to furnish two-thirds of the first legislature, both the *ultra* parties were dissatisfied, and the city of Paris was agitated to such an extent, that it organized an insurrection of forty thousand men, and threatened the destruction of the national convention. It was on this occasion, that Barras, who was commandant of the conventional forces, gave the management to young Bonaparte, who made the most skilful arrangements,—and on the 13th Vendemaire, (5th October, 1795,) he completely defeated the Paris mob with his volleys of grapeshot; and from this day forward, a new era opens in the French revolution. Paris ceases to be omnipotent, its mobs become overawed by regular troops, and lose their influence on the progress of events. The 13th Vendemaire is the true era of the overthrow of the rule of the mobs, and the establishment of that of the regular armies.

This victory of Bonaparte in Paris, caused the quiet establishment of the directorial government,—which seemed to work admirably well as long as there was harmony between the directory and the two councils. But, in the year 1797, the new third sent into the councils by the elections of that year, produced a majority adverse to the directory. This at once afforded a test for the strength of the government,—and the result proved, that parties were too violent to abide by the forms of the constitution. The directory thought, or pretended to think, that the royalists had triumphed in the councils, and would restore the Bourbons, and thereby destroy the whole work of the revolution. In this opinion the armies concurred, particularly that of Italy. Bonaparte sent Angereau to Paris, at the call of the directory. He was put at the head of the directorial forces, and on the 18th Fructidor, the directory struck another *coup d' etat*,—overthrew the party of the councils, and arrested and banished forty members of the council of five hundred, and eleven of the council of ancients. Here is a stroke in the retrograde movement of the revolution, exceedingly analogous to the fall of the Girondists in the forward movement. The conquering party, on the 18th Fructidor, were trying to keep the revolution from running backwards too fast,—on the 2d June, the conquering party were anxious to run it forward, and therefore they ran it over the Girondists, who were holding it back. This bold act of the directory has generally been justified by the republican historians of France, upon grounds of state policy.

The government, after the purging of the two councils, worked on tolerably well, until the elections of the year 1799 again produced a decided majority against the directory. By this time the directory had become too weak for another *coup d' etat*, and the councils now triumphed in turn, and expelled all the obnoxious members from the directory and put in their own favorites. From this period, it was seen that the directorial government must be a failure. Neither party would abide by the constitution, when the directory and two councils were at issue. The directory first set the example of using force, which we have just seen followed by the councils on the 30th Prairial, 1799.

In addition to these collisions between the executive and legislative branches, other causes were rapidly undermining the government. In the first place, the directory was generally an exceedingly weak body—the violence of faction had destroyed all the conspicuous talent of France, except that which was in the army. When the first election of directors took place, Carnot and Seyes were the only two men of France of any reputation out of the armies; and it was an established principle, not to put a military chieftain into the directory. But, again, the directory, during the absence of Bonaparte in Egypt, and after the accession of Russia to the alliance, became unfortunate. Suwarrow beat the French in Italy,—the Archduke Charles beat them in Germany; and although Massena, in Switzerland, by his masterly manœuvres, somewhat repaired the disasters of the campaign, yet it was evident that the enthusiasm of the French was wearing out. The tremendous force of the democratic spring, which never lost its power as long as the onward movement of the revolution lasted, was beginning to relax ever since the revolution had turned backwards. That hope of perfect liberty and perfect equality, which had fired all hearts and nerved all arms, was now gone,—the sweet dreams of *democracy* were past. The allies on the other hand, were coming upon France with renovated hopes and renovated strength. The campaign of 1799, had shown that a mixed government, like the directorial, without the enthusiastic support of the people, constantly divided against itself, could not save France from the tremendous array of foreign bayonets encircling its whole territory. The democratic vigor was gone; it was now necessary to have some mighty chief that could re-organize the government in all its departments, and concentrate the resources of France against Europe. Bonaparte, returning from Egypt, was that man. The 18th and 19th Brumaire had become necessary. "It was not," says Thiers, "liberty that he came to continue, for that could not yet exist. He came to continue, under monarchical forms, the revolution in the world; he came to continue it, by seating himself, a plebeian, on a throne; by bringing the Pontiff to Paris to anoint a plebeian brow with the sacred oil; by creating an aristocracy with plebeians; by obliging the old aristocracies to associate themselves with his plebeian aristocracy; by making kings of plebeians; by taking to his bed the daughter of the Cæsars, and mingling plebeian blood with that of one of the oldest reigning families of Europe; by blending all nations; by introducing the French laws in Germany, Italy and Spain; by dissolving so many spells; by mixing up together and compounding so many things. Such was the immense task which he came to perform; and meanwhile, the new state of society was to consolidate itself under the protection of his sword; and liberty was to follow some day."

4. *Concluding reflections.* We will close this long article, by some reflections growing out of the history of the great event which we have been describing, and 1st,—It may be well asked, how happened it that force was not sooner resorted to? Why did not the military chieftain sooner end the sanguinary conflict of domestic factions? How happened it that the central government, so cruel in its action, nevertheless sustained itself, not only without the aid of the military, but even brought the generals themselves to the scaffold? It is not enough to say, in answer to this, that there were no generals of sufficient distinction, and that the experiment was not made. La Fayette, Dumouriez, and at a later period, Pichegru, were all anxious to overthrow the government, and they were all popular with the army. Why then did they fail? Simply because the army deserted them the moment they turned against the government. In the onward progress of the revolution, there was an abiding confidence in the ultimate triumph of liberty. As long as the revolution had not run its entire course, no matter with what horrors it was attended,—still, men believed that all would one day come right. Even the enthusiastic prisoner did not lose his confidence and his patriotism in the hour of death; but cried *Vive la Republique* the moment before the fatal axe had fallen. As long as this hope, this enthusiasm lasted, no military chieftain could succeed. La Fayette was beloved by his army, and they had confidence in his virtue. But the moment he called on that army to support him against the revolution, he was obliged to flee from his country. The same fate attended Dumouriez, a much abler general. But when Bonaparte appeared, as we have just seen, the democratic spring had recoiled and lost its vigor. Democratic hope was gone,—the self-sustaining power of the revolution was lost,—all its forces had been successively evoked and worn out. France longed for order and tranquillity,—for a ruling power sufficient

to quell faction, protect property, and save the national glory. The hero of Italy and Egypt alone could save her from foreign bayonets,—the age of civil rule was past, and that of the military had come. Marengo and Austerlitz had become necessary to her political independence,—hence the wonderful popularity of the 18th Brumaire throughout all France.

2d. We can but be struck in contemplating the history of the revolution, with the fact, that every set of statesmen, until the time of Bonaparte, failed the moment they had a *system* to defend. They succeeded only whilst revolutionizing,—thus the constitutionalists succeeded against the old-fashioned royalists in the national assembly. But as soon as they adopted a constitution and set up a *system*, they were overthrown by the Girondists. As soon as the Girondists triumphed and set up their *system* of a republic, they in turn fell before the Jacobins. Then the Dantonists on one side, and the commune of Paris and the Hebertists on the other, both set up *their system*, and both fell before Robespierre. Robespierre had a *system* likewise, and as soon as established, he was overthrown. Lastly, the Thermidorians established a *system*,—the directorial government, which lasted a little longer than its predecessors; but was in the end subverted by Bonaparte. From these facts, we are enabled to make an important deduction, applicable to all governments based exclusively on popular support. The party in power, where there are manifold and complicated interests to provide for, labor under a great disadvantage, because they always have a *system* to defend. In such countries, it is really extremely difficult to rally on any one well-defined system of measures, a decidedly national majority. But whilst the government, *de facto*, labors under this disadvantage, it is, perhaps, in such countries as England and the United States, more than compensated for by the power which patronage confers. In France, this compensating advantage was lost amid the hurry and whirl of the revolutionary movements. As soon as government lost its popular support, every one knew that its doom was sealed. People did not bear with it, merely because the forms of the constitution guaranteed its power. That revolution was too great and too violent to be held back by mere technical formalities. In every great crisis, mere constitutional bonds proved as unavailing as the threads which bound the sleeping Samson. Never, perhaps, since the fall of the Roman Empire, has there existed a popular government in the world, save that of England and of the Unites States, whose excesses have been permanently restrained by constitutional checks, and whose aberrations have been corrected within the prescribed forms of law, by the peaceful action of a sound, temperate, public opinion. No one thing gives us more hope in the grand experiment we are trying in our own favored land, than the fact, that since the institution of our system, the vessel of state has several times been thrown, in mariner's phrase, on the *wrong tack*, and has, in every case, been brought back by peaceful agencies, exerted within the limits of legal forms. The silent, but mighty power of public opinion, in this country, has shown itself, thus far, capable of forcing our government from a bad position, or enabling it to regain a good one, —it has rebuked systems of immorality, and developed recuperative energies without the agencies of mobs and armies. When different branches of our system have been thrown into conflict with each other, however clamorous the parties may have been, they have yet been ever willing to abide by the forms and requisitions of the constitution, and have patiently waited for the great arbiter, public opinion, to settle the dispute between them.

In this respect, we look upon the late accession of an individual to the Presidential chair, without the support of either of the great parties in the country,—without the support of the press,—as being a most interesting experiment on our government; and, as already observed, the result has been such as to inspire increased confidence in the strength of our institutions. However successful our experiment may be thus far, we are forced, nevertheless, to confess, that the greatest strain on our institutions has not yet taken place; that must come when our land shall be filled up with a dense population,—when a strong line of demarkation shall be drawn between those who *have* and those who *have not*, and thousands shall be born who can only expect to live like their fathers, labor like their fathers, and die like their fathers, without being able to accumulate more than barely enough to support life. When the day shall come that this class shall form the numerical majority, as it did in France, then will the high pressure come on our institutions; and the reign of terror in France has presented, I fear, too faithful a picture of what a government *may be*, that shall fall *exclusively* into such hands. In the mean time, we may with confidence assert, that there can be no texture of society better calculated to ward, than that which exists uneer the much reviled, much slandered institutions of the South.

3d. The above speculations lead us to another, which cannot fail to impress itself on every mind, after an attentive perusal of the revolutionary history. The principal horrors of the French revolution proceeded from Parisian *sans-culottic* influence, which we have already fully explained, and from the interference of the Allies. If any one lesson can be learnt from the French revolution, it is that which teaches the danger and impolicy of nations *forcibly interfering in each other's domestic concerns*. Look at the most tragic scenes of the revolution, and you will find that the pressure of foreign force produced nearly all of them. It was the declaration of war by Austria and Prussia, that rendered the constitutional government of 1791 wholly impracticable. It was the irritating manifesto of the Duke of Brunswick in 1792, which produced the 10th August, the dethronement of the king, and the flight of Lafayette. It was his march on Paris, the taking of Longwi and Verdun, and the insurrection in La Vendée, which produced the September massacres. It was the loss of the great battle of Neer-Winden by Dumouriez, and his subsequent treason and flight from France, which led to the overthrow of the Girondists and the rule of the Jacobins, and when two-thirds of France were in open revolt at their high-handed measures. It was nothing but the fear that this revolt would inure wholly to the benefit of the Allies and the Bourbons, which quelled internal strife, reconciled the nation to the horrors of Jacobin rule, and united all arms and hearts once more against the foreign foe. It was the danger of this same foreign foe that produced the national intoxication of 1793,—the mad decree and order sent to the generals, that they should conquer the enemy in twenty days. It was this, too, that produced the levy *en masse*, and those splendid campaigns which will ever remain the admiration of the world. It was this same reason which Robespierre alleged as justificative cause for striking down the Hebertists and the Dantonists, almost at the same blow. It was, in fine, this same cause which made so many virtuous patriots cleave to the government, even whilst they were moaning over its excesses. The great principle of action was, let us first save France from the foreign foe, then let us save her from herself. The system of terror was used for the purpose of producing unity of counsel and unity of action, and to prevent the waste of national resources by internal feud; and if we look to the military operations, we shall find that they afforded a strong pretext for this system. At the commencement of the war in 1792, the generals were *constitutionalists*,—the ministry were Girondists. Lafayette, Rochambeau and Luckner, were always at variance with Dumouriez, Servan, Claviere and Roland; and at this time we find no energy in the armies,—they were beaten and dispirited. But, after the high-handed measure of the 10th August, when the constitutional generals were replaced by Dumouriez, Custine, Kellermann and Dillon, Girondists, then do we find for a season, unity of view and action between the army and the government; instantly the energy of the army augments, and the campaign of the Argonne, the victories of Valmi and Jemappe, and the invasion of Holland, were the splendid results. In a short time, however, we witness the violent dissensions between the Girondists and the Jacobins. This introduces again dissension between the army and the government; the army once more loses its energy, and experiences numerous reverses and defeats. Dumouriez turns traitor, and France for a moment seems lost. Then came the violent scenes of the 31st May and 2d June in Paris,—the overthrow of the Girondists and the rule of the Jacobins. A corresponding revolution takes place in the armies; the Girondist generals, Dumouriez, Custine, Houchard, Dillon, are replaced by the Jacobin generals, Pichegru, Jourdan, Moreau, Hoche. As soon as harmony is thus violently restored, we find brilliant victories and conquests again attendant every where on the French armies. Never was the world more astounded, nor the enemies of France more signally beaten, than during the dark days of the reign of terror. Upon the heads of the allies, then, must fall the chief responsibility of French excesses; and let this memorable example be ever a warning to nations, how they interfere forcibly in the domestic concerns of their neighbors. Those concerns they can rarely comprehend; and if they could, they can still more rarely administer relief by force. The patriotism of every high-minded people revolts at such interference, and will run into the wildest excesses at home, for the purpose of pushing back the impertinent *propagandism* from abroad. The result too often is, which happened in the French revolution, the destruction of that very party and that very system which the foreigner advocates.

4th. Let us now conclude by a few remarks on the benefits of the French revolution. In the first place, then, we may assert, that never in the history of the world has there been made a richer or more valuable experiment in government,—never has the democratic problem been more completely worked out than in France. There we have exhibited on a grand scale, in quick successions, all the phases of democracy, from the top to the bottom stratum of the social edifice. There we see, as by a sort of panoramic view, both the strong and the weak points of democratic rule. We behold the tremendous energy which it generates, and the rock on which it splits. Ignorant and obstinate must be that statesman, who has not profited by the history of the French revolution; and may we not hope that its lessons will prevent the recurrence of so awful a catastrophe in future. It has taught the true value and the true danger of the popular element, which will henceforth be the moving force in every civilized government, no matter what may be its form.

But, while the French revolution has furnished such a rich fund of political experience to the contemplation of the world, it has been of incalculable advantage to France. It broke down, with a rude hand, the abuses and evils consecrated by the sufferance of a thousand years,—it overthrew the systems of feudality and priestcraft,—it seized with unrelenting energy, on the property of the noble, the priest and the corporation, and distributed it amongst the people,—it broke down that miserable system of custom-houses, (*douanniers*,) which interrupted trade between province and province, and thus it diffused the blessings of free trade over a great nation.*

Lastly, we may assert, that however depraved the morals and manners of the French were during the progress of the revolution, that grea event has nevertheless operated a most beneficial change in this respect It has acted like the storm which has purified the atmosphere. The Bourbons, when they came back to Paris, were ashamed to act as their ancestors had done. The court of Louis Philippe is now one of the most decorous in Europe; and the profligate scenes of the regency, and of the reign of Louis XV., can never occur again in the history of France. If enlightened philanthropy, then, should be called on, in full view of all the evils and all the benefits resulting from the French revolution, to render up a final judgment, we can scarcely for a moment doubt that it would be in favor of the revolution and all its attendant horrors, if these were the *only condition* on which the benefits could be obtained.

* It is these beneficial influences which explain, in part, the mighty resources which France constantly exhibited during this period and under the empire, and by not sufficiently attending to them, Pitt was led into the mistake of almost constantly thinking, during the progress of the contest, that France was on the eve of national bankruptcy. In 1794 he was confident of this result,—so was he in 1799,—yet France moved on with gigantic energy, and six years afterwards, on the field of Austerlitz, broke to pieces the last and greatest coalition of Pitt, and no doubt sent that great minister to an untimely grave. While we are thus noticing the great mistake of Pitt in regard to France, it is curious to see that Napoleon was constantly making one as great in regard to England. He read the speeches of Fox and the journals of the opposition, and was constantly looking for the fall of the *anti-gallican* administration, judging merely by the virulence with which it was attacked. He never could understand the character of the British government.

THE END.

www.ingramcontent.com/pod-product-compliance
Lightning Source LLC
La Vergne TN
LVHW021050110826
845150LV00001B/34

* 9 7 8 1 4 2 5 5 6 7 8 5 9 *